F. P Healy, O. M. Healy

A Record of Unfashionable Crosses in Shorthorn Cattle Pedigrees

F. P Healy, O. M. Healy

A Record of Unfashionable Crosses in Shorthorn Cattle Pedigrees

ISBN/EAN: 9783337254179

Printed in Europe, USA, Canada, Australia, Japan

Cover: Foto ©ninafisch / pixelio.de

More available books at **www.hansebooks.com**

OF

UNFASHIONABLE CROSSES

IN

SHORT-HORN CATTLE PEDIGREES.

By
F. P. AND O. M. HEALY.

BEDFORD, IOWA:
PUBLISHED BY F. P. AND O. M. HEALY.
1883.

Entered according to Act of Congress, in the year 1883,
BY F. P. AND O. M. HEALY,
In the office of the Librarian of Congress, at Washington.

PRINTED BY JOHN H. PORTER,
MOLINE, ILLINOIS.

INTRODUCTION.

In issuing this work for the benefit of the breeders of Short-Horn Cattle, we believe we are supplying a book that has long been needed, especially by the younger breeders, or those not having the Herd Books at hand. Those conversant with Short-Horn pedigrees will readily understand the great amount of patient labor required in producing such a work. We have endeavored to make it as correct as possible, and believe we have succeeded—the typographical errors in the Herd Book rendering it quite difficult at times. Infallibility is not to be expected, however.

Those familiar with pedigrees may find crosses in this book that they think ought not to be here, and others not here that ought to be. To such we would say, do not judge too harshly until you are certain you are right. Many pedigrees in the earlier volumes of the Herd Book have been corrected in the later volumes, thereby changing the value of many pedigrees. For instance, Rover 931 (a bull quite extensively used), is not in. On examination of his pedigree, in Vol. II, we find he was sired by Selima 957. Selima's pedigree reads thus: "Bred by Col. Powell, Philadelphia; got by Emperor ———, out of Kate ———, both thoroughbred Short-Horns." Surely a very incomplete pedigree. But in Vol. XIV we find Selima corrected at number 20947, and it reads thus: "Bred by Col. Powell, Philadelphia, Pa.; got by Emperor 1511, out of Kate, by Raymond (1357); Martha, by Wye Comet (1591); Imported Laura, by Denton (198); Selina, by Wellington (687), by Danby (190)."

F. P. AND O. M. HEALY.

June 1st, 1883.

THE PATTON STOCK.

In 1783 Mr. Matthew Patton procured for use on his Virginia plantation a bull of the Long-Horned breed, imported from England by Mr. Gough, of Baltimore. In 1785 three of Mr. Patton's sons and his son-in-law, Mr. Gay, took several of the half-breed heifers — the get of this bull — with them to Jessamine county, Kentucky. In 1790 Matthew Patton himself moved to Clark county, Kentucky, taking with him several more half-blood calves of this same bull. These cattle were described as large and rangy, somewhat coarse, fattening slowly and late, but at maturity making excellent beef. Being well pleased with one cross of improved stock, Mr. Patton decided to try one more; and in 1795 bought of Mr. Miller, of Virginia, a bull and heifer of the Short-Horn breed (spoken of then as the Milk breed) named Mars 1850 (bred from Imported stock) and Venus. Mars is described as a deep red with white in the face, of good size, large bone, horns somewhat coarse. Venus was white with red ears, of fine form and good size, short horns turning downward. Venus produced but two calves — both bulls, by Mars — and then died. One of these calves went to Ohio, the other was retained in Kentucky, and with his sire, Mars, they made a marked improvement over the common stock. In 1803 a son and two sons-in-law of Mr. Patton sent to Mr. Miller, of Virginia, for another bull of the "Milk" (Short-Horn) breed, and got a two-year-old named Pluto, since recorded in the Herd Book as number 825, certified to be from Imported stock. He is described as dark red or roan, was quite large, with small head and neck, and light, short horns.

The calves from Pluto, out of cows sired by Mars and from the half-blood Long-Horns, were a superior class of cattle.

In 1812 Pluto went to Ohio, where he soon afterward died. In 1810 Capt. William Smith, of Fayette county, Kentucky, bought from the herd of Mr. Miller the bull Buzzard 304 (3253), who was himself of mixed blood, being by a Short-Horn bull (the sire of Pluto), and out of a grade Long-Horn cow which had been purchased of Mr. Patton, Sr., before his removal to Kentucky. He is described as large and coarse, taller but not so heavy as Pluto. He proved to be no advantage to the stock of the country. The two Short-Horn crosses on bulls, procurable from the Pattons, furnished a better basis for breeders. "Inksip's Brindle," taken to Kentucky in 1813, was of like breeding to Buzzard. In 1814 Mr. Daniel Harrison brought into the country a pair of "Pied red and white," rather small, light-fleshed, raw-boned animals which were not much used. In the same year Hutcheraft and Wilton bought from the Shakers, of Kentucky, the bull Shaker 2193, which had come from Mr. Miller's herd, and was doubtless a thoroughbred Short-Horn.

From this stock has descended what is known as the Patton Stock.

THE COX IMPORTATION.

In 1816 Mr. Cox, an Englishman, imported into Rensselaer county, near Albany, N. Y., a Short-Horn bull and two cows. They had no recorded pedigrees. They were put upon the farm of Mr. Colden, and there bred for several years. Mr. Bullock, of Albany county, afterward purchased some of this stock, which was locally termed the "Bullock Stock." Many pedigrees in the American Herd Book end in "of the Cox, Colden, and Bullock stock," or "The Cox Importation."

THE SEVENTEENS.

The question is often asked, "What are the 'Seventeens?'" and "Why such a prejudice against them?" That there is a prejudice against them, whether imaginary or real, no one will deny. Almost the first thing a new beginner learns is, that he must not buy Seventeens, or animals with pedigrees containing blood of that importation, and when asked why not, many can only answer, "They are not fashionable."

When we consider that some of the finest show cattle on the continent are "Seventeens" it seems this prejudice is only a fanciful one, and surely is, when viewed in a practical light. If the Short-Horns of the Seventeen Importation had all been kept pure, and some of their descendants not been bred to bulls of other breeds or mixed blood, we doubt whether this prejudice would ever have existed.

In 1817 Col. Lewis Sanders, of Kentucky, imported twelve head of cattle — eight Short-Horns — four bulls and four heifers; four Long-Horns — two bulls and two heifers. The Short-Horns had no pedigrees, as that was five years before there was such a thing as a Herd Book; but they were represented as pure and without a blemish of outside blood in their compositions, as true Short-Horns from near the River Tees, the ancient home of the race. The Short-Horn bulls were: San Martin (2599), Tecumseh (5409), Comet 1382. The fourth one appears not to have been recorded in either the English or American Herd Books, and nothing is further known of him. The Short-Horn heifers were: Mrs. Motte, the Durham Cow, and the Teeswater Cow. The fourth one died before reaching Kentucky. Of the Long-Horn bulls, one was called Bright and the other Rising Sun, and recorded in the English Short-Horn Herd Book as number (6386). The cows were called: "The Long-Horned Cow" and Georgia Ann. Mr. Warfield, in his history of the Kentucky Short-Horns, published in the "Breeders' Gazette" of April 27th, 1882, says: "After landing at Baltimore they were sent into the country to await Mr. Sanders' orders, and were there joined by a pair of Herefords, imported by Henry Clay, the bull of which is recorded in the English Short-Horn Herd Book as number (3711). With them, they made the journey to Kentucky. Mr. Sanders had, in the meantime, failed in business, and before the arrival of the stock had sold one-third interest in them to Capt. Smith, one-third to Dr. Tegarden, and subsequently the remaining third to James Munday. Capt. Smith shortly afterward died. Dr. Tegarden moved to the southern part of the State, and the consequence was the stock was almost immediately scattered into numerous hands. The original Short-Horn cows produced at least twenty-six calves — all from Short-Horn bulls, except Pink, who was one-half Long-Horn. In the meantime, the Hereford and the Long-Horn cows were being carefully bred also, and various crosses between the three races were being tested. Examples of the various crosses have, in their descendants, found permanent record in the American Herd Book. The choice cows of the old cattle of the country — the Patton stock — already showing from one to three improved crosses, were also bred to the new bulls." Thus, it will be seen, the Short-Horns were not all kept pure, and those that were, being of the same importation and in bad company, soon had a bad name.

THE DUN IMPORTATION.

In 1833 Mr. Walter Dun, of Kentucky, imported several Short-Horns from England; among them were the cows Red Rose, by Ernesty; Caroline, by Dashwood; and Daisy, by Wild. The sires of these cows — Ernesty, Dashwood and Wild — had no numbers in the English Herd Book, but were, no doubt, well-bred bulls. They have since been recorded, under a certificate, in the American Herd Book as Ernesty 10017, Dashwood 9731, and Wild 11134. The above families are considered unfashionable by a few of our breeders, simply because their descendants have been crossed on some other families of a higher character; otherwise, we doubt if there ever would have been a prejudice against them. Some of the most noted show animals in America are descendants of these cows. We believe there has never been three cows imported that have been of as much benefit to the Short-Horn interest of America as Red Rose, Caroline and Daisy.

EXPLANATION.

P S means Patton Stock; ***COX,*** the Cox Importation; ***M,*** Mrs. Motte; ***T.*** the Teeswater Cow; ***D,*** the Durham Cow (of the Seventeen Importation); ***K Y I,*** Kentucky Importation, many animals tracing to a cross of or ending in "Tracing to the Kentucky Importation," meaning the importation of 1817; ***DAISY,*** Daisy by Wild: ***C,*** Caroline; ***R R,*** Red Rose, of the Dun Importation. Where animals are marked as tracing to one of the last three named cows, they contain no other unfashionable blood than that of the Dun Importation. ***L R,*** Lost Record, many pedigrees ending in "From the Imported Stock of Mr. ——," without showing a direct descent from the Imported animals; ***WOODS,*** animals supposed to not trace to any Importation. Animals with —— after the name means that there is a trace of such blood in the pedigree of that animal. For example, 231 Barmpton ——M (although a direct descendant of Imported Clarksville by Lottery), the grand-sire of his sire is a Mrs. Motte; and those without—— are a direct descendant of such animal, thus: 286 Broomdale M, descends from Mrs. Motte on the Dam's side. Numbers in parenthesis refer to the English Herd Book; open, to the American Herd Book, thus: Nicholas 115 (6248) is recorded in both Herd Books.

ERRATA

To avoid confusion the following corrections should be carefully noted with a pen in their proper places:

1403	Crampton — M	83160	Major — Cox
4964	Lord Renfrew — M		

The above three bulls should have been included.

(3253) Buzzard P S, not L R.
8620 Meteor — R R, not P S.
8741 Oxford — C, not Cox.
11956 Financier — R R, not R R.
14502 Horace — C, not L R.
14503 Horace — L R, not M.
20033 Invincible Duke 5th, not Imperial Duke 5th.
20036 Invincible Duke 6th, not Imperial Duke 6th.
20293 Loyal Duke of Shawnee, not Loyal Duke of Shannon.
21532 2d Duke of Windingvale, should be 21533.
22695 5th Duke of Briggsdale, should be 22694.
25416 Morning Boxer, not Morning Star.
28552 4th Baron of Riverside —Cox, not C.
30260 Should be Malcom Duke.
30908 Should be Runnemede Duke.
31192 Star Duke of Oakland, not Star Duke of Oxford.
31382 Werner — Cox, not C.
34640 Bridesman 2nd C, not P S.
37977 Clinton Grand Airdrie, not Clinton Grand Duke.
38089 7th Earl of Cedar Lawn — P S, not R R.
41464 Babraham's Roan Duke, should be 41465.
41871 Should be 7th not 4th Earl of Grass Hill.
44596 Pretty Patsy, — P S.
44597 Pride of Barrington, Cox.
44598 Pride of Brimfield, — D.
45931 3d Duke of Sac, Ky I.
47796 Dick Willis, should be 47795.

The following animals are included as tracing to R R, but by a recent correction in the Herd Book they do not, and should be erased:

9246 U. S. Grant.	12377 Malcom Miller.	16319 Bob Miller 3rd.
10116 Gen. Rawlins.	14846 Malcom Miller.	16338 Bourbon Peabody
11416 Bob Miller.	16318 Bob Miller 2nd.	17990 Prince.
	19305 Daisy Duke 2nd.	28789 Capt. Miller.

A

List of Unfashionable Pedigrees

IN SHORT-HORN CATTLE.

No.	Name	Code	No.	Name	Code
5	Alexis	— M	271	Bolivar	— D
12	Balfour	Ky I	272	Bolmer	M
25	Boston	M	275	Borodino	M
27	Boxer	— M	278	Bourbon	T
29	Boz	M	281	Barmpton	— M
35	Cataract	— L R	283	Brigham Young	— M
42	Comac	L R	285	Brock	— D
43	Comet	M	286	Broomdale	M
45	Cornplanter	L R	288	Brother Jonathan	T
53	Dragon	D	290	Bruce	L R
57	Eclipse	— M	291	Bruce	T
70	Hannibal	L R	295	Brutus	Daisy
73	Hatney	M	304	Buzzard	P S
77	Herdsman	D	309	Captain	— M
78	Hero	L R	313	Carleton	— Cox
98	Marcellus	M	314	Carson	Woods
101	Mastodon	D	316	Cassius	Ky I
106	Young Monarch	L R	323	Challenger	Ky I
115	Nicholas	D	325	Champion	M
119	Orestes	M	329	Champion 2nd	M
135	Prince Charles	Ky I	330	Chancellor	— C
136	Prince Frederick	— M	335	Chieftain	— L R
147	Remus	L R	335½	Childs' Bull	M
150	Roanoke	D	336	Clarence	— P S
155	Rover	L R	338	Clark's Bull	Ky I
159	Sarpedon	M	339	Clayton	M
165	Sultan	M	342	Clifford	— L R
178	Voltaire	D	343	Clifton	C
191	Accident	T	344	Clinton	C
192	Accident, Jr.,	M	346	Clinton	— M
196	Acmon	— L R	351	Colonel	— Ky I
199	Advance	D	355	Comet	M
206	Allen	M	360	Comet 2nd	Daisy
207	Allen	— R R	361	Comet 2nd	T
214	Androscoggin	L R	364	Compromise	M
215	Angus	— L R	366	Compromise	— R R
223	Atlantic	D	368	Congo	L R
224	Auburn	M	371	Constitution	— Ky I
230	Baron Larry	P S	377	Cossack, Jr	M
231	Baron Steuben	M	379	Count	M
232	Barrington	L R	386	Crowder	M
239	Bedford Duke	Cox	390	Cumberland	— T
246	Belvedere	M	391	Cupid	— L R
247	Belvedere	— M	404	Daniel Boone	— M
252	Ben Gratz	— M	405	Daniel Boone 2nd	R R
253	Ben Hardin	C	406	Daniel Webster	— R R
258	Berthune	C	409½	Decatur	— Cox
260	Bertram	— R R	413	Denton	M
261	Bertram 5th	M	414	Derby	Cox
269	Bloodgood	Daisy	415	De Soto	Daisy
269½	Bolingbroke	M	418	Diamond	Cox

No.	Name	Code	No.	Name	Code
419	Diamond	— L R	641	Lilard	C
420	Dick	— M	648	Locomotive	Daisy
424	Don	R R	649	Locomotive, Jr	— Daisy
428	Don Juan	Daisy	651	Locum	— D
430	Don Juan	M	653	London Lad	— Cox
431	Don Juan	M	654	Lookont	T
433	Doubloon	Daisy	656	Lopez	M
437	Dudley	— M	659	Lord Barrington	— Cox
438	Duke	— M	667	Lord Stanley	C
439	Duke	— M	671	Luther	D
441	Duke	Cox	676	Madison	M
452	Duke of York	L R	677	Magyar	P S
454	Duroc	M	680	Major	Ky I
455	Duroc	R R	689	Marquis of Bute	L R
467	Eclipse 2nd	Cox	690	Mars	— R R
469	Eclipse 3rd	— C	692	Marshal Suwarrow	M
471	Elonzo	C	695	Matty	M
473	Eminence	— L R	701	Mercer	M
479	Enterprise	P S	703	Mercury	— C
482	Exchange	M	704	Messenger	C
485½	Exeter	L R	707	Meteor	Cox
498	Favorite	Cox	708	Miami	L R
501	Fear Not	M	710	Milo	M
503	Fillmore	— M	711	Milo	Wrong
504	Fillmore	T	714	Mingo	Ky I
505	Fillmore	— T	715	Mirandi	M
506	Financier	M	716	Misfortune	M
507	Florentine	— M	719	Monarch	— M
509	Ford	M	726	Mountaineer	L R
514	Franklinton	T	727	Munday's Bull	Long-Horn
518	Garret Davis	— R R	730	Myrum	— R R
522	Gen. Butler	M	735	Napoleon	— L R
523	Gen. Cass	— M	736	Napoleon	R R
524	Gen. Marion	— M	747	New Years Day	T
527	Gen. Scott	M	748	Ney	T
528	Gen. Washington	M	749	Niagara	— L R
529	Gen. Washington	L R	752	Nicholas, Jr	— D
531	Gen. Wool	M	756	Norfolk	— M
534	Gold Dust	— R R	757	Northern Light	Cox
535	Gold Eagle	— R R	760	North Star	Cox
536	Goldfinder	— C	764	Ohio	— L R
538	Gold Hunter	— R R	765	Ohio	Ky I
540	Good Isaac	C	769	Oliver, Jr	D
542	Governor	L R	770	Oliver, Jr	T
543	Gov. Morrow	M	773	Oregon	Wrong
546	Grand Duke	Cox	777	Oregon	Wrong
547	Grand Duke	— Cox	782	Orion	M
548	Grand Duke 2nd	Cox	787	Orphan	— P S
551	Gray Eagle	M	788	Osceola	M
554	Haggin	T	792	Othello	D
555	Haggin 2nd	Woods	793	Otley 2nd	T
561½	Harry Lorrequer	L R	796	Owasco	M
563	Hector	M	801	Partnership	Woods
571	Henry Clinton	L R	803	Partnership	T
574	Hero	— Cox	804	Pascal Bruno	D
576	Higby	L R	806	Paul	C
594	Jasper	D	810	Perfection	— M
598	Jim Cropper	M	811	Peter	M
598¾	John Bull, Jr	L R	812	Peter	P S
601	John O'Gaunt, Jr	T	818	Pioneer	— R R
604	John Sutton	Ky I	819	Pioneer	T
606½	Junius	— M	820	Pioneer	M
608	King Cyrus	Ky I	825	Pluto	P S
616	Kossuth	P S	828¼	Powell	L R
617	Kossuth	L R	833	President	M
624	Lamartine	— M	838	Prince	D
626	Lamplighter	— M	840	Prince	M
632	Leonidas	M	848	Prince Albert	M
637	Lewellyn	L R	863	Prince D'Joinville	M
640	Lieber	Cox	868	Prince Hal	T

SHORT-HORN CATTLE PEDIGREES. 11

No.	Name	Herd
870	Prince of Bourbon	M
871	Prince of Orange	— L R
875	Prince of Wales	C
882	Rampart	— M
884	Ranger	D
889	Red Comet	— M
895	Red Rover	Cox
896	Reform	T
897	Reformer	Wrong
901	Remus	C
903½	Rensselaer	Cox
905	Rialto	Ky I
907	Richard Morrison	M
909	Rip Van Winkle	— L R
912	Roanoke	Daisy
916	Robin Hood	Cox
920	Rocket	L R
921	Rocket	— M
926	Romulus	— R R
942	Sam Patch	M
945	Sanders	L R
949	Scioto	— M
952	Second Diamond	— Cox
969	Sir Alfred	R R
971	Sir Don	— Milo 711
972	Sir Henry	D
973	Sir Henry Vane Tempest	M
974	Sir Humphrey	T
975	Sir Philip	Sire, Oregon 777
979	Slider	M
984	Snowball	L R
987	Snowstorm	P S
988	Socrates	M
989	Soldier	— C
990	Soldier	— T
992	Son of Comet Halley, Jr	T
994	Son of Duke of York	L R
994½	Southard	M
997	Splendor	— Long-Horn
998	Sportsman	M
999	Spot	T
1000	Squire	— Ky I
1002	Stanley	— R R
1006	St. Quintin	C
1012	Sultan	M
1013	Sultan	C
1015	Summit	L R
1020	Symmetry	— R R
1023	Tariff	M
1024	Taylor	— T
1026	Telegraph	— T
1027	Tempest	P S
1037	Tomahawk	— Cox
1038	Tom Marshall	M
1042½	Tribune	Ky I
1043	Triumph	D
1045	Troye	M
1049	Twin	D
1053	Tyro	M
1054	Ulric	T
1055	Uncas	— L R
1059	Valentine	D
1063	Van Buren	M
1065	Vandal	C
1066	Vice President	— M
1068	Victor	— Cox
1071	Virginia Andes	Woods
1074	Walters' Bull	M
1078	Wasson	L R
1081	Waterloo	M
1088	Wellington	L R
1089	Wellington	L R
1090	Wetherell	— R R
1096	White Eagle	— R R
1097	White Eagle	— R R
1099	Wickliffe's Bull	D
1101	Wm. O. Butler	— D
1110	Wonder	D
1112	Worth	T
1115	Yarborough	T
1119	Yorkshireman	— Cox
1126	Young Baronet	Wrong
1132	Young Comet	C
1136	Young Duke of Exeter	M
1138	Young Exchange	M
1140½	Young Goldfinder	P S
1143	Young Kossuth	M
1144	Young Mario	Ky I
1145	Young Marius	D
1146	Young Matchem	T
1148	Young Meteor	— Cox
1153	Young Oliver	M
1154	Young Oliver	M
1159	Young Romeo	— Oregon 773
1164	Young Wisconsin	— L R
1167	Yusef	C
1172	Achmet	C
1173	Afton	R R
1174	Ajax	D
1175	Ajax	Cox
1176	Ajax	P S
1179	Albert	T
1180	Albert	Ky I
1180½	Albion	M
1183	Alexander 2nd	T
1184	Alfred	R R
1186	Alfred	T
1188	Allen	Ky I
1190	Almonte	L R
1191	Almonte	Daisy
1192	Alonzo	M
1194	Altona	D
1201	Andes 2nd	Ky I
1202	Andrew Jackson	M
1203	Antler 2nd	Ky I
1205	Apollo	Ky I
1207	Archer	— M
1210	Arthur	M
1211	Arctic	— Daisy
1212	Ashland	Ky I
1215	Atchison	L R
1216	Atholl	— M
1219	Autocrat	D
1221	Avon	— P S
1224	Baltimore	— Ky I
1228	Baron Balco	Ky I
1232	Beaufort	— Cox
1234	Belfounder	— P S
1235	Bellerman	— M
1236	Belmont	— R R
1240	Belvedere	M
1244	Bellville	D
1248	Bem	P S
1254	Bethlehem	Cox
1257	Burmingham	Ky I
1260	Blucher	T
1262	Bob	P S
1266	Bolivar	— L R
1267	Bolivar	— L R
1270	Boston	— M

No.	Name	Mark
1271	Boston 2nd	Woods
1272	Boswell	Ky I
1274	Barmpton	M
1275	Brandywine	P S
1276	Breckenridge	D
1276½	Bridegroom	Ky I
1277	Brilliant	L R
1278	Brilliant Beau	D
1284	Brutus	M
1285	Brutus	M
1286	Brutus	D
1287	Brutus	M
1289	Buchanan	M
1290	Buchanan	Ky I
1295	Buckeye	M
1297	Buckeye Boy	— M
1298	Buck Morris	Ky I
1299	Buckner 2nd	M
1299½	Buena Vista	T
1303	Bunyan	Ky I
1305	Byron	— C
1306	Byron	— M
1307	California	Cox
1308	Caliph	D
1315	Captain	T
1319	Capt. Mackachack	Daisy
1322	Capt. Shannon	— Wrong
1323	Capt. Smith	P S
1325	Capulet	D
1326	Capulet	P S
1327	Caractacus	D
1330	Carlos	P S
1332	Cassius	M
1333	Cassius	M
1337	Cato	T
1338	Cato	M
1343	Champion	— M
1344	Champion	Cox
1345	Champion 2nd	M
1348	Chaos	T
1349	Chapman	Cox
1350	Charlie	L R
1351	Cherokee	T
1353	Chicago	D
1358	Chilton 2nd	— M
1359	Christie	Ky I
1360	Cicero	L R
1361	Cicero	M
1364	Clay	L R
1365	Clayton	M
1367	Clemont Hero	T
1369	Clifford	L R
1370	Clifton	C
1371	Clifton	P S
1374½	Coke	— M
1377	Col. Fremont	Cox
1379	Col. Sage	M
1382	Imp. Comet	Imported in 1817
1386	Comet, Jr.	Daisy
1388	Commodore	— Ky I
1392	Contract	M
1393	Copson	Cox
1394	Copway	Ky I
1396	Cornplanter	M
1399	Cossack	T
1404	Creole	C
1406	Croton	— M
1407	Crown Prince	L R
1412	Crusade 3rd	— D
1416	Cunningham	L R
1418	Cupid	— M
1420	Czar	C
1421	Dagobert	M
1425	Darby	— Ky I
1426	Darius	— M
1429	Dayton	L R
1432	Decatur	M
1433	Delaware	L R
1434	Derby	L R
1436	Diamond	— L R
1437½	Dick Bates	M
1438	Dick Dudley	— M
1439	Dictator	— Long-Horn
1441	Dictator	M
1442	Dejalma	T
1446	Donnelson	M
1447	Don Juan	C
1451	Doremus	L R
1452	Douglas	— M
1453	Douglas	M
1456	Drummond	— Cox
1458	Dudley	— L R
1461	Duke of Bourbon	Ky I
1466½	Duke of Bourbon	M
1467	Duke of Bourbon	Ky I
1474	Duke of Indiana	— Ky I
1475	Duke of Lancaster	M
1476	Duke of Lexington	M
1480	Duke of Orleans	— Long-horn
1484	Duke of Warren	T
1489	Durham 1st	L R
1490	Durham 2nd	L R
1493	Eagle	— R R
1498	Earl of Richmond	D
1502½	Eclipse	M
1503	Elbert	— P S
1504	Elector	M
1505	Elector	Ky I
1508	Embryo	— P S
1510	Emperor	R R
1513	Enterprise	C
1514	Enterprise 2nd	M
1517	Eucles	M
1520	Evening Star	— C
1520½	Excel	— R R
1521	Excelsior	C
1522	Exception	P S
1524	Exchange	— Daisy
1525	Exeter 2nd	L R
1526	Exeter 3rd	— Cox
1527	Exeter 4th	L R
1528	Exeter 5th	L R
1529	Exeter 6th	L R
1532	Fantichini 3rd	M
1533	Farmer	— M
1535	Favorite	— D
1536	Favorite 2nd	M
1537	Favorite	— M
1537½	Favorite	C
1538	Fawkes	T
1539	Fayette	Ky I
1540	Fayette	D
1541	Fayette	D
1542	Fair Day	P S
1544	Fairfax	Ky I
1547	Felix	Ky I
1548	Ferguson	Ky I
1551	Fillmore	T
1552	Fillmore	M
1553	Fillmore	D

1554	Fillmore	T	1703	John Elick	M
1556	Fillmore	M	1704	John Moore 2nd	P S
1562	Foljambe	C	1705	John Moore, Jr	— M
1565	Fourth Colonel	C	1708	John O'Gaunt	L R
1566	Fourth Diamond	Cox	1713	John Smith	T
1568	Fox Hunter	— R R	1714	Johnson Boy	— M
1569	Frank	M	1715	Jonathan	M
1570	Frank	— Ky I	1717	Josh Bell	M
1573	Frank	— D	1718	Julius	M
1574	Franklin	T	1720	June Bug	— M
1575	Frederick 2nd	L R	1721	Junot	M
1577	Fremont	L R	1723	Jupiter	Daisy
1589	General Butler 1st	— P S	1724	Jupiter	M
1592	General Hardin	T	1725	Jupiter	Ky I
1593	Gen. Harrison	— M	1727	Jupiter	— L R
1594	Gen. Scott	— Ky I	1728	Jurat	P S
1595	Gen. Scott	P S	1729	Jurist	— M
1597	Gen. Taylor	D	1730	Justice	P S
1599	Gen. Taylor	P S	1733	Kentuckian	D
1601	Gen. Taylor	T	1734	Kentucky	D
1603	Gen. Washington	— Ky I	1736	Keokuk	— R R
1604	Gen. Wool	M	1737	King Fantichini	M
1605	Gen. Worth	T	1741	King William	— Ky I
1607	George	— D	1745	Kirwan	Ky I
1608	George Combe	M	1746	Knickerbocker	R R
1609	George O'Gaunt	C	1747	Knox	Ky I
1611	George Third	— D	1749	Kosciusko	— T
1612	George Washington	L R	1750	Kossuth	P S
1613	Gibralter	— L R	1755	La Fayette	D
1615	Godolphin	C	1756	La Fayette	P S
1619	Goldfinder, Jr	L R	1758	Laudable	M
1622	Governor Vance	M	1760	Lauderdale	L R
1627	Grand-Son of 3rd D. of Camb'g	Ky I	1761	Lawson	M
1630	Haggins' Comet	T	1769	Leopold	— C
1632	Hampden	— Cox	1770	Lexington	— D
1633	Hamlet	Ky I	1777	Littleton	M
1634	Hamlet 2nd	Ky I	1781	Locomotive	L R
1636	Hanover	— M	1782	Locum	M
1636½	Harrison	P S	1783	Logan	— M
1637	Harrison	Ky 1	1785	Logan	P S
1642	Hacienda	— C	1787	Logan	— M
1643	Hawthorn	— Daisy	1789	Lopez	P S
1645	Haymaker	Ky I	1790	Lord Aberdeen	— T
1648	Hector	Ky I	1793	Lord Barrington 4th	— Cox
1650	Henry	D	1794	Lord Dufferin	— M
1651	Henry	P S	1796	Lord Eglintoun	D
1652	Henry Clay	L R	1797	Lord Erroll	P S
1653	Henry Clay	L R	1799	Lord Fitzclare	M
1654	Henry Clay	Ky I	1801	Lord Kenton	P S
1660	Hero	Cox	1805	Lord Raglan	L R
1661	Hero	— C	1808½	Lord Phillipe	L R
1662	Hiawatha	C	1809	Lowder's Bull 1st	— M
1673	Hoosier	— M	1810	Lowder's Bull 2nd	— M
1679	Hurricane	— D	1811¼	Lowder's Bull 4th	L R
1681	Iceland	L R	1815	Macarthur	M
1682	Illinois Emigrant	P S	1816	Maclean	T
1684	Ingles	P S	1817	Mad Anthony	T
1685	Ion	L R	1825	Major	T
1687	Ivanhoe	C	1830	Malcom	P S
1688	Ivanhoe	L R	1831	Malcom	Wrong
1689	Jackson	M	1834	Marion	— M
1691	Jacob Strader	Ky I	1836	Marius 3rd	L R
1692	Jake	L R	1837	Marius 4th	L R
1693	James Buchanan	M	1839	Marius 6th	L R
1694	James Buchanan	Ky I	1840	Marmion	Cox
1695	Japhet	P S	1841	Marmion 3rd	Cox
1698	Jewel	— M	1842	Marmion	L R
1700	John Bascom	— D	1845	Marquis	L R
1701	John C. Fremont	— Daisy	1849	Mars	L R
1701½	John Dun	R R	1850	Mars	P S

1851	Martin	M
1854	Master Winfield	M
1855	Matson	— M
1857	May Duke	C
1861	Melville	T
1862	Melvin	M
1863	Meninger	— C
1864	Menchikoff	M
1866	Mercer	M
1867	Merlin	T
1868	Merlin	P S
1870	Meteor 2nd	— Cox
1871	Miami	D
1874	Mill Boy	P S
1875	Milo	M
1876	Milo 2nd	M
1879	Mohawk	M
1880	Mohican	— T
1881	Moleskin	L R
1882	Monarch	P S
1884	Monarch	L R
1885	Monarch	M
1887	Monterey	Cox
1890	Montezuma	— L R
1891	Montgomery	— Ky I
1892	Mordicai	D
1893½	Morteer	D
1894	Mt. Hope	Cox
1896	Murat	M
1899	Napoleon	D
1901	Napoleon	P S
1903	Napoleon 2nd	Ky I
1905	Napoleon	— Cox
1909	Nebraska	M
1911	Ned Buntline	P S
1912	Ned Forrister	— R R
1914	Nelson	Cox
(1914)	Dennis-De-La-Motte	M
1916	Neptune	L R
1918	Neptune	L R
1919	Nero	Cox
1920½	Nero	M
1921	Newton	— R R
1922	New Years Gift	— M
1923	Niagara	Cox
1924	Niagara	M
1925	Nicholas	D
1927	Nick	M
1928	Nimrod	L R
1930	Nimrod 2nd	Ky I
1931	Noble	— R R
1934	Nobleman	M
1935	Nobleman 2nd	D
1937	Norfolk	— R R
1942	North Star	Ky I
1943	North Star	R R
1945	Novice	— M
1945½	Nowlin's Splendor	L R
1947	Oakum 2nd	D
1949	Ohio	Daisy
1949½	Olanden	M
1950	Old Bullion	— Long-Horn
1950½	Old Virginia	M
1951	Oliver	T
1952	Oliver	T
1953	Oliver	— R R
1954	Oliver	— D
1956	Ophir	— Daisy
1958	Orator	— L R
1960	Oregon	T
1965	Orontes	— C
1968	Orphan	L R
1969	Orphan Boy	P S
1972	Osage	C
1973	Oscar	— M
1976	Osceola	— M
1980	Ostrogoth	C
1983	Otho	D
1984	Otho	L R
1985	Ozark	Cox
1986	Ozello	T
1987½	Pacificator	M
1988	Paddy	M
1990	Pandum	— L R
1991	Paragon	— T
1993	Paramount	Daisy
1994	Paris	— M
1995	Paris	M
1996	Paris	Daisy
1997	Parson Pratt	P S
2000	Passenger	M
2001	Pathfinder	L R
2002	Pathfinder	L R
2003	Pathfinder	Ky I
2005	Patrick Henry	— Long-Horn
2007	Patrick Henry	T
2008	Patriot	D
2009	Patriot	— Long-Horn
2011	Paul Jones	Woods
2014	Pendes	— D
2016	Percy	— Ky I
2017	Perfection	L R
2018	Perfection	M
2020	Perfection	— M
2024	Philip	M
2025	Pilot	P S
2026	Pilot	R R
2027	Pilot	T
2028	Pioneer	L R
2029	Plantaganet	— P S
2031	Plato	M
2034	Pluto	P S
2035	Pompey alias Moh'k	— Long-Horn
2037	Pontiac	L R
2040	Potiphar	P S
2042	Powhattan	D
2043	Prairie King	Ky I
2044	Prairie State	P S
2045	Prentice	— M
2046	President	M
2048	President	— Long-Horn
2050	President	P S
2051	President	Ky I
2053	Priam	L R
2054	Pride of the West	M
2059	Prince	P S
2060	Prince	— D
2062	Prince	Ky I
2063	Prince	— Cox
2066	Prince Albert	— Cox
2067	Prince Albert	L R
2068	Prince Albert	— Cox
2069	Prince Albert	— D
2070	Prince Albert	— M
2071	Prince Albert	P S
2072	Prince Albert	M
2075	Prince Albert 3rd	— Daisy
2075½	Prince De Joinville	L R
2077	Prince George	Ky I
2078	Prince John	M

2079	Prince of Orange	— R R	2221	Sir Isaac	— Wrong
2084	Prince Rasselas	— C	2222	Sir John	— Wrong
2089	Rama	L R	2223	Sir John	D
2092	Randolph	— M	2227	Sir Temple	L R
2094	Ranger	Cox	2229	Sir Thomas	T
2097	Reconcile	M	2230	Sir Thomas	M
2099	Red Comet	Ky I	2232	Sir Warrior	Ky I
2100	Red Duke	D	2233	Sir Worthy	C
2103	Red Jacket	— C	2234	Snowball	M
2104	Red Jacket	M	2237	Snow Cloud	— M
2105	Red Jacket	— R R	2239	Snowdrift	— M
2107	Red Rover	C	2242	Solon	— Ky I
2110	Red Rover	D	2246	Specie	Ky I
2113	Reformer	M	2248	Splendor	P S
2114	Reformer	M	2249	Splendor	— L R
2116	Regent	— L R	2250	Splendor	M
2117	Relief	— L R	2251	Spot	T
2119	Remus	Cox	2253	Spy	Wrong
2120	Renick 2nd	— M	2254	Squire	Ky I
2121	Renshaw's Bull	L R	2255	St. Albans	P S
2123	Reuben	— R R	2257	Stanhope Burley	M
2124	Reuben 2nd	Daisy	2260	Star of the West	D
2125	Richard, or R. G. Jackson's Bull	L R	2262	Stephen A. Douglas	— M
2126	Richmond	P S	2263	Streshley	— Long-Horn
2129	Roan Darby	P S	2267	Strakosch	Ky I
2130	Roanoake	L R	2268	Sultan	— R R
2133	Robin 2nd	— M	2269	Sultan	— R R
2134	Rob Roy	— R R	2271	Sunrise	T
2136	Rochester	P S	2273	Superior	D
2137	Rock	— M	2275	Suwaroff	Ky I
2139	Rockingham	L R	2279	Tamerlane	R R
2140	Rockingham	L R	2282	Tecumseh 2nd	T
2142	Rockland	— L R	2284	Texas	M
2146	Roland	D	2285	Texas	M
2149½	Romeo	— M	2286	Thaddeus	P S
2151	Romulus	P S	2287	The Duke	C
2158	Rover	P S	2288	The Duke	— R R
2158⅓	Royal Archer	L R	2290½	Third Baron Larry	— P S
2160	Rozelle	T	2291	Third Colonel	R R
2161	Ruby's Halton	— Cox	2293	Thomas Bates	— R R
2167	Saginaw	L R	2295	Thompson's Bull	— M
2169	Sam Houston	— L R	2296	Thornton	T
2169½	Sam Patch	P S	2299	Tom Clagget	— Ky I
2172	Sampson	— M	2302	Tom Walker	P S
2177	Scott	— Ky I	2303	Tony Lumpkin	P S
2177½	Scott's Snowball	D	2305½	Tranby	— M
2185	Senator	M	2309	Triumph	P S
2186	Senator	M	2310	Troy Lad	L R
2189	Senator 4th	M	2312	Turk	D
2190	Senator 5th	P S	2314	Tutor	— M
2191½	Sergeant Chilton	— P S	2316	Twin	T
2192	Sevastopole	M	2318	Twin Duke	L R
2193	Shaker	P S	2324	Uncle Sam	P S
2195½	Shakspeare	— L R	2325	Valentine	M
2198	Sort-Tail 2nd	— M	2326	Valentine 1st	— L R
2199	Shropshire	T	2327	Valentine 2nd	— L R
2200	Shylock	P S	2328	Valentine 2nd	M
2201	Sidney	M	2329	Valentine 3rd	M
2202	Simon	C	2330	Valentine 4th	M
2203	Simon Kenton	— R R	2331	Valentine 5th	M
2205	Siroco	D	2331½	Valentine	D
2206	Sissera	D	2333	Van Buren	M
2210	Sir Charles	P S	2335	Vanguard	Ky I
2211	Sir Colin Campbell	R R	2337	Vernon	Ky I
2212	Sir David	— Wrong	2341	Victor	M
2213	Sir George	C	2342	Victor	— D
2217	Sir Harry	L R	2343	Victor	P S
2218	Sir Harry	M	2346	Victory	M
2219	Sir Harry 2nd	— D	2349	Volney	M
2220	Sir Hinton	Ky I	2351	Voltaire	M

2352	Vulcan — Long-Horn	2490	Alfred 4th ...T
2354	Warfield ...T	2491	Aladdin ...D
2356	Warwick ...D	2493	Alton ...P S
2358	Washington ...P S	2495	America — Cox
2359	Washington — Cox	2498	Andrew ...T
2360	Waterloo — L R	2503	Ariel ...L R
2361	Waterloo ...Cox	2513	Balco ...Cox
2365	Wellington 2nd ...L R	2515	Balco ...Cox
2368	Wellington ...P S	2516	Balco ...D
2369	Wellington 2nd ...L R	2519	Banker ...Ky I
2371	Wellington Hero — Cox	2520	Barchus ...Ky I
2373	Wesley R. ...P S	2523	Baron DeKalb ...D
2374	Wheat Ear — Cox	2526	Baron French ...M
2378	Whiteface ...L R	2529	Beadle ...L R
2380	White Jacket ...M	2530	Bedford ...M
2383	White Warrior ...Ky I	2534	Belmont — T
2390	Wolverine ...Cox	2537	Benedict ...D
2394	Wright's Bull ...M	2540	Berlin ...M
2396	York ...Cox	2541	Berthier ...M
2397	York ...L R	2542	Bethune ...C
2399	Yorkshireman — L R	2543	Belvedere ...C
2405	Young America ...L R	2546	Birmingham 3rd ...L R
2406	Young America ...Ky I	2547	Blazing Star ...M
2407	Young America — D	2549	Blucher — L R
2407¾	Young Archer 3rd ...L R	2551	Blucher ...L R
2410	Young Bellville ...Ky I	2552	Boatswain 2nd ...L R
2412	Young Bourbon ...Ky I	2553	Bob Bates ...Ky I
2414	Young Brutus ...M	2555	Bolingbroke ...Cox
2415	Young Brutus ...M	2557	Bolivar — Cox
2416	Young Byron ...Cox	2559	Bouncer ...Ky I
2417	Young Chilton 2nd ...T	2561	Bourbon — D
2418	Young Comet ...L R	2562	Bourbon — R R
2419	Young Comet ...Cox	2565	Brent — R R
2422	Young Cossack ...Ky I	2567	Brilliant — L R
2423	Young Crescent ...L R	2573	Bruno — D
2425	Young Enterprise ...P S	2573½	Brutus ...Cox
2429	Young Golddust — R R	2574	Brutus ...M
2431	Young. Kirk — Cox	2575	Brutus ...M
2434	Young Matchem ...D	2577	Buckeye ...R R
2438	Young Nero ...Cox	2579	Buckeye — L R
2439	Young Oakum — M	2579½	Buckeye ...Ky I
2440	Young Oliver ...T	2580	Buckeye — Cox
2441	Young Oliver ...M	2582	Buckingham ...M
2442	Young Olympus — D	2584	Bugler ...Ky I
2445	Young Oregon ...M	2588	Cabell Breckenridge ...P S
2446	Young Prince ...M	2590	Calvin — L R
2451	Young Sheffielder ...D	2593	Camillus ...Ky I
2451½	Young Splendor ...L R	2597	Capt. Baird — D
2452	Young Sultan ...T	2598	Capt. Crusader — P S
2454	Young Tempest ...M	(2599)	San Martin ...Imp. in 1817
2455½	Young Townley ...M	2600	Capt. White ...L R
2456	Young Warrior ...M	2601	Carcase 3rd ...L R
2458	Young Whig ...P S	2602	Carrol — T
2461	Zack Taylor ...L R	2603	Cass ...M
2462	Zack Taylor ...L R	2604	Cassius Clay — L R
2463	Zero — M	2608	Cato — L R
2467	Zwornick ...M	2610	Challenge — R R
2468	Zybee ...Long-Horn	2611	Challenger ...Ky I
2469	Aageson ...D	2614	Champion — Cox
2474	Admiral 2nd ...P S	2615	Champion ...Ky I
2475	Admiral 3rd ...Ky I	2616	Champion ...D
2476	Agamemnon — L R	2619	Chase — M
2477	Agricola — Cox	2624	Chickasaw ...M
2480	Albion ...Ky I	2626½	Chillon ...Cox
2481	Albion ...M	2627	Chimborazo — R R
2484	Alexander ...M	2631	Clarendon ...L R
2485	Alexander ...M	2633	Clarendon 2nd ...L R
2487	Alfred 2nd ...R R	2635	Claudius ...D
2488	Alfred 2nd ...M	2636	Clearchus — Cox
2489	Alfred 3rd ...T	2641	Collossus — L R

No.	Name	Mark	No.	Name	Mark
2643	Colonel	— L R	2786	Duke of Shelby	M
2647	Col. Devore	P S	2793	Duke of Woodford	M
2648	Col. Pierce	— M	2799	Duroc	D
2652	Comet	— L R	2803	Earl Derby	M
2654	Comet	D	2805	Earl of Nicholas	— Daisy
2655	Comet	M	2808	Echo of Venice	M
2656	Comet	M	2811	Eglinton	— M
2658	Commodore	P S	2812	Eglinton	— M
2660	Conductor	— L R	2818	Emigrant, Jr	P S
2661	Conqueror	— P S	2819	Emperor	M
2662	Constitution	Cox	2820	Emperor	D
2663	Continental	M	2821	Emperor	D
2667	Cortez	P S	2822	Empire	Ky I
2670	Cotopaxi	— R R	2824	England	L R
2671	Count Piper	L R	2827	Erin	— Cox
2673	Cripple	— P S	2828	Eugene	— M
2674	Croghan	D	2829	Everett	D
2676	Crusoe	— L R	2830	Excelsior	— Cox
2680	Cultivator	Ky I	2831	Exception	P S
2681	Cupid	L R	2832	Exchange	M
2682	Cupid	M	2834	Exeter	Cox
2683	Curd	Ky I	2835	Exeter	Cox
2684	Czarina	— C	2836	Expectation	M
2686	Damon 2d	Cox	2838	Falstaff	D
2687	Damon 3d	— Cox	2840	Fancy Boy	— Long-Horn
2688	Damon 4th	— Cox	2844	Favorite	M
2689	Dandy	— T	2846	Favorite	— Cox
2690	Dandy	— Cox	2849	Fayette	M
2692	Daniel Boone	M	2850	Fayette Dudley	D
2694	Darby Duke	Ky I	2853	Fielding	— Long-Horn
2695	Darius	— M	2854	Fillmore	P S
2697	Darlington	— D	2855	Fillmore	M
2699	Darlington 2d	— R R	2857	Financier	M
2700	Davis	M	2859	Fisher	Ky I
2702	Decatur 2d	M	2861	Florizel	L R
2703	Deceiver 2d	T	2864	Forest	R R
2705	Defiance	Cox	2865	Fortunatus	— M
2707	Delhi	Ky I	2866	Frank	Ky I
2708	Denton	M	2867	Frank	M
2710	De Soto	— C	2869	Franklin	— M
2712	Diamond	M	2872	Fred Douglas	— M
2716	Dillard	M	2885	Fremont	P S
2717	Dion	Woods	2886	Fremont	— T
2722	Don Cossack	L R	2889	Fremont	— M
2723	Don John	— Ky I	2895	Gano	R R
2724	Don John	Ky I	2899	Gen. Darlington	L R
2731	Douglas	— Ky I	2902	Gen. Pilcher	M
2735	Dudley	— M	2903	Gen. Scott	P S
2737½	Duke 2d	M	2904	Gen. Scott	— D
2738	Duke	M	2906	Gen. Taylor	P S
2739	Duke	Cox	(2907)	Accommodation	— M
2740	Duke	M	2908	Gen. Washington	L R
2743	Duke of Airdrie	R R	2909	Gen. Washington	M
2749	Duke of Bourbon	Daisy	2911	Gen. Wool	M
2750	Duke of Bourbon	M	2914	George	— M
2751	Duke of Bourbon	— C	2915	Gladiator	C
2752	Duke of Bourbon	C	(2917)	Acteon	— L R
2753	Duke of Boyle	Ky I	2918	Glindower	— Cox
2754	Duke of California	— R R	2919½	Gold Dust	P S
2759	Duke of Exeter	M	2920	Gold Eagle	L R
2761	Duke of Fayette	Ky I	2921	Goldfinder	— L R
2762	Duke of Florence	D	2921½	Goldfinder 2nd	— Ky I
2769	Duke of Kentucky	— Ky I	2923	Governor	— Cox
2771	Duke of Madison	P S	2926	Governor Grimes	T
2772	Duke of Marlborough	— Cox	2927	Gov. Jones	M
2775	Duke of Nicholas	— M	2928	Gov. Jones of Tenn	Ky I
2776	Duke of Norfolk	— M	2929	Gov. Matteson	P S
2777	Duke of Northgrave	Ky I	2934	Grand Duke	— R R
2781	Duke of Oxford	— L R	2936	Grand Turk	— Ky I
2785	Duke of Rockland	M	2937	Grantley	— Cox

UNFASHIONABLE CROSSES IN

2938	Grey Eagle	Ky I
(2942)	Agricola	— L R
2942	Greenholm Experiment	D
2946	Halton 2nd	— Cox
2947	Hamed	Ky I
2948	Hamlet	— C
2952	Harold	D
2953	Harold	D
2956	Harry A. Wise	P S
2957	Harry Clay	P S
2960	Hawthorn Duke — Long-Horn	
2961	Hector	— M
2964	Henrico	Cox
2975	Highland Chief	— L R
2977	Hiram	Ky I
2981	Homer	— P S
2982	Hoosick	Cox
2983	Howard	— Cox
2984	Hubback	D
2985	Hudson	Cox
2987	Humphrey Marshall	M
2989	Independence	— M
2990	Independence	— L R
2991	Independence	— Cox
2993	Ion 2d	T
2994	Ira	Ky I
(2994)	Alfred Allen	T
2996	Irone	Cox
2998	Islander	— D
3000	Ivanhoe	Ky I
3001	Jack Falstaff	Ky I
3002	Jack Hare	M
3003	Jackson	— M
3004	James Douglas	Ky I
3005	James	Ky I
3007	Jason Wallner	— T
3008	Jasper	M
3009	Javelin	M
3010	Javelin	— D
3011	Javelin	Ky I
3012	J. B. Howell	T
3013	Jeddo	P S
3016	Jim Bell	Ky I
3018	Joe	T
3019	Joe Vance	Ky I
3028	John Diamond	T
3029	Johnny Bull	M
3031	John O'Gaunt	L R
3032	John Wesley	T
3033	Jonathan	M
3034½	Joseph Brant	— Cox
3035	Josephus	L R
3036	Joe Smith	Cox
3038	Julian	— P S
3039	Julian	L R
3041	Julius	T
3047	Kendrick	P S
3048	Kentucky	— Ky I
3049	Kentucky Boy	L R
3051	Keokuk	T
3052	King of Trumps 2nd	L R
3054	King William	L R
3055½	Kirk	P S
3056	Kirk	L R
3058	Kosciusko 2nd	— T
3060	Landseer	Daisy
3062	Lath	Ky I
3063	Lavengro	T
3067	Leviathan	— D
3068½	Lexington	Ky I
3069	Lightfoot	R R
3071	Lincoln	P S
3076	Loco	Ky I
3078	Locomotive	— P S
3081	Logan	Daisy
3082	Longfellow	— D
3086	Lord Derby	— R R
3087	Lord Ellington	— Cox
3088	Lord Kintore	— P S
3093	Lord Raglan	— Cox
3094	Lord Raglan	— Cox
3096	Lou Allen	L R
(3097)	Baron Steuben	— M
3098	Louis	— L R
3100	Lowder's Bull 5th	T
3101	Lowder's Bull 6th	L R
3102	Lowder's Bull 7th	T
3103	Lowder's Bull 8th	L R
3105	Lowder's Bull 10th	L R
3107	Lowder's Bull 12th	M
3108	Lowder's Bull 13th	L R
3110	Machinery	— L R
3111	Mack	L R
(3111)	Bates	— M
3113	Major Duncan	L R
3116	Marsellus	— R R
3117	Marion	Ky I
3118	Mario	— Cox
3123	Mars	D
3124	Mars	— D
3125	Marshall	P S
3126	Marshall	— L R
3127	Marshall	— M
3128	Marshal Blucher	— L R
3129	Marshal Ney	— L R
3132	Martin	— D
3137	Master Charlie	— L R
3142	Master Snowden	M
3144	Matchem	P S
3148	May Duke	— M
3149	Medalist 3rd	Daisy
3151	Menander	
3152	Menifee	M
3153	Menifee	P S
3156	Messenger	Cox
3157	Meteor 3rd	L R
3158	Meteor 4th	L R
3160	Miami	R R
3161	Micajah	M
3163	Milo	— L R
3167	Moctezuma	R R
3172	Monarch	— P S
3173	Monarch	Ky I
3176	Morgan	C
3177	Morgan	— M
3178	Morgan	M
3179	Moslem	Ky I
3180	Mountaineer	— Cox
3181	Mozart	— C
3182	Mudjeekeewis	Cox
3183	Musard	— Cox
3184	Napoleon	— L R
3186	Napoleon	P S
3188	Navajo	Cox
3189	Nelson	T
3190	Nelson	Ky I
3193	Neptune	— M
3194	Neptune	— L R
3197	Nero	— M
3200	New Years Day	— L R

SHORT-HORN CATTLE PEDIGREES. 19

No.	Name	Ref.	No.	Name	Ref.
3201	Nicholas	— R R	3322	Raphael	— L R
3202	Nimrod	L R	3327	Red Chief	— Cox
3203	Noble	L R	3330	Red Gauntlet	Daisy
3205	Norfolk	— D	3333	Red Perfection	M
3207	Normans Kill	Cox	3336	Red Simon	— C
3208	North Ben	Ky 1	3340	Renick 2nd	T
3210	Nortwick	Cox	3342	Renovator	T
3213	Oakdale	Ky I	(3344)	Charles	P S
3215	Olanden	— M	3344	Richard Booth	M
3215½	Old Defiance	— Cox	3346	Richard M. Johnson	L R
3216	Ole Bull	R R	3348	Richmond	D
3218	Olympus	R R	3352	Roan Pioneer	M
3219	Orator	D	3360	Roderick	Ky I
3221	Orion	— M	3361	Roderick	Ky I
3222	Orion	— L R	3363	Roderick Dhu	— M
3223	Orion	M	3364	Rodolph	L R
3232	Ossahinta	Cox	3365	Roebuck	Ky I
3234	Othello	T	3366	Roger D	— D
3235	Othello	— L R	3367	Roger Hanson	— M
3236	Otley	— M	(3369)	Chieftain	T
3237	Otley 2nd	— P S	3372	Rolland	M
3238	Oxford	— L R	3375	Romeo	Cox
3244	Panic	M	3376	Romeo	L R
3245	Paul Clifford	P S	3377	Romeo	— M
3247	Pawnee	D	3378	Romeo	Cox
3250	Pedro	Cox	3383	Roscius	D
3251	Pekin	Ky I	3384	Rosette's Cayuga	— Cox
3252	Pendleton	M	3385	Rover	M
3253	Perfection	M	(3387)	Clan Albin	An Ayershire Bull
(3253)	Buzzard	L R	3387	Rover	L R
3255	Perfection	— P S	3388	Rover	M
3256	Perfection	Ky I	3389	Royal Duke of White Hall	— T
3257	Perfection Jr	M	3390	Royal Favorite	D
3258	Perfect Perfection	D	3391	Royal George	Cox
3261	Peyton Castleman	Ky I	3392	Royal Matson	Ky I
3263	Pilot	R R	(3394)	Clarke	D
3264	Pilot	M	3396	Rudolph	— D
3266	Pindar	T	3397	Rush	M
3267	Planter	T	3398	Russian	Ky I
3268	Plato	L R	3402	St. Lawrence Jr	Woods
3270	Pontiac	M	3404	St. Louis	T
3271	Pope	Cox	3405	St. Louis	P S
3273	Powell	M	3406	St. Nicholas	P S
3274	Prentice	R R	3408	Sam	T
3275	Prentice	— M	3409	Sampson	L R
3276	President	M	3410	Sampson 2nd	Cox
3280½	Prince	L R	3411	Sam Slick	L R
3281	Prince	M	3414	San Juan	— P S
3283	Prince	L R	3415	Santa Anna	T
3286	Prince Albert	Cox	3416	Santa Claus	Ky I
3287	Prince Albert	M	3418	Scipio	P S
3289	Prince Albert	M	3420	Sebastopol	Ky I
3292	Prince Albert	P S	3422	Senator	M
3294	Prince Arthur	— Long-Horn	3423	Senator 6th	M
3299	Prince Edward	D	3424	Sevastopol	— C
3300	Prince Edward	— D	3426	Seward	— M
3304	Prince Logan	Daisy	3427	Sexton's Whittington	M
3305	Prince of Bourbon	C	3428	Seylon	Ky I
3309	Prince Oscar	— M	3429	Shepherd	— M
3310	Prince Royal	T	3430	Sherwood	M
3311	Printer	Ky I	3431½	Sir Arthur	— Ky I
3312	Prize Fighter	L R	3432	Sir John	Ky I
3313	Progress	Ky I	3433	Sir John	T
3313½	Punch	L R	3436	Sir Charles Napier	— Cox
3314	Punch	M	3438	Sir Henry Havelock	T
3316	Quality	— M	3439	Sir Robert 2nd	L R
3319	Rumbler	M	3440	Sir Robert Alexander	— R R
(3320)	Champion	T	3444	Snowball	— Cox
3321	Runwokx	P S	3444½	Snowball	Ky I
(3322)	Champion	M	(3448)	Commodore	D

UNFASHIONABLE CROSSES IN

No.	Name	Code
3449	Snowball	Cox
3450	Snowball	Ky I
3451	Snowball	P S
3455	Solon	T
3456	Son of Goldfinder	T
3459	Spencer	P S
3461	Splendor 2nd	— P S
3462	Sportsman	Ky I
3465	Spotted Rover	— T
3468	Starlight	D
3469	Star of the West	M
3470	Star of the West	L R
3472½	Sultan	Cox
3473	Summit	L R
3474	Sumner	— T
3474½	Sumner	— M
3476	Sun Rise	— Ky I
3477	Superior	Ky I
(3479)	Contention	— M
3479	Suwarrow	— Cox
3481	Tara	— C
3482	Tarlton	— T
3483	Tarquin	— D
3484	Telegraph	M
3485	Tempest	Wrong
3486	Tenbroeck	— P S
3487	Texas	M
(3492)	Corn Planter	M
3492	Thomas Marshall	— R R
3498	Tim Day	T
3500	Tolono	M
3501	Tom Crib	— Cox
3504	Townley Jr	Ky I
3505	Trenton	— P S
3507	Triumph	— R R
3508	Trumbull	M
3509	Trumpet	— L R
3510	Trumpeter	R R
3512	Turk	Ky I
(3513)	Cox Bull	L R
3515	Uncas	— L R
3516	Uncas	T
3517	Uncle Sam	M
3519	Uncle Sam	Cox
3521	Union	— D
3524	Valley Duke	M
3525	Vance	M
3526	Velvet Duke	— M
3528	Victor	— Cox
3529	Victor	Ky I
3530	Vitellus	— Daisy
3531	Volcano	— Daisy
3532	Von Rudolph	P S
3534	Wagner	— M
3537	Walton	— M
3538	Warburton	T
3538½	Warrior 2nd	— M
3539½	Washington	Cox
3543	Waubonsa	— M
3544	Wayne	Cox
3545	Wentworth	— Cox
3547	Western Chief	M
3548	Westerner	M
3551	White Comet	Daisy
3554	White Eagle	Ky I
3555	White Eagle	T
3556	White Otley	M
3558	Whitler	P S
3563	Winfield	Woods
3564	Winfield Scott	— L R
3565	Woodburn 2nd	M
3567	Wyandotte Hero	L R
3571	Young Accident	P S
3572	Young America	L R
3573	Young America	M
3575	Young America	Cox
3576	Young Andes	D
3577	Young Archer	— L R
3578	Young Baltimore	D
3580	Young Ben	D
3582	Young Buckeye State	Ky I
(3583)	Denton	M
3584	Young Colonel	— Daisy
3585	Young Crescent	P S
3586½	Young Defiance	— Cox
3587	Young Don	— R R
3590	Young Duke	Ky I
3590	Young Duke	M
3591	Young Exception	D
3592	Young Farmer	M
3593	Young Favorite	— Cox
3594	Young Gold Dust	— R R
3595	Young Governor	L R
3596	Young Halton	L R
3597	Young Highlander	L R
3606	Young Morgan	D
3607	Young Nero	Cox
3608	Young North Star	Cox
3610	Young Prince Albert	L R
3612	Young Symmetry	— M
3616	Young Wellington	D
3618	Zeodor 2nd	Ky I
3619	Zeodor 3rd	P S
3620	Zoroaster	P S
(3622)	Drone	Ky I
3623	Abdallah	Ky I
3625	Abe Lincoln	Ky I
3626	Abe Lincoln	M
3627	Abe Lincoln	P S
3628	Abe Lincoln	— P S
3631	Ajax	Cox
3632	Ajax	Ky I
3633	Albion	D
3634	Albinus	M
3635	Alexander	Ky I
3636	Alfred	T
3638	Alfred 2nd	— Ky I
3639	Alfred 5th	T
3640	Allardyce	M
3641	Alpha	— M
3642	Alpha	— Ky I
3644	American Eagle	Ky I
3645	American Comet	Cox
3646	American Comet	— Ky I
3647	Apollo	M
3648	Arbitrator	— P S
3652	Avon	T
3653	Balco	— P S
3655	Bandy	L R
3656	Banner Boy	Ky I
3657	Banta	M
3658	Barney	D
3659	Baron Martin 4th	— M
(3660)	Dumfries	An Ayershire Bull
3661	Barre	— L R
3663	Beau of Kilkerby	P S
3665	Belgrave	P S
(3666)	Duroc	M
3669	Belvedere	Cox
3670	Ben Fulton	— P S

3672	Benica Boy	Cox	
3673	Ben Wade	— M	
3678	Black Hawk	— T	
3679	Black Hawk	D	
3681	Blucher	— L R	
3682	Blucher	M	
3683	Blue Buck	— Cox	
3691	Bourbon	M	
3692	Bourbon	M	
3695	Brachman	— D	
3697	Bravo	— Cox	
3698	Breckinridge	P S	
3699	Breckinridge	T	
3700	Brian Born	D	
3701	Bridegroom	— Cox	
3708	Brother Jonathan	P S	
3709	Brunducium	— L R	
3710	Brutus	M	
(3711)	Embassador	A Hereford Bull	
3712	Brutus	— M	
3713	Buccancer	Ky I	
3714	Buchanan	P S	
3716	Buckeye Boy	— Long-Horn	
3717	Buckeye Boy	M	
3719	Buckonghelas	Ky I	
3721	Bullfinch	— Cox	
3722	Butterfly	— M	
3726	Captain	P S	
3727	Capt. Crusade 2nd	Ky I	
3728	Capt. Dalgetty	Ky I	
3729	Capt. Harper	P S	
3730	Capt. Lincoln	— L R	
3731	Capt. Lincoln	— L R	
3732	Capt. Moore 2nd	Daisy	
3734	Capt. Starlight	M	
3735	Cassius	M	
3736	Cassius M. Clay	Ky I	
3737	Cato	M	
3738	Cato 2nd	P S	
3740	Challenger 2nd	— R R	
3741	Champion	— D	
(3746)	Exception	Ky I	
3748	Chattanooga	R R	
3749	Chantauque	— L R	
3751	Chester	P S	
3756	Clarendon 2nd	T	
3757	Claridon	Ky I	
3758	Clay	— D	
(3760)	Fantastical	— M	
(3763)	Farmer	— P S	
3765	Col. Dunlap	P S	
3766	Col. Taylor	P S	
3767	Col. Wentworth	— Cox	
3769	Colusi	— M	
3770	Comet	Ky I	
3771	Comet	— T	
3773	Comet	Ky I	
3776	Commodore	D	
3778	Commodore	M	
3778½	Commodore Decatur	—. M	
3781	Conqueror	— L R	
3782	Conrad	T	
3784	Corsair	D	
3789	Crescent Duke	— D	
3791	Crittendon	— R R	
3792	Crowder	M	
(3794)	Financier	— D	
3794	Crusader	Ky I	
3795	Crusade 2nd	— L R	
3796	Cuba	— Cox	
3797	Cumberland	— T	
3799	Cyrus	— M	
3803	Daisy 7th's Echo of Oxford	— Cox	
3804	Damon	— Ky I	
3807	Dante	T	
3808	Darby 3rd	Ky I	
3809	Darby Duke	C	
3811	Darlington 2nd	— L R	
3812	Dave	— M	
3813	David Jones	P S	
3814	Day Break	— Daisy	
3815	Dean	P S	
3816	Deceiver	— M	
3817	Deceiver	T	
3819	Denton	— M	
3821	Dick Yates	Ky I	
3822	Dick Yates	— P S	
3824	Dillie Wiggand	M	
3826	Doctor	— Cox	
3827	Dr. Buckingham	P S	
3828	Dr. Johns	P S	
3829	Dr. Kane	M	
3830	Doesticks	Ky I	
3831	Don	— D	
3832	Doniphan	— T	
3834	Douglas	— L R	
3835	Douglas	M	
3836	Douglas	P S	
3838	Duke	— Cox	
3847	Duke of Athol	— R R	
3848	Duke of Andrain	P S	
3949	(Should be 3849) Duke of Bourbon	— M	
3860	Duke of Illinois	M	
3863	Duke of Licking	— D	
3864	Duke of Malakoff	— L R	
3867	Duke of Mellery	D	
3869	Duke of Newberry	T	
3874	8th Duke of Northumberland	L R	
3875	Duke of Ohio	M	
3876	Duke of New Orleans	M	
3877	Duke of New Orleans	— Cox	
3878	Duke of Oxford	Ky I	
3883	Duke of Plumwood	C	
3889	Duke of Southwick	— P S	
3892	Duke of the West	D	
3893	Duke of Waterloo	Cox	
3895	Duke of Windhane	Cox	
3898	Duncan Gray	— C	
3899	Duroc	M	
3905	Early Bird	Ky I	
3906	Eclipse	M	
3907	Edward Bates	P S	
(3909)	Gold Finch	T	
3910	Emperor	D	
3911	Emperor	M	
3912	Emperor	D	
3913	Enforcement	P S	
3914	Equinox	Ky I	
3915	Ernest	P S	
3916	Esterville	Ky I	
3919	Exile Jr	M	
3922	Fancy Boy	— M	
3924	Farmer Boy	— M	
3925	Favorite	— M	
3926	Favorite	— Ky I	
3927	Fayette	— Long-Horn	
3931	Field Marshall	P S	
3933	Fillmore Jr	M	
3937	Forest	M	

3938	Franc	M	(4070)	Independence	L R
3940	Frank	— R R	4070	John Cotton	M
3941	Frank	P S	4073	John M. Harlin	— M
3943	Frederick	M	4077	Julius	L R
3944	Gamboy	P S	4080	Kankakee	— Ky 1
3945	Garibaldi	D	4081	Kansas	M
3947	Garibaldi	P S	4082	Kenton	L R
3949	(Should be 3849) Duke of Bourbon	— M	4083	King Cup	R R
			4084	King Philip	— Cox
3949	Garibaldi	P S	4085	King William	M
3953	Garibaldi	— L R	4088	Kit Carson	Cox
3954	Garibaldi	— T	4093	Lawrence 5th	M
3955	Garibaldi	M	4095½	Lincoln	— M
3956	Garrard	M	4096	Lincoln	D
3958	Gen. Green	P S	4097	Lincoln	P S
3964	Gen. Taylor	M	4098	Lincoln	Cox
3967½	Geo. M. Patchin	Ky 1	4101	Lindsay's White Bull	M
3968	Gid Butler	M	4102	Linton	M
3969	Glaucus	M	4103	Lion	— P S
3972	Goldfinder	M	4104	Little Grant	T
3973	Governor	D	4106	Livandias	T
3975	Gov. Chase	T	4107	Livingston	M
3976	Gov. Dennison	— M	4108	Locomotive	— D
3977	Gov. Dennison	— M	4109	Logan	— P S
(3979)	Harrison	— P S	4110	Lord Byron	— Daisy
3979	Gov. Letcher	M	4111	Lord Eglinton 2nd	— D
3980	Gov. Wise	P S	4113	Lord Highland	— R R
3981	Gov. Wood	D	4116	Lord Mansfield	— M
3982	Gov. Worthington	M	4117	Lord Napier	— P S
3983	Gracchus	Ky 1	4120	Lord Renfrew	— M
3984	Grand Duke	D	4121	Lord Spencer	D
3985	Grand Duke	— R R	4123	Lotos	R R
3986	3rd Grand Duke	— Cox	4125	Lowder's Bull 14th	T
3995	Guthrie	M	(4126)	Julius Caesar	L R
3996	Hacker	P S	4126	Lowder's Bull 15th	— M
4002	Hannibal Hamlin	Ky 1	4127	Lowder's Bull 16th	L R
4007	Harrold	— R R	4128	Lowder's Bull 17th	M
4008	Hautboy	Cox	4129	Lowder's Bull 18th	M
4009	Havelock	M	4130	Lowder's Bull 19th	— L R
4010	Hawkeye	D	4132	Macduff	T
4012	Hector of Plymouth	M	4133	McGillvary Lad	— Cox
4013	Henderson	P S	4135	Magic	P S
4014	Hercules	Cox	4137	Major	— M
(4016)	Herdsman	D	4138	Major	— L R
4017	Hershel V. Johnson	M	4139	Major	Ky 1
4019	Hiawatha	P S	4141	Major Anderson	— M
4023	Hickory	P S	4143	Major Anderson	Ky 1
4024	Holland	— M	4147	Major Belleville	— D
4027	Honest Abe	M	4148	Major Worth	— Cox
4029	Horatio	L R	4151	Mariner	— M
4032	Hudson	— Cox	4153	Marion	— L R
4039	Independence	— D	4154	Marquis	— L R
4040	Independence	M	4155	Mars	— L R
4045	Italy	— T	4157	Master Butterfly	— Ky 1
4046	Ivanhoe 2nd	— L R	4160	Master Harry	— D
4049	Jack	M	4162	Matchem	— L R
4051	Jack Slaughter	— P S	4163	Maynard Upstart	— M
4052	Jackson	M	(4165)	Kleber	— Long-Horn
4053	Jackson	Ky 1	4166	Medalist	Ky 1
4054	Jack Tar	— Ky 1	4168	Merriman	D
4057	John	— M	4171	Miami 2nd	R R
4058	Jericho	Woods	4172	Miles Standish	— Cox
4060	Joe Helm	T	4173	Milton	M
4061	Joe Lane	— P S	4174	Minstrel	— M
4063	John Bell	P S	4176	Model	— L R
4064	John Bell	P S	4179	Monroe	M
4065	John Bell	M	4180	Montezuma	M
4066	John Bell	T	4181	Mortimer	— M
4067	John Bell	— R R	(4182)	Lannes	T
4069	John C. Heenan	— T	4187	Nero	— Cox

4189	Nimrod	— R R	4323	Roguish Roan	L R
4190	Nimrod	P S	4324	Romeo	P S
4191	Nobleman	T	4326	Romeo	M
4192	Norfolk	— D	(4327)	Magnum Bonum	— M
4197	Oakwood Duke	— M	4327	Roscoe	— M
4199	Odus	P S	4330	Rover	— D
4201	O K	P S	4331	Rover	L R
4202	Olentangy Duke	— Long-Horn	4332	Royal Butterfly	— Cox
4204	Omega	— M	4333	Royal Cambridge	— Cox
4206	Oregon	— L R	4335	Royal Duke	— Cox
4207	Oriole	D	(4336)	Majestic	— M
4210	Orontes of Nicholas	— R R	4339	Royal George	M
4212	Orphan Boy	— Daisy	(4340)	Major	T
4213	Orphan Boy	T	4340½	Ruby's Oxford	— Cox
4214	Orr	— M	4341	Sacramento	M
4222	Paragon	↝ R R	4343	St. John	— M
4223	Paris 2nd	— M	4344	Splendor	Ky I
4224	Patterson's 4th Duke of Airdrie	— D	4346	St. Lawrence	— M
4226	Peet	— Cox	4350	Sam	D
4227	Perfection	— P S	4352	Sam Slick	Ky I
4228	Perfection	M	4353	Santa Anna	P S
4230½	Peter	Ky I	4357	Senator	D
4232	Pilgrim	L R	4359	Shasta	Ky I
4234	Pilot	L R	4361	Shawnee	Ky I
4235	Planet	— P S	4363	Shelton	M
4236	Planet	— M	(4367)	Marion	— M
4237	Planet	— T	4369	Simon	M
4238	Planet	L R	4372	Sirius 2nd	M
4239	Planet	P S	4373	Sirius 3rd	M
4240	Plenipotentiary	Ky I	4375	Sirius	L R
4241	Plutarch	— M	4376	Sir Lesley	— M
4244	Porphyry	D	4377	Sirloin	— M
(4245)	Lofty	P S	4379	Sir William	— M
4245	Prairie Farmer	M	4382	Snowball	P S
4248	President	D	4383	Snowball	R R
4249	President	Ky I	4387	Solon	D
4251	President 2nd	M	4393	Squire John	— M
4256	Primus	— M	4394	Star	Ky I
4258	Prince	T	4395	Starled	D
4261	Prince Edward	— Ky I	4398	Starry	Ky I
4266	Prince of Clydesdale	— L R	(4399)	Marshal Suwarrow	L R
4267	Prince of Dubuque	P S	4401½	Steve Douglas	M
4268	Prince of Iowa	Ky I	4407	Summit	— Ky I
4269	Prince of Monroe	M	4410	Sumter	— D
4270	Prince of Ninevah	L R	4412	Tam O'Shanter	T
4271	Prince of Oakland	— T	4414	Tecumseh	L R
4277	Prince of Wales	P S	4415	Tempest	T
4278	Prince of Wales	— Cox	4416	Thames	M
4280	Prince of Wales	M	4417	The Duke	M
4281	Princeps	M	4418	The Duke	Ky I
4284	Prince Starlight	— M	4420	The Marquis 2nd	— D
4287	Punch	— M	4425	Tom Breeze	Ky I
4288	Rail Splitter	M	4426	Tom Corwin	P S
4290	Rambler	M	4428	Tom Corwin	Daisy
4291	Red Bill	— M	4429	Tom Sayers	— Cox
4294	Red Diamond	P S	4430	Trojan	— P S
4297	Red Ike	L R	4431	Trimble	— D
4298	Red Jacket	— L R	4432	Troubadour	— M
4302	Regent Prince	— Long-Horn	4433	Tunis	Cox
4304	Remus	— P S	4435	Uncas	— Long-Horn
4307	Renfrew	P S	4436	Uncle Bill	Ky I
4309	Rescue	Ky I	4437	Uncle Sam	Ky I
4310	Revenue	— P S	4438	Uncle Sam	— M
4314	Risingham	— L R	4440	Union	Ky I
4315	Roan	Ky I	4441	Union	M
4316	Roan Jasper	M	4442	Union	Ky I
4317	Robert	M	4446	Valley Prince	Ky I
4318	Rob Roy	— M	4449	Veritas	— M
4319	Rob Roy	— D	4450	Vermont	— P S
4322	Roger Williams	— Long-Horn	4451	Victor	— P S
			4453	Virginia	M

No.	Name	Code	No.	Name	Code
4456	Wagner 2nd	M	4583	Billy Bryant	M
4459	Warrior	M	4585	Blanchard	L R
4462	Washington	— M	4590	Boston	M
4463	Washington's Day	Daisy	4593	Boxer	Ky I
4464	Webster	— R R	4596	Brigadier	M
4465	Wellington	— D	4597	Brigadier	— D
4465½	Wellington	T	4599	Briton	Ky I
4466	Whig	T	4601	Bruce	M
4467	White Cloud	Ky I	4602	Bruce, Jr	Ky I
4468	White Cloud	M	4603	Brutus	— Daisy
4469	White Cloud	M	4604	Brutus	Cox
4471	White Flag	P S	4605	Brutus	— D
4475	White Oak	P S	4606	Brutus	Ky I
4476	White Rock	Ky I	4607	Buckeye	Cox
4477	White Stockings	L R	4608	Buckeye	Ky I
(4478)	Milo	T	4609	*Buckeye Lad	M
4478	White Stockings	P S	4613	Bullion	— Daisy
4479	White Warrior	— L R	4614	Bunker Hill	— L R
4481	Whittington 2nd	P S	4615	Burlington	M
4484½	Windsor 2nd	D	4622	Cambridge Duke	D
4485	Winfield	— Long-Horn	4624	Capt. Blue	— M
(4488)	Mirandi	T	4625	Capt. Clay	— Cox
4488	Wolviston	— Ky I	4632	Cedric	— Cox
4489	Woodland Duke	— M	4633	Champion	Cox
4490	Woodland Duke	M	4635	Champion	Cox
(4492)	Mohawk	M	4638	Chandler	— P S
4492	Wyoming	— L R	4642	Chevalier 2nd	Cox
(4493)	Monica	P S	4643	Chillicothe	Daisy
4493	Wysox	L R	4645	Clarendon 3rd	T
4493½	Wysox 2nd	L R	4647	Clay	— P S
4495	York	L R	4652	Col. Andrews	M
4496	Young America	P S	4653	Col. Barnes	— R R
4500	Young Champion	Ky I	4654	Col. Beaty	— M
4503	Young Comet	M	4655	Col. Candy	— L R
4507	Young D'Jalma	M	4656	Col. Croxton	— D
4509	Young Duke	M	4658	Col. Harlan	— C
4512	Young Exile	P S	4659	Col. Judy	— L R
4514	Young Governor	— M	(4661)	Paul Jones	
4518	Young Nelson	— M	4661	Col. Prall	— R R
4519	Young North Star	Cox	4662	Col. Warner	— R R
4521	Young Pilot	— D	4664	Comet	— R R
4526	Young Thornberry	— P S	4666	Commodore	— Cox
4527	Young Townley	Ky I	4670	Commodore Foote	— D
4533	Zack Taylor	M	4671	Commodore Gerrard	M
4537	Zip Coon	— M	4673	Conqueror	— L R
4538	Abe	Ky I	4674	Cornet	Cox
4539	Abe Lincoln	D	4676	Cortland	— Cox
4540	Abe Lincoln 2nd	M	4678	Count Starlight	— P S
4541	Accident	M	4679	Crittenden	— M
4542	Airdrie	⁓ D	4680	Cromwell	D
4543	Ajax	Cox	4681	Crusader	— M
4545	Alfred	T	4684	Cyrus	— R R
4547	Alfred of Mallery	P S	4685	Daisy Boy 2nd	P S
4548	Alonzo	— R R	4687	Delaware	L R
4549	Alpheus	M	4688	Dennis	L R
4550	Alphonso	— R R	4695	Doctor Franklin	Wrong
4551	Amazon	— Cox	4697	Don Pedro	C
4554	Ashtabula	— Ky I	4698	Douglass	T
4556	Balco	L R	4700	Drover	— L R
4561	Baron of Oxford 3rd	P S	4701	Drummer Boy	M
4564	Bassanio 4th	C	4702	Dubuque	M
4569	Beauregard	P S	4705	Duke	P S
4572	Belvedere	Cox	4706	Duke	Cox
4573	Belvedere	L R	4708	Duke	T
4575	Bem	— Ky I	4709	Duke	— Cox
4576	Ben Bolt	M	4716	Duke of Alva	D
4577	Ben Bolt	— M	4719	Duke of Berwick	D
4580	Bertrand		4722	Duke of Cumberland 2nd	— L R
4581	Billy Bluff	L R	4723	Duke of Cumberland 3rd	— L R
4582	Billy Bright	— M	4728	Duke of Gloster	— L R

SHORT-HORN CATTLE PEDIGREES. 25

No.	Name	Ref.
4731	Duke of Jefferson	— Cox
4734	Duke of Laurens	D
4735	1st Duke of Logan	Daisy
4736	2nd Duke of Logan	— R R
4737	3rd Duke of Logan	— R R
4738	4th Duke of Logan	— R R
4740	Duke of Manlius 2nd	L R
4750	Duke of Tecumseh	— Ky I
4754	Duke of Warren	— D
4756	2nd Duke of Waterloo	— Cox
(4762)	Priam	P S
4767	Earl Grey	— Long-Horn
4776	Earl of Stuyvesant	Cox
4779	Elbert (alias Mohammed Ali)	— P S
4781	Embargo	— Ky I
4782	Emperor	— Cox
4784	Enchanter	D
4785	Enchanter 2nd	M
4786	Endorser	— P S
4789	Ebulus	— L R
4790	Excelsior	R R
4792	Fairfax	— R R
4793	Fairy Boy	L R
4795	Favorite	— P S
4798	Foreman	Ky I
4799	Frank	M
4807	Garibalda	— R R
4810	Geo. B. McClellan	— R R
4811	Geo. Washington	R R
4812	General	— M
4813	Gen. Beatty	— M
4814	Gen. Beauregard	— C
4815	Gen. Buell	D
4816	Gen. Burdside	— M
4818	Gen. Butler	M
(4820)	Prince Frederick	M
4821	Gen. Fremont	— D
4822	Gen. Grant	R R
4823	Gen. Grant	— R R
4827	Gen. Halleck	M
4828	Gen. Hooker	D
4830	Gen. Hunter	Ky I
4831	Gen. Joe Hooker	— D
4832	Gen. Lyon	— Daisy
4833	Gen. McClellan	R R
4834	Gen. McClellan	— M
4835	Gen. Morgan	M
4836	Gen. Pope	— Cox
(4838)	Proclamation	M
4838	Gen. Rosecrans	R R
4839	Gen. Rosecrans	M
4842	Gen. Sigel	— P S
4843	Gipsey Boy	— Ky I
4844	Gloster	— T
4845	Goldfinch	P S
4846	Governor	— T
4850	Gov. Tod	— D
4851	Grand Admiral	— Daisy
4853	Grand Bashaw 2nd	— L R
4854	Grand Bashaw 3rd	— Cox
4855	Grand Bashaw 4th	Cox
4859	Grand Duke of Cambridge	Cox
4864	3rd Grand Turk	L R
4865	Granger	— L R
4866	Grantham	— D
4867	Grove	Cox
4869	Guelph	Cox
4870	Halleck	Ky I
(4871)	Ranter	— T
4872	Hamlet	M
4875	Hanover	— P S
4878	Harkaway	— Cox
4879	Harry	M
4880	Harve Edwards	M
4882	Hawkeye	M
4885	Hector	Ky I
4886	Henry 2nd	— L R
4887	Henry Clay	T
4888	Henry Clay	M
4889	Hero	— R R
4892	Hero	T
4893	Herod	T
4897	Highland Chief	— D
4899	Hooker	— D
4906	Independence	M
4907	Iowa	— T
4908	Ira Moore	M
4912	James	— L R
4914	Jeff Davis	Cox
4915	Jewell	— Long-Horn
4916	Jim Lane	D
4917	Joe	— M
4918	John Bell	— R R
4919	John Bell 2nd	— R R
4924	Joe Hooker	— M
4926	Julio	L R
4928	Jupiter	Ky I
4929	Kansas	— M
4931	Keokuk	M
4932	King Alfred 2nd	M
4933	King Corn	M
4934	King Cotton	M
4935	Lang	M
4936	Laramie	— M
4939	Lincoln	Ky I
4940	Lincoln	— T
4941	Lincoln	Cox
4942	Lincoln	L R
4943	Lippard	— R R
4943½	Little Bear	— R R
4944	Locomotive	Ky I
4945	Logan	M
4946	Logan	T
4947	Lorain	T
4948	Lord Barrington 2nd	— L R
4950	Lord Derby	— Cox
4951	Lord Lovat	M
4953	Lord Lyons	M
4955	Lord Monck	— Cox
4959	Lord Palmerston	— Cox
4960	Lord Portman	— Cox
4963	Lord Renfrew	— Cox
4965	Lord Vernon	— M
4966	Lord Walpole	M
4967	Lowder's Bull 20th	— T
4968	Lowder's Bull 21st	T
4969	Lowder's Bull 22nd	— T
4970	Lowder's Bull 23rd	— T
4971	Lowder's Bull 24th	— T
4972	Lowder's Bull 25th	T
4974	Loyalist	— P S
4977	Mac	P S
4979	McHenry Duke	Ky I
4980	Madison Duke	P S
4982	Major	— L R
4983	Major	— M
4984	Major	— L R
4987	Major Anderson	M
4989	Marco	T
4990	Marengo	M

4998	Marshall	P S	5147	Rosseau	L R
5004	May Duke	M	5148	Round Eye	P S
5007	Miami Duke	C	5149	Rousseau	— M
5011	Miner	— M	5150	Rover	— R R
5012	Mirandi	— M	5151	Rover	M
5015	Monarch	— Cox	5153	Rover	T
5018	Monitor	M	(5158)	Sir Henry	D
5020	Monitor	— L R	5159	Rutledge	— L R
5022	Monitor	— L R	5160	Sailor	— Cox
5024	Mortimer	Daisy	5161	Sam Patch	— L R
5028	Napoleon	M	5162	Sam Walker	Ky I
5030	Napoleon	M	5164	Sangamon Duke	P S
5031	Ned Buntline	L R	5165	Saurin	M
(5034)	Rufus	T	5166	Saxon Prince	P S
5034	Nero	Ky I	5169	Seneca	Ky I
5035	Nestor	L R	5170	Seneca Lad	Cox
5036	New Years Day	— D	5171	Sertorius	— L R
5038	Nimrod	— M	5173	Seward	— L R
5039	Noble	Ky I	5174	Sidney	M
5041	Northampton	T	5176	Sigel	T
5043	Odd Trick	D	5179	Sir Arthur	M
5044	Oliver	— R R	5183	Sir Henry Havelock	T
5044½	Opothobolo	— R R	5184	Sir Robert Alexander 2nd	— R R
5046	Orator	— Cox	5187	Sir William Wallace	M
5047	Oregon	— R R	5188	Shaker	M
5048	Organist	— Cox	5190	Shawnee Chief	C
5049	Orion	L R	5192	Sherman	— C
5052	Otho	Ky I	5193	Shiloh	— M
5054	Oxford	— Cox	5194	Sirloin 2nd	Cox
5059½	Pascoria	— R R	5196	Snowstorm	— M
5061	Pathfinder Jr	M	5197	Snowstorm	— M
5064	Perfection	M	(5198)	Sir Walter	— M
5065	Perfection 2nd	— Cox	5199	Son of Scottish Crusader	— R R
5068	Peter	M	5202	Speck's Orpheus	Ky I
(5069)	Sam Patch	M	5203	Splendor	— L R
5070	Peter	— Ky I	5208	Starlight 5th	— M
5072	Pioneer	M	5210	Starlight 7th	— M
(5073)	Sambo	P S	5211	Sterling	M
5073	Plato	— M	5212	Steve Douglass	M
5075	Pope	L R	5214	Stonewall	— M
5080	Primus	Cox	5215	Stonewall Jackson	— P S
5082	Prince	— Cox	5216	Stonewall Jackson	Ky I
5083	Prince	M	5219	Sumter	P S
5084	Prince Albert	M	5222	Taurus	— Long-Horn
5091	Prince of Cortland	— Cox	5224	Tippecanoe	M
5101	Prince Porter	P S	5229	Trabuc	M
5103	Progenitor	M	(5230)	Snowball	— Hereford
5104	Puritan	M	5233	Uncle Sam	— R R
5106	Rambler	Cox	5234	Union	M
5107	Rattler	Cox	5235	Union	— L R
5109	Rebel	— L R	5236	Union Duke	Cox
(5111)	Shannon	— L R	5237	Usurper	— Cox
5111	Red Count	M	5238	Utah	M
5112	Red Duke	— D	5243	Victor	M
5113	Red Duke	— M	5245	Victor Emanuel	— M
5114	Red Jacket	— Ky I	5246	Voucher	Ky I
5116	Red Jacket	— L R	5248	Wagram	— P S
5118	Red Prince	— Long-Horn	5251	Warrior	— Cox
5123	Reliance	— M	(5252)	Son of Cicero	L R
5124	Renick	— R R	5254	Washoe	L R
5125	Renick	P S	5256	Waterloo	— M
5127	Richard	— L R	5257	Waterloo	— Cox
5128	Ringold	— D	5259	Waxaw	— L R
5132	Roan Count	M	5263	White Count	M
5137	Robert Anderson	M	5266	Wm. Tell	M
5139	Rockland	L R	5268	Woodland Duke	M
5140	Roderick 2nd	L R	5270	Wrangler	— Cox
5143	Rosecrans	— L R	5274	Young America	— M
5145	Rosecrans	— D	5276	Young Comet	M
5146	Rosecrans	— M	5277	Young Comet	Ky I

No.	Name	Herd	No.	Name	Herd
5278	Young Daisy Boy	— Cox	5403	Bruce	— P S
5279	Young Duke	Cox	5405	Brutus	L R
5280	Young Duke	Ky I	5406	Bubona	Woods
5282	Young Marion	M	5407	Buckeye	— M
5283	Young North Star	Cox	5408	Buckeye Chief	— Long-Horn
5285	Young Townley	P S	(5409)	Tecumseh	Imp 1817
5286	Young Troubadour	M	5409	Bulwer	— L R
5292	Zeodor Jr	M	5412	Cadmus	L R
5293	Zollicoffer	D	5414	Comanche	— C
5298	Abe Lincoln	R R	5415	Canada Punch	— Cox
5299	Adam	M	5416	Canadian Chief	— Cox
5300	Admiral	— M	5417	Canefield 5th	C
5307	Aladdin	T	5419	Canefield 7th	C
5308	Albert	— D	5422	Canefield 10th	C
5309	Alexander	— R R	5425	Canefield 13th	C
5310	Alexander	— M	5427	Captain	— P S
5312	Alfred	— D	5428	Captain Gray	— Long-Horn
5315	America	M	5433	Casimar	R R
5316	Anderson	C	5434	Castor	— Cox
5318	Andover	— P S	5435	Cecil	— M
5319	Andy	M	5437	Cinnaminson	— L R
5320	Andy	— M	5444	Chevalier 2nd	Cox
5321	Ansel	— P S	5445	Chevalier 3rd	Cox
5322	Anson	— P S	5446	Chief Justice	— L R
5323	Anvill	— P S	5449	Clarendon 2nd	R R
5324	Apolacon 2nd	L R	5451	Clifton Duke 2nd	— C
5329	Artemus Ward	— R R	5455	Colonel	— M
5336	Bainbridge	— L R	5457	Col. Cunningham	M
5337	Balco	— Cox	5458	Col. Ellsworth	M
5338	Balco	M	5459	Col. Ellsworth	M
5339	Balco	Cox	5461	Col. Haskins	— M
5340	Baltic	T	5463	Col. Oakley	— R R
5342	Barnet	— M	5465	Col. Woodford	M
5344	Baron Bold	C	5468	Comet	C
5351	Bassanio 6th	C	5470	Comet	M
5353	Beauregard	P S	5473	Commodore	M
5354	Bedford	— T	5475	Conductor	— L R
5355	Belden	— L R	5476	Conjuror	L R
5356	Bell Balco	Ky I	5477	Conqueror 2nd	— L R
(5359)	Superior	— Long-Horn	5479	Conscript	— P S
5359	Belligerent	M	5480	Conservitude	— R R
5361	Belmont	M	5482	Consternation	— L R
5363	Belvedere	Cox	5483	Corinth	— Cox
5365	Ben Butler	— L R	5484	Count Pulaski	M
5366	Ben Butler	— D	5485	Coupon	— D
5367	Benham	— L R	5486	Crooktail	— M
5369	Berry Bolt	— M	5489	Crusader Boy	Ky I
5370	Bill Bolt	— M	5490	Crystal Count	— P S
5371	Billy	Cox	5491	Czar 2nd	— C
5372	Bill Martin	— L R	5492	Dairy Boy 3rd	P S
5373	Bill Rea	— P S	5495	Dan Sickles	Daisy
5376	Bob Dun	R R	5496	Dapple	C
5377	Bob Lee	Woods	5499	Deacon Dorset	Ky I
5378	Bob Lee	— P S	5500	Defiance	— L R
5379	Bob McGrew	M	5502	DeSoto	— C
5381	Bonaparte	T	5507	Dick Richardson	P S
5383	Bonny Chase	T	5509	Dick Whiting	P S
5384	Bon Ton	R R	5512	Douglas	— L R
5387	Boston	— Cox	5518	Duke	Ky I
5388	Bourbon	M	5519	Duke	— M
5389	Bourbon 2nd	— M	5520	Duke	— Long-Horn
5390	Bourbon 3rd	— M	5522	2nd Duke	M
5391	Bourbon Champion	— R R	5523	Duke Albert	— R R
5392	Bourbon Duke	— R R	5525	Duke Frederick	C
5393	Bourbon Duke	— M	5530	Duke of Airdrie Jr	M
5394	Boxer	M	5531	3rd Duke of Airdrie	M
5395	Boxer	R R	5538	Duke of Anderson	— Daisy
5396	Boyle	P S	5542	Duke of Avon	— D
5401	Briton	— P S	5544	Duke of Bedford	— C
5402	Bruce	Cox	5546	Duke of Bourbon	— R R

5547	Duke of Bourbon...M	5694	Gen. Legett...— R R
5551	Duke of Clark...— M	5696	Gen. Logan...— L R
5552	Duke of Clark 2nd...— R R	5697	Gen. Logan...— D
5554	Duke of Clifton...— D	5698	Gen. Moore...— P S
5555	Duke of Dundale...C	5699	Gen. R. E. Lee...— C
5556	2nd Duke of Dundale...P S	5702	Gen. Sheridan...— M
5558	Duke of El Hakim...— C	5704	Gen. Sheridan...M
5559	Duke of Exeter...— R R	5706	Gen. Sherman...— R R
5560	Duke of Fayette...— M	5707	Gen. Sherman...— L R
5565	Duke of Harrison...— R R	5708	Gen. Sherman...R R
5570	Duke of Highland...— R R	5710	Gen. Scott...M
5571	Duke of Iowa...— M	5712	Gen. Terry...L R
5572	Duke of Illinois...M	5713	Gen. Thomas...R R
5573	Duke of Kent...— R R	5714	Gen. Thomas...— R R
5574	Duke of Knox...P S	5715	Gen. Turk...— Cox
5576	Duke of Logan...M	5718	Gen. W. T. Sherman...— R R
5577	4th Duke of Logan...Daisy	(5720)	Aladdin...T
5578	5th Duke of Logan...Daisy	5721	Glasgow Duke...M
5579	6th Duke of Logan...Daisy	5723	Gold Duke...R R
5582	1st Duke of Madison...Ky I	5725	Gold Finder 3rd...— Ky I
5586	Duke of Marengo...Daisy	5729	Grand Duke...Ky I
5591	Duke of Millersburg...— D	5736	Granville Duke...— Ky I
5592	Duke of Montgomery...L R	5739	Groveland...— P S
5593	Duke of Norfolk...— C	5742	Gwynne Duke...— Cox
5594	Duke of Oak Grove...— R R	5754	Ham...M
5595	Duke of Oglesby...— Cox	(5755)	Andrew...D
5597	14th Duke of Oxford...L R	5758	Hancock...— D
5599	Duke of Park Farm...L R	5759	Hanson Jr...— L R
5603	Duke of Rosedale...— L R	5760	Hearts of Oak 2nd...Ky I
5604	Duke of Sharon...— L R	5762	Heber...M
5607	Duke of Stone...— R R	5764	Henderson...P S
5612	Duke of Wayne...— Cox	5765	Hendon...— P S
5613	Duke of Wellington...Daisy	5766	Henry 3rd...— L R
5615	Duncan's Airdrie...— R R	5767	Henry 4th...— L R
5616	Dunderberg...Ky I	5768	Henry Clay...M
5617	Dupage...Cox	5770	Hercules...— L R
5618	Earl...— L R	5771	Hercules...P S
5623	East Lick...— P S	5772	Herndon...— P S
5624	Eclipse 2nd...— D	5774	Hero...L R
5629	Emperor...— L R	5775	Hero...— Cox
5631	Enterprise...P S	5776	Hero...— Ky I
5632	Ericsson...Cox	5790	Highland Duke 2nd...— Daisy
5637	Fayette...— L R	5791	Highlander...Cox
5641	Field Marshal 2nd...P S	(5795)	Billy Button...P S
5644	Floriel...M	5795	Holkham...Cox
5649	Fox...L R	5796	Homer...T
5652	Franklin...— R R	5797	Hoosick...Cox
5654	Frederick...— L R	5800	Idaho...— M
5658	Gasquet...T	5802	Ike Marvel...M
5664	Gen. Fisk...— C	5804	Ingot...R R
5665	Gen. Franklin...— Daisy	5807	Israel...C
5667	Gen. Goe...— Cox	5810	Jack Bolt...Ky I
5668	Gen. Grant...— C	5811	Jack Cade...R R
5669	Gen. Grant...— R R	5812	Jack Frost...R R
5670	Gen. Grant...— L R	5814	Jackson...D
5672	Gen. Grant...— P S	5817	Jacob Strawn...— D
5673	Gen. Grant...M	5818	Jallapa 2nd...Ky I
5674	Gen. Grant...— D	5819	Jasper...— Daisy
5675	Gen. Grant...— R R	5820	Jeb Stuart...Woods
5676	Gen. Grant...L R	5821	Jeff...P S
5677	Gen. Grant...Cox	5822	Jeff Davis...R R
5681	Gen. Grant...— L R	5824	Jefferson...D
5682	Gen. Grant...Ky I	5826	Jim Bolt...Ky I
5684	Gen. Grant...— L R	5827	Jim Finley...— L R
5686	Gen. Grant 3rd...Cox	5828	Jim Lane...— M
5689	Gen. John H. Morgan...— C	5829	Jock...L R
5690	Gen. John Morgan...— M	5830	John Bell 2nd...— R R
5691	Gen. Lander...— Cox	5831	John Bell 6th...— R R
5692	Gen. Lander 2nd...— Cox	5832	John B Floyd...— M
5693	Gen. Lee...— M	5836	John C. Breckenridge...P S

No.	Name	Mark	No.	Name	Mark
5838	John M. Harlan	— M	6007	Octus	— L R
5841	John R. Bryant	— M	6008	Okalona	— Ky I
5847	Julian	L R	6010	Oliver	P S
5848	Junius	M	6011	Oliver	— L R
5849	Jupiter	P S	6012	Oliver 2nd	M
5851	Kelburne	— M	6014	Orphan Boy 3rd	— Daisy
5852	Kentucky	M	(6018)	Florain	Cox
5853	Kilpatrick	— D	6022	Patriot	Cox
5854	King George	M	6023	Perfection	T
5856	King of Kansas	Ky I	6026	Phil Sheridan	— D
5862	Klippart	— D	6028	Phil Sheridan	— D
5865	Lafayette	— T	6032	Planter	M
5868	Lame Broken Leg	— R R	6039	Powhatan	Daisy
5874	Letton	— M	6040	Prairie	— R R
5875	Lexington	— R R	(6042)	Gold Bud	T
5877	Liberator	Cox	6042	Prairie Duke	M
5880	Little Giant	M	(6044)	Gold Snap	T
5883	Little Phil	Cox	6045	Primus	— L R
5884	Locofoco	C	6048	Prince	— P S
5885	Logan	— M	6051	Prince	— Cox
5892	Lord John	— Cox	6052	Prince Ardee, Jr	Cox
5893	Lord John	— Cox	6054	Prince Ernest	Cox
5897	Lord Logan	— P S	6055	Prince Ernest	Cox
5905	Lord Willoughby	M	6058	Prince Louis	— R R
5908	Lowder's Bull 27th	— M	6059	Prince Napoleon	M
5909	Lowder's Bull 28th	L R	6060	Prince of Bourbon	— D
5910	Lowder's Bull 29th	— M	6065	Prince of Wales	M
5911	Lowder's Bull 30th	T	6066	Prince of Wales	— Cox
5913	Lowder's Bull 32nd	— M	6070	Prince Starlight	— L R
5914	Lowder's Bull 33rd	T	(6072)	Henry Clay	— L R
5915	Loyal Duke	— D	6073	Prince Virgil	M
5918	Mack-A-Cheek	R R	6079	Ralph	M
5919	Macaroni	— Cox	6080	Randolph	— P S
5921	Major	— L R	6082	Rebel	P S
5922	Major	— Ky I	6083	Rebel	P S
5923	Major	— M	6084	Red Diamond	P S
5925	Major Anderson	L R	6088	Red Duke	M
5926	Major Duncan	— R R	(6090)	Indian Chief	D
5927	Major Duncan	— R R	6090	Red Duke	M
5928	Malcom	M	6091	Red Duke	— T
5936	Marmion	— R R	6092	Red Duke	— L R
5938	Mars	P S	6094	Red Jacket	Cox
5948	May Duke	— D	6095	Red Jacket	— R R
5952	Melnotte	— M	6096	Red Jacket	— Cox
5955	Menifee	— M	6097	Red Jacket	— M
5957	Miami Duke	R R	6098	Red Jacket	— M
5958	Mike Hooter	R R	6100	Red Jacket 2nd	Cox
5960	Minstrel	— M	6102	Red Prince	— Long-Horn
5963	Monarch	— L R	6103	Red Rover	— Cox
5966	Monitor	Cox	6104	Red Rover	M
5967	Monitor	Ky I	6105	Red Rover	— R R
5968	Monitor	Ky I	6108	Reformer	P S
5969	Monitor 2nd	Cox	6109	Remus	— M
5970	Montezuma	Cox	6110	Renick	— T
5973	Morning Star	— L R	6111	Renick 2nd	— T
5974	Morris	— D	6113	Reuben	— M
5978	Mozart	— Cox	6114	Revenge	— R R
5979	Murat	Cox	6116	Richmond	— L R
5981	Mystic	— M	6117	Rickets	T
5982	Napoleon	— M	6122	Roan Duke 2nd	L R
5983	Napoleon	P S	6124	Rob Anderson	— M
5984	Neosho	— D	6125	Rob't Moorman	P S
5986	Neptune 2nd	— Cox	6126	Robin	T
5988	Nero	M	6127	Robin Hood	P S
5990	Nestor 2nd	L R	6129	Rob Roy	— Cox
5992	Newland	Daisy	6130	Roger	— L R
5993	Newton	— L R	6133	Roman	Ky I
5995	Nicholas	— Wrong	6134	Romeo	Cox
5996	Nicol Jarvie	— M	6135	Romeo	C
6004	North Star 2nd	Cox	6136	Romeo	P S

6137	Romeo 5th...Cox	6286	Washington 4th...Daisy
6140	Rosecrans...— L R	6290	Weah...M
6143	Rover...— M	6291	Wellington...Cox
6144	Rover...Cox	6294	White Cloud...L R
6148	Rover...— M	6295	White Duke...— P S
6153	Ruby...M	6296	White Jacket...— Cox
6154	Rush Floyd...P S	6308	Wellington...— T
6158	Sailor...— Cox	6309	Willis...M
6165	Schofield...M	6310	Wright...— M
6170	Senator...Daisy	6311	Yankee Boy...M
6173	Septus...— P S	6312	Yorick...— L R
6174	Seward...— Cox	6314	Young America...— M
6177	Sheridan...— R R	6315	Young America...M
6178	Sheridan...Cox	6317	Young Bourbon...M
6180	Sherman...— R R	6319	Young Chevalier...Cox
6181	Shinn...— R R	6324	Young Duke...— L R
6183	Sir Charles...— M	6325	Young Hendon...— M
6184	Sir Edwards...M	6326	Young Hero...Cox
6187	Sir Highland...— M	6327	Young Hickory...— P S
6188	Sir Roderick...— Cox	6329	Young North Star...Cox
6189	Sir Wm. Wallace...M	6336	Young Yorick...— L R
6190	Smiley...— P S	6337	Zinganee...R R
6191	Sky Rocket...D	6338	Andy Johnson...M
6192	Snowball...R R	6340	Clark's Duke...— R R
6196	Son of Wallace...L R	6341	Comet of Melleray...D
6198	Spartan...Cox	6342	Commodore...P S
6199	Spears Duke...M	6344	Diamond of Melleray...P S
6200	Splendor...Cox	6353	Gen. Grant...P S
6201	Splendor...— D	6354	General Sherman...D
6206	Star Duke...M	6355	Girard...L R
6207	Starlight...Ky I	6356	Glendale...— P S
6208	Starlight 3rd...D	6357	Illinois Duke...— M
6209	Starlight 3rd...— L R	6361	Major Anderson 2nd...— L R
6211	Starlight 11th...— M	6364	Nimrod...C
6213	Starlight Best...— Long-Horn	6365	Novus...— L R
6215	Statesman...Cox	6366	Orpheus 4th...Cox
6216	Steelyards...— M	6368	Red Prince...L R
6221	Stonewall Jackson...— P S	6373	Rover of Melleray...T
6223	Stonewall Jackson...T	6374	Sirius 3rd...Ky I
6224	Stonewall Jackson...— M	6375	Stephen A. Douglas...M
6225	Strafford...D	6378	Tycoon...T
6228	Sultan...L R	6380	U. S. Grant...— Ky I
6229	Superior...— M	6382	Abel...C
6231	Sylla...Cox	6383	Accident...Ky I
6238	Tecumseh...Cox	6384	Admiral...— L R
6239	Tennyson...T	6385	Admiral...— Daisy
6242	The Duke...M	(6386)	Rising Sun...Long-Horn
(6244)	Nero...P S	6386	Admiral...— C
6245	The Parson...Ky I	6387	Admiral 3rd...Ky I
6247	Thistle...— Cox	6388	Eneas...R R
(6248)	Nicholas...D	6389	Aid-De-Camp...P S
6251	Toland...— R R	6391	Airdrie...— R R
6252	Toland 2nd...D	6392	Airdrie Duke...— R R
6254	Tom Corwin...— R R	6393	Ajax...L R
6255	Tom Hood...— R R	6396	Albert...Daisy
6256	Tomogonops...— Cox	6397	Albert Victor...— Long-Horn
6257	Traveller...— L R	6399	Alexander...— Cox
6262	Trumbull Starlight...Cox	6400	Alexander...L R
6266	Union...— L R	6402	Alex. H. Stephens...M
6267	Union Duke 2nd...M	6404	Alfred...Ky I
6269	Van Buren...M	6405	Alhambra...C
6271	Victor...— M	6409	Andes...Ky I
6273	Victor...— M	6410	Andy Johnson...Cox
6274	Victor 7th...C	6411	Andy Johnson...P S
(6277)	Partnership...L R	6412	April Duke...Ky I
6277	Virginius...R R	6413	Arbie...L R
6278	Volunteer...C	6415	Argus...P S
281	Wappello Duke...M	6416	Armedale...— L R
6284	Washington...P S	6418	Arthur...— Ky I
6285	Washington 3rd...Daisy	6419	Astute...— Cox

6421	Atlantic	— R R	6521	Cassius	— R R
6422	Atlantic	— D	6524	Cato	P S
6423	Atlantic Duke	Daisy	6525	Cato	Ky I
6424	Australian Tom	— L R	6527	Cedric	R R
6425	Azrim	— Daisy	6528	Champaign	Ky I
6426	Badger Boy	Ky I	6529	Champion	— M
6428	Barney	— L R	6529½	Champion	Cox
6429	Baron Hylton	P S	6531	Charles Garrard	M
6433	Basil	— M	6532	Charlie	— T
6435	Basil Duke	M	6533	Charlton 2nd	— M
6437	Basil Duke	P S	(6534)	Splendor	P S
6441	Bassanio 11th	C	6534	Chatsworth	M
6444	Beck	M	6536	Cherokee	— R R
6445	Belfast	M	6539	Chieftain	T
6446	Bell	M	6540	Chieftain	— R R
6447	Bell Duke	— R R	6541	Cicero	— R R
6448	Bell Duke 2nd	— L R	6542	Claret	— Daisy
6450	Belvedere	Ky I	6544	Clifton	M
6451	Ben Nevis	M	6545	Clifton	— R R
6452	Bentley	M	6547	Clinton Duke 2nd	Cox
6453	Benton	Cox	6549	Colfax	C
6454	Ben Wade	M	6550	Col. Humphreys	— Long-Horn
6456	Berthola	— L R	(6552)	Sultan	P S
6457	Big Bolt	— M	6553	Colorado	— M
6458	Bill	Ky I	6554	Columbus	— M
6459	Bill	— Long-Horn	6556	Comet	— D
6460	Bill Arp	Ky I	6558	Comet	L R
6461	Billy	L R	6559	Comet	Ky I
6462	Billy	T	6560	Comet	— M
6465	Billy Grey	— Long-Horn	6561	Comet	— Cox
6467	Billy Smith	— T	6562	Comet	— M
6468	Billy Smith	— T	6563	Comet	T
6470	Bismarck	— Cox	6565	Commodore	— Cox
6473	Blazing Star	M	6566	Commodore	D
6474	Blinker	P S	6567	Commodore	L R
6475	Blucher	L R	6569	Copernicus	Cox
6476	Blucher	— M	6570	Corax	— L R
6477	Blucher	— D	6570½	Cortes	M
6479	Bon Ton	— R R	6574	Count Bismarck	M
6482	Bourbon	M	6575	Count Bismarck	— L R
6483	2nd Bourbon	M	6576	Count Bismarck	D
6484	Bourbon 3rd	— M	6577	Count Fathom	M
6486	Bowman	M	6584	Crown Prince	— C
6487	Brandon	M	6586	Cupid	C
6488	Break of Day	Cox	6590	Dandy	L R
6490	Brick Pomeroy	M	6591	Dandy Jack	Cox
6493	Bright-Eyes Duke	— M	6592	Darling	Cox
6494	Brutus	— C	6595	Democrat	— R R
6495	Brutus	M	6595½	Democrat	D
6496	Buck Creek	— M	6596	Dexter	C
6497	Buckeye	— L R	6597	Dexter	— D
6498	Buckeye Boy	C	6599	Diamond	M
6499	Bugle	— Daisy	6600	Diamond Duke	— C
6500	Burr Oak	— M	6601	Dick Yates	P S
6501	Butman	— L R	6602	Dictator	— M
6502	Butterfly	— Cox	6603	Don	Cox
6503	Butterfly	— M	6604	Don Juan	— M
6504	Byron	— M	6606	Double Massie	C
6505	Cable	— Daisy	6607	Douglas	M
6506	Calculator	— L R	6608	Duchess Duke	— Cox
6507	Cambrian Prince	— Long-Horn	6609	Dudley	— R R
6507½	Cambridge 2nd	— M	6610	Duke	— L R
6509	Captain	— M	6612	Duke	— M
6510	Captain	Cox	6612½	Duke	— M
6511	Captain	P S	6614	Duke 2nd	— M
6513	Captain Gwynne	— Cox	6617	Duke Auvergne 2nd	D
6514	Captain Jack	— L R	6623	2nd Duke of Airdrie	— R R
6515	Captain John Brown	P S	6625	3rd Duke of Airdrie	— T
6517	Capt. Pike	P S	6631	Duke of Bedford	— C
6518	Capt. Shafto	— M	6632	Duke of Bourbon	— M

6633	8th Duke of Cambridge .... Cox	6755	Gen. Butler .... M
6634	Duke of Ceresco .... Cox	6756	Gen. Cass .... L R
6635	1st Duke of Claremont .... Cox	6757	Gen. Custer .... Cox
6636	Duke of Clarence .... — M	6758	Gen. Grant .... — M
6639	Duke of Cowassalon .... — Cox	6759	Gen. Grant .... — D
6640	Duke of Cumberland 4th .... — L R	6760	Gen. Grant .... Ky I
6641	Duke of Derby .... Cox	6762	Gen. Grant .... P S
6643	Duke of Dundale 3rd .... P S	6763	Gen. Grant .... L R
6644	4th Duke of Dundale .... P S	6766	Gen. Grant .... L R
6645	5th Duke of Dundale .... P S	6769	Gen. Harriman .... Cox
6646	Duke of El Hakim .... — C	6770	Gen. Joe Hooker .... — R R
6648	Duke of Exeter .... Ky I	6771	Gen. Lee .... — Ky I
6651	Duke of Galesburg .... D	6772	Gen. Lee .... M
6652	Duke of Genesee .... — Cox	6773	Gen. Lee .... Ky I
6655	Duke of Hamilton .... Cox	6774	Gen. Logan .... M
6657	Duke of Hancock .... P S	6775	Gen. Logan .... Ky I
6658	Duke of Harrison .... T	6777	Gen. Reno 2nd .... M
6659	Duke of Homer .... T	6778	Gen. Reno 3rd .... — P S
6662	Duke of Lorain .... — D	6780	Gen. Sheridan .... T
6663	7th Duke of Logan .... Daisy	6781	Gen. Sheridan .... — Cox
6664	8th Duke of Logan .... Daisy	6783	Gen. Sherman .... Ky I
6665	Duke of Madison .... — R R	6784	Gen. Sherman .... — D
6667	2nd Duke of Malakoff .... Daisy	6785	Gen. Sherman .... M
6668	Duke of Marshall .... Cox	6786	Gen. Sherman .... Ky I
6668½	Duke of McDonough .... P S	6787	Gen. Stewart .... M
6669	Duke of McDonough .... D	6791	Gen. Tuttle .... — Ky I
6671	3rd Duke of Menard .... Ky I	6792	Gen. Warner .... — D
6672	Duke of Menard's Son .... M	6794	George .... M
6674	Duke of Mercer .... — M	6799	Gladiator .... — P S
6675	Duke of Montgomery .... — L R	6800	Glaucus .... — Daisy
6676	Duke of Oak Home .... D	6802	Gold Drop .... M
6677	2nd Duke of Oak Home .... — D	6803	Goldfinch .... Ky I
(6678)	White Cloud .... — Hereford	6805	Governor .... — Daisy
6683	Duke of Paris .... — M	6806	Gov. Brough .... — L R
6684	2nd Duke of Paris .... M	6808	Gov. Helm .... — C
6685	Duke of Pickaway .... D	6809	Gov. Yates .... — Daisy
(6686)	Winder .... D	6810	Gramp .... — T
6687	Duke of Roses .... — M	6811	Grand Duke .... — R R
(6687)	Winfield .... T	6812	Grand Duke .... — L R
6688	Duke of Rothsay .... P S	6813	Grand Duke 1st .... — Cox
(6689)	Wonder .... — Long-Horn	6814	2nd Grand Duke .... L R
6691	Duke of Stoner .... — R R	6815	Grand Duke of Airdrie .... — R R
6692	2nd Duke of Stoner .... — R R	6816	Grand Duke of Marshall .... Cox
6696	Duke of Trumwell .... M	6817	Grand Master .... — Cox
6698	Duke of Wayne .... L R	6820	Grant .... — P S
6700	Duke of Wellington .... — P S	6823	2nd Great Republic .... — Woods
6702	Duroc .... L R	6824	3rd Great Republic .... — P S
6705	Earl of Cornwall .... Cox	6828	7th Great Republic .... — R R
6711	Easton Duke .... — Cox	6833	Halton .... Cox
6713	Edward Bates .... P S	6834	Hamlet C
6714	Egleston .... — M	6835	Hamlet .... P S
6715	Election .... Ky I	6836	Hampden .... Ky I
6717	Elsie's Duke of Airdrie .... — D	6838	Hannibal .... — R R
6718	Emigrant .... — M	6840	Harold .... D
6719	Emmett .... — P S	6842	Harrison .... D
6721	Engineer .... R R	6843	Harry .... — L R
6722	Ensign .... — R R	6845	Hazle Duke .... — M
6723	Enterprise .... — D	6846	Hearts .... Ky I
6724	Erastus .... M	6847	Hector .... Cox
6727	Excelsior .... — Cox	6851	Heir of Atha .... — D
6728	Favorite .... — R R	6853	Henry .... — D
6731	Fairy Boy .... — M	6855	Henry Clay .... — R R
6734	Fenian .... M	6857	Hero .... — M
6737	Fillmore .... M	6858	Hero .... — R R
6739	Flying Cloud .... — D	6861	Hero .... — T
6741	Fortune .... — L R	6862	Herschel .... M
6744	Franklin .... P S	6863	Higby 2nd .... Ky I
6745	Frederick .... — R R	6864	Highland Chief .... — R R
6750	Garibaldi .... — R R	6866	Highland Duke 4th .... — L R
6752	Gen. Buford .... — L R	6867	Highland Duke 5th .... — L R

SHORT-HORN CATTLE PEDIGREES.

No.	Name	Code
6868	Highland Duke 6th	P S
6869	Highland Duke of Airdrie	— L R
6871	Highland Lad	P S
6873	Hiram Abiff	— D
6874	Hitt	Ky I
6875	Holofernes	— C
6877	Honest John	— R R
6879	Hugh Crozer	M
6880	Hugh Miller	— D
6881	Huguenot	C
6886	Ike Curran	M
6887	Illinois Starlight	— R R
6890	Imperial Duke	— R R
6895	Jack Spratt	R R
6896	James Beck	— R R
6901	Jeff Davis	— P S
6902	Jeff Davis	— Cox
6904	Jeremiah Duncan	— P S
6905	Jerry Linton	M
6906	Jerome	Ky I
6908	Jester	R R
6909	Jew	— L R
6911	Jim	— P S
6914	John Brown	— P S
6918	John Franklin	M
6919	John Grey	— Long-Horn
6921	John Hancock	Ky I
6925	Joseph Hooker	— M
6926	Josh Billings	Cox
6927	Jugurtha	— M
6928	Julian	— M
6929	Junius	— C
6930	Junius Brutus Booth	— R R
6933	2nd Kentucky Duke	M
6934	King Cyrus	Daisy
6936	Labolt	— M
6937	Lafayette	M
6938	Lame Bull	D
6942	Lee	M
6943	Legal Tender	M
6945	Leonidas	R R
6946	Leroy	— M
6949	Lexington	Ky I
6950	2nd Liberator	— Daisy
6951	Liberty	— R R
6952	Lincoln	— D
6953	Lincoln	— D
6954	Live Oak 1st	Ky I
6955	Live Oak 2nd	Ky I
6957	Locomotive	Ky I
6959	Logan	— L R
6961	London Billy	— D
6962	Longfellow	— D
6964	Lookout, Jr	— Wrong
6965	Lord Lathan	— D
6972	Lord Valentine 2nd	P S
6973	Lord Valentine 3rd	P S
6974	Lord Valentine 4th	P S
6975	Lorenzo Dow	Ky I
6977	Loyal Duke of Oakland	— R R
6978	Lucifer	C
6980	Mack-A-Chack	R R
6981	McHenry	M
6982	Mad River Duke	M
6983	Magic	Woods
6985	Magnus	— P S
6986	Mahogany	M
6989	Major Anderson	— P S
6991	Major Bedford	D
6992	Major Downing	— R R
6999	Marius	C
7000	Marius 3rd	D
7001½	Marquis	D
7002	Marquis	Cox
7003	Marquis 2nd	Cox
7008	Massasoit	— L R
7010	Masterman	— M
7012	Maximilian	— Cox
7014	Maximilian	— P S
7015	May Boy	T
7016	May Boy	M
7017	May Boy	— Cox
7018	May Day	M
7019	May Duke	— M
7021	May Duke	— Cox
7022	Maynard	— L R
7026	Metamora	— R R
7027	Miami Chief	D
7028	Miami Duke	Ky I
7030	Midwinter	— R R
7033	Milt	M
7035	Mingo	R R
7039	Mississippi	— R R
7040	Molecatcher	— Ky I
7041	Monarch	L R
7042	Monarch	M
7043	Monitor	Cox
7045	Monitor	— Long-Horn
7046	Monitor	Ky I
7048	Montauk	P S
7051	Morning Star	M
7052	Mortimer	Daisy
7053	Mountaineer	M
7054	Mountaineer	— D
7055	Mountain Lad	— Cox
7059	Muskingum Duke	M
7061	Mystery	— P S
7063	Napoleon	— Daisy
7064	Napoleon	— Cox
7065	Nelson Starlight	Cox
7066	Nero	— M
7071	Oakland	D
7073	Oconee	M
7074	Ohio Lad	— Cox
7075	Omaha	R R
7076	One Horn	M
7079	Orman	— Daisy
7080	Orphan Boy	L R
7081	Orphan Boy 5th	— C
7084	Oscar	M
7086	Osway	M
7087	Otto	— M
7089	Oxford Boy	— Cox
7091	Paley Starlight	— D
7092	Panick	Ky I
7093	Park Farm Prince	L R
7095	Patrick Henry	— D
7096	Peacock	— P S
7097	Pedro	M
7099	Percy	L R
7100	Perfection	D
7101	Perfection	T
7103	Perfection 2nd	Ky I
7106	Phil Sheridan	P S
7107	Phil Sheridan	Daisy
7109	Planet	P S
7110	Pollock	— Daisy
7111	Pontiac	— M
7112	Pontiac	— Ky I
7113	Pope	— M

7114	Portsmouth	— L R	
7115	Potawatomie	— M	
7116	Powhattan	M	
7118	Prep	R R	
7122	Pride of the West	— P S	
7123	Prince	L R	
7124	Prince	— C	
7126	Prince	Ky I	
7127	Prince	C	
7129	Prince Albert	Cox	
7132	Prince Ernest	— L R	
7133	Prince Fairland	— M	
7137	Prince Imperial	— L R	
7141	Prince of Bourbon	— D	
7142	Prince of Clark	— M	
7143	Prince of Cowassalon	— Cox	
7145	Prince of Licking	— D	
7149	Prince of Wales	— R R	
7152	Prince Thorne	— Cox	
7153	Princeton Count	M	
7155	Prior	— M	
7157	Railway 2nd	Daisy	
7158	Rama	— L R	
7160	Rattler	— R R	
7163	Red Bill	L R	
7164	Red Billy	— M	
7165	Red Bull	M	
7167	Red Duke	— R R	
7168	Red Gauntlet	— M	
7169	Red Ike	— C	
7171	Red Jacket	T	
7174	Red Leaf	M	
7177	Red Prize	— Long-Horn	
7180	Red Star	Cox	
7183	Renick	M	
7184	Renick	— P S	
7184½	Renick McAfee	D	
7186	Republican	M	
7188	Richmond	M	
7190	Roan Duke	— Ky I	
7193	Roan Duke	— D	
7196	Roan Duke	D	
7200	Roan Comet	— P S	
7201	Roan Oak	— M	
7204	Robin Grey	M	
7205	Robin Grey	— Long-Horn	
7206	Robin Hood	R R	
7208	Rob Roy	M	
7209	Rob Roy 2nd	— M	
7210	Rochester 2nd	M	
7211	Rocket	Ky I	
7213	Roderick	R R	
7215	Rolla	M	
7217	Romeo	— Ky I	
7218	Romeo	— R R	
7219	Romeo	— D	
7223	Ross	— P S	
7225	Rover	— Cox	
7226	Rover 1st	M	
7227	Rover 2nd	M	
7228	Rover 3rd	M	
7233	Royal Duke	Cox	
7234	Royal Duke of Delaware	P S	
7238	Royal Sangamon	— Long-Horn	
7239	Royalton	— M	
7240	Royal Turk	L R	
7241	Rupee	M	
7242	Sachem	— Cox	
7243	Sugar	— Cox	
7245	Salmon Chase	P S	
7246	Sam Patterson	M	
7247	Sam Pomeroy	— M	
7248	Sampson	Cox	
7251	Sarpedon	— C	
7252	Saxon	R R	
7253	Scotchman	— M	
7256	Senator 3rd	— R R	
7257	Seth	Cox	
7259	Shelby	M	
7262	Sheridan	P S	
7263	Sheridan	D	
7265	Sherman	P S	
7266	Sherman	M	
7267	Sibley	Cox	
7268	Sigel	— Cox	
7271	Sir Grant	— L R	
7272	Sirius 3rd	Ky I	
7273	Sir John	— M	
7275	Sir Morton Peto	T	
7276	Sir Richard	P S	
7277	Sir Robert	— R R	
7278	Sir Robert	M	
7280	Skylight	R R	
7282	Snowball	L R	
7283	Snowball	L R	
7284	Stowstorm	— L R	
7285	Soft Jacket	R R	
7286	Soldier	— Cox	
7289	Splendor	— D	
7290	Splendor	— T	
7291	Squibob	Cox	
7292	Star	— Cox	
7295	Starlight 13th	— M	
7296½	Star of Hoosick	Cox	
7298	Stevenson's Bull 1st	— T	
7299	Stockton	— D	
7300	Stonewall	— P S	
7302	Sultan	— L R	
7307	Tarlton	— Cox	
7308	Tay Fisher	— M	
7309	Tecumseh	— R R	
7310	Telegraph	— Daisy	
7311	Tempest	— D	
7312	Templar	C	
7312	Terre Coupee Duke	— Ky I	
7314	Thane of Boscobel	— C	
7315	The Bishop	— L R	
7317	The Earl	C	
7322	Thornton	M	
7324	Toland 3rd	— D	
7325	Toland 4th	— R R	
7326	Tom Benton	— D	
7327	Tom Fisher	— L R	
7328	Tommy	L R	
7331	Trebel Gloster	— Cox	
7332	Triumph	Daisy	
7333	Triumphant	— L R	
7336	Troubadour	M	
7337	Troubadour	Daisy	
7338	Tuscola	— C	
7340	Umpire	— L R	
7343	Vallandingham	P S	
7344	Valentine	— Cox	
7346	Vantrump	R R	
7351	Veteran	— M	
7352	Victor	— M	
7353	Victor	L R	
7354	Victor	— M	
7356	Victor	P S	
7357	Victor	Ky I	

SHORT-HORN CATTLE PEDIGREES. 35

No.	Name	Herd
7359	Victor	— D
7360	Victor 12th	C
7362	Vidaurri, Jr	M
7363	Wade Hampton	— M
7366	Warren	— R R
7367	Warren	M
7368	Washington	— L R
7370	Waverly	M
7371	W. D. Jacobs	M
7372	Webster	P S
7374	Wellington	P S
7375	Wellington 3rd	Cox
7378	Wellington	— Ky I
7379	Wellington	— M
7381	Wellington	— D
7385	White Duke	— L R
7386	White Flag	P S
7387	White Jacket	Cox
7388	White Oxford	Ky I
7389	White Prince	M
7392	Wildeyes 2nd	M
7397	Windsor Duke	— C
7398	W. L. Vance	— P S
7401	Xenophon	R R
7402	York	L R
7403	Young America	M
7404	Young Bell	C
7405	Young Bell 2nd	M
7406	Young Bell 3rd	— R R
7412	Young Exeter	L R
7414	Young Hendon 2nd	— M
7416	Young Minister	Ky I
7417	Young Orpheus	Cox
7418	Young Orpheus	Cox
7419	Young Prince of Wales	M
7423	Young Sweepstakes	C
7424	Young Tecumseh	L R
7425	Young Wellington	Cox
7426	Zeno	— P S
7428	Ben Lomond	L R
7429	Champion	L R
7432	Huntsman	— D
7433	Lord Lambton	D
7434	Marvel	D
7435	Peveril	— Cox
7436	Prince	P S
7437	Tam O'Shanter	— M
7438	Young Herald	P S
7439	Aaron Harden	— M
7441	Abe	— M
7443	Accident	D
7445	Acolyth	C
7446	Adam	M
7447	Adam Clark	L R
7448	Admiral	— M
7449	Admiral	— Daisy
7450	Advance	— Cox
7451	Agamagrir	C
7458	Airdrie Duke	— M
7459	Airdrie's Duke of Illinois	— R R
7463	Airdrie of Durham Valley	— Ky I
7465	Airdrie of Paxton	— R R
7466	Airdrie of Paxton	— R R
7472	Alaska	Ky I
7474	Alaska	— T
7476	Alban	— D
7477	Albert	— D
7478	Albert	— D
7481	Alex	— R R
7483	Alexander	Ky I
7487	Alfred	T
7492	Allen	— M
7493	Alpine	L R
7494	Althorp	Ky I
7497	Andy	— M
7498	Andy Johnson	T
7499	Andy Johnson	Ky I
7500	Andy Johnson	— M
7502	Apis	M
7503	Apollo	T
7506	Arch Duke	— R R
7508	Argus	D
7513	Ashby	— T
7516	Atholl	— M
7517	Atlanta	— R R
7518	A. T. Stewart	— M
7519	Augustus	— M
7520	Australian Tom 2nd	— Long-Horn
7521	Auvergene Chief	Ky I
7523	Azim	R R
7525	Balco	P S
7526	Bamburg	— M
7527	Bandola	— M
7528	Banner Duke	— D
7529	Barkley	M
7536	Baron Munchausen	D
7541	Baron of Woodstock	— M
7542	Baron's Trump	— Long-Horn
7543	Barto	T
7544	Basil Duke	— C
7545	Baton Rouge	— P S
7546	Baxter	Ky I
7547	Beauregard	Ky I
7548	Beauregard	D
7551	Bell Duke	— D
7552	2nd Bell Duke of Airdrie	— R R
7553	Bell Plain	— D
7558	Belvedere	— M
7560	Belvoir	Ky I
7561	Ben Adin	Cox
7562	Ben Bertrand	M
7563	Ben Butler	— R R
7564	Ben Butler	— Long-Horn
7566	Ben Butler	Ky I
7567	Ben Butler	— D
7569	Ben Butler	— L R
7570	Ben Butler	— T
7571	Ben Butler	— R R
7572	Benjamin Butler	— Cox
7574	Ben Gray	— Long-Horn
7579	Bertram	— D
7580	Better Dun	L R
7581	Bill Anderson	— P S
7582	Billy Boy	— D
7585	Bismarck	M
7587	Bismarck	P S
7588	Bismarck	— L R
7589	Bismarck	— M
7592	Blanco	L R
7594	Bob Alexander	— R R
7595	Boffin	L R
7598	Bolivar	— M
7600	Bourbon Jr	— M
7601	Bourbon Duke	— M
7603	Boxer	— M
7604	Bradford Prince	Cox
7605	Bradshaw	— M
7606	Barmpton	M
7607	Brandywine	— L R
7610	Brick Pomeroy	Ky I

7612	Bright Eyes Lad	— M	
7615	Brock	— Cox	
7616	Brodick	— L R	
7618	Bruce	— L R	
7619	Bruce	Ky I	
7621	Brutus	M	
7622	Brutus	M	
7623	Brutus	— M	
7624	Brutus	— M	
7625	Bub	— R R	
7626	Buckeye	— R R	
7627	Buckeye Boy	— T	
7628	Bullet	Cox	
7630	Burnside Wiley	— M	
7631	Burnet	— Long-Horn	
7632	Burns	M	
7633	Burton	L R	
7634	Butler	— M	
7638	Byron	M	
7640	Byron	Daisy	
7641	Cadmus	— Daisy	
7644	Calypso	— L R	
7645½	Cambridge 2nd	— M	
7649	Canonchet	P S	
7650	Captain	— Cox	
7652	Capt. Balco	— L R	
7653	Capt. Brown	— P S	
7654	Capt. Coulter	— Cox	
7655	Capt. Duncan	— R R	
7657	Capt. Kibler	— D	
7660	Capt. Shaftoe	D	
7662	Carnival	— T	
7666	Cassander	Cox	
7667	Cassius	— R R	
7669	Cecil	— M	
7671	Champion	M	
7672	Champion	D	
7673	Champion	— D	
7674	Champion	D	
7676	Champion Duke	— Ky I	
7677	Charley	M	
7678	Charley Gray	— Long-Horn	
7679	Cherry Duke	— R R	
7680	Cherubusco	— L R	
7683	Chieftain	— L R	
7684	Christmas Duke	— Cox	
7685	Christmas Eve	Cox	
7687	Christopher	Cox	
7689	Cicero	— R R	
7694	Claremont	— D	
7696	Clarence	— M	
7697	Clarence 2nd	— C	
7701	Clark Duke of Austinburg	— R R	
7704	Clifton	— R R	
7705	Clifton	— Ky I	
7706	Clifton	M	
7707	Clifton	— M	
7709	Clifton Duke	L R	
7710	Clifton Duke	— M	
7712	Clifton Duke 3rd	— R R	
7714	Clyde Duke	M	
7715	Clyde Lad	M	
7716	Clyde Prince	M	
7718	Colfax	D	
7720	Colfax	M	
7721	Colfax	L R	
7722	Colfax	M	
7723	Colfax	Ky I	
7724	Colfax	— D	
7725	Colfax	— D	
7726	Colfax	Cox	
7728	Colfax	T	
7730	Colonel	Ky I	
7732	Col. Dahlgren	— D	
7733	Col Dick Johnson	M	
7734	Col. Holladay	M	
7735	Col. Knox	— L R	
7737	Colorado	— M	
7738	Columbus	M	
7739	Comet	M	
7740	Comet	— L R	
7742	Comet	— Cox	
7743	Comet Airdrie	— M	
7744	Comet Airdrie 2nd	— M	
7746	Commodore	— L R	
7747	Commodore Perry	— D	
7751	Conscript	R R	
7752	Conservative	M	
7757	Copson	Cox	
7759	Corn Cracker	— Daisy	
7761	Corydon	M	
7764	Count Fathom	— D	
7766	Count of Atha	— R R	
7767	Coupon	T	
7769	Creston Duke	— T	
7769½	Cripple	— Cox	
7770	Crowder	Daisy	
7772	Crusader	— Ky I	
7773	Crusader	— Cox	
7774	Crusader Boy	Ky I	
7775	Crystal Drop	— M	
7776	Crystal Duke	— M	
7778	Crystal Prince	— Long-Horn	
7779	Cuba	— Daisy	
7780	Cultivator	— L R	
7782	Dacotah	M	
7783	Dairy Boy	— M	
7785	Dandy	— T	
7786	Dandy	— M	
7787	Darb	Ky I	
7788	Darbyite	Daisy	
7789	Darlington	— R R	
7790	Dave	Ky I	
7791	David	Ky I	
7792	David Crocket	M	
7793	Daybreak	— Daisy	
7794	Day's Duke	P S	
7796	December Duke	— Cox	
7797	Defender	— D	
7799	Denton	Cox	
7801	Derby	— M	
7802	Derby	— M	
7804	De Soto	— D	
7807	Dexter	Ky I	
7808	Dexter	— M	
7809	Dexter	— M	
7810	Dexter	— T	
7812	Diamond	D	
7814	Diamond	— M	
7815	Diamond	P S	
7817	Diamond	— D	
7820	Dickens	— D	
7821	Dick Gray	— Long-Horn	
7822	Dick Mitchell	— D	
7823	Dick Rover	M	
7826	Dick Yates	— Daisy	
7828	Dictator	Cox	
7829	Dimple	Ky I	
7830	Dingle	— M	
7831	Dock	M	

SHORT-HORN CATTLE PEDIGREES.

No.	Name	Source
7832	Doctor	— L R
7835	Dominion Prince	— Cox
7836	Don Cubano	— D
7837	Don John	C
7838	Don Juan	R R
7839	Don Juan	— C
7840	Don Lonanjo	R R
7842	Donzales	R R
7843	Douglas	D
7844	Douglas	— L R
7846	Douglas 2nd	P S
7847	Draco	— Cox
7848	Druid	P S
7848½	Duchess Lord Valentine	— P S
7849	Duke	L R
7851	Duke	— T
7853	Duke	Ky I
7854	Duke	— D
7855	Duke	— P S
7856	Duke	— M
7857	Duke 3rd	P S
7858	Duke 4th	Ky I
7861	Duke Comet	— D
7862	Duke Imperial 2nd	— Long-Horn
7864	1st Duke of Abingdon	— M
7864½	2nd Duke of Abingdon	— P S
7865	Duke of Acworth	Cox
7866	Duke of Adams	— Cox
7868	4th Duke of Adams	— Cox
7871	Duke of Airdrie	— C
7872	Duke of Airdrie	— M
7875	4th Duke of Airdrie	M
7876	4th Duke of Airdrie	D
7877	5th Duke of Airdrie	— L R
7881	Duke of Alleghany	— M
7882	Duke of Allen	P S
7884	Duke of Arlington	— M
7886	Duke of Audrain	D
7887	Duke of Blue Mound	— R R
7888	Duke of Boscobel	— C
7889	Duke of Bourbon	— D
7890	Duke of Bourbon	— M
7896	Duke of Cass	Ky I
7900	Duke of Claremont	Cox
7901	Duke of Clarion	T
7902	Duke of Clark 3rd	— R R
7903	Duke of Clark 4th	— R R
7905	Duke of Clifton	— D
7911	2nd Duke of Cowassalon	— Cox
7912	Duke of Dearborn	— R R
7913	Duke of Dimmick	— Cox
7918	Duke of Dorset 2nd	M
7919	6th Duke of Dundale	P S
7920	Duke of Eckford	L R
7923	Duke of Electa	— M
7926	Duke of Fauholme	— P S
7927	Duke of Fayette	— M
7929	Duke of Forest Hill	— M
7938	2nd Duke of Goodness	— R R
7939	3rd Duke of Goodness	— R R
7941	Duke of Greenbush	— Cox
7944	2nd Duke of Hamilton	Cox
7945	Duke of Harrison	— R R
7946	Duke of Henderson	M
7947	Duke of Heindoka	P S
7954	3rd Duke of Kansas	L R
7955	4th Duke of Kansas	L R
7958	7th Duke of Kansas	T
7960	9th Duke of Kansas	L R
7962	11th Duke of Kansas	T
7964	Duke of Kenosha	— L R
7966	Duke of Kirk	— M
7967	Duke of Knoxville	— M
7970	Duke of Lancaster	L R
7971	Duke of Lockport	Daisy
7972	Duke of Licking	— D
7973	Duke of Logan	— R R
7974	8th Duke of Logan	Daisy
7975	Duke of Louisa	— P S
7979	2nd Duke of McDonough	D
7980	3rd Duke of McDonough	D
7981	Duke of McLean	M
7983	2nd Duke of McLean	M
7985	5th Duke of Menard	M
7986	7th Duke of Menard	M
7989	Duke of Morgan	— D
7992	Duke of Muerkirk	— L R
7996	Duke of Ninevah	— R R
7998	Duke of Novi	L R
7999	Duke of Oakland	L R
8001	Duke of Ohio	Ky I
8003	Duke of Orleans	Cox
8006	Duke of Paint	R R
8007	Duke of Paris	— R R
8009	Duke of Paxton	— R R
8010	Duke of Pike	M
8011	Duke of Portage	M
8012	Duke of Prospect Farm	— M
8013	Duke of the Rock	— R R
8014	Duke of Ross	D
8015	Duke of St. Clair	— Cox
8016	Duke of St. Clair 2nd	L R
8017	Duke of Salem	— L R
8018	Duke of Saltville	Cox
8019	Duke of Sciota	— D
8022	Duke of Shrewsbury	— Cox
8023	Duke of Silas	R R
8024	Duke of Sumerset	— T
8026	Duke of Springdale	D
8027	Duke of the Meadow	— M
8028	Duke of the Pines	P S
8029	Duke of the Valley	— Ky I
8032	Duke of Townsend	M
8033	2nd Duke of Townsend	M
8034	Duke of Wabash	M
8034½	Duke of Wabash County	— R R
8036	Duke of Warren	— M
8037	Duke of Wayne	D
8038	2nd Duke of Wayne	L R
8043	Duke of Wheatland	— M
8044	Duke of Winchester	M
8049	Duke of Woodford	— C
8050	Duke Pierce	C
8052	Duke Royal	M
8055	Duncan	R R
8056	Duncan's General Grant	— R R
8057	Duroc	Ky I
8058	Duroc	— Ky I
8059	Earl	P S
8067	Earl of Cleveland	— D
8070	Earl of Glasgow	— D
8083	Ebenezer	M
8085	Echo	— L R
8086	Echo	— L R
8087	Eclipse	— C
8089	Economist	Ky I
8091	Elkhorn	L R
8094	Eminence	— M
8095	Emmet	— P S
8096	Emmet	T

No.	Name	Herd
8098	Emperor of China	— Cox
8098½	Emperor of China 2nd	— Cox
8099	Emperor of China 3rd	— L R
8100	Engineer	P S
8102	Enterprise	M
8103	Enterprise	— Cox
8104	Enterprise	Ky I
8105	Erie	— Cox
8110	Eureka	— L R
8113	Exception	P S
8114	Exchequer	— R R
8115	Experiment	— R R
8116	Falconbridge	— M
8119	Fancy Boy	— M
8121	Farmer Boy	— M
8122½	Favorite	— Cox
8124	Favorite	— M
8128	Felix	M
8130	Ferguson	L R
8131	F. F. V	— M
8135	Fillmore	— L R
8138	1st Duke of Yuba	Ky I
8140	Five Twenty	— R R
8141	Five Twenty 2nd	— R R
8147	Fox	D
8149	Frank	Ky I
8151	Frank Blair	— T
8154	Franklin Duke	D
8155	Fremont	M
8157	Friday	— P S
8159	Fulton	— D
8161	Fusileer	L R
8163	Galena Duke	— P S
8167	Gen. Brent	— R R
8168	Gen. Brock	— Cox
8169	Gen. Butler	— M
8172	Gen. Dale	Ky I
8173	Gen. Early	D
8174	Gen. Garfield	Cox
8175	Gen. Grant	— L R
8177	Gen. Grant	— Cox
8179	Gen. Grant	T
8180	Gen. Grant	M
8181	Gen. Grant	M
8184	Gen. Grant	P S
8186	Gen. Grant	Cox
8188	Gen Grant	— L R
8189	Gen. Hancock	— R R
8191	General Issimo	P S
8192	Gen. Jackson	— P S
8194	Gen. Lee	M
8196	Gen. Logan	— Daisy
8197	Gen. Lyon	— L R
8198	Gen. Lyon 2nd	M
8200	Gen. Napier	— C
8205	Gen. Sheridan	Wrong
8206	Gen. Sherman	D
8212	Gen. Strickler	M
8214	Gen. Terry	L R
8215	Gen. Thomas	— C
8216	Gen. Thomas	Cox
8217	Gen. Washington	— M
8218	Gen. Woolford	M
8219	George	Cox
8221	George Washington	— C
8222	Gladiator	P S
8225	Glencoe	— P S
8226	Glencoe	— C
8229	Gold Coin	R R
8230	Gold Duke 2nd	— R R
8232	Governor	P S
8233	Governor	— M
8234	Governor	M
8235	Governor	— Daisy
8236	Governor Floyd	— P S
8237	Gov. Hayes	— D
8238	Gov. Morton	— M
8239	Gov. Morton	Ky I
8240	Gov. Oglesby	— M
8242	Gov. White	Ky I
8243	Gov. Smith 2nd	L R
8244	Grandee	Daisy
8248	Grand Duke 2nd	— Cox
8248½	Grand Duke 3rd	— Cox
8249	Grand Duke of Eckford	L R
8254	Grand Duke of Oakland	— R R
8256	Grand Turk	M
8257	Grand Turk	— Daisy
8259	Granger	M
8261	Grant	Daisy
8263	Grant	Cox
8264	Grant	— P S
8265	Grant	M
8266	Grant	P S
8267	Grant	— P S
8268	Granville Duke	— Ky I
8271	Greenback	— L R
8277	Green Mountain Boy 2nd	Cox
8280	11th Great Republic	— Daisy
8282	13th Great Republic	— R R
8283	14th Great Republic	— R R
8285	16th Great Republic	— R R
8291	22nd Great Republic	M
8292	23rd Great Republic	M
8293	24th Great Republic	— Daisy
8295	26th Great Republic	— R R
8298	29th Great Republic	— R R
8300	Grouseland Duke	P S
8303	Gurth	— D
8307	Hamburg	— M
8310	Hamlet	— M
8311	Handy	M
8312	Hannibal	— M
8313	Happy Day	M
8314	Harbinger	Cox
8315	Harlen	M
8316	Harold	— D
8318	Harpoon	R R
8319	Harry Bluff	— C
8320	Hawkeye	— T
8321	Hector	Cox
8322	Hector	Cox
8323	Hector	— P S
8324	Heenan	Cox
8326	Hendon	— P S
8327	Henry	M
8328	Henry	— P S
8329	Henry	L R
8331	Herdsman	— D
8333	Hero	— R R
8334	Hero	P S
8335	Hero	— T
8336	Hero of Magdala	T
8337	Hiawatha	— Cox
8341	Highflyer 4th	— L R
8343	Highland Chief	— L R
8344	Highland Duke	P S
8345	Highlander	— C
8350	Hoosier Boy	— Long Horn
8351	Hopefull	— R R

SHORT-HORN CATTLE PEDIGREES.

No.	Name	Code
8352	Hotspur 2nd	Cox
8353	Hotspur 3rd	Cox
8355	Hubback	D
8356	Hubback	L R
8357	Hub Hollester	Ky I
8360	Humboldt	— D
8362	Hylas Primus	D
8363	Idaho	M
8364	Ida's Valentine	— Cox
8365	Idlewild	— M
8368	Imperial Duke	— P S
8372	Independence	Ky I
8373	Independence	M
8375	Index	Ky I
8377	Indian Chief 8th	— C
8378	Indian Chief 9th	— C
8379	Indian Chief 10th	— C
8380	Indian Chief 11th	— C
8383	Inventor	— Ky I
8384	Invincible Duke	— R R
8385	Ioan	— M
8386	Irenack	— Cox
8388	Ivanhoe	Ky I
8391	Jack Malone	— P S
8392	James Dudley's Roan Bull	— C
8393	Jason	R R
8394	Javelin	— D
8395	J. Brown	— Cox
8396	Jem Clay	Ky I
8401	Jerry Dodge	Ky I
8402	J. H. Bruce	— L R
8403	J. I. Dudley's Red Bull	Ky I
8405	Jim Clay	Ky I
8406	Jim Giddings	Ky I
8408	Jim Lane	M
8409	Jim Lang	D
8410	Joe Hardy	D
8412	Joe Hooker	Ky I
8415	John Booth	P S
8416	John Bright	M
8417	John Bright	— M
8418	John Bright	— M
8421	John C. Breckenridge	— T
8423	John Gilpin	Ky I
8425	John Martin	— D
8426	John Morgan	C
8427	John Morgan	— P S
8428	John O'Gaunt Jr	P S
8429	John Ward	C
8430	Johnny-Jump-Up	C
8431	Johnny Reb	— M
8432	Johnny Temple	M
8433	Jolly Boy	P S
8435	Joe Shelby	P S
8437	Josh Bell	D
8438	Jouel	D
8439	Julian	L R
8440	Julius	M
8441	Julius Cæsar	M
8442	Junius	— R R
8444	Jupiter	M
8450	Kennebec Lad	— M
8458	Kentucky	— D
8459	King Alfred 3rd	L R
8460	King Duke	— M
8463	King Lear	C
8464	King Lear	Ky I
8466	King of the Short-Horns	— L R
8467	King of the West	— L R
8468	King of Trumps 2nd	Ky I
8470	Kirkwood	— R R
8474	Knight of the Garter	— R R
8475	Koran	— C
8476	Kosciusko	— C
8477	Kriss Kringle	— Cox
8478	La Crosse	— M
8479	Lame Bull	— Daisy
8480	Larry Doolan	D
8483	Legal Tender	R R
8489	Leonine Crusade	— D
8491	Leopard 2nd	— D
8492	Leopard	C
8493	Letton 2nd	P S
8494	Letton 3rd	— M
8495	Letton 4th	— M
8496	Letton 5th	— M
8497	Levento	— L R
8498	Lexicon	— Daisy
8502	Lincoln	— T
8503	Linger	— L R
8504	Little Grant	— L R
8505	Little John	— L R
8506	Live Oak 3rd	Ky I
8507	Locomotive	C
8508	Locomotive	— Cox
8509	Logan	P S
8510	Logan	— P S
8515	Lord Arthur	— Cox
8516	Lord Baltimore	— T
8517	Lord Blithe	— R R
8518	Lord Byron	D
8519	Lord Byron	M
8521	Lord Derby	— R R
8525	Lord John Gordon	— P S
8527	Lord Lyndhurst	— M
8530	Lord of Oxford	— L R
8531	Lord Napier	— D
8532	Lord Nelson	M
8534	Lord Sweepstakes	P S
8535	Lord Sweepstakes 2nd	P S
8537	5th Lord Valentine	P S
8538	Lord Wellesley	M
8542	Loudon Duke 3rd	— R R
8543	Lowder's Bull 34th	— M
8544	Lowder's Bull 35th	— T
8545	Lowder's Bull 36th	L R
8546	Lowder's Bull 37th	L R
8547	Lowder's Bull 38th	— T
8548	Lowder's Bull 39th	L R
8549	Lowder's Bull 40th	— T
8550	Lowder's Bull 41st	— M
8551	Lowder's Bull 42nd	L R
8552	Lowder's Bull 43rd	— M
8553	Lowder's Bull 44th	L R
8554	Lucifer	C
8557	Luminary	— M
8558	Lucurgus	C
8559	Lucurgus	— M
8564	Macochee	— M
8569	Major	T
8570	Major	Cox
8571	Major	— R R
8573	Major Anderson 2nd	— D
8574	Major Duncan	— R R
8575	Major Grey	L R
8577	Major Story	— R R
8580	Manlius	— L R
8583	Mariner	Ky I
8586	Marius 4th	D
8589	Marmion	— M

UNFASHIONABLE CROSSES IN

No.	Name	Code
8591	Marquis of Quebec	— M
8593	Mars	R R
8595	Marshal Ney	— C
8596	Martagon	M
8598	Martin Welker	— M
8601	Master John	— L R
8602	Master Oxford	L R
8604	Master Rain	D
8607	Matthew 3rd	— M
8612	May Duke	T
8614	McMillan	R R
8615	Medalist	— M
8617	Mercer	Daisy
8618	Metamora	— Cox
8619	Meteor	P S
8620	Meteor	— P S
8622	Miami Lad	Ky I
8624	Michael	L R
8625	Michigander	Cox
8631	Milo	— R R
8632	Milton	— M
8633	Milwaukee	M
8636	Minister of Oxford	Ky I
8640	Miser	— M
8641	Mississippi	— R R
8642	Mississippi 2nd	— R R
8644	Mohawk	— Long-Horn
8645	Molunke	— M
8646	Monaduock	— Cox
8648	Monarch	— P S
8651	Monitor	M
8652	Monitor	Ky I
8654	Monitor	D
8655	Monitor	— P S
8656	Monroe	M
8658	Montana	Daisy
8659	Montezuma	M
8660	Montezuma	— D
8661	Montezuma 2nd	Cox
8663	Morning Star	— P S
8664	Morning Star	Ky I
8665	Morning Star	L R
8666	Morton	— M
8667	Moses	M
8669	Mountain Boy	— D
8674	Mt. Vernon Duke	— M
8678	Nabob	T
8681	Nelson	— L R
8682	Nelson	M
8683	Nelson	— Cox
8685	Nero	— Cox
8686	Nero	— Cox
8688	Nero	Cox
8690	New Hampshire	L R
8691	Newton	— M
8692	New Years Day	— M
8693	New Years Day	— M
8695	Nicholas 2nd	— D
8696	Nimble Boy	Cox
8703	Noble Festus	Ky I
8704	Nonesuch	Cox
8706	Noras Airdrie	— M
8713	Northman	L R
8715	North Star 3rd	Cox
8717	Norwood	— Cox
8719	Oakland Favorite	— R R
8720	Oakland Lad	L R
8721	Oakley	— R R
8722	Otaka	— Cox
8723	Oceanus	R R
8724	Officer	— D
8726	Onondago	— Cox
8727	Ontario Farmer	— M
8731	Orphan Boy	— C
8732	Orphan Boy	— M
8733	Orphan Boy 7th	— C
8734	Orphan Boy 8th	— C
8735	Orpheus 2nd	Ky I
8736	Ossian	P S
8737	Othello 2nd	P S
8739	Ottawa	T
8741	Oxford	— Cox
8751	Oxford Renick	P S
8754	Pacific	T
8757	Paris	— D
8759	Pat Maloy	R R
8760	Pat Maloy	— P S
8762	Patrick Henry	Daisy
8765	Peer	— Ky I
8766	Peerless	— R R
8770	Perfection	— Daisy
8771	Perfection	D
8775	Perruque	— M
8776	Pertilla	M
8778	Phaeton	R R
8779	Philip	M
8781	Philip Le Bell	Ky I
8783	Phil Sheridan	R R
8784	Phil Sheridan	— Long-Horn
8785	Photograph 2nd	M
8786	Pike	Ky I
8789	Pilot	Cox
8790	Pioneer	M
8792	Pirate	Cox
8793	Planet	Ky I
8797	Plumwood Lad	— R R
8798	Plumwood Oxford	— R R
8799	Podunk	— Cox
8801	Pomeroy	— M
8802	Pomp	— D
8803	Poney	— D
8808	Prairie Boy	— Ky I
8809	Prairie Chief	Ky I
8811	Prairie King	Ky I
8811½	Premier 2nd	Cox
8812	President	— P S
8813	President	— D
8814	President	D
8815	President Grant	— T
8817	Pride of Indian Point	— P S
8818	Prime Duke	— L R
8823	Prince	— P S
8824	Prince	Cox
8825	Prince	— M
8826	Prince	— L R
8827	Prince	Cox
8829	Prince	Cox
8830	Prince	M
8831	Prince	M
8835	Prince Albert	— C
8837	Prince Albert	M
8838	Prince Albert	— L R
8839	Prince Albert	D
8844	Prince Darling	D
8845	Prince Ernest 2nd	Cox
8846	Prince Frederick	— D
8853	Prince Imperial	— C
8858	Prince of Carroll	M
8859	Prince of Clyde	M
8860	Prince of Tardenne	— M

SHORT-HORN CATTLE PEDIGREES.

No.	Name	Code
8861	Prince of Lorain	— D
8862	Prince of McLean	M
8865	Prince of Plumwood	R R
8867	Prince of Shelby	M
8870	Prince of the Glen	— M
8872	Prince of Wales	M
8877	Princeton	Ky I
8881	Punch	— D
8883	Quality	Daisy
8886	Radical	— L R
8887	Ramadan	Ky I
8888	Rambler	T
8889	Rambler	— C
8891	Ranger	— L R
8892	Ranger	— M
8893	Ranger	— L R
8894	Ranger	— Cox
8895	Ranger	Cox
8896	Rantipole	M
8897	Raphael	Daisy
8898	Rasper	P S
8899	Ratler	Cox
8901	Real Admiral	— R R
8902	Rebel Duke of Plumwood	C
8903	Receiver	Cox
8907	Red Duke	Ky I
8910	Red Duke	M
8911	Red Duke of Harristown	Daisy
8912	Red Duke	M
8914	Red Gauntlet	Daisy
8916	Red Jacket	— Ky I
8917	Red Jacket	Cox
8918	Red Jacket	P S
8919	Red Jacket 2nd	— R R
8920	Red Jacket 3rd	— R R
8921	Red Knife	P S
8923	Redman	— M
8924	Red Mario	L R
8925	Redmond	Cox
8929	Red Oak	— P S
8931	Red Robin	— Long-Horn
8934	Red Rover	— R R
8935	Red Rover	L R
8936	Red Victor	C
8937	Reformer	Ky I
8938	Relentless	Ky I
8939	Reliance	Ky I
8940	Relic	— M
8941	Remus	— M
8942	Remus	T
8943	Renick	— R R
8945	Reno	P S
8946	Reuben	M
8948	Rice	M
8949	Richard	P S
8950	Richard	M
8951	Richland	— M
8954	Ringleader	R R
8955	Rising Star	Cox
8962	Roan Duke	D
8963	Roan Duke	P S
8967	Roan Moscow	— M
8971	Roan Star	— L R
8974	Robert Burns	C
8977	Robin Hood	— M
8981	Rob Roy	— Cox
8982	Rob Roy	— P S
8983	Rob Roy	— R R
8987	Roderick Dhu	P S
8989	Rogers	P S
8990	Rolla	— R R
8993	Romeo	R R
8995	Romeo	P S
8999	Romulus	T
9001	Roscoe	Cox
9002	Roscoe	— Cox
9005	Rover	Ky I
9006	Rover	— P S
9008	Rover	Cox
9009	Rover Duke	— R R
9016	Royal Charley	— L R
9017	Royal Duke	C
9022	Royal Durham	— D
9024	Royal George	Ky I
9026	Royal George of Greenbush	L R
9031	Royal King	— Ky I
9033	Royal Oak	T
9036	Royal Prince	— C
9037	Royal Turk 2nd	L R
9038	Roy Cluke	— R R
9039	Ruba	L R
9040	Rustic	Ky I
6041	Saccus	— M
9043	Saginaw	C
9044	Sailor	— Cox
9047	Samaritan	M
9048	Sam Maud	— Woods
9049	Sam Patch	M
9050	Sampson	M
9051	Sam Slick	M
9052	Saracen	— M
9056	Schofield	M
9057	Schuyler	— R R
9058	Scioto	— L R
9061	Scott Wike	— D
9065	Secundus	M
9068	Senator	T
9069	Senator	C
9070	Senator	— L R
9071	Senator	— Ky I
9072	Senator	— Ky I
9073	Senator	— P S
9075	Senator	— M
9076	Senator	— L R
9078	Senator Pomeroy	— Ky I
9079	Seneca 2nd	— Long-Horn
9081	Sergeant	— M
9082	Seven Thirty	— R R
9083	Seymour	— C
9086	Sheffielder Duke	— D
9087	Shellbark	— Long-Horn
9090	Sheridan	M
9092	Sheridan	— C
9094	Shiloh	D
9095	Signal Light	— R R
9098	Silver Dick	— R R
9099	Silver Duke	M
9101	Simple Tom	M
9103	Sir Bob. Peel	P S
9104	Sir Charles	— Ky I
9105	Sir Edwin Landseer	— Daisy
9108	Sir Guy	— L R
9109	Sir Henry	D
9111	Sirius	— Cox
9112	Sir John Franklin	— Cox
9113	Sir Robert Alexander	— R R
9114	Sir Robert Alexander 2nd	D
9116	Sir Roger Ascot	— M
9117	Sir Walter	C
9118	Sir Walter Scott	— R R

9120	Snowball	— L R	9248	Valley Farmer	M
9122	Snowball	M	9253	Vermont Boy	— Cox
9123	Snowball	— P S	9254	Veto	M
9124	Snowball	L R	9257	Victor	— P S
9125	Snowball Duke	M	9258	Victor	Ky I
9127	Snowflake	D	9260	Victor	Cox
9133	Speculator 2nd	C	9263	Victor	P S
9134	Speculator 3rd	C	9265	Victor 3rd	— M
9138	Springland	M	9266	Victor 15th	C
9139	Squire	— T	9267	Victor Hugo	M
9140	Stamford	— D	9268	Victor of Orleans	— Long-Horn
9142	Star	M	9270	Vindicator	— T
9143	Star	Cox	9271	Virgil	— L R
9145	Star Gazer	L R	9272	Vivion	— M
9147	Starlight 5th	— L R	9274	Vulcan	— M
9148	Star of Hendon	— M	9275	Vulcan	— Daisy
9151	Star of the West	— Ky I	9276	Wallace 4th	— M
9152	St. Charles	— M	9277	Walsh	Ky I
9156	St. Elmo	M	9280	Warfield Duke	R R
9157	Stephen A. Douglas	— D	9282	Warren	Ky I
9158	Steward of Hope	— M	9285	Washington 11th	Daisy
9159	Stevenson's Bull 2nd	— T	9289	Wellington	— M
9160	Stevenson's Bull 3rd	— T	9290	Wellington	Daisy
9162	Stonewall	M	9291	Wellington	— D
9163	Stonewall	— M	9293	Wellington	— D
9164	Stonewall 1st	— P S	9297	Western Prince	— M
9165	Stonewall 2nd	— P S	9299	White Bob	— Daisy
9166	Stonewall 3rd	— P S	9301	White Comet	— L R
9167	Stonewall 4th	— P S	9302	White Duke	D
9168	Stonewall Jackson	— M	9303	White Duke	C
9170	Styx	— L R	9311	1st Wilderburg Duke	P S
9171	Sucker Boy	— R R	9312	Wildair	Daisy
9172	Sultan	— M	9313	Wild Eyes	M
9173	Sultan	— L R	9314	William Wallace	— C
9174	Sultan	L R	9315	Willis Shumate	— M
9175	Sultan	— Ky I	9316	Wisconsin	— M
9180	Sweden	M	9317	White Foot	Ky I
9184½	Tancred	T	9318	Windsor	P S
9185	Tanner	M	9322	Woodland Duke 2nd	M
9186	Tarquin	P S	9323	2nd Woodlawn Duke	M
9187	Tasso	— Cox	9325	4th Woodlawn Duke	M
9190	Temptation	C	9328	Woodstock	— L R
9191	Texas	Ky I	9329	Wynyard	Cox
9193	The Baron	Ky I	9330	Xerxes	— R R
9194	The Baron	L R	9331	Yorkshireman 2nd	M
9196	The Bishop	M	9332	Young Admiral	M
9197	The Czar	P S	9337	Young America	Cox
9202	The Pearl	— M	9339	Young Ascot	— P S
9206	Thomas Jones	M	9340	Young Ascot	M
9207	Thompson	— P S	9341	Young Balco	Cox
9212	Thorne's Carlisle	— Cox	9344	Young Comet	Cox
9213	Thurman	M	9345	Young Comet	— D
9215	Tinker	— Cox	9346	Young D'Israeli	— M
9216	Tiptop	— L R	9347	Young Duke	Cox
9218	Tom Corwin	— Ky I	9348	Yorick Duke	— M
9221	Tom Jones	M	9352	Young Grampion	— P S
9222	Tom Marshall	Daisy	9353	Young Hamilton	Cox
9223	Tom Moore	D	9359	Young Marske	— C
9224	Tommy Smith	— T	9364	Young Norwood	M
9226	Tragedian	R R	9369	Young Prince	Ky I
9227	Triumph	— T	9370	Young Prince	M
9228	Triumph	P S	9374	Young Rover	— Cox
9232	Turk	Ky I	9376	Young Sangamon	C
9234	Twin Boy	D	9377	Young Sheffielder	— D
9238	Tymochetee	M	9387	Zingance 2nd	— R R
9239	Ulysses	— Cox	9390	Bruce	— Ky I
9240	Umpire	L R	9392	Coleridge	M
9244	Uncas	— Cox	9394	Grant	— Wrong
9245	Upper Ten	C	9395	Jupiter	— C
9246	U. S. Grant	— R R	9396	Rob Roy 2nd	— D

SHORT-HORN CATTLE PEDIGREES. 43

9397	Royal Duke	M		9516	Benton Lad	— M
9398	Young Minister	Ky I		9517	Berlin Boy	— R R
9401	Abe	Ky I		9518	Berthas Oxford	— M
9402	Abe Renick	M		9519	Bertram	D
9403	Accident 2nd	P S		9520	B. H. Hill	— M
9404	Adam	P S		9521	Bill Anderson	— M
9405	Adam Creston	— L R		9523	Billy Boy	L R
9406	Admiral	— M		9527	Bismarck	Ky I
9408	Admiral 2nd	— P S		9528	Bismarck	P S
9409	Adonis	— Cox		9531	Bishop	D
9410	Acolus	— Daisy		9532	Blackhawk	— T
9411	Airdrie	— M		9533	Blanco	— M
9413	Airdrie 3rd	— M		9534	Blondin	M
9414	Ardrieago	— M		9535	Blood Royal	— L R
9417	Airdrie Duke	D		9538	Bluff Airdrie	— R R
9420	Agnew	— Cox		9539	Boanerges	Daisy
9421	Alaska 2nd	— T		9540	Bob Lee	— M
9424	Albert Rice	Ky I		9541	Bob McAfee	— D
9426	Alexander	— M		9542	Bob McGroty	— D
9427	Alfred	— Cox		9543	Bonaparte	M
9428	Alfred	T		9544	Bolden	— M
9429	Alhambra	Woods		9545	Bolingbroke	M
9430	Aliaro Duke	D		9546	Bon Ben	C
9431	Allan A. Dale	— D		9547	Bonder	M
9433	Alpha	— R R		9548	Bonnie Barney	— L R
9435	Althorp	— Cox		9549	Boone	P S
9438	Americus	— L R		9551	Boreas	— L R
9439	Anda	P S		9552	Bourbon	— M
9440	Andrew Jackson	M		9554	Boyd Allen	M
9441	Andrew Johnson	D		9555	Brack	Ky I
9442	Andy Johnson	— M		9557	Brick Pomeroy	D
9443	Anson, Jr	M		9558	Brick Pomeroy	— D
9444	Antrim Lewis 2nd	P S		9559	Bridesman	— R R
9445	Antrim Lewis 3rd	— C		9561	Brigham	M
9447	Arbaces	M		9563	Brighton	M
9448	Arizona	— Cox		9565	Brock	— R R
9449	Ashburnham	M		9568	Buckeye	D
9452	Assewamsit	— Cox		9569	Buckeye Boy	— R R
9453	Athabasca	Ky I		9570	Buckingham	M
9454	Atholl Duke	— R R		9573	Bullfinch	— Cox
9456	Attica	— Cox		9575	Burley	— Cox
9457	Auctioneer	— M		9577	Burnett	— P S
9459	Aurelius	— M		9578	Burnett	T
9460	Australian Tom 2nd	D		9580	Burnside 2nd	P S
9464	Badger	— M		9581	Burnside 3rd	M
9465	Baldwin's Favorite	— M		9582	Burnside, Jr	M
9469	Barkis	— L R		9584	Butler	M
9470	Barnaby	— R R		9587	Butternut	R R
9471	Barney	— Cox		9588	Cadet	— M
9475	Baron	T		9589	Cadmus	P S
9479	Baron Booth of Canna	C		9590	California	— R R
9480	Baron Booth of Woodford	M		9591	Caliph	C
9482	Baron Grey	— Long-Horn		9594	Canuck	L R
9485	Baron Mack	— M		9595	Captain	— C
9487	Baron Oakland	— D		9596	Captain Bravo	— M
9488	Baron of Belview	C		9598	Captain Dale	Ky I
9492	Baron Waldo	— M		9599	Captain Jenks	M
9493	Barrington	M		9600	Captain Jenks	— M
9494	Barrister	— T		9601	Captain Jenks	P S
9496	Barton 2nd	L R		9602	Captain Jenks	— M
9497	Basil Duke	— M		9603	Captain Jenks	— R R
9501	Bazaine	— L R		9605	Captain Terry	Ky I
9502	Bazaine	— P S		9606	Captain Williams	— D
9504	Beauty's Grant	— M		9607	Captive	— M
9505	Belligerant	— M		9608	Cardinal	— R R
9509	Belvedere Oxford	M		9613	Cato	Ky I
9511	Ben Bolt	L R		9614	Cato	Ky I
9512	Ben Butler	— Cox		9615	Caucasian	— P S
9513	Benj. Franklin	T		9617	Challenger	M
9514	Benoni	D		9618	Champaign Charlie	R R

UNFASHIONABLE CROSSES IN

No.	Name	Code
9619	Champaign Duke	Ky I
9620	Champion	C
9621	Champion	Ky I
9622	Champion 2nd	M
9623	Champion Starlight	— D
9624	Chance Clyde	M
9625	Chancellor	Ky I
9626	Charles Dickens	— R R
9627	Charlie	P S
9628	Charlie Clyde	M
9629	Cherokee	Ky I
9631	Chevalier	T
9632	Chicago	T
9634	Chieftain	— C
9636	Chieftain	R R
9637	Christmas	— M
9639	Cicero	— T
9640	Clarence 2nd	— C
9641	Clarence 3rd	— C
9642	Clark Duke	— C
9644	Cleveland Lad	P S
9645	Clifton	— M
9648	Climax 3rd	— L R
9650	Clinker	M
9653	Clydesdale 2nd	— L R
9653½	Clydesdale 3rd	— L R
9654	Col. Crawford	— M
9656	Colfax	D
9657	Colfax 2nd	L R
9658	Col. Foote	— R R
9659	Col. Grimshaw	P S
9661	Col. Lloyd	M
9662	Col. Nelson	Woods
9664	Col. Ramsdell	Ky I
9665	Columbus	Cox
9666	Col. Williams	— R R
9668	Comet	M
9669	Comet	— R R
9671	Comet	P S
9672	Comet	— D
9674	Comet	Ky I
9675	Comet	— L R
9678	Commodore 3rd	L R
9679	Commodore Decatur	— M
9680	Commodore Farragut	Ky I
9686	Cophetua	— Ky I
9688	Cotton Plant	Ky I
9690	Count Fathom	— M
9691	Count of the Park	— R R
9694	Count Tagenet	— R R
9695	Coy	M
9697	Crowder	Woods
9698	Crown Duke	P S
9699	Crown Prince	— M
9702	Crown Prince 2nd	— Cox
9704	Crown Prince of Oakland	→ R R
9705	Cromwell	— R R
9706	Crusader	Woods
9711	Cunningham	— R R
9712	Curd	T
9713	Cyrus	— D
9715	Dairy Boy	L R
9716	Dairy Lad	— P S
9719	Dandy	Cox
9720	Dandy Duke	C
9722	Daniel Webster	Ky I
9729	Darling Duke of Solway	— R R
9730	Darwin	Cox
9731	Dashwood	L R
9732	Dashwood	— Ky I
9734	Dave	— M
9737	Daylight	— M
9738	D. D. Bell	— P S
9740	Derby	— R R
9742	Dexter	M
9743	Dexter	P S
9744	Dexter	— M
9745	Dexter	T
9746	Diamond	Cox
9747	Diamond	— Ky I
9748	Diamond Duke	— M
9750	Dictator	— C
9751	Dictator	— P S
9752	Dictator	— P S
9753	Dick Johnson	— R R
9757	D'Jalma 2nd	P S
9759	Dombey	R R
9760	Dombey	P S
9761	Dombey	— L R
9762	Dominion	— M
9763	Dominion	L R
9764	Dominion Boy	— T
9767	Don Blanco	— Ky I
9769	Don Juan	— M
9770	Don Zales	R R
9771	Double Duke	P S
9773	Dr. Bennett	Ky I
9776	Driver	R R
9779	Duke	Ky I
9780	Duke	L R
9781	Duke	— Wrong
9782	Duke	— R R
9783	Duke	C
9784	Duke	Ky I
9786	Duke	D
9787	Duke	— R R
9788	Duke 3rd	— P S
9789	Duke, Jr	— L R
9790	Duke Airdrie 2nd	M
9791	Duke Anthony	— Long-Horn
9792	Duke Ardale	— R R
9794	Duke John	— R R
9799	Duke of Airdrie	— R R
9800	Duke of Airdrie	Daisy
9804	Duke of Atha	— R R
9805	Duke of Atholl	— R R
9807	Duke of Aurora	— Cox
9808	Duke of Bath	— Cox
9809	Duke of Bedford	— C
9810	Duke of Belfield	D
9811	1st Duke of Belle Vert	— D
9812	3rd Duke of Belle Vert	— T
9814	Duke of Bloomfield	— L R
9815	Duke of Boone	— R R
9816	Duke of Bourbon	— M
9817	Duke of Bourbon	— M
9820	Duke of Burnett	R R
9822	Duke of Carroll	— P S
9823	Duke of Champaign	P S
9824	Duke of Clarrendon	P S
9826	Duke of Clark 3rd	— R R
9828	Duke of Clyde	M
9829	Duke of Corinth	— R R
9830	Duke of Cowassalon	— Cox
9831	Duke of Crawford	R R
9832	Duke of Delaware	— Cox
9833	Duke of Dimons	M
9835	Duke of Edinburg	Daisy
9836	Duke of Erie	— T
9837	Duke of Essex	— M

SHORT-HORN CATTLE PEDIGREES.

No.	Name	Herd
9838	Duke of Fayette	— R R
9839	3rd Duke of Forest Hill	...M
9841	Duke of Galesburg	P S
9845	Duke of Goodness	— R R
9846	2nd Duke of Goodness	— R R
9847	3rd Duke of Goodness	— R R
9848	4th Duke of Goodness	— R R
9849	5th Duke of Goodness	— R R
9850	6th Duke of Goodness	— R R
9852	Duke of Grand Prairie	— D
9853	Duke of Greenbush	— M
9854	2nd Duke of Greenbush	— T
9856	Duke of Hamilton	L R
9859	1st Duke of Hancock	— Cox
9860	3rd Duke of Hendon	— M
9861	Duke of Henry	P S
9872	Duke of Howland	L R
9873	Duke of Iowa	P S
9875	Duke of Jesse	D
9876	12th Duke of Kansas	L R
9877	13th Duke of Kansas	L R
9879	15th Duke of Kansas	L R
9880	16th Duke of Kansas	L R
9881	17th Duke of Kansas	L R
9883	19th Duke of Kansas	L R
9884	20th Duke of Kansas	L R
9886	Duke of Leatherwood	— R R
9889	2nd Duke of Liberty	P S
9890	3rd Duke of Liberty	P S
9891	4th Duke of Liberty	— L R
9892	Duke of Linwood	— Long-Horn
9894	2nd Duke of Mahaska	T
9896	Duke of Maplewood	P S
9901	Duke of McDonough	P S
9902	9th Duke of Menard	M
9904	Duke of Monroe	Ky I
9905	2nd Duke of Monroe	Ky I
9906	3rd Duke of Monroe	Ky I
9908	Duke of Montrose	R R
9909	Duke of Morgan	P S
9911	2nd Duke of Muirkirk	— L R
9912	Duke of Nicholas	— R R
9913	Duke of Nicholas	— M
9915	Duke of Nineveah	— R R
9917	Duke of North Bend	— D
9918	Duke of Norwood	— M
9919	2nd Duke of Novi	L R
9921	1st Duke of Oakhill	— R R
9922	3rd Duke of Oak Home	— L R
9923	Duke of Ohio	Ky I
9924	2nd Duke of Onondaga	Woods
9928	Duke of Orleans	P S
9932	Duke of Paris	— R R
9933	Duke of Paris	— P S
9934	Duke of Poland	— L R
9935	Duke of Poplar Farm	— R R
9937	Duke of Racine	T
9938	Duke of Randolph	— Ky I
9942	Duke of Rutland	L R
9945	Duke of Saline	— M
9946	2nd Duke of Saltville	L R
9947	3rd Duke of Saltville	P S
9949	Duke of Scioto	— D
9950	Duke of Shelby	M
9951	Duke of Shrewsbury 2nd	— Cox
9952	Duke of Slausondale	— Wrong
9953	2nd Duke of Somerset	— T
9954	3rd Duke of Somerset	— T
9955	Duke of Springdale	— P S
9957	Duke of Stark	— D
9958	2nd Duke of Stoner	— R R
9962	2nd Duke of the Pines	— R R
9964	Duke of Vance Herd	R R
9965	Duke of Virginia	M
9966	Duke of Wapsie	Woods
9969	Duke of Wellington	M
9971	Duke of Wildwood	— M
9972	Duke of Wildwood 2nd	Ky I
9973	2nd Duke of Woodford	— C
9974	Duke of Woodland	— P S
9976	Duke of Woodland 2nd	— P S
9977	2nd Duke of Yates	— M
9978	3rd Duke of Yates	— M
9980	Durock	T
9981	Earl	— M
9988	Earl of Waltham	— T
9990	Echo of Oakland	— R R
9992	Eclipse	— C
9993	Eclipse	D
9996	Edwin Drood	D
9997	Edwin Drood	— L R
9998	Egmont	— M
9999	Election	— L R
10000	El Hakim 2nd	— Long-Horn
10001	Elmerton	— T
10002	Elyra Duke	T
10003	Eminence	Ky I
10004	Emperor	P S
10005	Emperor	T
10007	Emperor	— P S
10008	Emperor	M
10010	Emperor	D
10012	Empress Airdrie	D
10013	Emmet	— C
10014	Enchanter	Ky I
10015	E. P. Jones	— D
10016	Ernest	P S
10017	Ernesty	L R
10018	Escort	— R R
10021	Exchequer	— R R
10022	Exeter	L R
10024	Expectation	— Cox
10025	Extra	— Cox
10026	Euclid	M
10030	Fairfax	— L R
10031	Fairfax	— M
10034	Falstaff	— Cox
10036	Fancy	— M
10038	Fancy Jim	Ky I
10040	Fandango	Cox
10041	Farmer	D
10042	Farmer Boy	Cox
10043	Farmer Boy	M
10044	Farmer Boy	C
10045	Favorite	— P S
10046	Favorite	— Cox
10047	Favorite 3rd	L R
10048	Favorite 3rd	— M
10049	Favorite 4th	— M
10050	Fawn's Major	M
10052	Fayette	— D
10054	Fayette Chief	— D
10055	February	P S
10058	Filligree's Oxford 2nd	— C
10059	Filligree's Oxford 2nd	— M
10060	Financier	Ky I
10062	Fireball	M
10063	Flame	— P S
10065	Forest	M
10066	Forest Duke	— P S

No.	Name	Code
10070	Fourth of June	— R R
10071	Frank	— L R
10072	Frank Leslie	— D
10073	Frantic's Pride	— Cox
10074	Frontier	T
10077	Gaban	— P S
10078	2nd Gaban	— P S
10079	3rd Gaban	— P S
10081	Gay Lothario	— L R
10083	Geauga Duke	M
10084	Gem	Ky I
10087	General	— T
10088	Gen. Boynton	Ky I
10089	Gen. Buckingham	D
10091	Gen. Cass	— L R
10092	Gen. Grant	— M
10093	Gen. Grant	— Cox
10095	Gen. Grant	— T
10097	Gen. Grant	— T
10098	Gen. Grant 2nd	Ky I
10099	Gen. Hancock	L R
10101	Gen. Howard	M
10103	Gen. Logan	— L R
10104	Gen. Lee	T
10105	Gen. Logan	M
10106	Gen. Logan	— P S
10107	Gen. Mahone	P S
10108	Gen. McClellan	Ky I
10109	Gen. Morgan	M
10110	Gen. Morgan	M
10111	Gen. Muster	— L R
10112	Gen. Napier	— Cox
10114	Gen. Prim	P S
10116	Gen. Rawlins	— R R
10117	Gen. Reno 4th	— Cox
10120	Gen. Sherman	P S
10122	Gen. Stark	— D
10123	Gen. Thomas	D
10126	Gen. Webster	— L R
10127	Geneva	M
10130	Genius	T
10131	George	— M
10132	George Peabody	— M
10133	George Washington	M
10134	Gestor's Gloster	— Cox
10139	Gloster's Echo	— Cox
10140	Gloster of Pine Grove	— Cox
10142	3rd Golden Duke	— M
10144	Golddust	M
10145	Golddust	Ky I
10147	Goldfinder 2nd	P S
10148	Goldhunter	— M
10149	Gold of Hendon	— M
10150	Gold Panic	M
10151	Gold Smith	T
10152	Good Friday	Cox
10153	Governor	D
10154	Governor	— T
10155	Governor Butler	P S
10157	Gov. Reeder	R R
10160	Grand Duke 4th	— Cox
10161	1st Grand Duke of Oakland	L R
10164	Grant	— Cox
10165	Grant	— L R
10167	Granite	— C
10168	Grassfield Lad	L R
10169	Great Otley	— R R
10174	Grimes Bull	L R
10176	Gunsale	— C
10184	Hannibal	— D
10185	Hannibal	D
10186	Hannibal 2nd	M
10187	Hannibal 3rd	L R
10188	Hannibal 4th	— T
10189	Hannibal 5th	L R
10192	Harry Bennett	Ky I
10193	Harry Fenn	C
10194	Hartford Lad	M
10196	Hartwell	— R R
10198	Hawkeye	— Cox
10199	Hazel Baron	— P S
10200	Hazelwood Duke	C
10201	Hearts of Oak	— R R
10202	Hector	Cox
10203	Hector	— Woods
10205	Henchman	— Cox
10207	Henry Clay	— Cox
10208	Henry Duke	— C
10209	Hermit	Woods
10210	Hercules	— D
10212	Hero	— M
10214	Hero 2nd	— L R
10215	Hero of Yates	— M
10217	Herzog	M
10220	Highlander	Ky I
10222	Highland Duke	— Woods
10225	Highland Duke	L R
10226	Highland Duke	L R
10228	Highland Prince	L R
10229	Hingston Duke	— C
10230	Hole in the Day	M
10231	Honest John	— R R
10232	Honey Lad	Ky I
10233	Hopeful	Wrong
10234	Hopewell	— Cox
10235	Hopewell	P S
10236	Horace	— M
10239	Hotspur	Woods
10241	Hoyle's Duke	— D
10242	Huron	M
10243	Hyacinth	C
10245	Idaho	— R R
10246	Ides of March	P S
10248	Ike Kalock	Ky I
10250	Imperial Duke	M
10251	Independence	D
10252	Independence	— D
10253	Independence	— D
10255	Index	— M
10256	Indian Chief	— P S
10258	Indian Chief 15th	— C
10259	Indian Chief 16th	— C
10261	Invincible	D
10262	Invincible Duke 2nd	— R R
10264	Island Duke	P S
10266	Iowa King	M
10267	Iowa Ascot	— D
10269	Jackson	Cox
10270	Jackson	— M
10271	Jackson	Ky I
10272	Jacob Pierce	C
10273	James Rainey	R R
10274	January	P S
10276	Jeff	Ky I
10277	Jeff Davis	— T
10278	Jeff Davis	M
10280	Jeffries	D
10281	Jerry Clyde	M
10282	Jerry Duncan	D
10283	Jerry Duncan	D

SHORT-HORN CATTLE PEDIGREES.

No.	Name	Herd
10284	Jerry Lancaster	— M
10286	Jimmie Ransom	D
10289	Joe Brady	— L R
10290	Joe Davis	Ky 1
10291	Joe Hidy	Ky 1
10292	Joe Hooker	Ky 1
10293	Joe Hooker	M
10295	Joe McAllister	M
10296	John	— R R
10298	John Allen Gano	— C
10301	John Bell	M
10302	John Brown	Ky 1
10303	John Marshall	— P S
10304	John Maxwell	— Long-Horn
10306	Johnson's White Bull	— P S
10309	Judge of Tuscarawas	M
10311	Jupiter	L R
10312	Kankakee Duke	M
10316	Kansas Boy	M
10317	Kansas Chief	L R
10318	Kelvinside	— C
10319	Kent Champion	— Cox
10320	Kentuckian	— T
10321	King Cyrus	P S
10322	King of Diamonds	— C
10324	Kirkbridge	— R R
10325	Kirklevington	— D
10329	Kossuth	L R
10330	Koscinsko	— C
10331	Lad of Forest Hill	— Ky 1
10332	Lagonda	R R
10335	Launes	— P S
10338	Lee	— D
10339	Lee	— Long-Horn
10340	Leg Horn	Woods
10341	Leamington	— D
10343	Leopard Duke	— D
10344	Leopard	D
10346	Letton 6th	P S
10347	Lexington	P S
10348	Lexington	— M
10349	Lexington	— R R
10351	Limerick	L R
10352	Linden	— M
10353	2nd Linden	— M
10355	Lippard 2nd	— R R
10356	Lippard	T
10358	Little John	L R
10359	Livingston	Cox
10360	Longfellow	— Cox
10362	Lorainet	— C
10364	Lord Booth	M
10365	Lord Byron	Ky 1
10367	Lord Derby	Wrong
10368	Lord Derby	— L R
10374	Lord Nelson	Cox
10377	Lord of Linville	— R R
10378	Lord of Sangamon	— R R
10379	Lord of the Isles	T
10380	Lord of the Manor	— R R
10381	Lord of Oakhurst	— T
10383	Lord Palmer	Cox
10386	Lord Wenlock	P S
10388	Lost Boy	— D
10389	Lothair	— P S
10392	Lothair	— R R
10394	Louan Duke	— M
10395	Louan Duke	— R R
10397	Loudon Duke 1st Ohio	R R
10399	Loudon Duke 6th	— R R
10404	Louni	— L R
10405	Lowder's Bull 45th	— T
10406	Lowder's Bull 46th	— T
10407	Lowder's Bull 47th	— M
10409	Loyal Duke	— R R
10410	Loyal Duke	Wrong
10412	Macbeth	— M
10414	Maddox	— D
10415	Madison	L R
10416	Manouver	— Daisy
10417	Magenta Duke	— M
10424	Major	— D
10425	Major	— R R
10428	Major	Ky 1
10429	Major 1st	Ky 1
10430	Major 2nd	— D
10431	Major Jones	— R R
10432	Major Ringgold	M
10433	Major Ringgold	P S
10435	Major Whartdale	Ky 1
10439	Maranon	— R R
10441	Marengo	— Cox
10442	Mario 5th	P S
10444	Marion	Ky 1
10445	Marks Rocket	L R
10446	Mark Tapley	R R
10447	Mark Twain	— T
10448	Mark Twain	P S
10449	Marquis	P S
10450	Marquis	— M
10452	Marquis of Lansdown	— M
10454	Mars	Ky 1
10455	Marshal	M
10459	Master Durham	— R R
10460	Master Lownds	P S
10462	Matchless	— L R
10463	Matthew 4th	— M
10464	Mauvaisterre	P S
10465	Maxim	L R
10466	May Duke	M
10467	May Duke	— D
10471	Maynard	— D
10473	Mayor of Oakkurst	— Ky 1
10481	Meddlesom	— Cox
10482	Melvin	T
10483	Merryman	— P S
10484	Meteor	— L R
10485	Mickey Free	— Cox
10487	Milwaukee	M
10488	Milo	— M
10492	Minister	P S
10493	Minnesota 1st	Ky 1
10494	Minstrel Boy	L R
10497	Miss Wiley's Oxford	— Wrong
10498	Moffat	— Cox
10499	Monarch	Ky 1
10500	Monarch	D
10503	Monitor 2nd	P S
10504	Monkey John	— P S
10505	Mono	— Ky 1
10506	Monroe	M
10507	Monte Cristo	Ky 1
10508	Montezuma	— M
10509	Morgan	— M
10510	Morgan	P S
10511	Morgan	— M
10513	Morning Star 2nd	L R
10514	Moses	T
10515	Mountain Chief	— Cox
10516	Mountaineer Jr	Daisy

10517	Muirkirk Laddie......P S	10627	Prairie Duke........— Long-Horn
10520	Naples..............M	10628	Prairie Duke.............— Cox
10522	Napoleon ....L R	10629	Prairie Duke.............M
10524	Nelson..............P S	10630	Premier.................C
10526	Nero................Ky I	10631	Premier 2nd.............D
10527	Nero................Cox	10633	Priam...................R R
10528	Nero................Ky I	10634	Pride of Wapsie.........— T
10529	Nero 2nd............Ky I	10635	Prince..................— Cox
10532	Nevada..............— L R	10636	Prince..................T
10534	Noah................— M	10638	Prince..................— Cox
10538	Noble John..........— Ky I	10643	Prince..................M
10539	Norfolk..............—D	10645	Prince 2nd..............M
10542	North Star..........— Long-Horn	10646	Prince 2nd..............L R
10544	Nonconformist.......— D	10647	Prince Airdrie..........— R R
10545	Novelty.............— Long-Horn	10648	Prince Alamayou........— D
10546	Oakland Favorite....— R R	10649	Prince Albert...........T
10547	Ohio Duke...........— R R	10650	Prince Albert..........— P S
10548	Olander.............C	10651	Prince Albert..........— P S
10552	Ole Bull............Daisy	10652	Prince Albert..........— R R
10553	Ole Bull............C	10653	Prince Albert..........M
10554	Oliver Twist........Ky I	10654	Prince Albert..........M
10555	Oliver Twist........M	10655	Prince Albert..........Cox
10557	Oneida..............— Cox	10656	Prince Albert..........D
10559	Orpheus.............— T	10657	Prince Albert..........— L R
10560	Orphan Boy..........T	10659	Prince Albert..........M
10561	Orphan Boy..........— R R	10662	Prince Arthur..........— M
10563	Orphan Boy 11th.....— C	10663	Prince Arthur..........— M
10565	Orpheus.............— T	10664	Prince Arthur..........— M
10566	Orpheus.............P S	10665	Prince Charlie.........M
10569	Oxford..............Ky I	10670	Prince Louanjo........R R
10573	Oxford Boy..........— R R	10672	Prince of Avilla.......P S
10575	Oxford Lad..........— T	10675	Prince of Glady........C
10579	Paradol.............— C	10677	Prince of Langdon.....— L R
10580	Pat.................— M	10685	Prince of Wales........M
10581	Patchen.............— P S	10686	Prince of Yates........— M
10582	Pathfinder..........— Wrong	10687	Prince Regent.........— R R
10583	Pat Molloy..........Ky I	10688	Prince Royal..........— M
10584	Paul Jones..........— C	10689	Prince St. Valentine...— Cox
10586	Paxton Duke.........— C	10691	Princeton..............M
10587	Pearl...............— P S	10692	Princeton..............— R R
10589	Peck................— Daisy	10696	Proctor................M
10590	Pegasus.............C	10697	Proctor................P S
10591	Pelham..............— M	10705	Rambler................— M
10593	Perfection..........L R	10706	Rambler................D
10594	Perfection..........— M	10707	Random.................M
10595	Perfection..........P S	10709	Rank...................— T
10596	Perfection..........P S	10711	Rascal.................Cox
10599	Phaeton.............— T	10712	Raymond................M
10600	Philip..............M	10714	Red Bill...............— M
10602	Phil Sheridan.......— M	10715	Red Billy..............— M
10603	Phil Sheridan.......— Ky I	10716	Red Bud................— M
10604	Phil Sheridan.......P S	10717	Red Bud Duke..........— M
10606	Phoenix.............— Ky I	10719	Red Champion..........M
10607	Phoenix Clyde.......— M	10720	Red Cliff..............— M
10609	Pilot...............L R	10722	Red Cloud..............L R
10610	Pilot...............Woods	10723	Red Cloud..............— T
10611	Pilot...............— M	10724	Red Cloud..............P S
10612	Pilot 2nd...........— D	10726	Red Cloud..............— M
10613	Pilot...............— R R	10727	Red Cloud..............— R R
10614	Pioneer.............D	10728	Red Cloud..............— M
10615	Pipes...............M	10729	Red Diamond...........Cox
10616	Planet..............— R R	10730	Red Duke...............— P S
10618	Plumwood Boy........— R R	10732	Red Duke...............— C
10619	Pluto...............R R	10733	Red Duke...............— T
10620	Pompey..............L R	10734	Red Duke...............— M
10621	Pontefract..........Ky I	10736	Red George.............Ky I
10622	Poplar Lad..........— C	10737	Red Jacket.............— M
10623	Portage Starlight...Cox	10738	Red Jacket.............— C
10625	Prairie Boy.........— R R	10739	Red Knight.............D
10626	Prairie Boy.........P S	10740	Red Lad................P S

No.	Name	Code	No.	Name	Code
10741	Red Oak	— D	10933	Royalty	P S
10742	Red Oak	— M	10934	Rubicon	— T
10742½	Red Oak	— R R	10935	Rusticus	— P S
10744	Red Rover	P S	10936	Rutledge 2nd	— L R
10745	Red Rover	M	10937	Sailor	P S
10747	Red Rover	M	10939	Sam	P S
10748	Red Rover	— Long-Horn	10940	Sam	P S
10750	Red Sheridan	Ky I	10941	Sam Houston	— Long-Horn
10751	Red Star	— D	10942	Samson	P S
10752	Red Stockings	— T	10943	Samson	— Cox
10753	R. E. Lee	P S	10945	Samuel 2nd	M
10754	R. E. Lee	— P S	10947	Sancho Panza	T
10755	Reliance	— R R	10948	San Lorenzo	— M
10756	Relief	Ky I	10949	Sarpedon	— D
10757	Remus	— M	10950	Scipio	— Cox
10759	Remus	P S	10952	Scottish Chief	— M
10761	Remus	P S	10955	Selim	— Long-Horn
10763	Renick Wiley	P S	10956	Senator	M
10764	Reno	Cox	10957	Senator	— C
10765	Reno	P S	10958	Seventy	— L R
10766	Reuben	M	10959	Sheffield	— D
10769	Richland Lad	— L R	10960	Sheffielder Eclipse	— D
10770	Ringgold Duke	L R	10962	Sheridan	— M
10771	Ring Master	R R	10963	Sheridan 2nd	— L R
10772	Rip Van Winkle	P S	10964	Sheridan 2nd	M
10775	Roan	— R R	10965	Sheridan 3rd	M
10776	Roan Bull	Cox	10966	Sherwoods	L R
10777	Roan Chief	L R	10967	Shoo Fly	Ky I
10778	Roan Clyde	— M	10970	Sid Clark	— M
10779	Roan Duke	— R R	10973	Silver Cloud	M
10781	Roan Duke	M	10974	Simon Kenton	— M
10784	Roan Duke	— R R	10976	Sir Charles	— L R
10785	Roan Duke	P S	10978	Sir E. W. Gladstone	— Cox
10876	Roan Duke	P S	10979	Sir Francis	— D
10878	Roan Knight	L R	10983	Sir John	— D
10879	Red Knight 2nd	L R	10984	Sir Knight	P S
10880	Roan Lad	P S	10987	Sir William Temple	— Cox
10881	Roan Prince	— L R	10988	Sir William Wallace	— P S
10882	Roan Star 2nd	— L R	10989	Skipton	— Ky I
10883	Robert Bonner	L R	10990	Skylark	L R
10884	Robert E. Lee	— Cox	10991	Snowball	— L R
10886	Robin Hood	M	10993	Snowbank	— R R
10888	Rob Roy	— T	10994	Snowboy	— D
10889	Robin Hood	— P S	10998	Son of Renick's Airdrie	— Ky I
10890	Rocky Mountain	M	11000	Speculator	Woods
10891	Roger Hanson	T	11004	Spot	— D
10892	Roger	P S	11006	Spotted Tail	— M
10894	Romeo	L R	11007	Spotted Tail	— M
10896	Romeo	M	11008	Spotted Tail	T
10897	Romeo	— P S	11009	Springfield	— R R
10898	Romeo	— Cox	11011	Squire	D
10899	Romeo	P S	11014	Star	Cox
10900	Romeo	— Cox	11015	Star Duke	— R R
10902	Romulus	— L R	11017	Starlight	D
10903	Romulus	M	11018	Starlight	Daisy
10904	Roscoe	P S	11019	Starlight	Cox
10905	Rosecrans, Jr	Ky I	11020	Star of Logan	Daisy
10906	Rosedale	M	11022	Star of the West	M
10908	Rough	— M	11025	Staunton	M
10909	Rover	T	11026	St. Cuthbert	P S
10910	Rover	Cox	11027	St. Elmo	P S
10911	Rover	D	11028	St. Elmo	R R
10912	Royal Allepo	— L R	11031	St. John	P S
10915	Royal Competitor	— R R	11032	St. Lawrence	— D
10917	Royal Duke of Gloster, Jr	— Cox	11033	St. Patrick	Ky I
10918	Royal Duke 2nd	P S	11035	Stockstry	L R
10924	Royal Knight	L R	11036	Stoner	M
10925	Royal Lad	Cox	11038	Stonewall	— P S
10926	Royal Lad	M	11040	Stonewall	M
10930	Royal Oxford, Jr	P S	11041	Stonewall	D

11042	Stonewall 7th	— M	11148	Worth 2nd	— T
11044	Stonewall Jackson	T	11150	York	L R
11046	Strawberry Duke	M	11152	Young America	Cox
11047	Surprise	P S	11153	Young America	— M
11048	Sweden 2nd	M	11154	Young America	— R R
11049	Sweepstakes	Ky I	11155	Young Cambridge	C
11050	Sweepstakes, Jr	C	11156	Young Comet	— R R
11051	Sweepstakes of Well Dun	— L R	11157	Young Duke	L R
11052	Sydney P. Cunningham	— R R	11158	Young Duke	M
11053	Symmetry	M	11159	Young Duke	Ky I
11055	Taylor	— T	11160	Young Duke of Stark	— M
11056	Temple	— M	11162	Young Geo. O'Gaunt	P S
11059	The Czar	— P S	11163	Young Grant	Ky I
11060	The Jerker	— R R	11164	Young Lord	Daisy
11061	The Lad	P S	11165	Young Marshall	— P S
11062	The Pearl	— M	11166	Young Napier	— Cox
11064	Thomas	Cox	11167	Young Perfection	Ky I
11066	Toledo	— P S	11168	Young President	Ky I
11067	Tom	— P S	11169	Young Sam	C
11068	Tom Brown	— Long-Horn	11170	Young Sam 2nd	D
11070	Tom Jones	M	11172	Young Saxon	P S
11072	Tom Lang	— R R	11173	Young Senator	M
11074	Tompkins	L R	11174	Young Shakespeare	Daisy
11077	Topeka Duke	— R R	11175	Young Townley	P S
11078	Tot	— D	11176	Young Renick	— D
11079	Trojan	L R	11179	Young Woodland Duke	M
11081	Trochu	— L R	11181	Zilpha's Belleville	— Ky I
11083	Trumbull	Cox	11182	Zygler	— P S
11084	Trumbull, Jr	L R	11183	Zopyrus	— T
11085	Trunnion	M	11184	Zouave	— P S
11087	Tuscoon	— D	11185	Zephyr 2nd	— P S
11089	Utoka's Paragon	— R R	11187	Alex	L R
11091	Valentine, Jr	M	11189	Artemus	— L R
11092	Vandal	Ky I	11191	Basil Duke 2nd	P S
11095	Valor	— L R	11192	Ben Butler	L R
11096	Vanderbilt	P S	11194	Brant	— Cox
11097	Vanderbilt	— D	11196	Candidate	— Cox
11099	Velocipede	— R R	11197	Cantrell	D
11100	Vermillion	— D	11198	Captain	— Cox
11101	Vermillion Duke	Daisy	11199	Chesterfield	— T
11102	Vermont Boy	Cox	11201	Crown Prince of Oakland	Cox
11103	Victor	— R R	11202	1st Duke of Vermillion	— R R
11104	Victor	M	11207	Fred	— Cox
11105	Victor	— P S	11208	Frederick 2nd	M
11106	Victor	Daisy	11210	Gen. Grant	Ky I
11107	Victor	— Cox	11211	Gen. Sherman	— L R
11110	Victor 17th	C	11213	Glenwood	M
11111	Victor 18th	C	11214	Good Boy	— M
11112	Victor Emanuel	— L R	11217	Hannibal	T
11113	Vidauri Prince	M	11218	Hawkeye	— Cox
11116	Wakefield	D	11219	Illinois	— D
11117	Walnut Chief	P S	11225	Major	— Cox
11119	Wanderer	— M	11226	Malahide	— Cox
11120	Warlaby	— R R	11228	Oleander	— T
11121	Warneater	— R R	11229	Matthew 3rd	D
11122	Warwick	Woods	11230	Orphan Boy	Ky I
11123	Washtenaw 2nd	Ky I	11231	Our Fritz	— M
11126	Western Duke	— P S	11232	Ozark	M
11127	Western Duke 2nd	M	11236	Prince of Newton	— L R
11129	White Duke	L R	11238	Putnam Duke	P S
11132	Whiteside	— Cox	11244	Heridan	T
11134	Wild	L R	11245	Son of Gwynne's Marmion	— Cox
11135	Wild	Daisy	11246	Tempest	— Cox
11138	Winfleigh Duke	M	11247	Thornleigh	C
¶11139	Winneconnet	— Cox	11251	Young Wellington	L R
11142	Woodburn	Ky I	11252	Zygonya	Ky I
11143	Woodburn Prince	M	11254	Abe Hitt	D
11145	Woodford Lad	M	11255	Abe Lincoln	M
11146	Woodland Duke, Jr	M	11257	Accident	L R
11147	Woods	— M	11258	Ad	— Ky I

No.	Name	Code	No.	Name	Code
11260	Admiral	— T	11365	Bellville 3rd	Daisy
11261	Admiral	Ky I	11367	Ben	M
11262	Admiral 2nd	M	11368	Ben	— D
11264	Admiral, Jr	T	11369	Ben Booth	D
11265	Ah-Sin	— M	11370	Ben' Butler	— D
11266	Airdrie	— C	11371	Ben Butler	T
11267	Airdrie 2nd	— R R	11372	Ben Butler	— L R
11269	Airdrie Duke	M	11375	Ben Carlton	— D
11272	Airdrie Duke of Iowa	— Wrong	11376	Ben Clyde	— L R
11273	Airdrie Lad, Jr	P S	11377	Ben Etherlind	Ky I
11274	Airdrie Lee	— M	11379	Ben Lathrop	D
11275	2nd Airdrie of Paxton	— R R	11380	Ben McCullough	— M
11277	Albert	M	11381	Ben Wade	M
11280	Albus	M	11382	Ben Wade	— P S
11282	Alexander	— C	11385	Beverly of Logan	Daisy
11283	Alexander	Ky I	11387	Bill	M
11284	Alexander	M	11388	Bill Anderson	C
11285	Alexander	M	11389	Bill Van Horn	Ky I
11286	Alexander	— D	11390	Billy C.	— R R
(11287)	Clayton	M	11391	Billy Harrison 2nd	T
11287	Alexis	M	11392	Billy Harrison 3rd	T
11289	Alfred	L R	11393	Billy Harrison 4th	Ky I
11290	Alfred Vargrave	— R R	11394	Billy Harrison 5th	T
11292	Algoma	C	11395	Billy Harrison 6th	T
11295	Althorp Lad	— P S	11396	Billy Mack	— M
11296	Andrew	M	11397	Billy Sherman	Ky I
11298	Andrew Jackson	— R R	11398	Bishop Royal	M
11299	Andrew Johnson	— M	11400	Bismarck	M
11300	Andy Johnson	Ky I	11401	Bismarck	M
11301	Anthony	— R R	11403	Bismarck	M
11302	Antony	— P S	11404	Bismarck	— T
11303	Arch Duke's Favorite	— R R	11407	Blucher	— D
11304	Archy	— Cox	11408	Blucher	Ky I
11305	Arcola	— D	11411	Bobby Burns	— P S
11306	Arden	— P S	11412	Bob Lee	— P S
11307	Ardrosen	— P S	11414	Bob Lee 2nd	— P S
11308	Argyll	L R	11415	Bob Lincoln	— L R
11309	Arion	L R	11416	Bob Miller	— R R
11313	Astor	— P S	11417	Bob Walker	C
11314	Atholl Duke	M	11418	Bob White	M
11315	Audrain	Daisy	11420	Bolivar	M
11318	Australian Tom 2nd	— P S	11421	Boudholder	— M
11319	Australian Tom 3rd	— L R	11422	Bonny Barney	— L R
11320	Authority	— L R	11423	Booth	— M
11321	Bacchus	L R	11432	Bret Harte	Cox
11322	Bainbridge	— R R	11434	Brick Pomeroy	— Cox
11323	Balco	Daisy	11436	Brigham	M
11324	Baltic, Jr	P S	11441	Britton	— P S
11327	Banner Boy	Ky I	11442	Brooklyn Boy	— D
11328	Banquo	— C	11444	Brutus	M
11329	Barclay	C	11445	Brutus	— Long-Horn
11330	Barlow	M	11446	Brutus	D
11333	Baron Bedford	— C	11448	Brutus J. Clay	M
11335	Baronet	— P S	11449	Buckeye	M
11336	Baronet	— M	11450	Buckeye	M
11340	Baron Hudson	P S	11451	Buckeye Boy	M
11341	Baron Louanjo	— R R	11452	Buckeye Lad	— Long-Horn
11343	Baron Martin	— D	11453	Buckeye Lad	— R R
11347	Beauregard	Ky I	11454	Buckingham	— R R
11348	Beauty's Gloster	L R	11455	Bucyrus	M
11350	Bedford	— M	11456	Buddha	D
11351	Bedford	P S	11457	Bully Boy	P S
11353	Beddington	M	11459	Burnell	— Ky I
11355	Bell Duke	— P S	11460	Burns	M
11356	Bell Duke	R R	11462	Bush	— T
11357	Bell Duke	— D	11463	Butcher Boy	— Cox
11358	Bell Duke B	— R R	11464	Butcher Boy	— Cox
11360	Belgium	Ky I	11467	Butter Duke	Ky I
11361	Belmont	— P S	11468	California Duke	— L R
11362	Belmont	P S	11470	Camillus	— C

No.	Name	Code		No.	Name	Code
11472	Candidate	M		11575	Crown Duke	M
11473	Captain	L R		11576	Crown Prince	— M
11474	Captain Arno	P S		11579	Crown Prince	T
11476	Captain Jenks	— P S		11580	Crown Prince	M
11477	Capt. Ned	— L R		11582	Cuddie	— M
11478	Capt. Nero 2nd	D		11583	Cupid	D
11479	Capt. of Willow Shade	M		11584	Cupid	— M
11480	Capt. Scott	— R R		11586	Cypher	— C
11481	Capt. Shaftoe 2nd	— D		11589	Cyrus	D
11482	Capt. Shaftoe 3rd	T		11590	Cyrus	Ky I
11483	Capt. Waxam	L R		11591	Cyrus	— M
11484	Carl	— D		11592	Dairy Boy	D
11486	Carlisle	— M		11593	Dairy Boy 2nd	— L R
(11487)	Fortune	— Cox		11595	Dairyman	— Cox
11487	Carlisle Carlton	— M		11598	Dairyman	— M
11488	Carlotta's Airdrie	— R R		11599	Daisy	— R R
11490	Cassius	— P S		11601	Dandy Jim	R R
11491	Cato	Ky I		11602	Daniel Boone	— R R
11493	Charles	— Cox		11604	Daniel Boone	— R R
11495	Champion	P S		11606	Dan Rice	M
11496	Champion	M		11607	Dantilla	L R
11498	Champion 2nd	Ky I		11608	Dan Tucker	— M
11499	Charles Dickens	M		11609	Darby	R R
11500	Charles Dickens	M		11610	Darien	Ky I
11502	Chautauqua 2nd	— L R		11612	Dave	Ky I
11504	Cherry 3rd's Son	— M		11613	David Copperfield	M
11506	Chikarora	Ky I		11615	Davy Crockett	— M
11507	Chief of Trumbull	P S		11616	Dean	— L R
11513	Clarence, Jr	— C		11617	Defiance	— L R
11516	Clay	— L R		11618	Democrat	M
11522	Clinton	— R R		(11619)	John Moore	— M
11523	Clinton	— M		11620	Derby 2nd	— M
11525	Clipper	M		11622	Dexter	— P S
11526	Clydesdale 4th	— L R		11623	Dexter	— R R
11527	Colfax 3rd	L R		11625	Diamond	M
11528	Colossus	— C		11626	Diamond 2nd	M
11529	Colonel	— M		11628	Dick Derby	— T
11530	Colonel	L R		11629	Dick Johnson	— M
11531	Col. Baker	— L R		11630	Dick Swiveller	M
11533	Col. Crocket	— R R		11632	Dick Watson 2nd	D
11534	Col. Kinsman	— L R		11634	Diamond	L R
11535	Col. Talbutt	C		11635	Dixie	Ky I
11536	Col. Trimble	— R R		11636	Dixie Duke 1st	— R R
11538	Colorado	D		11638	Doctor	— L R
11539	Columbus	P S		11639	Domby	— L R
11541	Comet	M		11640	Don	— M
11542	Comet	L R		11641	Don Bernardo	— R R
11543	Comet	Cox		11642	Donn Piatt	— M
11544	Comet	— L R		11643	Dot	Cox
11545	Comet 2nd	Ky I		11644	D'Otley	Ky I
11546	Comet 2nd	— M		11646	Douglass	— L R
11547	Comet, Jr	Ky I		11647	Douglass	— L R
11548	Commodore	— L R		11648	Douglass	Daisy
11551	Compromise	— M		11653	Duke	P S
11552	Compton Lad	Cox		11654	Duke	Ky I
11557	Corporal Try	— Ky I		11655	Duke	Ky I
11558	Cossack	— Ky I		11656	Duke	Cox
(11559)	Harry of the West	— M		11657	Duke	— M
11560	Counsellor	— P S		11659	Duke 2nd	— R R
11561	Count Bismarck	Cox		11660	Duke 3rd	— D
11562	Count Bismarck	M		11661	Duke 4th	— D
11563	Count Fathom 3rd	M		11662	Duke 5th	— D
11566	Count Fosco	— T		11663	Duke 6th	— D
11567	Count of Monte Cristo	M		11664	Duke Jr	— L R
11568	Country Gentlemen	M		11666	Duke of Airdrie 3rd	M
11570	Coupon	M		11667	Duke of Airdrie 4th	— M
11571	Crescent	— M		11668	Duke of Airdrie 5th	— L R
11572	Crockett	— T		11669	Duke Bell	— R R
11573	Cromwell	— L R		11670	Duke Calemes	— C
11574	Crowder	— P S		11671	Duke Charles	L R

SHORT-HORN CATTLE PEDIGREES.   53

No.	Name	Mark		No.	Name	Mark
11673	Duke De Lavois	— R R		11773	27th Duke of Kansas	L R
11675	Duke Jubilant	— R R		11774	28th Duke of Kansas	L R
11676	Duke Morton	— M		11776	Duke of Kewanee	— Ky I
11677	Duke of Airdrie	— R R		11777	Duke of Knox	M
11682	3rd Duke of Ashland	M		11778	Duke of Licking	M
11685	Duke of Barrington	L R		11779	1st Duke of Little Pine	— M
11686	Duke of Bellview	M		11781	3rd Duke of Mahaska	T
11687	Duke of Berwick	Woods		11785	Duke of Marlborough	— M
11688	Duke of Blanchard	— D		11788	9th Duke of Menard	M
11690	Duke of Boone	M		11789	Duke of Melbourne	— M
11691	Duke of Beaver	— R R		11790	Duke of Meritt	Ky I
11692	Duke of Brockland Farm	— R R		11792	1st Duke of Mill Run	P S
11694	Duke of Burnett 2nd	P S		11793	Duke of Monmouth	Wrong
11695	Duke of Burnett 3rd	— R R		11794	Duke of Morgan	Daisy
11696	Duke of Burnett 4th	— P S		11795	Duke of Morgan	— Daisy
11697	Duke of Cambridge	— R R		11796	Duke of Nelson	M
11699	Duke of Cedar	Wrong		11801	3rd Duke of Onondaga	Woods
11700	Duke of Cherry Valley	— R R		11802	4th Duke of Onondaga	P S
11701	Duke of Clarence	D		11803	5th Duke of Onondaga	Cox
11702	2nd Duke of Clarendon	P S		11804	Duke of Orange	— L R
11704	Duke of Clinton	Cox		11807	Duke of Oregon	P S
11705	Duke of Crawford	— M		11808	Duke of Orleans	D
11706	Duke of Crescent Hill	C		11809	Duke of Orleans	— P S
11707	Duke of Cross Creek	Ky I		11810	Duke of Orleans	P S
11708	Duke of Colusa	— Ky I		11811	1st Duke of Paris	— P S
11709	Duke of Coshocton	— R R		11812	Duke of Parke	Ky I
11711	1st Duke of Edgar	— R R		11813	1st Duke of Patterson Dale	— R R
11713	3rd Duke of Edgar	— Long-Horn		11815	Duke of Pike	P S
11716	6th Duke of Edgar	— D		11817	Duke of Pike	— Ky I
11718	8th Duke of Edgar	— L R		11818	Duke of Portage	— L R
11719	9th Duke of Edgar	M		11819	Duke of Poweshiek	— D
11720	10th Duke of Edgar	— R R		11820	2nd Duke of Prospect Farm	— C
11721	Duke of Elgin	— P S		11822	2nd Duke of Randolph	— P S
11722	2nd Duke of Elgin	— P S		11823	Duke of Ravenswood	— M
11725	Duke of Fairview	— C		11824	Duke of Richmond	— R R
11726	Duke of Fairview	D		11825	Duke of Richmond	— D
11727	Duke of Fayette 2nd	L R		11826	Duke of Roseville	M
11730	1st Duke of Garnaville	— D		11827	Duke of Ruth	Ky I
11733	2nd Duke of Glendale	— M		11828	Duke of Rutland	L R
11734	7th Duke of Goodness	— R R		11829	4th Duke of Saltville	— Cox
11735	8th Duke of Goodness	— R R		11830	Duke of Shannon	— M
11737	3rd Duke of Greenbush	— Cox		11832	Duke of Somers 2nd	— P S
11738	4th Duke of Greenbush	T		11833	4th Duke of Stanstead	L R
11739	5th Duke of Greenbush	T		11835	Duke of Sugar Grove	— R R
11740	6th Duke of Greenbush	— L R		11837	Duke of Sunbeam	Ky I
11741	7th Duke of Greenbush	— Cox		11838	Duke of Syracuse	Cox
11742	8th Duke of Greenbush	— Cox		11839	2nd Duke of Tecumseh	Ky I
11743	Duke of Greenlawn	— D		11840	3rd Duke of Tecumseh	M
11744	Duke of Greenwick	Ky I		11841	4th Duke of Tecumseh	— Ky I
11745	Duke of Greenwood	D		11842	5th Duke of Tecumseh	D
11747	Duke of Guilford	— L R		11843	Duke of the Meadows	T
11749	Duke of Harrison	— R R		11844	3rd Duke of the Pines	— R R
11750	Duke of Hazel Dell	— M		11845	4th Duke of the Pines	C
11751	Duke of Hazelwood	— M		11846	5th Duke of the Pines	Daisy
11752	2nd Duke of Hazelwood	— M		11847	Duke of the Plains	M
11753	2nd Duke of Hemdoka	— P S		11848	Duke of the Valley	— R R
11754	Duke of Hemp Ridge	M		11849	Duke of the Valley	Cox
11755	Duke of Henderson	M		11850	Duke of the Woods	— R R
11756	4th Duke of Hendon	— M		11852	2nd Duke of Thornvale	L R
11757	Duke of Hickory Grove	M		11853	3rd Duke of Townsend	— M
11758	Duke of Highland	— M		11854	Duke of Troy	— D
11761	Duke of Hinkston	— R R		11855	Duke of Trumbull	— M
11762	Duke of Huron	M		11859	Duke of Wayne	L R
11763	Duke of Iowa	M		11862	Duke of Wilson	— D
11764	Duke of Iowa	M		11864	Duke of Woodland	Ky I
11766	Duke of Johnson	— P S		11865	Duke of Woodside	Daisy
11768	22nd Duke of Kansas	T		11866	Duke of York	— R R
11770	24th Duke of Kansas	T		11868	2nd Duke of Yuba	Ky I
11771	25th Duke of Kansas	T		11869	3rd Duke of Yuba	Ky I
(11772)	Major Bragg	D		11871	Duke of Princeton	Ky I

11873	Duke of Winchester	— M	11998	Galba ... — Daisy
11874	Duncan	M	12001	Garrett Davis ... — M
11875	Dunglen Boy	R R	12002	Garry Owen ... L R
11876	Dun Major	— Cox	12005	Gen. Baker ... D
11877	Dusty Miller	D	12006	Gen. Beauregard ... — P S
11878	Dutch	— L R	12007	Gen. Brent ... R R
11879	Earl 2nd	P S	12010	Gen. Crocker ... — L R
(11889)	Patrick Henry	P S	12011	Gen. Forrest ... R R
11891	Earl Littleton	— R R	12013	Gen. Grant ... — Cox
11893	Earl of Durham	D	12014	Gen. Grant ... — L R
11894	1st Earl of Elevay	P S	12015	Gen. Grant ... — T
11903	Ester	— L R	12016	Gen. Grant ... M
11905	Echo of Saltville	L R	12017	Gen. Grant ... M
11906	Eclipse	P S	12018	Gen. Grant ... M
11908	Edwin	— Daisy	12020	Gen. Grant ... — D
11910	Elisha	L R	12021	Gen. Grant ... M
11911	Elton Boy	— L R	12026	Gen. Lee ... — P S
11912	Emmett 2nd	— Daisy	12027	Gen. Lee ... — P S
11913	Emperor	— L R	12029	Gen. Lee ... — M
11914	Emperor	— Ky I	12030	Gen. Logan ... — R R
11915	Emperor 2d	D	12031	Gen. Morgan ... M
11919	Emperor William	— Cox	12032	Gen. Morgan ... — L R
11921	Ensign	P S	12033	Gen. Muster ... — L R
11924	Erastus	— M	12034	Gen. Putnam ... P S
11925	Erie	— M	12035	Gen. Russell ... M
11927	Esquire Anderson	— R R	12036	Gen. Scott ... D
11928	Ethan Allen	— M	12039	Gen. Sherman ... — L R
11931	Eureka	Daisy	12040	Gen. Sherman ... L R
11932	Everett	— P S	12041	Gen. Sherman ... L R
11934	Exception	— P S	12043	Gen. Sherman ... — M
11935	Excelsior	— R R	12044	Gen. Taylor ... T
11936	Exception	— P S	12045	Gen. Thomas ... Cox
11940	Fancy	— Ky I	12046	Gen. Tom Duncan ... — M
11943	Farmer's Boy	Ky I	12047	Gen. Wallace ... M
11945	Fashion's Admiral	Ky I	12050	Genoe Hill ... — T
11946	Fauquier	— L R	12052	George Hill ... — T
11949	Favorite 5th	— M	12053	George H. Thomas ... T
11952	Fearnaught	— M	12054	George Mansfield ... — Cox
11954	Fifteenth Amendment	M	12056	Gilbert ... — M
11955	Fillmore	L R	12057	Gillroy ... — C
11956	Financier	R R	12058	Gilson's Duke ... Ky I
11957	Fine Times	M	12059	Gip ... L R
11958	Firby	— R R	12060	Glencoe ... M
11959	Fitz Lee	— P S	12061	Glen Owen ... Ky I
11960	Five Forty	M	12064	Gloster of Pine Grove ... — L R
11961	Five Twenty 4th	M	12065	Gloster's Oxford ... — Cox
11962	Five Twenty 5th	— R R	12066	Godolphin ... M
11963	Five Twenty 6th	— R R	12068	Gold Duke 2nd ... — R R
11964	Flash	— P S	12069	Gold Dust ... M
11965	Fletcher Johnson	— M	12072	Goldfinch 2nd ... — Ky I
11966	Floral Duke	— D	12074	Gov. Baker ... — M
11968	Florian	— Cox	12075	Governor ... L R
11969	Florisant	— Ky I	12076	Governor ... R R
11977	Fortunatus	— M	12077	Governor ... — T
11978	Frank	— Ky I	12078	Governor ... Ky I
11980	Frank Forrester	— L R	12080	Governor 2nd ... — Daisy
11982	Franklin	P S	12081	Gov. Joe Duncan ... — M
11983	Franklin Boy	— M	12082	Gov. Leslie ... — M
11984	Franklin Duke	Ky I	12083	Gov. Morrow 2nd ... — L R
11985	Franky	— M	12087	Grand Duke 2nd ... — R R
11987	Frederick	— Cox	12090	Grand Duke 5th ... — Cox
11989	Fritz	D	12091	2nd Grand Duke of Airdrie ... — R R
11990	Fritz	— M	12093	1st Grand Duke of Bureau ... D
11991	Fulton Lad	D	12094	Grand Duke of Elm Grove ... — R R
11992	2nd Gaban	— P S	12095	5th Grand Duke of Moreton ... M
11993	4th Gaban	— P S	(12007)	Sir Thomas ... M
11994	5th Gaban	— P S	12097	Grand Prince ... — C
11995	6th Gaban	— P S	12098	Grant ... — Cox
11996	7th Gaban	— P S	12099	Grant ... P S
11997	8th Gaban	— P S	12102	Grafton ... — Cox

SHORT-HORN CATTLE PEDIGREES.

No.	Name	Herd
12103	Great Expectations	— L R
12104	Greenbush	— M
12105	Groveland Duke	D
12107	Gue	— Ky I
12109	Guy Devereux	— L R
12110	Hal Walters	— M
12111	Hall's Bull 1st	— T
12112	Hamiltonian	— R R
12114	Hampton Boy	M
12115	Hannibal	Ky I
12117	Hannibal 6th	L R
12118	Hannibal 8th	— R R
12119	Hannibal 9th	— T
12120	Hannibal 10th	L R
12121	Hannibal 11th	L R
12122	Hansiro	T
12124	Harrold	— P S
12125	Harry	— L R
12126	Harry	— R R
12128	Harry Hershey	— R R
12130	Hawkeye	M
12131	Hazelwood Duke 2nd	C
12133	Hector	L R
12134	Hector	T
12137	Henry Clay	M
12138	Henry Clay	T
12139	Henry Clay	M
12140	Henry Clay	— Ky I
12141	Herbert	M
12143	Hero	— P S
12144	Hero	— R R
12146	Hiawatha	P S
12147	Hickory	P S
12150	Highflyer 5th	— L R
12151	Highland Chief	L R
12153	4th Highland Duke	— P S
12154	Hokie	— M
12155	Holland	L R
12156	Homer	— R R
12157	Honest John	— M
12159	Hopewell	— R R
12160	Horace	— L R
12161	Homer	— M
12162	Howard	L R
12164	Hurricane	Daisy
12165	Idas Cayuga	— Cox
12167	Illinois Duke	— P S
12168	Imperial	— M
12169	Imperial Grey	— Long-Horn
12170	Imperial Oakland	— R R
12171	Independence	— D
12173	Independence	— M
12174	Indian Chief 17th	— C
12178	Ira	— L R
12179	Iron Duke	L R
12181	Itaska	— L R
12185	Ivanhoe	— M
12186	Ivanhoe	P S
12187	Jack Ketch	— M
12188	Jackson	— P S
12189	Jackson Lad	Ky I
12191	James Duke	Ky I
12192	James Smith	— T
12193	Jamesville Duke	L R
12194	January	— M
12195	Janus	— Ky I
12198	Jeff Davis	— L R
12199	Jeff Davis	M
12200	Jeff Davis	— Ky I
12201	Jeff Davis	— M
12203	Jeff Davis Jr	L R
12204	Jerome	C
12206	Jerry	— P S
12209	Jim	— M
12210	Joe	D
12211	Joe Bowers	T
12212	Joe Johnson	— R R
12213	John Anderson	— P S
12215	John Gilpin	— M
12216	John Loui	— M
12217	John Martin	M
12218	John Morgan	Ky I
12219	Johnny Barlow	— T
12222	John Simms	— Long-Horn
12223	Joker	— M
12224	Jordan	— P S
12225	Joseph John Gurney	Ky I
12227	Joy	— M
12228	Judgson	M
12229	Junius	— T
12230	Jupiter	— M
12231	Jupiter	— M
12233	Kaiser	P S
12234	Kenny	T
12236	King Cyrus	— R R
12237	Kingfisher	D
12238	King of Prussia	M
12240	King William	M
12241	King William	— P S
12243	King William	— Long-Horn
12244	King William	— M
12245	King William	M
12246	King William	Cox
12247	King William	Cox
12248	King William 2nd	— M
12251	King William	L R
12252	King William 2nd	L R
12253	King William 3rd	— P S
12254	Kinikinick	M
12256	Kit Carson	— Ky I
12257	Kit Carson	— Ky I
12260	Know Thyself	— M
12262	Ku-Klux	— Daisy
12263	Ku-Klux	D
12264	Ku-Klux	— R R
12265	Lady Jefferson's Son	D
12267	Laird of Muirkirk	P S
(12268)	Victor	— Cox
12270	Lancer	C
12271	Lansing	C
12272	Laocoon	— R R
12273	Last Grand Duke of Airdrie	— D
12274	Last Sensation	Ky I
12275	Latham	— M
12276	Laudable	T
12277	Lavengro	— D
12278	Lawson	M
12279	Legal Tender	— T
12280	Legal Tender 2nd	P S
12281	LeGrand	— Ky I
12282	Leo	— T
12283	Leonard	— T
12284	Leonard	M
12285	Leonidas	T
12287	Leopard 2nd	— R R
12289	Leslie	L R
12290	Leslie	— M
12291	Leyden	— Cox
12292	Liberty Duke	— R R
12293	Liberty London	— M

12294	Lieut. Gage	— P S
12295	Lincoln	— L R
12297	Lincoln	— M
12298	2nd Linden	— M
12299	3rd Linden	— M
12301	Little Giant	M
12302	Little Mac	L R
12305	Llewellyn 2nd	L R
12306	Locomotive	C
12307	Logan	— D
12310	Longstreet	Ky I
12311	Lorain Prince	— C
12312	Lord Baltimore	— T
12313	Lord Baltimore 2nd	P S
12315	Lord Clifton	— M
12316	Lord Danby	P S
12317	Lord Douglass	— M
12320	Lord John	C
12323	Lord Lorne	— R R
12325	Lord Marmion	M
12328	Lord of Lorne	P S
12329	Lord of Oxford 3rd	— L R
12331	Lord of the Manor	L R
12333	Lord of the Valley	Ky I
12334	Lord Oxford	M
12338	Lothair	M
12339	Louan Duke of Woodlawn	— M
12340	Louanjo	— L R
12341	Louan's Oakland	— R R
12344	Loudon Duke of Fairview	— R R
12345	Louis	P S
12346	Lucy's Oxford	C
12347	Loyal	Ky I
12348	Maccaroon	Ky I
12349	Macomb Duke	P S
12350	Mad Anthony	— D
12354	Major	— P S
12355	Major	— Daisy
12356	Major	— L R
12357	Major	— Daisy
12358	Major	M
12359	Major	— P S
12360	Major	D
12361	Major	Ky I
12362	Major	— M
12364	Maj. Anderson	Ky I
12365	Maj. Andre	— T
12366	Maj. Butterfly	— R R
12367	Maj. Duke	— Ky I
12368	Maj. Duncan	— R R
12370	Maj. Sheridan	— R R
12371	Maj. Stark	— Ky I
12372	Maj. Stonewall	D
12373	Maj. Wheeler	M
12374	Major	Ky I
12376	Malcolm Jr	P S
12377	Malcolm Miller	— R R
12380	Magnet	R R
12381	Maple Grove	— M
12384	Marblewald	P S
12385	March Earl	— R R
12386	March Marston	Ky I
12390	Marion Duke of Airdrie	M
12391	Mark	Ky I
12394	Mark Antony	— D
12397	Mark Twain	— M
12398	Marlborough	— R R
12399	Marmaduke Jr	— Cox
12400	Marmion	Ky I
12402	Marquis	— C
12403	Marquis	Ky I
12404	Marquis	— D
12405	Marquis of Lorne	— M
12406	Marquis of Lorne	— R R
12407	Mars	— C
12408	Marshal Bazaine	— M
12410	Marvello	Ky I
12412	Master Airdrie 2nd	— T
12415	Masterman	— R R
12419	Maximillian	Ky I
12420	May Boy 2nd	— Cox
12421	May Duke	— M
12422	May Duke	— P S
12423	May Duke	Daisy
12425	Mazurka Duke of Airdrie	C
12427	Mazurka's Heir	— Cox
12432	McDonough Duke	— M
12433	Melodeon	— M
12434	Melrose	— M
12435	Mercer	C
12436	Merrill	— Cox
12437	Merry Boy	— M
12438	Merry Duke	Ky I
12439	Mike	— P S
12440	Mike Davison	— R R
12441	Mike Girty	T
12442	Mike Maloney	— L R
12445	Milo	— Daisy
12446	Milton	— M
12447	Minister	— P S
12448	Miral	— Ky I
12449	Mogul	— P S
12450	Mohawk	— P S
12452	Monarch of the Plains	— D
12453	Money Maker	L R
12454	Monitor	— M
12456	Monitor	— Cox
12457	Monitor	P S
12458	Monitor	M
12459	Monitor 2nd	— Ky I
12460	Monroe	M
12461	Monroe Duke	Ky I
12462	Montana	T
12463	Montana	Daisy
12465	Montezuma 2nd	— L R
12466	Montgomery	M
12469	Morning Star	— M
12470	Moscow Duke	— R R
12472	Mountaineer	— T
12473	Mohawk	Ky I
12474	Mr. Boffin	— R R
12476	Mr. Toots	M
12480	Napier	— Cox
12481	Napier Jr	— Cox
12483	Nebraska	— Ky I
12484	Nebraska Boy	M
12487	Neptune	D
12488	Neptune	— C
12489	Neptune	— P S
12493	Newton	— P S
12494	Newton	— R R
12496	New Years Gift	M
12497	New Years Lad	— M
12498	Nimrod	— P S
12499	Nimrod	— R R
12500	Nimrod	Ky I
12501	Nimrod Long	— M
12502	Noble 3rd	D
12503	Noble 4th	— C
12504	Noble Airdrie	— P S

No.	Name	Herd	No.	Name	Herd
12505	Noble Duke	— M	12618	Prairie Starlight	— R R
12506	Noble Duke	— L R	12619	Preacher	— R R
12507	Nonconformist	— D	12620	President	P S
12514	Oakland Starlight	— L R	12621	President 15th	— M
12517	Ocean Boy	Ky I	12622	President Barrett	P S
12518	Octo	— M	12623	Priam	— M
12519	Ohio Prince	— D	12625	Pride of Camden	— Cox
12521	Old Hundred	— R R	12626	Pride of Jefferson	T
12524	Ole Bull	Ky I	12627	Princeton	— D
12525	Oliver	Ky I	12628	Prince	M
12526	Oliver Twist	M	12631	Prince	L R
12528	Onondaga's Lad	P S	12632	Prince	Cox
12529	Orange	— P S	12634	Prince	Ky I
12530	Oregon	— P S	12635	Prince	— R R
12531	Oregonian	P S	12636	Prince 3d	L R
12532	Orion Boy	M	12637	Prince Albert	C
12533	Orphan Boy	P S	12638	Prince Albert	P S
12534	Orphan Boy	Ky I	12639	Prince Albert	M
12535	Orphan Boy	P S	12641	Prince Albert	M
12537	Oscar	C	12643	Prince Albert	— L R
12538	Oscar	T	12644	Prince Albert 2nd	— Ky I
12539	Osceola	— M	12646	Prince Arthur	— M
12542	Otley	— M	12648	Prince Arthur	— R R
12544	Oxford	D	12649	Prince Atha	— M
12549	Oxford Boy	C	12650	Prince Bismarck	C
12550	Oxford Gywnne	— Cox	12651	Prince Charles	— L R
12555	Oxford Lad	L R	12654	Prince Edward	P S
12557	Oxford of Cedar Nook	— Cox	12655	Prince Frederick	M
12558	Oxford of Mercer	— L R	12660	Prince Imperial	— D
12559	Oxford Prince	M	12661	Prince John	— M
12561	Oxford Duke of Atholl	— R R	12661½	Prince John 2nd	— M
12563	Oxford Vann	— M	12662	Prince John	— R R
12564	Palmyra	Ky I	12668	Prince of Buchingham	— R R
12565	Paragon	— Cox	12670	Prince of Sharon	— L R
12567	Parson Booth	— R R	12672	Prince of Oakhill	— M
12569	Pat Molloy	— R R	12673	Prince of Oakland	L R
12572	Pat Sanford	— L R	12674	Prince of Orange	M
12573	Paul Jones	M	12679	Prince of Wyoming	— M
12574	Paul Pry	— M	12683	Prince Royal	Ky I
12578	Pearl Duke	— R R	12687	Princeton Count 2nd	P S
12580	Persimmon	D	12688	Prince William	— M
12582	Petroleum V. Nasby	M	12689	Prince William	— M
12584	Phil Sheridan	R R	12690	Prize Duke	M
12585	Phil Sheridan	T	12691	Prospect Duke	— C
12586	Pickwick	Ky I	12692	Prussian King	— D
12587	Pike	— M	12693	Pulaski	Woods
12588	Pilgrim	— M	12694	Punch	M
12589	Pilot	M	12695	Punch	— P S
12590	Pilot	— R R	12696	Purcell	— M
12592	Pilot	— Ky I	12698	Quilp	— R R
12594	Planchette	M	12699	Quincy	— C
12595	Plantaganet Lad	— R R	12701	2nd Ranger	— Cox
12596	Plebiscite	T	12705	Red Airdrie of Elm Grove	— M
12598	Plumwood A	Ky I	12707	Rod Bill	— D
12599	Plumwood B	C	12708	Red Robbie	— Cox
12600	Plumwood C	R R	12712	Red Buckingham	— M
12601	Plumwood D	R R	12713	Redbud	P S
12602	Plumwood E	Ky I	12714	Red Bull	— R R
12603	Plumwood Boy	R R	12715	Red Chief	P S
12604	Plumwood Lad 2nd	R R	12716	Red Cloud	Ky I
12605	Pole Star	— Daisy	12717	Red Cloud	— L R
12606	Polydore	M	12718	Red Cloud	— Cox
12607	Polypus	— M	12719	Red Cloud	D
12608	Pony	— Cox	12721	Red Cloud	— P S
12611	Potosi	— Ky I	12722	Red Cloud	— M
12612	Powhatan	— M	12723	Red Cloud	M
12613	Prairie Bird	Cox	12724	Red Davy	— T
12614	Prairie Boy	— T	12726	Red Douglas	Ky I
12616	Prairie Boy	— M	12729	Red Duke	Ky I
12617	Prairie Duke	— P S	12730	Red Duke	Ky I

No.	Name	Code
12735	Red Duke	Cox
12736	Red Duke	— M
12739	Red Duke	M
12743	Red Duke of Woodford	C
12744	Red Favorite	L R
12745	Red Ike 2nd	— C
12746	Red Jacket	— M
12747	Red Jacket	T
12748	Red Jacket	— R R
12750	Red Lion	— L R
12751	Red Major	— D
12752	Red Oak	D
12753	Red Oak	— L R
12754	Red Prince	L R
12755	Red Prince	C
12756	Red Ranger	— D
12757	Red Rocket	L R
12758	Red Rover	M
12759	Red Rover	— C
12760	Red Rover	— Ky I
12761	Red Rover	— Cox
12762	Red Rover	— L R
12763	Red Rover	Ky I
12764	Red Rover	— P S
12766	Red Rover	— P S
12767	Red Star	— M
12768	Red Star	— M
12769	Red Wiley	— R R
12770	Redwing	— Cox
12771	Reformer	P S
12772	Regium Donum	— M
12774	Remus	— L R
12775	Remus	— Ky I
12777	Renick Duke 1st	R R
12778	Reon	M
12779	Rescue	Ky I
12780	Reuben 2nd	M
12783	Richland Duke	Daisy
12784	Richmond	— T
12785	Richmond	M
12786	Richmond Lad	— L R
12787	Rinaldo	T
12788	Ringgold	Ky I
12789	Roan Billy	M
12790	Roan Chief	L R
12792	Roan Duke	— R R
12794	Roan Duke	D
12795	Roan Lad	P S
12796	Roan Prince	Daisy
12798	Roan Rover	L R
12800	Roan Star 3rd	— L R
12801	Robert Burns	C
12802	Robert Scott	T
12803	Robin Grey	— Long-Horn
12804	Rob Roy	D
12805	Rob Roy	— D
12807	Rob Roy	— D
12808	Rocket	M
12809	Roderick	Ky I
12810	Roderick Dhu	P S
12811	Rodman	— M
12813	Rodolph	M
12814	Roger Hanson	— R R
12815	Roland	M
12816	Roland	Ky I
12817	Rolin	— M
12818	Romeo	Cox
12819	Romeo	Ky I
12823	Romulus	— L R
12824	Roscoe	— Wrong
12827	Rosendale	— P S
12828	Rosendale 1st	— M
12829	Rosendale 2nd	— L R
12830	Rosendale 3rd	— M
12831	Rosendale 4th	— L R
12832	Rosendale 5th	— L R
12833	Rosendale 6th	— M
12834	Rosendale Laddie	— P S
12835	Rose's Duke	— D
12836	Rosseau	— M
12837	Rossiter	— M
12839	Rover	M
12840	Rover	Ky I
12841	Rover	— L R
12842	Royal	T
12848	Royal Commander	T
12850	Royal Duke 3rd	P S
12851	Royal Duke of Moreton	M
12852	Royal Forth Jr	M
12853	Royal George	— D
12857	Royal Nero	— Cox
12861	Royal Prince of Fairview	— R R
12863	Royal William	— L R
12864	Row Boy	L R
12866	Rubicund	— P S
12867	Rudolph	— R R
12868	Rush	— P S
12871	Sam	— Cox
12875	Sampson	— L R
12876	Sampson	— Cox
12877	Sam Slick	Ky I
12878	Sam Slick	M
12879	Sam Sly	— L R
12883	Sandy Hook	P S
12886	Santa Anna	P S
12888	Sargeant	M
12889	Saturn	— Cox
12890	Schuyler	Ky I
12895	Seeley	Ky I
12896	Senator	M
12897	Senator	P S
12898	Senator	P S
12900	Senator 4th	— Wrong
12902	Seven Thirty 3rd	— L R
12903	Seventy	— L R
12904	Shakespeare	D
12905	Shamrock	— C
12907	Shannon	M
12908	Ben Sheffield	— M
12909	Shelby	— M
12910	Shenango Boy	M
12912	Sheridan	— Ky I
12914	Sherman	— Ky I
12915	Sherman	Ky I
12916	Sherman	M
12918	Shropshire	— D
12921	Sinbad	— Cox
12922	Sir Alfred	— C
12924	Sir Anthony	Ky I
12925	Sir Colin Campbell	— Ky I
12926	Sir Frederick	— R R
12927	Sir John	T
12928	1st Sir Knox	M
12929	2nd Sir Knox	M
12930	3rd Sir Knox	— L R
12931	Sir Walter	— L R
12932	Sir William Pinckney	Ky I
12934	Smike	— M
12935	Snowball	— D
12936	Snowbank	T

12937	Snowdon — L R	13054	Trouble — P S
12938	Snowdrop's Duke — Ky I	13055	Trumpeter — M
12939	Snowflake — Wrong	13056	Tudor — Ky I
12940	Sockburn Duke 2nd — M	13058	Turk — M
12941	Solitaire — D	13059	Twanky — M
12942	Solomon — L R	13061	Tycoon — R R
12943	Son of Douglas — L R	13063	Tyrone — P S
12944	Son of Premier — Cox	13064	Ulysses — M
12946	Southerner — P S	13065	Ulysses — D
12950	Sportsman — M	13067	Union Jack — P S
12954	Star — M	13068	Vallandigham — R R
12955	Star — M	13069	Valentine — D
12956	Stanley Waterloo — M	13070	Valley Duke — Ky I
12957	Star Davis — D	13071	Vassal — Ky I
12959	Star Duke — Ky I	13074	Velocipede 1st — M
12960	Star Duke — D	13075	Velocipede 2nd — Wrong
12962	Star in the West — M	13077	Veni-Vidi-Vici — R R
12964	Starlight — M	13078	Vermillion Duke — R R
12966	Starlight of Pickaway — C	13080	Veto — Ky I
12967	Starlight of Ross — C	13084	Victor Duke — R R
12968	Star of Hope — Cox	13085	Viceroy — M
12969	Star of Oxford — Cox	13086	Vim — M
12971	Star of the East — L R	13089	Vispring — M
12973	Star of the West — M	13090	Von Moltke — L R
12974	Star of Towanda — M	13092	Von Moltke — L R
12976	Steerforth — T	13093	Von Moltke — C
12977	Sterling — M	13094	Volberg — L R
12978	Sterling — P S	13096	Wallace — M
12980	St. Elmo — P S	13097	Walnut Grove Duke — M
12983	St. Lawrence, Jr — P S	13099	Wapsie Count — M
12985	Stock Duke — R R	13100	Wapsie Duke — L R
12989	Stonewall Jackson — P S	13101	Wapsie River — R R
12991	Storm — M	13103	Warrior — L R
12992	St. Patrick — D	13105	Warwick — D
12993	St. Switson — P S	13106	Warwick — L R
12994	Strawberrys Duke — Ky I	13107	Washington — D
12995	Sucker Boy — D	13108	Washington — M
12996	Summit Chief — P S	13109	Washington 12th — Daisy
12998	Sumter — D	13117	Welcome Guest — R R
12999	Sunlight — M	13119	Wellington — M
13000	Sutherland — L R	13120	Wellington — P S
13001	Swiss Boy — M	13121	Welrose — C
13002	Sidney Carton — Ky I	13122	Weston — T
13003	Sylvan Duke — Ky I	13123	Western Chief — Ky I
13004	Sylvester Strong — D	13124	Western Lion — L R
13005	Talanka — T	13125	White Cloud — M
13007	Taurus — D	13126	White Cloud — Ky I
13008	Tempest 1st — M	13127	White Comet — M
13009	Tempest 2nd — Ky I	13128	White Eagle — L R
13010	Tempest 3rd — Ky I	13130	White Rover — L R
13011	Tempest Duke — D	13131	White Stockings — M
13012	Ten-Forty — R R	13132	Wild Edgerton — Daisy
13014	Ten-Forty — P S	13133	Wild Moor — M
13015	Ten-Forty 2nd — M	13134	Wiley — Ky I
13016	Terrapin — M	13138	William — P S
13017	Teeswater — Cox	13140	Willie — P S
13020	The Doctor — C	13141	Windsor — Cox
13026	Theodrick — P S	13143	Winnisheik — R R
13027	The Monk — C	13147	Wissahikon 2nd — M
13029	Thor — R R	13149	Woodlawn — M
13036	Thornton — L R	13150	Woodlawn Duke — Ky I
13037	Thoroughby — L R	13151	Woodlawn Duke — M
13038	Tipton — M	13152	Woodlawn Prince — Ky I
13039	Toldy — R R	13153	Woodman Duke — P S
13041	Tom Corwin — Ky I	13154	Yankee Boy — R R
13042	Tom Moore — D	13155	Yarborough 2nd — T
13045	Tom Wappet — P S	13156	Yarborough 3rd — P S
13047	Toulon Lad — P S	13160	Young Arthur — Ky I
13051	Triumph — R R	13162	Young Banner Boy — M
13052	Trojan — L R	13163	Young Emigrant — M

13169	Young Empire	Ky I	13288	Red Rover — M
13170	Young Exile	P S	13291	Sheldon — Daisy
13172	Young John O'Gaunt	P S	13295	Starlight of Madison — L R
13175	Young Mozark 2nd	— Ky I	13301	Victor — Daisy
13176	Young Norwood 2nd	— M	13302	Victory — Cox
13178	Young Prince	— D	13303½	William Owsley — M
13179	Young Rafe	L R	13304	Wolverine — Ky I
13181	Young Roderick	T	13305	Young Alpha M
13185	Zadig	— M	13306	Young Duke of Scioto — Cox
13186	Zeb	Ky I	13307	Zeb Dun — C
13187	Zero	Cox	13308	Abdallah M
13188	Zareb	— R R	13309	Abe — D
13189	Zealot	— R R	13310	Accident 3rd — P S
13190	Zero	M	13311	Acteon R R
13193	Adonis	— Cox	13312	Adam M
13195	Alexander The Great	— D	13313	Adam Clark — D
13197	Argyll Duke	D	13315	Admiral M
13200	Baron Sheffelder	— D	13316	Admiral 2nd P S
13208	Ben Bolt	— R R	13317	Admiral 3rd — Daisy
13204¼	Bill Arp	— P S	13322	Airdrie Boy Cox
13205	Billy	— M	13324	Airdrie Duke of Linwood — R R
13206	Bishop	T	13326	Airdrie's Duke of Kansas P S
13210	Bridesman 2nd	— R R	13329	Airdrie Sweepstakes M
13214	Canadian Boy	— R R	13330	A. J. Dunlap Ky I
13215	Capt. Booth	— L R	13335	Aleck — T
13216	Carlotta Duke	D	13336	Aleck Anderson D
13217	Cass Co. Boy	T	13340	Alexander M
13218	Castile	— T	13341	Alexander P S
13223	Colfax	T	13342	Alexis — Wrong
13224	Col. Hanna	M	13343	Alexis — M
13225	Comet	M	13347	Alexis M
13226	Crœsus	Cox	13349	Alexis L R
13227	Daylight	D	13350	Alexis R R
13228	Duke	— R R	13351	Alexis — Cox
13229	Duke of Airdrie 2nd	T	13352	Alexis — P S
13231	11th Duke of Edgar	— R R	13353	Alexis — P S
13232	12th Duke of Edgar	— R R	13354	Alexis 2nd Ky I
13233	13th Duke of Edgar	— M	13355	Alexis Mason — R R
13234	14th Duke of Edgar	Daisy	13359	Alonzo — T
13235	15th Duke of Edgar	— P S	13360	Alpha P S
13235½	Duke of Fairview	— M	13362	Alton — D
13239	Duke of Pendleton	L R	13363	Altona M
13240	Duke of Starlight	D	13365	Amazon Duke — D
13243	Elmwood Favorite	Daisy	13366	Ambassador P S
13244	Fairholme Duke of Atholl	— R R	13367	Andes M
13245	Fairy Duke	— R R	13368	Andy Ky I
13247	Five-Twenty, Jr.	M	13369	Andy Johnson — M
13248	Fourth of July	— D	13371	Anthony Ky I
13249	Gen. Grant	T	13372	Antioch Duke — R R
13250	Gen. Opdyke	L R	13374	Apollo — D
13251	Gen. Grant	M	13375	April Fool — M
13252	Gen. Sherman	M	13377	Arcas — Daisy
13253	Gov. Vance	M	13380	Arcola Prince M
13254	Gov. Worthington	M	13385	Astoria L R
13256	Hoosier Boy	T	13386	Atholl Duke — D
13257	Joe Dwyer	D	13387	Athelstaneford — L R
13258	Joel	— M	13388	Atholston — M
13261	Kentucky	— T	13390	Augustus T
13262	Kilpatrick	T	13392	Augustus P S
13264	Leonidas	— L R	13393	Aurora Duke T
13269	Louan Duke	— R R	13394	Aurora Lad M
13270	Louan's Airdrie	— M	13397	Balla Bolt Ky I
13271	Louan's Imperial	— M	13398	Banta Tim M
13273	Major Booth	— L R	13399	Barclay C
13274	Major Brent	— Long-Horn	13401	Barnum D
13277	Meteor	Daisy	(13403)	Ohio — M
13279	Mountaineer 2nd	— M	13404	Baron Atholl Ky I
13282	Perfection 2nd	T	13408	Baron Bertram — Long-Horn
13283	Perfection 3rd	T	13409	Baron Bertram 2nd — P S
13287	Red Jacket	M	13411	Baron Booth of Linwood —P S

SHORT-HORN CATTLE PEDIGREES. 61

No.	Name	Herd
13412	Baron Dun	— M
13417	Baron Gwynne 4th	— Cox
13421	Baron Kirk	— C
13425	Baron Louanjo 2nd	— R R
13426	Baron Louanjo 3rd	— R R
13429	Baron of Fairview	— D
13430	Baron of Fairview	R R
13432	Baron of Franklin	Ky I
13433	Baron of Leroy	— M
13438	Baron Raglan	— C
13440	Baron Sheldon	L R
13441	Baron Starlight	— D
13442	Baron Unus	— Ky I
13445	Basil Duke 2nd	— P S
13447	Baxter	Cox
13448	Beacon	— L R
13450	Beauregard	Ky I
13451	Bell Duke	— L R
13452	Bell Duke 2nd	— D
13454	Bell Duke D	— R R
13455	Bell Duke E	— R R
13456	Bell Duke of Airdrie	— R R
13461	Belle's Duke	M
13465	Belvedere	Ky I
13468	Bem Ranels	M
13470	Ben Berther	— M
13471	Ben Butler	M
13472	Ben Clyde	M
13473	Ben F. Dodson of Poplar Farm	— C
13474	Ben Forrester	— R R
13476	Beppo	Ky I
13478	Berkshire Boy	Cox
13479	Berlin	— C
13485	Bill Arp	— M
13486	Billy	— M
13487	Billy	Ky I
13488	Billy Barlow	— R R
13489	Billy Bishop	M
13490	Billy Baskins	— M
13491	Billy Button	M
13492	Billy Rogers	— P S
13493	Billy Sherman	— R R
13494	Bill Waddy	P S
13496	Bismarck	M
13499	Bismarck	M
13500	Bismarck	D
13501	Bismarck	— P S
13502	Bismarck	— P S
13503	Bismarck	— D
13504	Bismarck	— R R
13505	Bismarck	Ky I
13506	Bismarck	— L R
13507	Bismarck	— R R
13508	Blanco 2nd	— L R
13512	Blazing Star	— L R
13514	Bloom's Vandal	— T
13515	Blucher	— Cox
13518	Bob	— Ky I
13520	Bob Breckenridge	— P S
13521	Bob Lee	— P S
13523	Bob Lee 3rd	— P S
13524	Bob Schenck	— P S
13525	Bob Taylor	— M
13531	Bonaparte	— L R
13533	Boreas	Daisy
13534	Boston	— M
13535	Boston	— P S
13536	Boston	— C
13537	Botheration	L R
13538	Bourbon Duke	— D
13540	Bourbon Duke	Daisy
13541	Bourbon Lad	— Ky I
13544	Brakeman	P S
13546	Bravo	— L R
13547	Breckenridge	— L R
13548	Brick Pomeroy	— Cox
13549	Brick Pomeroy	P S
13550	Bridegroom	— R R
13552	Brigham	T
13553	Brigham	M
13555	Brighton Lad	— M
13559	Brother Jonathan	Ky I
13561	Brutus	P S
13562	Brutus	— M
13563	Brutus	— R R
13564	Brutus	— M
13565	Buena Vista	— R R
13566	Buccaneer	Ky I
13568	Buckeye	M
13569	Buckeye Chief	— Long-Horn
13570	Buckeye Boy	D
13571	Buckingham	— R R
13572	Bullet	— Cox
13573	Bullion	— D
13575	Burlington	— R R
13576	Burnside	— L R
13577	Burnside	— M
13579	Burton	— P S
13580	Buttercup	M
13581	Butterdale	L R
13585	Byron	— M
13586	Cadet	— P S
13588	Calhoun	— D
13589	Caligula	— M
13590	Callippus	— D
13591	Camelia's Oxford	— M
13592	Canada	— M
13593	Canadian Chief	— Cox
13594	Canada Duke	M
13597	Captain	L R
13598	Captain	L R
13599	Captain Absolute	R R
13600	Capt. Acres	— Wrong
13601	Capt. Airdrie	C
13602	Capt. Ascot	— M
13603	Capt. Coulter	M
13604	Capt. Creigh	T
13605	Capt. Hope	— Cox
13606	Capt. Kidd	— Long-Horn
13607	Capt. Jenks	Ky I
13608	Capt. Jenks	— L R
13609	Capt. Leonard	— L R
13610	Capt. Pervis	M
13612	Capt. Smith	— R R
13614	Cardinal	— R R
13621	Carmel Duke	— L R
13622	Cassander	P S
13623	Cato	— L R
13624	Cato 2nd	Ky I
13625	Cavagna	— M
13628	Challenger	Ky I
13629	Champion	D
13631	Champion 2nd	M
13635	Charley Austin	— L R
13636	Charles Edward	— L R
13637	Cherry 2nd's Australia	— L R
13638	Cherry 3rd's Ascot	— D
13642	Cherokee	C
13644	Chester	— R R
13647	Chieftain	Ky I

No.	Name	Code
13649	Chief of McKee's Creek	M
13654	Christopher Duke	M
13655	Christmas Day	Wrong
13662	Claude	P S
13664	Clermont	— R R
13665	Cleveland Lad	— D
13666	Clifton Duke 4th	R R
13668	Climax	Ky 1
13671	Colfax	— D
13672	Colfax	L R
13673	Colfax	Daisy
13674	Colfax 4th	L R
13675	Colfax 5th	M
13676	Col. Boone	— T
13677	Col. Breckenridge	— P S
13678	Col. Clark	— R R
13682	Col. Jas. W. Judy	— P S
13684	Col. Judy	Ky 1
13685	Col. Jilt	— Long-Horn
13689	Col. R. W. Davis	T
12693	Colorado	— P S
13695	Columbus	— D
13696	Columbus	M
13699	Comet	Cox
13700	Comet	— P S
13701	Comet 2d	C
13702	Comet Halley	D
13703	Commodore	— M
13704	Commodore 4th	L R
13706	Commodore	— D
13707	Compromise	P S
13708	Comus	Daisy
13712	Cooper	M
13716	Cortland	P S
13717	Cosmos	— M
13718	Councillor	— L R
13719	Count	C
13721	Count Atholl	— R R
13722	Count Bismarck	L R
13724	Count Cavour	L R
13727	1st Count of Oneida	— R R
13729	Crooker	R R
13731	Cream of the West's Ascot	M
13732	Cream's Ascot	M
13733	Creston Chief	— D
13734	Creston Lad	— L R
13737	Crown Prince	— M
13738	Crown Prince	— D
13739	Crown Prince	L R
13740	Crusader	Ky 1
13741	Crusader	— M
13742	Crusader 2d	Ky 1
13744	Cycle	R R
13747	Dairyman	— Cox
13748	Dairyman 2d	— Cox
13749	Daisy Bull	— R R
13750	Daisy Duke	M
13751	Daisy Duke	Ky 1
13752	Daisy Duke	— R R
13753	Daisy Duke	— Ky 1
13754	Dandy	— D
13756	Dandy	D
13757	Dandy Clyde	M
13759	Dandy Jim	Ky 1
13762	Dan Griffin	— R R
13763	Dan Harrison	— R R
13764	Daniel Boone	T
13765	Dan McMillan	M
13766	Dan O'Connell	L R
13767	Dan Tucker	L R
13769	David Davis	— L R
13770	Darby Lad 2d	— P S
13772	Darby Lad 4th	— P S
13774	Dardeene	— M
13775	Darling Duke	P S
13778	Dave	Cox
13779	Dave Mosier	— R R
13780	David Copperfield	— R R
13781	David Wilson	— D
13782	Davie Grant	— R R
13784	Davy	M
13785	Daybreak	M
13786	Dean's Prince of Oxford	M
13787	Decori	— M
13788	Deerfoot	— Cox
13789	Defender	— Cox
13792	Defiance	— L R
13793	Delver (or Drone)	M
13794	Derby Duke	— R R
13795	Der Graf Von Wilderberg	P S
13797	Dewey	— Ky 1
13799	Dexter	P S
13800	Dexter	Ky 1
13801	Dick Clyde	M
13802	Dick Clarence	— Cox
13803	Dickens	Cox
13807	Dick Oglesby	— T
13808	Dick Taylor	— D
13809	Dick Taylor	C
13811	Dick Turpin	Ky 1
13812	Dick Watson 2d	— D
13813	Dimple	Ky 1
13815	Dr. Durbin	— Ky 1
13817	Dr. Lacy	Ky 1
13818	Domino	— P S
13819	Don	— M
13820	Donax	Cox
13821	Don Carlos	— Cox
13822	Don Carlos	P S
13824	Don Pedro	— R R
13827	Doublet	— L R
13828	Douglas 3d	P S
13831	Dred	— L R
13832	Drover	— M
13833	Drusus	— Daisy
13834	Duchess 5th's Ascot	— D
13835	Duchess Oxford's Bull	— D
13837	2d Duke	M
13839	Duke	R R
13840	Duke	— M
13841	Duke	Ky 1
13843	Duke	— R R
13844	Duke	Ky 1
13845	Duke Airdrie 6th	T
13846	Duke Airdrie 7th	— M
13847	Duke Alexis	— M
13848	Duke Alexis	— M
13849	Duke Alexis	T
13850	Duke Alexis	P S
13851	Duke Alexis	P S
13852	Duke Alexis	L R
13853	Duke Alexis	— P S
13854	Duke Alexis	— M
13855	Duke Alexis	M
13856	Duke Alexis	M
13858	Duke Alexis	— Ky 1
13863	Duke Elick	M
13864	Duke Forrester	— R R
13865	Duke John	— T
13871	5th Duke of Airdrie	— M

SHORT-HORN CATTLE PEDIGREES.

No.	Name	Owner
13874	Duke of Animus	— Cox
13877	Duke of Annapolis	P S
13878	Duke of Arlington	T
13879	4th Duke of Ashland	P S
13885	Duke of Booth	M
13886	Duke of Brant	— Cox
13889	Duke of Burnett 5th	— C
13890	Duke of Burnett 6th	— R R
13891	Duke of Burnett 7th	— R R
13892	Duke of Burnett 8th	— M
13893	Duke of Burnett 9th	P S
13894	Duke of Burnett 10th	— M
13896	Duke of Burnett 13th	— R R
13898	Duke of Burnett 14th	— R R
13899	Duke of Burnett 15th	— R R
13900	Duke of Burnett 16th	— R R
13902	Duke of Camden	— Cox
13905	Duke of Cartright Valley	— R R
13906	Duke of Cedar Nook	— Cox
13910	4th Duke of Clarendon	P S
13911	Duke of Clay	— R R
13913	Duke of Cleveland	P S
13914	Duke of Cumberland	— R R
13915	2nd Duke of Dallas	— D
13916	1st Duke of Deerpark	— D
13917	2nd Duke of Deerpark	— D
13918	3rd Duke of Deerpark	— D
13919	4th Duke of Deerpark	P S
13921	Duke of Durham Farm	— M
13922	1st Duke of East Side	— M
13923	Duke of Edgwood	C
13924	Duke of Elmgrove	— M
13925	Duke of Eminence	T
13928	Duke of Fairview	L R
13929	2nd Duke of Fairview	— R R
13930	Duke of Fashion	Cox
13931	Duke of Fayette	P S
13932	Duke of Fayette	— D
13933	Duke of Fayette	D
13934	Duke of Florence	— D
13935	Duke of Ford	— Daisy
13939	2nd Duke of Garnaville	— P S
13940	Duke of Genesee	— Cox
13941	Duke of Glen Echo	— M
13942	Duke of Gloster	L R
13944	7th Duke of Goodness	— R R
13945	10th Duke of Goodness	— R R
13946	11th Duke of Goodness	— R R
13947	12th Duke of Goodness	— R R
13948	13th Duke of Goodness	— R R
13949	14th Duke of Goodness	— R R
13952	1st Duke of Granville	— R R
13953	2nd Duke of Granville	— R R
13959	8th Duke of Granville	— R R
13962	9th Duke of Greenbush	L R
13963	10th Duke of Greenbush	T
13965	12th Duke of Greenbush	— P S
13966	13th Duke of Greenbush	— L R
13968	2nd Duke of Greenlawn	— M
13969	3rd Duke of Greenlawn	— D
13970	4th Duke of Greenlawn—Long-Horn	
13971	5th Duke of Greenlawn	— M
13972	6th Duke of Greenlawn	— M
13973	8th Duke of Greenlawn	— M
13974	9th Duke of Greenlawn	— M
13975	Duke of Grenville	— D
13980	Duke of Hazelland	Ky I
13981	Duke of Hellena	Daisy
13983	Duke of Highland	— D
13985	Duke of Hillsdale 2nd	R R
13988	Duke of Independence	P S
13991	Duke of Industry	— M
13996	Duke of Johnson	— D
13997	1st Duke of Kalamazoo	Ky I
13998	2nd Duke of Kalamazoo	Ky I
13999	3rd Duke of Kalamazoo	Ky I
14000	Duke of Kansas	— R R
14001	Duke of Kenton	— T
14002	Duke of Knox Grove	— M
14003	Duke of Lancaster	— L R
14004	2nd Duke of LaSalle	— Cox
14005	3rd Duke of LaSalle	— M
14006	Duke of Lee	— M
14007	Duke of Lee	— M
14008	Duke of Lee	D
14010	Duke of Liberty	P S
14011	Duke of Liberty	— Cox
14013	6th Duke of Liberty	T
14014	7th Duke of Liberty	Ky I
14015	8th Duke of Liberty	— M
14016	9th Duke of Liberty	Ky I
14017	10th Duke of Liberty	Ky I
14018	11th Duke of Liberty	Ky I
14019	12th Duke of Liberty	Ky I
14020	13th Duke of Liberty	T
14021	Duke of Limestone	M
14022	Duke of Livingstone	— Cox
14023	Duke of Lone Elm	Ky I
14024	Duke of Muscatreek	— D
14025	Duke of Madison	— P S
14026	Duke of Mad River	— M
14027	Duke of Malakoff 3d	— Cox
14028	Duke of Mansfield	— R R
14029	Duke of Maple Grove	— M
14031	Duke of Marrowbone	— R R
14033	Duke of Maudville	— R R
14035	Duke of May	— D
14036	2nd Duke of May	— P S
14037	3rd Duke of May	— P S
14038	4th Duke of May	— D
14039	5th Duke of May	— D
14040	Duke of Mercer	Ky I
14042	9th Duke of Morgan	Daisy
14045	Duke of Nicholas	Woods
14047	Duke of Oakdale	— R R
14048	3rd Duke of Oakland	L R
14049	4th Duke of Oakland	L R
14050	5th Duke of Oakland	L R
14051	6th Duke of Oakland	L R
14053	Duke of Okaw	— M
14054	Duke of Omaha	M
14055	1st Duke of Omaha	— M
14057	6th Duke of Onondaga	Cox
14058	7th Duke of Onondaga	Woods
14059	8th Duke of Onondaga	Woods
14060	9th Duke of Onondaga	Woods
14061	Duke of Orleans	M
14062	Duke of Osage	— P S
14063	2nd Duke of Osage	— P S
14064	Duke of Oxford	— Cox
14065	Duke of Ozark	— M
14066	Duke of Paris	Ky I
14067	2nd Duke of Paris	— P S
14069	Duke of Putnam	Daisy
14070	3rd Duke of Randolph	Ky I
14071	4th Duke of Randolph	Ky I
14072	5th Duke of Randolph	Ky I
14076	Duke of Riggston	Ky I
14077	Duke of Rutland	Ky I
14078	Duke of Salem	R R

14079	5th Duke of Saltville	P S	14187	Elias Brown — Long-Horn
14080	Duke of Saratoga	— M	14191	Emerald M
14081	Duke of Seaham	— C	14192	Emmett D
14082	2nd Duke of Shannon	— P S	14193	Emmett 3rd — C
14083	3rd Duke of Shannon	— L R	14195	Emperor Cox
14084	3d Duke of Silverwood	M	14196	Emperor — Cox
14086	Duke of Simpson	Daisy	14199	Emperor 2nd — P S
14087	Duke of Solway	— M	14200	Emperor 3rd D
14088	Duke of Stoner	M	14202	Eneas R R
14091	3rd Duke of Sullivan	— Ky I	14203	Engineer Cox
14094	7th Duke of Sullivan	Daisy	14205	Erin Duke Ky I
14098	6th Duke of Tecumseh	Ky I	14206	Ernesty Ky I
14100	Duke of the Hills	— Long-Horn	14208	Euclide — T
14101	Duke of the Vale	— R R	14209	Eureka M
14102	Duke of the Valley 2nd	Cox	14212	Everett M
14103	Duke of the Woods	— R R	14213	Excelsior T
14104	Duke of Townsend	— D	14214	Excelsior — M
14105	Duke of Townsend 2nd	— D	14215	Excelsior 2nd — M
14106	Duke of Trumbull	— M	14216	Excelsior 3rd — M
14107	2nd Duke of Trumbull	— M	14219	Exeter — M
14108	Duke of Union	Ky I	14220	Fabricius — R R
14110	Duke of Valley View	— R R	14221	Fairfax L R
14111	1st Duke of Vermillion	— R R	14223	Fairview — D
14112	2nd Duke of Vermillion	— R R	14224	Fairview 2nd — D
14113	Duke of Vermillion	Ky I	14225	Fancy Boy — D
14114	2nd Duke of Vermillion	P S	14226	Fancy Boy — M
14115	2nd Duke of Vermillion	— R R	14227	Fancy Boy — D
14116	3rd Duke of Vermillion	Ky I	14228	Fancy Boy 2nd — D
14117	4th Duke of Vermillion	— R R	14230	Fancy York T
14118	Duke of Viola	Ky I	14232	Farmer Boy Daisy
14119	2nd Duke of Wabash Co	— R R	14236	Faust D
14121	Duke of Wapello	D	14237	Favorite — M
14123	Duke of Waverland	— R R	14238	Fearless — D
14126	1st Duke of Wayne	Cox	14239	Felix — Long-Horn
14128	Duke of Wellington	Daisy	14242	Festus — P S
14129	Duke of Wesley	— Ky I	14247	Fidus 3rd — C
14132	Duke of Woodland 3rd	— D	14248	Figaro C
14133	Duke of Woodland 4th	— D	14251	Finance — R R
14134	2nd Duke of Woodside	Daisy	14253	Fitzroy — T
14136	4th Duke of Woodside	Daisy	14254	Five Twenty — R R
14137	Duke of Wyandott	D	14256	Flash — M
14138	Duke of Yolo	— P S	14257	Flash — M
14139	Duke Wayne 2nd	Cox	14258	Flashy Arab — M
14140	Duncan 2nd	— T	14261	Flinny — Long-Horn
14142	Duncan of Oakdale	C	14262	Flora Temple's Airdrie D
14143	Dundee	R R	14265	Forest Duke — R R
14144	Dunglen Boy 2nd	R R	14266	Forester M
14145	Dunning's Duke	P S	14267	Fortune — M
14146	Duroc	Ky I	14268	Fourth of July — D
14147	Eager	R R	14269	Frank — P S
14148	Eagle	L R	14270	Frank — M
14152	Earl of Cleveland 2nd	Ky I	14271	Frank Blair — Wrong
14153	Earl of Cleveland 3rd	Ky I	14273	Franklin Duke Ky I
14155	Earl of Gloster	— Cox	14274	Franklin Duke 2nd Ky I
14156	Earl of Gloster	— Cox	14277	Frank Watson — R R
14159	Earl of Oxford	P S	14282	Fruitland Prince — D
14162	Earl of Lakeview	— M	14284	3rd Gaban — P S
14163	5th Earl of Lakeview	R R	14285	4th Gaban — P S
14165	7th Earl of Lakeview	— M	14286	5th Gaban — P S
14166	8th Earl of Lakeview	— D	14287	6th Gaban — P S
14168	Earl of Lyttleton	— R R	14288	7th Gaban — P S
14171	Earl of Saltville	L R	14289	9th Gaban — P S
14174	Earl of Warwick	P S	14291	Gallio M
14176	Early	R R	14295	Gallatin Chief — M
14179	Echo	— M	14296	Gambetta — Long-Horn
14180	Eclipse	— D	14297	Gamester — R R
14181	Edin Boy	L R	14299	Gareth Daisy
14183	Edward Bates	Ky I	14302	Gay Cloud Ky I
14184	Edwin Gay	— C	14305	Geneva Daisy
14186	Elgin	— M	14311	George — C

No.	Name	Herd
14312	George	— Cox
14313	George 2nd	— Ky I
14314	George Block	C
14315	George Scott	— L R
14316	George Thorndale	— Cox
14317	George Washington	M
14318	George Washington	— R R
14320	General	P S
14321	Gen. Anderson	— M
14322	Gen. Ascot	M
14324	Gen. Clare	Ky I
14326	Gen. Grant	Cox
14327	Gen. Grant	— M
14328	Gen. Grant	P S
14329	Gen. Grant	Ky I
14330	Gen. Grant	M
14332	Gen. Grant	— T
14333	Gen. Grant	— P S
14334	Gen. Grant	Ky I
14336	Gen. Grant	Ky I
14337	Gen. Grant, Jr.	— M
14338	Gen. Harding	— P S
14339	Gen. Jackson	M
14340	Gen. Knox	P S
14341	Gen. Lee	P S
14343	Gen. Lyon	— T
14344	Gen. McGrant	— M
14345	Gen. Putnam	— T
14346	Gen. Sherman	— M
14347	Gen. Sherman	— M
14348	Gen. Stark	— Ky I
14349	Gen. Taylor	R R
14350	Gen. Thomas	M
14351	Gen. Thomas	M
14355	Giant	P S
14356	Gil Blas	— L R
14358	Gipsy Duke	Ky I
14361	Glenwood Duke	— R R
14362	Glory	L R
14364	Gloster Duke	L R
14365	Gloster Duke of Morton	— M
14366	Gloster's Airdrie	— Cox
14367	Goddard	— M
14368	Golddust	R R
14370	Golddust	M
14371	Golden Crown	P S
14374	Golden Prince	— M
14376	Goldfoil	— R R
14378	Gonzola	— T
14379	Gossamer	— M
14380	Gov. Joe Johnson	— T
14381	Gov. Walker	— M
14383	Grand Duke	— C
14385	Grand Duke	— M
14386	Grand Duke 7th	M
14387	Grand Duke Alexis	— Ky I
14390	Grand Duke Alexis	— D
14391	2nd Grand Duke of Airdrie	— R R
14392	5th Grand Duke of Moreton	— Cox
14393	2nd Grand Duke of Oakland	L R
14395	Grand Cloud	Ky I
14396	Grandee	— C
14397	Grand Master	M
14399	3rd Grand Turk of Oak Home	— L R
14400	4th Grand Turk of Oak Home	— M
14401	6th Grand Turk of Oak Home	L R
14402	7th Grand Turk of Oak Home	L R
14403	8th Grand Turk of Oak Home	— D
14404	9th Grand Turk of Oak Home	— L R
14405	Granger	— M
14406	Granite	— C
14407	Grant	T
14408	Grant	Cox
14409	Grant	— M
14410	Grant	Cox
14411	Grant	— T
14413	Gratz	M
14414	Gratz Brown	— D
14415	Gravious	M
14416	Greeley	— M
14417	Greeley	— M
14418	Greeley	— M
14419	Greeley	D
14420	Greenback	— C
14422	Greenlawn Lad	— Ky I
14424	Greenwood Boy	— M
14425	Greenwood Lad	— C
14429	Guy	— D
14430	Hafed	P S
14432	Hancock 1st	— P S
14433	Hancock 2nd	— P S
14434	Handy	M
14435	Hank Ford	— T
14436	Hannibal	D
14437	Hannibal 11th	L R
14438	Hanson	— P S
14439	Hardscrabble	— M
14442	Harold	D
14445	Harrington	Cox
14446	Harry	Cox
14447	Harry	— P S
14448	Harry	— M
14450	Harry Basset	— D
14451	Harveys Duke	Ky I
14452	Hawthorne	— R R
14454	Hazlewood Duke 3d	C
14455	Hearts of Oak	P S
14456	Hebron	— T
14457	Hector	Ky I
14459	Helena Prince	— M
14460	Henry	P S
14461	Henry	— L R
14462	Henry	— L R
14465	Hero	Cox
14467	Hero	— M
14468	Hero	— C
14469	Hero	— T
14470	Hero	Ky I
14475	Hero of Turkey Run	Daisy
14476	H. G.	— R R
14477	H. G.	— M
14478	Highflyer 6th	— L R
14479	Highland Boy	— Cox
14481	Highland Duke	— M
14484	Highland Duke	— Ky I
14485	Highlander	T
14486	Highlander 2nd	— Ky I
14487	Highland Lad	D
14488	Highland Lad	— Ky I
14490	Highland Minister	— Ky I
14491	Highland Prince	— R R
14492	Highland Prince	— L R
14493	Highland Senator	— Ky I
14494	Hillsborough	— R R
14495	Hillsdale	— D
14496	Hiram	— Daisy
14499	Honest John	— R R
14500	Honey Lad 2nd	— Ky I
14501	Hop Shrivers	— R R
14502	Horace	— L R

No.	Name	Code
14503	Horace	— M
14504	Horace	Daisy
14505	Horace G.	Ky I
14506	Horace Greeley	— T
14507	Horace Greeley	— M
14508	Horace Greeley	— M
14510	Horace Greeley	— M
14511	Horace Greeley	Cox
14512	Horace Greeley	Ky I
14513	Horace Greeley	— P S
14514	Horace Greeley — Woods	
14515	Horace Greeley	Ky I
14516	Horace Greeley	— P S
14517	Horace Greeley	M
14518	Horace Greeley	Ky I
14519	Horace Greeley	— L R
14520	Horace Greeley	— D
14521	Honest Abe	— P S
14522	Horace Mann	— R R
14524	Hotspur 2nd	— R R
14525	Hoyle's Duke	— D
14526	Hubback	— R R
14528	Humboldt	— M
14531	Hunter	T
14532	Idan 3rd	— R R
14537	Imperial Buck	— D
14543	Independence	— P S
14545	Independence	— P S
14546	Indian Chief 18th	— C
14549	Invincible 2nd	— R R
14551	Iron Duke	M
14552	Ivanhoe	M
14553	Ivanhoe	— R R
14554	Ivy 2nd's Ascot	M
14555	Ivy 3rd's Ascot	M
14556	Izetta's Oxford	— M
14557	Jack Frost	— M
14558	Jackson	— P S
14560	Jacocoy	Ky I
14561	Jake	— Ky I
14562	James	M
14564	James N. Brown	— R R
14565	January	— Ky I
14567	Jay Gould	— R R
14569	Jere Duncan	— R R
14570	Jeremiah D.	— M
14571	Jerome 2nd	— Cox
14572	Jerome	— P S
14573	Jerry	Ky I
14574	J. Horace	D
14578	Jim Craig	— D
14579	Jim Crow	L R
14581	Jim Fisk	— M
14582	Jim Fisk	— D
14583	Jim Fisk	— R R
14584	Jim Fisk — Long-Horn	
14585	Jim Fisk — Cox	
14586	Jim Green — Long-Horn	
14587	Jim Logan	Ky I
14588	Jim Stephens	— P S
14589	Jim Stephens 2nd	— P S
14590	Jim Robinson	— Ky I
14593	Joe Batchelder	M
14594	Joe Croxton	Daisy
14595	Joe Dudley	— Ky I
14597	Joe Grant	— R R
14598	Joe Hooker	R R
14599	Joe Hucker	— R R
14601	Joe Johnson	— M
14605	Joe Kerby	— D
14606	John Ascot	— D
14607	John Bright	P S
14608	John Bronaugh	M
14612	John Dudley	— M
14613	John G. Whittier	— R R
14614	John Kent	— D
14615	John Moore	— D
14617	John Odin	— D
14618	John O'Gaunt Jr	P S
14619	John O'Gaunt 3rd	L R
14621	John Tucker	— R R
14622	Jolly Albert	— L R
14623	Jolly Jim	— L R
14624	Jolly Pike	— M
14625	Jonathan	T
14626	Joseph White	Ky I
14627	Juan	— M
14628	Judge	— C
14629	Judge Buckner	Ky I
14630	Jupiter	— M
14631	Jupiter	— D
14634	Kane	Ky I
14635	Kansas	— P S
14636	Kansas Duke	T
14637	Kansas Goldfinch	— Ky I
14638	Kearsarge	— M
14641	Kentucky	— M
14642	Kentucky	C
14644	Kentucky Clyde	M
14645	Kentucky Lad	— P S
14647	Kewanee Chief	— Daisy
14648	King George	— Daisy
14649	King John	D
14651	King Philip	— C
14652	King Philip	— M
14653	King Richard	— Daisy
14654	King of Diamonds	— C
14655	King of Forest	— R R
14657	King of Paint Valley	D
14658	King of Stark	— Ky I
14660	King William	— T
14661	King William	— D
14662	King William	— D
14663	King William 2nd — Long-Horn	
14669	Kinnellar 4th	M
14670	Kirkwood Duke	— R R
14675	Knight of the Lodge	— R R
14676	Knight of the Plains	— R R
14677	Lady Blanche 4th's Ascot	— D
14678	Lady Oxford	— P S
14679	Laertes	— R R
14680	Lafayette	— P S
14681	Lake	— L R
14683	Lancaster	— D
14684	Lancaster	M
14686	Langar	— M
14687	Larboard	Ky I
14688	Last Chance of Poplar Farm	— R R
14689	1st Laudable of Pattersondale	— R R
14690	Lawrence	— P S
14691	Lawson	D
14693	Lazy Lad	— D
14695	Legal Tender	— Ky I
14696	Lee, Jr	— M
14697	Leno Duke	— M
14698	Leo	— Ky I
14703	Leonidas	— C
14705	Leopard	— M
14706	Le Roy Chief 2nd	— M
14707	Leslie's Duke	— T

SHORT-HORN CATTLE PEDIGREES.

No.	Name	Herd
14708	Lester	Daisy
14709	Letton 2nd	— M
14710	Lewis Hill	— R R
14711	Lexington	Daisy
14712	Lexington	— R R
14713	Lexington	— P S
14714	Lexington	Ky I
14717	Lieutenant Joe	— P S
14718	Light Cloud	— P S
14720	Lilac Duke	— M
14721	Lincoln	— Cox
14723	Linden Duke	— C
14724	Linwood Lad	M
14727	Little York	T
14728	Live Oak	— M
14731	Locomotive Jr	Ky I
14732	Locomotive	— P S
14733	Lodown	— P S
14734	Lofty	Cox
14735	Logan	Ky I
14736	Logan	— L R
14737	Logan	— P S
14738	Logan	Ky I
14739	Logan	— R R
14740	Logan	Ky I
14741	Lone Star	— P S
14742	Lone Star	— R R
14744	Longfellow	M
14745	Longfellow	Ky I
14747	Longfellow	— D
14748	Longfellow	T
14749	Longfellow	— P S
14751	Longstreet	Ky I
14753	Lord Baltimore	— M
14754	Lord Baltimore 3rd	— T
14755	Lord Beverly	— R R
14756	Lord Blythe	— R R
14757	Lord Butte	P S
14758	Lord Byron	— T
14760	Lord Byron	— Cox
14761	Lord Byron	— L R
14762	Lord Byron	— Daisy
14763	Lord Byron	— R R
14769	Lord Essex	— D
14772	Lord Highland	— M
14774	Lord Lieutenant 3rd	— M
14776	Lord Monmouth	M
14777	Lord Nelson	— C
14778	Lord Nelson	P S
14779	Lord Nelson	— D
14780	Lord of Hemp Ridge	M
14781	Lord of Lorne	— R R
14787	Lord of the Valley	P S
14790	Lord Sweepstakes 3rd	— P S
14792	Lothair	— Cox
14793	Louan Duke 2nd	— R R
14794	Louan Duke 3rd	— R R
14795	Louan 35th's Gold Leaf 1st	— R R
14796	Louan's Duke	— R R
14797	Louan's Mazurka	— M
14798	L. of Waverland's Geneva	— R R
14799	Loudon	— C
14800	Loudon Bob	M
14801	Loudon Duke 7th	D
14803	Loudon Gem 2nd	Ky I
14804	Loudon Lad	— Cox
14806	Louis	Ky I
14807	Lucky Boy	— R R
14808	Lucky Boy	— P S
14810	Lucretius	— R R
14811	Lucullus	— R R
14812	Luke Stanley	Ky I
14813	Luke	— D
14815	Mackinac	— Cox
14816	Macvey	— D
14818	Madrigal	— Cox
14820	Magician	— L R
14823	Magnet Duke of Moreton	— M
14824	Magnum	Ky I
14826	Major	— L R
14827	Major	— C
14828	Major	D
14829	Major	Ky I
14830	Major Ascot, Jr	Ky I
14831	Major Bullock	P S
14832	Major Dobbin	P S
14833	Major Elder	— Ky I
14835	Major Handy	— M
14836	Major Hill	— R R
14837	Major Hunt	M
14840	Major Lee	— Daisy
14842	Major Rice	Cox
14844	Major Worlledge	— M
14846	Malcom Miller	— R R
14850	Mansfield	— R R
14852	Marigold's Duke of Fairfield	— M
14855	Mariner 3rd	M
14859	Mark Twain	— D
14860	Mark Twain	— D
14861	Marlborough	R R
14862	Maroon	— R R
14865	Marquis 2nd	— D
14868	Marquis of Hope	— Cox
14869	Marquis of Le Roy	— M
14870	Marquis of Lorne	— D
14873	Mars 8th	— Daisy
14877	Master Bellville 2nd	— T
14881	Master Maynard	— C
14883	Master Republic	M
14884	Mat Johnston	— P S
14885	Matthew 5th	— M
14886	Matties Royal	— P S
14887	Master Tom	T
14888	Maximillian	— M
14889	Max Kramer	— C
14890	Maxwell	Woods
14892	May Boy	Ky I
14893	May Duke	M
14896	Mayflower's Prince	— D
14897	Maynard Duke	— C
14902	McComet	— M
14903	McCoy	— Ky I
14904	McDaniels	Woods
14907	Mead	— Cox
14908	Meadow Duke	— P S
14909	Mercer's Lad	Ky I
14911	Meridean	— T
14912	Merry Boy	M
14914	Messenger	— P S
14915	Messenger	C
14916	Meteor	P S
14917	Meteor	T
14918	Metzs Bull	M
14919	Miami Duke 2nd	— M
14920	Macawber	P S
14922	Middlesbro	— R R
14924	Milburn	— M
14925	Milton	— T
14926	Minister	Ky I
14928	Minister of the West	— R R

UNFASHIONABLE CROSSES IN

No.	Name	Code
14931	Minstrel 2nd	— M
14932	Missouri Duke	— C
14933	Missouri Prince	— P S
14936	Mohawk	— Daisy
14937	Mohawk	— D
14938	Mohican	— M
14939	Molecatcher	— D
14940	Momence Duke	— T
14942	Monarch	— R R
14943	Monitor	— Daisy
14944	Monitor	L R
14945	Monitor	M
14946	Monitor	— M
14947	Monmouth Lad	— Wrong
14948	Monroe Chief	— D
14949	Monroe Duke	— P S
14950	Montana Duke	— L R
14951	Montgomery	— M
14952	Montgomery Duke	— M
14954	Morgan	T
14955	Morning Prince	L R
14957	Morning Star	M
14958	Morning Star	— M
14959	Morning Star	Cox
14960	Morning Star 3rd	L R
14961	Morrow	M
14963	Motley's Duke	— Cox
14965	Mountaineer	— P S
14968	Mozart	— L R
14970	Mr. Dick	Daisy
14972	Muscatoon	M
14976	Muskingum Prince	M
14979	Napoleon	— Cox
14982	Narragansett	— Cox
14983	Nathan	Cox
14984	N. B. Forrest	— M
14985	Ned	M
14986	Ned Walraven	Ky I
14987	Neptune	— Daisy
14988	Neptune	— M
14990	Nero	L R
14991	Nero	— M
14992	Nestor	R R
14993	Newtonian	— M
14996	Nevada	L R
14997	Niagara	— Cox
14998	Niantic	— M
14999	Nicator	R R
15001	Nimrod	Ky I
15003	Nimrod	— Cox
15004	Noble Duke	— Cox
15006	Noggs	— M
15008	Norris	— M
15009	Northern Light	L R
15010	Northern Light	— L R
15012	North Star	— Cox
15020	Oakdale	L R
15021	Oakland	Cox
15022	Oakland 2nd	— M
15023	Oakland 2nd	P S
15024	Oakland 3rd	— T
15025	Oakland 4th	— P S
15026	Oakland Chief	L R
15027	Occident	M
15028	Odean	— M
15031	Ohio Lad	— D
15032	Oleander	C
15033	Olena Duke	— P S
15035	Oliver	M
15036	Olympus	R R
15038	Omer	P S
15039	Onondaga Chief	— Cox
15042	Ored Cloud	— M
15044	Orion	— Ky I
15045	Orion	— D
15046	Orion	— Ky I
15047	Orion Chief	— M
15048	Orion Duke	— M
15049	Orlando	Ky I
15050	Orlando	M
15051	Orleans Lad	— L R
15052	Orphan Boy 16th	— C
15054	Orphan Boy 18th	— C
15056	Ossawattomie	— M
15058	Othello	D
15059	Othello	— Ky I
15060	Othello 3rd	— P S
15061	Otho	— T
15062	Otley	— R R
15063	Oxford	L R
15065	Oxford	— P S
15067	Oxford Anson	— M
15070	Oxford Boy	P S
15072	Oxford Chief	— M
15073	Oxford Duke	Ky I
15074	Oxford Duke	— Cox
15075	Oxford Duke	— R R
15078	Oxford Hero	— Cox
15079	Oxford Imperial	— T
15080	Oxford Lad	L R
15081	Oxford Lad	— D
15082	Oxford Lad	— Cox
15085	Oxford Major	Cox
15086	Oxford Morgan	M
15087	Oxford of Deerfield	— D
15088	Oxford of Hickory Grove	— M
15089	Oxford Prince	— Cox
15090	Oxford Prince	— C
15091	Oxford Star	Cox
15092	Oxford Wiley	— M
15093	Oxonion	— Cox
15097	Paola	— R R
15098	Parish Arthur	Ky I
15101	Pat	R R
15103	Pat Maloy 2nd	P S
15104	Pat Murphy	— Ky I
15105	Patrick Henry	Cox
15107	Paul Jones	P S
15113	Peerless	— R R
15114	Peerless	— L R
15115	Perfect	M
15116	Pennsylvania	L R
15117	Perfection	L R
15118	Perfection	—R R
15119	Perfection	— D
15122	Peter Boyd	Ky I
15123	Peter Galute	L R
15131	Phil Sheridan	— P S
15133	Pilot	L R
15134	Pilot	— Long-Horn
15135	Pilot	— R R
15136	Pilot	P S
15137	Pilot	— D
15139	Pilot	— M
15140	Pineapple's Airdrie	— Wrong
15141	Pioneer	— D
15142	Pioneer	— P S
15143	Planet	C
15144	Planet	M
15145	Plantagenet	— M

SHORT-HORN CATTLE PEDIGREES. 69

No.	Name	Code
15147	Plumwood	— P S
15148	Plumwood F	R R
15149	Plumwood G	— R R
15151	Plumwood H	Daisy
15152	Plumwood I	Ky I
15153	Plumwood J	R R
15154	Plumwood K	R R
15155	Plumwood L	Ky I
15156	Plumwood M	C
15157	Plumwood N	R R
15158	Plumwood O	R R
15159	Plumwood P	Ky I
15160	Plumwood Q	R R
15161	Plumwood R	C
15162	Plumwood S	R R
15163	Plumwood T	C
15164	Plymouth	M
15165	Pony	— D
15166	Port Welch	T
15167	Prairie Banner Boy	M
15168	Prairie Duke!	— P S
15169	Prairie Duke	P S
15171	Prairie Rambler	Ky I
15175	Pride	L R
15177	Prince	— Ky I
15178	Prince	— M
15179	Prince 3rd	P S
15180	Prince 2nd	Ky I
15181	Prince 3rd	Ky I
15182	Prince 4th	P S
15183	Prince 5th	P S
15184	Prince Abram 2nd	D
15187	Prince Albert	T
15188	Prince Albert	R R
15189	Prince Albert	L R
15190	Prince Albert	M
15191	Prince Albert	R R
15192	Prince Albert	— C
15195	Prince Arthur	— M
15196	Prince Atha	— M
15198	Prince Dufferin	— Cox
15200	Prince Edward	— M
15201	Prince Frederick Charles	— D
15204	Prince Hanibal	— L R
15205	Prince Harold	— M
15208	Prince John	— M
15210	Prince of Forest Hill	— R R
15212	Prince of Montana	— C
15213	Prince of Paley	— D
15216	Prince of Reeder	— P S
15217	Prince of Rosendale	— P S
15218	Prince of the Bluff	— R R
15219	Prince of Wales	M
15220	Prince of Wales	Cox
15222	P. of Washington	— Long-Horn
15224	Prince Royal	Ky I
15225	Prince Royal	— Daisy
15228	Prince Geneva	— C
15229	Princess Upstart's Ascot	— D
15231	Princeton	M
15233	Princeton	— C
15234	Prince Taylor	— R R
15235	Princeton Lad	— M
15237	Prince William	M
15238	Prior	— M
15239	Procknott	— R R
15240	Profiter	Ky I
15241	Prosper Duke	— R R
15243	Punch	— Wrong
15245	Quintin	R R
15246	Railway	— M
15248	Ranchero	— Cox
15249	Random	— D
15250	Ranger	— D
15251	3rd Ranger	— Cox
15253	Ralston	— P S
15254	Rattler	L R
15257	Richmond Lad	— R R
15259	Rip Van Winkle	— P S
15260	Rising Sun	P S
15261	Rising Sun	— D
15262	Reavias	— T
15263	Reconstruction	Ky I
15265	Red Bird	— Woods
15267	Red Bird	— D
15268	Red Boy	— P S
15270	Red Butterfly	— M
15271	Red Chief	Ky I
15272	Red Cloud	— Ky I
15274	Red Cloud	— R R
15275	Red Cloud	— M
15276	Red Cloud	L R
15277	Red Cloud	— M
15278	Red Cloud	P S
15279	Red Cloud	— D
15280	Red Cloud 2nd	— M
15281	Red Cliff	— M
15282	Red Commoner	— D
15284	Red Dick	Ky I
15287	Red Duke	— Long-Horn
15288	Red Duke	— T
15289	Red Duke	M
15290	Red Duke 2nd	M
15291	Red Duke of the West	— P S
15293	Red Jacket	T
15296	Red Jacket	L R
15297	Red Jacket	P S
15298	Red Jacket	— L R
15299	Red Jacket	— Ky I
15301	Red Jacket 5th	— R R
15302	Red Jacket 7th	— R R
15304	Red Jacket 9th	— R R
15305	Red Jacket 12th	— R R
15306	Red Joe	T
15307	Red Lion	L R
15309	Red Medalist	Daisy
15311	Red Oak	M
15312	Red Oak	— Ky I
15313	Red Oak	M
15314	Red Prince	— Daisy
15316	Red Renick	M
15317	Red Rose's Son Peter	Ky I
15318	Red Rover	T
15319	Red Rover	P S
15320	Red Rover 2nd	— R R
15321	Red Rover 2nd	M
15322	Red Samson	Ky I
15324	Red Stockings	— D
15325	Redwood	P S
15328	Remus	— R R
15330	Reno	— L R
15331	1st Reserve Duke	— L R
15332	1st Reserve Prince	— L R
15333	Revenue	— P S
15335	Roan Duke	— R R
15336	Roan Duke	Ky I
15338	Roan Duke	— M
15339	Roan Medalist	M
15340	Roanoke	— L R
15342	Roan Prince	— D

15345	Roan Prince 2nd — Ky I	15454	Seven Forty ...D
15346	Roan Rover — L R	15455	Seymour's Ahrdrie — R R
15347	Roan Star Ky I	15456	Shamrock — C
15348	Roan Star 4th — L R	15457	Shawnee Duke Ky I
15349	Robert Bruce — Cox	15458	Shawnee Chief M
15350	Robert Claude — M	15459	Shawnee Duke M
15351	Robert Electa — D	15460	Shelby P S
15352	Robert Emmett — R R	15461	Shelby 2nd — M
15353	Robert Gale — M	15463	Sheridan L R
15354	Robby Burns — Cox	15464	Sheridan Cox
15355	Robbin — P S	15465	Sheridan Ky I
15357	Rob Roy — L R	15467	Sheridan 3rd — L R
15358	Rob Roy — Cox	15470	Shiloh — T
15359	Rob Roy Ky I	15471	Short Ears — D
15360	Rocket — P S	15472	Short Tail — C
15361	Rockingham — R R	15474	Short Tail M
15362	Rodolph — R R	15475	Silas — C
15363	Rokeby Cox	15476	Simon Peter — L R
15366	Romau M	15478	Sir Charles — M
15368	Romano — Cox	15479	Sir Charles Napier — R R
15369	Romeo — R R	15480	Sir Collin Campbell — M
15371	Romeo — L R	15482	Sir Frederick — R R
15373	Romeo Oxford — T	15483	Sir George M
15374	Romulus 2nd M	15484	Sir Hubbell Ky I
15375	Rosco M	15485	Sirius — R R
15376	Rosco — C	15486	Sir John Franklin — M
15379	Rosewood — D	15487	Sirloin M
15381	Rosy Boy L R	15488	Sir Noel — M
15383	Rosy Lad — M	15489	Sir Renick D
15384	Rousey — Daisy	15490	Sir Rupert Ky I
15385	Rousseau — C	15491	Sir William — M
15386	Rover 2nd Ky I	15492	Sir Wm. Wallace P S
15394	Royal Buck — R R	15497	Snowball — T
15395	Royal Duke — D	15499	Snowball — R R
15397	Royal Duke — D	15500	Snowball's Ascot — D
15398	Royal Duke Ky I	15503	Somerset — M
15402	Royal George — L R	15504	Somerset Lad — M
15403	Royal George 2nd — D	15506	Southerner — P S
15404	Royal Gloster — Cox	15508	Spanker T
15405	Royal Goldfinch — Ky I	15509	Spectator — L R
15406	Royal Hotspur L R	15510	Speculation Ky I
15408	Royalist Ky I	15511	Splendor — C
15409	Royal Lad — Cox	15512	Spondulix — C
15413	Royal Oxford 3rd Ky I	15513	Sportsman — D
15414	Royal Red M	15514	Spotted Chief — D
15418	Royal Wood — R R	15515	Spotted York — R R
15420	Rubin R R	15516	Sprightly's Gloster — Cox
15421	Ruric M	15517	Stafford — C
15423	Russian Duke — M	15518	Stanhope — L R
15424	Ryburn Duke Ky I	15519	Star Duke C
15425	Sailor L R	15520	Star Duke T
15426	Saladin 2nd L R	15523	Star Duke of Belleville—Long-Horn
15428	Sam Ky I	15524	Starlight — M
15429	Sam — M	15525	Starlight — Cox
15430	Sam — P S	15526	Starlight — M
15432	Sam Calwell — M	15527	Starlight 5th Cox
15433	Sam Grundy — M	15528	Starlight of Fortland D
15434	Sam Patch — L R	15529	Starlight of Linwood — P S
15435	Sam Patch — M	15533	Star of Fairview — D
15436	Sampson — D	15534	Star of the Realm D
15437	Sampson Ky I	15535	Star of the West — Cox
15438	Sampson — L R	15536	Star of the West — D
15439	Samson Duke — P S	15537	Star of the West Daisy
15440	Samson's Duke Ky I	15538	Star and Garter — M
15441	Sancho Panza M	15540	St. Clair — M
15442	San Luis — M	15541	Steamboat P S
15444	Scottish Chief M	15543	St. Joe — P S
15447	Senator Ky I	15545	St. Nick M
15450	Senator 4th L R	15546	Stonewall Ky I
15451	Seneca 3rd — Long-Horn	15547	Stonewall D

SHORT-HORN CATTLE PEDIGREES. 71

No.	Name	Code
15548	Stonewall	— P S
15550	St. Patrick	— Cox
15552	Strawberry Duke	P S
15553	Style	Daisy
15555	Sultan	— Cox
15556	Sultan 2nd	— M
15557	Summit Athelstane	— L R
15559	Sunshine	— Cox
15560	Superior	— D
15562	Surprise	— C
15563	Swan	— M
15564	Sylla 2nd	— M
15565	Sylla 3rd	— Daisy
15566	Symmetry Minister	— Cox
15567	Syntax	— Daisy
15568	Tanner	M
15569	Tartar	R R
15570	Tazewell	— M
15571	Tecumseh	Ky I
15572	Tecumseh	— M
15573	Tecumseh	M
15575	Tempest	Ky I
15576	Tenantry	L R
15579	The Baron	— P S
15581	The Czar 2nd	— P S
15583	The Governor	L R
15586	The Poor House Bull	L R
15587	The Young Republic	— R R
15588	Thomas Nast	T
15596	Thurlow Weed	— Long-Horn
15597	Tiger	M
15599	Tip	— P S
15600	Toby	R R
15601	Tom Anderson	— Long-Horn
15602	Tom Anderson	— M
15603	Tom Bascom	— M
15605	Tom Duke	— P S
15606	Tom Hixon	— R R
15607	Tom Kelley	P S
15608	Tom Long 2nd	D
15611	Tom Moore	— M
15612	Tom Taylor of Poplar Farm	— R R
15613	Townsend	— C
15615	Tulips Grant	Ky I
15616	Trouble	— P S
15617	Turk	— M
15618	Turley 2nd	Daisy
15621	Upstart's Ascot	— P S
15623	Uncle Lewis	— Cox
15624	Uncle Ned	— P S
15625	U. S. Grant	— L R
15626	Utah	T
15627	Vain Boy	— R R
15629	Valley Boy	— M
15630	Valley Princeton	— M
15631	Vanderlyn	— Ky I
15633	Vanmeter	— M
15635	Venture	D
15637	Veritas	— M
15638	Vermillion Lad	— M
15639	Veteran	M
15644	Victor	D
15645	Victor	— M
15646	Victor	— R R
15650	Volunteer	— M
15653	Waddy's Duke of Moreton	M
15654	Wade Hampton	— D
15656	Walker	— T
15657	Wallace	M
15658	Wallace	Ky I
15660	Wapello Chief	D
15661	Wapsie River 2nd	— L R
15662	Wapsie River 3rd	Cox
15662½	Wapsie River 4th	— L R
15663	Wapsie River 5th	Cox
15664	Wapsie River 6th	— L R
15665	Wapsie River 7th	Cox
15666	Wapsie River 8th	Cox
15667	Wapsie River 9th	Ky I
15668	Warren	— L R
15669	Young Warrior	— R R
15670	Warrior	— D
15672	Warwick 3rd	L R
15673	Washington	P S
15675	Washington 9th	Daisy
15676	Washington 13th	Daisy
15678	Washington Duke	— R R
15680	Washtenaw 3rd	Ky I
15681	Washtenaw 4th	Ky I
15683	Waterloo	M
15685	Waverly	— R R
15687	Weehawken, Jr	— Long-Horn
15693	Wellington	M
15695	Wellington	— R R
15696	Welton	— P S
15699	Western Lad	— P S
15700	Western Minister	R R
15701	Western Star	Ky I
15704	Whetsel	Ky I
15706	White Cloud	— L R
15708	White Duke	P S
15709	White Eagle	Ky I
15710	White Eagle 2nd	M
15712	White Oak	— D
15714	White Side	L R
15715	White Stockings	— M
15716	White Stocking	R R
15717	White Stockings	R R
15718	White Tail	— P S
15722	Wiley 2nd	L R
15723	Wiley 3rd	L R
15724	Wiley 4th	L R
15727	Wiley Duke	— R R
15729	Wilson	Ky I
15731	Winnebago	— L R
15733	Wilson Kendall	P S
15736	Wisewall	— Ky I
15739	Woodford 2nd	— M
15741	Woodlawn	T
15743	Woodlawn Chief	— L R
15744	6th Woodlawn Duke	P S
15745	Xerxes	Ky I
15747	York	— R R
15748	Yorkshire Lad	T
15749	Yosemite	— P S
15750	Yosemite	T
15751	Young America	Ky I
15752	Young America	M
15756	Young Bourbon	— M
15757	Young Butcher Boy	— Cox
15760	Young Chicago	P S
15761	Young Chilton 2nd	R R
15763	Young Duke	— Cox
15764	Young Duke	— D
15765	Young Duke	M
15766	Young Goldfinder	Ky I
15767	Young Hero	— D
15770	Young Marlboro	— M
15771	Young Minister	D
15772	Young Nero	D

15773	Young Nero 2nd..........Ky I	15875	Figg..........M
15774	Young Norwood 3rd..........— M	15876	Fortune..........M
15775	Young Norwood 4th..........— M	15879	Gen. Barnett..........T
15778	Young Peerless.....— Long-Horn	15880	Gilli's President..........M
15780	Young Prince..........L R	15881	Glen Dandy..........L R
15783	Young Reno..........— T	15882	2nd Grand Duke of Bureau......D
15784	Young Rover..........M	15884	Grinder..........— T
15785	Young Rover..........— Cox	15886	Hero..........— Cox
15786	Young Sattelite..........P S	15887	Hidalgo..........M
15787	Young Shelton..........D	15888	Highland Lee..........— R R
15788	Young Senator..........P S	15889	Hunter..........— T
15790	Young Starlight..........Cox	15891	Invincible Duke 10th..........— R R
15791	Young Sultan..........— D	15892	Iron Duke..........L R
15793	Young Victory..........L R	15893	Jeems Giles..........— R R
15794	Young Warrior..........Cox	15894	Jerry..........— Cox
15797	Young William..........— L R	15896	Joe Goodness..........— M
15798	Yuba Boy..........— P S	15897	Joe Prince..........— D
15799	Zoe Pope..........— Long-Horn	15898	John A. Logan..........M
15800	Zebulon..........— R R	15899	John A. Logan 2nd..........— M
15801	Zenas King..........— C	15902	Keystone..........L R
15802	Zero..........Ky I	15905	Lambert..........Cox
15803	Zilpha's Prince..........Ky I	15906	Last of the Presidents..........M
15805	Airdrie 3rd..........— P S	15907	Leroy..........M
15810	Albert..........— Cox	15909	Lord Lisgar..........— D
15811	Alexander..........Ky I	15912	McLean Co. Boy..........— M
15812	Alexander..........— Cox	15913	Major Spears..........Ky I
15814	Alonzo..........C	15914	Mankato..........D
15815	Al Raschid..........Cox	15915	Mapleton Duke 1st..........— R R
15817	Argyll..........L R	15918	Marion..........— C
15819	Augustus Cæsar..........P S	15921	Maroon..........— T
15820	Azim..........— Cox	15924	Matchless..........Cox
15822	Baron's Cab..........— L R	15925	May Duke..........— M
15823	Benton..........— Cox	15926	Maximillian..........L R
15827	Bowen..........— C	15929	Merritt..........— M
15828	Brigham..........M	15930	Monarch 2nd..........Cox
15829	Brigham Young..........— Cox	15931	Moreau..........— T
15831	Calumet..........P S	15934	Muirkirk Laddie 2nd..........— L R
15832	Carlottas Duke..........— R R	15936	New Years Day..........— P S
15833	Chaplain..........T	15937	Nimrod..........T
15834	Charley..........— M	15939	Oakland Lad..........— R R
15835	Charley O'Malley..........P S	15940	Orphan Lad..........— M
15836	Clinton..........— D	15942	Ozark..........P S
15837	Col. White..........M	15944	Paul Jones..........T
15838	Col. Judy..........— R R	15945	Pearl..........— D
15839	Columbus..........Ky I	15947	Pilot, Jr..........Cox
15840	Comet..........L R	15949	Premo..........M
15842	Com. Perry..........Cox	15950	Prince..........— R R
15843	Com. Porter..........D	15951	Prince Albert..........— P S
15844	Compromise..........M	15952	Prince Alfred..........M
15846	Crown Prince..........Cox	15953	Prince John..........— L R
15848	Deacon..........— T	15955	Princess Geneva 2nd..........— C
15849	Destination..........— M	15961	Red Duke..........D
15851	Don Juan 2nd..........D	15963	Roan Duke..........— R R
15852	Duke Alexis..........T	15965	Roderick..........— Ky I
15853	Duke of Anderson..........— R R	15967	Royal Baron..........— L R
15854	Duke of Bloomfield..........— R R	15968	Royal George..........T
15855	Duke of Carthage..........P S	15969	Royal John..........T
15856	Duke of Columbus..........L R	15970	Roxbury..........L R
15857	1st Duke of Holmes..........Cox	15971	Sam Brady..........— R R
15859	Duke of Linwood..........— Daisy	15972	Second to None..........— M
15861	Duke of Midway..........— R R	15973	Shakespare..........M
15865	El Hakim 2nd..........P S	15974	Sharon Red..........— R R
15866	Elkanah..........— D	15975	Sharon Roan..........— R R
15867	Elmador..........— Cox	15976	Sharon Twin..........— R R
15868	Enchanter..........— R R	15979	Shylock..........— L R
15869	Esther Duke..........— M	15980	Sir John..........— P S
15871	Fairy Duke..........— M	15982	Son of Starlight 2nd..........— L R
15872	Farmer..........— Cox	15983	Spring Hill Lad..........Ky I
15873	Favorite..........— D	15984	Squire..........T
15874	Field Marshal..........P S	15987	Ticonic..........— M

SHORT-HORN CATTLE PEDIGREES.

No.	Name	Code	No.	Name	Code
15988	True Blue	— R R	16110	Agricola	T
15989	Trump	Ky I	16111	Ah Sin	— Cox
15992	Victor 16th	C	16112	Airdrie	M
15998	Wellington	M	16113	Airdrie	— P S
16002	Zeb	— T	16115	Airdrie Atholl	— R R
16003	Zeador 2nd	— M	16117	Airdrie Duke 3rd	— T
16004	Abraham Lincoln	— R R	16118	Airdrie Duke	T
16005	Advance	— Cox	16124	Airdrie of Cedar Nook	— Cox
16011	Bellevue Lad	P S	16126	Aladden	— M
16012	Billy Boice	— P S	16128	Albert	T
16014	Bismark	— D	16129	Albert	Ky I
16015	Bob Lee 2nd	— P S	16130	Albert	— L R
16016	Bridgenorth	— P S	16132	Albert	P S
16017	Castle Duke	— D	16133	Albert Edward 2nd	— L R
16020	Charles	— L R	16135	Albert Edward 4th	P S
16021	Cherry Grove Duke	— T	16136	Albert Edward 5th	L R
16023	Colfax	Ky I	16137	Albert Edward 6th	P S
16024	Colfax	M	16139	Albion	P S
16025	Colfax 3rd	M	16142	Alexander	L R
16026	Conawagus	— Cox	16143	Alexander	L R
16028	Dick Taylor	— D	16144	Alexis	Ky I
16030	Duke of Bloomfield	— M	16145	Alexis	M
16032	Duke of Fox Run	P S	16146	Alexis	D
16033	Duke of Herr	— R R	16147	Alexis	M
16034	Duke of Louan	— R R	16148	Alexis	M
16035	Duke of Southerland	M	16149	Alexis	P S
16036	Earl of Leicester	— Cox	16150	Alfred	Ky I
16037	Echo	L R	16151	Alfred 2nd	L R
16038	Ellington's 1st Duke	— M	16152	Alma's Duke	— Cox
16039	Ellington's 2nd Duke	— D	16153	Alma's Grand Duke	— Cox
16041	Fisher	— M	16154	Almont	M
16042	Frederick	— L R	16155	Alonzo	— Ky I
16043	Gambetta	— Long-Horn	16156	Alpheus	— L R
16044	Garibaldi 2nd	— M	16157	Ambassador	M
16045	Gen. Grant	— M	16160	Ames	P S
16046	Glenbrook	— M	16161	Amos Lad	— Daisy
16047	Gloster's Ivanho	— Cox	16162	Andrew Johnson	— Ky I
16048	Goldfinder	Ky I	16163	Andrew Johnson	— L R
16049	Huron	Ky I	16164	Annie's Atholl	— Ky I
16050	Imperial	— L R	16166	Antietam	M
16052	John Morgan	— P S	16167	Anti-Monopoly	Ky I
16055	King of Mown	P S	16168	Anti-Monopoly	— P S
16056	Lamartine	— L R	16169	April Fool	— L R
16057	Longfellow	— R R	16171	Arch	— M
16058	Lord Alexander	P S	16172	Archie Riley	— M
16059	Lord Nelson	Daisy	16173	Arctic	— P S
16062	Mahan	— T	16174	Argive	Cox
16065	Palmetto Chief	Ky I	16175	Aristides	— M
16068	Prince Imperial	— M	16176	Ashby	— P S
16072	Resolution	M	16178	Askaross	M
16073	Roan Prince	— L R	16180	Atlanta 2nd	D
16074	Royal Oakland 2nd	— R R	16181	August Duke	L R
16078	Stock Exchange	— M	16182	Augustus Cæsar 2nd	P S
16081	Young Favorite	L R	16183	Aurelius	— L R
16086	Highland Duke	— T	16184	Australian	— L R
16089	Abe Lincoln	— M	16185	Autocrat	— R R
16090	Abe Lincoln	— R R	16186	Aysgarth	— M
16092	Accident 4th	P S	16187	Badger Boy	L R
16094	Adair	— Cox	16188	Badger Boy	— P S
16095	Adam of Woodlawn	— M	16189	Bailey	P S
16097	Addison	— C	16190	Baker	P S
16098	Admiral	T	16191	Balco	— M
16099	Admiral	— C	16192	Balco	Ky I
16100	Admiral 4th	— Daisy	16193	Bald Eagle	M
16101	Admiral	Ky I	16196	Banjo	— C
16103	Admiral	— R R	16197	Barkis	M
16104	Admiral Roscawen	Cox	16198	Barningham	P S
16106	Admiral Stark	— M	16199	Barnum	Ky I
16108	Advance	— L R	16200	Barnum	Ky I
16109	Afton	— M	16201	Barnum	— D

16202	Baron Augustus	M	16318	Bob Miller 2nd — R R
16205	Baron Bedford — R R		16319	Bob Miller 3rd — R R
16207	Baron Bertram 4th — P S		16320	Bob Morrison — Ky I
16208	Baron Blossom Ky I		16322	Bob Ridley — T
16210	Baron Boone 2nd M		16324	Bob Tucker D
16213	Baron Booth of Glenn Farm — D		16325	Boldon Ky I
16215	Baronet Ky I		16326	Bonner — Ky I
16217	Baronet — L R		16327	Bonner — D
16219	Baron French — Daisy		16328	Bonnie Boy M
16220	Baron Gwynne 3rd — Cox		16329	Bonum — M
16221	Baron Gwynne 5th — Cox		16330	Boone 2nd — R R
16222	Baron Gwynne 6th — Cox		16331	Booth M
16223	Baron Gwynne 7th — Cox		16332	Boreas — Daisy
16232	3rd Baron of Oakwood R R		16333	Boston Ky I
16235	Baron of Sunside Ky I		16334	Boston Ky I
16236	Baron of the Pines C		16335	Boston Duke — R R
16242	Baron Rene — M		16337	Bound Boy M
16244	Baron Sheffielder 2nd — D		16338	Bourbon Peabody — R R
16245	Baron Unus — Ky I		16339	Boxer M
16248	Barton Duke Ky I		16340	Boxer — D
16250	Beauregard — L R		16341	Boyle M
16251	Bedford Chief — Ky I		16342	Boyle Duke — M
16252	Bedington M		16346	Brigadier — L R
16254	Bell Duke of Airdrie — D		16348	Brigham — D
16255	Belle's Duke — L R		16349	Brigham Young Cox
16256	Belleville Lad — P S		16350	Brigham Young — M
16257	Bellfounder Cox		16352	Bright Eye's Duke — R R
16258	Belle Royal — R R		16354	Brighton Lad — M
16259	Belus R R		16355	Bristol P S
16260	Belleville Hall — Ky I		16358	Britton — M
16264	Ben Airdrie Ky I		16360	Brummell — M
16265	Ben Butler D		16361	Brutus Cox
16266	Ben Butler T		16364	Buey — M
16267	Ben Butler Ky I		16365	Buford — P S
16268	Ben Butler Daisy		16366	Bulwer P S
16269	Ben Butler — D		16367	Bummer Ky I
16270	Ben Dodson — R R		16368	Bummer — L R
16272	Ben Garret — L R		16369	Bummer — R R
16274	Ben Sea — D		16370	Burgess M
16276	Ben Wade — R R		16371	Burgoyne — M
16277	Bernadott — Cox		16372	Burns — Daisy
16278	Bernard — M		16374	Buster — L R
16279	Bernardo D		16375	Butler — M
16280	Bertha's Royal — M		16376	Butter Ball Ky I
16283	Bill Allen T		16378	Butterfly — L R
16285	Bill Hill Ky I		16379	Button — P S
16286	Bill Jones — M		16380	Calm Duke — D
16287	Bill Seaham — D		16381	Cambria's Mazurka — Long-Horn
16288	Billy Beverly Daisy		16382	Cambridge Duke 2nd — R R
16289	Billy Bishop 2nd M		16383	Cambridge Duke 3rd Ky I
16290	Billy Boston Cox		16384	Cambridge Duke 4th Ky I
16291	Billy Duncan P S		16385	Cambridge Prince — M
16292	Billy Harrison T		16386	Camden — M
16293	Billy Pickerell M		16388	Cap-a-pie T
16295	Birdwood — M		16389	Capital State D
16298	Bismark T		16390	Captain M
16299	Bismark — C		16391	Captain D
16300	Bismark M		16392	Captain — P S
16301	Bismark M		16393	Captain Bates — P S
16302	Bismark D		16394	Captain Claude — P S
16304	Blanch's Belleville — R R		16396	Captain Cook M
16306	Blossom's Duke — M		16397	Captain Fry — M
16308	Blucher — R R		16399	Captain Gall M
16309	Blue Grass — D		16400	Captain Gunter — R R
16311	Bob M		16401	Captain Hood M
16312	Bob Campbell — M		16402	Captain Jack T
16313	Bob Forsyth — P S		16403	Captain Jack — D
16314	Bob Ingersoll Daisy		16404	Captain Jack — L R
16315	Bob Kelly P S		16406	Captain Jack P S
16316	Bob Lee — P S		16408	Captain Jack — C

SHORT-HORN CATTLE PEDIGREES. 75

No.	Name	Herd
16409	Capt. Jack	— L R
16410	Capt. Jack	— M
16411	Capt. Jack	— Cox
16412	Capt. Jack	— T
16413	Capt. Jack	D
16414	Capt. Jack	Ky I
16415	Capt. Jack	— L R
16416	Capt. Jack	D
16417	Capt. Jack	T
16418	Capt. Jack	— M
16419	Capt. Jack	— M
16420	Capt. Jack	M
16421	Capt. Jack	— M
16422	Capt. Jack	— D
16423	Capt. Jack	— Ky I
16424	Capt. Jinks	L R
16425	Capt. Jinks	M
16426	Capt. Jinks	D
16427	Capt. Jinks 2nd	— M
16429	Capt. Neal	— P S
16430	Capt. Neal 2nd	Ky I
16431	Capt. Pope	D
16432	Capt. Sandy	M
16433	Capt. Shaftoe 2nd	Ky I
16434	Capt. Tapscott	— Daisy
16436	Carlisle Ascot	M
16437	Carmalt	L R
16438	Carmine	— R R
16439	Carrollion Lad	— P S
16440	Carter's Bull	— T
16441	Cassius 1st	— D
16442	Cassius 2nd	— M
16443	Cassius 3rd	— M
16444	Cassius 4th	— M
16445	Cassius 2nd	— M
16446	Castelar	— R R
16448	Cavalier	Cox
16452	Champion	Ky I
16453	Champion 3rd	M
16455	Champion	— Cox
16456	Charity's Atholl	Ky I
16457	Charles	P S
16458	Charles Dahler	— M
16459	Charley Davis	— L R
16460	Charley Harden	— P S
16461	Charley Innes	T
16463	Charlie	— M
16464	Charlie Clark	— R R
16465	Chautauqua Duke	— L R
16469	Cherry's Duke	— M
16472	Cherub Louanjo	— R R
16473	Cherub of Cornwell	P S
16474	Chester Red Cloud	D
16476	Childe Harold	Wrong
16477	Christmas Day	— M
16478	Christmas Day	— L R
16480	Chub	T
16481	Cincinnatus 2nd	M
16485	Clay	Cox
16486	Clement 2nd	— R R
16487	Clendening	— Ky I
16488	Cleveland	— R R
16489	Clifton	— M
16491	Clifton Duke	— T
16492	Clifton Lad	— D
16493	Climax	— R R
16494	Climax	— L R
16497	Clinton Duke	M
16498	Clipper	T
16499	Clipton Duke	— Ky I
16500	Cloud	— Long-Horn
16502	Colfax 2nd	— M
16503	Colfax	— P S
16504	Colfax	— D
16505	Colfax	— M
16506	Colfax, Jr.	M
16509	Collin	Ky I
16510	Colonel	— C
16511	Colonel	D
16513	Colonel	Cox
16514	Colonel	P S
16515	Colonel	— R R
16516	Colonel	Ky I
16517	Colonel Buckner	— M
16518	Colonel Claude	— P S
16519	Colonel Hood	M
16520	Colonel Moore	— D
16521	Colonel Morgan	— P S
16527	Colorado	— P S
16528	Colorado	L R
16531	Columbus	— D
16533	Comanche	M
16534	Comet	— C
16535	Comet	M
16538	Commodore	L R
16539	Commodore	— C
16540	Commodore	— L R
16541	Commodore	M
16542	Com. Owens	— M
16543	Commodulation	— M
16544	Competitor	— R R
16546	Compton	Cox
16547	Congress	— M
16548	Conqueror 3rd	— Cox
16550	Constantina's Oxford	— R R
16552	Consul	— P S
16553	Continental	— L R
16554	Cornell	— Ky I
16555	Cossair	— M
16557	Coshocton Duke of Airdrie	— P S
16558	Cottage Prince	C
16559	Comet Atholl	— R R
16566	1st Count of Oneida	— R R
16569	Count Rumford	— L R
16570	Cowan's Duke 1st	— M
16571	Craco	— M
16572	Crescent Hill Booth	— R R
16573	2nd Crescent Hill Booth	M
16574	3rd Crescent Hill Booth	— M
16575	4th Crescent Hill Booth	— R R
16576	5th Crescent Hill Booth	— T
16577	6th Crescent Hill Booth	— D
16578	Cross Hill Duke	L R
16579	Crowder	— R R
16581	Crown Prince	— Cox
16582	Crown Prince	P S
16583	Crown Prince 2nd	M
16584	Crown Prince	— T
16586	Crusade	L R
16587	Crusade	M
16588	Crystal Lesley	— Long-Horn
16589	Cuban	— M
16590	Cupid	— T
16591	Cypria's Heir	— R
16592	Cyrus	— R R
16594	2nd Daisy's Duke	— R R
16595	Daisy Prince	— C
16597	Damascus	P S
16599	Dan	— Cox
16600	Danby	Cox

16601	Danby ... L R	16700	Duke of Altaham ... — M
16602	Dandy ... — P S	16701	Duke of Andrew ... L R
16603	Dandy ... — M	16702	2nd Duke of Aninas ... — Cox
16604	Daniel ... P S	16703	5th Duke of Ashland ... — M
16606	Daniel Boone ... — P S	16705	2nd Duke of Atholl ... R R
16607	Daniel Drew ... — R R	16706	3rd Duke of Athol ... — M
16608	Dan Pratt ... P S	16707	6th Duke of Athol ... — P S
16609	Dan Price ... L R	16709	Duke of Bedford ... — M
16610	Dan Rice, Jr ... D	16710	Duke of Bellevue ... D
16611	Darby Lad 5th ... — P S	16713	Duke of Bourbon ... — R R
16612	Darby Lad 6th ... — P S	16715	2nd Duke of Briggsdale ... — C
16614	Datura ... M	16717	Duke of Bristol ... — P S
16615	David ... P S	16719	Duke of Brush Creek 2nd ... — M
16616	Davis ... — Ky I	16720	Duke of Buckingham ... P S
16617	De Benuet ... Ky I	16721	Duke of Burnett 17th ... — R R
16618	Decimus ... — L R	16722	Duke of Burnett 18th ... — R R
16620	Denmark ... — P S	16724	Duke of Burnett 20th ... T
16622	Des Soto ... — Ky I	16725	Duke of Burnett 21st ... — R R
16623	Dexter 2nd ... — M	16727	Duke of Cherry Grove ... — R R
16624	Dexter ... Ky I	16728	Duke of Cherry Thicket ... — D
16625	Dexter ... M	16730	Duke of Clarence 2nd ... D
16626	Dexter ... Ky I	16731	Duke of Clark ... — R R
16628	Diamond ... — M	16732	Duke of Clark 2nd ... C
16630	Dick ... Ky I	16733	Duke of Clark 3rd ... — C
16631	Dick ... — M	16734	Duke of Cliftondale ... — P S
16632	Dick Johnson ... — P S	16735	Duke of Cliff Grange ... — D
16633	Dick Johnson ... M	16736	2nd Duke of Cliff Grange ... — D
16634	Dick Pomeroy ... — M	16737	Duke of Congress ... — M
16638	Dick Taylor ... C	16738	Duke of Crawford ... — R R
16639	Dick Taylor 2nd ... Ky I	16740	Duke of Dallas 3rd ... — M
16640	Dick Yates ... Ky I	16741	Duke of Dallas 4th ... — L R
16641	Dictator ... C	16742	Duke of Dallas 5th ... M
16644	Dixie Duke 6th ... — R R	16743	Duke of Dallas 6th ... — D
16645	Dixon Chief ... — R R	16744	Duke of Dallas 8th ... — L R
16646	Doctor ... P S	16745	Duke of Dallas 9th ... — L R
16647	Doctor Goddard ... — L R	16746	Duke of Dallas 10th ... — L R
16649	Doctor Livingston ... Ky I	16747	Duke of Dallas 11th ... — L R
16651	Doctor Prewitt ... M	16748	Duke of Dallas 12th ... M
16652	Don Carlos 2nd ... — Cox	16749	Duke of Deer Lodge ... — M
16654	Don Duchess ... — M	16750	Duke of Desmoius ... — L R
16655	Don Juan ... Ky I	16751	1st Duke of Downs ... — R R
16656	Don Juan 2nd ... M	16752	2nd Duke of Downs ... — R R
16660	Double Knight ... — D	16753	2nd Duke of East Side ... — M
16661	Douglas ... C	16754	16th Duke of Edgar ... M
16662	Douglas ... Ky I	16755	17th Duke of Edgar ... Daisy
16664	Dayle ... C	16756	18th Duke of Edgar .. — Long-Horn
16665	Draco ... — L R	16757	19th Duke of Edgar .. — Long-Horn
16666	Drona's Airdrie ... P S	16758	20th Duke of Edgar ... — P S
16667	Dronas 3 d's Duke ... P S	16759	21st Duke of Edgar .. — Long-Horn
16669	Duane's Duke 2nd ... Cox	16760	22nd Duke of Edgar ... Daisy
16670	Duchess Duke ... Ky I	16761	Duke of Edgwood 2nd ... — C
16672	Duchess Duke ... — P S	16762	Duke of Ellison ... — D
16673	Duff Green ... M	16764	Duke of Erie ... — P S
16674	Dugdale ... — M	16765	Duke of Esmere ... D
16675	Duke ... — M	16766	Duke of Fairfax ... — C
16677	Duke ... Ky I	16767	Duke of Fairfield ... — M
16679	Duke ... — D	16768	Duke of Fairview ... — M
16682	Duke ... — T	16769	Duke of Fairview 2nd ... — R R
16683	Duke Alexis ... — L R	16770	Duke of Fairview 3rd ... — R R
16684	Duke Alexis ... — M	16771	4th Duke of Fairview ... — R R
16687	Duke Alexis ... — Long-Horn	16772	Duke of Fayette ... — R R
16688	Duke Captain ... M	16773	Duke of Fayette ... — R R
16689	Duke Dunmore ... — M	16774	Duke of Five Twenty ... — R R
16690	Duke Forester 2nd ... — R R	16775	Duke of Flint ... P S
16691	Duke George ... C	16776	3rd Duke of Forest ... — R R
16693	Duke of Napier ... — M	16779	10th Duke of Forest Hill ... — C
16696	Duke of Airdrie ... P S	16780	Duke of Four Mile ... — Ky I
16697	Duke of Albemarl ... — M	16781	Duke of Franklin ... — P S
16698	Duke of Alexander ... Ky I	16782	Duke of Garrard ... — M
16699	1st Duke of Alexis ... — R R	16786	Duke of Glendale ... — Ky I

SHORT-HORN CATTLE PEDIGREES.

16787	3rd Duke of Glendale	— M	16879	Duke of Merced	L R
16789	Duke of Glenwood 1st	— L R	16880	Duke of Montgomery	P S
16790	Duke of Glenwood	M	16883	Duke of New London	— Ky I
16791	Duke of Glenwood	— M	16884	Duke of Niagara	Ky I
16793	Duke of Goodness	— R R	16885	2nd Duke of Oakdale	— R R
16795	2nd Duke of Granville	— R R	16886	7th Duke of Oakdale	L R
16796	4th Duke of Granville	— R R	16887	9th Duke of Oakdale	L R
16797	9th Duke of Granville	— R R	16888	10th Duke of Oakdale	L R
16798	10th Duke of Granville	— R R	16889	Duke of Old Virginia	L R
16799	11th Duke of Granville	— R R	16890	Duke of Oleutangy	Ky I
16801	13th Duke of Granville	— R R	16891	2nd Duke of Omaha	M
16805	15th Duke of Greenbush	— P S	16892	Duke of Orangedale	M
16806	Duke of Greenlawn	— M	16893	Duke of Orleans 2nd	P S
16807	2nd Duke of Greenlawn	— M	16894	Duke of Orleans	Ky I
16808	12th Duke of Greenlawn	— M	16895	3rd Duke of Osage	— P S
16809	13th Duke of Greenlawn	— L R	16900	Duke of Palmyra	D
16810	14th Duke of Greenlawn	— M	16903	Duke of Parker	D
16811	15th Duke of Greenlawn	— M	16905	Duke of Pleasant Hill	— R R
16812	16th Duke of Greenlawn	— M	16906	Duke of Plymouth	— L R
16813	Duke of the Valley	— M	16907	Duke of Polk	— M
16814	Duke of Greenville	— R R	16908	Duke of Portage	P S
16815	Duke of Grovedale	— Cox	16909	Duke of Proctor	P S
16816	2nd Duke of Grovedale	— Cox	16910	2nd Duke of Proctor	P S
16819	Duke of Hamilton	Ky I	16911	2nd Duke of Putnam	— M
16822	Duke of Hardingdale	— L R	16912	Duke of Pythia	— P S
16823	Duke of Harrison	T	16913	Duke of Richardson	P S
16824	2nd Duke of Harrod's Creek	— R R	16914	Duke of Riverside	— M
16825	Duke of Hazel Dell	— M	16915	Duke of Romulus	— R R
16826	Duke of Highland	— M	16917	Duke of Rushfield	— L R
16831	Duke of Henuloka 2nd	— P S	16918	Duke of Rutland	— L R
16833	3rd Duke of Holt	— R R	16919	2nd Duke of Saratoga	— M
16834	Duke of Howland	— L R	16920	Duke of Saybrook	D
16835	Duke of Humphry	— R R	16922	Duke of Seneca	— M
16836	Duke of Huron	— Long-Horn	16924	Duke of Silverdale	— L R
16837	2nd Duke of Huron	M	16925	Duke of Skaneateles	— Cox
16838	Duke of Indian Creek	— R R	16929	3rd Duke of Stark	— Ky I
16839	Duke of Ionia	— L R	16930	4th Duke of Stark	— M
16840	Duke of Iroquois	— P S	16932	8th Duke of Sulivan	— D
16842	Duke of Jackson	Ky I	16933	9th Duke of Sulivan	M
16843	Duke of Jefferson	P S	16935	Duke of Sumner	— P S
16844	Duke of Jordan	P S	16937	Duke of Swezyana	Wrong
16845	4th Duke of Kalamazoo	Cox	16938	7th Duke of Tecumseh	D
16846	5th Duke of Kalamazoo	Cox	16939	8th Duke of Tecumseh	— Ky I
16847	Duke of Kensington	— T	16940	9th Duke of Tecumseh	— T
16848	1st Duke of Lakeside	D	16941	10th Duke of Tecumseh	— Ky I
16849	3rd Duke of Lee	— M	16942	11th Duke of Tecumseh	D
16850	2nd Duke of Lee	D	16943	12th Duke of Tecumseh	— Ky I
16851	2nd Duke of Lexington	Ky I	16944	13th Duke of Tecumseh	— Ky I
16852	Duke of Lincoln	— M	16945	Duke of the Forest	— M
16853	Duke of Livingston	— M	16947	Duke of the Meadows	C
16854	Duke of Livingston	— M	16948	Duke of the Meadows	— R R
16855	Duke of Locust Hill	D	16949	6th Duke of the Pines	— R R
16856	Duke of Loda	M	16950	7th Duke of the Pines	Daisy
16857	Duke of Loudon	— R R	16951	8th Duke of the Pines	— R R
16859	Duke of McDowell	— R R	16952	9th Duke of the Pines	— R R
16860	Duke of Macoupin	M	16953	10th Duke of the Pines	— M
16861	Duke of Mahaska	— M	16954	11th Duke of the Pines	— R R
16862	Duke of Mauscarido	— Wrong	16955	Duke of the Pines	— P S
16863	2nd Duke of Mauscarido	— Wrong	16956	2nd Duke of the Pines	Ky I
16864	Duke of Marion	— M	16957	Duke of the Reserve	— M
16865	Duke of Marion	— D	16960	Duke of the Union Coal Farm	Cox
16866	Duke of Marlboro	— M	16961	Duke of the Valley	— R R
16869	6th Duke of May	— P S	16962	Duke of the Valley	— R R
16870	7th Duke of May	— D	16963	Duke of the West	— M
16871	8th Duke of May	— P S	16964	Duke of Thorndale 2nd	— L R
16872	9th Duke of May	— D	16966	Duke of Tuscarawas	Cox
16873	10th Duke of May	— P S	16967	Duke of Vermillion 2nd	— M
16874	Duke of May	— D	16968	Duke of Vernon	M
16875	Duke of Maynard	— C	16970	Duke of Walburg 3rd	M
16876	3rd Duke of Meadows	— R R	16971	Duke of Washington	C

No.	Name	Code	No.	Name	Code
16972	Duke of Washington	D	17083	Feld Spar	— L R
16974	Duke of Waverly	— R R	17088	Fidget's Oxford	— R R
16976	3rd Duke of Waverly	— M	17091	Filligree Prince	Ky I
16978	Duke of Wellington	— C	17092	Fillmore	P S
16979	Duke of Wellington	M	17093	Finance	— R R
16982	5th Duke of Woodside	Daisy	17094	Financier 2nd	— R R
16984	6th Duke of Yates	— M	17096	4th Fisherman's Pride	— Cox
16986	4th Duke of Yuba	Ky I	17098	6th Fisherman's Pride	— Cox
16987	5th Duke of Yuba	Wrong	17099	Fitzroy	— T
16988	6th Duke of Yuba	Ky I	17101	Five Twenty 4th	Ky I
16989	7th Duke of Yuba	Ky I	17102	Flash	Ky I
16990	8th Duke of Yuba	Ky I	17103	Flower Chief	— M
16991	9th Duke of Yuba	Ky I	17106	Forest	— R R
16992	10th Duke of Yuba	Ky I	17107	Forest Duke	Ky I
16993	11th Duke of Yuba	Ky I	17108	Forester	— P S
16994	12th Duke of Yuba	Ky I	17110	Forest	Ky I
16995	Duke Red	— M	17111	Fortunate	Ky I
16998	Duncan	— L R	17112	Fortunatus 2nd	L R
17001	Durock	— M	17113	Foster	— C
17002	Dutch Boy	— M	17114	Found Out	— M
17004	Earl Barrington	— L R	17115	Frank	— L R
17005	Earl Gwynne	— Cox	17116	Frank	— T
17006	Earl Louan	— R R	17117	Frank Kinkhead	— M
17013	Earl Exeter	— R R	17118	Franklin Duke 3rd	Ky I
17014	Earl of Fairbury	P S	17119	Franklin Duke 4th	Ky I
17016	Earl of Greenbush	— T	17121	Fred Airdrie	M
17018	Earl of Hamilton	P S	17122	Fred Hooper	Ky I
17020	Earl of Mozart	— C	17123	Fred Power	P S
17021	2nd Earl of Mozart	— C	17126	Fritz	— M
17022	3rd Earl of Mozart	— M	17127	Fruitland Duke	— Daisy
17027	Earl of Sturgis	— P S	17128	Fulton	T
17029	Earl Sisson	— P S	17129	Fulton Prince	Ky I
17030	Eclipse	D	17130	9th Gaban	— P S
17031	Eclipse	D	17131	11th Gaban	— P S
17033	Eclipse	— R R	17132	12th Gaban	— P S
17034	Eildon	Ky I	17133	13th Gaban	— P S
17035	Eldorado	— P S	17134	Galletty's Bull	Ky I
17036	Eldorado	M	17135	Gamester 2nd	— R R
17037	Electa's Antony	— P S	17138	Gem Airdrie 2nd	— C
17038	Election	— Daisy	17144	Gen. Canby	Ky I
17039	Elijah	— L R	17145	Gen. Canby	— M
17041	Elliott's Red Duke	— Ky I	17146	Gen. Ernesty	— Ky I
17043	El Rey	M	17147	Gen. Gill	Cox
17044	Elriver Duke	— M	17148	Gen. Grant	M
17045	Elva's Duke	— R R	17149	Gen. Grant	M
17049	Emperor	— P S	17150	Gen. Grant	— D
17051	Enchanter	Ky I	17151	Gen. Grant	M
17053	Eric	M	17152	Gen. Grant	— Cox
17055	Esquire	— T	17153	Gen. Grant, Jr	Daisy
17059	Euparca's Red Jacket	D	17154	Generalissimo	P S
17060	Eureka	D	17155	Gen. Jackson	— Cox
17061	Eureka 2nd	— L R	17156	Gen. Lee	— Cox
17062	Eutaca	M	17157	Gen. Lee	— P S
17063	Excalibar	R R	17158	Gen. Porter	R R
17064	Excelsior 5th	— M	17160	Gen. Riggs	— M
17065	Excelsior 6th	— M	17162	Gen. Sheridan	Ky I
17066	Excelsior 7th	— M	17163	Gen. Sherman	— M
17067	Excelsior 8th	— M	17164	Gen. Singleton	— M
17068	Excelsior	Ky I	17166	Gen. Stewart	R R
17069	Excelsior	L R	17167	Gen. Washington	— M
17070	Excelsior Duke	— M	17168	Gen. Worth	D
17071	Exception	— M	17173	Geneva Lad	— C
17072	Exchange	— D	17175	Gentry	C
17073	Fair Eclipse	— R R	17177	George	L R
17074	Fair Mount Duke	— M	17178	George Bright	— M
17076	Famosa Chief	— R R	17179	George Creek	Ky I
17077	Fantana	M	17180	George Washington	— M
17080	Fearnaught	— M	17181	Gerard	— T
17081	Fearnaught	— P S	17183	Gibralter	— R R
17082	February Snowball	T	17184	Gilcher	— Long-Horn

No.	Name	Herd	No.	Name	Herd
17185	Ginger Blue	D	17276	Hannibal 13th	— M
17186	Glendower	Cox	17277	Hannibal 14th	— T
17188	Gloster	— D	17278	Hannibal 15th	C
17189	Gloster of Ingham	— Cox	17279	Hannibal 16th	— M
17190	2nd Gloster of Pine Grove	— Cox	17280	Hannibal 17th	— D
17191	Gloster's Duke	— Cox	17281	Hannibal 18th	— D
17192	Godfrey	— L R	17282	Hannibal 19th	— M
17194	Gold Dust	M	17283	Hannibal 20th	L R
17195	Gold Dust	M	17284	Hannibal 21st	— M
17196	Gold Dust	— R R	17285	Hannibal 22nd	— D
17198	Gold Finder	Ky I	17286	Hannibal	T
17199	Gold Finder	— P S	17287	Happy Jack	— P S
17200	Goodness of Florentia	— R R	17289	Harry Todd	— M
17202	Governor	— P S	17290	Hartington	— P S
17204	Governor 1st	— M	17291	Hartland	— P S
17205	Gov. Allen	— Woods	17292	Hastings	— M
17206	Gov. Carpenter	M	17293	Hazelwood Duke 4th	C
17207	Gov. Noyes	— Woods	17294	Hazum	— P S
17208	Gov. Noyes	— D	17295	Heart-breaker	— D
17209	Gov. Woodson	M	17296	Hector	L R
17210	Gov. Woodson	— P S	17297	Hector 3rd	Cox
17212	Grafton Lad	— Cox	17298	Hector	D
17213	Granady	— Cox	17301	Henselman	— M
17214	Grand Central	— R R	17303	Hematite	— R R
17215	Grand Duke	— M	17304	Henry	L R
17216	Grand Duke	— M	17305	Henry	— M
17217	Grand Duke 2nd	— R R	17306	Henry	— R R
17218	Grand Duke	— P S	17307	Henry's Thanksgiving — Long-Horn	
17220	Grand Duke of Alexis	R R	17308	Henry Wilson	— R R
17221	Grand Duke of Geneva	— M	17310	Hercules	— M
17223	6th Grand Duke of Moreton	— Cox	17312	Herkimer	M
17224	Grandee	— M	17313	Hermit	— M
17225	Grand Royal Duke	P S	17314	Hermit	— R R
17226	Grand Turk	— Cox	17315	Hero 2nd	— P S
17227	Grand Turk of Alameda	— M	17318	Hero	— Ky I
17228	11th Grand Turk of Oak Home	L R	17319	Hero	— M
17229	12th Grand Turk of Oak Home	L R	17320	Hero	— Ky I
17230	17th Grand Turk of Oak Home	L R	17321	Hiawatha	— Daisy
17231	18th Grand Turk of Oak Home	— M	17322	Hickory Duke	T
17232	19th Grand Turk of Oak Home	— M	17323	Hidalgo	— M
17233	Grand Turk of Sonoma	L R	17324	Highland Chief	D
17234	Granger	Daisy	17325	Highland Chief	— Ky I
17235	Granger	M	17326	Highland Chief	D
17236	Granger	Ky I	17327	Highland Chief	— C
17237	Granger	— M	17329	Highland Duke	— M
17239	Granger	L R	17330	Highland Duke	— C
17240	Granger	Ky I	17331	5th Highland Duke	P S
17241	Granite Boy's Son	Cox	17332	Highlander	D
17242	Granite Rock	— L R	17333	Highlander	T
17243	Grant	Ky I	17334	Highland Lad	— R R
17244	Grant 2nd	Ky I	17335	Highland Lad	T
17245	Grant	— D	17337	Highland Lad	M
17248	Gratz Brown	— P S	17338	Highland Prince	— L R
17249	Gratz Brown	Ky I	17340	Hiram Powers	Cox
17250	Great Fragrant	— R R	17341	Honest John	— Ky I
17251	Great Turley	— R R	17342	Hoosier Boy	D
17252	Greeley	— Cox	17344	Hope of Princess	— Cox
17254	Greeley	— D	17345	Hopewell	— Cox
17255	Greeley	M	17346	Horace Greeley	— Daisy
17256	Greenback	M	17347	Horace Greeley	P S
17257	Greenmountain Boy 2nd	P S	17348	Horace Greeley	— Cox
17259	Greenwood Airdrie	— C	17349	Horace Greeley	— P S
17261	Grey Duke	— Daisy	17350	Horatio	— R R
17263	Grinell Goldfinch	— M	17352	Hotspur	— M
17265	Guardsman, Jr	— C	17354	Hubbacks Oxford	— Cox
17269	Hail Columbia	— M	17355	Hughs	M
17272	Hamburg	Ky I	17356	Humbolt	— P S
17273	Hamlet	— P S	17358	Hunter	— C
17274	Hannibal 7th	— R R	17359	Hunter	L R
17275	Hannibal 12th	— L R	17360	Huston	— P S

17361	Ida's Duke — Ky I	17462	King George 1st — M
17362	Ike Stone — M	17464	King John — Ky I
17366	Improver — D	17465	King Lear — L R
17367	Independence — Ky I	17468	King of the Prairie — D
17368	Independence — M	17471	King's Loudon Duke — R R
17370	Indian Chief 24th — C	17472	King William — M
17371	Invincible — M	17473	King William — L R
17372	Invincible — R R	17474	Kirklivington — R R
17374	Invincible Duke 4th — R R	17477	Kit Carson — Cox
17377	Irene's Duke — M	17480	Knight — P S
17378	Iris — M	17482	Knight of Gloster — Ky I
17379	Islander — L R	17484	Knight of Garter — R R
17380	Ivanhoe — M	17485	Knox — P S
17381	Ivy's Duke — M	17486	Lafayette — Cox
17382	Jack — L R	17487	Lancaster 2nd — D
17383	Jack — T	17489	Laramie Chief — Ky I
17384	Jack Cade 2nd — C	17490	Lasalle — M
17385	Jack Cade — M	17492	Laudable 2nd — R R
17386	Jack Chinn — M	17493	Laudable — R R
17388	Jack Reed — L R	17494	Lee Cox — P S
17389	Jackson — M	17495	Legal Tender — M
17392	James Giles — R R	17497	LeMont — D
17394	January — Ky I	17498	Leo — Cox
17395	Jason — Ky I	17501	Leopard — C
17396	Jason E — M	17502	Leopold — R R
17397	Javert — Ky I	17503	Leopard — R R
17398	Jay Cooke — T	17504	Leopard — Ky I
17401	Jerry — L R	17506	Level Best — Cox
17402	Jerry — Ky I	17509	Lexington — M
17403	Jerry Taylor — R R	17510	Liberty — D
17404	Jesse — D	17511	Liberty — M
17405	Jewell — R R	17512	Lieutenant — P S
17407	Jim Ashley — M	17513	Lieutenant Fred Grant — M
17408	Jim Fisk — M	17515	Lieutenant Hood — P S
17409	Jim Potts — M	17516	Lillia Duke — Daisy
17413	Joe Brown — R R	17517	Lilly's Gloster — Cox
17414	Joe Cloyd — T	17518	Limber Jack — R R
17415	Joe Goodwin — Ky I	17519	Limerock — L R
17417	Joe Red Cloud — P S	17520	Lincoln — P S
17419	John — M	17521	4th Linden — M
17424	John Bull — P S	17524	Lisle — M
17425	John Bull — P S	17525	Lisle Lad — M
17427	John Dawson — Daisy	17526	Little Mac — P S
17428	John Fern — Cox	17527	Lochiel — Ky I
17429	John Haley — M	17528	Locomotive — T
17430	John Halifax — M	17529	Logan — C
17431	John Langdon — L R	17531	Logan — D
17433	Johnny Grant — M	17532	Logan — Ky I
17434	John of Cleveland — M	17533	Logan's Airdrie — C
17437	John Wesley — T	17534	Logan's Duke — C
17438	Josh Javish — P S	17535	Logan's Star — M
17439	Joker — M	17536	Lollo Booth — Wrong
17440	Jolly 2nd — M	17537	Lone Elm Prince — P S
17441	Jolly 2nd — M	17538	Lone Jack — P S
17442	Jolly, Jr — M	17540	2nd Lone Star — R R
17443	Jolly Boy — P S	17541	Longfellow — M
17445	Josh Billings — M	17542	Longfellow — M
17446	Jubilee — L R	17544	Longfellow — Daisy
17448	Judge Critchfield — T	17545	Long John — M
17449	Judge Lawrence — P S	17548	Lord Airdrie — C
17450	Judson — Ky I	17549	Lord Alexander — P S
17451	June Flower — T	17551	Lord Beetive — Daisy
17452	Jupiter — C	17553	Lord Blythe 2nd — R R
17455	Kent — Long-Horn	17556	Lord Chancellor — M
17456	Kentucky 2nd — Ky I	17558	Lord Chiltren — P S
17457	Kentucky Duke — T	17564	Lord Erin — M
17458	Keros — P S	17568	Lord John — P S
17459	Keystone State — Cox	17570	Lord Lieutenant 5th — P S
17460	King Alfred — T	17571	Lord Lieutenant 6th — M
17461	King George — M	17572	Lord Lieutenant 7th — P S

No.	Name	Herd
17574	Lord Lovell	M
17577	Lord Munson	Ky I
17582	Lord of Sutter	Wrong
17584	Lord of the Valley	— Cox
17587	Lord Oxford	— L R
17588	Lord Penrhyn	— R R
17589	Lord Roy	— R R
17590	Lord Stanley	— D
17593	Lothario	— Cox
17595	Lothario	— M
17596	Louan Duke of the Pines	P S
17597	Louanjo	— R R
17598	Louan's Airdrie	— R R
17599	Louan's Cherube	M
17600	Louan Duke of Geneva	— M
17601	Louan 10th's Duke	— R R
17602	Louan Thorndale	— R R
17603	Loudon Airdrie	— R R
17604	Loudon Duke 8th	— R R
17606	Loudon Duke 10th	— R R
17607	Loudon Gem 2nd	— M
17608	Loudon Gem 3rd	— M
17609	Louis	Ky I
17611	2nd Loyal Duke of Oakland	Wrong
17612	Loyal Duke of Richland	Wrong
17614	Lucius	M
17615	Lucky Lad	— P S
17616	Lucretius	— R R
17617	Lucullus	— Cox
17618	Luke Lincoln	— M
17619	Luniska	— M
17621	Lyman	Ky I
17622	McClellan	— L R
17624	Macedonia Chief	— R R
17626	MacMahon	— Cox
17627	Macomb Duke	— P S
17628	Macoupin Chief	— M
17630	Madison	— T
17631	Madison	— L R
17632	Madison Duke	— M
17636	Maquoketa Duke	— Ky I
17637	Magnolia	— M
17639	Maid's Airdrie	M
17640	Major	— Cox
17641	Major	L R
17643	Major	— M
17644	Major	P S
17645	Major	— P S
17646	Major	— M
17647	Major	Ky I
17649	Major Anderson	— R R
17650	Major Claude	— P S
17651	Major General	M
17652	Major Hood	M
17653	Major Kay	— R R
17654	Major Long	— M
17655	Major Long	— D
17657	Major Monroe	— R R
17658	Major Mungall	P S
17659	Major Muscatoon	— C
17660	Major of Hilldale	— P S
17661	Major Ooutlet	— L R
17662	Major Prindle	P S
17665	Major Rollins	Ky I
17666	Major Rollins	T
17667	Major Story 2nd	— R R
17670	Major Wilson	M
17671	Major Wadsworth	L R
17672	Malachi	— M
17673	Manfred	— D
17675	Manlius	Cox
17676	Manly	— Cox
17678	Marcus	Cox
17679	Margrave	— R R
17680	Mariner	— R R
17681	Mariner	Daisy
17683	Marion	P S
17686	Marksman	— Cox
17687	Mark Twain	C
17688	Mark Twain	— P S
17690	Marquis	— D
17691	Marquis O'Gaunt	— C
17692	Marquis of Langdon	— L R
17695	Mars 6th	— Daisy
17697	Martin's Imperial	M
17698	Master Agate	— M
17703	Master General	M
17704	Master Granger	— L R
17705	Master Man	— M
17707	Master of Ravenswood	— R R
17708	Master Story	M
17711	Matchem	L R
17712	Matchem	L R
17713	Matt Logan	— C
17714	Matt Cullen	— Daisy
17715	Mauna Lau	R R
17716	Max	— L R
17717	Max Bromer	— C
17719	May Duke	— Ky I
17720	May Duke	— R R
17721	May Duke	— M
17723	Mayor of Linn	— M
17725	Mazeppa	Ky I
17728	Mazurka Prince	— Long-Horn
17729	Mazurka Prince of Airdrie	R R
17736	2nd Meadow Duke	— M
17737	Medora Duke	— R R
17741	Merit	— L R
17742	Merry Duke	Ky I
17743	Merry Monarch	— M
17744	Miami Duke	T
17745	Miami Goodness	T
17748	Milton	M
17749	Minister 2nd	Ky I
17750	Minister	— L R
17751	Minister	— M
17752	Minister	— D
17753	Minna's Antony	— P S
17755	Minstrel Dun	Daisy
17757	Miss Gilkey's Oxford	M
17758	Missouri Chief	— P S
17760	Modoc	— P S
17761	Modoc	— L R
17762	Modoc	— Ky I
17763	Modoc	— L R
17764	Modoc	— L R
17765	Modoc Chief	— P S
17769	Monarch	Ky I
17773	Monitor	M
17773½	Monitor 2nd	— M
17774	Monkey John 2nd	Ky I
17775	Monopoly	Ky I
17777	Montezuma	L R
17778	Montezuma	M
17779	Montgomery	— R R
17780	Moonlight	— M
17781	Morello	— D
17783	Morgan	— M
17784	Morgan	— P S
17785	Moscow 4th	— R R

17786	Moscow 5th — R R	17885	Oxford Hero 2nd — Cox
17787	Moscow Duke 2nd — R R	17886	Oxford Lad — D
17788	Moscow Duke 3rd M	17887	Oxford Lad — M
17790	Mountain Boy Cox	17888	Oxford Lad L R
17791	Murat — M	17889	Oxford Linn Ky I
17792	Musco Duke — C	17891	Oxford Prince — D
17793	Muscatoon's Duke P S	17892	Oxford's Echo — D
17794	Music's Airdrie L R	17893	Oxford's Von D
17797	Nannie Williams' Mazurka — R R	17894	Oxford's Zab — R R
17799	Napoleon 2nd M	17895	Oxide R R
17804	Ned Buntline — P S	17896	Oxly Daisy
17805	Ned Forrester — P S	17897	Pacific — P S
17806	Neontichus Ky I	17898	Palmer M
17807	Nelson Ky I	17899	Palo Alto M
17808	Nelson P S	17900	Panic — Daisy
17809	Neptune 2nd — M	17901	Panic — R R
17810	Nero — M	17902	Paragon — M
17811	Nero Ky I	17903	Paragon — D
17812	Nero Cox	17904	Pathfinder, Jr M
17814	Newpin L R	17905	Pat O'Neal P S
17815	Newton Ky I	17906	Patrician R R
17816	Newton Booth D	17912	Patsey P S
17818	New Year's Gift — R R	17914	Peacock L R
17819	Niagara — L R	17917	Pearl Duke 2nd — R R
17820	Nicholas Duke — R R	17918	Pearl of Oakland 3rd — Long-Horn
17821	Niskayuma Cox	17919	Pearl of Oakland 4th M
17822	Noble Duke Ky I	17923	Perfection — P S
17823	Noble Duke — M	17926	Peter Parley L R
17824	Nobleman — P S	17927	Peter Lehigh — T
17825	Nora's Duke — M	17929	Phil Dennis — D
17826	Northerner — D	17931	Philip Lee — C
17828	North Star 2nd — P S	17932	Philo — P S
17829	North Star M	17933	Phil Sheridan M
17831	Norwood — P S	17934	Pilgrim — Long-Horn
17833	Oakalona — Ky I	17935	Pilgrim Cox
17834	Oakhill Airdrie P S	17936	Pilot — M
17835	Oakland 6th M	17937	Pilot P S
17836	Oakland 8th L R	17938	Pilot Ky I
17836½	Oakland 9th P S	17939	Pilot — M
17837	Oakland Fancy — R R	17940	Pilot — L R
17838	Oakwood Duke Ky I	17941	Pilot M
17839	Oakwood Laddie — L R	17942	Pioneer — T
17840	Oakwood Louanjo 4th R R	17943	Pioneer D
17842	Occident — Cox	17944	Pioneer Duke — R R
17843	Ocean Boy Ky I	17945	Pioneer of Deer Lodge — M
17845	Ogle Airdrie Ky I	17947	Pixot R R
17846	Old Abe P S	17949	Planet — P S
17848	Old Sally's Gloster L R	17951	Plantagenet P S
17849	Olena Duke — P S	17952	Plantagenet, Jr — Wrong
17850	Olena Duke 2nd — P S	17953	Plantagenet of Deerfield — D
17851	Oliver — P S	17954	Plantagenet of Green Lawn — D
17852	Oliver 2nd M	17956	Pleasant Duke — L R
17853	Oliver Twist — M	17957	Pliny P S
17854	Olathe Minister — Ky I	17958	Plumwood U R R
17855	Omar Pacha — Cox	17959	Plumwood V R R
17861	Orphan Boy 21st — C	17960	Plumwood W C
17862	Orphan Duke — P S	17961	Plumwood X C
17863	Orpheus — M	17962	Plumwood Y Ky I
17865	Oscar — M	17963	Pluto Ky I
17867	Osceola — Ky I	17964	Pluto P S
17869	Osceola — M	17965	Pocahontas — L R
17870	Othello Cox	17967	Pomp — L R
17872	Ottawa Duke — Cox	17968	Pompeii Ky I
17873	Owen's Bull — M	17970	Ponto M
17874	Oxford — M	17971	Popcorn — D
17876	Oxford Boy — L R	17972	Poplar Lad — P S
17879	Oxford Chief M	17973	Porter — M
17880	Oxford Chief 2nd — Cox	17974	Poser P S
17882	Oxford Don R R	17976	Prairie Boy — P S
17883	Oxford Duke — M	17977	Prairie Boy — P S

SHORT-HORN CATTLE PEDIGREES.

No.	Name	Ref.	No.	Name	Ref.
17978	Prairie Duke	L R	18077	Pulaski	— Ky I
17979	Prairie Duke	— D	18079	Putnam Boy	D
17980	Premier Gladstone	Cox	18080	Quartz	— L R
17981	Prentice	— M	18081	Queen of Iowa's Ascot	— M
17982	Presbyter	— T	18082	Queen's Duke	— M
17984	President	Cox	18084	Quantius	— L R
17985	Preston	— D	18085	Quantius	M
17986	Pride of Cortland	— Cox	18086	Raccoon	M
17987	Pride of Muskingum. — Long-Horn		18087	Radical	Ky I
17988	Priest	M	18090	Ralph	— M
17989	Priest	Ky I	18092	Ranchero 2nd	— Cox
17990	Prince	— R R	18093	Ranger	D
17993	Prince	— L R	18094	Ranger 2nd	D
17994	Prince	— P S	18096	Ravenswood	— R R
17995	Prince	M	18097	Rebellion	P S
17996	Prince	— Cox	18098	Rebellion	— M
17997	Prince	— M	18099	Red Airdrie	Daisy
17999	Prince	M	18101	Red Airdrie	R R
18000	Prince	D	18102	Red-and-White Prince	— L R
18001	Prince	— R R	18103	Red Atholl	Ky I
18004	Prince Albert	M	18104	Red Bird's Atholl	Ky I
18005	Prince Albert	M	18105	Red Buck	M
18006	Prince Albert	M	18106	Red Cap	— R R
18007	Prince Albert	P S	18107	Red Cloud	— R R
18008	Prince Albert	L R	18108	Red Duke	M
18010	Prince Albert	M	18109	Red Duke	M
18012	Prince Arthur	— M	18110	Red Duke	— M
18014	Prince Charles	— M	18113	Red Duke	— P S
18016	Prince Ernest 2nd	— L R	18114	Red Duke 5th	M
18019	Prince Gerold	M	18115	Red Duke	P S
18021	Prince Imperial	Ky I	18116	Red Duke	— D
18023	Prince Marg	— M	18117	Red Duke	M
18024	Prince May	— D	18118	Red Duke of Linwood	— R R
18026	Prince Napier	D	18119	Red Duke of Oxford	— C
18027	Prince Nicholas	L R	18120	Red Duke of The Valley	— D
18028	Prince of Bourbon	— P S	18121	Red Gloster	M
18030	Prince of Boyle	— M	18122	Red Jacket 6th	— R R
18031	Prince of Buckingham	— R R	18123	Red Jacket 10th	— R R
18034	Prince of Cortland	— P S	18124	Red Jacket 12th	D
18035	Prince of Elm Grove	— Ky I	18125	Red Jacket 15th	— R R
18036	Prince of Glady	C	18126	Red Jacket	L R
18040	Prince of Knox — Long-Horn		18127	Red Jerry	— D
18041	Prince of Lomo	— Wrong	18128	Red Knight	— Cox
18042	Prince of Virginia	L R	18130	Red Oak	P S
18043	Prince of Orangedale	— T	18133	Red Prince	— P S
18044	Prince of Putnam	— M	18134	2nd Red Prince	— Daisy
18046	Prince of The Grange	D	18138	Red Rose Airdrie	— P S
18050	Prince of The West	— R R	18140	Red Rover	— M
18051	Prince of Tonica	— M	18141	Red Rover	M
18053	Prince of Wales 1st	— M	18142	Red Rover	Ky I
18054	Prince Woodland	— D	18144	Red Star	Ky I
18055	Prince of Yuba	Ky I	18145	Red Star	— Cox
18056	Prince Otho	M	18146	Red Wiley	— T
18057	Prince Oxford 2nd	— Cox	18148	Reformer	— P S
18059	Prince Persia	— M	18149	Regent	L R
18060	Prince Porter	— P S	18150	Regent	T
18061	Prince Redwood	— Wrong	18151	Regent	P S
18062	Prince Royal	Ky I	18152	Regent Duke	T
18063	Prince Royal 2nd	Ky I	18153	Reginold	— L R
18064	Prince Royal	— R R	18154	Regulator	— M
18065	Princess' Airdrie	— D	18155	Remus	— M
18066	Prince Taylor	— R R	18156	Remus	— C
18067	Prince Taylor	— R R	18157	Renfro	P S
18068	Princeton	— D	18158	Renick	M
18069	Prince Zil	— Ky I	18159	Renick	— P S
18071	Prospect	— Woods	18160	Renick Wiley 2nd	T
18072	Proxy	Ky I	18161	Reno	P S
18074	P. T. Barnum	— M	18162	Reno	— R R
18075	Pueblo	— P S	18163	Reuben 3rd	Woods
18076	Pulaski	M	18164	Reuben 4th	M

18165	Reuben 5th	— M	18268	Royal Pansey ... — Long-Horn
18166	Reuben	Ky I	18269	Royal Prince ... — D
18167	Rex	Ky I	18273	Ruby ... — R R
18168	Rhoderick	— M	18274	Rufus B. ... Ky I
18169	Richard	— R R	18276	Rupee ... M
18170	Richard 3rd	— Daisy	18277	Rural ... T
18172	Rigdon	— P S	18278	Sadorus ... — D
18173	Rinaldo	— D	18281	St. Bernard ... — T
18174	Ringleader	— M	18284	St. Elmo ... — M
18176	Rising Sun	— L R	18285	St. Joe ... — R R
18177	Rival	— M	18287	St. Lawrence, Jr ... M
18178	Roan Buck	— D	18288	St. Malo ... — M
18181	Roan Knight	L R	18289	St. Nicholas ... — P S
18182	Roan Major	Cox	18290	St. Patrick ... C
18184	Roan Prince	— D	18293	Sam ... — R R
18186	Roan Prince 3rd	— L R	18296	Sam Weller ... Ky I
18187	Roan Rover	— Long-Horn	18298	Santa Claus ... — D
18188	Rob Anderson	— M	18299	Sanford ... M
18191	Robert Napir	D	18302	Schenectady ... Cox
18192	Robert Smith	— M	18304	Sculptor ... — D
18193	Robert The Bruce	— Cox	18306	Senator ... Cox
18195	Robbin	Cox	18308	Shabony ... — M
18196	Robbin Grey	— Daisy	18309	Shabony ... — M
18197	Robbin Hood	— P S	18310	Shakespeare ... T
18198	Rob Roy	— T	11311	Shanarke Chief ... — L R
18199	Rob Roy	— T	18313	Shawnee Chief 2nd ... M
18200	Rob Roy	— R R	18314	Shawnee Lad ... Ky I
18201	Rob Roy	— M	18316	Sherman ... — P S
18202	Rob Roy	D	18318	Sherman ... Ky I
18203	Rob Roy	Cox	18320	Shipwreck ... Ky I
18204	Rock Bridge	P S	18321	Sidney Johnson ... Ky I
18205	Rockingham	— R R	18322	Silver Duke ... P S
18206	Roderick	Ky I	18323	Simon ... P S
18207	Roderick 2nd	L R	18324	Sir Alfred ... — M
18209	Rodney	— C	18325	Sir Benjamin ... — P S
18210	Roebuck	D	18327	Sir Frederick 3rd ... — R R
18211	Rogers	— M	18328	Sir Frederick ... Ky I
18212	Rokeby	— L R	18329	Sir George ... — Long-Horn
18215	Romeo	M	18330	Sir Harrold ... — M
18216	Romeo	— M	18331	Sir Henry ... — Cox
18218	Romulus	— M	18332	Sir Henry 2nd ... — Cox
18219	Romulus	— M	18333	Sir Henry ... Cox
18220	Romulus	Daisy	18334	Sir Henry ... — Ky I
18222	Rosco	— L R	18337	Sir Nicholas ... — Cox
18226	Rosendale 7th	— M	18338	Sir Robert ... Ky I
18227	Rosendale 8th	— L R	18340	Sir Thomas ... C
18228	Rosendale 10th	— M	18341	Sir Walter ... — Cox
18229	Ross	Ky I	18342	Sir Walter Scott ... L R
18230	Rosy Duke	— P S	18343	Sir William ... — Cox
18231	Rotterdam	— L R	18344	Sir William Pinckney 2nd ... Ky I
18233	Rover 2nd	Ky I	18345	Sir Wm. Wallace ... — L R
18235	2nd Royal Airdrie	— M	18346	Sir Wm. Wallace ... — Ky I
18237	Royal Arch	— C	18347	Sir Will Skiff ... Ky I
18239	Royal Barrister	— M	18348	Smuggler ... — L R
18240	Royal Chief	— R R	18349	Snowball ... T
18244	Royal Duke	— R R	18350	Snowball ... M
18245	Royal Duke	— P S	18352	Solomon ... — Cox
18248	Royal Duke of Austinburg	— R R	18353	Solomon 2nd ... — Cox
18249	Royal Duke of Claremont	Cox	18354	Son of Favorite ... — Cox
18251	Royal Duke of Gloster, Jr	— Cox	18355	Son of Squire ... L R
18252	Royal Duke of Waterloo	— R R	18356	Samona ... — R R
18254	Royal Frith	— P S	18358	Southern Duke ... — P S
18255	Royal Gem	Ky I	18360	Sovereign ... — M
18257	Royal George	L R	18361	Speculator ... — R R
18258	Royal George 2nd	Ky I	18362	Spence Dabeny ... — R R
18259	Royal George 3rd	T	18363	Splendor ... Ky I
18261	Royal John	— D	18364	Splendor ... L R
18262	Royal Justice	M	18365	Spot ... — D
18263	Royal Lad	— Cox	18366	Spotted Oxford ... — L R
18264	Royal Lonanjo	— D	18367	Spotted Prince ... — L R

SHORT-HORN CATTLE PEDIGREES.

18368	Springdale Duke	Ky I
18368½	Springdale Duke 2nd	Ky I
18369	Springdale Duke 3rd	Ky I
18371	Spurgeon	P S
18374	Stanley	— D
18378	Star Duke	— P S
18379	Star Duke	D
18381	Star in the East	T
18382	Stark	— M
18383	Star King	— M
18384	Starlight	M
18386	Star of Glendale	— L R
18387	Star of Medling	— M
18388	Star of Peace	— D
18389	Star of the East	— L R
18390	Star of the West	— P S
18391	Star of the West	M
18392	Star of the West	— M
18393	Star of the West	— P S
18395	State Forester	Ky I
18396	Stately Hero	— Cox
18397	Staver	M
18400	Stoner 2nd	— R R
18401	Stonewall	— D
18402	Stonewall	M
18403	Stonewall 2nd	— P S
18406	Stonewall	— L R
18407	Stonewall Jackson	— T
18409	Stonewall Jackson	P S
18410	Storm	— T
18411	Storm	Ky I
18413	Sullivan	Cox
18414	Sultan	— M
18417	Swiss Boy	M
18418	Switzer Boy	— D
18420	Sycum	T
18422	Taurus	— T
18424	Tecumseh	— R R
18426	Texas	— L R
18427	Thackaray	P S
18428	Thad. Stevens	— D
18429	Thad. Stevens	— L R
18430	The Cardinal	— D
18434	The Lad	M
18435	The Meadow's Duke 2nd	— M
18438	The Sultan	M
18439	Thomas Bates	Ky I
18443	Tim Bunker	P S
18445	Timothy Titcomb	P S
18446	Tippecanoe	M
18447	Tippecanoe Prince	Ky I
18448	Tiptoe	L R
18450	Toledo	— P S
18452	Tom	Cox
18453	Tom	— M
18454	Tom Handy	— L R
18455	Tomlinson	— M
18456	Tom McCarty	— D
18457	Tom Wonder	— P S
18458	Tom Payne	P S
18459	Tonawanda	— Cox
18460	Tornado	M
18461	Tornado	— Cox
18462	Toulon	— T
18464	Traveler	— Cox
18466	Triumph	— C
18468	Trumbull	M
18470	Tuleboy	— D
18471	Tulip's Baron Booth	Ky I
18472	Turley	D
18473	Tycoon	— M
18474	Uncle Sam	M
18475	Uncle Sam 2nd	D
18476	Uncle Sam 3rd	— D
18477	Union Duke	— R R
18478	Valentine	Ky I
18480	Valley Forge	Ky I
18481	Valley Ridge Prince	L R
18484	Vandal	— M
18487	Velocipede	— M
18488	Vermillion Charley	M
18489	Vermillion Duke	— L R
18490	Vermillion Duke 2nd	Cox
18491	2nd Vermillion Lad	— M
18492	Vermillion Sucker Boy	— T
18493	Vermont	Ky I
18494	Vesper	— Cox
18495	Vicar of Wakefield	L R
18496	Vick	— Cox
18497	Victor	— M
18498	Victor	— M
18499	Victor	L R
18500	Victoria's Duke	— P S
18501	Vidette	— C
18502	Vigilance	— L R
18503	Villisca Chief	P S
18504	Vinca	M
18505	Violet's Airdrie	— D
18509	Von Moltke	— D
18511	Wallace	D
18512	Wallace	Ky I
18513	Wallace	M
18514	Walter B. Dance	— D
18516	Waushara	L R
18519	Warren Davis	— M
18521	Warrior	L R
18522	Warrior Boy	— R R
18523	Warwick	M
18524	Washington	Daisy
18525	Washington 1st	— R R
18527	Washington Duke	— R R
18532	Waverly	— Ky I
18536	Western Duke	— D
18537	Western Duke	— R R
18538	Western Duke	Ky I
18539	Western Hunter	— Ky I
18540	Western Jim	Ky I
18541	Western Prince	P S
18542	Western Star	M
18546	Wharfdale Hero	— M
18547	W. H. Hendricks	— M
18549	Whitefoot	— D
18551	White Prince	— D
18552	Whittier	P S
18553	Wild Billy	— Ky I
18555	Wild Star	— D
18556	Wild Woods	C
18557	Wiley 5th	L R
18558	Wiley 6th	L R
18559	Wiley 7th	L R
18560	Wiley 8th	L R
18561	Willow Duke	— T
18562	Wilton	M
18565	Winnebago Chief	— C
18567	Wisconsin 2nd	— M
18568	Wiseton Lad	— M
18569	Witness	— M
18574	Woodford Airdrie	— M
18575	Woodland Duke	— M
18576	Woodland Duke	— R R

18577	Woodland Echo	M	18688	Duke of Polk	— L R
18579	Woodson	— M	18689	Duke of Princeton 2nd	Ky I
18583	Xerxes	Ky I	18690	Duke of Ramsey	— P S
18587	Young America 2nd	P S	18691	Duke of Walnut Grove	Ky I
18590	Young Argyll	— Cox	18692	Duke of Wellington	— Cox
18591	Young Baltic	L R	18693	Duke of York	M
18592	Young Baron Lewis	— M	18694	Earl Goodness	— R R
18593	Young Beauty	M	18698	Eliab	— P S
18594	Young Butterfly	M	18699	Emperor Alexander	L R
18595	Young Chief	T	18701	Evening Star	Ky I
18596	Young Comet	— Ky I	18702	Excelsior	— R R
18597	Young Goldfinder	— M	18703	Fanchon's Duke	R R
18598	Young King	— M	18706	Field Marshal	— Cox
18599	Young Leopard 3rd	P S	18707	Filligree Prince	M
18602	Young Minister	— M	18708	Fisherman's Pride	L R
18603	Young Monitor	D	18709	Forest	— R R
18605	Young Oxford	— M	18710	Fortune	L R
18606	Young Prairie Chief	D	18711	Frank	— M
18607	Young Prince	— P S	18712	Fred	— D
18608	Young Republic	M	18714	Fremont	D
18609	Young Sam	M	18716	Gen. Decatur	P S
18614	Zack Taylor	M	18724	Grant, Jr,	L R
18615	Ziba	Ky I	18726	Grenadier	— R R
18616	Agassiz	— R R	18727	Gulliver	— L R
18617	Alexander	— L R	18728	Harrold	D
18619	Althorp Lad	— P S	18729	Harry Airdrie	— C
18621	Arlington	M	18730	Honest John	— T
18627	Baron of Australia	— Cox	18732	Jack Harrison	— M
18628	Baron of Australia 2nd	— Cox	18734	Jury	— R R
18629	Baron of Australia 3rd	— Cox	18735	Joe Shaw	— T
18630	5th Baron of Oakwood	R R	18738	Kirklivington 3rd	— Cox
18634	Baron Romeo	Ky I	18739	Kokoma	Ky I
18635	Bell Duke Des Moines	— L R	18740	Lee Irvin	— M
18637	Ben	— D	18744	Lord Duke 2nd	— M
18638	Ben Bolt	Ky I	18745	Lord of Lorne	— R R
18639	Billy	M	18747	Lord Trimble	— R R
18641	Booth Lad	M	18748	Louan Duke of Deer Park	— D
18643	Boston Charlie	L R	18749	Mack	— M
18646	Bronte	— Cox	18750	Madison Duke	— C
18647	Buckeye Boy	— R R	18751	Major	— M
18648	Burnside	— Cox	18752	Major Burnside	— Cox
18649	Canadian Boy	— M	18755	Mate	D
18651	Captain Cook	— M	18756	May Duke	— M
18652	Captain Jack	L R	18757	3rd Meadow Duke	— M
18653	Captain Jack	— M	18758	Medallion	— M
18655	Captain Starlight	— R R	18759	Milton	— Cox
18656	Castelar	D	18760	Minnas Duke	— T
18657	Champaign Duke 2nd	Ky I	18762	Modoc	— P S
18659	Chief of Knox	— D	18764	Morning Star	M
18662	Climax	L R	18765	Murat	D
18663	Colfan	T	18766	Napoleon	— Cox
18666	Count Bismarck	Cox	18768	Nero	— P S
18667	Crown Prince	D	18769	Noble Airdrie	M
18668	Darlington	— M	18771	Oakland 9th	P S
18669	DeGraw	— T	18773	Ontario John	— Cox
18670	DeGraw 2nd	— T	18774	Our Fritz	— Cox
18671	Dick Pomeroy	— M	18778	Pere Hyacinth	Ky I
18672	Dixie Duke	M	18779	Pickwick	— R R
18673	Dixie Duke 2nd	— R R	18780	Pluvius	— Cox
18674	Don Juan	D	18781	Prairie Boy	— P S
18675	Don Piatt	D	18782	Prince	— M
18676	Duke of Avondale	Ky I	18782½	Prince	Daisy
18677	Duke of Bedford	— Cox	18783	Prince Albert	— Cox
18679	5th Duke of Deer Park	— L R	18787	Ravenswood Favorite	— M
18680	Duke of DesMoines	— L R	18789	Red Boy	Ky I
18681	Duke of Douglas	— M	18791	Red Cloud	L R
18682	Duke of Eddington	— L R	18792	Remus	— Cox
18684	Duke of Garden Grove	— M	18794	Robert Lee	M
18686	Duke of Illinois	— M	18795	Rob Roy	— L R
18687	Duke of Montrose	L R	18801	Russell	L R

SHORT-HORN CATTLE PEDIGREES.

No.	Name	Ref.
18803	Sir Francis	— Cox
18804	Sir Henry	— Cox
18806	Sovereign	— M
18807	Spotswood Lad	— D
18808	Stanton	L R
18811	Tecumseh	P S
18812	Tiger	M
18813	Tweedside	— M
18814	Valliant	— Cox
18815	Vanguard	— Cox
18816	Victor 8th	— C
18820	White Stocking	— T
18821	Wolf Run	— R R
18828	Abb Duke	— R R
18829	Abe	Ky I
18831	Adair	M
18832	Adam	M
18834	Ada's Mazurka	— Cox
18835	Admiral	— Cox
18836	Admiral 2nd	Ky I
18838	Admiral 4th	— Daisy
18839	Admiral 5th	— Daisy
18840	Admiration	— M
18841	Adolfo	— Cox
18842	Agassiz	— P S
18846	3rd Airdrie Duke	— D
18848	Airdrie Grant	T
18851	Airdrie Lad	— Cox
18852	Airdrie Pike	M
18854	Airdrie Thorndale	L R
18857	Airdrie of Glenecho	— M
18858	Airdrie of Riverside	— Cox
18859	Airline 1st	— Cox
18860	Airline 2nd	— Cox
18861	Ajax	— M
18862	Aladdin	— Cox
18863	Alaric	— Cox
18864	Albert	— C
18866	Albion	Cox
18867	Albion	— R R
18869	Aldebairn	— D
18870	Aledo Lad	Ky I
18871	Alexis	P S
18872	Alexander Favorite	L R
18873	Alhasson	P S
18874	Allbeach	— R R
18875	Allen	Ky I
18877	Alonzo	— Cox
18878	Alpha	— R R
18881	Althorp Lad	— P S
18883	Ambition	— Cox
18885	Americus	— M
18886	Americus	Ky I
18888	Antoine	— D
18889	April Fool	— P S
18890	Aram	T
18891	Arctic	— L R
18894	Ascot, Jr	Ky I
18895	Ashland Prince	— M
18897	August Boy	M
18900	Autum Prince	T
18901	Baby Boy	Cox
18902	Baby John	— D
18903	Bacchus	— M
18904	Bachelor	— M
18905	Ballard	M
18906	Balloon	Ky I
18908	Banner Boy	Cox
18909	Barbarossa	— L R
18910	Barber	— P S
18911	Barlow	— Cox
18912	Baron	— M
18913	Baron	P S
18914	Baron	Ky I
18915	Baron	— L R
18916	Baron Airdrie 2nd	— R R
18921	Baron Bedford 2nd	— R R
18923	Baron Bertram 6th	— R R
18924	Baron Boone 8th	— D
18926	Baron Booth's Commander	— D
18929	Baron Booth of the Valley	— M
18930	Baron Booth of Woodlawn	— M
18933	Baron Clyde	— M
18934	Baron De Kalb	— Cox
18935	Baron Gloster	— Cox
18939	Baron Gwynne 8th	— Cox
18940	Baron Gwynne 9th	— Cox
18941	Baron Gwynne 10th	— Cox
18942	Baron Gwynne 11th	— Cox
18943	Baron Gwynne of Hardin	— T
18944	Baron Humbolt	R R
18945	Baron Konutz	Cox
18948	Baron Louanjo 4th	— R R
18950	Baron Mazurka	— R R
18959	Baron Starlight	— Daisy
18960	Baron of Australia 4th	— Cox
18961	Baron of Australia 5th	— Cox
18962	Baron of Carlisle	M
18963	Baron of Crethmere	— C
18968	Baron of Oakhill	— C
18969	2nd Baron of Oakhill	— C
18970	3rd Baron of Oakhill	— C
18971	3rd Baron of Oakwood	R R
18972	4th Baron of Oakwood	— M
18973	Baron of Riverside	— Cox
18977	Barry Cornwall	— M
18981	Batavia Duke	— R R
18982	Baxter	— M
18985	Bearl 3rd	— Cox
18988	Beauty's Duke	M
18989	Beauty's Duke	M
18990	Beverwyck	Ky I
18992	Bedford	— R R
18993	Bedford	— P S
18994	Bedford	T
18995	Beecher	— C
18996	Beecher	Ky I
18997	Beecher	Ky I
18998	Beecher	— M
18999	Bell Duke	T
19000	Bell Duke	— R R
19001	Bell Duke	— M
19004	Bell Duke F	— R R
19005	Bell Duke of Airdrie 2nd	P S
19010	Bellevue Lad	P S
19012	Bell Muscatoon	M
19017	Ben Bolt	— L R
19018	Ben Butler	— Cox
19019	Ben Butler	— C
19020	Ben Franklin	— M
19022	Ben Wade	— D
19023	Ben Wade	— D
19025	Benzine	M
19026	Berthune	— P S
19028	Bill	— T
19029	Bill Anderson	— Long-Horn
19030	Bill Thompson	— M
19031	Billie Hunt	— D
19032	Billy Barlow	— M
19033	Billy Burton	— L R

19034	Billy Shakespeare — D	19130	Captain Woods
19035	Billy Sherman Ky I	19131	Captain — L R
19036	Bishop — R R	19132	Capt. Billy Ford P S
19037	Bishop Ky I	19133	Capt. Buckland — M
19038	Bismarck M	19136	Capt. Gay Ky I
19039	Bismarck — R R	19137	Capt. Gay Ky I
19040	Bismarck — P S	19138	Capt. Innis — R R
19042	Black Hawk Chief M	19139	Capt. Jack — Long-Horn
19046	Bloom's Baron — R R	19140	Capt. Jack — P S
19047	Bloom's Gloster — L R	19141	Capt. Jack — M
19048	Blossom's Boy L R	19142	Capt. Jack Cox
19050	Blucher — Cox	19144	Capt. Kidd — L R
19051	Blucher T	19146	Capt. Steele — P S
19054	Bob Pitman — L R	19148	Caliph — M
19056	Bolivar — Cox	19149	Calloway Duke — M
19057	Bolivar Graves T	19152	Cambria Duke — R R
19058	Bolton — L R	19156	Canadian Chief — Cox
19059	Bonner — M	19159	Canova — P S
19061	Bonny Boy 2nd — Ky I	19160	Carnival — T
19062	Bonny Scotland — M	19161	Carnival 2nd — T
19063	Bonny Doon — R R	19162	Cashier — R R
19064	Booker P S	19163	Casket's Napier — R R
19065	Boone — D	19164	Cassander — M
19066	Boss — P S	19166	Catawba Duke — M
19067	Boss Allen — P S	19167	Cerro Gordo Chief — T
19069	Boston Duke 4th — T	19168	Cicero — M
19070	Boston Lad Ky I	19169	Cinnabar L R
19071	Bouncer — Cox	19171	Champaign — M
19072	Bourbon M	19176	Champion — P S
19074	Bourbon Duke Ky I	19177	Champion — P S
19076	Bourbon Grampion — P S	19179	Champion — M
19077	Bourbon Prince — T	19180	Champion C
19079	Bourbon Star 2nd — P S	19181	Champion — D
19080	Bovis 1st Ky I	19183	Chancellor — M
19081	Bovis 2nd Ky I	19185	Chandler's Airdrie — D
19083	Boxer L R	19186	Charles — C
19084	Boxer — L R	19188	Charley R R
19085	Boyd's Airdrie R R	19189	Charley — Cox
19086	Boyle Duke, Jr. — M	19190	Charley M
19089	Breastplate Louanjo — R R	19191	Chatham's Boy — M
19091	Brent — C	19192	Chatham's Duke — M
19092	Bret Harte M	19193	Chatham's Duke 2nd — M
19094	Bride's Duke of Thorndale — R R	19197	Cherry's Mazurka T
19095	Bride's Red Jacket — R R	19199	Cheyenne — T
19096	Brides Thorndale — R R	19200	Chief of the Short-Horns — L R
19097	Brigham Ky I	19202	Chieftain M
19098	Brigham — P S	19203	Chieftain — M
19099	Brigham Green — M	19204	Chieftain 2nd — M
19100	Brigham Young Ky I	19205	Chieftain 3rd — R R
19101	Bright Eye — P S	19206	Childe Harold R R
19102	Bright Eye Gloster — Cox	19207	Chillingworth L R
19104	Bright Lad — Cox	19212	Chuck Anderson D
19105	British Baron 2nd — R R	19213	Clarence — C
19108	Brilliant — Cox	19214	Clarence — C
19109	Bro. Beecher Daisy	19215	Clarence — Cox
19110	Bruce M	19216	Clarendon — R R
19111	Bruce's Corporal — M	19220	Cleome M
19113	Buckeye Boy — D	19221	Clifton L R
19114	Buckeye Lad L R	19222	Clifton Duke — Cox
19115	Buckeye State — Long-Horn	19223	Clifton Duke 3rd — P S
19116	Buffalo Duke Ky I	19234	Clifton Duke 4th Ky I
19117	Buford — P S	19235	Climax — M
19118	Bullion — R R	19226	Clinton Chief — D
19119	Buncomb M	19228	Cochrane Ky I
19121	2nd Burnside Duke D	19230	Colonel Ky I
19122	3rd Burnside Duke — D	19231	Col. Clay T
19123	Burrett Lad L R	19232	Col. Hamer — Long-Horn
19125	Byron P S	19233	Col. Hankins — D
19127	Byron Ky I	19236	Col. Montague — Daisy
19129	Captain R R	19238	Col. Rhodes Bull M

SHORT-HORN CATTLE PEDIGREES. 89

No.	Name	Herd
19239	Col. Standish	— Ky I
19242	Comanche	— R R
19243	Comet	— Cox
19245	Comet	M
19246	Comet	— Cox
19247	Comet	Cox
19248	Comet	— R R
19249	Comet 2nd	Ky I
19251	Commodore	— T
19252	Commodore	T
19253	Commodore	M
19254	Commodore	— P S
19256	Commodore 2nd	— D
19259	Connaught	Ky I
19260	Conqueror 2nd	M
19263	Constantina's Oxford 2nd	— R R
19265	Constitution	— P S
19268	Corporal 2nd	— R R
19269	Count Athol	— R R
19271	Count Bismarck	— M
19273	Count Fathom	— M
19274	Count Fathom	D
19276	Count Llewellyn	— R R
19277	Count of Onawa	— M
19279	5th Count of Oneida	— D
19281	Crescent Favorite	— M
19282	Crittendon	— M
19284	Crown Prince	— Long-Horn
19286	Crown Prince 2nd	P S
19287	Crown Prince 3rd	M
19288	Crown Prince 4th	M
19289	Crusader	— R R
19290	Crusader 3rd	Ky I
19291	Cuban	— M
19293	Currency	— D
19294	Cypress Airdrie Duke	— D
19296	Czar	— Ky I
19297	Dairy Boy	M
19298	Daisy Bull	— M
19299	Daisy Bull 2nd	M
19300	Daisy Bull 3rd	— M
19302	Daisy Duke	— R R
19305	Daisy Duke 2nd	— R R
19308	Dan Rice	— M
19309	Dandola	— M
19311	Dandy	— Cox
19312	Daniel Carmine	Cox
19314	Daniel Webster	— M
19315	Darby Lad 7th	— P S
19316	Darby Lad 8th	— P S
19319	Dean Swift	T
19320	Deacon Bross	Ky I
19321	Decatur	— M
19324	Defender	M
19325	Defender	— R R
19326	Delia's Boy	— D
19327	Denham Duke	M
19328	Derby, Jr	— M
19330	Dexter	— R R
19331	Dexter	Ky I
19332	Dexter	— M
19334	Dexter 2nd	— R R
19335	Dexter 2nd	M
19336	Diadelphian	L R
19337	Diamond Duke	M
19338	Dick	P S
19339	Dick	— T
19340	Dick	M
19342	Dick Long	— D
19343	Dick Napier	— Daisy
19344	Dick McGrath	— M
19345	Dick Taylor, Jr	— C
19349	Dillard Duke	M
19350	Dimmitt	— M
19351	Diomede	— M
19352	Dixie Clyde	M
19354	Dixie Duke 2nd	— R R
19355	Dixie Duke of Augusta	— P S
19356	Doctor	— M
19357	Doctor Stevenson	— R R
19359	Don	M
19361	Don Juan	— Cox
19363	Don Louan	— R R
19364	Don Pedro	— P S
19365	Don Quixote	— P S
19366	Double Duke	L R
19367	Double P. of H	— D
19368	Doubloon	D
19369	Dr. Montgomery, Jr	— M
19370	Draco	— Ky I
19371	Driver	M
19373	Duff	— R R
19375	Duguescline	— D
19376	Duncan's Bull	— R R
19377	Duke	Cox
19378	Duke	P S
19379	Duke	— L R
19380	Duke	— R R
19381	Duke	— M
19382	Duke 2nd	— Cox
19384	Duke 2nd	D
19385	Duke 2nd	Ky I
19386	Duke Alexis	— M
19387	Duke Mercer	D
19388	Duke Alexis 2nd	Ky I
19389	Duke Alexis 2nd	P S
19395	Duke of Austin	— P S
19396	Duke of Arcola	M
19398	Duke of Arkell 2nd	— Cox
19399	Duke of Armwell	— T
19400	6th Duke of Ashland	— M
19401	7th Duke of Ashland	— M
19402	8th Duke of Ashland	— M
19403	9th Duke of Ashland	— P S
19404	4th Duke of Atholl	— Long-Horn
19405	5th Duke of Atholl	C
19406	6th Duke of Atholl	— R R
19407	Duke of Avon	— C
19408	Duke of Ayr	M
19409	Duke of Barton	L R
19410	Duke of Belmont	— M
19412	Duke of Bourneville	— D
19415	Duke of Burnett 23rd	— R R
19417	Duke of Casey	— M
19418	Duke of Cedar Grove	— M
19419	1st Duke of Cedar Spring's Farm	M
19422	Duke of Clearfield	— L R
19424	Duke of Como	R R
19427	Duke of Cumberland	M
19428	Duke of Dayton	— D
19429	Duke of December	— M
19430	6th Duke of Deer Park	— L R
19433	Duke of Earlville	— C
19434	Duke of East Lincoln	T
19435	Duke of Edinboro	— P S
19436	Duke of Edinburg	M
19437	Duke of Edinburg	— M
19440	Duke of Ellison	— D
19441	Duke of El Paso	— P S
19442	Duke of Exeter	— R R

19443	2nd Duke of Fairfield — M	19533	Duke of Mercer — M
19444	Duke of Fairview — M	19534	Duke of Millington — M
19445	1st Duke of Fairview M	19536	4th Duke of Millington — P S
19446	2nd Duke of Fairview — M	19537	5th Duke of Millington — M
19447	Duke of Fayette — D	19538	Duke of Mogul L R
19448	Duke of Finley — D	19543	Duke of Mt. Airy — R R
19449	Duke of Flat Lick — M	19545	2nd Duke of New London — Ky I
19452	Duke of Fountain Daisy	19546	Duke of Oakland L R
19453	2nd Duke of Fountain — R R	19547	Duke of Oakland — L R
19456	Duke of Freedom — Ky I	19548	11th Duke of Oakland L R
19458	Duke of Fulton — D	19549	12th Duke of Oakland L R
19459	3rd Duke of Garnaville — Ky I	19550	13th Duke of Oakland L R
19461	3rd Duke of Geneva — P S	19551	14th Duke of Oakland L R
19462	4th Duke of Geneva P S	19552	15th Duke of Oakland L R
19464	Duke of Gloster Ky I	19553	2nd Duke of Ogle Ky I
19466	2nd Duke of Goodness T	19554	Duke of Okaw 3rd Ky I
19467	3rd Duke of Goodness T	19555	2nd Duke of Omaha — P S
19469	22nd Duke of Goodness — R R	19556	Duke of Onawa — T
19470	Duke of Grangers — P S	19557	4th Duke of Oneida — R R
19471	14th Duke of Granville — Ky I	19558	5th Duke of Oneida — R R
19473	Duke of Green — M	19559	Duke of Oran T
19474	3rd Duke of Greenlawn — M	19560	1st Duke of Oran — M
19475	Duke of Hallsville T	19561	4th Duke of Osage — P S
19477	2nd Duke of Hancock — Cox	19563	Duke of Oxford — M
19478	Duke of Hardwick M	19565	Duke of Oxford — P S
19479	Duke of Hartford — P S	19566	Duke of Oxford — P S
19481	3rd Duke of Harristown — T	19569	Duke of Parke 2nd — Ky I
19482	Duke of Harrod's Creek — R R	19570	Duke of Paris — C
19483	1st Duke of Hawksbill Valley — T	19571	Duke of Pittsfield T
19484	Duke of Hazel Dell — M	19572	Duke of Plane P S
19487	5th Duke of Hendon — M	19573	Duke of Pleasant Hill — Cox
19488	Duke of Henry M	19574	Duke of Pleasant Ridge — M
19489	2nd Duke of Highland — M	19575	1st Duke of Pleasant View — D
19492	1st Duke of Hinsdale M	19576	Duke of Princeton — T
19493	Duke of Houston T	19577	Duke of Princeton — D
19494	1st Duke of Huron — Ky I	19578	Duke of Princeton Ky I
19495	Duke of Iowa Ky I	19581	6th Duke of Randolph Ky I
19496	Duke of Jackson — P S	19582	7th Duke of Randolph Ky I
19497	Duke of Jamestown — M	19583	8th Duke of Randolph Ky I
19499	Duke of Kent Ky I	19584	Duke of Rock — Cox
19500	Duke of Kent — R R	19586	Duke of Ruralusia — P S
19501	Duke of Knox — M	19589	4th Duke of Salem P S
19502	Duke of Knox — D	19590	Duke of Salina L R
19503	Duke of Lancaster Ky I	19591	Duke of Saunders — Ky I
19504	Duke of Lapwing Farm — M	19592	Duke of Saxon P S
19505	Duke of Lenox — M	19593	1st Duke of Scioto — R R
19507	Duke of Liberty P S	19594	2nd Duke of Scioto D
19508	Duke of Liberty — M	19595	Duke of Seneca M
19509	1st Duke of Lincoln Ky I	19598	Duke of Shawnee L R
19510	Duke of Locust Grove — P S	19602	Duke of Solway — R R
19511	Duke of Locust Grove Cox	19603	Duke of Southwick — M
19513	2nd Duke of Locust Lawn — R R	19604	Duke of Springbrook 1st — R R
19514	4th Duke of Locust Lawn — Daisy	19605	Duke of Springbrook 2nd — R R
19515	5th Duke of Locust Lawn M	19607	6th Duke of Sulivan Ky I
19516	6th Duke of Locust Lawn — Ky I	19608	Duke of Sunnyside D
19517	1st Duke of Louan — R R	19611	Duke of Tama — M
19518	Duke of Lyons — L R	19612	15th Duke of Tecumseh D
19519	Duke of Maple Avenue — P S	19613	Duke of the Grove L R
19520	2nd Duke of Maple Avenue — L R	19615	Duke of the Lake L R
19521	3rd Duke of Maple Avenue — P S	19617	Duke of the Prairies Ky I
19522	Duke of Maple Hill — M	19618	Duke of the Valley — R R
19523	Duke of Maple Hill — M	19621	Duke of Tipton D
19524	Duke of Maple Lawn — D	19623	Duke of Townsend — R R
19525	Duke of Maple Wood R R	19624	Duke of Tuscumbia — T
19526	Duke of Marion P S	19625	2nd Duke of Valley Ridge L R
19527	2nd Duke of Marlborough — D	19626	Duke of Vermillion — R R
19528	3rd Duke of Marlborough — Cox	19628	2nd Duke of Vinewood — Ky I
19529	Duke of McLean — M	19629	2nd Duke of Vinewood — Long-Horn
19530	Duke of Meadow Lawn M	19632	Duke of Wadsworth — Cox
19531	Duke of Mecca — D	19633	Duke of Wadsworth 2nd — Cox

19634	Duke of Walnut Hill ...... M	19749	Fancy's Boy ...... T
19636	3rd Duke of Wapsie ...... Ky I	19750	Fancy's Boy ...... — L R
19637	Duke of Wayne ...... — M	19752	Fanny's Heir ...... — R R
19638	Duke of Wea ...... M	19756	Fat Boy ...... — L R
19639	Duke of Wellington ...... — P S	19757	Favorite ...... — Cox
19640	Duke of Wild Rose ...... — R R	19759	Favorite ...... — R R
19641	2nd Duke of Wilton ...... — Ky I	19760	Favorite ...... — R R
19642	Duke of Woodstock ...... — M	19761	Fennimore Lad ...... — P S
19643	Duke of Woodstock 2nd ...... — M	19767	Financier ...... — R R
19644	Duke of Woodson ...... Ky I	19776	Forester ...... — P S
19645	Duke of York ...... — P S	19777	Forester ...... — L R
19646	Duke Orontes ...... Daisy	19778	Forester ...... P S
19647	Duke Royal ...... — R R	19783	Frank ...... — D
19649	Duncan ...... D	19784	Frank ...... — Cox
19650	Duncan Airdrie ...... Ky I	19785	Frank Clyde ...... M
19651	Dunglen Airdrie ...... — Daisy	19786	Frank Collins ...... — D
19652	Dunglen Prince ...... — Daisy	19787	Franklin Kidd ...... — M
19653	Duroc ...... — R R	19788	Franklin P. Bedford ...... — R R
19654	Dusty Bob ...... — Daisy	19789	Fred ...... — Cox
19655	Dutch Boy ...... — R R	19790	Fred ...... M
19656	Dutch John ...... — R R	19792	Fremont ...... D
19657	Dutchman ...... — M	19793	Fremont Duke ...... — M
19658	Earl ...... — D	19794	Fritz ...... — Ky I
19662	Earl Moscow ...... P S	19795	Frogtown ...... — R R
19667	Earl of Cold River ...... — L R	19796	Frontier Duke ...... R R
19671	Earl of Elm Grove ...... — P S	19797	Frosty ...... — T
19674	2nd Earl of Gloster ...... — Cox	19798	Fullington ...... M
19675	3rd Earl of Gloster ...... — Cox	19800	14th Gaban ...... — P S
19676	2nd Earl of Greenbush ...... — R R	19801	15th Gaban ...... — P S
19677	3rd Earl of Greenbush ...... — P S	19802	Galva Prince ...... Ky I
19678	4th Earl of Greenbush ...... — P S	19804	Gamester 3rd ...... — R R
19679	5th Earl of Greenbush ...... — Cox	19805	Garland's Son ...... — M
19680	6th Earl of Greenbush ...... — Cox	19808	Gay Boy ...... — R R
19681	7th Earl of Greenbush ...... T	19810	General ...... — D
19682	8th Earl of Greenbush ...... — M	19811	General ...... — D
19683	Earl of Hanover ...... — P S	19812	Gen. Butler ...... — L R
19684	2nd Earl of Hanover ...... — R R	19813	Gen. Butler ...... — M
19694	4th Earl of Mozart ...... — M	19814	Gen. Coburn ...... — M
19696	10th Earl of Oxford ...... P S	19816	Gen. Cooney ...... Ky I
19697	Earl of Proctor ...... — P S	19817	Gen. Ellsworth ...... — M
19698	2nd Earl of Proctor ...... P S	19818	Gen. Forrest ...... — L R
16704	2nd Earl of Sturgis ...... — P S	19819	Gen. Forrest ...... Ky I
19705	Earl of the Pines ...... — Cox	19821	Gen. Grant ...... P S
19709	Echo ...... — Cox	19822	Gen. Grant ...... — L R
19711	Echo ...... Woods	19823	Gen. Grant ...... — M
19712	Echo 2nd ...... Ky I	19825	Gen. Howard ...... Cox
19713	Earl of Cedar ...... — R R	19828	Gen. Lee ...... R R
19716	Eclipse 4th ...... M	19830	Gen. Marion ...... — P S
19717	Ed Davison ...... — Long-Horn	19831	Gen. Morgan ...... — R R
19719	Edward ...... — R R	19832	Gen. Palmer ...... M
19720	Eiland Duke ...... — D	19833	Gen. Prim ...... — Daisy
19721	Elmwood Lad ...... P S	19835	Gen. Stark ...... — Cox
19722	El Nath ...... — Ky I	19836	Gen. Stark ...... — D
19724	Elwell ...... — L R	19837	Gen. Washington ...... — L R
19725	Emerson ...... — C	19838	Gen. Worth ...... — M
19726	Emmet ...... — C	19840	Geneva Boy ...... — C
19728	Emperor William ...... — R R	19842	Geneva Lad of Pattersondale ...... R R
19729	Enoch Arden ...... P S	19844	George ...... — Cox
19731	Esquire Gillett ...... — R R	19845	George Ann's Oxford ...... T
19732	Ethan Allen ...... — M	19846	George Ann's Oxford 1st ...... T
19734	Eureka 2nd ...... Daisy	19847	George Green ...... — M
19735	Eva's Airdrie ...... — P S	19848	George Herd ...... P S
19736	Excelsior ...... — D	19849	George Peabody ...... — L R
19737	Expansion ...... R R	19850	George Snider ...... P S
19738	Fair Play ...... M	19851	George Washington ...... — M
19739	Fairview ...... D	19856	Glenbrook ...... — R R
19741	Fairy Duke ...... — R R	19857	Glen Lad ...... — D
19746	Fancy Duke ...... Ky I	19858	Glenwood Boy ...... M
19747	Fancy Duke 2nd ...... — M	19859	Gloster ...... — Cox
19748	Fancy Lad ...... — L R	19860	Gloster ...... — R R

19861	Gloster's Duke	P S	19957	Harrison Duke	— R R
19863	Gloster's Surprise	— Cox	19958	Harrison Hero	M
19864	3rd Gloster of Pine Grove	— Cox	19959	Harry	— Daisy
19866	Gold Beater	— Cox	19961	Hardin of Oakland	— P S
19867	Gold Coin	P S	19963	Harley	M
19871	Gold Dust	— Cox	19965	Harrold of Santa Clara	L R
19872	Gold Dust	— T	19967	Hatties Duke	Ky I
19873	Gold Dust	— R R	19969	5th Hazelwood Duke	C
19877	Goldfinch, Jr	M	19970	Hearts of Oak 3rd	Cox
19878	Goldfinder	— D	19971	Hearty Boy	— Cox
19879	Goldfinder	— P S	19972	Heber 2nd	M
19880	Goldfinder	L R	19974	Hebron 2nd	— D
19881	Gold Plait	L R	19975	Hector	— Cox
19882	Gonzalvo	— M	19977	Heenan	M
19883	Goodspeed	Ky I	19978	Hendricks	— P S
19884	Governor	— Daisy	19979	Henrico	Cox
19885	Governor	— D	19980	Henrietta's Duke	— P S
19886	Governor	— M	19981	Henry	M
19887	Governor	P S	19982	Henry	— Daisy
19890	Gov. Hardin	— Ky I	19983	Henry	— P S
19891	Gov. Helm	D	19985	Henry Clay	Ky I
19892	Gov. Stevenson	— R R	19986	Henry Duke	— M
19893	Graceful Duke	— C	19987	Henry Ward	— Daisy
19895	Grand Duke	— P S	19988	Henry Ward Beecher	T
19896	Grand Duke	— R R	19989	Henry Ward Beecher	P S
19898	Grand Duke 9th	— T	19991	Hero	M
19899	Grand Duke of Clay	Daisy	19992	Hero	Ky I
19901	Grand Duke of Green Lawn	— R R	19993	Hero of Macomb	R R
19902	Grand Duke of Oakland 2nd	— M	19994	Hickory Fearless	M
19904	Grand Duke of Thorndale	— Ky I	19996	Highlander	— L R
19905	Grand Master	— M	19999	Highland Duke	Ky I
19906	Grand Royal Duke	P S	20002	Highland Rover	D
19908	Granger	P S	20004	Hogarth	— R R
19909	Granger	— T	20005	Holt Co. Star	— M
19910	Granger	— M	20006	Honest John	P S
19911	Granger	M	20007	Honest John	R R
19912	Granger	— Ky I	20008	Hoosier Lad	T
19913	Granger	— T	20009	Hope of Princess 2nd	— Cox
19914	Granger	Ky I	20010	Horace Greeley	— L R
19916	Granger	— T	20011	Horace Greeley	— M
19917	Granger	— M	20012	Horace Miller	— R R
19918	Granger Boy	— R R	20013	Hotspur 4th	— M
19919	Granger Frank	Ky I	20014	Hotspur 5th	— R R
19921	Grant	L R	20016	Hudson	Cox
19922	Grant	Ky I	20017	Huguenot	— M
19923	Grant	— D	20018	Humbolt	P S
19924	Grant	L R	20019	Huron	Cox
19925	Grass Hopper Duke	— Ky I	20020	Huron's Duke 2nd	— Long-Horn
19928	Greeley	M	20021	Ides of November 2nd	— Ky I
19929	Greeley	T	20022	Illinois	— C
19930	Greeley 2nd	P S	20025	Imperial Duke	M
19931	Grey Coat	M	20026	Imperial Gloster	— Cox
19932	Grinell Favorite	— L R	20028	Independence	— C
19933	Gunsaule Duke	— C	20029	Independence Duke	— R R
19937	Gwynne Duke	M	20030	Indian Chief	Cox
19939	Gwynne of Orchard Farm	— Cox	20031	Indian Chief	— C
19940	Hack Driver	P S	20032	Indianola	— R R
19943	Hamlet	D	20034	Invincible Duke 3rd	— R R
19944	Hannibal	Ky I	20035	Imperial Duke 5th	Ky I
19945	Hannibal	— R R	20036	Imperial Duke 6th	Ky I
19946	Hannibal 18th	— D	20037	Iowa	Ky I
19947	Hannibal 23rd	M	20038	Iowa Boy	— P S
19948	Hannibal 24th	— R R	20039	Iowa Lad	— P S
19949	Hannibal 25th	— T	20043	Ivan	— Cox
19950	Hannibal 26th	— D	20045	Jack	M
19951	Hannibal 27th	— M	20046	Jack Rogers	Daisy
19952	Hannibal 28th	— C	20047	Jackson	— T
19953	Hannibal 29th	— D	20051	Janus 2nd	— C
19954	Hannibal 30th	C	20052	Janus 3rd	— M
19955	Hannibal 31st	L R	20053	Janus 4th	— C

SHORT-HORN CATTLE PEDIGREES.

20054	Janus 5th	— C
20055	Janus 6th	— C
20056	Janus 7th	— C
20057	Jeff Davis	— P S
20058	Jenkin's Duke	— D
20059	Jerry	— Ky I
20060	Jessamine's Duke	— R R
20061	Jesse Meadows	— M
20062	Jim Byram	M
20065	Jim Fisk	— M
20066	Jimmie	— P S
20069	John, Jr	— D
20070	John White	P S
20071	Josh Javish	P S
20073	Joe	— T
20074	Joe	— M
20076	Joe Croxton 3rd	Daisy
20077	Joe Goodness	— M
20078	Joe Johnson 4th	Cox
20079	Joe Johnson 5th	Cox
20081	Joe Porter	Ky I
20086	John	M
20087	John	M
20088	John, Jr	— M
20089	John Alden	— L R
20091	John Barnum	Ky I
20092	John Bull	M
20093	John C Bagby	Ky I
20094	John Haley	— C
20095	John Hareland	— M
20096	John M. Stevens	M
20100	John Oakhurst	— Long-Horn
20102	John T.	— P S
20103	John T. Morgan	Ky I
20105	Josie's Son	— Daisy
20107	Jubilee Duke	— Ky I
20109	Jubilo	— Cox
20112	Judge Craig	— L R
20113	Judge Douglas	— L R
20115	Julius	— M
20117	Junius	— M
20120	Jupiter	— M
20121	Juryman	— M
20122	Kaiser	Cox
20124	Kate's Duke	— R R
20125	Kearsarge	— L R
20126	Kemper	— P S
20127	Kenosha Duke	— Cox
20129	Ketton	— L R
20131	Kewanee Duke	M
20132	Killmer	— Ky I
20133	King Albin	— D
20134	King Arthur	— Cox
20135	King Kalakaua	M
20136	King Knox	— T
20142	King of Oakwood	Ky I
20144	King of the Ocean	— M
20145	King of the Prairie	— Ky I
20146	King of the West	M
20147	King of Walnut Hill	P S
20149	King Richard	M
20150	King's Loudon Duke 2nd	— R R
20153	King Wood	Ky I
20154	Kinloch	— R R
20157	Kit Carson	D
20158	Kit Clay	— M
20159	1st Knight of Hazlewood	— Daisy
20160	2nd Knight of Hazlewood	— Daisy
20161	Knight of Rose Hill	— L R
20164	Lacteal Duke	L R
20165	Lacteal O !	L R
20166	Lad Leo	M
20167	Lad Napo	M
20168	Lad Renick	M
20169	Lafayette	— Ky I
20171	Lancaster	— P S
20172	Lancet	— P S
20173	Langton 2nd	— M
20174	Lantern	— Cox
20175	Lapeer	— P S
20177	Laureled Duke	P S
20179	Leamington	— R R
20180	Leando	M
20181	Leatherstocking	— Long-Horn
20182	Lee's Gloster	— Cox
20183	Leighton	— Ky I
20184	Lentullus	R R
20185	Leo	P S
20187	Leopard	— M
20189	Leopold	P S
20191	Leonardo De Vinci	— P S
20192	Leonidas	M
20193	Leopard 2nd	— D
20194	Levering	— Ky I
20195	Lewis	— L R
20196	Lewis Hill 2nd	— R R
20197	Lewis Hill 3rd	— R R
20198	Lexington	D
20199	Licking Duke	— D
20200	Light Roan Duke 5th	M
20201	Lillie's Greek	— M
20202	Lincoln Granger	— P S
20203	2nd Linden	— M
20204	Linesman	— Cox
20205	Little Jack	— M
20207	Lizzie's Oxford	— M
20208	Lockhart	P S
20209	Locomotive	— P S
20210	Locomotive	Ky I
20211	Locomotive	— C
20212	Lofty	— R R
20213	Logan	D
20216	Logan Duke	T
20217	Logan Yeazell	— D
20218	Lone Gem's Airdrie	D
20219	Lone Star	— D
20220	Longfellow	Daisy
20221	Longfellow	L R
20222	Longfellow	— M
20223	Long John	— Ky I
20225	Lord Alabaster	D
20227	Lord Baltimore	— P S
20228	Lord Baltimore 4th	M
20229	Lord Baltimore 5th	Ky I
20231	Lord Beck	— L R
20233	Lord Devon	P S
20234	Lord Erne	— P S
20237	Lord Granville	— M
20238	Lord Gwynne	— Cox
20243	Lord Monmouth	— M
20244	Lord Mortimer	Ky I
20245	Lord of Carroll	— Cox
20247	Lord of Fashion	— Cox
20248	Lord of Lorne	— Cox
20252	Lord of the Valley	M
20253	Lord Ormsby	T
20255	Lord Rodney	— D
20256	Lord Scattergood	M
20258	Lord Thorn	M
20262	Lonan Chief	— R R

20263	Louan Duke — M	20365	Master Claron — P S
20264	Louan Grant — R R	20366	Master Dick — P S
20265	Louanjo — R R	20367	Master Doc Golder — D
20266	Louan's Booth — M	20369	Master Grange — Ky I
20267	Louan's Clifton — M	20370	Master Lang — D
20268	Louan's Duke of Geneva 3rd — M	20372	Master of Arts — Cox
20269	Louan's Mazurka — D	20374	Master Sharon — Cox
20270	Louan's Oxford — M	20375	Master Star P S
20271	Loudon Duke — R R	20379	Matt Ransom P S
20272	Loudon Duke — P S	20380	Maumee Cox
20273	Loudon Duke Jr — R R	20383	May Duke — M
20275	Loudon Duke 15th C	20385	May Duke — D
20277	1st Loudon Duke of Shannon — R R	20388	May Hugh M
20278	2nd Loudon D. of Shannon — Cox	20390	Mazurka Duke C
20279	3rd Loudon D. of Shannon — R R	20394	Mazurka's Rose of Sharon — P S
20280	4th Loudon D. of Shannon — R R	20398	McClellan — L R
20281	5th Loudon D. of Shannon — L R	20399	McCune of Perry — M
20282	6th Loudon D. of Shannon — R R	20400	McDonough Boy — T
20283	7th L. D. of Shannon — Long-Horn	20401	McDonough Lad — P S
20284	8th L. D. of Shannon — Long-Horn	20402	McDonough Star — T
20285	9th Loudon D. of Shannon — R R	20403	McGinnis — C
20286	10th Loudon D. of Shannon — R R	20404	Miami Duke — P S
20287	11th Loudon D. of Shannon — R R	20405	Miami Duke Ky I
20288	12th L. D. of Shannon — Long-Horn	20406	Midas — M
20289	13th Loudon D. of Shannon — R R	20407	Midshipman — Cox
20293	Loyal Duke of Shannon M	20409	Mike D
20294	Lucien — R R	20410	Miles Standish — M
20297	Lucy's Duke P S	20411	Milford M
20299	Lysander — L R	20412	Milliner 2nd Ky I
20300	Macbeth — M	20415	Millington Prince M
20301	Mack Clyde M L	20416	Millington Prince 2nd M
20303	Madison's Duke 2nd — P S	20417	Milo Ky I
20305	Maggie's Airdrie P S	20418	Minister of Sunbeam — M
20306	Magic — R R	20419	Minister's Treasure — M
20308	Magician — Cox	20423	Mirza — D
20310	Major Woods	20424	Mischief's Boy — Cox
20311	Major — P S	20425	Missouri Granger Daisy
20312	Major — Cox	20426	Meadow's Duke 2nd — R R
20313	Major Ky I	20427	4th Meadow Duke — M
20314	Major — D	20429	Megibben M
20315	Major P S	20430	Melvin 2nd P S
20316	Major — Daisy	20432	Merriman — L R
20317	Major Brent — Ky I	20433	Meteor — P S
20318	Major Coy — T	20434	Minna Muscatoon — M
20319	Major Dibble L R	20435	Modoc Cox
20321	Major Hill — R R	20436	Modoc P S
20323	Major Jones M	20437	Modoc — T
20325	Major Townley 2nd — D	20438	Modoc — M
20326	Major Wiley — R R	20440	Monarch — M
20331	Maquoketa Monarch — Cox	20442	Monarch Ky I
20332	Marathon — C	20443	Monarch Ky I
20333	Marengo — D	20446	Monitor 3rd M
20334	Marigold's King — M	20447	Monona Lad — P S
20336	Mariner 5th — C	20448	Monroe T
20337	Mario — R R	20449	Montana — Cox
20338	Marion Duke of Airdrie 2nd M	20450	Montana — P S
20340	Mark — Ky I	20451	Montgomery Duke Daisy
20342	Marquis — L R	20452	Moreton — Daisy
20345	Marquis of Goodness — R R	20453	Moreton — R R
20347	Marquis of Lorne — D	20454	Morgan Chief — D
20348	Marquis of Oakwood — D	20455	Morley — M
20350	Marquis of Stonebank — R R	20456	Morning Star — Ky I
20351	Marshall — M	20458	Morton's Hillhurst — L R
20352	Marshall Ky I	20462	Mount Jack — Ky I
20353	Marshal Serranno — C	20463	Mountain Chief — M
20355	Martin Duke 2nd M	20465	Mowder's Bull L R
20357	Master Airdrie 3rd — R R	20466	Muscatine Ky I
20358	Master Balco M	20468	Musket — T
20363	Master Butterfly 2nd — L R	20470	My Favorite P S
20364	Master Charley — M	20471	Nabob — M

20474	Napoleon — L R	20586	Phil. Lee — Long-Horn
20476	Nellino — Wrong	20588	Pilgrim — Ky I
20478	Nelson Duke M	20589	Pilgrim — M
20479	Neptune L R	29590	Pilot D
20480	Nero P S	20591	Pilot M
20481	Nero — L R	20592	Pioneer — M
20482	Nero P S	20594	Pioneer M
20484	New Lenox Duke Ky I	20595	Pioneer Duke of Mesquite — M
20485	Newton — M	20596	Pirate — R R
30486	Newton's Grant T	20597	Planet T
20488	New Years Day M	20598	Plato Daisy
20489	Nimrod 2nd — R R	20600	Plato Ky I
20491	Noble M	20601	Play Boy Ky I
20492	Noble — C	20602	Plowman P S
20493	Noble Airdrie — C	20603	Plumwood M
20494	Noble Duke M	20604	Plumwood Lad A C
20497	Norfolk — D	20605	Plumwood Lad B C
20501	North Star — M	20606	Plumwood Lad C R R
20502	North Star — P S	20611	Pompey Ky I
20503	No Surrender — P S	20612	Pompey Boy L R
20505	Oakland 9th P S	20613	Positive — M
20506	Oakland 10th L R	20615	Praetor — L R
20507	Oakland Boy — L R	20616	Prairie Boy — P S
20508	Oakwood Gwynne 3rd — D	20617	Prairie Boy — P S
20510	Ohio — M	20618	Prairie Duke — R R
20511	Ohio Chief — P S	20619	Prairie Farmer Ky I
20512	Ohio Duke — L R	20620	Prairie King — D
20514	Old Bullion R R	20621	Prairie Lad P S
20515	Oleander — M	20622	Pre-Emption Duke — P S
20520	Onward — L R	20623	Premier — L R
20521	Orean's Booth M	20624	President D
20522	Orion — P S	20625	President — P S
20523	Orlando P S	20626	President 2nd M
20524	Orphan Boy — T	20627	President Grant Daisy
20525	Orphan Boy Ky I	20628	Preston — C
20528	Oscar — Cox	20629	Pride of Somerset — L R
20530	Otho — Daisy	20630	Pride of the West D
20532	Otley Duke M	20633	Prince — Long-Horn
20537	Oxford Chief 3rd — M	20634	Prince — P S
20539	Oxford Duke L R	20635	Prince — L R
20540	Oxford Duke 2nd — Cox	20636	Prince — D
20541	Oxford Gem — L R	20637	Prince — L R
20544	Oxford Gwynne — M	20638	Prince Abram 3rd D
20545	Oxford Heir — M	20639	Prince Abram 4th T
20546	Oxford Hero 3rd — M	20640	Prince Airdrie — M
20547	Oxford J — L R	20642	Prince Albert Ky I
20548	Oxford Lad — M	20643	Prince Albert M
20549	Oxford Lad T	20644	Prince Albert M
20551	Oxford Lee — T	20648	Prince Alfred M
20553	Oxford of Brush Creek M	20649	Prince Arthur — T
20554	Oxford of Walnut Grove — R R	20650	Prince Arthur P S
20555	Oxford of Walnut Grove 1st — M	20651	Prince Arthur 2nd — M
20557	Oxford Patroon — Cox	20653	Prince Bismarck — M
20560	Oxford Wiley 2nd L R	20654	Prince Bismarck M
20561	Oxford's Duke — M	20655	Prince Cambria — M
20562	Panic — M	20656	Prince Charles — C
20563	Pat Dyer — M	20658	Prince Clyde 2nd M
20564	Pat Flynn — R R	20660	Prince Cundiff — L R
20565	Pat Maloney R R	20661	Prince Edward Ky I
20566	Patrick — M	20663	Prince Hal M
20570	Pawnee — R R	20665	Prince John P S
20571	Paxton's Duke R R	20666	Prince John — C
20574	Peacock 2nd — Cox	20667	Prince Leon — P S
20576	Pearl Duke 4th — R R	20669	Prince Louan — R R
20578	Pearson L R	20671	Prince Napier — M
20579	Peerless — M	20673	Prince Napoleon — Ky I
20580	Perfection P S	20674	Prince of Airdrie M
20581	Peregrine — R R	20677	Prince of Empire — D
20583	Perry — Ky I	20679	Prince of Henry P S
20584	Pete Helm — M	20682	Prince of Mercer — M

No.	Name	Herd
20683	Prince of Mercer 2nd	— M
20684	Prince of Momence	— P S
20685	Prince of Oakland	Ky 1
20686	Prince of Oakshade	Ky I
20687	Prince of Orange	Cox
20693	Prince of Plymouth	M
20694	Prince of Sharon	— L R
20695	Prince of Tecumseh	R R
20697	Prince of the Prairie	— M
20698	Prince of the Realm	Cox
20700	Prince of Wales	— Cox
20701	Prince of Wales	— M
20703	Prince of Winnebago	L R
20704	Prince of Oxford 4th	— D
20706	Prince Royal	T
20708	Prince Sam	— R R
20709	Princeton	— P S
20713	Prince Vanmeter	— R R
20715	Prince William	M
20718	Promise	L R
20719	Protumna	P S
20724	Punch	— M
20722	Putnam Lad	D
20723	Quaker Boy	— Ky 1
20727	Ralston	M
20730	Rattler	— M
20734	Red Billy	P S
20735	Red Bird	Ky 1
20737	Red Buck	— P S
20739	Red Challenger	— R R
20740	Red Clarence	Ky 1
20741	Red Cloud	— P S
20742	Red Cloud	— R R
20744	Red Cloud	— D
20745	Red Cloud	— M
20746	Red Cloud	— P S
20747	Red Cloud	— Ky 1
20748	Red Cloud 2nd	— M
20749	Red Cloud 3rd	— M
20751	Red Count	— M
20752	Red Dick	— R R
20755	Red Duke	— P S
20757	Red Duke	— P S
20758	Red Duke	M
20759	Red Duke	— R R
20761	Red Duke	— R R
20762	Red Duke	— D
20763	Red Duke	Ky 1
20764	Red Duke	— R R
20765	Red Duke 2nd	— R R
20766	Red Gallant	— M
20767	Red Gauntlet	— M
20768	Red Goldfinder	— R R
20769	Red Jacket	P S
20770	Red Jacket	— D
20771	Red Jacket	Ky 1
20772	Red Jacket	— D
20773	Red Jacket	M
20774	Red Jacket	— Long-Horn
20776	Red Jacket 16th	Ky 1
20777	Red John	— P S
20778	Red John	P S
20779	Red Knight	— M
20780	Red Lion	M
20781	Red Monarch	— P S
20784	Red Prince	— M
20785	Red Prince	T
20786	Red Prince	— M
20788	Red Ranger	— T
20789	Red Ratler	— M
20790	Red Roan Duke 7th	M
20791	Red Rope	— D
20793	Red Rouster	— M
20794	Red Rover	Woods
20795	Red Rover	— M
20796	Red Rover	— L R
20797	Red Rover	— P S
20800	Red Rover 2nd	M
20802	Red Thorndale	M
20803	Red Tiger	— P S
20804	Red Townley	D
20805	Red Turk	— L R
20806	Reflector	— M
20807	Reformer	— D
20808	Regulator 2nd	Cox
20809	Regulator 3rd	Cox
20810	Remington	— Cox
20813	Remus	M
20814	Renick	— P S
20817	2nd Reserve Duke	— P S
20818	Ribbon's Duke	P S
20819	Richland Lad	— D
20820	Rigdon	M
20821	Rinaldo	— Cox
20822	Ringmaster	— M
20824	Roan	— Cox
20827	Roan Bull	M
20829	Roan Duke	C
20830	Roan Duke	M
20831	Roan Duke	— P S
20832	Roanoke	M
20833	Roanoke	— L R
20834	Roan Oxford	— Cox
20835	Roan Prince	M
20837	Robin Hood	— M
20838	Robin Hood	— Cox
20839	Rob Roy	— M
20840	Rob Roy	L R
20842	Rob Roy	T
20843	Rob Roy	Ky 1
20844	Rob Roy	M
20845	Rob Roy	— Daisy
20846	Rockford	— L R
20847	Rock River Gloster	— Cox
20848	Rock River Lad	— D
20849	Rock River Lad 2nd	L R
20850	Rock River Lad 3rd	— D
20851	Roderick	— M
20854	Rodman	— M
20855	Rollin P. Saxe	M
20858	Romeo	— M
20859	Romeo	— M
20860	Romeo 2nd	— P S
20861	Romeo 2nd	Cox
20862	Romeo 3rd	Cox
20863	Romulus	— Daisy
20864	Romulus	M
20865	Romulus 3rd	Ky 1
20866	Rondale	— L R
20867	Rosa's Airdrie	M
20868	Rosa Duke	T
20869	Rosa Lee's Airdrie	— T
20870	Rose Duke	— R R
20871	Rose Duke	T
20872	Rose's Duke	— C
20873	Rose's Duke	D
20874	Rose's Duke	M
20875	Rosette's Duke	— R R
20877	Rosendale 11th	— M
20879	Rosser	— P S

20880	Rosy Duke	— Long-Horn		20974	Silver Mine	— L R
20882	Rothschild	— C		20976	Simple Tom	M
20883	Rover	— P S		20977	Sirius 2nd	— R R
20884	Rover	P S		20978	Sir Albert	— Daisy
20886	Rover Duke	— R R		20980	Sir Charles	M
20887	Rowena's Airdrie	M		20981	Sir Charles	— Cox
20888	Royalist 2nd	— Cox		20982	Sir Child	— P S
20889	Royal Airdrie	— T		20983	Sir Garnet Wolseley	P S
20890	Royal Arthur	— Cox		20984	Sir George	— Cox
20894	Royal Booth 3rd	— P S		20985	Sir George	M
20895	Royal Buckingham	— R R		20986	Sir Gregory	Ky I
20897	Royal Dale	— M		20987	Sir Henry	P S
20898	Royal Duke	— P S		20989	Sir John	— P S
20899	Royal Duke	— Daisy		20991	Sir John Booth	— D
20902	Royal Frantic	— Cox		20992	Sir Knox 4th	M
20904	Royal George 2nd	— L R		20994	Sir Peter	— M
20905	Royal George 3rd	— D		20995	Sir Robert	M
20906	Royal Gwynne	Cox		20997	Sir Walter	D
20909	Royal Louan	— M		21000	Snowball	— C
20910	Royal Master	M		21001	Snowball	— Long-Horn
20911	Royal Oak	P S		21003	Snow Prince	— T
20913	Royal Prince of Randolph	— M		21004	Snowstorm	— Ky I
20914	Royal Princeton	— M		21005	Sockburn Lad	M
20915	Royal Richmond	— L R		21006	Solicitor	— L R
20916	Royal Rose	— Ky I		21007	2nd Son of Josie	— Daisy
20917	Royal Rose	— Cox		21008	Son of Stonewall	M
20918	Royal Rose of Princeton	— M		21009	Son of Wiley 3rd	— Ky I
20920	Ruby Dick Taylor	— P S		21115	Sovereign	— L R
20921	Rudolph	Ky I		21117	Spangler	M
20922	Rufus	— Cox		21118	Specie Payment	M
20923	Rugby	— P S		21119	Spotted Chief 2nd	M
20924	Rupee	M		21120	Spotted Duke 2nd	— M
20925	Russell	L R		21121	Spotted Oxford 2nd	— L R
20926	Rustic's Duke	M		21123	Spring Valley Monarch	— L R
20927	Rutledge	— M		21125	Squire Perkins	M
20928	St. Bernard	— T		21126	Standard	— M
20930	St. Lawrence 2nd	M		21129	Star Chief	— L R
20931	St. Lawrence 3rd	— R R		21131	Star Duke of Hendon	— M
20932	St. Ouge	— C		21133	Star Gazer	Ky I
20933	St. Patrick	M		21134	Starlight	— P S
20934	Sailor	— D		21135	Starlight	— D
20935	Sallie's Jubilee	M		21138	Starlight 5th	D
20937	Sampson	— L R		21139	Starlight 6th	— R R
20938	Sampson	P S		21142	Starlight 9th	— R R
20939	Sam White	M		21143	Starlight 10th	— M
20940	Savanavola	M		21144	Starlight Airdrie	M
20941	Schalk's Duke	M		21145	Star of Bruce	L R
20942	Scotsman, Jr	— M		21146	Star of Fairview	D
20944	Scotsman 3rd	— Cox		21148	Star of the West	M
20949	Sensation	— Cox		21149	Star Taylor	— D
20950	Sentinel	— M		21151	Stoner	T
20951	Seymour Duke	D		21154	Stonewall	M
20952	Shaker Boy	— D		21156	Stonewall Jackson	— P S
20955	Shakespeare	— Long-Horn		21157	Strathallan Chief	— D
20956	Shamrock	— R R		21158	Strawberry Duke	— C
20957	Shamrock 2nd	— C		21159	Strawberry's Airdre	— T
20958	Sharon	— Long-Horn		21160	Stunner	Ky I
20960	Shelly Duke	— M		21161	Sturdy	M
20961	Shell Bark	T		21162	Stuyvesant	— D
20962	Sheridan	T		21164	Sucker Boy	— Long-Horn
20964	Sherman	Ky I		21165	Sultan	— L R
20965	Sherman	Ky I		21166	Sultan	— M
20966	Sherman 2nd	M		21168	Sunrise 2nd	L R
20967	Short Eared Duke	P S		21169	Superlative	M
20968	Shylock	— M		21170	Sweepstakes	M
20969	Siegel	— M		21171	Swift	P S
20970	Silas	D		21172	Symmetry	— M
20971	Silas Gale 2nd	— M		21174	Talbutt's Bull	M
20972	Silver Cloud	— C		21176	Tamerlane	M
20973	Silver Heels	— Cox		21177	Tasso	M

21179	T. D. Campbell...................D	21285	Washington Duke.............. — D
21180	Tea Rose of Walnut Hill....... — C	21286	Washington Duke 2nd....... — R R
21182	Temescal......................L R	21290	Waukegan..................... — M
21183	Teneriffe..................... — P S	21292	Wellington...................Ky I
21186	The Colonel.....................T	21293	Wellington................... — L R
21187	The Grand Duke of Thorndale — R R	21294	Wellington Duke.............. — D
21188	The Lad..........................M	21295	Wenonga..................... — Cox
21189	The Monk..................... — C	21297	Wentworth Airdrie........... — L R
21190	The Prior..................... — R R	21298	Western Duke.................Ky I
21191	Theodore 1st.....................D	21299	Western Duke.................Ky I
21192	Thornberry.......................D	21300	Western Duke 1st of Oakland. — P S
21193	Thornburg.................... — Ky I	21301	Western Lad................. — P S
21199	Thorndale's Wiley 2nd........ — M	21302	Western Lad 2nd.............Ky I
21202	Tiger......................... — Ky I	21305	Whitebait.................... — P S
21203	Tipler........................ — M	21306	White Bull................... — Daisy
21204	Tip Tyler..................... — L R	21307	White Boy................... — D
21205	Toby..........................Ky I	21308	White Chief.................. — T
21207	Tom...........................Ky I	21310	White Cloud................. — P S
21208	Tom, Jr..........................M	21311	White Cloud................. — M
21209	Tom Austin......................M	21312	White Cloud..................M
21210	Tomboy....................... — L R	21314	White Duke.................. — Ky I
21211	Tom Coleman................ — M	21315	White Princeton.............. — M
21212	Tom Collins.................. — Ky I	21317	White Stockings.............Woods
21213	Tom Corwin.................. — Ky I	21318	White Stockings............. — Cox
21214	Tom Moore................... — R R	21319	Whiting...................... — T
21215	Tommy....................... — P S	21320	Whitman's Duke of Geneva. — Cox
21217	Tom Sayers................... — Cox	21321	Whitsitt's Duke.............. — P S
21218	Tom Scott.................... — P S	21322	Whittington.................. — R R
21220	Toto.............................M	21324	Wild Eyes.....................M
21221	Towanda..................... — R R	21326	Wiley Cherry................. — R R
21223	Trafalgar........................M	21332	Wimpell......................Ky I
21224	Tranquil...................... — R R	21333	Winnebago Duke............. — R R
21225	Transit....................... — T	21334	Winsor....................... — P S
21227	Troy..........................Ky I	21335	Wolverine.................... — L R
21229	Turk.......................... — M	21337	Woodland B.................. — L R
21230	Twilight......................Ky I	21339	Woodland Duke...............M
21233	Twin Brother....................C	21340	Woodland Duke.............. — P S
21234	Twin Duke......................P S	21342	Woodman.....................P S
21237	Twin of Oakwood.............Ky I	21346	Worthington................. — M
21238	Twin Roan................... — M	21347	Wright's Bull................ — Ky I
21239	Tyro.......................... — Daisy	21350	Yankee Jim.................. — M
21240	Tyrol............................D	21351	Yankee Boy.................. — Cox
21241	Uncle Abe.................... — R R	21352	Yankee Pedler............... — Ky I
21242	Union.........................Ky I	21353	Young Alfred..................T
21243	Union Duke.................. — R R	21357	Young Berkshire Boy..........Cox
21245	Valliant...................... — M	21358	Young Burnside.............. — P S
21247	Vandyke...................... — M	21359	Young Burnside 2nd..........Ky I
21249	Vatican....................... — M	21361	Young Chief................. — Cox
21250	Vera Cruz.......... — Long-Horn	21364	Young Copson................Cox
21251	Vermont Boy................. — M	21365	Young Corporal..............Ky I
21252	Verner....................... — Cox	21366	Young Corwin...............Ky I
21253	Vernon Duke................. — R R	21367	Young Cuthbert.............Ky I
21254	Vespasian 2nd...................D	21368	Young De Gray..............P S
21255	Vespasian 3rd...................D	21372	Young Gledhow.............. — C
21257	Veto.......................... — D	21376	Young Minister...............D
21259	Viceroy 2nd.................. — Cox	21377	Young Perfection.............P S
21260	Viceroy 3rd.................. — P S	21378	Young Prince.................M
21261	Victor........................ — R R	21379	Young Prince................Cox
21262	Victor........................ — T	21380	Young Richard............... — L R
21264	Victor........................ — D	21381	Young Richland.............. — Daisy
21265	Victor 2nd.................... — Ky I	21382	Young Royal.................P S
21269	Victoria's Oxford.................C	21384	Young Sheffielder............ — D
21271	Vulcan....................... — M	21385	Young Sheffielder 2nd....... — D
21273	Wade Hampton............. — P S	21386	Young Sheffielder 3rd....... — D
21274	Wallace..........................M	21387	Young Sir Humphry...........M
21275	Walter Scott................. — P S	21389	Young Townly............... — M
21276	Weltham Lad................ — M	21390	Young Warrior.............. — M
21277	Wapsie Gwynne............. — Cox	21391	Zack......................... — M
21278	Warrior...................... — L R	21392	Zachary..................... — M
21279	Warrior...................... — P S	21393	Zack Taylor..................Ky I

SHORT-HORN CATTLE PEDIGREES.

No.	Name	Code
21395	Zolicoffer	T
21397	Admiral	— R R
21401	Albion	— L R
21402	Alexander 2nd	L R
21403	Anchor	— Cox
21406	Atha's Duke	Ky I
21407	Barnum	— T
21411	Ben Butler	— L R
21417	Billey	— D
21418	Billy Prendergast	— L R
21419	Bismarck	— Cox
21421	Bobtail	— M
21422	Bois D' Ark	— Long-Horn
21425	Bourbon	— D
21426	Bride's Boy	— R R
21427	Brigadier	— M
21428	Bruno	— M
21433	Buzzard	— Cox
21435	Cambrian	— Cox
21438	Capt. Allan	— Cox
21439	Capt. Carlos	L R
21440	Capt. Mac	L R
21441	Carson	L R
21442	Cashier	— Cox
21444	Charlie	R R
21445	Chautauqua 2nd	— L R
21449	Chilesburg	— M
21453	Comet	— Cox
21457	Cornet	— Long-Horn
21450	Cossack	P S
21462	Count De Grey	— Long-Horn
21463	Crab	— M
21467	Crusoe	L R
21469	Dairyman 1st	Ky I
21470	Dairyman 2nd	Ky I
21472	Dan	— Cox
21474	Defiance	— L R
21475	Denver	Ky I
21477	Diamond	R R
21478	Diana's Duke of Oxford	L R
21480	Don	L R
21482	Douglas	— M
21484	Duke of Humphry	— R R
21486	Duke of Bedford	— M
21488	Duke of Boardman	P S
21490	Duke of Carlinville	Ky I
21491	Duke of Chartiers	— T
21492	Duke of Chautauqua	L R
21493	Duke of Chautauqua 2nd	M
21495	Duke of Clarence	— R R
21497	Duke of Como	R R
21498	Duke of Edinburg	— Cox
21499	Duke of Franklin	— T
21500	17th Duke of Greenlawn	— D
21501	18th D. of Greenlawn	— Long-Horn
21502	19th Duke of Greenlawn	— M
21503	20th Duke of Greenlawn	— M
21504	21st Duke of Greenlawn	— M
21505	22nd Duke of Greenlawn	— M
21506	Duke of Hamburg	P S
21511	2nd Duke of LaSalle	— Cox
21512	4th Duke of Lee	— M
21513	5th Duke of Lee	— M
21515	Duke of Medina	— D
21516	Duke of Melrose	P S
21517	Duke of Oakland	— R R
21518	1st Duke of Odell	T
21519	2nd Duke of Odell	T
21521	Duke of Orange	M
21522	Duke of Osage	— D
21524	Duke of Poland	— L R
21526	Duke of Roscoe	L R
21532	1st Duke of Windingdale	— R R
21532	2nd Duke of Windingdale	— C
21537	Duncan	— T
21538	Durham Hill Star	D
21540	Earl Fox	L R
21541	Earl of Athol	— D
21542	Earl of Highland	— R R
21543	Earl of Platt	— D
21546	Fairy Duke	— R R
21548	Fashion	L R
21549	Fashion	— Ky I
21552	Financier 2nd	M
21556	Frank	— D
21558	Frank Leslie	Ky I
21559	Frederick	— L R
21560	Fred Grant	— D
21561	Freedom	L R
21563	1st Gaban of Eastville	— P S
21565	Gen. Brecenridge	— P S
21566	Gen. Dix	— Cox
21567	Gen. Grant	— Cox
21570	Gen. McClellan	— M
21571	Gen. Sheridan	— T
21572	Gen. Webster 2nd	— L R
21573	Gen. Webster 4th	— L R
21574	Gen. Wise	Woods
21575	George	— D
21576	George Washington	P S
21578	Golddust	Ky I
21579	Golden	Woods
21580	Golden Louan Duke	— R R
21585	1st Grand Duke of Ellsworth	P S
21586	Grand Son of Squire	— Cox
21587	Granger	— Ky I
21588	Granger	— R R
21589	Granger	— M
21592	Guy	L R
21593	Hannibal 32nd	— M
21596	Helmet	— P S
21597	Hero 2nd	— P S
21599	Highland Lad	— R R
21603	Inca	P S
21604	Investor	— P S
21605	Iowa	Cox
21606	Iron Duke 2nd	L R
21607	Iron Duke 3rd	L R
21608	Joe Stoner	— M
21609	Johnnie Husband	— Cox
21611	John Hull	P S
21612	John Milton	R R
21613	John Oxford	— P S
21614	Johnny R	— D
21616	Julius Cæsar	— M
21618	J. W. Barlow	— R R
21619	Kentuckian	M
21620	Kentucky	D
21628	Leap Year	— R R
21630	Lehigh Chief	— Cox
21631	Letton Roseleaf	— M
21633	Lightning	— Cox
21634	Logan	L R
21635	Logan	— M
21636	Logan	C
21637	Logan Duke	— P S
21640	Lord Byron	— T
21641	Lord Byron	M
21648	Lord Lander	P S
21654	Lord Sweepstakes	P S

No.	Name	Code	No.	Name	Code
21657	Louan Duke 3rd	— M	21792	Royal Duke	D
21658	Louanjo	— R R	21798	St. Nicholas	— D
21659	Louan Prince of Randolph	— M	21801	Senator	P S
21661	Lucretius 2nd	— Ky I	21802	Senator	— M
21664	Mad Anthony	— Cox	21804	Shakespeare	— M
21666	Mahoning	P S	21805	Sheridan	— Cox
21670	Major Wayne	— Cox	21806	Short Tail	— Cox
21674	Mark Twain 2nd	— T	21810	Sir Daniel	Ky I
21675	Mark Twain 3rd	— Cox	21812	Sir George	— M
21680	Master Rope	— Cox	21813	Sir Ralph	L R
21681	May Duke	— M	21814	Sir Robert Alexander 2nd	— R R
21683	McDonald	— M	21816	Sir Rupert	L R
21684	Meadow's Duke	— R R	21817	Sir Thomas	— Cox
21685	Messenger's Boy	— L R	21818	Sir Walter	— M
21687	Midland	— L R	21821	Spotted Bull	— L R
21688	Mike Hutton	— L R	21824	Stanley	— Cox
21690	M. M. Pomeroy	L R	21825	Starlight	— Cox
21691	Modoc Chief	— Cox	21826	Star of Hope 2nd	— Cox
21692	Monument	— D	21828	Storm Duke	— T
21693	Morgan Jubilee	T	21829	Sultan	— L R
21694	Morn Duke	— D	21830	Tempest	P S
21696	Morning Star 4th	L R	21834	Tige	— Cox
21700	Napoleon Bonaparte	D	21835	Tremendous Bob	— P S
21701	Ned Collins	— Cox	21836	Tricks	— M
21703	Neptune	— M	21838	Twin Lad	P S
21704	Nichol	— Cox	21839	Tymoch	R R
21705	Nicholas	— T	21843	Victor	— T
21706	North Star	D	21846	Warfield Airdrie	— Daisy
21709	November Duke	— M	21847	Washington	— D
21710	Oakland Chief	Ky I	21849	Winongan	Ky I
21713	Orange	Cox	21851	Young Clinton Duke	— T
21714	Orphan Lad	— M	21855	Young Farmington	L R
21715	Orpheus	— Cox	21858	Young Viscount	M
21716	Oxford	Cox	21861	Abe Bute	P S
21719	2nd Oxford of Vermillion	— R R	21862	Abe Ireland	— T
21721	Phil Sheridan	D	21863	Adam	T
21723	Plumwood E.	Ky I	21864	Adam	Cox
21724	Plymouth Lad	— R R	21866	Adaline's Duke	— R R
21725	Pontoon	— L R	21867	Adalaid's Duke	— M
21726	Primus	— T	21868	Admiral	— L R
21727	Prince	— L R	21869	Admiral	— Daisy
21728	Prince	— M	21870	Admiral	— P S
21730	Prince	— L R	21871	Admiral 6th	— R R
21732	Prince Albert	R R	21872	Admiral Boscawen	Cox
21736	Prince Edward	— Cox	21873	Admiral Hardy	— P S
21738	Prince George 2nd	— M	21877	Afton Pride	P S
21744	Prince of Clyde 2nd	M	21880	Airdrie Jr	— M
21745	Prince of Sugar Grove	L R	21881	Airdrie 2nd	T
21748	Prince of Wales	— Cox	21882	Airdrie 3rd	— M
21754	Ranger	— R R	21887	Airdrie Chief	— Ky I
21758	Red Boy	— M	21888	Airdrie Duke	— Cox
21760	Red Bud	— M	21890	Airdrie Duke	— R R
21761	Red Cloud	D	21894	Airdrie D. of the Evergreens 3d	P S
21762	Red Duke	— D	21895	Airdrie Duke of Goodness	— R R
21763	Red Duke	— M	21896	3d Airdrie Duke of Sciota	— R R
21766	Red Jacket	— P S	21897	4th Airdrie Duke of Sciota	D
21767	Red Jacket	— L R	21898	Airdrie Duke of Spencer	M
21768	Red Rover	— L R	21901	Airdrie Grant	— Ky I
21769	Red Rover 2nd	— Long-Horn	21902	Airdrie Muscatoon	— R R
21770	Red Rover 2nd	— Cox	21908	Airdrie Sharon	— R R
21771	Red Russell	L R	21909	Airdrie Thorndale	— M
21772	Red Stillwater	— Cox	21912	Alaric	— M
21777	Rip Van Winkle	— T	21913	Albert	T
21780	Roan Duke	— T	21914	Albert	Ky I
21781	Roan George	— Cox	21915	Albion	— Cox
21782	Ronoake	Ky I	21918	Albert Edward	— L R
21783	Robert	Ky I	21919	Albert Edward 7th	L R
21786	Rock	— Ky I	21920	Albert Edward 8th	L R
21788	Rover	P S	21921	Albert Edward 9th	Cox
21789	Row Boy	L R	21922	Albert Edward 10th	L R

SHORT-HORN CATTLE PEDIGREES.

No.	Name	Herd
21923	Albert Edward 11th	L R
21924	Albert Edward 12th	P S
21925	Albert Edward 13th	Woods
21926	Alexander	— M
21927	Alexis	L R
21928	Alexis	— R R
21930	Alfred	P S
21932	Allen	— Ky I
21934	Alpheus	L R
21938	America	Cox
21939	American	— Cox
21940	American John Bull	L R
21941	Amicus	— Long-Horn
21942	Amos Lad 2nd	— M
21943	Andrew Johnson	— P S
21945	Andy Johnson	— D
21949	April Boy	Ky I
21950	April Boy 2nd	— P S
21951	April Snowstorm	— M
21953	Arch Duke	— R R
21957	Arch Duke of Goodness	— R R
21958	Archer	— R R
21959	Archibald	— Ky I
21960	Archy 2nd	Cox
21964	Aristocrat	— Ky I
21965	Arizona	— C
21966	Arlington	Ky I
21968	Artemus	— D
21969	Arthur	— Cox
21972	Atholl	— R R
21973	Atholl Baron	Ky I
21974	Atholl Duke	— R R
21975	Atholl Duke	— R R
21976	Ashland Prince	— M
21977	Astoria Boy	T
21981	Aurora Duke	T
21982	Austin	— L R
21983	Aram 2nd	T
21986	Aztec	R R
21989	Balance	M
21990	Ballankeel	— M
21991	Balloon	— L R
21993	Banker	— Ky I
21994	Banter	— L R
21995	Bardolph	L R
21996	Barkis	Ky I
21999	Barmpton	— R R
22000	Barnum 2nd	— L R
22001	Barnum 2nd	— Ky I
22002	Barnum 3rd	— Ky I
22004	Baron Airdrie	— M
22007	Baron Airdrie 3rd	— R R
22008	Baron Bates	L R
22012	Baron Biern	— P S
22013	Baron Blithe	— R R
22014	Baron Bloom	— L R
22015	Baron Boone	— Cox
22016	Baron Boone 7th	— P S
22017	Baron Booth of Calumet	Ky I
22018	Baron Booth of Greendale	— M
22019	Baron Booth of Nebraska	— C
22021	Baron Duke	— M
22022	Baron Duke 2nd	— M
22023	Baron Duke 3rd	— M
22024	Baron Elva	— C
22026	Baron Fairfax	— D
22029	Baron Hubbock 3rd	— Cox
22030	Baron Gwynne 2nd	Ky I
22031	Baron Gwynne of Springdale	— Cox
22032	Baron Lakeview	— D
22035	3rd Baron Louan	— R R
22036	Baron Louan of Middle Creek	— M
22037	Baron Louan of Springdale	— R R
22038	4th Baron Mazurka	— R R
22041	Baron Oakdale	— R R
22043	Baron of Australia 7th	— Cox
22044	Baron of Australia 8th	— Cox
22045	Baron of Australia 9th	— Cox
22048	Baron of Exira	— Cox
22049	2nd Baron of Grasshill	— Cox
22050	Baron of Grovedale	— Cox
22052	Baron of Lee	— C
22053	3rd Baron of Oakwood	— Cox
22056	2nd Baron of Riverside	— Cox
22057	Baron of Terrace Hill	— L R
22058	Baron of Runnemede	— L R
22060	Baron Oxford	— P S
22064	Baron Peabody	M
22065	Baron Pickrell	— C
22067	Baron Richard	— Ky I
22068	Baron Rose	M
22069	Baron Secundus	— Ky I
22071	Baron Starlight	— L R
22073	Baron Thornapple	— L R
22077	Baron Whitsitt	— P S
22082	Baron Wynnstay	C
22085	Barrington	M
22088	Bashan	— L R
22093	Baxter	P S
22096	Beauregard	— D
22097	Beauty	M
22098	Beauty's Duke	P S
22099	Beauty's Duke	— R R
22100	Beauty's Duke	T
22101	Beauty's Duke 2nd	M
22102	Bee Bread	— M
22104	Beecher	— P S
22105	Beecher Boy	— L R
22106	Bell Duke	— M
22108	Bell Duke	— R R
22109	Bell Duke 3rd	M
22111	Bell Duke H	— R R
22115	Belle's Airdrie	Ky I
22117	Belle's Airdrie	C
22119	Belle's Duke	C
22120	Belles Duke	— M
22121	Bella Duke 2nd	T
22122	Bell Townley	T
22124	Belmont of Delhi	— Cox
22127	Blus	— Cox
22129	Belvoir	— L R
22130	Ben	— M
22132	Ben Allen	— M
22133	Ben Allen 2nd	— M
22134	Ben Butler	— L R
22135	Ben Butler	— Ky I
22136	Ben Butler	— D
22137	Ben Butler	Cox
22138	Benevolence	— R R
22140	Ben Ledi	— P S
22141	Ben Lomond	— P S
22142	Ben Nevis	— P S
22145	Ben Wade	Ky I
22146	Ben Wade	— R R
22148	Beppo 2nd	Ky I
22149	Berlin 2nd	M
22152	Bertram	— Wrong
22153	Bertrand	— P S
22155	Bifrous 2nd	— M
22157	Big Fellow	— M

22159	Billy — Cox	22266	Buey — M
22160	Billy Boy D	22268	Burnside — R R
22161	Bill Percy Ky I	22269	Buster Duke L R
22162	Billy Airdrie M	22270	Butler Cox
22163	Billy Boice — P S	22271	Butler — M
22164	Billy Hise — Long-Horn	22272	Buttercup — Cox
22165	Billy Pavor — Cox	22273	Butterfield — M
22166	Billy Pavor 2nd — Cox	22276	Butterfly's Favorite — M
22168	Bishop Ky I	22278	Cadmus — L R
22169	Bishop Royal M	22279	Cæsar T
22171	Bismarck M	22280	Caledonia — P S
22172	Bismarck Ky I	22282	Callies Red Cloud T
22173	Bismarck — D	22285	Calvin — M
22174	Bismarck M	22286	Camargo T
22175	Bismarck R R	22287	Cambria's Chief — D
22176	Black Hawk — M	22289	Cambridge Duke — L R
22177	Blanchard Boy M	22297	Camilla's Prince — Cox
22178	Blaize — D	23301	Candidate — Cox
22179	Blenheim Star — Cox	22303	Captain P S
22180	Bloom's Baron — Ky I	22304	Captain L R
22183	Blondin M	22305	Captain — Cox
22185	Blucher — L R	22306	Captain — M
22188	Bob — Ky I	22308	Captain 2nd R R
22189	Bob Johnson — Ky I	22309	Capt. Allen — Cox
22190	Bob Landis — C	22310	Capt. Brown — R R
22191	Bob Lee — C	22311	Capt. Easter — L R
22192	Bob Price — R R	22312	Capt. Fisher M
22193	Bob Samuels M	22313	Capt. Gardner — D
22196	Bogardus — Cox	22314	Capt. Jack — T
22198	Bolivar — M	22315	Capt. Jack M
22201	Bonanza — D	22316	Capt. Jack — D
22206	Booth 2nd T	22317	Capt. Jack Cox
22207	Boreas — L R	22318	Capt. Jack — C
22208	Boss — Ky I	22319	Capt. Jack M
22209	Boss Hesing — D	22321	Capt. Jack — R R
22210	Boston — C	22322	Capt. Jack — M
22212	Boston — Cox	22324	Capt. Kidd — L R
22214	Bourbon Duke Ky I	22325	Capt. Kidd M
22216	Bovis 3rd Ky I	22327	Capt. Napier M
22217	Boxer M	22328	Capt. Renic 2nd T
22219	Braceville Louanjo — M	22329	Capt. Tom L R
22221	Bradley L R	22331	Carlos — Cox
22222	Brassfield's Airdrie — M	22332	Carleton — L R
22226	Breastplate 3rd — D	22333	Caroline's Favorite — M
22228	Breastplate Louanjo 2nd — R R	22340	Cato — P S
22230	Breckenridge — P S	22341	Cato or Katto — T
22231	Brick Pomeroy — D	22343	Cayuga Lad — Cox
22232	Brick Pomeroy — M	22346	Champion — M
22233	Bridegroom — D	22347	Champion — L R
22234	Brigham — Cox	22349	Champion of Rose Mound — C
22235	Brigham Young — L R	22352	Charlatan — D
22236	Brigham Young — M	22357	Carles Darwin — P S
22237	Brigham Young — D	22358	Charles Dickens — L R
22238	Brigham Young — P S	22359	Charles Lewis — C
22239	Brigham M	22360	Charlestown M
22240	Bright Ky I	22361	Charley Goodnight P S
22241	Bright Eyes — P S	22362	Charley — T
22242	Bright Eyes Duke — Daisy	22364	Charley Long — Ky I
22245	Brilliant — M	22365	Charley Porter — P S
22246	Brilliant Lad — P S	22367	Charon — Daisy
22251	Bro. Beecher — P S	22368	Chatham's Comet — M
22254	Bruce Bull L R	22370	Chatham Star — M
22255	Brush Creek Thorndale — Ky I	22371	Chautauqua King L R
22256	Brush Creek Thorndale 2nd — Ky I	22372	Cherry Duke — M
22257	Brutus — M	22377	Cherry Prince — M
22258	Brutus — M	22378	Cherry Royal — D
22260	Bub L R	22379	Cherry's Gloster — Cox
22261	Buckeye M	22382	Cherub's Chief — C
22262	Buckeye Boy — L R	22383	Cherub's Cousin — L R
22263	Buckeye Lad M	22384	Chesapeak L R

SHORT-HORN CATTLE PEDIGREES. 103

No.	Name	Herd
22385	Chester	D
22386	Chief	— D
22387	Chief Airdrie	— Cox
22388	Chief of the Pines	— P S
22389	Chief of the Sharons	— P S
22390	Chieftain	L R
22391	Chieftain	— M
22393	Childers Breastplate	P S
22398	Christmas	— R R
22408	Clark	— P S
22409	Clark's Duke	— M
22410	Claude Watson	— R R
22412	Clay Cockrell	— C
22413	Clay Wright	— T
22414	Clearmont	R R
22416	Clifton	R R
22417	Clifton 3rd	— T
22418	Clifton Duke	— M
22419	Clifton Duke 2nd	— M
22420	Climax 2nd	— L R
22421	Climax Palmer	L R
22422	Clinton Duke of Airdrie	— M
22425	Colenso	— P S
22426	Colfax	M
22429	Colonel	M
22430	Colonel	— Daisy
22431	Colonel	— L R
22435	Col. Boutt	Ky I
22436	Col. Breckenridge	— P S
22437	Col. Buckner	— P S
22438	Col. Croxton 2nd	— D
22440	Col. Hull	Ky I
22441	Col. Lincoln	M
22442	Col. Muir	— M
22443	Col. Philipps	— D
22444	Col. Pierce	T
22445	Col. Ritchie	P S
22446	Col. Smith	— T
22448	Col. Tim Reeves	P S
22449	Col. Wiley	L R
22450	Colarado	T
22451	Colarado Mazurka 1st	— Cox
22452	Colarado Mazurka 2nd	— Cox
22453	Colarado Mazurka 3rd	— Cox
22455	Comack	— M
22457	Comet	— L R
22458	Comet	R R
22459	Comet	— Cox
22460	Comet	— Ky I
22461	Comet 2nd	— D
22463	Coming Comet	Ky I
22464	Commander	Daisy
22465	Commodore	Cox
22466	Commodore 2nd	M
22468	Complete	M
22469	Comus	R R
22471	Consul	— M
22473	Congressman	— M
22477	Constantina's Oxford 3rd	— R R
22479	Corporal Nym	L R
22482	Count Atholl	— R R
22484	Count of Spring Hill	— D
22485	Count Piper	— P S
22486	Counterpart Duke	M
22488	Crescent Booth	— R R
22489	7th Crescent Hill Booth	— D
22490	8th Crescent Hill Booth	L R
22491	Creston Chief	— M
22492	Cricket	P S
22494	Cromwell	— Cox
22497	Crowder	Ky I
22498	Crown Prince	M
22500	Crown Prince	— Cox
22503	Crown P. of Athelstane 3d	— M
22504	Cumberland	— L R
22508	Cyclops	— L R
22509	Cypress	Ky I
22511	Cypress Duke	Daisy
22512	Cypress Duke of Nebraska	M
22513	Cypress Grant	— M
22514	Cypress Lad	M
22515	Cyrus Booth	— M
22516	Dairy Boy	— L R
22517	Dairyman	— Cox
22518	Dairyman 2nd	— R R
22519	Daisy Boy	— M
22520	Daisy Duke	— P S
22522	Daisy Lad	P S
22523	Daltona	L R
22524	Danby 2nd	Cox
22525	Dandy	— Cox
22526	Dandy Jim of Etna	— Daisy
22527	Dan White	— M
22528	Daniel Mason	Woods
22529	Daniel Webster	— L R
22530	Darby	— P S
22531	Darby Jr	M
22532	Darby Duke	R R
22533	Darby Duke 2nd	— P S
22534	Darby Duke 3rd	R R
22535	Darlington 2nd	— M
22537	Davis Thorndale	— T
22540	Dean Jr	L R
22541	Decoration	— L R
22542	Defiance	— L R
22543	Delhi	Cox
22544	Della's Booth	— M
22545	Dell Byrns	P S
22546	Deputy Sheriff	— D
22549	Derby	— L R
22551	Derby 3rd	T
22552	Derby Jr	— M
22553	Derby Chief	— D
22554	Derby of Hillside Farm	— L R
22555	Derby 2nd of Hillside Farm	— L R
22556	Dewitt	— Ky I
22558	Dexter	— M
22559	Dexter 3rd	M
22561	Diamond Duke	— R R
22562	Diamond Duke 2nd	Wrong
22563	Diamond Duke 2nd	— M
22564	Diamond Joe	— L R
22565	Dick	Ky I
22566	Dick Erickson	— T
22567	Dick Johnson	Cox
22569	Dick Naylor	— Cox
22570	Dickson's Airdrie	Ky I
22571	Dick Turpin	Cox
22572	Dick Yates	L R
22574	Dictator	P S
22577	Dixon Boy	— D
22578	Doctor	P S
22582	Doctor Jackson	— Ky I
22586	Doctor Prewitt	— T
22587	Doctor Scott	— Daisy
22588	Dollys Duke	— P S
22589	Domino	P S
22590	Domino 2nd	— P S
22591	Domino 3rd	— P S
22595	Don John	— M

22596	Don Juan — D	22693	Duke of Branch — Ky I
22598	Don Juan — Ky I	22695	5th Duke of Briggsdale — C
22599	Dom Pedro — M	22697	Duke of Brown — P S
22600	Double Louanjo — Ky I	22699	Duke of Burlington — M
22602	Douglass — Cox	22701	Duke of Canton — T
22603	Dover Duke — Ky I	22702	2nd Duke of Cedar Springs Farm — T
22604	Dowley's Oakland — R R	22703	Duke of the Center — Cox
22605	Dronas Airdrie — P S	22704	Duke of Chance — P S
22606	Duane's Duke 4th — L R	22708	1st Duke of Chico — Ky I
22608	Duchess Gem — Cox	22709	2nd Duke of Chico — T
22610	Duenna Duke 3rd — R R	22710	3rd Duke of Chico — D
22611	Duenna Duke 3rd — R R	22711	Duke of Clarence 3rd — D
22615	Duke — D	22714	2nd Duke of Cliff Grange — D
22616	Duke — L R	22715	3rd Duke of Cliff Grange — D
22618	Duke 3rd — T	22716	Duke of Clinton — Cox
22619	Duke 4th — D	22719	Duke of Columbus — L R
22620	Duke 5th — T	22720	Duke of Commodore — L R
22621	Duke Airdrie — Ky I	22721	Duke of Cross Hill — L R
22623	Duke Alexis — Ky I	22724	Duke of Darby — M
22624	Duke Alexis — T	22727	Duke of Duenna 1st — R R
22626	Duke Booth — P S	22728	Duke of Dunglow Farm — C
22628	Duke De La Vois 2nd — P S	22729	Duke of Dunstable — M
22629	Duke Doublet 2nd — D	22730	Duke of Earl — R R
22630	Duke Doublet 3rd — T	22731	Duke of Edinburg — L R
22632	Duke Imperial — T	22732	Duke of Edinburg — Ky I
22633	Duke Lang — R R	22734	Duke of Elkhart — T
22635	Duke Mack — Ky I	22737	Duke of Erin — M
22636	Duke of Adams — M	22738	3rd Duke of Etna — Daisy
22637	1st Duke of Adams — Long-Horn	22739	Duke of Evergreen — P S
22638	3rd Duke of Adams — Cox	22740	Duke of Evergreen Hill — L R
22639	Duke of Adams County — M	22741	2nd Duke of Evergreen Hill — L R
22641	Duke of Airdrie — Daisy	22742	Duke of Exeter — Ky I
22642	Duke of Airdrie 2nd — P S	22743	2nd Duke of Exeter — Ky I
22644	23rd Duke of Airdrie's Son — Cox	22744	3rd Duke of Exeter — Ky I
22646	Duke of Albermarl 2nd — P S	22745	Duke of Fairview — P S
22650	Duke of Altaham — M	22746	Duke of Fairview — M
22651	Duke of Alto — D	22747	1st Duke of Fairview — M
22652	Duke of Applewood — M	22748	2nd Duke of Fairview — R R
22653	Duke of Arcola — Cox	22749	Duke of Farmville — M
22655	3rd Duke of Armada — Cox	22750	Duke of Fayette 2nd — P S
22656	Duke of Arthur — M	22751	1st Duke of Fennimore — C
22657	5th Duke of Ashland — M	22754	Duke of Freeport — M
22658	10th Duke of Ashland — M	22757	2nd Duke of Gabilan — R R
23659	11th Duke of Ashland — P S	22758	4th Duke of Garnaville — Ky I
22660	12th Duke of Ashland — M	22761	Duke of Glendale — L R
22661	13th Duke of Ashland — M	22762	2nd Duke of Glenwood — Cox
22662	14th Duke of Ashland — M	22766	Duke of Goodness — R R
22663	15th Duke of Ashland — Ky I	22767	Duke of Goodness — Daisy
22664	16th Duke of Ashland — D	22768	4th Duke of Goodness — T
22665	17th Duke of Ashland — M	22769	5th Duke of Goodness — T
22667	Duke of Athens — D	22771	23rd Duke of Goodness — R R
22668	6th Duke of Atholl — R R	22772	24th Duke of Goodness — R R
22669	7th Duke of Atholl — R R	22773	25th Duke of Goodness — R R
22670	10th Duke of Atholl — M	22774	Duke of Graingers — R R
22671	11th Duke of Atholl — Long-Horn	22775	16th Duke of Granville — R R
22672	12th Duke of Atholl — R R	22776	1st Duke of Greendale — L R
22673	13th Duke of Atholl — C	22777	2nd Duke of Greendale — L R
22674	Duke of Australia — Cox	22778	Duke of Greenfield — D
22676	Duke of Baden — M	22779	23rd Duke of Greenlawn — M
22677	Duke of Beaverhead — D	22780	24th Duke of Greenlawn — M
22679	Duke of Bedford — R R	22781	25th Duke of Greenlawn — M
22681	Duke of Bellview — P S	22782	26th Duke of Greenlawn — M
22682	1st Duke of Benton — Ky I	22783	27th Duke of Greenlawn — M
22683	Duke of Blackhawk — Ky I	22784	28th Duke of Greenlawn — M
22684	Duke of Blanchard 2nd — D	22785	29th Duke of Greenlawn — M
22685	Duke of Blanchard 3rd — D	22786	1st Duke of Grinell — M
22688	2nd Duke of Bluffdale — R R	22787	2nd Duke of Grinell — R R
22689	3rd Duke of Bluffdale — R R	22788	Duke of Groton — Cox
22691	5th Duke of Bluffdale — R R	22789	4th Duke of Grovedale — Cox
22692	6th Duke of Bluffdale — C	22790	3rd Duke of Grovedale — Cox

SHORT-HORN CATTLE PEDIGREES.

No.	Name	Breeder
22791	2nd Duke of Hamilton	L R
22792	3rd Duke of Hamilton	L R
22794	Duke of Habdusburg	— M
22795	Duke of Harlem	D
22796	Duke of Harmony	— Cox
22797	Duke of Harrison	M
22798	Duke of Hawthorn Hill	M
22799	Duke of Hazelhurst	— Ky I
22802	Duke of Hermon	— M
22803	Duke of Hickory Grove	— Ky I
22804	Duke of Highland 2nd	— R R
22807	Duke of Hillsdale	— Cox
22811	Duke of Howard	— P S
22812	Duke of Howard	M
22813	Duke of Ingham	L R
22814	1st Duke of Iowa	— M
22815	2nd Duke of Iowa	— P S
22816	3rd Duke of Iowa	— P S
22817	Duke of Iroquois	— L R
22818	Duke of Irwin	M
22821	6th Duke of Kalamazoo	Cox
22822	7th Duke of Kalamazoo	Cox
22823	Duke of Kent	— P S
22830	1st Duke of Lake Forke	— D
22831	4th Duke of La Salle	— M
22833	Duke of Legged Grove	— P S
22835	Duke of Leon	T
22836	8th Duke of Liberty	— M
22837	2nd Duke of Licking	— M
22838	3rd Duke of Licking	— M
22840	Duke of Livingston	Ky I
22841	7th Duke of Locust Lawn	— Ky I
22842	8th Duke of Locust Lawn	M
22843	Duke of Macon	— P S
22844	Duke of Madison	— L R
22846	Duke of Malakoff 3rd	— Cox
22847	1st Duke of Maplewood	M
22849	2nd Duke of Marion	P S
22852	Duke of Mercer	— M
22854	Duke of Monroe	— R R
22855	1st Duke of Monroe	— Ky I
22856	5th Duke of Monterey	Ky I
22857	6th Duke of Monterey	— P S
22859	1st Duke of Morgan	M
22860	2nd Duke of Morgan	M
22861	Duke of Morrison	D
22862	1st Duke of Moss Side	P S
22865	Duke of New Castle	— M
22866	3rd Duke of New London	— Ky I
22867	Duke of North Buffalo	L R
22869	Duke of Oakland	— R R
22870	Duke of Oakland	Ky I
22871	19th Duke of Oakland	L R
22873	3rd Duke of Omaha	— P S
22874	3rd Duke of Omaha	M
22876	3rd Duke of Oran	M
22877	4th Duke of Oran	Ky I
22879	5th Duke of Osage	— T
22887	3rd Duke of Paris	— C
22889	Duke of Phalanx	Cox
22890	Duke of Pigeon Run	Cox
22891	Duke of Pleasant Hill	M
22893	Duke of Polo	— Daisy
22894	Duke of Portage	— M
22895	Duke of Portage 2nd	M
22896	1st Duke of Redwood	— P S
22898	Duke of Ridgeland	— R R
22899	5th Duke of Ripley	— T
22900	6th Duke of Ripley	M
22902	Duke of Rutland	Ky I
22903	Duke of Rutland	— L R
22906	5th Duke of Salem	P S
22907	Duke of Sandusky	— Long-Horn
22908	Duke of Scott	Ky I
22909	2nd Duke of Seneca	— M
22911	Duke of Seville	— Cox
22912	4th Duke of Shannon	— P S
22914	Duke of Sharon 2nd	T
22915	Duke of South Valley	M
22921	Duke of Springhill	— R R
22922	1st Duke of Springvale	— L R
22923	Duke of Stanstead	L R
22924	Duke of Stark	Cox
22925	Duke of Steadman	— L R
22926	1st Duke of Stones Prairie	Ky I
22927	Duke of Strouds Creek	— R R
22929	Duke of Sunny Side	Cox
22931	1st Duke of Sycamore	— L R
22932	2nd Duke of Sycamore	— L R
22933	17th Duke of Tecumseh	M
22934	18th Duke of Tecumseh	— M
22935	19th Duke of Tecumseh	Ky I
22936	20th Duke of Tecumseh	D
22937	21st Duke of Tecumseh	— Ky I
22938	Duke of the Crossing	Ky I
22941	Duke of the Pines	L R
22942	12th Duke of the Pines	— R R
22943	13th Duke of the Pines	— R R
22944	14th Duke of the Pines	— R R
22945	15th Duke of the Pines	C
22946	2nd Duke of the Prairies	L R
22947	Duke of the Valley	— D
22949	Duke of the Valley	— R R
22953	Duke of Thornhill	D
22956	3rd Duke of Townsend	— M
22957	1st Duke of Trenton	Ky I
22958	2nd Duke of Trenton	Ky I
22959	3rd Duke of Trenton	— D
22960	4th Duke of Trenton	Cox
22961	6th Duke of Trenton	Cox
22965	Duke of Unity	— C
22966	2nd Duke of Unity	— C
22967	Duke of Union Grove	D
22969	2nd Duke of Vermillion	— R R
22970	Duke of Waldburg 3rd	— D
22972	2nd Duke of Warner	— L R
22973	Duke of Warren	— T
22974	Duke of Washington	— Ky I
22975	Duke of Washington	— M
22976	Duke of Washington	— M
22977	2nd Duke of Washington	— M
22979	3rd Duke of Wayne	— M
22982	Duke of Wheatland	— L R
22983	Duke of Wilder	— R R
22984	3rd Duke of Wilton	— P S
22987	Duke of Wisedale	— M
22988	Duke of Wolf Creek	— D
22991	9th Duke of Yates	— M
22992	Duke Renick	M
22993	Duke Stoner 2nd	— R R
22996	Duke Wiley 2nd	— C
22997	Duke William	— M
22999	Dumplin	— M
23000	Duncan Duke	— R R
23001	Duncan's Glen Airdrie	— R R
23003	Dunlap	D
23004	Durham Hill Duke	D
23005	Duroc	M
23306	Duroc	Ky I
23007	Dutch	— M

23009	Earl	— P S	23128	Fairfield	— Cox
23010	Earl	— D	23130	Fancy Duke 2nd	Ky I
23011	Earl Duchess	— R R	23132	Farina's Duke	— R R
23013	Earl Duke	— R R	23133	Farmer	— M
23015	Earl Eph	— P S	23134	Farmer	M
23016	Earl of Augusta	M	23136	Farmer Boy	— Ky I
23028	Earl of Fayette	R R	23137	Farnsworth	— Cox
23029	Earl of Forest Dale	— R R	23138	Fashion	— M
23034	5th Earl of Gloster	— Cox	23139	Favorite	Ky I
23035	6th Earl of Gloster	— Cox	23140	Favorite	Cox
23036	7th Earl of Gloster	— Cox	23141	Favorite	— L R
23039	Earl of Goodness	— Cox	23142	Favorite	Daisy
23040	9th Earl of Greenbush	— Cox	23144	Favorite	— M
23041	10th Earl of Greenbush	— P S	23145	Favorite	— T
23042	11th Earl of Greenbush	— P S	23146	Favorite Duke	— R R
23043	12th Earl of Greenbush	— R R	23149	Fear Naught	L R
23048	1st Earl of Kalamazoo	Cox	23150	Felix	M
23051	Earl of Maplelawn	— Ky I	23158	Fidgets Duke of Oakland	— R R
23052	Earl of Meadow Lawn	— M	23156	Fillpail Senator	Cox
23055	Earl of Oakland	— C	23160	Florence Duke	— C
23058	Earl of Pembroke	— D	23161	Florence Duke 2nd	— C
23060	Earl of Shannon	— M	23162	Florence Duke 3rd	— C
23061	Earl of Sharon	— D	23163	Florence Duke 4th	— C
23064	Earl of Stanford	P S	23164	Florence Duke 5th	— C
23065	3rd Earl of Sturgis	— P S	23165	Florentia's Double Duke	— C
23066	Earl of Tennessee	— R R	23166	Florentina's Oakland	P S
23068	Earl of Woodlawn	— M	23168	Florin's Bridegroom	M
23069	Earl of Thornapple	— Cox	23171	Fordham Duke 7th	— C
23070	Earl Richmond	— L R	23175	Forester	— M
23072	Echo of the Tree	— M	23176	Forester	— M
23074	Eclipse 2nd	— D	23178	Fortunate	L R
23075	Eclipse	— C	23179	Fosters Beauty	— P S
23076	Ed Blinn	T	23180	Fourth of July, Jr.	— D
23077	Ed Jacobs	— M	23181	Francis	— Cox
23079	Ed of Maple Hill	— R R	23183	Frank	Ky I
23080	Edward Bates	— M	23184	Frank	D
23081	Edwin	T	23185	Frank	— M
23084	Elgin	— Ky I	23186	Frank Cockerell	— M
23085	El Hakim	L R	23187	Frank Conklin	— R R
23086	Elias Brown	— Long-Horn	23188	Frank Moulton	Daisy
23087	Ella's Duke	P S	23189	Frank Potter	R R
23088	Ellsworth	Cox	23190	Frank Webber	P S
23091	Emma's Sheriff	D	23191	Frank Whipple	M
23092	Emma's Thorndale	— Cox	23194	Fred Joiner	L R
23094	Emperor	— R R	23196	Frederick	M
23095	Emperor	— T	23197	Frederick	— T
23096	Emperor	— M	23199	Freeborn County's First	D
23098	Emperor	— M	23202	Frontier Granger	— M
23099	Emperor 4th	D	23203	Frosty's Duke	P S
23100	Emperor of Pleasant View	— M	23205	17th Gaban	— P S
23102	Engineer	Ky I	23206	2nd Gaban of Eastside	— P S
23103	Engineer	— Ky I	23209	Gambetta	— M
23104	Enoch	— L R	23210	Gamester 4th	— R R
23105	Enterprise	Ky I	23211	Garrett Davis	— C
23106	Eric	D	23213	Gayest Boy	— D
23109	Ernesty	— D	23214	Gem's Alert	— Cox
23110	Ethelbert	— Cox	23216	Gen. Bates	Ky I
23111	Etna Oxford	— P S	23217	Gen. Belknap	P S
23112	Euclide	M	23218	Gen. Butler	— C
23113	Eudora's Lad	— R R	23219	Gen. Clifton	L R
23114	Eugene	T	23222	Gen. Custer	— Cox
23115	Eugene Airdrie	L R	23223	Gen. Goe	— L R
23118	Ex	— M	23224	Gen. Grant	Ky I
23119	Excellent	Ky I	23225	Gen. Grant	P S
23120	Excelsior	— M	23226	Gen. Grant	Ky I
23121	Exception	T	23228	Gen. Hancock	— Cox
23122	Exchange	— R R	23230	Gen. Hurlbut	— D
23123	Exchange	L R	23232	Gen. Jackson	— M
23126	Experiment	L R	23234	Gen. Logan	— M
23127	Fairfax	— R R	23235	Gen. Marion	— D

SHORT-HORN CATTLE PEDIGREES.

No.	Name	Mark
23236	Gen. Marshall	— Daisy
23237	Gen. Napier	— Cox
23238	Gen. Reno	Ky I
23239	Gen. Rice	Daisy
23240	Gen. Rosecrans	P S
23241	Gen. Scott	Ky I
23242	Gen. Sherman	M
23243	Gen. Sumner	M
23245	Gen. Taylor	— R R
23246	Gen. Thomas	— T
23247	Gen. Vanderbilt	— M
23248	Gen. Washington	P S
23251	Gen. Williams	— M
23254	Geneva Airdrie	M
23257	Geneva Boy 2nd	Ky I
23260	Geneva Duke	— R R
23262	Geneva Duke of Springdale	— M
23263	Geneva Lad	— C
23266	Genier Duke	— D
23269	George	R R
23270	George	— L R
23271	George	— Cox
23272	George	— Cox
23273	George	M
23274	George	M
23275	George	— P S
23276	George Boydon	T
23277	George Linn	— M
23279	Gerald	Daisy
23280	Gerald	Ky I
23284	Giltners Commodore	T
23285	G. Jules Germain	— M
23286	Gladley	Ky I
23289	Glen Count	M
23290	2nd Glen Count	M
23291	3rd Glen Count	M
23292	4th Glen Count	M
23293	2nd Glen Dandy	L R
23294	Glen Duke 14th	M
23295	Glen Farm Duke	— R R
23296	Glen Hannibal	— L R
23297	2nd Glen Hannibal	— L R
23298	Gloster	D
23300	Gloster 2nd	D
23301	Gloster Chief	— Cox
23303	Gloster Hero	— Cox
23304	Gold Dust	Ky I
23306	Goldfinder	— P S
23307	Goldleaf 2nd	— R R
23310	Goodness Duke	Daisy
23311	Goodness Prince	— R R
23312	Governor	Cox
23313	Gov. Allen	— R R
23314	Gov. Carpenter	T
23315	Gov. Dix	— Cox
23316	Gov. Hardin	Ky I
23317	Gov. Hayes	T
23318	Gov. Hayes	— P S
23319	Gov. Hayes	Ky I
23320	Gov. Kirkwood	— D
23321	Gov. Kirkwood	— P S
23323	Gov. Stone	Daisy
23324	Gov. Stone	— C
23325	Gov. Taylor	— M
23326	Gov. Tod	— P S
23327	Gracie's Duke	— P S
23328	Grandee	— M
23330	Granger	L R
23331	Granger	— M
23333	Granger Boy	M
23334	Granger Boy	M
23335	Granger Boy	D
23336	Granger Duke	Ky I
23337	Grand Duke 6th	— L R
23341	Grand Duke of Anderson	— M
23346	Grand Duke of Goodness	— R R
23347	2nd Grand Duke of Greenlawn Daisy	
23360	Grand Oxford	P S
23362	Grant	Ky I
23363	Grant	Cox
23364	Grant	L R
23365	Grant	— T
23366	Granite	D
23368	Gratz Brown	— P S
23369	Great Bend	— M
23370	Greely 3rd	P S
23371	Green Hill Lad	M
23373	1st Greenwood Lad	— R R
23374	2nd Greenwood Lad	— R R
23375	3rd Greenwood Lad	— R R
23376	4th Greenwood Lad	Daisy
23377	Guizot	— M
23379	Gulover	— R R
23380	Gus Johnson	L R
23381	Guy	— Cox
23383	Gwynne Duke 2nd	M
23385	Gwynneth	— Cox
23387	Haines	M
23389	Hankins Loudon Duke 2nd	— M
23392	Hannibal	— L R
23393	Hannibal 32nd	— M
23394	Hannibal 33rd	— R R
23395	Harewood	T
23396	Harmony	L R
23397	Harold	Ky I
23398	Harold	D
23400	Harrison Taylor	— M
23401	Harry	— M
23402	Harry Bassett	— R R
23403	Harry Clay	— L R
23405	Harvey	M
23407	Harvest Duke	M
23408	Hattie Harrison's Duke	T
23409	Hawkeye Boy	— Cox
23410	Hawkeye Boy	— R R
23411	Hazelland	— L R
23412	Hector	— M
23413	Hector	— Cox
23414	Hector	P S
23415	Hector	D
23416	Hector Clyde	M
23418	Helmet	— R R
23419	Helmet	— P S
23420	Henry	Ky I
23423	Henry Clarion	— M
23424	Henry Clay	— M
23425	Henry Clay	Ky I
23426	Henry Clay	L R
23427	Henry Ward Beecher	— P S
23428	Henry Ward Beecher	— P S
23429	Henry Ward Beecher	P S
23430	Henry Ward Beecher	— M
23432	Hercules	— Cox
23433	Hero	D
23437	Hero 3rd	— Cox
23438	Hero Clyde	M
23439	Hero of Fairview	M
23440	Hero of Oakland	D
23441	Heterogene	— Cox
23442	Hickory	— D

23443	Hiffy — C	23549	Joe Davis — M
23445	High Henry — R R	23550	Joe Hooker — M
23447	Highland Duke — Ky I	23551	Joe Hooker — Ky I
23448	Highlander — Cox	23552	Joe Johnson 2nd — T
23449	Highland Scott — D	23554	Joe Luckie — M
23452	Hillside — L R	23556	Joe Nelson — M
23456	Homepark Napier — M	23557	Joe Nelson — M
23460	Honey Lad 2nd — Ky I	23558	Joe — T
23461	Hoosier Boy — P S	23559	John — P S
23462	Hoovers Breastplate — P S	23560	John — L R
23464	Hopewell Duke — R R	23562	John C. Breckenridge — R R
23465	Hopson — Ky I	23563	John Diamond 3rd — R R
23467	Horace Greeley — M	23564	John Diamond 4th — R R
23468	Horatio 2nd — R R	23565	John Dodge — P S
23470	Hotspur 4th — M	23566	John D. Gillett — T
23471	Hotspur 5th — M	23567	John Harris — R R
23473	Howard — C	23568	John Malcom — T
23475	Hughs — M	23569	John McCoy — M
23476	Humbolt — L R	23570	John of Maple Hill — R R
23477	Humbolt Chief — Cox	23571	John Oxford — P S
23478	Humbug — M	23574	John Wyatt — T
23479	Hunter's Duke — M	23575	Johnny — M
23480	Huron's Duke 2nd — Long-Horn	23576	Johnny — R R
23482	Idler — M	23578	Johnny Bull — R R
23484	Imperial — M	23581	Johnny Mac — Cox
23487	Imperial Duke — L R	23582	Jolly — Cox
23489	Imperial Prince — M	23583	Joseph — T
23490	Indian Chief — M	23584	Joseph E. Johnson — Ky I
23493	Invincible Duke — Daisy	23585	Joseph Reiter — C
23494	Invitress Duke — M	23587	Josephus — Ky I
23495	Iowa — L R	23588	Josie Duke — T
23496	Iowa Chief — T	23589	Juba — L R
23498	Iowa Duke — M	23592	Judge Comstock — R R
23499	Iowa Eclipse — M	23593	Judge Craig — L R
23500	Iowa Roan — P S	23594	Judge Gill — L R
23501	Irenus — M	23595	Judge Prescott — D
23503	Iris Favorite — M	23596	Julia's Son — R R
23504	Iron Duke — M	23597	Julius — M
23505	Iron Duke — M	23600	Juno — M
23507	Ivanhoe — Cox	23601	Jupiter — R R
23509	Jack Frost — Ky I	23604	Juvenal — Cox
23510	Jack Hays — T	23605	Kates Duke — R R
23511	Jack Hays 2nd — M	23608	Kent — Ky I
23512	Jackson — Ky I	23609	Kentucky Boy — P S
23513	Jackson — T	23612	Keokuk — M
23515	Jacob — P S	23613	King — D
23517	Janizary — L R	23614	King — P S
23518	Janus — Cox	23615	King David — P S
23520	Janus 9th — C	23616	King David — M
23521	Janus 10th — C	23617	King Fisher — Cox
23522	Janus 11th — C	23621	Kings Loudon Duke 3rd — R R
23524	Jason — Cox	23622	King of Leroy — Cox
23525	Javelin — Cox	23625	King of the West — R R
23527	Jeff — M	23626	King William — L R
23529	Jeff Davis — Ky I	23627	King William — Cox
23530	Jeff Davis 2nd — T	23630	Kitty's Duke — P S
23533	Jeff Pool — R R	23632	Knightly — R R
23534	Jenny's Duke — R R	23637	Knight of Allendale — P S
23535	Jenny's Duke — P S	23639	Knight of Chautauqua — Cox
23536	Jenny 2nd's Duke — P S	23640	Knight of Green — M
23537	Jim — R R	23641	Knight of Maryland — M
23538	Jim Bridgeford — P S	23642	Knight of Nashville — D
23540	Jim Fisk — Ky I	23643	Knight of Nebraska — M
23542	Jimmy — D	23649	Knight of the Thistle — R R
23543	Jim Sanders — M	23651	Kosciusko — P S
23544	Joaquin Miller — D	23653	Lacteal Duke — L R
23545	Joe — Ky I	23654	Lad Duke — R R
23546	Joe Airdrie 1st — L R	23655	Lad of Shawnee — R R
23547	Joe Batchelder — M	23656	Lad's Son — C
23548	Joe Bell 2nd — T	23657	Lady Harriet's Duke — T

SHORT-HORN CATTLE PEDIGREES.

No.	Name	Mark	No.	Name	Mark
23659	Land Seer	— R R	23782	Lord Nelson	M
23660	Lantice	— Daisy	23783	Lord of Cedar	— R R
23661	Lara	— D	23784	Lord of Fitchburg	— Cox
23663	Latimer's Breastplate	— Daisy	23785	Lord of Rose Hill	— Cox
23664	Laura Ascot's Cherub	— T	23786	Lord of Sharon	— M
23666	Lawrence	— M	23790	Lord of the Manor 2nd	— M
23668	Layton	— L R	23791	Lord of the Pines	— R R
23669	Leander	— C	23794	Lord of the West	— Cox
23670	Leander	P S	23802	Lord Rivers	— M
23671	Lee	Ky I	23805	Lord Sheffielder	— D
23672	Legal Tender	— M	23806	2nd Lord Sheffielder	— D
23673	Legal Tender	M	23807	3rd Lord Sheffielder	— D
23674	Lemma's Duke	Ky I	23812	Lord Wiley	— M
23675	Lemma's Monarch	— L R	23816	Louan Clement	— R R
23678	Leo	Cox	23817	Louan Duke 5th	— M
23679	Leon	— R R	23818	Louan Duke 6th	— M
23681	Leonidas	— C	23819	2nd Louan Duke of Deer Park	— D
23683	Leopard 3rd	D	23820	Louan Duke of Fairview	— R R
23684	Leopard 4th	D	23821	Louan Prince of Randolph	— M
23686	Leopold	— C	23822	Louan's Airdrie	— R R
23687	Leslie Duke	— T	23823	Louan's Booth	— M
23691	Lewis Brentwood	M	23824	Louan's Duke	— M
23692	Lewis Hampton	P S	23825	Louan's Duke of Oneida	— R R
23693	Lewis Jones	M	23826	Louan's Geneva	— R R
23694	Lexington	Ky I	23827	Louan's Magic	— R R
23696	Liberator	— Cox	23828	Louan's Muscatoon	— R R
23697	Liberty	— L R	23829	Louan's Napier	— R R
23698	Lillas Airdrie	— D	23832	Louan's Sucker Boy	— M
23699	Lillas Airdrie 2nd	— D	23833	Lou Angeline's Airdrie	— R R
23700	Lily Dales Duke	M	23834	Louanjo	— R R
23701	Lily's Duke	— M	23835	Louanjo	— R R
23703	Lincoln	— Cox	23836	Louanjo	M
23706	Linden	M	23837	Louanjo 2nd	D
23707	8th Linden	— M	23838	Louanjo 3rd	— R R
23708	Linn Home	— R R	23839	Louanjo 4th	— R R
23710	Lionel	— M	23840	Louanjo 5th	— R R
23711	Little Chief	M	23841	Louanjo 6th	D
23712	Little Dorritt's Anthony	P S	23842	Louanjo of the Evergreens	R R
23714	Little Giant	M	23843	2nd Louanjo of the Evergreens	R R
23715	Little Giant	— L R	23844	3rd Louanjo of the Evergreens	Ky I
23716	Little John	P S	23845	4th Louanjo of the Evergreens	P S
23717	Lobo Lad	— D	23846	5th Louanjo of the Evergreens	R R
23718	Locomotive	M	23847	Loudon Duke 12th	— R R
23719	Locomotive	M	23848	13th Loudon Duke	D
23721	Locum	— R R	23849	Loudon Duke 18th	— R R
23723	Lofty	Ky I	23851	Loudon Duke 22nd	— R R
23724	Lofty	D	23852	Loudon Duke of Belmont	— T
23725	Logan	— L R	23855	Loudon Duke of Linwood	— R R
23727	Logan Chief	— L R	23859	Lucky Boy	Ky I
23728	London Duke	— Cox	23860	Lucky Boy	— D
23729	Lone Star	— Cox	23861	Lucretius of Oakland	— R R
23730	Longfellow	— M	23863	Lulu's Duke	— R R
23731	Longfellow	R R	23864	Lustful Turk	L R
23732	Longfellow	Ky I	23865	Luxembourg	M
23733	Lorain Duke	— Cox	23866	Lynn Duke	— D
23736	Lord Baltimore 3rd	— P S	23867	Madison Duke 3rd	P S
23737	Lord Barmpton	— Daisy	23868	Madrid 2nd	— Daisy
23739	Lord Bates	— R R	23871	Magnolia's Gwynne	— Cox
23747	Lord Byron	— R R	23872	Maid's Duke	M
23740	Lord Chancellor	— M	23875	Major	— Cox
23752	Lord Derby	— R R	23877	Major	— Cox
23753	Lord Derby 2nd	— L R	23878	Major	— R R
23754	Lord Duke	M	23880	Major	— D
23759	Lord Ellington	— Cox	23881	Major	Ky I
23762	Lord Fawsley	— Cox	23883	Major Balco	— Ky I
23767	Lord Graham	— R R	23884	Major Bedford	— R R
23768	Lord Gwynne of Riverside	— Cox	23885	Major Burns	— L R
23772	Lord John	— Ky I	23886	Major Clarion	C
23775	Lord Baltimore	— P S	23887	Major Coomes	T
23779	Lord Napier	— M	23888	Major Cowan	M

23889	Major Duffy	P S
23890	Major Hill 2nd of Springdale	Ky I
23891	Major Hill 3rd of Springdale	Ky I
23892	Major Hill 4th of Springdale	Ky I
23893	Major Hill 5th of Springdale	Ky I
23894	Major Lang	— R R
23895	Major Morrell	— D
23896	Major Mills	M
23897	Major Ringgold	— P S
23898	Major Rollins	— P S
23899	Major Stephens	— T
23900	Major Story 3rd	M
23902	Major Vanmeter	— R R
23903	Major Wadsworth	Ky I
23904	Major Warnock	M
23905	Major White	Cox
23908	Maple Hill Duke	— R R
23909	Marcellus	— R R
23910	Marcus	— P S
23911	Marg's 1st Duke	— P S
23914	Marion of Sugar Grove	L R
23916	Mark Anthony	— R R
23919	Mark Twain	— M
23922	Marquis of Goodness	— R R
23924	Marquis of Lorne	Ky I
23926	Marquis of Lorne	— D
23927	Marquis of Minglewood	— C
23928	2nd Marquis of Oakwood	— D
23932	Marquis of Tennessee	— R R
23934	Mars	Ky I
23935	Mars	— L R
23936	Marshal Chapman	— M
23937	Marshal Clyde	M
23939	Martha's Duke	— P S
23940	Martial	P S
23941	Marvin	— M
23945	Master Butterfly	— R R
23949	Master Fairfax	P S
23950	Master Fortunatus	— Cox
23953	Master Geneva 4th	— M
23955	Master Gwynne	— Cox
23956	Master Hopewell	— R R
23958	Master Jim	M
23959	Master Mac	— M
23963	2nd Master of Ravenswood	— R R
23964	Master of the Prairie	Cox
23965	Master Robbie	— Cox
23966	Master Scooty	— Cox
23969	Master Wilderberg	M
23973	May Day	— Cox
23974	May Day's Duke	— Ky I
23975	May Duke	— M
23976	May Duke	— P S
23978	Mayflower's Oakland	L R
23979	Mayflower Lad	— Cox
23980	Mayor	— T
23981	Mayor Baugh	T
23982	Major Hill of Middle Creek	Ky I
23983	Maximilian 3rd	— M
23984	Maximilian	— Cox
23988	Mazurk Baron 3rd	— C
23995	Mazurka's Duke	C
23997	Mazurka Gwynne 2nd	— Ky I
23998	Mazurka Gwynne 3rd	— Ky I
23999	Mazurka Lad	— R R
24003	5th Meadow Duke	— M
24004	Mecosta	— Cox
24007	Messenger Earl	Cox
24008	Messenger Knight	— D
24010	Messenger Lord 2nd	— D
24014	Mike	— R R
24015	Mike Carr	— R R
24016	Milander	— C
24017	Milley's Duke	— P S
24018	Milley 2nd's Duke	— P S
24019	Millington Chief	M
24020	Milo	— P S
24021	Milo 2nd	— P S
24022	Mina's Gwynne	— Cox
24023	Minglewood Fancy Boy	L R
24024	Minna's Antony 2nd	— P S
24026	Minnesota Duke	— D
24029	Minor of Poplar Grove	— P S
24031	Mirza	— D
24034	Miss Electa's Antony	— P S
24035	Mississippi 2nd	T
24036	Missouri Jim	— C
24037	Missouri Lad	D
24041	Moberly	— T
24044	Modoc	Ky I
24045	Modoc	M
24047	Modoc	— D
24048	Modoc	— R R
24049	Modoc	Daisy
24050	Modoc Chief 2nd	— R R
24051	Mogul	P S
24052	Mohawk	— Daisy
24053	Mollie's Duke	— Ky I
24054	Monarch	— P S
24055	Monarch	— Ky I
24056	Monarch	— D
24059	Monarch	M
24060	Monarch 3rd	— Cox
24062	Monarch's Favorite	— M
24063	Moniteau's Favorite	P S
24067	Monoch	— M
24068	Monroe Duke	M
24069	Monta Chief	Ky I
24070	Montgomery Lad	— M
24071	Monti Jo	Ky I
24072	Morgan Monarch	P S
24073	Mormon Tom	— D
24074	Morning Boxer	M
24075	Morning Star	Cox
24076	Morning Star	— L R
24078	Morrison	— D
24080	Moses	— D
24085	Moulton	— Cox
24087	Mountaineer	M
24091	Mugg's Son	— R R
24093	Muscatoon 3rd	— P S
24094	Muscogee	— P S
24096	Myall	D
24097	My Choice	— M
24098	My Maryland	— L R
24099	Myris	Ky I
24100	Nabal	— P S
24101	Nabob	M
24103	Nannie's Bridegroom	M
24104	Napier	— L R
24105	Napier	— T
24106	Napier of Sugar Grove	Long-Horn
24107	Nellie's Duke	— M
24108	Nellies Duke	P S
24109	Nelson	L R
24110	Nelson	— P S
24113	Nero	— Wrong
24114	Nepther	Cox
24116	Nero	— M
24117	Nero	L R

SHORT-HORN CATTLE PEDIGREES.   111

No.	Name	Herd
24118	New Years Day	— P S
24119	New Years Day 2nd	— P S
24120	New Years Duke	— M
24121	New Years Red Jacket	— R R
24123	Ney	Woods
24124	Nick Hazelhurst	— D
24125	Nigel	Ky I
24126	Ninevah's Booth	— R R
24128	Noble Breastplate	— Daisy
24129	Noble Duke	— T
24130	Noble Duke	— L R
24131	Noble Duke	— Ky I
24134	Noble Master	— M
24137	Nora's Duke 2nd	— M
24138	Nora's Leo	— M
24139	North Briton	— Cox
24140	North Briton, Jr	— Cox
24142	North Star	— C
24145	Northumberland	— D
24147	Nowlan's Roan Bull	L R
24148	Okaola	— R R
24149	Oakdale	R R
24150	Oakdale Lad	— R R
24151	Oak Grove Duke	C
24152	Oakland 10th	P S
24156	Oakland Star	— P S
24157	Oakley	P S
24158	Oakum	— T
24159	Oakwood Louanjo	R R
24160	Odd Fellow	M
24161	Ogden	— P S
24162	Ohio	— Cox
24163	Ohio Lad	— L R
24165	Ole Bull	— T
24166	Oliver	— M
24167	Oliver	— T
24170	Oliver Twist 2nd	— M
24172	Oneida Chief	L R
24173	Oneida Chief 3rd	L R
24174	Oneida Chief 4th	— Cox
24177	Ontario	— Cox
24178	Onward	— M
24179	Olite	— M
24181	Orator	Ky I
24182	Orator	M
24183	Orient	— Ky I
24184	Oriole	— M
24185	Orion	— Ky I
24186	Oronte's Duke	— R R
24187	Orphan Boy	M
24188	Orphan Boy	— M
24189	Orphan Boy	M
24190	Orphan Boy	— M
24191	Orphan Boy 13th	— C
24192	Orphan Boy of Bath	— M
24193	Orphan Lad	Ky I
24194	Orpheus 2nd	— P S
24195	Oscar	— M
24196	Osceola	M
24198	Othello	Ky I
24200	Othello 4th	P S
24201	Otho	— Cox
24202	Otto	— M
24203	Ottumwa Chief	— P S
24204	Oxford	— M
24205	Oxford	Ky I
24206	Oxford 2nd	Ky I
24207	Oxford 3rd	Ky I
24208	Oxford 4th	Ky I
24209	Oxford Argyll 2nd	Cox
24218	Oxford Duke	— M
24219	Oxford Duke	P S
24223	Oxford Gwynne	— Cox
24224	Oxford Hero	— Cox
24226	Oxford Lad	— Cox
24228	Oxford Leo	L R
24229	Oxford Marquis	— M
24234	4th Oxford of Vermillion	— R R
24235	5th Oxford of Vermillion	— M
24236	6th Oxford of Vermillion	— T
24237	7th Oxford of Vermillion	— R R
24238	Oxford Patroon	— Cox
24239	Oxford Prince	— L R
24245	Oxmore	P S
24247	Ozark	— M
24248	Ozena's Duke	M
24249	Pacific	M
24251	Parson Brownlow	— D
24253	Paragon Boy	— R R
24254	Parish Arthur	— M
24257	Patterson Duke	— M
24258	Pat Husband	M
24264	Patrick of Sugar Grove	— Ky I
24266	Patriot	Ky I
24267	Patroon	— Long-Horn
24268	Paul Boynton	L R
24269	Paul Jones	Ky I
24272	Paymaster	— Ky I
24275	Pearl	— Ky I
24279	Pedro	— L R
24280	Pedro	Ky I
24281	Peerless Louan Duke	— R R
24282	Peleg	— Cox
24283	Pelham	— R R
24284	Peregrine Pickel	P S
24285	Perfect Duke	— R R
24286	Perfection	Ky I
24288	Perfection	— M
24291	Peri Duke	— L R
24296	Phil Sheridan	— M
24297	Phœnix Oakland	— R R
24298	Photograph	— M
24301	Pilate	— M
24302	Pile's Roan Bull	P S
24303	Pilgrim	Cox
24304	Pilot	— T
24306	Pilot	— D
24310	Pippin's Grant	T
24314	Planet	M
24315	Plano Duke	T
24316	Pleasant Star	— R R
24318	Plumwood F	R R
24319	Plumwood Z	R R
24320	Plumwood Boy	C
24321	Plumwood Lad D	R R
24322	Plumwood Lad K	R R
24323	Plumwood Lad L	— R R
24324	Plumwood Lad M	— R R
24325	Plumwood Lad N	R R
24326	Plumwood Rosecrans	M
24327	Pollock	Ky I
24329	Pompey	— L R
24330	Pontiac	— T
24331	Popcorn	— D
24332	Porter	— L R
24333	Porter	T
24334	Porter	— M
24335	Potomac Duke	— M
24336	Pottawattamie	M
24337	Poweshiek	— L R

24339	Prairie Boy	— M	24459	Profitable of Cleona — R R
24340	Prairie Boy	M	24461	Promise — M
24341	Prairie Boy	T	24462	Promise Ky I
24342	Prairie Chief	— Cox	24465	Proud Duke of Fairview 2nd — R R
24343	Prairie Chief	— Cox	24466	Prune Hubback R R
24344	Prairie Chief	— Ky I	24467	P. T. Barnum — Cox
24347	Prairie Flag	R R	24468	Pulaski — T
24348	Prairie King	— M	24469	Pythias 2nd — P S
24349	Premium	— C	24470	Queen's Duke T
24351	Pride's Alfred	— P S	24471	Queen Harrison's Duke T
24352	Prides Prince	L R	24472	Queen's Oxford Lad — M
24354	Pride of the West	M	24473	Quickstep — Cox
24357	Prince	T	24474	Rainbow M
24359	Prince	L R	24476	Ralph Cato P S
24360	Prince	— M	24477	Ralston — D
24361	Prince	— D	24478	Rama 3rd — D
24362	Prince	D	24479	Rambler — M
24363	Prince	L R	24481	Randolph — C
24365	Prince, Jr	— Cox	24482	Random — Cox
24367	Prince Airdrie	C	24483	Ranger — Cox
24368	Prince Albert	R R	24485	Ranger — M
24369	Prince Albert	M	24486	Ranger 4th — Cox
24370	Prince Albert	— L R	24487	Ransom Cox
24372	Prince Albert	— L R	24488	Rasselas M
24374	Prince Albert	— T	24489	Rasselas 2nd M
24377	Prince Alphonso	— M	24490	Rattler — L R
24378	Prince Alvah	M	24491	Rattler — C
24380	Prince Arthur	— C	24492	Ravenwood — D
24381	Prince Arthur, Jr	M	24496	Red M
24383	Prince Carnival	— M	24498	Red Airdrie P S
24384	Prince Charles	M	24499	Red Ambo — M
24385	Prince Charles	C	24500	Red Banker — Ky I
24387	Prince Climax 2nd	Ky I	24501	Red Baron M
24388	Prince De Joinville	— M	24502	Red Baron M
24389	Prince Edward	— P S	24503	Red Bill D
24390	Prince Frederick	— M	24504	Red Boy M
24393	Prince George	P S	24505	Red Bracelet's Duke — R R
24394	Prince George	— R R	24506	Red Buck T
24395	Prince Gwynne	— Cox	24507	Red Buck — P S
24396	Prince Imperial	L R	24508	Red Buck — M
24398	Prince John	— P S	24509	Red Bud — M
24399	Prince Lewis	— L R	24511	Red Bully — M
24400	Prince Louis	— R R	24512	Red Chief — Cox
24401	Prince Mazurka	— R R	24515	Red Cloud — D
24402	Prince Mazurka 2nd	— R R	24516	Red Cloud — M
24403	Prince Norman	— L R	24517	Red Cloud P S
24405	2nd Prince of Ashland	— M	24518	Red Cloud — R R
24406	Prince of Atha	— R R	34519	Red Cloud T
24409	Prince of Benton	— T	24520	Red Cloud — M
24412	Prince of Clarendon	Ky I	24521	Red Coat — R R
24413	Prince of Cobourg	— L R	24523	Red Dick — P S
24414	Prince of Freehold	— L R	24524	Red Duke — P S
24415	2nd Prince of Grasshill	— Cox	24526	Red Duke — P S
24416	Prince of Goodness	— R R	24527	Red Duke — T
24422	Prince of Lakeside	— Cox	24528	Red Duke — R R
24423	Prince of Logan	— P S	24529	Red Duke M
24424	Prince of Momence	— D	24530	Red Duke of Linwood — R R
24426	Prince of Orleans	— M	24531	Red Duke — M
24430	Prince of Richland	C	24532	Red Duke — L R
24435	Prince of Tennessee	D	24534	Red Duke — M
24438	Prince of Wales	D	24535	Red Duke P S
24444	Prince Royal	Ky I	24536	Red Duke Cox
24445	Prince Royal	— Cox	24538	Red Duke — R R
24446	Prince Royal	T	24541	Red Duke 2nd — D
24447	Prince Royal	— R R	24543	Red Havelock P S
24449	Prince's Profitable	— R R	24544	Red Jacket — Cox
24452	Princeton	L R	24545	Red Jacket — Cox
24453	Princeton's Duke of Airdrie	— Cox	24546	Red Jacket — Cox
24457	Profit	— M	24547	Red Jacket M
24458	Profitable 5th's Louanjo	— R R	24548	Red Jacket P S

SHORT-HORN CATTLE PEDIGREES.

No.	Name	Ref.
24549	Red Jacket	— L R
24552	Red Jacket 10th	— R R
24553	Red Jacket 12th	D
24554	Red Jacket 15th	— R R
24555	Red Jacket 17th	— R R
24556	Red Joe	— C
24557	Red John	M
24558	Red John	M
24561	Red Louan of Maplehill	— P S
24562	Red Meteor	Cox
24564	Red Oak	Ky I
24565	Red Oak	T
24566	Red Oak 2nd	Ky I
24567	Red Oak 3rd	P S
24568	Red Prince	R R
24569	Red Prince	L R
24570	Red Rambler 2nd	M
24571	Red Ribbon	— T
24573	Red Robin	P S
24575	Red Rover	M
24576	Red Rover	M
24577	Red Rover	— P S
24578	Red Rover	Ky I
24580	Red Rover	M
24581	Red Rover 2nd	— Cox
24582	Red Roy	— M
24583	Red Star	C
24584	Red Wiley	— R R
24585	Red Wing	— M
24586	Reed Marquet	T
24588	Rembrandt	— M
24589	Remus	— D
24593	Renick Sharon	T
24594	Renick's Duke of Airdrie	— M
24596	Republican	— R R
24597	Reuben	P S
24598	Richard 4th	— M
24599	Richard 5th	Cox
24600	Richard 6th	Cox
24601	Richmond	— R R
24602	Rigdon	— P S
24606	Rio Grande	— M
24607	Rival Clarion	— P S
24608	Roan Airdrie	— Ky I
24609	Roan Baron	— R R
24610	Roan Reddy's Duke	— P S
24611	Roan Boy	D
24614	Road Duke	— D
24615	Roan Duke	— Cox
24616	Roan Duke	M
24617	Roan Duke	M
24618	Roan Duke	— P S
24619	Roan Duke	P S
24624	Roan Duke of Kansas	— M
24625	Roan Joe	— T
24628	Roan Napier	— R R
24630	Roan Prince	— D
24632	Roan Prince	M
24633	Roan Prince	— Cox
24634	Roan Star	— L R
24635	Roan Star 4th	— L R
24636	Rob	— L R
24638	Robert E. Lee	— P S
24639	Robert Fulton	— Cox
24640	Robert Napier	— M
24641	Robinson Crusoe	T
24642	Rob Roy	— Cox
24645	Rock Island Chief	— M
24646	Rock River Lad 4th	— Cox
24647	Rock River Lad 5th	— Cox
24648	Rock River Lad 6th	— Cox
24649	Rock River Lad 7th	— Cox
24650	Rock River Lad 8th	— Cox
24651	Rock River Lad 9th	— Cox
24652	Rock River Lad 10th	— Cox
24653	Rock River Lad 11th	— Cox
24654	Rock River Lad 12th	— Cox
24655	Rock River Lad 13th	L R
24656	Rockville	— M
24657	Roderick	— M
24658	Roderick 2nd	L R
24660	Romeo	— L R
24661	Romeo	— M
24662	Romeo	M
24663	Romeo	— P S
24664	Romeo	M
24671	Rosabella's Duke	M
24673	Rosalie's Lad	— R R
24674	Rosa's Duke	— M
24675	Rosco	— R R
24680	Rose Hill Duke 3rd	— C
24681	Rose's Duke	— Cox
24682	Rosie Duke	R R
24685	Rosy Duke	— M
24688	Rosy Knight	— R R
24690	Rothschild 2nd	R R
24691	Rover	M
24692	Rover	M
24693	Rover	— Cox
24695	2nd Rover Duke	— R R
24699	Roxa's Chatham	— M
24702	Royal Airdrie 2nd	— M
24707	Royal Briton 2nd	M
24708	Royal Briton 2nd	M
24716	Royal Duke	— R R
24717	Royal Duke	M
24718	Royal Duke	— T
24719	Royal Gem	Ky I
24720	Royal George	— R R
24721	Royal George	— M
24722	Royal George 3rd	— L R
24723	Royal Gwynne	— Cox
24724	Royal Jim	— Cox
24726	Royal Lang	— R R
24728	Royal Muscatoon	— R R
24731	Royal Oxford	L R
24735	Royal Prince	— P S
24737	Royal Rose	— M
24739	Royal Saxon	L R
24740	Royal Sharon	— R R
24742	Ruby Chief	Daisy
24744	Ruby's Vandal	— D
24745	Rufus	— R R
24746	Rural Boy	P S
24749	Rustic	— L R
24750	Rutledge	— R R
24751	St. Albans	— R R
24754	St. Elmo	— Long-Horn
24756	St. John's Sharon	— D
24757	St. Lawrence	— Cox
24759	St. Patrick	— M
24760	St. Patrick	— M
24761	St. Patrick	— D
24762	St. Vincent	M
24764	Sam	M
24766	Sam Clover	P S
24767	Samp's Talbot	P S
24768	Sam Stone	— R R
24770	Sankey	M
24775	Sartoris	— D

24777	Saturn	P S	24886	Springer's Duke — P S
24783	Saxon Keith of Oakland	R R	24889	Spring Valley Monarch 2nd — L R
24784	2nd Saxon Keith of Oakland	Ky I	24893	Standard Bearer — M
24785	Scioto Airdrie	R R	24894	Stanley — M
24786	Scioto Prince	R R	24898	Star Duke — D
24787	Scotland John	D	24900	Star Duke — R R
24788	Scotland's Oxford	P S	24901	Star Duke — R R
24789	Scotsman, Jr	M	24902	Star Duke — Ky I
24790	Scotsman 2nd	M	24903	Star Duke 2nd — R R
24791	Scotsman's Lad	Cox	24904	Star Duke of Tecumseh — Ky I
24792	Scotsman's Snowball	Cox	24906	Starlight Daisy
24793	Scott	P S	24907	Starlight Ky I
24794	Scott Duke	C	24908	Starlight — M
24798	Sedley	Daisy	24909	Starlight — Cox
24799	Senator	Cox	24911	Starlight 3rd C
24800	Senator	Cox	24912	Starlight 4th — M
24801	Seneca	Cox	24913	Starlight 4th — R R
24802	Seneca Prince	R R	24914	Starlight Keith of Oakland — Ky I
24806	Shamrock 3rd	D	24915	2nd Starlight Keith of Oakl'd — Ky I
24807	Shanarke Chief	L R	24916	Starling — M
24808	Sharon	D	24918	Star of East Concord — L R
24809	Sharon Boy	T	24920	Star of Iowa M
24810	Sharon Boy	Daisy	24922	Star of Sugar Grove — Ky I
24811	Sharon Duke	T	24924	Star of the Empire — C
24814	Sharon Mazurka	R R	24926	Star of the Tree M
24815	Sharon Rose	P S	24932	Stonewall M
24817	Sheridan's Duke	Cox	24933	Stonewall — C
24819	Sheriff Jones	M	24934	Stonewall, Jr D
24820	Sherman	M	24936	Stonewall Jackson — R R
24821	Sherman	T	24938	Stonewall Jackson of Springdale M
24824	Sil Beason	T	24939	Strawberry Prince P S
24825	Silas Brent 2nd	M	24940	Stunner — D
24826	Sinbad	Ky I	24942	Sucker Boy 2nd — R R
24827	Sir Alfred	R R	24943	Sudduth — C
24829	Sir Charles	M	24944	Sulphur Spring Duke — P S
24838	Sir Henry 2nd	P S	24945	Sultan Cox
24839	Sir Isaac	T	24953	Summit Duke of Elm Grove — M
24841	Sir Jesse	L R	24954	Sumner P S
24843	Sir Normal	Long-Horn	24955	Sunlight — P S
24844	Sir Oliver	P S	24956	Sunlight — Daisy
24845	Sir Richard	D	24957	Sunrise Duke — R R
24846	Sir Robert Alexander 3rd	R R	24958	Surprise — M
24850	Sir Triplette	L R	24959	2d Surprise Gloster of Ingham Cox
24853	Skillet Duke	M	24961	Sweet Duke — Cox
24854	Slashum	Ky I	24962	Sweepstakes — Ky I
24855	Sleete	M	24969	Syphax L R
24857	Snowball	P S	24970	Tabby's Duke P S
24859	Snowball	Ky I	24973	Tam O'Shanter Ky I
24860	Snowball	P S	24975	Tarlton — T
24861	Snowbank	L R	24976	Tasso — P S
24862	Snowbound	Ky I	24977	Taurus — L R
24863	Snowboy	Cox	24981	Tazurka L R
24865	Snowdrop	P S	24982	Teaser L R
24866	Snowflake	P S	24983	Tempest — D
24868	Snyder	Ky I	24985	Thad Stevens — Ky I
24869	Solon	Cox	24986	Thanksgiving L R
24870	Solon	Woods	24987	Thanksgiving Lad M
24871	Solon Boy	M	24988	The Barber Bull C
24872	Son of Dexter	Cox	24989	The Beau — Cox
24874	Son of Viscount	M	24992	The Earl — R R
24876	Spectator	M	24993	The Earl — M
24877	Sperry	T	24995	Theodore Tilton — P S
24878	Spie Buck	P S	24996	Theodore Tilton — R R
24879	Spilman	M	24997	Third Term Ky I
24880	Spot	L R	24998	Thirsty — T
24881	Splendor	Cox	24999	Thomas Burch — T
24882	Spotted Boy	P S	25001	Thorndale — C
24883	Spotted Duke	T	25002	Thorndale — C
24884	Spotted Tail	Cox	25003	Thorndale Boy — C
24885	Spotted Tail	D	25006	Thorndale Lad — L R

25007	Thorndale Wiley	— Cox		25122	Washington	Cox
25008	2nd Thorne of Mt. Zion	— M		25123	Washington	— Ky I
25011	Ticonderoga	M		25124	Washington 14th	Daisy
25012	Tilton	— P S		25125	Washtenaw Chief	— M
25014	Tilton	Ky I		25127	Waterloo	— M
25016	Tilton	L R		25132	W. B. Arnold	— M
25017	Timbunker	— T		25135	Wellington	— D
25019	Tip	Cox		25140	Wellington 2nd	— M
25023	Tipton Duke	— M		25143	Western Duke	P S
25024	Tom	P S		25144	Western Earl	— Cox
25026	Tom Bailey	— M		25145	Western Lad	— R R
25027	Tom Boy	— M		25146	Western Monarch	— M
25029	Tom Casey	— C		25147	W. H. Crawford	— M
25030	Tom Corwin	— R R		25149	White Cloud	— Cox
25031	Tom Gadd	T		25150	White Cloud	M
25032	Tom Hendricks	P S		25151	White Cloud	— R R
25033	Tom Marshall	— P S		25153	White Duke	— L R
25035	Tom Taylor 2nd	— R R		25154	White Duke	— D
25037	Tom Windle	T		25155	Whitefaced Bill	— M
25038	Tom Wonder	— P S		25156	White Jacket	— T
25039	Topeka	— M		25157	White Jubilee	— Ky I
25042	Trafalgar	— Cox		25158	White Lad	— T
25046	Triton	R R		25160	White Sam	P S
25047	Triumph	L R		25161	White Stockings	— M
25048	Trochee	M		25162	Whitsitts Duke 2nd	— P S
25049	Trojan	— P S		25164	Whopper	— M
25051	True Blue	— Cox		25165	Wild Chief	— L R
25052	Trueman	D		25168	Wild Rover	— M
25053	Trunnion 2nd	— M		25170	Wm. Chenault	— C
25054	Turbine	— M		25171	Wm. Henry	— M
25055	Turley 3rd	Daisy		25172	Wm. Sharon	— L R
25056	Tully	— L R		25177	Wiley 7th	— M
25057	Twain	— T		25178	Wiley Duke	— M
25058	Twilight	— M		25180	Wiley Oxford, Jr	— R R
25059	Twilight's Gwynne	— Cox		25182	Wilton Lad	— Ky I
25060	Twin Napier 1st	— Cox		25186	Winfield Lad	R R
25061	Twin Napier	— Cox		25187	Winfield's Pearl	— M
25063	Uncle Sam	— T		25189	Wiseton Lad 2nd	— M
25070	Val	— P S		25191	W. K. Rodway	— K I
25073	Valentine 2nd	— Cox		25194	Woodland Duke	— M
25075	Valiant	— R R		25195	Woodlawn Duke	— R R
25076	Valley Duke	— M		25198	Woodland Star 3rd	— M
25081	Vasco	— D		25199	Wyandotte Lad	— R R
25082	Velvet Jacket	— Cox		25202	Yara	Ky I
25083	Vendome	— D		25204	Yellow Bill	— T
25086	Vermont	— D		25205	Yellow Jacket	L R
25087	Vermout	— C		25206	Yellow Robert	— L R
25088	V. Duke	— Cox		25207	York Lady's Prince	Ky I
25091	Victor	— L R		25208	Yorkshire Duke	Ky I
25092	Victor	Cox		25209	Young Airdrie Duke	— D
25093	Victor	Ky I		25210	Young America	Ky I
25094	Victor	P S		25211	Young America	— L R
25095	Victor	— M		25213	Young America	M
25097	Victoria's Gloster	L R		25214	Young Belmont of Lakeside	— Cox
25098	Victory	— Cox		25216	Young Clarno	— M
25100	Viola Duke	D		25217	Young Clifford	— M
25101	Virgil 2nd	P S		25218	Young Comet	Ky I
25102	Viscount	— D		25219	Young Comet	Ky I
25104	Viscount of Tennessee	— T		25220	Young Crusader	Ky I
25105	Volunteer	R R		25221	Young Czar	Ky I
25106	Volunteer	— Cox		25222	Young Darlington	T
25107	Vulcan	— M		25223	Young Duke	Ky I
25108	Wakamo	M		25224	Young Duke	— P S
25109	Walker's Duke	— M		25226	Young Derby	— M
25111	Walter	— Long-Horn		25229	Young Farmer	— D
25115	Warrior	— T		25230	Young Fawsley	— Cox
25117	Warrior	— P S		25232	Young Gold Dust	Ky I
25118	Warwick	— L R		25233	Young Hannibal	Wrong
25120	Warwick's Duke	— R R		25234	Young Huber	M
25121	Waseca Lad	Ky I		25235	Young Kitt	P S

UNFASHIONABLE CROSSES IN

25236	Young Loudon Duke — R R		25334	Duke of Platte — M
25237	Young Loudon P S		25335	1st Duke of Pine Hill — D
25238	Young Minister M		25336	1st Duke of Ridgeland — L R
25239	Young Nebraska Ky I		25337	2nd Duke of Ridgeland — L R
25240	Young Monarch — M		25338	3rd Duke of Ridgeland M
25241	Young Oxford — D		25339	4th Duke of Ridgeland M
25244	Young Remus — M		25340	5th Duke of Ridgeland — L R
25246	Young Rover Ky I		25341	6th Duke of Ridgeland — L R
25248	Young Selim — Long-Horn		25344	Duke of Sharon — P S
25249	Young Tommy — T		25345	Duke of Springbrook 3rd — R R
25252	Young Windsor — Cox		25346	Duke of Springbrook 4th — R R
25253	Yuba Ky I		25347	Duke of Springbrook 5th — P S
25254	Zack — T		25348	Duke of Springbrook 6th — R R
25255	Zack — T		25349	Duke of Springbrook 7th — R R
25256	Zack Chandler L R		25350	Duke of Springbrook 8th — R R
25257	Zack Taylor T		25351	Duke of Springbrook 9th — R R
25258	Zack Taylor 2nd — R R		25352	Duke of Springbrook 10th — R R
25259	Zadig — M		25353	Duke of Springbrook 11th — R R
25260	Zadig M		25354	Duke of Springbrook 12th — P S
25261	Zadoc M		25356	Duke of Syracuse M
25263	Zeb Moore — Daisy		25358	Duke 1st of Wheatland — Ky I
25264	Zeb Ward — C		25359	Duke 2nd of Wheatland C
25267	Zero M		25360	Duke 3rd of Wheatland — R R
25268	Zip M		25361	Duke of Wilchester — R R
25269	Zora Duke — R R		25363	Dutch John — T
25271	Zouave — Cox		25366	Excelsior — Cox
25272	Addison — C		25367	Fanny's Son — R R
25275	Alexander — C		25369	Frank Clay M
25276	Alexander — P S		25370	Fred — T
25277	August Duke — M		25371	Gen. Grant — Cox
25278	Badger — D		25372	Gen. Sheridan T
25279	Baltimore Ky I		25373	Gen. Sherman T
25280	Baron Stewart M		25374	Gen. Scott — R R
25281	Baron Stowe Ky I		25375	George Thomas — M
25282	Beauty's Valentine — Cox		25377	Good Friday — M
25283	Beaver Boy M		25379	Grant — Cox
25284	Belle's Duke — L R		25380	Hannibal — D
25286	Belted Will — Cox		25382	Henry Thomas — D
25288	Benness M		25383	Henry Ward Beecher — T
25289	Bismarck — M		25386	Imperial Harrison — T
25290	Blucher — M		25388	Kansas Mauvaisterre T
25291	Bonner — D		25389	King Duke — M
25292	Brother to Young America — M		25390	King of the Dairy — Cox
25294	Capt. Jack — Ky I		25391	Lady's Duke — D
25295	Charley Russell — D		25392	3rd Linden — M
25299	Cicero 2nd Daisy		25393	Logan — C
25300	Clara's Son — C		25395	Lord Darnley — Cox
25301	Clinton — M		25396	Lord Delaware — R R
25302	Clinton Duke — R R		25398	Lord Zetland — M
25306	Crusader — M		25399	Louans Duke P S
25307	Dairy Boy R R		25400	Louan Duke 4th — R R
25308	Dan Rice Jr Ky I		25401	Loudon Boy — R R
25310	Diamond 2nd — L R		25403	Louis Philipp — D
25311	Diamond Duke — D		25404	Major Anderson — M
25313	Dr. Todd Ky I		25405	March — P S
25314	Drover — M		25406	Mark Twain — M
25316	Duke Daisy		25410	Mayflower's Duke — Cox
25318	Duke 2nd — R R		25411	Medoc — R R
25319	Duke 6th — D		25412	Monarch — D
25320	Duke of Australia — Cox		25415	Monroe Duke M
25321	Duke of Black Hawk — P S		25416	Morning Star M
25322	Duke of Bulbona M		25419	Napoleon — Cox
25323	5th Duke of Clark — R R		25422	Otaka Boy — L R
25324	2nd Duke of Erie — M		25424	Orleans — Cox
25325	2nd Duke of Etna — R R		25426	Oxford Airdrie M
25326	20th Duke of Goodness — R R		25428	Oxford of Abingdon 2nd — Daisy
25327	Duke of Goodness of Pomona — R R		25430	Phyllis Duke of Goodness — R R
25331	Duke of Orleans M		25432	Prince — T
25332	Duke of Oxford P S		25434	Red Duke M
25333	Duke of Oxford — P S		25435	Red George — T

25436	Red Prince	— Cox	25538	Alvaro	— R R
25439	Reformer	R R	25541	Andrew Johnson	— M
25440	Rip Van Winkle	— P S	25542	Andy Johnson	— P S
25441	Rob Roy	— Woods	25547	Architect	— P S
25442	Rosebrook 3rd of Mansfield	— Cox	25548	Argyle	L R
25443	Rosebrook 4th of Mansfield	— Cox	25549	Arm Chair	L R
25444	Rowdy	R R	25553	Ascot Airdrie	— P S
25445	Royal Cardiff	— P S	25554	Ascot Duke	— P S
25447	Sartoris	— M	25555	Aster	— Cox
25450	Shakespeare	D	25557	Atholl Duke	— R R
25451	Shylock	— Cox	25558	Avalanche	D
25453	Sir William	D	25559	August	Ky I
25455	Snowball 2nd	— Cox	25560	Aurum Duke	— M
25456	Snowball	Ky I	25561	Australias Duke	— Cox
25457	Solana	— M	25562	Australian Tom	— D
25458	Soldier Boy	P S	25563	Autocrat	— M
25459	Son of 11th Bell Duchess	— R R	25565	Aztec	R R
25460	Star	P S	25566	Baileys Duke	— R R
25461	Star Duke	— Ky I	25567	Balco	— Ky I
25462	Statesman 1st	— M	25568	Balco Starlight	Ky I
25463	Stephen A. Douglass	— M	25569	Baldwin	— Cox
25464	Sultan	— D	25571	Bandoola	— Cox
25466	Tom Hines	— M	25572	Banker	P S
25467	Tornado 2nd	M	25573	Barmpton Duke	— R R
25468	Vanguard	— Cox	25574	Barney	— M
25469	Victor	— Cox	25575	Barnum	M
25472	Walter Scott	— M	25576	Barnum 4th	— M
25474	Western Gentleman	P S	25578	Baron	— R R
25478	Wyoming Lad 2nd	P S	25582	Baron Airdrie 2nd	— P S
25479	Young Boone	R R	25586	Baron Bates 2nd	— M
25480	Young Maguet	— Cox	25588	Baron Bates of Plumwood	— R R
25481	Aaron 2nd	Woods	25590	Baron Booth	— M
25482	Aaron Burr	— M	25591	Baron Booth 2nd	— R R
25483	Abe	— D	25592	Baron Booth of Peoria	— M
25484	Abilene	L R	25593	Baron Booth of Woodlawn	— R R
25485	Abul-Hacen	R R	25595	Baron Clark	— R R
25487	Actor	— Cox	25596	Baron Coxcomb	L R
25488	Adam	R R	25599	Baron Duke	— R R
25489	Adelaid's Duke	— P S	25602	Baron Gwynne	— Cox
25491	Adjutant	— R R	25604	Baron Gwynne 5th	— P S
25492	Admiral	— Cox	25613	Baron Lad	— M
25494	Admiral 3rd	Cox	25614	Baron Leathana	Ky I
25495	Admiral 4th	Ky I	25615	Baron Lewis	— D
25497	Afton	— M	25616	Baron Louan	— R R
25498	Al	— P S	25618	Baron Louan 3rd	— R R
25499	Airdrie	— P S	25619	Baron Louan 4th	— R R
25502	Airdrie Jr	— M	25620	Baron Louanjo 2nd	— D
25505	5th Airdrie Duke of Scioto	— D	25622	Baron Mazurka of Kengrove	— R R
25506	6th Airdrie Duke of Scioto	— R R	25623	Baron New Castle 2nd	— Cox
25507	7th Airdrie Duke of Scioto	— R R	25625	Baron of Lancaster	— R R
25508	8th Airdrie Duke of Scioto	D	25627	Baron 2nd of Maple Grove	— M
25509	9th Airdrie Duke of Scioto	— M	25629	Baron of Osage	L R
25510	10th Airdrie Duke of Scioto	D	25630	Baron of Oxford	L R
25511	Airdrie Goodness	— R R	25631	3rd Baron of Riverside	— Cox
25513	Airdrie Lad	— T	25633	2nd Baron of Vermillion	— P S
25516	Albert	L R	25645	Baron Taylor	P S
25517	Albert	M	25651	Baron Wynnstay 3rd	C
25518	Albert	— L R	25653	Baxter	— Cox
25519	Albert	— Cox	25654	Beau of Lafayette	M
25520	Albert Lea	M	25655	Beauty	M
25521	Alameda	L R	25656	Beauty's Duke	D
25523	Alex, Jr	— Cox	25659	Bedford	— M
25526	Alexander	M	25661	Beecher	— T
25528	Alexis	T	25662	Beecher	— M
25529	Alexis	— M	25663	Beecher	P S
25530	Al Princeton	— C	25664	Beecher	— T
25531	Alfonso	— T	25665	Beecher	P S
25532	Alfred	P S	25666	Beecher	— D
25533	Alice Maud's Cherub	— R R	25668	Bell Duke	— P S
25534	Allen	Ky I	25669	Bell Duke	— R R

25670	Bell Duke	— M	25765	Bourbon Duke 2nd	— L R
25671	Bell Duke I	— R R	25766	Bourbon Star	— L R
25673	Bell Duke of Maplewood	— M	25767	Boxer	Ky I
25675	Bell's Loudon Duke	— R R	25768	Boxer 2nd	Daisy
25677	Bellville Duke — Long-Horn		25769	Brandywine	P S
25678	Bellville Lee	— P S	25770	Brant Chief	— Cox
25679	Bellville Stark	— Ky I	25771	Breastplate 3rd	M
25680	Bellville Waldburg	— Ky I	25775	Bride Duke	— R R
25681	Belshazzar	P S	25778	Bright Duke	P S
25682	Belshazzar	— Cox	25783	Brilliant	— M
25683	Belmont	— R R	25784	Briscoe	P S
25684	Belvedere	— P S	25785	Bristow	P S
25685	Belvedere	— M	25786	Bristow	Ky I
25688	Ben Bristo	— D	25790	Briton	— R R
25689	Ben Butler	— M	25792	Brose Carroll	— M
25692	Benefactor	— C	25793	Bruce	— M
25693	Ben Franklin	— R R	25794	Bruce	— R R
25698	Bertha's Boy	— M	25796	Brutus	M
25699	Beverly	Daisy	25797	Brutus	M
25700	Bifrou's 3rd	— M	25799	Brutus	P S
25701	Billy	L R	25800	Buck	— T
25704	Billy	Ky I	25801	Buckalew 2nd	Ky I
25705	Billy Boy	— Cox	25802	Buckeye 2nd	Cox
25706	Billy Boy	— M	25803	Buckeye Chief	Ky I
25707	Billy Bright	P S	25804	Buckeye Lad	— L R
25708	Billy Hise — Long-Horn		25805	Buckingham	P S
25709	Bill King	— Cox	25806	Bullion	— P S
25710	Bill Oliver	— M	25808	Burdick's Breastplate	— P S
25711	Billy Pickrell	M	25809	Burme's Duke	— M
25713	Bismarck	T	25811	Butman	— R R
25714	Bismarck — Long-Horn		25812	Buster	M
25715	Bismarck	— R R	25813	Bute	L R
25716	Bismarck	— Cox	25814	Butler	D
25717	Blackhawk Bates	— R R	25817	Buttercup 2nd	— Cox
25718	Blain	— D	25818	Buttercup's Son	Daisy
25719	Blair	— Cox	25819	Butterfly Duke	Ky I
25720	Bloomfield Airdrie 2nd	— R R	25820	Butterfly's Duke	— R R
25721	Blossom's Airdrie	— R R	25821	Byram's Goodness	— M
25722	Blucher	P S	25822	Byron	— Ky I
25723	Blucher 2nd	— M	25826	Cadwell Duke	M
25725	Blue River Duke	L R	25827	Cæsar	M
25726	Blue River Prince	— C	25829	Cairn Gorm	— P S
25727	Blunder	Ky I	25831	Calumet Lad	— M
25728	Bluster	— R R	25834	Cannan Boy	P S
25729	Bob Ayers	— P S	25835	Canada Duke 2nd	— C
25730	Bobby Burns	— L R	25837	Canton	— M
25731	Bobby Burns	— P S	25838	Captain	— M
25732	Bobby Burns 2nd	M	25839	Captain	— D
25734	Bob Ingersoll	— M	25840	Captain	— M
25735	Bob Lee	M	25841	Capt. Bates	— Ky I
25736	Bob Phillips — Long-Horn		25842	Capt. Bates 2nd	— Ky I
25738	Bolivar	— P S	25844	Capt. Jack	— Woods
25742	Bolton	R R	25845	Capt. Jack	— R R
25743	Bona Lad	— C	25848	Capt. Kidd	D
25744	Bonaparte	— M	25849	Capt. Lail	T
25745	Boniface	— C	25850	Capt. Maynard	— D
25746	Bonnie Lad	— D	25851	2nd Capt. Maynard	— D
25747	Boojum	L R	25852	Capt. Seacord	M
25750	Bosco 2nd	T	25853	Capt. Shaftoe	— P S
25751	Bosco 3rd	T	25854	Capt. Sherron	— Ky I
25752	Bosco 4th	T	25855	Capt. Wm. Chambers	L R
25753	Bosco 5th	T	25857	Cardinal	Ky I
25754	Bosco 6th	T	25860	Carlton Lad 2nd	M
25755	Boscobel	T	25861	Carnival 3rd	— T
25757	Boss Twede	— D	25862	Carpenter	— M
25760	Boston Duke 7th	— T	25865	Cato	— M
25761	Botheration	— R R	25867	Caucassian	— L R
25762	Boquet Louanjo	Ky I	25868	Cavalier	— R R
25763	Bourbon	M	25870	Centennial	M
25764	Bourbon	— Ky I	25871	Centennial	M

SHORT-HORN CATTLE PEDIGREES. 119

No.	Name	Herd
25872	Centennial	P S
25873	Centennial	Ky I
25874	Centennial	Ky I
25875	Centennial	— Cox
25876	Centennial	R R
25877	Centennial	— M
25878	Centennial	— Cox
25880	Centennial	— L R
25881	Centennial	— P S
25882	Centennial	C
25883	Centennial	— Cox
25884	Centennial	— R R
25885	Centennial	— P S
25887	Centennial	M
25888	Centennial 2nd	— M
25889	Centennial 3rd	M
25890	Centennial 4th	Ky I
25891	Centennial 5th	M
25892	Centennial 6th	Ky I
25894	Centennial 8th	M
25895	Centennial 9th	— P S
25896	Centennial 10th	— P S
25897	Centennial Duke	L R
25898	Centennial Duke	— Long-Horn
25899	Centennial Duke	— M
25900	Centennial Duke	M
25901	Centennial Hero	— Cox
25902	Centennial Prince	— M
25903	Centennial Prince	L R
25906	Champion	— L R
25907	Champion	— L R
25908	Champion	M
25910	Champion	M
25911	Champion	L R
25912	Champion Duke	L R
25917	Charles	L R
25918	Charles	P S
25920	Charles 2nd	M
25921	Charles 3rd	M
25922	Charles Clyde	— M
25923	Charles Henry	M
25924	Charles Napier	— M
25925	Charley	— Cox
25926	Charley Woods	— L R
25927	Charlie	— Long-Horn
25928	Charlie	— Cox
25929	Charlotte's Duke	— R R
25930	Chatham's Duke	— M
25931	Chatham's Earl	— M
25932	Chautauqua Prince	— Cox
25935	Chicago Duke	— Cox
25936	Chief	— Cox
25937	Chief Justice	— M
25938	Chieftain	— D
25941	Chilco	T
25944	Cicero	— M
25945	Cincinnati	— M
25947	Clara's Duke	Ky I
25948	Clarion	— Cox
25950	Clement	D
25951	Clifton 4th	— T
25953	Clinton Duke	— D
25956	Coburne	L R
25957	Colfax	— M
25959	Colfax 2nd	Ky I
25960	Coloma Duke	T
25962	Col. Duncan	— R R
25963	Col. Duncan	— R R
25965	Col. Hall	— Ky I
25966	Col. Hays	— R R
25969	Col. John	P S
25970	Col. Jones	P S
25971	Col. Kountz	— Cox
25972	Col. Redman	R R
25973	Col. Ringo	— M
25975	Col. Thorndale	— Cox
25976	Colossus	— M
25978	Columbus Duke	— D
25979	Comet	P S
25980	Comet	— P S
25981	Comet	— D
25982	Comet	M
25983	Comet	M
25984	Comet 4th	— M
25985	Comet Halley	— R R
25986	Commodore	— Daisy
25987	Commodore	— M
25988	Commodore	— Cox
25989	Commodore	— P S
25990	Commissary	— M
25991	Conaly Pitkin	— L R
25992	Conductor	— Daisy
25994	Conqueror 3rd	R R
25995	Conqueror 4th	R R
25997	Conrad	Ky I
26001	Cooper	— Cox
26003	Coronet	— M
26004	Corporal 2nd	— M
26005	Corporal 3rd	M
26007	Cottonwood Louan 1st	M
26009	Count	— M
26011	Count Bismarck	Ky I
26012	Count Brant	— Cox
26014	Counterpart 3rd	— M
26015	Count Fosco	Ky I
26017	Count Mapleton	— C
26019	5th Count of Oneida	— R R
26020	Count of Woodside	Cox
26021	Count Rumford	L R
26025	Crown Prince	— R R
26026	Crown Prince	— Cox
26027	Crown Prince 3rd	— C
26028	Crown Prince 5th	M
26030	Crusoe	— R R
26033	Custer	M
26034	Cypria's Airdrie	T
26035	Cypress Duke	Ky I
26036	Cypress Wiley	Daisy
26037	Cyrus	T
26038	Cyrus	P S
26039	Cyrus Duke	C
26041	Daisy Bull 3rd	— M
26046	Dalton Duke	— Cox
26047	Dan	Cox
26048	Dan Rice 2nd	P S
26049	Dandy Jim	— Cox
26051	Darby	P S
26052	Darlington	L R
26054	Dash	— M
26055	Dauntless	— L R
26056	David Crockett	T
26057	David McNeil	Ky I
26058	Daylight	— M
26059	Decatur	— M
26060	Dekotah	— M
26061	Democrat	M
26062	Deronda	— Daisy
26063	Detective	— Daisy
26064	Dewdrop's Oxford	— Cox
26065	Dewitt Clinton	— T

26066	Dexter.................— Cox	26154	Duke Merrywether............:— C
26067	Dexter.................P S	26155	Duke of Airdrie.............— M
26068	Diamond................P S	26157	Duke of Afton..............— Ky I
26070	Diamond................—L R	26158	Duke of Allen..............C
26071	Diamond Duke...........— C	26161	4th Duke of Armada.........— Cox
26072	Diamond Duke...........P S	26162	6th Duke of Armada.........— Cox
26073	Diaz...................— C	26163	Duke of Arthur 3rd..........— M
26074	Dick...................Ky I	26167	Duke of Berea..............P S
26075	Dick...................— M	26168	Duke of Bethel.............P S
26078	Dick Johnson............— C	26169	Duke of Blanchard 4th......— M
26079	Dick Long 2nd...........— D	26170	7th Duke of Bluffdale.......— C
26080	Dick Yates..............— T	26171	Duke of Boston.............— Cox
26082	Dictator 2nd............—P S	26172	1st Duke of Boston..........— Ky I
26083	Dion....................— Cox	26173	Duke of Bourbon............—R R
26084	Dixie...................M	26174	Duke of Bradford...........Wrong
26085	Dixon...................L R	26176	1st Duke of Brookside.......— D
26087	Dom....................— M	26177	Duke of Butler..............M
26088	Dom Pedro..............M	26178	1st Duke of Cambridge......— Cox
26089	Dom Pedro..............T	26180	Duke of Carroll.............L R
26090	Dom Pedro..............T	26181	Duke of Cass..............P S
26091	Dom Pedro..............— P S	26182	Duke of Centerville..........T
26092	Dom Pedro..............— T	26184	1st Duke of Charter Oak....—M
26093	Dom Pedro..............L R	26185	2nd Duke of Charter Oak...— M
26094	Dom Pedro..............— L R	26187	Duke of Chester............— L R
26095	Dom Pedro..............— Cox	26190	Duke of Cloverdale..........P S
26097	Dom Pedro..............L R	26192	Duke of Concord............P S
26098	Dom Pedro..............— M	26193	Duke of Cornwall............D
26099	Dom Pedro..............— M	26194	Duke of Dallas..............R R
26100	Dom Pedro..............L R	26195	Duke of Decatur............R R
26101	Dom Pedro..............— M	26196	Duke of Delaware...........— L R
26103	Dom Pedro..............Daisy	26198	Duke of Dover..............— Cox
26104	Dom Pedro..............R R	26199	3rd Duke of Downs.........— R R
26105	Dom Pedro..............— Cox	26200	Duke of Dryden.............— Cox
26106	Dom Pedro..............—L R	26204	2nd Duke of Essex..........— Ky I
26107	Don Alfonso.............R R	26205	3rd Duke of Evergreenhill...— L R
26108	Don Cameron............M	26206	3rd Duke of Fairfield........— M
26109	Don Carlos..............M	26207	Duke of Fairplains..........L R
26110	Don Chatham............M	26208	2nd Duke of Fairplains......L R
26112	Don Scott...............— R R	26209	3rd Duke of Fairview........— M
26113	Donavan's Duke.........P S	26210	4th Duke of Fairview........— M
26114	Double Airdrie...........— L R	26211	5th Duke of Fairview........M
26115	Double Airdrie...........— L R	26212	2nd Duke of Fennimore.....— C
26118	Double Star..............M	26213	3rd Duke of Five-twenty....— Cox
26120	Downhorn's Duke........Daisy	26215	Duke of Floyd..............M
26121	Drummer Boy...........— R R	26216	Duke of Floyd..............Ky I
26122	Daune's Duke 9th........— L R	26217	3rd Duke of Fountain.......— M
26125	Duchess Duke of Tecumseh....R R	26218	Duke of French Grove.......Ky I
26127	Duke....................L R	26219	Duke of Fulton.............— T
26128	Duke....................— L R	26220	4th Duke of Gabilan.........— R R
26129	Duke 2nd................— L R	26224	8th Duke of Gabilan.........Ky I
26130	Duke 3rd................P S	26225	9th Duke of Gabilan.........Ky I
26131	Duke 3rd................— M	26226	10th Duke of Gabilan........— R R
26132	Duke 5th................M	26227	Duke of Garden City........— M
26133	Duke 7th................Ky I	26232	Duke of Glencoe............— P S
26134	Duke 8th................T	26233	Duke of Gloster.............— D
26135	7th Duke................Ky I	26234	Duke of Goodness 3rd.......— L R
26136	Duke 13th...............— R R	26236	20th Duke of Goodness.....— Wrong
26137	Duke Albert..............— R R	26238	Duke of Goshen............— L R
26138	Duke Alexis..............M	26239	Duke of Grand Prairie.......T
26139	Duke Barmpton..........— C	26240	Duke of Greenside..........— Cox
26140	Duke Bright Eyes.........— M	26241	Duke of Greenvalley........— Cox
26143	Due DeSavoie............Ky I	26242	2nd Duke of Greenvalley....— Cox
26145	Durand.................T	26244	1st Duke of Greenwood.....— R R
26147	Duke Franklin............—C	26245	Duke of Groton 2nd.........— Cox
26148	Duke Geoffrey...........— Daisy	26246	Duke of Hamilton..........Ky I
26149	Duke Goodness..........— R R	26247	3rd Duke of Hamilton.......Cox
26150	Duke Goodness 2nd......R R	26248	3rd Duke of Hancock.......— T
26151	Duke Goodness 4th.......— T	26249	4th Duke of Harlem........— M
26152	16th Duke's Grand Son...Daisy	26250	Duke of Hastings...........—P S
26153	Duke John...............M	26251	Duke of Hawkeye..........Ky I

26252	Duke of Hawley — Cox	26345	Duke of Orange M
26254	2nd Duke of Hazelhurst Daisy	26346	Duke of Orleans M
26255	6th Duke of Hazelwood C	26353	Duke of Peru — M
26258	Duke of Hickory Grove — M	26354	Duke of Pettis — M
26259	7th Duke of Highland — Cox	26355	Duke of Pine Hill D
26260	8th Duke of Highland — Cox	26356	Duke 2nd of Pine Hill — Wrong
26261	Duke of Hoosier Ky I	26357	Duke 3rd of Pine Hill — D
26262	Duke of Howard — P S	26358	1st Duke of Pleasant Valley — Cox
26263	Duke of Huntington — Cox	26359	1st Duke of Plum Creek — P S
26264	2nd Duke of Huron Ky I	26361	Duke of Pollywogg — R R
26265	Duke of Jackson — M	26362	1st Duke of Post Road — M
26266	2nd Duke of Jasper P S	26365	1st Duke of Raisin — M
26267	3rd Duke of Jasper P S	26367	2nd Duke of Richland — D
26268	4th Duke of Jasper P S	26368	Duke of Richmond — D
26269	Duke of Johnson — M	26370	Duke of Rich Valley — R R
26270	Duke of Jonesville Ky I	26371	Duke of Rick Valley Ky I
26272	6th Duke of Jonesville — R R	26372	Duke of Riverside Ky I
26277	1st Duke of Lagrange Ky I	26373	2nd Duke of Rockland M
26280	Duke of Leicester — M	26375	Duke of Rose Hill — L R
26281	2nd Duke of Lenox — M	26377	Duke of Salinas — P S
26282	3rd Duke of Lenox P S	26378	Duke of San Jose T
26283	Duke of Lewisburg P S	26379	Duke of Schuyler — P S
26284	Duke of Liberty — Long-Horn	26380	Duke of Scotland P S
26285	Duke of Lincoln — M	26381	Duke of Sharon — M
26286	Duke of Lincoln — R R	26382	5th Duke of Shannon — P S
26287	Duke of Livingston M	26383	Duke of Shelbina P S
26288	3rd Duke of Loamland — Daisy	26384	Duke of Shelby Woods
26289	4th Duke of Loamland — R R	26385	2nd Duke of Shiawasse Ky I
26290	9th Duke of Locust Lawn M	26386	Duke of Silas — C
26291	10th Duke of Locust Lawn — Ky I	26387	2nd Duke of Skaneateles — Cox
26292	Duke of Lombard — C	26388	Duke of Smithville — M
26293	2nd Duke of Loudon — R R	26391	Duke of Stark R R
26294	2nd Duke of Louisa — P S	26392	1st Duke of Sunbury D
26295	1st Duke of Macomb L R	26393	Duke of Sylvester — R R
26296	2nd Duke of Macomb L R	26394	Duke of Tallmadge — Cox
26297	3rd Duke of Macomb L R	26395	22nd Duke of Tecumseh — T
26298	Duke of Madison — M	26396	23rd Duke of Tecumseh D
26300	Duke of Mahoning L R	26397	24th Duke of Tecumseh Ky I
26303	Duke of Maplewood — Woods	26398	1st Duke of Tekamah R R
26305	2nd Duke of Maplewood — M	26400	Duke of The Manor — Daisy
26306	3rd Duke of Maplewood M	26402	16th Duke of the Pines C
26307	Duke of Marion 3rd M	26403	17th Duke of the Pines — R R
26308	4th Duke of Marion M	26404	18th Duke of the Pines — R R
26309	Duke of Marshall Daisy	26405	Duke of the Tree M
26310	Duke of Maryland M	26407	Duke of Tinkins C
26312	Duke of Mayslick — P S	26409	3rd Duke of Valley Ridge L R
26314	Duke of Meadow Valley D	26410	Duke of Vergennes Ky I
26315	Duke of Mecca 2nd — D	26411	Duke of Walnut Grove Ky I
26316	2nd Duke of Melleray — M	26413	Duke of Waterford — Cox
26317	Duke of Miami M	26414	Duke of Wellington Ky I
26318	2nd Duke of Miami T	26417	1st Duke of Wheatfield Ky I
26320	Duke of Monmouth D	26418	2nd Duke of Wheatfield Ky I
26321	Duke of Monroe Ky I	26419	3rd Duke of Wheatfield Ky I
26322	Duke of Monroe Ky I	26420	Duke 4th of Wheatland — Ky I
26323	Duke of Monterey — P S	26421	Duke 5th of Wheatland — R R
26324	8th Duke of Monterey — P S	26422	3rd Duke of Wicken — M
26326	Duke of Morgan P S	26423	2nd Duke of Wild Eyes — C
26327	Duke of Morgan — Daisy	26424	2nd Duke of Wildwood — M
26328	2nd Duke of Moscow — L R	26425	Duke of Williams — P S
26329	Duke of Moss Rose — M	26426	3rd Duke of Windingvale — R R
26332	Duke of New Castle — M	26427	Duke of Winehill — M
26333	Duke of New Castle P S	26429	3rd Duke of Woodson Ky I
26334	Duke of New Castle P S	26431	Duke of Wyaconda — M
26335	4th Duke of New London M	26432	2nd Duke of Wyaconda — P S
26336	1st Duke of Noble Glen M	26433	Duke of York — R R
26338	1st Duke of Oakland C	26435	Duke Sowdowsky M
26339	2nd Duke of Oakland — R R	26436	Duke Taylor — R R
26340	Duke of Old Town — L R	26439	Dunbar — D
26342	Duke of Oneida — Long-Horn	26440	Duncan's Airdrie — R R
26344	6th Duke of Oran M	26442	Dunglen Prince 2nd — Daisy

26443	Duplain Lad — Ky I	26570	Florence Duke 2nd — C
26444	Dwight Coburn — D	26571	Florentias Duke — C
26445	Earl P S	26573	Flotilla's Don — M
26464	Earl of Gainsborough P S	26574	Flying Cloud 2nd — D
26465	Earl of Garden City — Cox	26575	Ford Airdrie M
26469	4th Earl of Gloster — Cox	26577	Forester 2nd — P S
26471	13th Earl of Greenbush — Cox	26580	Forrest Hill 2nd — C
26473	Earl of Hammond L R	26582	Fortune — Cox
26477	2nd Earl of Kalamazoo Cox	26583	Foulks — M
26479	Earl of Manchester — Ky I	26585	Fourth of July — Daisy
26482	1st Earl of Martin Cox	26588	Frank Forest — Cox
26484	Earl of Oakdale — R R	26589	Frank Moulton — R R
26485	2nd Earl of Oxford — Cox	26591	Frank Wilson — T
26487	11th Earl of Oxford P S	26593	Franklin Duke 9th Ky I
26488	Earl of Pleasant Hill M	26594	Fred M
26489	Earl of Pleasant Valley P S	26595	Fred Grant Cox
26492	3rd Earl of Raisin — M	26596	Fred Linn M
26493	4th Earl of Raisin — R R	26597	Fred Napier Ky I
26495	Earl of Riverside — P S	26598	Fred Star — Cox
26498	Earl of Sharon — C	26600	Frederick — R R
26500	Earl of Wilmount — C	26601	Frederick — P S
26502	Easton Lad — C	26603	French Lad Ky I
26503	Easton Lad 2nd — C	26604	Frendship — D
26504	Ebon L R	26605	Frontier Lad Ky I
26505	Eclipse — M	26606	Frontier Lad 2nd — Ky I
26506	Eclipse — R R	26607	Front Rank P S
26508	Eclipse — M	26608	Fulton — M
26510	Ed Bower — M	26610	Galesburg — P S
26511	Edison P S	26611	Gallant Duke M
26512	Eighteen Seventy-Six — Daisy	26612	Gallant Knight — R R
26514	Elias — Cox	26613	Garland's Duke — M
26517	Ella Clyde's Son M	26617	General P S
26518	Ella's Duke — L R	26618	General — M
26519	Ella's Duke — Ky I	26619	Gen. Belknap Cox
26520	Ella's Duke — M	26621	Gen. Blucher — P S
26521	Ellwood — T	26622	Gen. Brock — M
26523	Elmwood Lad — M	26622½	Gen. Brock — D
26524	Emerald Ky I	26623	Gen. Butler — Cox
26525	Emigrant Ky I	26624	Gen. Carr — Wrong
26530	Emperor 5th — P S	26626	Gen. Custer — L R
26531	Equinox R R	26627	Gen. Custer — L R
26533	Eucalyptus — T	26628	Gen. Custer P S
26534	Eureka — P S	26629	Gen. Custer M
26535	Europa — Ky I	26630	Gen. Custer — R R
26536	Excelsior T	26631	Gen. Custer L R
26537	Exciption — P S	26633	Gen. Crook — R R
26538	Exchequer — M	26635	Gen. Dix — T
26539	Expectation M	26636	Gen. Garfield Cox
26540	Fabius Cox	26637	Gen. Grant — M
26541	Fairfax — M	26638	Gen. Grant Ky I
26542	Fairview — M	26639	Gen. Grant — L R
26545	Fairy Lad — P S	26640	Gen. Hayes — T
26550	Fancy M	26641	Gen. Hayes — R R
26551	Fannie's Duke Ky I	26642	Gen. Hayes — M
26553	Fashion's Royalist — Cox	26643	Gen. Hayes D
26555	Favorite — L R	26644	Gen. Hayes Ky I
26556	Favorite Ky I	26645	Gen. Houston T
26557	Favorite — C	26646	Gen. Knox M
26558	Favorite — Cox	26647	Gen. Logan — Cox
26559	Favorite — R R	26648	Gen. McClellan — Cox
26560	Favorite Daisy	26649	Gen. McPherson — T
26561	Favorite 3rd — M	26650	Gen. Morgan 2nd — L R
26562	Favorite Duke — R R	26651	Gen. Palmer M
26563	Feland — P S	26653	Gen. Scott — R R
26564	Fernando — R R	26655	Gen. Sheridan — D
26565	Fidus 4th D	26655	Gen. Sheridan — P S
26566	Field Marshall — Cox	26657	Gen. Sherman — P S
26567	Financier 2nd — L R	26658	Gen. Sherman — D
26568	Fitchburg Lad P S	26659	Gen. Simpkins — M
26569	Fletcher — T	26660	Gen. Stark — D

SHORT-HORN CATTLE PEDIGREES. 123

No.	Name	Code
26662	Gen. Thornton	— M
26663	Gen. Tracy	— Ky I
26664	Gen. Washington	M
26665	Gen. Washington	— Ky I
26666	Genesee	— M
26667	Geneva	— M
26668	Geneva Duke	— R R
26670	Geneva Earl	M
26673	Geneva's Oxford	Daisy
26674	George	— M
26676	George Cyrus	— M
26677	George Jones	P S
26679	George Washington 2nd	— R R
26683	2nd Glen Airdrie Duke	L R
26684	Glen Buchan	— R R
26685	Glen Cairn	— D
26686	Glencoe	M
26687	5th Glen Count	M
26688	3rd Glen Dandy	— T
26690	Glen Duke 9th	— P S
26691	3rd Glen Hannibal	— R R
26694	Gloster Duke	— L R
26695	Gloster Duke	— Cox
26696	Gloster of Fairplains	— M
26697	Gloster of Oakland	L R
26699	Goatee	M
26700	Golddrop	M
26701	Gold Duke 2nd	— R R
26702	Golden Crown 2nd	— R R
26703	Golden Duke	— M
26705	Goldfinder	M
26706	Goldfinder	Ky I
26707	Goldfinder 2nd	Ky I
26708	Goldfinder 3rd	— Ky I
26709	Goldfinder 4th	— Ky I
26710	Golding	P S
26711	4th Gold of Hendon	— M
26712	Goodness Duke	— R R
26713	Goodness Duke	— R R
26714	Goodness Duke	R R
26715	Cordo	R R
26716	Governor	— Cox
26717	Governor	Woods
26720	Gov. Hayes	— P S
26721	Gov. Hayes	L R
26722	Gov. Hayes	— T
26723	Gov. Hayes	— P S
26724	Gov. Hayes	T
26725	Gov. Hayes	— P S
26726	Gov. Helm 2nd	— T
26727	Gov. Irwin	— D
26728	Gov. Kirkwood	P S
26729	Gov. Ludington	— M
26730	Gov. Palmer	T
26731	Gov. Tilden	M
26732	Gov. Tilden	— P S
26733	Gov. Tilden	Cox
26734	Grand Airdrie of Valley Farm	Ky I
26735	Grand Alexis	L R
26736	Grand Chunk	— R R
26740	Grand Duke 3rd of Elm Grove	— R R
26741	Grand Duke of Goodness	— M
26744	2nd Grandson of Minister	— D
26745	Grandson of Starlight	— L R
26747	Granger	— R R
26748	Granger	P S
26749	Granger	— Cox
26750	Granger	— R R
26752	Grant	— P S
26753	Grant	— L R
26757	Green Mountain Prince 2nd	— C
26758	Greenwich Duke	M
26759	Greenwood Favorite	— R R
26760	Greenwood Favorite 2nd	— R R
26761	Greenwood Favorite 3rd	— R R
26762	5th Greenwood Lad	— R R
26763	6th Greenwood Lad	— R R
26764	7th Greenwood Lad	— R R
26765	8th Greenwood Lad	— R R
26766	9th Greenwood Lad	— R R
26767	Guardsman	— Cox
26770	Gwynne-Gwynne	— Cox
26771	Hamilton	— M
26772	Hamlet	— R R
26774	Hampton	M
26775	Hankins Luodon Duke 1st	— R R
26776	Hanley	— C
26777	Hannibal	— M
26778	Hannibal	— C
26780	Happy Jack	— T
26782	Harrison Taylor, Jr	— M
26783	Harry O.	— M
26784	Harry of the West	P S
26785	Harry Peyton	— M
26788	Harvey	Ky I
26789	Harvey Shields	— R R
26791	Hayes	L R
26792	Hayes	— T
26793	Hayes	— P S
26794	Hector	— M
26796	Hector	— P S
26797	Hector	— M
26798	Hector 2nd	— M
26802	Helmer	Ky I
26805	Hendon Duke	— M
26806	Hendricks	— M
26807	Hendricks	Ky I
26808	Hendricks	P S
26809	Henry D.	— C
26810	Henry Glazier	M
26811	Henry Porter	— P S
26812	Henry Wilson	— R R
26815	Hero	Ky I
26817	Hero of McDonough	— T
26821	Highland Chief	L R
26822	Highland Chief	P S
26824	Highland Chief 2nd	T
26825	Highland Duke	— M
26826	Highlander	— D
26827	Highland Joe	L R
26831	Hillside Lad	— P S
26832	Hoffman	L R
26833	Honest Ben	Daisy
26834	Honest John	P S
26835	Hoosier Boy	L R
26836	Horace Greeley	T
26839	Hubback	— R R
26840	Hudson	L R
26841	Humbo	Ky I
26842	H. W. Beecher	L R
26845	Idris	— P S
26846	Ike Lee	— M
26850	Imperial Grey	— Long-Horn
26854	Independence	— R R
26855	Independence	Ky I
26856	Independence	— Cox
26858	Indian Boy	— C
26859	Indian Prince	— C
26860	Infant	— Ky I
26861	Ingobard	M

124 UNFASHIONABLE CROSSES IN

No.	Name	Code
26862	Ingomar	— Long-Horn
26864	Invincible Monarch	— R R
26865	Iowa Ruck	— Ky I
26866	Iowa Chief	M
26868	Iron Duke 4th	L R
26869	Isham	— Ky I
26870	Jack Horner 2nd	P S
26871	Jaco	P S
26872	Jackson	— R R
26873	Jackson	P S
26874	Jackson	M
26875	Jackson	M
26876	Jack Tar 4th	— M
26877	Jack Tar 5th	— M
26878	Jack Tar 6th	— M
26879	Jack Tar 7th	— R R
26880	Jack Tar 8th	— M
26881	Jake	— R R
26882	Jake Foster	L R
26883	James Ransdel	D
26884	Janus 12th	— C
26888	Janus 16th	— C
26889	Janus 17th	— C
26891	Jeff	— Ky I
26892	Jeff Davis	— L R
26893	Jeff Davis 2nd	— T
26894	Jennie 4th's Son	— R R
26895	Jerico	P S
26896	Jerry	Ky I
26899	Jim Crane	P S
26900	Jim Fisk	L R
26901	Jim Hughs	Ky I
26902	Jimmie Boy	D
26904	Joaquin	— D
26905	Joe	— R R
26906	Joe Atholl	— R R
26907	Joe Bell 2nd	— R R
26908	Joe Daviess	M
26909	Joe Duncan	— M
26911	Joe Hooker	D
26912	Joe Johnson 2nd	T
29914	John Fry	P S
26915	John Hancock	P S
26916	John Harris	P S
26917	Joe Hooker	T
26918	John Martin 2nd	— Ky I
26919	Johnny May	— R R
26920	Johnny May 2nd	— R R
26921	John Morrissey	Ky I
26923	John Paragon	— R R
26925	John Robinson	— M
26926	John Robinson	Daisy
26928	Jolly	— Cox
26929	Jolly Duke	Ky I
26930	Josephine's Duke	— C
26932	Josh	— M
26934	Judge Lowe	— M
26935	Judge Van Sicklen	P S
26938	Jupiter	— R R
26939	Jupiter	— T
26940	Jupiter	D
26942	Jupiter 2nd	— Cox
26943	Jupiter Clyde	M
26944	Kankakee Prince	— C
26945	Kansas Boy	— P S
26946	Kansas Chief	— M
26947	Kansas Ranger	Ky I
26948	Keno	P S
26951	Kentucky Belle Duke	M
26952	Kentucky Duke	M
26953	Kaintone	— Cox
26955	Killington	M
26956	King	— M
26959	King David	M
26960	King Derby 3rd	— M
26962	King George	L R
26963	King James	— L R
26964	King Lewis	L R
26966	King of Liberty	— Cox
26968	King of the Meadows	L R
26970	King of the West	Ky I
26972	Kingsley	— M
26973	Kings Loudon Duke 4th	— R R
26974	Kings Loudon Duke 5th	— R R
26975	Kingston	— R R
26978	King William	Ky I
26985	Kirk White	L R
26993	Knight of Lingwick	L R
26994	Knight of Maple Hill	— R R
26995	Knight of Marion	— M
26997	Knight of the Ridge	— M
26998	Kokosing	— M
26999	Kokosing Duke	— T
27001	Laclede	C
27002	Lad of the Hills	— P S
27003	Lady Bride's Breastplate	— R R
27004	Lady Byron's Duke	— R R
27005	Lady's Sheriff	— P S
27007	Land Ranger	— Ky I
27008	Lansing	Ky I
27009	Lascar	Ky I
27011	Lavinium Louanjo	— R R
27012	Lawrence 2nd	P S
27013	Leader	— L R
27014	Leamington	— P S
27016	Leapyear Lad	— Ky I
27017	Lebanon	— Long-Horn
27018	Le Beau	— R R
27019	Lee	— M
27020	Lee	D
27021	Legal Tender	M
27022	Leon	— P S
27023	Leonard	— M
27025	Leopard	— C
27026	Leslie Chief	— T
37027	Lewis 1st	— R R
27029	Liberator	L R
27031	Lictor	— C
27032	Lieut. General	P S
27033	Lilac's Duke	— P S
27034	Lila's Breastplate	P S
27035	3rd Linden	— M
27037	Linganore	P S
27038	Lion	Ky I
27039	Lionel	Ky I
27040	Little Giant	— T
27044	Lizzie's 2nd Ardrie	— M
27047	Logan	— T
27048	Logan	— M
27049	Logan Bouquet	— D
27050	Logan Prince	— D
27051	Lone Star	— L R
27052	Longfellow	P S
27053	Longfellow	— R R
27054	Longfellow 2nd	— Cox
27055	Lord Albert	— Cox
27060	3rd Lord Barmpton of Cleona	— R R
27063	Lord Beacher	D
27064	Lord Bellville	— R R
27065	Lord Blithe 2nd of Forrest Hill	— D

No.	Name	Herd
27066	Lord Blithe 3rd of Forrest Hill	D
27067	Lord Blithe 4th of Forrest Hill	L R
27068	Lord Byron	Ky I
27074	Lord Delaware	L R
27075	Lord Elgin	D
27076	Lord Ellington 2nd	Cox
27077	Lord Ellington 3rd	Cox
27078	Lord Erne 2nd	P S
27080	Lord Frontier	R R
27086	Lord Lieutenant 7th	P S
27090	Lord Mansfield	L R
27093	Lord Mortimer	C
27094	Lord Napier	M
27097	Lord of Oak Grove	M
27102	Lord Oxford	M
27103	Lord Raglan	Cox
27104	Lord Sharon	R R
27105	Lord Stanley 2nd	M
27106	Lord Swan	M
27107	Lord Valiant	L R
27109	Lord Wetherby	R R
27110	Lord Wheatland	R R
27111	Lord Whittington	R R
27115	Louander	R R
27116	Louan's Breastplate	R R
27117	Louan Chieftain 2nd	R R
27118	Louan's Duke	R R
27119	Louan's Duke	T
27120	Louan Duke 4th	R R
27121	Louan's 5th Duke	R R
27122	Louan Duke of Fairview 2nd	R R
27123	Lonanjo	R R
27124	Louan's Lord Oxford	R R
27125	Louan's Oxford	M
27126	Loudon	T
27127	Loudon Airdrie 2nd	R R
27128	Loudon Belle Duke	R R
27130	Loudon Duke 24th	R R
27135	Louisa's Cherub	P S
27137	2nd Loyal Duke of Oakland	P S
27138	3rd Loyal Duke of Oakland	M
27140	Lucille's Peabody	C
27142	Lucretius 2nd	R R
27143	Lucretius 3rd	R R
27144	Lucretius Butterfly	R R
27145	Lustre	Ky I
27146	Lyman Sheffelder	D
27147	Mac Buchan	D
27148	Mac Oxford	D
27150	Madison	D
27152	Maggie's Rosebud	Daisy
27155	Major	L R
27156	Major	Cox
27158	Major	Ky I
27159	Major	M
27160	Major	Ky I
27163	Major Hill	Ky I
27164	Major Hood	Long-Horn
27165	Major Huntly	Ky I
27166	Major Jack Downing	T
27167	Major Knox	M
27169	Major Long	R R
27170	Major Loop	Cox
27171	Major Prim	Ky I
27172	Major Ringold	M
27173	Major Rollins	P S
27174	Major Rose	T
27176	Major Wilcox	Ky I
27180	Maple Hill Duke	C
27182	Mario	R R
27185	Mariposa	L R
27187	Mark Twain	T
27188	Marks	Ky I
27189	Marksman	Cox
27190	Marlborough 2nd	P S
27192	Marmion	C
27193	Marmion	T
27194	Marquis	L R
27196	Marquis	Cox
27197	2nd Marquis of Bute	R R
27201	Marquis of Liberty	Cox
27203	Marquis of Lorne	L R
27203½	Marquis of Lorne	Cox
27206	Marquis of Sugar Grove	Daisy
27207	Marquis of Valley Ridge	L R
27208	Marquis Petitt	Cox
27209	Mars 4th	Daisy
27211	Marshall Ney	Ky I
27212	Mary's Breastplate	C
27213	Mary Lee's Don	R R
27215	Master Airdrie 2nd	Cox
27216	Master Airdrie 3rd	R R
27217	Master Airdrie 4th	Daisy
27219	Master Airdrie 6th	Daisy
27222	Master Geneva 8th	R R
27224	Master Harris	P S
27225	Master Mack, Jr	T
27226	Master Renick	R R
27227	Master Spilman	M
27228	3rd Master Wiseton	P S
27229	4th Master Wiseton	P S
27230	Matchem's Prince	Cox
27231	Matchless 2nd	L R
27232	Matilda's Airdrie	R R
27233	Matthew	Daisy
27234	Maximillian	M
27235	Maximillian	D
27238	May Boy 2nd	M
27239	May Duke	L R
27240	Mayflower	Ky I
27241	Mayflower 2nd	P S
27242	Mayflower 2nd	R R
27243	May Lad	M
27244	Maynard Duke	C
27250	Mazurka Lad 2nd	R R
27251	Mazurka of Walnut Grove	L R
27252	Mazurka's Oxford 2nd	Ky I
27253	Mazurka's Oxford 3rd	Ky I
27254	Mazurka's Oxford 4th	Ky I
27257	Meadow's Duke 2nd	M
27258	6th Meadow Duke	M
27259	Medalist 2nd	R R
27260	Medora Chief	R R
27261	Mendota	M
27262	Mendoza	R R
27263	Merry Boy	P S
27264	Messenger	Cox
27266	Meteor	Cox
27267	Milford	L R
27268	Miller's Duke	P S
27269	Milo	D
27270	Milton	M
27276	Minnesota	Cox
27277	Minna's Loudon Duke	R R
27278	Model	D
27279	Modoc	Daisy
27281	Modoc	L R
27282	Modoc 2nd	M
27283	Mohawk 2nd	Ky I
27284	Mohawk 3rd	Ky I

27285	Monarch .... Wrong	27391	Oxford Duke 6th............ — M
27286	Monarch Lad .... — M	27393	Oxford Goodness .... R R
27287	Mon. of Pattersondale 2nd.. — R R	27394	Oxford Gwynne .... — Cox
27288	Mon. of Pattersondale 3rd..... — C	27396	Oxford Jenner .... — Cox
27289	Mon. of Pattersondale 4th... — R R	27398	Oxford Lad................ — M
27290	Mon. of Pattersondale 5th.. — R R	27400	Oxford of English Farm...... — M
27291	Mon. 6th of Pattersondale .... — C	27401	7th Oxford of Vermillion.....— R R
27292	Monday Duke .... Cox	27402	Oxford Prince .... — Cox
27294	Monitor....................... — M	27406	Oxford Wiley .... Ky I
27295	Monitor..................... Ky I	27409	Pacific....................... P S
27296	Monroe Counterpart .... — M	27410	Pageant................... — T
27297	Mont .... — Cox	27413	Palmetto .... — Cox
27298	Montana .... Ky I	27415	Partner .... — L R
27299	Montezuma Duke .... — L R	27416	Patch .... — L R
27300	Monticello Prince............ Cox	27417	Pat Malloy................ R R
27301	Montrose.................. — D	27418	Patron.................... — D
27302	Moody..................... — D	27420	Paymaster .... — M
27303	Moody..................... — T	27421	Pearl .... — M
27304	Moresby Knight .... L R	27422	Pearl Drop .... — M
27305	Morgan.................... — M	27423	Pedro..................... — L R
27306	Morgan................... — L R	27424	Penfield's Duke of Hillsdale, — Cox
27308	Mountain Dew .... M	27426	Penola.................... — C
27309	Mountaineer .... P S	27427	Perfect Duke .... — M
27312	Mozart of Watertown............C	27428	Peter Cooper...............M.
27313	Muldoon................. — Cox	27429	Peter Cooper .... Ky I
27317	Napoleon .... — Ky I	27430	Peter Cooper .... — P S
27318	Napoleon.................. — M	27431	Peter Cooper .... — Cox
27322	Nebraska Lad 1st .... L R	27432	Peter Cooper .... Ky I
27323	Nelson .... — Cox	27433	Peter Cooper .... M
27324	Nelson Rowland............. — T	27435	Phil Sheridan .... — Cox
27325	Nelson Rowland 2nd .... — T	27436	Phil Sheridan .... — L R
27326	Nero .... — L R	27437	Phil Sheridan .... — M
27327	Nero .... — Cox	27439	Phyllis Goodness........... — R R
27328	Nettie's Baron.............. — T	27440	Pierce C
27329	Nevada Duke................C	27441	Pilgrim................... — L R
27330	Newell..................... L R	27442	Pilot 2nd................... M
27331	New Years Lad.............. Cox	27443	Pilot 2nd................... P S
27332	Nicati Duke .... P S	27444	Pilot 2nd................. — C
27334	Nicodemus .... P S	27446	Pioneer................... — D
27335	Noble Duke................ Ky I	27447	Pioneer..................... P S
27336	Nonsuch...................— P S	27448	Pioneer................... Ky I
27340	North Star................. — T	27449	Planet 2nd................ L R
27344	Oakey Hall .... — T	27450	Plumwood Duke C
27345	Oakhill Favorite............ — M	27451	Plumwood A. A........... Daisy
27346	Oakland Duke.............. — M	27452	Plumwood B. B.............. R R
27347	Oakland's Duke 2nd.......... — R R	27453	Plumwood Lad K .... R R
27348	Obispo....................— D	27454	Plumwood Lad O C
27349	Occult.................... Ky I	27455	Plumwood Lad P.......... Daisy
27352	Olie .... D	27456	Plumwood Lad Q.............C
27353	Oliver..................... P S	27457	Plumwood Lad R............ R R
27355	Oneida .... — Cox	27458	Plumwood Lad S............ R R
27358	Oneida Duke 2nd............ — R R	27459	Plumwood Lad T........... R R
27361	Orchard Duke............... — M	27460	Plumwood Lad U............ Ky I
27362	Origin .... — L R	27461	Plumwood Lad V............ R R
27363	Orontes Clyde .... M	27462	Plumwood Lad X........... R R
27365	Orphan Boy................ — C	27463	Plumwood Lad Y............ C
27366	Orphan Boy................. P S	27464	Plumwood Lad Z........... R R
27367	Orphan Boy .... — T	27465	Pluto..................... L R
27368	Orphan Boy............... — M	27466	Polk............... — Long-Horn
27370	Orphan Boy............... — T	27467	Pompey .... — Daisy
27372	Osceola .... M	27468	Pompey .... — M
27374	Othello .... P S	27469	Pope Pius .... — D
27375	Otis Bunker................ P S	27472	Prairie Duke...............—.L R
27377	Otter King .... M	27474	Prairie Duke............... D
27378	Oxford .... — D	27475	Prairie Duke 2nd........... — R R
27379	Oxford 2nd................ L R	27477	Prairie King................ M
37380	Oxford 3rd .... — D	27479	Prairie Lawn Duke........... P S
27386	Oxford Duke.............. — C	27481	Pride of Saline............ Woods
27387	Oxford Duke............... P S	27482	Pride of Woodland......... — P S
27389	Oxfords Duke.............. — R R	27483	Prima Donnas Duke......... — R R

27484	Prince	— D		27597	Rainstorm	Ky I
27485	Prince	— Ky I		27599	Rambler	— Cox
27486	Prince	— Woods		27600	Rambler	M
27487	Prince	— L R		27601	Randall	— R R
27488	Prince	— D		27602	Randolph	C
27490	Prince	L R		27603	Ranger	— R R
27491	Prince	— R R		27604	Raspberry Duke of Geneva	— D
27492	Prince	Ky I		27605	Ratler	T
27493	Prince	— P S		27606	Ratler	P S
27495	Prince Albert	Daisy		27607	Rawlston	— M
27497	Prince Albert	D		27608	Reckless	D
27498	Prince Albert 2nd	P S		27609	Recruit	M
27500	Prince Albert 2nd	Daisy		27610	Red Airdrie	— Cox
27502	Prince Alfred	Daisy		27611	Red Airdrie	— C
27503	Prince Ambrose	— Long-Horn		27612	Red Ambo	— M
27504	Prince Arnold	— L R		27613	Red Baron	— L R
27507	Prince Atha, Jr	L R		27614	Red Baron	— R R
27508	Prince Bellville	— M		27616	Red Boy	— P S
27512	Prince Charles	— M		27617	Red Boy	— P S
27513	Prince Charles	— M		27618	Red Buck	Ky I
27517	Prince Drakeo	— L R		27619	Red Bud	— M
27518	Prince Frontier	R R		27620	Red Bud	Ky I
27519	Prince George	L R		27621	Red Bull	M
27520	Prince Gwynne	— D		27622	Red Chief	L R
27523	Prince Jubilant	M		27623	Red Chief	— R R
27524	Prince's Knight	— P S		27624	Red Chief	— M
27527	Prince Macacheek	— M		27625	Red Cloud	P S
27528	Prince Napier	— M		27626	Red Cloud	P S
27530	Prince of Argyll	— R R		27627	Red Cloud 2nd	P S
27531	Prince of Ashbrook	— D		27628	Red Deputy	— P S
27532	Prince of Atha 3rd	— R R		27629	Red Dexter	— M
27533	Prince of Australia	— Cox		27630	Red Duke	— R R
27534	2nd Prince of Australia	— Cox		27632	Red Duke	C
27535	3rd Prince of Australia	— Cox		27634	Red Duke	— M
27538	Prince of Busti	— Cox		27635	Red Duke	— Ky I
27539	Prince of Carroll	L R		27636	Red Duke	L R
27542	2nd Prince of Grass Hill	— Cox		27637	Red Duke	— R R
27543	Prince of Green Valley	— Cox		27638	Red Duke	Ky I
27549	Prince of Neshannock	— M		27639	Red Duke 2nd	— P S
27550	Prince of Oakhill	— P S		27640	Red Duke 3rd	— T
27551	Prince of Oakland	— Cox		27641	Red Duke of Oakland	P S
27554	Prince of Queen Anne's	Cox		27642	Red General	— P S
27556	Prince of Rochester	— M		27643	Red Jacket	— P S
27557	Prince of Scott	Ky I		27644	Red Jacket	M
27559	Prince of Stark	— Ky I		27645	Red Jacket	D
27561	Prince of the Maples	Cox		27646	Red Jacket	L R
27562	Prince of the West	— D		27647	Red Jacket	— P S
27565	Prince of Tuscany	L R		27648	Red Joe	Ky I
27566	Prince of Wales	— P S		27649	Red Knight	M
27568	Prince of Wales, Jr	— Cox		27650	Red Lad	— Ky I
27569	Prince of Wales	— L R		27651	Red Mammoth	M
27570	Prince of Wales 2nd	— L R		27652	Red Napier	— Ky I
27572	Prince of Wales 3rd	M		27653	Red Pilot	— L R
27575	Prince Oxford	— Cox		27654	Red Prince	— Ky I
27576	Prince Royal 2nd	— Ky I		27655	Red Prince	— M
27577	Princeton	M		27656	Red Prince	L R
27579	Prince Taylor	— R R		27657	Red Prince	L R
27580	Prince Wiley	— M		27658	Red Prince	— P S
27581	Proctor	Ky I		27659	Red Ribbon	Ky I
27582	Proctor Knott	Ky I		27662	Red Rose Louanjo	— R R
27583	Professor	D		27663	Red Rose Louanjo 2nd	— R R
27584	Prospect	— Cox		27666	Red Rover	Ky I
27586	Proud Undine	— Cox		27667	Red Westward	— Cox
27587	Priest of Boone	— P S		27669	Redwing	— Cox
27588	P. T. Barnum	— M		27670	Reform	Cox
27589	Publicola	Ky I		27671	Reformer	M
27591	Quatennial	— C		27672	Reformer	— R R
27593	Queen's Duke	P S		27675	Renick	— D
27594	Queen's Duke of Geneva	— R R		27677	Republic	— M
27596	Quincy Duke	— P S		27678	Reveler of Pleasant View	— M

27679	Revenue	— M	27772	Rover	L R
27680	Revenue	M	27773	Rover	L R
27681	Rex	— P S	27774	Rover 2nd	— P S
27683	Richard	P S	27777	4th Royal Airdrie	— M
27684	Richard	— M	27781	Royal Briton 2nd	M
27685	Richard 1st	Ky I	27782	Royal Briton 2nd	M
27686	Richard 2nd	M	27784	Royal Cherub 2nd	— Ky I
27688	Richard Raymond	— R R	27785	Royal Chief 2nd	— P S
27689	Richelieu	Ky I	27788	Royal Duke	M
27690	Richmond	— D	27790	Royal Duke	D
27691	Richmond	M	27791	Royal Duke	M
27692	Rio Dan	— P S	27794	Royal Duke of Melleray	— M
27693	2nd Rio Dan	— P S	27795	Royal Duke of Sutherland	— M
27694	Rival	— L R	27796	Royal Duke of Waterloo	M
27695	Roan	— M	27800	Royalist 2nd	T
27696	Roan Boy	P S	27801	Royal Lad	— M
27697	Roan Chief	M	27804	Royal Maynard	— R R
27699	Roan Duke	C	27805	Royal Oak	P S
27700	Roan Duke	L R	27806	Royal Oxford	— R R
27702	Roan Duke	— M	27807	Royal Oxford	— M
27704	Roan Duke	— Woods	27809	Royal Prince	— R R
27705	Roan Duke	M	27810	Rose Prince 2nd	— R R
27709	Roan Duke of Tecumseh	— Ky I	27811	Royal Prince 3rd	C
27710	Roan Geneva	M	27814	Royal Tiger	— T
27712	Roan Jacket	T	27815	Royal Viscount	M
27713	Roan Lad	M	27817	Rozellas Airdrie	Ky I
27714	Roan Major	— Cox	27818	Rufus	P S
27715	Roan Oxford	— M	27820	Rustic	— Cox
27717	Roan Prince	— Cox	27821	Sadie's Duke	P S
27718	Roan Star	M	27822	St. Clair	R R
27719	Rob Roy	Cox	27823	St. Croix	Cox
27720	Rob Roy	— Cox	27826	2nd Saladin	— T
27721	Rob Roy	— D	27827	Sally Anne's Bridegroom	— Cox
27723	Robert Bruce 2nd	— R R	27829	Sam Carey	Ky I
27724	Robert Burns	— R R	27830	Sam Grundy	— M
27725	Robert F. Ayers	M	27831	Sam Lang	— R R
27726	Robin Hood	M	27832	Sam Marmion	L R
27727	Rockford Duke	P S	27833	Sampson	L R
27728	Rockingham	— L R	27834	Sam Tilden	— M
27729	Rockingham 2nd	— R R	27835	Sam Tilden	Cox
27730	Rock River Lad 13th	— Cox	27836	Sam Tilden	—Long-Horn
27731	Rock River Lad 14th	— Cox	27837	Sam Tilden	Cox
27732	Rock River Lad 15th	— Cox	27840	Samuel J. Tilden	— P S
27733	Rock River Lad 16th	— Cox	27841	Sam Wiley's Duke	— R R
27734	Rock River Lad 17th	— Cox	27842	Sandy Lookout	— Cox
27735	Rock River Lad 18th	— Cox	27843	Sangamon Duke	P S
27736	Rock River Lad 19th	— Cox	27844	Santa Anna	M
27737	Rock River Lad 20th	— Cox	27845	Santa Claus	— Ky I
27738	Rock River Prince	T	27847	Saratoga	T
27739	Rodolph	M	27848	Sartoris	T
27740	Roe Sheffelder	— D	27849	Saturn	— P S
27741	Roger Williams	— R R	27850	Savannah Duke of Valley Farm	— C
27742	Rokeby	— L R	27851	Saxe Coburg	— P S
27744	Rolling Stone	— T	27852	Scotia Lad	— R R
27745	Rolo	— C	27853	Scotia Lad 2nd	— D
27746	Roman	— R R	27854	Sea Gull	— Wrong
27747	Romeo	— Cox	27855	Seigal	P S
27749	Romeo	— P S	27856	Senator	M
27751	Romulus	— Cox	27857	Senator	— R R
27752	Romulus	Ky I	27860	Seneca Duke	— Cox
27754	Rosa's Airdrie	— R R	27862	September	R R
27758	Rosa's Duke	— M	27864	Seventy-Six	— M
27759	Rose Duke	L R	27865	Seventy-Six	— T
27760	Rose Duke	— L R	27867	Seymour	M
27765	Rosyman 2nd	M	27869	Shaker R.	— M
27766	Rosy Lad	— R R	27870	Shakespeare	— Cox
27767	Rosy Lad	— Cox	27872	Shakespeare	— D
27769	Rothschild	— M	27876	Sharon Blue	— D
27770	Rover	M	27877	Sharon Duke	— R R
27771	Rover	L R	27878	Sharon's Duke	— R R

No.	Name	Code	No.	Name	Code
27880	Sharon Duke	— R R	27978	Summit Duke	— L R
27882	Sheboygan	— M	27979	Summit Star	— P S
27884	Shelby Duke	— R R	27981	Sunflower	M
27885	Sherman	— M	27982	Sunny Eye	— P S
27886	Sheridan	— M	27983	Sunny South	T
27887	Sheridan	Ky I	27984	Sunshine	P S
27890	Sheridan 1st	— R R	27985	Superb	P S
27891	Sheridan 2nd	M	27986	Surprise	P S
27892	Shorttail	— L R	27987	Susan's Strathallan	— C
27894	Signet	— L R	27988	Sweepstakes	Ky I
27895	Silas Woodson	Daisy	27989	Sweepstakes	— M
27896	Sir Bellville	— P S	27990	Swimmer	P S
27897	Sir Charles	— R R	27991	Sylvester	M
27898	Sir Edward	L R	27992	Tacuya	— M
27900	Sir Henry	— P S	27993	Tamerlane	M
27901	Sir Henry	— Cox	27994	Tam O'Shanter	M
27905	Sir Ponsonby	— R R	27996	Tecumseh	— M
27906	Sir Renick	— R R	27997	Tecumseh Sherman	T
27908	Sir Robert	D	27998	The Boss	— L R
27909	Sir Roderick	R R	28002	The Young Pope	— Cox
27910	Sir Roger	L R	28003	Thos. Bates 2nd	— Ky I
27913	Sir William	— P S	28004	Thos. J. Hendricks	— Ky I
27914	Sir William	— M	28006	Thorndale	T
27915	Sir Wm. Wallace	M	28008	Thorndale Duke	— C
27917	Silver Cloud	— Cox	28010	2nd Thorndale Duke	— Daisy
27918	Silver Duke	— P S	28014	Thurbassett	— L R
27920	Sitting Bull	P S	28015	Thurlow	— L R
27921	Sitting Bull	— D	28016	Tice	M
27922	Sleeping Joe	— M	28020	Tilden	P S
27923	Smith Duke	M	28021	Tim Finnegan	T
27924	Snowball	Ky I	28022	Timour	— Cox
27928	Snowstorm	— M	28023	Tilden	— P S
27930	Solicitor 2nd	— L R	28024	Tilden	— P S
27931	Sophia's Sam	— M	28025	Tilden	— P S
27932	Speaker Chief	L R	28027	Tilden	— P S
27934	Splendor	M	28028	Tilden	— Cox
27935	Splendor	— R R	28030	Token 2nd	P S
27936	Splendor	M	28031	Tom	Ky I
27937	Splendor	L R	28032	Tom	— C
27938	Splendor	— Cox	28033	Tom	M
27939	Spot	— T	28034	Tom Benton	Cox
27940	Spotted Dick	— P S	28037	Tom Benton 2nd	Cox
27941	Spotted Tail	P S	28038	Tom Boyd	M
27942	Squire Bellville	M	28039	Tom Brown	— Long-Horn
27943	Standard Bearer	— R R	28041	Tom King	Ky I
27944	Stanford	M	28042	Tommy Bates 1st	— R R
27945	Stanford	L R	28043	Tommy Bates 2nd	— R R
27947	Starlight	— R R	28045	Tompkins	L R
27948	Starlight	Ky I	28046	Tom Shanty	— R R
27949	Starlight 2nd	M	28048	Tom Vanmeter	— D
27950	Starlight 3rd	— R R	28049	Townley	— P S
27953	Star of Hope	Ky I	28050	Travis Austin	— T
27954	Star of Oakland	P S	28051	Trenton Duke	— P S
27955	Star of Richland	D	28052	Triumph	— M
27956	Star of Tama	— Cox	28054	Turk	— M
27957	Star of Traer	R R	28055	Turner's Duke	— C
27958	Star of the Valley	— P S	28058	Twilight	— M
27960	Star of the West	— R R	28059	Tychunkus	— M
27963	Star of Woodlawn	L R	28060	Tyrone	P S
27965	Stonehill	— R R	28061	Uncle John	— P S
27966	Stonewall	— M	28062	Uncle Sam	— Cox
27967	Stonewall J.	C	28063	Undine Prince	— Cox
27968	Stonewall Jackson	— P S	28064	Union Duke	— Ky I
27970	Strawberry Duke	— M	28065	Union Duke	P S
27971	Substantial	L R	28067	Ursa Major	— Cox
27972	Success	L R	28068	Valentine	— Cox
27973	Sucker Boy, Jr	L R	28070	Valley Chief	P S
27974	Sultan	— R R	28071	Valley Duke	— D
27975	Sultan Cubano	— D	28072	Valverde	— P S
27976	Sultan Louanjo	— Ky I	28075	Vandal	— D

28079	Velvet Jack ....Ky I	28176	W. T. Sherman............T
28080	Vermillion Lad............—C	28179	Wyoming's Pride............P S
28081	Vermont............—M	28185	Young America............— L R
28083	Veto............M	28186	Young Badger............— P S
28084	Victor............— Ky I	28187	Young Barney............— L R
28087	Victor............M	28188	Young Baron............— P S
28088	Victor............M	28189	Young Beck............— P S
28089	Victor............L R	28190	Young Bellville............— Ky I
28090	Victor Hugo............D	28192	Young Breastplate............— D
28092	Virginia Duke............— M	28194	Young Chatham............— M
28093	Viscount............P S	28197	Young Earl Duchess............— P S
28096	Volney............— L R	28198	Young Farmer............— P S
28097	Volunteer............— P S	28199	Young Ira............Cox
28098	Vulcan............— P S	28200	Young Jupiter............— R R
28099	Wade Hampton............— P S	28203	Young Monitor............— Ky I
28100	Wade Hampton............L R	28205	Young Paley............— L R
28101	Waitman............— P S	28207	Young Peabody............— P S
28102	Wallace............— L R	28209	Young Professor............— Ky I
28103	Wallace............M	28211	Young Romeo............M
28104	Wallace............L R	28212	Young Sampson............L R
28105	Wallace............—M	28213	Young Seagull............— R R
28106	Wallflower's Jupiter............— Cox	28217	Young Wellington............—M
28107	3rd Walnut Grove Duke............— M	28218	Young Wilson............— M
28108	Walnut Lad............—D	28219	Young Zeno............— R R
28111	Wapsie Duke............— P S	28220	Zaccheus............— D
28112	Wapsie Duke 2nd............— M	28221	Zack Taylor............P S
28113	Wapsie Duke 3rd............— M	28226	Zero............— Cox
28114	Ward............—M	28227	Zero............L R
28115	Ward Beecher............R R	28228	Zingaroo............— Cox
28116	Warden............— R R	28232	Albert............— Cox
28119	Warrior............M	28235	Baron Booth of Elm Grove............D
28120	Washington............— Ky I	28236	Baron of Oakland............— Cox
28121	Washington............— L R	28238	Belmont 2nd............— R R
28126	Wat............— M	28241	Bob Nettie............— M
28127	Watchman............R R	28242	Bounty............P S
28129	Waterloo............— R R	28244	Buckner............— D
28131	Webster............— M	28245	Buckram............Cox
28132	Wellington............D	28246	Bulldozer............— P S
28133	Welland............— Cox	28247	Bulldozer............P S
28135	Western Duke............— P S	28248	Cavagna's Airdrie............D
28137	Western Prince............— M	28250	Centennial Duke............— D
28138	Western Star............M	28251	Chief of Warren............— Long-Horn
28139	Westward Ho!............— Cox	28252	Clifton Duke............— T
28140	Wheeler............M	28253	Col. Carter............— M
28141	Wheeler............— P S	28254	Comet............C
28144	White Bon Ton............M	28255	Crown Prince 6th............M
28145	White Cloud............Ky I	28256	Crown Prince 7th............M
28146	Whitefoot Prince............— M	28258	Dandy Jack............— Long-Horn
28147	White Jacket............Cox	28259	Dardenne............— T
28148	White Plume............Ky I	28263	Don............C
28149	White Prince............— L R	28265	Duke Goodness 5th............— D
28151	White Stockings............— P S	28266	Duke of Allen............Ky I
28152	White Stockings............— M	28268	Duke of Fairview............— M
28153	Whitie............— T	28270	18th Duke of Granville............— R R
28154	Whitsitt's Duke 3rd............— P S	28271	2nd Duke of Jonesville............Ky I
28155	Wiley............D	28272	Duke of Knox............— D
28156	Wiley 8th............— M	28273	Duke of Moscow............— M
28157	Wiley 9th............— M	28278	4th Duke of Wheatfield............— Ky I
28158	Wiley Duke............— R R	28279	2nd Duke of Woodson............Ky I
28159	Wiley Duke............— R R	28283	Favorite............— R R
28161	Willie............P S	28285	Frank............P S
28162	Willie............— R R	28286	Fulton............P S
28163	William E. Ray............— M	28289	Gen. Lee............C
28165	Winchester............— L R	28290	Gen. Logan............— M
28169	Wolverton............— M	28291	Gilmore's Duke............Ky I
28170	Woodland Chief............Daisy	28292	Gov. Allen............— M
28172	Woodland Star 2nd............— R R	28293	Gov. Hayes............— Long-Horn
28173	Woodlawn Chief 2nd............— Ky I	28294	Gov. Tilden............— Long-Horn
28174	Woodside Duke............Cox	28298	Happy Sam............— Daisy
28175	Worthy............P S	28301	Hokie............— M

28302	Invincible	— M	28412	14th Airdrie Duke of Scioto ..... D
28306	Lee	— Ky I	28413	15th Duke of Scioto ..... — M
28309	Lincoln	— L R	28414	16th Airdrie Duke of Scioto ..... D
28311	Logan	— M	28415	17th Airdrie Duke of Scioto ..... D
28312	Logan Lad	...M	28416	Airdrie of Emerald Valley .... — C
28313	5th Lone Star	— R R	28418	Airdrie Jackson ..... — P S
28317	2nd Loudon Duke of Elmwood .. — M		28419	Airdrie Joe C
28320	Martial	— M	28420	Airdrie Muhlenberg ..... — C
28321	Master Clark	— R R	28424	Airdrie of Springdale ..... — M
28322	Miami Chief	... — C	28425	Airdrie of Twin ..... — R R
28324	Modoc	— D	28426	Ajax ..... — M
28325	Moody	— Cox	28429	Albert ..... — Ky I
28326	Mountain Boy	Ky I	28430	Albert ..... — D
28328	Mozelle	— T	28431	Albert ..... — L R
28329	Ned	— M	28432	Albert Duke ..... — P S
28330	Noble Duke	— P S	28433	Albert Edward 14th ..... L R
28331	Nobleman, Jr	— P S	28434	Albion ..... — T
28334	Organ	— M	28435	Albion ..... D
28336	Prince Albert	— C	28437	Alexander ..... Ky I
28338	Prince Duncan	— T	28438	Alexander ..... M
28341	Prince Oxford	Ky I	28439	Alexander ..... — R R
28342	Ranger	— Cox	28440	Alexander ..... — Cox
28344	Red Cloud	— Long-Horn	28441	Alexander ..... — M
28345	Red Duke	— T	28443	Alex Ward ..... — M
28346	Red Prince	— Cox	28444	Alexis ..... Ky I
28347	Resumption	— M	28445	Alexis ..... M
28348	Roan Comet	Ky I	28447	Alexis ..... M
28349	Roan Dick	M	28449	Alfred Nier ..... P S
28350	Robert	— D	28450	Allanbane ..... — R R
28352	Roseboy	— M	28451	Allen Boy ..... — Cox
28353	Royal Hotspur	L R	38452	Allen's Oxford ..... — Cox
28354	Royal Knight	L R	28453	Allie's Scott ..... — L R
28355	Sam Patch	— D	28454	Almont ..... — R R
28358	Seneca Hero	Cox	28455	Alpha ..... — P S
28360	Sir John Franklin	— L R	28459	Amateur ..... — L R
28361	Sir Walter Scott	— Cox	28462	American Flag ..... T
28362	Slasher	— D	28465	Andrew Johnson ..... — D
28364	Starkey Chief	Cox	28466	April Lad ..... — C
28365	Star of Lebanon	— Cox	28467	Aramis ..... — P S
28366	Strawberry Duke	Daisy	28468	Arch Duke ..... — Cox
28367	Thorndale 2nd	— D	28469	2nd Arch Duke of Goodness .. — R R
28370	Thornton	— Cox	28470	3rd Arch Duke of Goodness .... — T
28372	Tilden	— M	28471	4th Arch Duke of Goodness .. — P S
28373	Valley Chief	— R R	28472	5th Arch Duke of Goodness .. — P S
28374	Vernon Duke	— D	28473	Archy ..... — C
28375	Wade Hampton	— L R	28474	Aristocrat ..... — M
28377	Waseca Boy	— Ky I	28476	Arnott ..... L R
28378	Wellington	— R R	28480	Austin ..... Ky I
28381	Wild Idle	— P S	28481	Autum Lad ..... — M
28385	Yonng Dan	— Cox	28482	Aztec ..... R R
28386	Young Loudon Duke	— D	28484	Balco ..... — Cox
28388	Aaron 3rd	D	28485	Ball Hornet ..... — P S
28389	Abel	— T	28486	Ballston Prince ..... — M
28391	Ad	— D	28487	Banker ..... Cox
28392	Adam	— D	28489	Banks ..... — M
28393	Adam	— T	28490	Banner Bearer ..... M
28394	Admiral	— Cox	28491	Barmpton Boy ..... — R R
28395	Admiral	— Cox	28492	Barmpton Duke ..... — D
28396	Admiral	— R R	28493	2nd Barmpton Duke of L ..... — R R
28397	Admiral	— Cox	28494	3rd Barmpton Duke of L ..... — R R
28398	Admiral 2nd	M	28495	Barney Boy ..... Ky I
28399	Admiral 5th	— Daisy	28496	Barnum ..... P S
28400	Admiral 7th	— R R	28497	Barnum ..... — Cox
28402	Adrian Duke	Ky I	28498	Baron ..... L R
28403	Aid-de-Camp	— L R	28500	Baron ..... — L R
28405	Airdrie	P S	28501	Baron of Anoka ..... L R
28406	Airdrie Duke	— R R	28503	Baron Bates ..... — R R
28409	11th Airdrie Duke of Scioto	D	28505	Baron Bates 2nd ..... — M
28410	12th Airdrie Duke of Scioto ..	— M	28506	Baron Bates of Towanda ..... M
28411	13th Airdrie Duke of Scioto ..	— R R	28507	Baron Beresford ..... — R R

28509	Baron Booth	— C	28635	Bettie's Mazurka	— M
28510	Baron Breastplate	— C	28636	Bifrous 4th	— M
28513	Baron of Cloverdale	— P S	28637	Bill	Cox
28515	Baron De Palm	— M	28639	Billy	— M
28516	Baron Duke	— Ky I	28641	Billy Barlow	— M
28517	Baron Duke 4th	— M	28642	Billy Bowman	— Ky I
28519	Baron Geneva	— C	28643	Billy Boy	— Cox
28522	Baron Gwynne	— Cox	28644	Billy Hise 2nd	— Long-Horn
28524	2nd Baron of Hillsdale	— M	28645	Billy O'Brien	— R R
28530	Baron Lewis	M	28646	Billy O'Sheridan	M
28531	Baron Lischer	L R	28647	Billy Patterson	T
28532	Baron Lyndale 4th	— R R	28648	Bishop Duke	C
28533	Baron Lyndale 5th	— R R	28649	Bismarck	— M
28534	Baron Manlius	— L R	28650	Bismarck	— M
28535	2nd Baron Manlius	— Cox	28651	Bismarck	T
28542	Baron of Mount Airy	— Cox	28652	Bismarck	— M
28543	Baron of New Castle	— Cox	28653	Bismarck	— T
28544	Baron Oakland, Jr	— D	28654	Bismarck	— M
28545	Baron Oakland 7th	— Cox	28655	Bismarck	— D
28546	Baron Oxford	P S	28656	Bismarck	— L R
28550	Baron Pierce	C	28657	Bismarck 2nd	— M
28552	4th Baron of Riverside	— C	28658	Bismarck Shaw	— T
28553	Baron Sheffielder	— D	28659	Blackhawk	— D
28556	Baron of the Bluffs	M	28663	Bloom Duke	— Cox
28558	3rd Baron of Vermillion	— L R	28664	Bloom's Duke	M
28559	4th Baron of Vermillion	— L R	28667	Blondin	— M
28561	Baron White	D	28668	Blood Chief	— M
28564	Barrington	— Cox	28660	Blood Chief	— R R
28565	Basil Duke 3rd	M	28671	Blucher	— Cox
28566	Bates Barmpton	— R R	28673	Blucher 2nd	— M
28568	Bates Rose	— M	28674	Blue Cap	— R R
28569	Beau of Oakland	— R R	28675	Blue Jeans	— P S
28570	Beau of Oxford	L R	28676	Blue Jeans Williams	T
28571	Beau of Oxford	— Cox	28677	Boaz	— M
28572	Beauregard	— C	28678	Bobalid	— P S
28574	Beautys Mazurka	— R R	28679	Bobb	D
28575	Beautys Peabody	— M	28680	Bob Grey	M
28577	Beaver Duke 1st	T	28681	Bob Ingersol	— P S
28578	Beaver Duke 2nd	— P S	28682	Bob Lamech	C
28579	Beaver Duke 3rd	— P S	28685	Bonaparte	— Cox
28580	Bedford Chief	— Cox	28686	Bonaparte	— D
28581	Bedford Lad	Cox	28688	Bonner 2nd	— D
28582	Beecher	Ky I	28689	Bonner 2nd	— M
28583	Beecher	— M	28691	Bonnie Lad	— D
28584	Beecher	Cox	28692	Bonnie Scotland	M
28586	Bells Airdrie	— M	28693	Broderick	— R R
28587	Belle Duke	Daisy	28695	Booth of Concord	— D
28591	Belle Duke	— Cox	28698	Boston Duke	— M
28592	Belle Duke	M	28700	Bourbon Duke 2nd	— L R
28593	Belle Duke	Ky I	28701	Boze	M
28596	Belle Duke, J	— R R	28702	Bravo	Ky I
28597	Belle Duke K	— R R	28704	Breastplate	L R
28598	Belle Duke L	R R	28705	Breckenridge 2nd	— P S
28599	Belle Duke M	— R R	28707	Brigham	— C
28602	Bell's Duke of Brookvale	— M	28708	Brigham 2nd	— P S
28604	Belle Duke of Magnolia	— T	28709	Brigham Young	— M
28605	Belle Duke of Riverside	— L R	28710	Bright Eye	— Ky I
28608	Bellevue's Duke	P S	28712	Brilliant Crown	— M
28610	Belmont	— Cox	28713	Bristow	— P S
28616	Ben Butler	— P S	28714	Bristow	P S
28617	Ben Butler	L R	28716	British Beau	— R R
28619	Ben Butler	— Cox	28717	British Bridegroom	— R R
28620	Ben De Bar	M	28718	Britton 1st	— L R
28621	Ben De Bar	M	28719	Britton 2nd	— L R
28622	Ben Duke	— M	28720	Britton 3rd	— R R
28625	Ben Geneva	— M	28722	Broken Leg	— P S
28626	Ben Green	M	28723	Bruce	— T
28628	Ben Ledi	— P S	28724	Bruce of Spring Lake	Cox
28631	Ben Wheeler	M	28725	Brutus	— P S
28632	Berkshire Limerock	L R	28727	Brutus	— M

SHORT-HORN CATTLE PEDIGREES. 133

28728	Brutus	— D		28814	Challenger	P S
28729	Brutus	M		28817	Champion	— R R
28730	Brutus	— L R		28819	Champion	Ky I
28732	Butler	— M		28820	Champion	— Ky I
28733	Buckeye Boy	— M		28821	Champion	P S
28734	1st Bull of Kentucky Home	D		28822	Champion Lad	— D
28735	2nd Bull of Kentucky Home	D		28824	Charles the Bold	— R R
28736	Bunksey	— L R		28825	Charley	— M
28737	Bushnell	— D		28827	Charlotte's Duke	Wrong
28738	Buster	P S		28828	Cherry Duke	M
28740	Butler	M		28830	Cherry Duke 3rd	— D
28741	Butte	— P S		28831	Cherry Duke	— L R
28742	Buttercup's Duke	Daisy		28833	Cherub 4th	— Ky I
28743	Butterfly	— L R		28834	Cherub Echo	— M
28745	Butterfly's Duke	— M		28836	Chetopa	Woods
28746	Butterfly's Duke	Cox		28837	Chicago Duke	T
28748	Byram Goodness	Daisy		28839	Chief	— M
28750	Cæsar	— M		28840	Chief of Atholl	P S
28751	Cain	— T		28841	Chief Joseph	— P S
28752	Calhoun	— D		28843	Chieftain	M
28753	Calhoun	— D		28844	Chieftain	P S
28754	Caliph 2nd	— M		28846	Chilton 4th	L R
28755	Caliph 3rd	— M		28847	Chilton's Duke	— M
28759	Cambridge Jubilee	— R R		28848	Chimborazo	Cox
28760	Cambridge Lad	— R R		28849	Chippewa Duke	— Cox
28763	Captain	P S		28858	Cicero 2nd	— C
28764	Captain	P S		28851	Clara's Duke	T
28765	Captain 3rd	— Ky I		28852	Clarence	— P S
28766	Capt. Allen	— Cox		28854	Clarks Cherub	— M
28767	Captain Brown	— M		28855	Clay Muscatoon, Jr	Ky I
28768	Capt. Clark	R R		28857	Cleasby Louanjo	— R R
28769	Capt. Costigan	P S		28858	Clifford	— M
28770	Capt. Derby	Cox		28862	Clifton Duke of Airdrie 2nd	D
28771	Capt. Dick	— P S		28864	Clio	Ky I
28772	Capt. Hall	Ky I		28866	Cobbossecontee	— L R
28773	Capt. Hayes	M		28868	Colonel	L R
28774	Capt. Holland	Ky I		28869	Colonel	C
28775	Capt. Hood	— P S		28870	Colonel	Daisy
28776	Capt. Jack	P S		28871	Col. Balco	P S
28777	Capt. Jack	L R		28872	Col. Booth, Jr	— L R
28778	Capt. Jack	L R		28873	Col. Brewster	Ky I
28779	Capt. Jack	Ky I		28874	Col. Crisp	P S
28780	Capt. Jack	M		28875	Col. Debolt	Ky I
28781	Capt. Jack	M		28877	Col. Ellsworth	— Cox
28782	Capt. Jack	— Ky I		28878	Col. Foot	— M
28783	Capt. Jack	Daisy		28879	Col. Hazzard	— L R
28785	Capt. Jack	— D		28880	Col. Hill	— Ky I
28786	Capt. Jamison	— P S		28881	Col. Judy	— R R
28788	Capt. Kountz	Cox		28882	Col. Judy	— Cox
28789	Capt. Miller	— R R		28883	Col. Knapp	T
28790	Capt. Parker	— M		28884	Col. Lynch	Ky I
28791	Capt. 1st of Richland	— P S		28885	Col. Mac	— Cox
28792	Capt. Roberts	— L R		28887	Col. Muir 2nd	— R R
28794	Carlovingian	— C		28888	Col. Pluck	— M
28795	Carnival 4th	— T		28889	Col. Richmond	— C
28796	Cashier	— Cox		28890	Col. Shaw	— T
28799	Cassabianca	Ky I		28892	Col. Duke	P S
28800	Cato	— M		28895	Comb's Duke	M
28801	Cavalier	— M		28897	Comet	M
28802	Cedar Prince	— P S		28898	Comet	P S
28803	Cedar Township Duke	— R R		28900	Comet	— M
28804	Centennial	Ky I		28901	Comet	— M
28805	Centennial	Woods		28902	Comet	Cox
28806	Centennial	— M		28903	2nd Comet	— L R
28807	Centennial 12th	Ky I		28904	Commander	— M
28808	Centennial 13th	— M		28907	Commander Bruce	M
28810	Centennial Duke	— L R		28908	Commodore	M
28811	Centennial Duke	— T		28909	Commodore 3rd	M
28812	Centennial Duke	— Cox		28910	Commodore Trunyon	P S
28813	Challenger	— R R		28911	Commodore Vanderbilt	Cox

28912	Commodore Vanderbilt........Ky I	29013	Diamond ....— R R
28913	Competitor................— P S	29015	Diamond of the Brook........Ky I
28921	Cornell....................P S	29016	Diamond Duke..............M
28922	Corning Lad...............— Cox	29017	Dick.....................— M
28923	Corporal 2nd..................T	29018	Dick Byron 2nd............— R R
28924	Corporal 3rd..............— D	29019	Dick Cool.................— L R
28925	Corporal 4th.................M	29021	Dick Gano................— C
28926	Corporal 5th..............— L R	29022	Dick Oakley...............— P S
28927	Corporal 6th..............— M	29023	Dick Rowett....................T
28928	Corporal 7th..............Ky I	29024	Dick Taylor...............— C
28929	Corporal 8th..............— D	29025	Dick Taylor...............Cox
28930	Corporal 9th..............— M	29026	Dick Taylor 2nd...........— C
28931	Corporal 10th.............— L R	29027	Dick Taylor 2nd............Woods
28932	Corporal 11th.............Ky I	29028	Dick Thompson............— R R
28933	Corporal 12th.............— M	29029	Dick Turpin...............— P S
28934	Corporal 13th.............— M	29930	Dick Turpin...............— Cox
28935	Corporal 14th.............— M	29031	Dick Warren..............P S
28936	Cosmo...................— P S	29032	Dictator..................— M
28938	Cottonwood Louan 2nd..— Woods	29033	Dictator..................Daisy
28939	Cottonwood Louan 3rd......— D	29035	Dine....................— Cox
28940	Cottonwood Louan 4th.........M	29037	Dixie's Airdrie..............C
28941	Cottonwood Louan 5th.........M	29039	Doctor..................— Cox
28942	Cottonwood Louan 6th.........M	29040	2nd Doctor..............— C
28946	3rd Count of Oneida........— R R	29041	Doctor Darwin............— Cox
28947	Count Rumford 2nd........— L R	29042	Doctor Day...............— R R
28948	Country Gentleman..........Ky I	29044	Dr. Vincent..............— Cox
28949	Crescent Oxford..............M	29045	Dr. Wiley................— R R
28954	Cronin...................— R R	29046	Dom Pedro...............— C
28955	Crown Prince.............— M	29047	Dom Pedro...............— R R
28958	Cruso...................— R R	29048	Dom Pedro...............— Cox
28962	Cuyahoga Chief.............Ky I	29049	Dom Pedro...............— M
28963	Cyrus...................— R R	29050	Dom Pedro...............P S
28964	Cyrus 2nd..................M	29052	Dom Pedro...............— M
28968	Cypress Duke.................T	29053	Dom Pedro...............Ky I
28969	2nd Cypress Duke of Airdrie....M	29054	Dom Pedro...............P S
28970	Dairyman................— Cox	29055	Don 1st..................— L R
28971	Daisy Duke...............— Cox	29056	Don A....................— L R
28972	Daisy Duke................P S	29057	Don B....................— L R
28973	Daisy's Duke of Goodness.....Ky I	29058	Don S....................— L R
28974	Daisy's Duke of Spring Lake..Cox	29059	Don Bernardo 2nd.........— M
28975	Dale Airdrie..............— M	29060	Don Cæsar...................T
28976	Dalton Duke..............— R R	29061	Don Carlos...............— M
28977	Dan.....................— M	29062	Don Carlos...............— R R
28979	Dandy...................— P S	29063	Don John................— R R
28980	Dan Huffman................M	29064	Don Juan................— M
28982	Daniel Boon..................M	29065	Don Juan................Ky I
28983	Daniel Deronda............— C	29066	Don Juan 3rd............— Ky I
28984	Dan Morgan..................T	29067	Don Sharon..............— R R
28985	Dan O'Leary..............— Cox	29068	Dorcas..................— L R
28986	Dan Rice.................— D	29069	Dorset....................M
28987	Darby Duke 4th...........— P S	29072	Doubloon................— Cox
28988	Darby Duke 5th............R R	29073	Douglass................— M
28989	Darby Duke 6th............R R	29074	Dover..................— L R
28990	Darby Duke 7th............R R	29075	Downey.................— R R
28991	2nd Darlington of RoseMound—Cox	29076	Druid....................Ky I
28992	3rd Darlington of Rose Mound..—M	29078	Duke...................— Cox
28993	Dave Renick..............— R R	29079	Duke...................— Cox
28994	David Copperfield..........P S	29080	Duke...................— M
28995	David Lewars 2nd.........Ky I	29082	Duke......................D
28997	Deano..................— L R	29084	Duke...................— M
28998	Decatur..................P S	29088	Duke of Airdrie...........— M
28999	Deception..................M	29089	Duke of Airdrie 8th.......— T
29002	Dellie's Duke.............— T	29091	Duke Alexis..............— M
29004	Deputy Sheriff 2nd.........— P S	29092	1st Duke of Alfred.........L R
29005	Derby....................P S	29093	Duke of Alma............— M
29006	De Soto.................— L R	29094	4th Duke of Altaham......— R R
29008	Dewdrops Oxford 2nd......— Cox	29095	Duke of Amity............P S
29009	Dexter 2nd................Ky I	29096	2nd Duke of Arcadia.........M
29011	Dexter 4th................L R	29097	Duke of Argyll............Ky I
29012	Diamond................— M	29098	Duke of Argyll..............M

SHORT-HORN CATTLE PEDIGREES.

29099	7th Duke of Armada	L R	29186	Duke of Fayette	— Ky I
29100	Duke of Armstrong	— R R	29187	Duke of Fayette	— D
29101	Duke of Armstrong	Ky I	29189	2nd Duke of Fayette	R R
29102	19th Duke of Ashland	— M	29190	2nd Duke of Fayette	M
29103	20th Duke of Ashland	M	29192	2nd Duke of Five-Twenty	Ky I
29104	Duke of Athens	— R R	29193	Duke of Forest Cove	— M
29106	Duke of Auvergne 2nd	— R R	29194	2nd Duke of Forest Home	M
29107	Duke Baden	— R R	29198	4th Duke of Fountain	— R R
29108	Duke Balder 3rd	Ky I	29199	5th Duke of Fountain	— R R
29109	Duke Balder 4th	Ky I	29200	Duke of Franklin	L R
29110	Duke Balder 5th	Ky I	29202	12th Duke of Gabilan	— R R
29111	Duke Bell 2nd	— M	29204	14th Duke of Gabilan	Ky I
29112	Duke of Belgrade	— Cox	29205	Duke of Garth	M
29113	Duke of Bellvue	Daisy	29206	Duke of Genesee	L R
29114	1st Duke of Belvue	— M	29207	Duke of Genesee	L R
29115	2nd Duke of Belvue	— M	29208	Duke of Genesee	L R
29116	2nd Duke of Bellevue	— M	29210	Duke of Gibson	T
29117	Duke of Benton	— T	29211	2nd Duke of Glendale	L R
29118	2nd Duke of Benton	— Ky I	29212	3rd Duke of Glendale	R R
29120	Duke of Berkshire	— L R	29213	4th Duke of Glendale	L R
29121	Duke of Berkshire	T	29214	5th Duke of Glendale	L R
29125	Duke of Big Creek	P S	29215	5th Duke of Glendale	M
29126	Duke of Boone	P S	29216	Duke of Glen Rock	P S
29127	Duke of Bourbon	— C	29217	3rd Duke of Glenwood	M
29128	Duke of Bradford	M	29218	4th Duke of Glenwood	M
29130	Duke Bright Eyes	M	29219	Duke of Gloster	P S
29131	Duke of Brighton	— P S	29220	Duke of Gloster 4th	— C
29132	Duke of Buffalo	— M	29222	11th Duke of Goodness	— R R
29133	Duke of Bureau	M	29224	28th Duke of Goodness	— R R
29134	Duke of Butler	M	29225	31st Duke of Goodness	— R R
29138	Duke of Callaway	D	29227	5th Duke of Greendale	L R
29139	1st Duke of Canehill	M	29228	Duke of Greenlawn	L R
29140	2nd Duke of Canehill	M	29229	30th Duke of Greenlawn	— M
29143	Duke of Carlotta	M	29230	31st Duke of Greenlawn	— M
29144	Duke of Cass County	Cox	29231	32nd Duke of Greenlawn	— M
29145	Duke of Cedar	— R R	29232	33rd Duke of Greenlawn	Ky I
29146	Duke of Center	T	29233	34th Duke of Greenlawn	— M
29147	Duke of Chaplain	— P S	29234	35th Duke of Greenlawn	— M
29148	Duke of Chestnut	— Ky I	29235	36th Duke of Greenlawn	— M
29150	5th Duke of Chico	Ky I	29236	37th Duke of Greenlawn	— D
29151	6th Duke of Chico	— P S	29237	38th Duke of Greenlawn	— M
29152	7th Duke of Chico	— P S	29238	1st Duke of Green Mountain	L R
29153	Duke of Clarence	M	29239	Duke of Grove Place	M
29154	3rd Duke of Clay	— M	29240	Duke of Grundy	M
29155	4th Duke of Cliff Grange	— P S	29241	Duke of Guernsey	— R R
29157	Duke of Clinton	— M	29242	Duke of Gustavus	M
29158	Duke of Coal Creek	— R R	29244	Duke of Hanover	— M
29159	Duke of Colebrook	Cox	29245	6th Duke of Harlem	M
29160	Duke of Cornland	Ky I	29246	Duke of Harrison	— M
29161	Duke of Copley	— L R	29247	Duke of Harrison 2nd	— C
29162	Duke Cornwall	P S	29249	Duke of Hayes	R R
29163	Duke of Cortland	Ky I	29250	Duke of Hiram	— L R
29164	1st Duke of Craincreek	— R R	29251	Duke of Hickory Grove	— L R
29165	Duke of Crow Farm	— D	29252	Duke of Hickory Grove	Daisy
29166	Duke Dallas 2nd	T	29253	Duke of Hickory Orchard	— P S
29168	Duke of Devonshire	M	29254	Duke of High Prairie	— R R
29169	Duke of Downey	— R R	29255	5th Duke of Hillsdale	— Cox
29170	Duke Drummond	M	29257	Duke of Holmes	M
29171	1st Duke of Dubuque	— R R	29258	2nd Duke of Huntington	— Cox
29172	2nd Duke of Dubuque	— R R	29260	2nd Duke of Iroquois	Daisy
29173	3rd Duke of Eastside	— M	29261	Duke of Iroquois	R R
29174	Duke of Edinburg	Ky I	29262	Duke of Jackson	— Ky I
29175	Duke of Elkhorn Valley	Ky I	29263	Duke of Jackson	— P S
29176	Duke of Elmwood 3rd	— R R	29265	Duke John	M
29178	1st Duke of Ensley	M	29266	Duke John	M
29181	Duke of Erie	— P S	29268	Duke of Kirkwood	— P S
29182	Duke of Erie 2nd	— P S	29270	Duke of Labette 2nd	— Ky I
29183	3rd Duke of Erie	— M	29271	Duke of Labette 3rd	— Ky I
29184	4th Duke of Evergreen Hill	— L R	29272	Duke of Lafayette	— P S
29185	Duke Fairfax	M	29273	Duke of Lamville	— M

No.	Name	Code	No.	Name	Code
29274	Duke of Lagrange	— R R	29363	Duke of Sharon	— D
29275	Duke of Lenox	M	29365	3rd Duke of Skaneateles	— Cox
29277	Duke of Liberty	— D	29366	1st Duke of Skara Glen	— D
29278	1st Duke of Lima	— L R	29367	4th Duke of Springdale	P S
29279	1st Duke of Locust Grove	— M	29368	5th Duke of Springdale	P S
29280	2nd Duke of Locust Grove	— M	29370	2nd Duke of Springwood's Son	— C
29281	Duke of Lodi	— M	29371	Duke of Suez	D
29282	2nd Duke of Lucknow	Cox	29373	2nd Duke of Sunny Side	— D
29283	Duke of Macomb	— Cox	29374	Duke of Superior	M
29284	Duke of Mahaska 2nd	— M	29375	Duke of Sutherland	— R R
29285	Duke of Mahoning	L R	29377	Duke of Sylvan	M
29286	4th Duke of Maple Avenue	— P S	29378	25th Duke of Tecumseh	Ky I
29289	1st Duke of Marlboro	— P S	29379	27th Duke of Tecumseh	— Ky I
29290	2nd Duke of Marlboro	— R R	29380	19th Duke of the Pines	— R R
29292	Duke of McDonough	— P S	29381	20th Duke of the Pines	— R R
29293	Duke Meredith	— C	29382	21st Duke of the Pines	— R R
29295	Duke of Midland	T	29383	Duke of the Plains	— R R
29296	Duke of Midway	— R R	29384	Duke of Thorne	— M
29298	9th Duke of Montery	— T	29385	Duke of Thorndale	M
29300	3rd Duke of Moscow	— M	29387	1st Duke of Tulare	Ky I
29301	Duke of Mt. Algor	— R R	29390	3rd Duke of Unity	— M
29305	Duke of Muskoda	— C	29391	Duke of Valley View, — Long-Horn	
29307	Duke of Nippersink	— L R	29392	5th Duke of Vermillion	— R R
29308	Duke of Noble County	D	29393	1st Duke of Vernon	T
29309	1st Duke of Nora	— T	29394	1st Duke of Victor	T
29310	Duke of North Buffalo	Ky I	29395	2nd Duke of Victor	T
29313	Duke of Oakgrove	— D	29396	3rd Duke of Victor	T
29314	Duke of Oakland	— M	29397	Duke of Viola	Ky I
29315	Duke of Oakland	— M	29398	Duke of Wahoo Valley	M
29316	1st Duke of Oakland	— R R	29399	Duke of Walnut Grove	L R
29318	Duke of Oakland 2nd	— L R	29400	Duke of Walnut Grove	— P S
29319	Duke of Oakland 3rd	— D	29401	2nd Duke of Walnut Grove	— P S
29320	22nd Duke of Oakland	— C	29402	Duke of Walton	R R
29321	Duke of Oakridge	— L R	29405	1st Duke of Waveland	— R R
29322	3rd Duke of Oakwood	Ky I	29406	2nd Duke of Waveland	— R R
29323	15th Duke of Onondaga	P S	29407	3rd Duke of Waveland	— R R
29324	17th Duke of Onondaga	— Cox	29408	4th Duke of Waveland	— R R
29325	18th Duke of Onondaga	L R	29410	Duke of Wayne	— T
29326	2nd Duke of Orleans	P S	29412	Duke of Westfield	— L R
29327	3rd Duke of Orleans	T	29413	Duke of West Lawn	— M
29328	4th Duke of Orleans	— R R	29419	5th Duke of Windingvale	R R
29329	Duke of Ottawa	— D	29420	8th Duke of Windingvale	— R R
29331	Duke of Oxford	— D	29421	1st Duke of Woodbine	R R
29332	Duke of Oxford 2nd	M	29422	1st Duke of Woodbine	P S
29335	Duke of Palestine	— C	29423	2nd Duke of Woodbine	— M
29336	Duke of Paris	— R R	29425	3rd Duke of Woodbine	— M
29337	Duke of Peoria	— M	29426	1st Duke of Woodside	— M
29338	Duke of Petrolia	Cox	29428	Duke of Yates 10th	M
29339	Duke of Pettis	— Ky I	29429	Duke of Yates 16th	— Cox
29340	Duke of Pike	— P S	29430	Duke of Yates 17th	M
29341	Duke of Pine Mound	— M	29432	Dun Allen	— C
29342	Duke of Plainsview	— R R	29435	Durango	— M
29343	Duke of Platte City	— R R	29436	Dutch Ben	— L R
29344	Duke of Princeton 2nd	Ky I	29437	Dutch Bill	P S
29345	Duke of Princeton 3rd	Ky I	29439	Earl of Argyll 2nd	Ky I
29346	Duke of Portage	Ky I	29441	Earl of Bedford	M
29347	1st Duke of Portage	M	29443	1st Earl of Boston	— Cox
29349	Duke of Putnam	— R R	29444	Earl of Calumet	— M
29350	Duke of Red Ex	— R R	29449	2nd Earl of Exeter	— R R
29351	2nd Duke of Rubenia	M	29452	4th Earl of Grasshill	— Cox
29352	Duke of Richland	M	29454	16th Earl of Greenbush	— P S
29354	Duke of Ridgevale	— T	29455	17th Earl of Greenbush	— R R
29355	Duke of Rio	— M	29456	18th Earl of Greenbush	D
29356	Duke of Robinson'	L R	29457	19th Earl of Greenbush	— R R
29357	1st Duke of Rosedale	— Cox	29465	3rd Earl of Kalamazoo	Cox
29358	Duke of Rose Hill	M	29466	4th Earl of Kalamazoo	Ky I
29359	Duke of Rush	— R R	29467	5th Earl of Kalamazoo	Cox
29360	2nd Duke of Seaham	P S	29468	6th Earl of Kalamazoo	Cox
29361	Duke of Seventy-Six	— T	29469	Earl of Kent	— L R
29362	Duke of Sharon	M	29472	3rd Earl of Lombardy Park	— R R

SHORT-HORN CATTLE PEDIGREES. 137

No.	Name	Ref.
29473	Earl of Maple Lawn	— Cox
29474	2nd Earl of Martin	— Cox
29475	Earl of Mason	— Cox
29476	Earl of McLean Park	— Cox
29478	Earl of Oxford	— Cox
29479	Earl of Palestine	— T
29483	Earl of Sharon	— C
29486	Earl of Spencer	— M
29489	1st Earl of Waveland	— R R
29491	1st Earl of Willow Street	— T
29492	2nd Earl of Willow Street	— Cox
29493	Earl of Winwood	Daisy
29494	Earl of Woodbine	— R R
29495	Easter	M
29496	Easter	— M
29497	Echo	M
29498	Echo	— L R
29499	Eclipse	L R
29500	Eclipse	M
29501	Eclipse	M
29505	Effie's Duke	Ky I
29506	Eglintoun Duke	— M
29509	Eldred	M
29511	Elgin Prince	— C
29514	Elmore	Ky I
29516	Emma Rue's Oxford	— C
29517	Emmett 3rd	T
29519	Emperor	D
29520	Emperor 6th	— P S
29521	Enoch	— T
29523	Enterprise	— Cox
29524	Ernestine's Prince	P S
29525	Eureka	M
29527	Excelsior	T
29528	Excelsior 3rd	— M
29529	Excelsior 4th	— M
29531	Excelsior Muscatoon	P S
29536	Fairys Breastplate	— M
29538	Fancy Bill	P S
29541	Farmer	— Cox
29542	Faust	— M
29543	Favorite	— D
29544	Favorite	— D
29545	Favorite	— M
29546	Favorite	M
29549	Fawsley Goodness	— D
29551	Fearnaught	— Cox
29552	Feland's Duke	— M
29554	Fidget's Airdrie	— D
29555	Fidget's Hayes	— Cox
29556	Fillmore	Ky I
29557	Fillmore Duke 2nd	— M
29559	Financier 3rd	— M
29560	Fin-Ma-Coul	M
29561	Fisher Boy	— Daisy
29562	Fisher Sharon	— Daisy
29563	Flag	— L R
29565	Flora's Mazurka	M
29566	Flower Boy	M
29568	Forester	— Cox
29569	Foreston Prince	Ky I
29570	Fortunatus	Daisy
29571	Fortune	— L R
29572	Frank	Ky I
29574	Frank	M
29575	Frank	— M
29576	Frank	— M
29577	Frank Huff	M
29578	Frank McCague	— P S
29579	Franklin	— L R
29580	Franklin Chief	Cox
29581	Franklin Duke 10th	— L R
29582	Franklin Duke 11th	C
29583	Frank Taylor	— Ky I
29584	Fred	— M
29585	Fred	Ky I
29586	Fred Clyde	M
29587	Fred Douglas	P S
29588	Fred Dudley	M
29590	Fred Renick	— P S
29591	Fremont	M
29592	Fritz	D
29593	Fulton Duke 2nd	— P S
29594	22nd Gaban	— P S
29596	3rd Gaban of Eastside	— P S
29598	Gambetta	— P S
29599	Gambetta	— R R
29600	Gambetta	— R R
29603	Garnet	Ky I
29606	Gayoso	— M
29607	Gem Duke	M
29608	Gem's Duke	— Cox
29611	Gen. Custer	— M
29612	Gen. Custer	— R R
29613	Gen. Custer	C
29615	Gen. Custer	D
29616	Gen. Custer	— M
29617	Gen. Custer	M
29619	Gen. Forest	— M
29620	Gen. Garfield	Ky I
29622	Gen. Grant	— Cox
29623	Gen. Grant	M
29624	Gen. Grant	— D
29625	Gen. Grant	M
29626	Gen. Grant	L R
29628	Gen. Hayes	Ky I
29629	Gen. Hayes	Ky I
29630	Gen. Hayes	— T
29631	Gen. Hood	Ky I
29632	Gen. Lee	M
29633	Gen. Lippincott	— R R
29634	Gen. Meredith	Ky I
29635	Gen. Morgan	M
29636	Gen. Oakland	— M
29637	Gen. Price	— P S
29639	Gen. Scott	L R
29640	Gen. Scott	Ky I
29641	Gen. Sheridan	— P S
29642	Gen. Sheridan	D
29643	Gen. Sherman	Ky I
29649	Geneva Duke	P S
29650	Geneva Duke 2nd	M
29654	3rd Geneva Lad	— Cox
29655	Geneva Otley of Mt. Zion	— M
29657	Gentle Duke 4th	— R R
29661	George	— Cox
29662	George Craggs	— Cox
29663	George Royal	— L R
29664	George Walker	M
29665	George of Wesley	M
29668	Gideon	— M
29669	Gideon	— M
29670	Gifford	— L R
29671	Gilmore's Duke	Ky I
29672	Gipsey Duke	R R
29673	Gladiator	— L R
29674	2nd Glen Airdrie Duke	L R
29675	3rd Glen Airdrie Duke	— M
29677	5th Glen Airdrie Duke	M
29678	6th Glen Airdrie Duke	— D

10

UNFASHIONABLE CROSSES IN

29679	7th Glen Airdrie Duke	L R
29680	8th Glen Airdrie Duke	— L R
29681	5th Glen Connt	M
29682	Glendola's Oxford	— R R
29683	Glen Duke 4th	M
29684	4th Glen Hannibal	— D
29685	5th Glen Hannibal	— D
29686	6th Glen Hannibal	— D
29688	Glenn	L R
29690	Glyndon	L R
29691	Gold Dust	— R R
29696	5th Golden Duke	— M
29700	Goldfinder	— P S
29701	Goldfinder, Jr	— M
29702	2nd Gold of Hendon	— M
29703	Golden Leaf	— R R
29704	Goldsmith	L R
29705	Goldwing	— Cox
29706	Gompachi	— C
29707	Goodness of Oak Hill	— M
29708	Goshen	— D
29709	Goshen Duke	D
29710	Governor 2nd	— M
29712	Gov. Cullom	— M
29713	Governor's Duke	— T
29714	Gov. Hayes	M
29715	Gov. Hayes	— Cox
29716	Gov. Helm 3rd	— T
29717	Gov. McClelland	M
29719	Gov. Woodson	M
29720	Grafton	Cox
29721	Grand Airdrie	— Cox
29722	Grand Airdrie 2nd	P S
29727	Grand Cambridge	— R R
29728	Grand Commander 2nd	— M
29729	Grand Duke	— M
29730	Grand Duke	— Cox
29733	Grand Duke of Clinchdade	— P S
29735	6th Grand Duke of Moreton	— Cox
29736	Grand Duke of Nicholas	— Cox
29741	2nd Grand Duke of Wytheville	P S
29742	Grand Master	P S
29744	Grandson of Premier	— Cox
29745	13th Grand Turk of Oakhome	I. R
29746	22nd Grand Turk of Oak Home	— M
29747	27th Grand Turk of Oak Home	L R
29748	Granger	— T
29749	Granger	Ky I
29751	Granger	— Ky I
29752	Granger	M
29754	Grant	— M
29755	Grant	T
29756	Grant	P S
29758	Grant	— L R
29759	Grape Grove Duke of Goodness	R R
29762	Greenwood Duke of Goodness	R R
29763	Greenwood D, of Goodness 2nd	R R
29764	Greenwood D, of Goodness 3rd	R R
29765	Greenwood Favorite 4th	Daisy
29767	Grenadier	— L R
29768	Grimes	— D
29769	Gringo	T
29770	Gulliver	T
29772	Gwynne's Duke of Oxford	— Cox
29774	Gwynneth 2nd	— Ky I
29776	Handy	D
29777	Hannibal	— P S
29778	Hannibal 34th	— R R
29779	Hannibal 36th	— M
29781	Harkaway	— P S
29782	Harold	— M
29785	Harrison Pierce	— D
29786	Harrison Pierce 3rd	— D
29787	Harrison Pierce 4th	— M
29788	Harrison Taylor 3rd	— P S
29789	Harry Loveland	Daisy
29791	Hawkeye Prince	— P S
29792	Hayes	M
29793	Hayes	P S
29794	Hayes	Ky I
29795	Hayes	— M
29796	Hayes	— P S
29797	Hayes	— Cox
29798	Haze	— Cox
29799	7th Hazelwood Duke	C
29801	Heartsease's Booth	— Ky I
29802	Hebron	Cox
29804	Hedgerow	— T
29807	Henderson Boy	— M
29808	2nd Hendon Duke	— M
29809	Hendon's Loudon Airdrie	— M
29810	Hendricks	Ky I
29811	Hendricks	— P S
29812	Henry	— M
29813	Henry	Ky I
29814	Henry Clay	T
29815	Henry Clay	— R R
29816	Henry Jim	Ky I
29817	Henry Pickrell	T
29818	Henry Ward Beecher	— M
29819	Henry Ward Beecher	M
29820	Hercules	— L R
29821	Hercules	M
29823	Hero	M
29824	Hero	— Ky I
29825	Hero	— T
29826	Hero	— M
29829	Hickory	L R
29830	Higgins' Starlight	D
29831	Highland Chief 2nd	— M
29832	Highland Duke	— Ky I
29833	Highland Duke	P S
29834	Highland Duke	P S
29835	Highland Lad	— T
29836	Highland Lad	Cox
29837	Highland Prince	P S
29838	Highland Prince	C
29839	High Standard	Ky I
29840	Hillsdale	— M
29842	2nd Hilldale Prince	— M
29844	Hinckley Duke	— L R
29846	Hippias	— L R
29847	Hiram Boy	— L R
29849	Home Park Duke	— M
29850	Homer	T
29851	Honest Joe	— Cox
29852	Honest John	P S
29853	Honest Tom	P S
29854	Hopeless Lad	— M
29855	Hope of Princess 3rd	— Cox
29856	Hotspur 1st	— Cox
29857	Howell Duke	— Ky I
29860	Hubert	C
29861	Hugh Despencer	— C
29862	Humbolt	Ky I
29864	Huron Chief	— R R
29865	Huxley	T
29867	Ike Loder	— C
29868	Ike Woodyard	Ky I
29872	Imperial Prince	M

SHORT-HORN CATTLE PEDIGREES.

No.	Name	Mark
29873	Indale	— P S
29874	Independence	— L R
29875	Independence	L R
29876	Indian Chief	— M
29877	Indian Chief	— L R
29878	Indian Dick	— C
29881	Iowa Boy	P S
29882	Iowa's Cap Sheaf	— L R
29883	Iowa Chief	M
29887	Ivanhoe	Ky I
29890	Ivanhoe	— C
29891	Jack Frost	M
29892	Jack Lorne	— M
29893	Jackson	— R R
29894	Jackson	P S
29896	Jake	— P S
29897	Jason 2nd	— Ky I
29898	Jason 3rd	— Ky I
29902	Jay Gould	— M
29904	Jeff Davis	— M
29905	Jeff Davis	Ky I
29906	Jeff Davis	— C
29907	Jefferson	— P S
29908	Jefferson Climax	— R R
29909	Jeff Pool	— R R
29910	Jem Cooper	— M
29911	Jenner	— Cox
29912	Jenner Boy	— Cox
29914	Jerry	— Cox
29915	Jerry	— Cox
29916	Jerry Duke	M
29917	Jerry Duncan	Ky I
29918	Jesse	— D
29919	Jessie's Duke 2nd	Ky I
29920	Jo Barber	L R
29921	Joe Bunker	— P S
29922	Joe Daviess	— R R
29923	Joe Hayes	M
29924	Joe Hixon's Boy	M
29925	Joe Miller	Ky I
29926	Joe Scott	— R R
29928	Jim	M
29929	Jim	Cox
29930	Jim	— L R
29931	Jim Blaine	— R R
29932	Jim King	Ky I
29933	Jim Taylor	— M
29934	John	— L R
29935	John Airdrie	P S
29936	John A. Logan	M
29937	John Backus	— R R
29938	John Brown	— D
29939	John Clark	— M
29940	John Hope	— M
29943	Johnny	— M
29948	John O'Gaunt	— Cox
29949	Johnston	Ky I
29950	John Whipple	— Cox
29951	Jolly	— Cox
29953	Joseph	P S
29955	Josh Billings	— Cox
29956	Josie's Duke of Richmond	— C
29957	Journal Prize	— R R
29960	Judge Davis	— L R
29961	Judge Dix	— P S
29962	Judge Savage	P S
29963	Judge Turner	— L R
29965	Julius	— M
29967	Jupiter	P S
29970	Kalos	— D
29971	Kazaar	M
29974	Keepsake	— L R
29976	Kenoma Duke	— M
29977	Kent	Ky I
29978	Kentucky	— M
29979	Kentucky	— R R
29980	Kentucky Duke	— R R
29981	Kentucky Jim	R R
29982	Kentuck Red Duke	— C
29983	Keokuk	Ky I
29984	Kil Patrick	Ky I
29985	King	Ky I
29986	King	P S
29987	Kings Airdrie	— R R
29990	King of LaGrange	T
29991	King of Lawrence	P S
29992	King of Liberty	Ky I
29993	King's Loudon Duke 6th	— R R
29994	King of Maple Grove	— Ky I
29995	King of Oakwood	Ky I
29996	King of Polk	— M
29997	King Philip	Ky I
29998	King Philip	— Cox
29999	1st King Red Rose	— D
30000	King of the Lake	— Cox
30001	King William	— M
30002	King William	M
30003	Kingston Duke	— M
30017	Kossuth	D
30019	Kuruk	— D
30020	Lad	P S
30021	Lady's Baron	— D
30022	Lady Jane's Duke	— R R
30024	Lady's Napier	M
30025	Lafayette	— M
30026	Lafayette	— D
30028	Laird of Waverly	L R
30029	Late Boy	— T
30030	Lammis	— M
30031	Lancaster	— Cox
30032	Lancaster 2nd	Ky I
30035	Lantz's Bourbon	— R R
30036	Larry	— R R
30037	Laudable	— R R
30039	Laudable Star	Woods
30040	Leander	— P S
30041	Ledge Duke 2nd	R R
30042	Ledge Duke 2nd	M
30043	Ledge Duke 3rd	— L R
30044	Ledge Duke 4th	R R
30045	Ledge Duke 5th	Ky I
30046	Lee	— M
30048	Legal Tender	Ky I
30049	Legal Tender	— R R
30050	Legal Tender	Woods
30052	Le Grand Sweepstakes	— P S
30053	Lehigh Chief	— D
30054	Lena's Duke	P S
30055	Leno Duke 3rd	M
30056	Lenox	P S
30057	Leo	— M
30058	Leo	— P S
30060	Leonard	— M
30063	Leopard 5th	D
30064	Leopard 6th	D
30067	Leopold	— P S
30069	Le Rue	Ky I
30070	Leslie Hall	— P S
30071	Lettie's Prince	— M
30072	Lewis Breastplate	— P S

UNFASHIONABLE CROSSES IN

30073	Lewis Orontes	— D		30172	Louan's Beau	— R R
30074	Lexington	— R R		30173	Louans Commander	— M
30075	Lexington	M		30174	Louan Duke	— M
30076	Liberty	— L R		30175	Louan Duke	— D
30077	Liberty Prince	— M		30176	Louan Gwynne	— R R
30078	Lieut. Darby	L R		30177	Louanjo	— R R
30079	Lightfoot	Woods		30178	Louanjo of Bloomfield	— M
30080	Lily's Duke	— R R		30179	Louan's Milander	— M
30081	Lincoln	M		30180	Louan Muscatoon	— M
30083	Lincoln Chief Waveland	— R R		30181	Louan's Nimrod	— M
30084	Lincoln's Duke of Locust Grove	— M		30182	2nd Louan's Oxford	— M
30085	Linwood Gloster	— Cox		30183	Louan's Prince	— D
30086	Little Giant	P S		30184	Louan Prince	— R R
30087	Little Mac	M		30185	Loudon Duke	— M
30088	Live George	M		30187	Loudon Duke 15th	— R R
30089	Live Oak	M		30189	Loudon Duke of Indiana	— R R
30091	Louan's Duke	— M		30195	Loveland Prince	— Cox
30092	Locomotive	— Ky I		30196	Lowther	— R R
30093	Locomotive 2nd	— R R		30197	Loyal	— R R
30094	Locomotive 3rd	— R R		30198	4th Loyal Duke of Oakland	— P S
30095	Locum	— R R		30199	5th Loyal Duke of Oakland	M
30096	Lofty	Ky I		30200	Loyal Prince	— R R
30097	Lofty	Ky I		30201	Louan's Duke	— D
30098	Lofty Duke	— R R		30202	Lucretius, Jr	— R R
30100	Logan	— Ky I		30203	Lucretius 2nd	— R R
30101	Logan	— L R		30204	Lucy Bly's Airdrie	— R R
30102	Logan	M		30205	Lucy's Red Boy	L R
30103	Logan Bull	— M		30206	Lyndale Baron	— M
30104	Logan's Masterpiece	T		30207	Lyndale Duke	— C
30105	Lone Star	M		30208	Mac Alva	— M
30106	Lone Star	— D		30209	McComb	M
30108	Longfellow	— P S		30210	MacDonough	P S
30109	Longfellow	— D		30211	McDuff	Ky I
30110	Long John	M		30212	McGregor	C
30111	Longstreet	Ky I		30213	McGregor	— M
30113	Lorainer	— D		30215	McGregor	— Cox
30114	Lord Aylesby	— R R		30216	MacMahon	— D
30118	Lord Bright Eyes	— M		30217	McMillen	— M
30120	Lord Byron	P S		30218	Mack Clyde	M
30123	Lord of Cedar	— R R		30219	Madison	M
30124	Lord Chatham 3rd	P S		30220	Madison	— M
30128	Lord Darby	— R R		30221	Madison Duke	— M
30130	Lord Derby	— M		30222	Magenta	— R R
30133	Lord Douglass	Cox		30223	Maggie's Duke	— C
30135	Lord Eglintoun 2nd	Daisy		30226	Magnum Opus	— M
30138	Lord Fragrant	— P S		30227	Majestic	— M
30139	Lord Gloster	— Cox		30228	Majestic	P S
30140	Lord Graham	— R R		30229	Major	— T
30142	Lord Hopewell	M		30230	Major	— Cox
30144	Lord John 2nd	— C		30231	Major	D
30145	Lord John of Clyde	M		30232	Major	Daisy
30146	Lord Layton	— Long-Horn		30234	Major	— Cox
30147	Lord Leslie	M		30235	Major	P S
30148	Lord London	— Ky I		30236	Major Airdrie	— M
30149	Lord Lovel	M		30237	Major Anderson	Cox
30150	Lord Lyons	— Daisy		30238	Major Anderson	— M
30151	Lord of Michigan	Ky I		30239	Major Booth	T
30153	Lord Nelson	— Cox		30241	Major Bullock	— M
30154	Lord Nero	— Ky I		30242	Major Butler	P S
30155	Lord Newham	— R R		30245	Major Downing	— M
30156	Lord North	— Long-Horn		30246	Major John	M
30158	Lord Ravenel	— M		30248	Major Moorhead	M
30160	Lord Russell	— M		30249	Major Morris	— P S
30161	Lord Strathallen 2nd	Ky I		30250	Major Pollard	Ky I
30162	Lord of the Larches	D		30251	Major Princeton	— C
30163	Lord of the Valley	— Ky I		30252	Major Prine	— R R
30166	2nd Lord Wheatland	— R R		30254	Major Rose	— D
30167	3rd Lord Wheatland	— R R		30255	Major Saxe	— P S
30170	Lotta Marsden	— M		30256	Major Saxe	— P S
30171	Louan's Airdrie	— R R		30257	Major Stewart	L R

No.	Name	Code
30258	Malchus	— T
30259	Malcolm	— D
30260	Malcolm	— M
30261	Malcolm Favorite	— L R
30264	Manfred	— Cox
30267	Maple Prince	— D
30268	March's Oakland	L R
30269	Marengo	— M
30270	Marietta's Son	— M
30272	Mark Anthony	— Cox
30274	Mark Twain	— Cox
30275	Marlborough Duke	— P S
30277	Marquis	— M
30278	Marquis 2nd	Ky I
30283	Marquis DeBute	— Cox
30286	Marquis of Linwood	— M
30288	Marquis of Wynnstay	C
30289	Mars	D
30291	Martha's Airdrie	— R R
30296	Master Airdrie 9th	Daisy
30297	Master Airdrie 11th	— M
30298	Master Airdrie 12th	Daisy
30299	Master Airdrie 13th	— M
30300	Master Airdrie 14th	— Cox
30305	Master Geneva 3rd	— C
30307	Master Geneva 12th	— M
30308	Master Green	P S
30313	Master Sharon	— C
30315	Matchless	— T
30316	Matchless	M
30317	Matchless 3rd	— L R
30318	Matilda's Airdrie	— Long-Horn
30319	Matilda's Oxford	— Long-Horn
30320	Matildas Thorndale	— R R
30321	Mat's Lancaster	D
30322	Max	— L R
30323	Max Sheffielder	D
30324	May Day	— R R
30325	May Duke	— Ky I
30331	Mazurk Hood	— M
30332	Mazurka Lad	Daisy
30333	Mazurka's Oxford 5th	— Ky I
30334	Mazurka's Oxford 6th	Ky I
30335	Mazurkas Oxford 7th	— Ky I
30337	6th Meadow Duke	— M
30338	8th Meadow Duke	— M
30340	Medoc	Ky I
30341	Medoras Nimrod	— R R
30342	Melodeon	— M
30344	Merry Monarch, Jr	— M
30345	Metamora	— Cox
30347	Meteor 3rd	Cox
30348	Meteor 5th	Cox
30349	Miami Duke	— D
30350	Michigan Prince	— M
30352	Mike Morris	— C
30353	Mill Brook, Jr	— C
30354	Milpeta's Duke	— L R
30356	Minister Duke	M
30360	Minnie's Duke	— M
30362	Miss Wiley's 2nd Baron	— M
30365	Modoc	M
30366	Modoc	M
30367	Modock Chief	Cox
30368	Modoc Chief	P S
30369	Modoc Chief	— R R
30371	Mogul	P S
30372	Mohawk 4th	Ky I
30374	Monarch	P S
30375	Monarch 2nd	— M
30376	Monarch of Pattersondale 4th	— R R
30377	Monarch of the Plains	— P S
30379	Monegaw	— M
30381	Monona 1st	— L R
30382	Moody	P S
30383	Moody	P S
30384	Moonlight	— M
30386	Morgan	Ky I
30391	Moss Rose Cherub 3rd	— M
30394	Moxiey Duke	— M
30395	Mozart	— M
30396	Murphy	— Long-Horn
30397	Music 4th	— Cox
30398	Musician	— Cox
30399	Muscatoon	— M
30401	Muscatoon 2nd	M
30402	Muscatoon 4th	P S
30403	Muscatoon of Oakland	— R R
30406	Napier	P S
30407	Napier Duke	— M
30409	Napoleon 2nd	C
30411	Napoleon 4th	— L R
30412	Nebraska Duke	— L R
30413	Nebuchadnezzar	— M
30416	Ned	M
30417	Ned Parker	Ky I
30419	Nels	M
30420	Nelson	P S
30421	Nelson	P S
30422	Nellie's Duke	— L R
30423	Nellies Headlight	P S
30424	Nemacolon	— T
30425	Nero	— M
30426	Nero	— Cox
30427	Nero	— P S
30428	Nevada	— L R
30430	New Years Day	— T
30431	Niagara Chief	— D
30433	Nickel	— Cox
30434	Nimble Will	— L R
30435	Nimrod	— Cox
30436	Niota	Ky I
30437	Noble Duke 2nd	— L R
30438	Nod	— Ky I
30439	Noel's Fridget	— Cox
30440	Nominee	— T
30441	Nonsuch	— M
30446	North Star	T
30447	Northumberland	— Ky I
30448	November Lad	— P S
30451	Oak Grove Boy	— M
30452	Oak Hill	— Cox
30455	Oakland Lad	Ky I
30456	Oakwood	— M
30457	Octo Duke	L R
30458	Ohio Boy	M
30459	Oleander	L R
30460	Ole Bull	P S
30461	Omoo	— R R
30462	One Eyed Riley	M
30463	Oneida 2nd	— Cox
30464	Oneida's Lad	— R R
30466	Onondaga	— Cox
30467	Orange Billey	— Cox
30470	Orange Lad	— Ky I
30473	Oreb	— M
30474	Orlando 2nd	M
30475	Orphan Boy	M
30476	Orpheus of Spring Lake	Cox
30477	Oscar 1st	M

30479	Osco Lad	— R R	30580	Plumwood F F	Ky I
30480	Osman Pasha	— M	30581	Plumwood G G	C
30481	Osman Pasha	— M	30582	Plumwood H H	Daisy
30482	Osman Pasha	— R R	30584	Plumwood I I	Ky I
30483	Osman Pasha	P S	30585	Plumwood J J	R R
30484	Osman Pasha	— P S	30586	Plumwood L, Jr	— Ky I
30485	Oswi	— Long-Horn	30587	Polo	Ky I
30486	Othello	— M	30588	Pomeroy	M
30487	Otho	M	30589	Pontiac	P S
30490	Oxford	— P S	30592	Porter	— M
30491	Oxford	, L R	30593	Prairie Chief	— T
30492	Oxford 7th	Ky I	30594	Prairie Duke	— Ky I
30493	Oxford 8th	Ky I	30595	Prairie Duke	— M
30495	Oxford Atha	— M	30596	Prairie King	— R R
30501	Oxford Boy	Cox	30597	Prairie King	— L R
30503	Oxford Boy	— R R	30598	Prairie Prince	— Cox
30506	Oxford Chief	— D	30600	President	M
30507	Oxford Duke	— M	30601	President	L R
30510	Oxford Duke	— P S	30603	President Hayes	— R R
30511	Oxford Duke	— R R	30605	Preston	— D
30514	Oxford Gwynne 2nd	— Cox	30610	Pride's Lord Abraham	Woods
30518	1st Oxford of Kane	— D	30612	Prince	— L R
30521	Oxford Lad	L R	30613	Prince B.	— L R
30522	Oxford Lad	M	30614	Prince	— L R
30523	Oxford Lad	— Cox	30615	Prince	D
30524	Oxford London	— M	30617	Prince	Ky I
30525	Oxford's Prince	— P S	30618	Prince	Ky I
30526	Oxford Prince 2nd	— M	30619	Prince	P S
30528	8th Oxford of Vermillion	— R R	30620	Prince	— M
30529	9th Oxford of Vermillion	— R R	30622	Prince	— P S
30530	10th Oxford of Vermillion	— R R	30623	Prince	— P S
30533	Palmyra Duke	M	30624	Prince	— M
30534	Paragon	— M	30625	Prince	— D
30535	Paragon	— P S	30626	Prince	— Ky I
30536	Parda 5th's Oxford	— D	30627	Prince	— R R
30538	Pasha	Ky I	30629	Prince Albert	— L R
30539	Patchin Duke	— L R	30630	Prince Albert	— Ky I
30540	Paul	— T	30636	Prince Arthur	— Cox
30541	Pauline's Duke	P S	30638	Prince Arthur	— D
30542	Pearl's London Duke	— T	30639	4th Prince of Australia	— Cox
30544	Peerless 2nd	— L R	30640	5th Prince of Australia	— Cox
30548	Perfection	— M	30641	Prince Bismarck	— L R
30549	Perry	— R R	30642	Prince of Bourbon	— M
30550	Peter Cooper	— M	30643	Prince of Bourbon	Daisy
30551	Peter Cooper	— P S	30644	Prince Charles	— T
30552	Peter Cooper	— M	30645	Prince Climax 3rd	— D
30553	Peter Cooper	Ky I	30646	Prince Climax 3rd	M
30554	Peter Cooper	— Cox	30648	Prince Edward	Ky I
30555	Petroleum	Ky I	30649	Prince of Elmwood	Ky I
30556	Phalanx Lad	Cox	30652	Prince Gwynne	— D
30557	Phenomenon	— Cox	30654	Prince Henry	— M
30558	Phil Sheridan	— Ky I	30661	Prince Kerby	— Cox
30559	Phil Sheridan	— Cox	30662	Prince of Lake	— D
30560	Phil Sheridan	— Cox	30663	Prince of Livingston	— M
30561	Pilot	Ky I	30664	Prince of Logan	Ky I
30562	Pilot	Ky I	30665	Prince of Louan	— R R
30563	Pilot	P S	30666	Prince Louan of Brookvale	— R R
30565	Pioneer	— T	30667	Prince McDougal	— L R
30566	Pioneer	Cox	30669	Prince of Minglewood	— T
30568	Pioneer Chieftain	M	30671	Prince Mazurka Rose	— M
30569	Pioneer Duke	M	30673	Prince of Monroe	R R
30570	Planet	— T	30674	Prince of Oakwood	— Ky I
30571	Playfellow	— M	30675	Prince Olive	P S
30572	Pleasant	R R	30676	Prince of Ontario	— Cox
30573	Plenary	R R	30677	Prince Oxford	— C
30575	Plumblick Thorndale 2nd	— Ky I	30680	Prince of Palestine	— T
30576	Plumblick Thorndale 3rd	— Ky I	30681	Prince of Pre-Emption	— P S
30577	Plumwood	— Ky I	30682	Prince's Profitable	— R R
30578	Plumwood C C	R R	30683	2nd Prince of Rochester	— M
30579	Plumwood E E	— R R	30685	Prince Royal	Ky I

SHORT-HORN CATTLE PEDIGREES.

30686	Prince Royal	— P S	30777	Red Duke	M
30687	Prince of Sanilac	M	30778	Red Duke	M
30688	Prince of Seaham 2nd	— C	30779	Red Duke 3rd	— L R
30689	Prince Shaw	— L R	30782	Red Duke of Turkey Run	Daisy
30690	Prince of Spring Plains	— M	30783	Red Granger	M
30691	Princess' Duke	— P S	30784	Red Jacket	— Cox
30692	Prince of the Dells	— M	30788	Red Jacket	L R
30693	Prince of the Meadows	— M	30789	Red Jim	L R
30694	Prince of the West	— M	30790	Red Jim	M
30695	Prince of Thorndale	— C	30791	Red John	— P S
30696	Princeton	D	30792	Red Knight	M
30697	Princeton Lad	— D	30793	Red Light	— P S
30699	Prince of Wales	M	30794	Red Lion	— Cox
30700	Prince of Wales	— L R	30795	Red Logan	R R
30701	Prince of Wales 2nd	— L R	30798	Red Muscatoon	— Daisy
30702	Prince of Walnut Grove	— M	30799	Red Prince	R R
30703	Prince Wiley of Hilldale	— M	30801	Red Oak	— Cox
30704	Prince William	P S	30802	Red Ranger	Ky I
30705	Prince William	P S	30803	Red Roan	— M
30706	Prince of Winfield	— R R	30804	Red Robin	— P S
30710	Procurator	— Daisy	30805	Red Roan	M
30714	Punch	— P S	30811	Red Rover	— T
30715	Puritan	— M	30812	Red Rover	— R R
30716	Putnam	— M	30813	Red Rover	— D
30719	Ralph	Cox	30814	Red Rover	Ky I
30720	Rambler	D	30815	Red Wellington	— D
30721	Rambler	— Cox	30816	Red Wing 2nd	— T
30722	Rande	— D	30817	Red Star	— Cox
30723	Ranger	D	30818	Red Star	P S
30724	Ranger	— P S	30821	Reformer	Ky I
30725	Ranger	Ky I	30822	Renick	— M
30726	Ranger	— Wrong	30823	Renick 2nd	— Daisy
30727	Ranger Prince	— R R	30824	Reno	— L R
30728	Ranger	M	30827	Richard 1st	— M
30729	Ranger	— M	30828	Richmond	— M
30730	Raritan Lad	— P S	30829	Richmond	— P S
30731	Raspberry Allen	— D	30831	Riley Duke	— M
30732	Rattler	— P S	30832	Rinaldo	— P S
30733	Ratler	M	30833	3rd Rio Dan	— P S
30738	Rebel Chief	— R R	30835	Roan	— Woods
30740	Red Airdrie	— R R	30841	Roan Dick	Ky I
30741	Red Airdrie 2nd	— C	30842	Roan Dick	— M
30743	Red and White Duke	M	39844	Roan Duke	— M
30744	Red Ben	M	30845	Roan Duke	— P S
30745	Red Berry	— P S	30846	Roan Duke	— P S
30746	Red Boy	M	30847	Roan Duke	— D
30748	Red Breastplate	— C	30848	Roan Duke	— L R
30749	Redbud	— D	30851	Roan Duke	— T
30750	Redbud	— P S	30853	Roan Duke	— P S
30751	Redbud	— Cox	30856	Roan Golden	— Cox
30752	Redbud	— M	30857	Roan Granger	— Cox
30753	Red Chief	— M	30858	Roan Knight	— Cox
30754	Red Chief	— Cox	30860	Roanoke	— L R
30755	Red Cloud	M	30861	Roan Prince	— M
30756	Red Cloud	Ky I	30862	Roan Prince	P S
30757	Red Cloud	P S	30863	Robert Bell	Ky I
30758	Red Cloud	T	30864	Robert Bruce	— Cox
30759	Red Cloud	— Cox	30865	Robert Bruce	— M
30760	Red Cloud	— D	30866	Robert Dhu	— M
30761	Red Cloud	— C	30867	Robert Ellington	— D
30762	Red Cloud	— K I	30868	Robert Fulton	— L R
30763	Red Cloud	— D	30869	Robert Hood	— M
30765	Red Daisy Duke	— R R	30870	Robert Lee	L R
30768	Red Duke	— M	30871	Rob Roy	— R R
30769	Red Duke	Daisy	30872	Rob Roy	— M
30770	Red Duke	— M	30873	Robert Sherman	M
30772	Red Duke	— M	30874	Robertson Favorite	— R R
30773	Red Duke	— M	30876	Robin	— M
30774	Red Duke	— D	30877	Robin Adair	— M
30776	Red Duke	P S	30878	Roderick	L R

30879	Roderick Dhu	Ky I	30986	Samuel J.	L R
30880	Rodolphus	— R R	30987	Samuel J. Tilden	— T
30881	Roland	— Cox	30988	Samuel J. Tilden	— D
30882	Roland	— Cox	30989	Sam J. Tilden	— P S
30883	Rolla	Ky I	30990	Samuel J. Tilden	— M
30884	Romeo	Ky I	30992	Samuel Kenton	— M
30885	Romeo	P S	30993	Sam Lord	L R
30886	Romeo	M	30994	Sam Patch	Cox
30887	Romeo	— D	30995	Sampson	— R R
30889	Romeo	D	30997	Sam Tilden	— T
30890	Romeo	L R	30998	Sam Tilden	— R R
30892	Romulus	— M	30999	Sam Tilden	— M
30897	Rose Chilton's Son	— R R	31000	Sam Weller	— M
30899	Rose Duke	R R	31001	Sankey	— C
30900	Rose Duke	— D	31002	Sarcoxie Chief	— Cox
30901	Rose's Duke	— P S	31003	3rd Saxon Keith of Oakland	— Ky I
30903	Rose Duke	— R R	31004	Scarlet Duke of Goodness	— M
30905	Rosy Duke 3rd	— M	31005	Scio Duke 2nd	Ky I
30906	Rosy Duke of Winfield	— Cox	31006	Scipio Lad	— M
30908	Rosamond's Duke	— R R	31008	Scottish Crown 2nd	— L R
30909	Rosamond Duke	— M	31009	Senator	— M
30912	Rose's Oxford	— R R	31112	Seneca Duke	— L R
30914	Rosy Prince 2nd	C	31114	Seth	— T
30916	Rosette's Grand Duke	— R R	31116	Shaker	— M
30917	2nd Rose of Waveland	— R R	31117	Shaker Boy	— L R
30918	Rosewood	— L R	31118	Sharon Blue	— D
30919	Rothsay	— L R	31120	Sharon Duke of Granite Farm	— C
30920	Rounder	— L R	31122	Sharon Prince	— L R
30921	Rover	— Cox	31123	Shawnee	— L R
30922	Rover	T	31124	Sheffielder	— D
30923	Rowena's Duke	— R R	31125	Sheffielder	— D
30924	Rowzer	Ky I	31126	Shelly	— L R
30925	Roxbury	M	31127	Sleepy Jim of Syene	P S
30926	Roy	Ky I	31128	Shelton	— T
30927	Royal	— Cox	31129	Sheridan	M
30932	Royal Briton	— R R	31130	Sherman	— M
30934	Royal Dick	M	31131	Sherwood	— P S
30935	Royal Duke	— M	31133	Simon Kenton	— M
30936	Royal Duke	— M	31134	Sir Arthur	— Cox
30937	Royal Duke	Ky I	31137	Sir George	— Ky I
30938	Royal Duke	M	31138	Sir George	Ky I
30940	Royal Duke John	— M	31139	Sir George	M
30941	Royal Favorite	— R R	31141	Sir Robert	Ky I
30943	Royal Gem	— Daisy	31143	Sir Robert	— R R
30945	Royal George 2nd	— L R	31144	Sir Roger Tichborne	— M
30946	Royal George 2nd	— M	31148	Sir Walter	L R
30948	Royal Hope 2nd	M	31150	Sir Wilfred	— Cox
30949	Royalist 2nd	M	31151	Sir William	— M
30952	Royal Napier	M	31152	Sir William	— D
30953	Royal Oakland	M	31154	Sitting Bull	— Ky I
30957	Royal Prince	D	31155	Sitting Bull	R R
30958	Royal Renick	T	31156	Sitting Bull	T
30960	Royalton Duke	— R R	31157	Sitting Bull	— M
30963	Ruby's Booth	— L R	31159	Sitting Bull	— P S
30964	Ruby's Prince of Orange	— L R	31160	Sitting Bull	M
30966	Rudolph	M	31161	Smuggler	Ky I
30967	Rulo	— M	31162	Smuggler	P S
30968	Runnemede	— L R	31163	Snowball	— D
30969	Ruralusia Duke	— R R	31164	Snowdon	— R R
30971	St. Cloud	— R R	31165	Snowflake	P S
30972	St. Crispin	P S	31166	Snowflake	— T
30974	St. Elmo 3rd	— R R	31167	Son of Airdrie	P S
30975	St. James Duke	— P S	31168	Son of Grey Jenner 4th	— Cox
30976	St. Joe	— T	31169	Sparkle	L R
30977	St. John's Duke	— L R	31170	Sportsman	— Cox
30978	St. Patrick	— Cox	31172	Spotted Duke	— M
30981	Sam	P S	31173	Spotted Mac	— R R
30983	Sam 3rd	Ky I	31175	Spotted Oxford	Ky I
30984	Sam Deering	— Cox	31176	Sprightly	Ky I
30985	Sam Hickory	— L R			

31177	Springfield — M	31273	Tilden — M
31178	Springfield Laird — Cox	31274	Tilden — C
31180	Stanley — L R	31275	Tilden — P S
31181	Stanley — Ky I	31276	Tilden — M
31182	Stanley 3rd — M	31277	Tim Day — M
31184	Stanwaittie — P S	31279	Tom Benton — L R
31186	Star — T	31280	Tom Benton — M
31188	Star Duke — Ky I	31281	Tomboy — Ky I
31189	Star Duke — Daisy	31284	Tom Hendricks — T
31190	Star Duke — D	31285	Tom Miller — R R
31191	Star Duke — P S	31289	Tom Scott — P S
31192	Star Duke of Oxford — R R	31290	Tom Wallace — P S
31193	Starlight — M	31292	Tongonoxie — Cox
31194	Starlight — Cox	31293	Towanda 2nd — R R
31195	Starlight — M	31294	Townley Gem 2nd — Cox
31196	Starlight — Ky I	31295	Townsend Lad — M
31197	Starlight — Ky I	31300	Triumph — Ky I
31198	Starlight 2nd — P S	31301	Triumph — M
31199	Starling — L R	31303	Tube Duke — P S
31200	Star Napier — Ky I	31304	Tube Duke 2nd — P S
31201	Star Prince — Ky I	31305	Twilight — Ky I
31202	Star of Ridge Grove — D	31306	Typee — R R
31203	Star of Spring Grove — P S	31307	Tyrannus — C
31206	Star of the Realm 5th — C	31310	Ulysses — P S
31207	Star of the West — M	31313	Undine's Oxford — Cox
31208	Star of the West — Cox	31314	Unser Fritz — T
31209	Star of the West — Cox	31316	Usurper — M
31210	Star of the West — M	31318	Vallandigham — Ky I
31211	Star of the West — Cox	31319	Valley Chief — R R
31214	Stentor — R R	31320	Valley Duke — R R
31215	Sterling — M	31321	Van 2nd — M
31219	Stonewall Jackson — Cox	31323	Vanderbilt — R R
31220	Storm — M	31324	Vanguard — P S
31221	Studley — M	31325	Vera Cruze — M
31222	Success — P S	31326	Vermillion Boy — Ky I
31223	Succor Boy — L R	31327	Vermont — M
31225	Sullivant — C	31328	Verulam — Cox
31227	Superb — Cox	31329	Vespasian 4th — P S
31228	Surprise — T	31330	Victor — T
31229	Surprise — M	31331	Victor — L R
31231	Swamp Duke — L R	31333	Victor — R R
31232	Sweetbriar's Kerklevington — Cox	31337	Violet 2nd — Cox
31235	Sylvia's Duke — L R	31338	Viscount 3rd — Ky I
31236	Symmetry Duke — R R	31340	Von Moltke — L R
31237	Talmage — D	31342	Vulcan — L R
31238	Tama Chief — Ky I	31344	Wade Hampton — T
31239	Tasso — C	31345	Wade Hampton — D
31240	Tecumseh — Cox	31346	Wade Hampton — P S
31241	Tempest — Ky I	31347	Wade Hampton — P S
31242	Tenbroke — P S	31348	Wallace — C
31243	Ten Mile — M	31349	Walnut Hill Duke 1st — R R
31244	Texas Beau — R R	31350	Walnut Hill Duke 2nd — M
31245	Texas Lad — P S	31351	Walnut Hill Duke 3rd — Ky I
31246	Thair — M	31352	Walnut Hill Duke 4th — M
31248	The Captain — P S	31356	Warren — M
31249	The Doctor — M	31358	Warrior Duke — R R
31252	The Judge — T	31361	Warwick — Cox
31253	Theodore Bates — D	31362	Warwick — P S
31254	The Pride of Como — C	31367	Washington Mazurka — P S
31255	The Sheriff — M	31371	Waterloo's Jupiter — R R
31258	Theta's Hillhurst — L R	31372	Watonwan — P S
31261	Thomas Henry Huxley — L R	31373	Waveland Chief — R R
31262	Thorndale — C	31375	W. C. Kent — M
31263	Thorndale — M	31376	Webster Duke 4th — Ky I
31264	Thorndale, Jr — C	31381	Wenzel — C
31268	6th Thorndale Duke — M	31382	Werner — C
31269	Thrifty — P S	31383	Western Boy — M
31270	Tilden — R R	31384	Western Chief — P S
31271	Tilden — Ky I	31385	Western Lad — R R
31272	Tilden — Ky I	31386	Western Prince — R R

31387	Western Prince .... Woods	31488	Duke of Irvington .... — M
31388	Wheeler .... P S	31489	Duke of Leinster .... M
31389	Wheelers Profitable .... — R R	31491	Duke of Oakland .... — D
31391	White Cloud .... M	31492	2nd Duke of Oakland .... — D
31393	Whiteface .... — M	31493	3rd Duke of Oakland .... — Cox
31394	White Favorite .... — M	31496	Eclipse .... M
31395	White Stockings .... — M	31500	Emperor .... — P S
31396	White Tail .... Ky I	31501	Fairview .... — D
31397	White Turk .... — Cox	31502	Fawn Prince .... — L R
31399	Wild Bill of Syene .... P S	31503	Fillmore .... Ky I
31402	Wiley's Baron .... — M	31505	Gallant Duke 2nd .... — D
31404	William Albert .... — P S	31506	Gen. Marion .... — T
31405	William Kent .... P S	31507	Gen. Tyner .... — C
31406	William Morton .... — L R	31508	Gloster .... L R
31407	William Wallace .... — L R	31509	Grant .... Ky I
31408	Winneshiek .... — Ky I	31512	Haystack .... — Cox
31409	Wisconsin .... M	31513	James Thorndale .... — P S
31410	Wolverine .... — T	31515	Jim Bell .... — Ky I
31411	Woodford .... — L R	31516	Jim Blaine .... — L R
31412	Woodlawn Duke .... — R R	31517	Kansas Sam .... D
31415	Wyoming Comet .... — P S	31518	Laird of Leamington .... — Cox
31417	Wyoming's Challenger ...... P S	31519	Laudable .... — R R
31418	Wyoming Duke .... P S	31521	Lord Anderson .... — C
31419	Wyoming's Excelsior .... — P S	31522	Lord Bluebell .... — P S
31420	Yakima Duke C	31523	Lord of Knox .... — D
31421	Young Andy .... — M	31524	Lord Levy .... — M
31422	Young Baron .... — R R	31526	Louander .... — R R
31424	Young Canada .... — Cox	31527	Louanjo .... — R R
31425	Young Chatham .... — M	31528	Major .... Ky I
31426	Young Duke of Hendon ...... — M	31529	Mason .... — R R
31427	Young Earl of Bourbon ...... P S	31531	Maynard .... — C
31429	Young George .... — Cox	31532	Miami Lad .... Ky I
31430	Young Hercules .... — P S	31533	Monarch 2nd .... — C
31431	Young Hero .... — Ky I	31534	Monarch 3rd .... — M
31432	Young Hero .... — M	31535	Monkey John 11th .... — P S
31433	Young Hero .... — T	31536	Nimrod .... — M
31434	Young Hiram .... — P S	31538	Norwood, Jr .... — D
31435	Young John .... Cox	31539	Oakland Lad .... M
31436	Young Larimore .... — P S	31541	Phil Sheridan 2nd .... M
31437	Young Locomotive .... — M	31545	Prince of Helm .... — P S
31439	Young Nimrod .... — P S	31546	Prince of Wales .... — Cox
31440	Young Octo .... L R	31547	Prince of Wales 3rd .... — M
31442	Young Renick .... Ky I	31548	Red Henry .... — D
31444	Young Stanley .... — M	21549	Roan Barmpton C
31445	Young Starlight .... — Daisy	31551	Roan Duke .... — M
31446	Young Waterloo .... Ky I	31552	Roan Maid's Grand Duke .... M
31449	Zahra .... — M	31553	Robert Bruce .... — M
31451	Zabulon .... — M	31554	Roderick .... — R R
31456	Zollicoffer .... — M	31555	Royal Duke .... Ky I
31460	Adina's Duke .... — M	31556	Sam Tilden .... D
31463	Baron Leonard .... — M	31557	Sarah's Earl .... — Cox
31465	Belle Duke .... — P S	31558	Sir Wellington .... — Cox
31466	Belzoni 2nd .... L R	31564	Tom Vanmeter .... — D
31467	Brutus .... — M	31565	Tom Warren .... L R
31468	Caithness .... L R	31566	Triumph .... — D
31469	Capt. Jack .... L R	31567	Sultan .... M
31470	Carthage .... — Cox	31568	Western Prince .... — Cox
31471	Cassius .... — M	31571	Williams Center Prince ...... Ky I
31472	Catkin .... Daisy	31572	Yankee .... L R
31473	Clear Spring Duke .... D	31573	Young Albion .... — M
31474	Clinton .... L R	31574	Young Baron .... — R R
31475	Colonel .... — R R	31575	Young Townley .... — D
31479	Daniel Boon .... — M	31576	Abe Renick .... M
31480	Diamond .... Ky I	31577	Achan .... — R R
31481	Don Juan .... M	31578	Achilles .... — T
31482	5th Duke .... Ky I	31579	Adair .... — M
31483	Duke Alexander .... — M	31580	Adelaid's Goodness .... — R R
31484	3rd Duke of Elmwood .... — M	31581	Adelaid's Grand Duke ...... — L R
31485	Duke of Fairview .... — L R	31582	Adolthe Thiers .... Ky I
31487	5th Duke of Hillsdale .... — Cox	31586	Aesop .... — Cox

31587	Afghan — L R	31713	Baron Lisger 2nd — Cox
31588	Agamemnon Ky I	31714	Baron of Locust Lawn M
31589	Agates Airdrie — M	31715	2nd Baron of Locust Lawn — R R
31590	Ahab — R R	31716	3rd Baron of Locust Lawn,— Daisy
31592	Airdrie Bates — L R	31718	5th Baron of Locust Lawn M
31593	Airdrie Duke — D	31721	Baron Louis — Ky I
31595	Airdrie Duke — M	31724	Baron Mazurka of the Oaks, — Cox
31596	Airdrie Duke P S	31725	Baron Newcastle 4th — Cox
31598	19th Airdrie Duke of Scioto, — R R	31726	Baron Newcastle 5th — Cox
31599	20th Airdrie Duke of Scioto D	31727	2nd Baron of Oakwood — Cox
31600	21st Airdrie Duke of Scioto D	31730	Baron Sharon 6th — P S
31601	22nd Airdrie Duke of Scioto — M	31736	Baron Wabash — D
31602	23rd Airdrie Duke of Scioto, — R R	31737	Baron Wadsworth 1st Cox
31603	24th Airdrie Duke of Scioto D	31738	Baron Wadsworth 2nd Cox
31604	25th Airdrie Duke of Scioto D	31739	Baron Wadsworth 3rd Cox
31605	26th Airdrie Duke of Scioto D	31742	Baron Wiley Ky I
31606	Airdrie D. of Evergreens 2nd,—Ky I	31749	Bartlett Ky I
31610	Airdrie Knight — Daisy	31750	Bas Blue — D
31613	Alamo — C	31751	Bastrope Prince — R R
31615	Albert Edward — R R	31752	Bates — M
31616	Albert Marlatt P S	31758	3rd Bates of Oak Hill P S
31618	Albion Gwynne — Cox	31759	4th Bates of Oak Hill — M
31620	Alexander — Ky I	31761	6th Bates of Oak Hill — R R
31621	Alexander 4th L R	31762	7th Bates of Oak Hill P S
31622	Alexander 3rd L R	31763	8th Bates of Oak Hill — M
31623	Alexander 5th L R	31765	Beaconsfield — M
31624	Alexander 6th L R	31766	Beaconsfield — D
31625	Alexander — Cox	31770	Beauty's Baron Clark Ky I
31625	Alexis — Cox	31771	Beauty Duke — M
31626	Alphonso Ky I	31772	Beaver Duke R R
31627	Alfred — M	31773	Beecher — Cox
31628	Allen T	31774	Beecher — Long-Horn
31629	Allendale — R R	31775	Beecher T
31630	Allen's Gloster — Cox	31776	Beecher L R
31631	Allen's Lad D	31777	Beecher P S
31632	Alma's Duke — R R	31778	Beecher P S
31638	Andover — Cox	31779	Bedford Duke P S
31639	Annandale — D	31783	Bell Duke — R R
31641	Anthony — L R	31784	Bell Duke 2nd Ky I
31643	Arabella Duke — D	31787	Bell Duke N — R R
31644	Aradus P S	31790	Bell Duke of Wauatoosa — P S
31645	Arator Lad — M	31791	Bellflower's Duke — M
31647	Arcola P S	31792	Belle's Goodness — R R
31648	Ariadne's Prince — D	31794	Bellevue's Duke M
31649	Armada L R	31795	Belmont C
31650	Arnon P S	31798	Belvedere — L R
31650	Atica Granger L R	31799	Belvedere 3rd — M
31662	Augustus — L R	31801	Ben Airdrie P S
31664	Avon Booth T	31802	Ben Allen — M
31665	Avondale P S	31803	Ben Butler — P S
31668	Baby — M	31804	Ben Butler P S
31669	Badger P S	31805	Ben Butler — M
31671	Baker's Red Oak — D	31806	Ben Butler 2nd — M
31672	Baldwin — T	31807	Ben Clyde M
31673	Barmpton Oxford — P S	31809	Ben Franklin — P S
31674	Barnum P S	31810	Ben Franklin P S
31675	Barnum P S	31811	Ben Hadad — R R
31683	Baron Airdrie 2nd — Long-Horn	31812	Ben Nora — M
31684	Baron Airdrie of the Oaks — Cox	31813	Ben Porter M
31685	Baron Bates Ky I	31814	Benton — Cox
31687	Baron Beirn 2nd — P S	31815	Benton T
31689	Baron of Bluffdale — D	31818	Berlin — M
31690	Baron Booth — M	31819	Besek Boy 3rd — D
31691	Baron Booth of Bluff Creek — T	31820	Bexar Ky I
31692	Baron Butterfly — Cox	31821	Bill Burgess — M
31696	Baronet — L R	31822	Bill Stone — M
31697	Baron of Fairview Cox	31823	Billy Boner L R
31707	Baron Hubback 3rd — R R	31824	Billy Guy 2nd — M
31708	Baron Jubilee Gwynne — R R	31826	Billy Lewis L R
31712	Baron Leonard 1st — M	31827	Billy McD Ky I

No.	Name	Code	No.	Name	Code
31829	Billy Root	— Cox	31923	Calla's Duke	— R R
31832	Billy Thorndale	— C	31927	Cambria Duke	— Long-Horn
31834	Bismarck	— P S	31930	2nd Cambridge Lad	— R R
31835	Bismarck	— M	31934	Captain 4th	— Ky I
31836	Bismarck	— Cox	31935	Captain 5th	— Ky I
31838	Bismarck	M	31937	Captain Dumars	— R R
31839	Bismarck	— L R	31938	Captain Eads	— C
31840	Bismarck	P S	31940	Captain Kidd	M
31841	Bismarck	L R	31941	Captain Jack	M
31842	Bismarck 2nd	— T	31942	Captain Jack	— M
31843	Bismarck Boy	M	31943	Captain Parker 2nd	— M
31844	Black Hawk	— D	31944	Captain Prim	M
31847	Blanchard	— M	31945	Captain Smith	— M
31848	Bland	— P S	31946	Captain Turbett	— R R
31849	Blazing Star	— P S	31947	Carew	Ky I
31852	Blucher	— L R	31948	Carey Lad	— P S
31853	Blucher	M	31949	Carlisle	— L R
31854	Blucher Underedge	— D	31950	Carlo	— M
31855	Bluejeans	— M	31951	Caroline's Duke	— Cox
31856	Blush's Breastplate	— D	31952	Carroll	M
31859	Bob	P S	31953	Casper Lewis	— R R
31860	Bob Ingersoll	— P S	31956	Cassius	— T
31861	Bob Ingersoll	P S	31959	Cataract	Cox
31862	Bob Reneck	— Ky I	31960	Cato	— M
31863	Bob Walker	Wrong	31962	Cattinat	— D
31864	Bogard	M	31963	Cavagna's Mazurka	D
31865	Bolivar	Ky I	31965	Cayuga Chief	Cox
31867	Bolton	— C	31966	Cecil	— T
31868	Bon-gre	— D	31967	Centaur	— M
31869	Bonner 3rd	— D	31968	Centennial Bill	Ky I
31870	Bonnie Boy	— R R	31969	Center Boy	— M
31871	Bonny Boy	M	31970	Centipede	— P S
31872	Bonnie Lad	Cox	31971	Cerberus	— R R
31873	Booth	Ky I	31972	Cere's Duke	T
31874	Bosphorus	— T	31973	Cerro Gordo Boy	— M
31875	Boss	Cox	31974	Cethegus	— T
31876	Bosseau	— M	31975	Challenger	— M
31877	Boss Keyes	— R R	31977	Champion	— M
31878	Boston Duke 10th	— T	31978	Champion	R R
31879	Boston Duke	L R	31979	Champion	— Cox
31881	Bourbon Duke 3rd	— M	31980	Champion	— Cox
31882	Bourbon Wonder	— M	31981	Champion	— L R
31883	Bowman's Oxford 2nd	— M	31983	Champion Duke of Madison	— M
31884	Boyle Duke	— M	31984	Champion Rose's Prince 1st	— L R
31885	Boyle Lad	— M	31985	Champion of Summit	— Cox
31886	Braceville Louanjo 2nd	— Cox	31987	Charles	D
31888	Breastwork 2nd	— M	31988	Charlie Green	— C
31889	Breckenridge	— Long-Horn	31989	Chautauqua Lad	— L R
31890	Bridal Duke	— R R	31990	Chenango	— Cox
31891	Bride's Shamrock 2nd	— R R	31994	Cherub Second	Ky I
31892	Brigham Young	M	31999	Chief of Pecatonica	M
31893	Brigham Young	P S	32000	Chief of Peoria	D
31895	Bright Light	R R	32001	Chieftain	— L R
31898	Briton	L R	32002	Chixon	— R R
31899	Briton Boy	— L R	32003	Chubby	— Cox
31900	Bronte	M	32005	Claudius	— R R
31901	Brooklyn Duke	— R R	32006	Clay Duke	D
31902	Brooklyn Duke 2nd	— R R	32008	Cleopatra Duke	— M
31905	Buchan Laddie	M	32009	Clifton 5th	— T
31906	Buckeye	Ky I	32010	Clifton Duke	— C
31907	Buckeye Boy	L R	32011	Clifton Duke	— Cox
31908	Buckeye Boy	Cox	32012	Climax 3rd	— P S
31910	Buck Irvine	— T	32013	Climeteor	— R R
31911	Buena Vista	Ky I	32015	Clinton Duke	— R R
31912	Budd	— L R	32017	Clyde Dimmitt	— P S
31915	Busento 2nd	— C	32018	Clyde Oxford	M
31916	Butcher Boy	— Ky I	32019	Codrus	P S
31919	Byron Oxford		32020	Colfax 2nd	— Ky I
31921	Calchas	— R R	32022	Colonel	Cox
31922	Caledonia Duke	— P S	32024	Colonel Bell's Duke	Daisy

SHORT-HORN CATTLE PEDIGREES. 149

No.	Name	Code
32028	Colonel Fremont	M
32029	Colonel Gloster	— Cox
32030	Colonel Ingersoll	— D
32032	Colonel Lewis P. Muir	— R R
32033	Colonel Marsh	P S
32034	Colonel Nibling	— D
32035	Colonel Nip	— T
32036	Colonel Phillips	Ky I
32037	Colonel Rawett	M
32038	Colonel Redman	R R
32039	Colonel Sanders	Ky I
32040	Colonel Scott	— M
32041	Colorado	— Wrong
32042	Columbus	— L R
32043	Comet	— M
32044	Comet	— T
32046	Comet Sharon	— D
32047	Commander	— R R
32048	Commander	— Daisy
32049	Commander	— M
32050	Commodore	— R R
32051	Commodore	— T
32052	Commodore	— M
32061	Consul	Cox
32062	Cora's Duke	M
32065	Count Bismark	D
32066	Counterpiece	R R
32068	Count of Orange	— T
32070	Count Strawberry	— Long-Horn
32073	Courage	— Cox
32075	Cowslip's Duke of Geneva	— M
32077	Cresco	M
32079	Cringle	— P S
32084	Crown Prince	— P S
32085	Crown Prince	— P S
32086	Crown Prince	— T
32087	Crown Prince	D
32088	Crown Prince 2nd	D
32089	Crusader	— Cox
32090	Cusey	— M
32092	Custer	— M
32094	Cypress Duke	— M
32097	Czar	— T
32098	2nd Daisy's Airdrie	— R R
32099	Daisy Bull	— M
32100	Daisy Champion	— L R
32101	Daisy Duke	— R R
32103	Daisy's Duke	— R R
32104	Daisy Duke of Orange	M
32105	Dalton Duke	— R R
32107	Dandy	— M
32108	Dandy Anderson	M
32109	Daniel	— D
32110	Daniel	— M
32111	Daniel Booue	C
32113	Dan Grady	— Wrong
32114	Dan McIntyre	— P S
32115	Dan Moore	— M
32116	Dan Pierson	Ky I
32117	Dan Riley	— P S
32118	Dan Ross	M
32119	Dan Tucker	Cox
32120	Darby	— R R
32121	Darius	— P S
32126	Dave Walker	— T
32127	Davy Crocket	— T
32128	December Lad	— M
32129	Decoration	M
32130	Defiance	L R
32132	Dellona	— M
32133	Denny	L R
32134	De Sota 2nd	— R R
32135	Dexter	— Cox
32136	Dexter	— Cox
32137	Dexter 2nd	— L R
32138	Dexter Prince	Ky I
32140	Diamond	— P S
32143	Diamond Joe	— M
32144	Dick	— Cox
32145	Dick Haworth	— D
32146	Dick Oglesby	— Cox
32147	Dick Rowett	M
32148	Dick Sharon	— R R
32149	Dick Taylor	— T
32150	Dick Taylor	Ky I
32154	Dock Reed	— M
32156	Doctor	— M
32157	Doctor Brown	— R R
32158	Doctor Finley	— Ky I
32161	Doctor Watts	— P S
32162	Doctor Watson	— R R
32163	Dom Pedro	— T
32164	Dom Pedro	C
32166	Dom Pedro	— T
32168	Dom Pedro	M
32169	Dom Pedro	— T
32170	Don Bernardo 2nd	— M
32171	Don Carlos	— P S
32172	Don Gale	— M
32173	Don Giovanni	M
32174	Don Juan	— R R
32176	Double Athol	— R R
32178	Double Prince	— M
32179	Dougan	— M
32180	Douglass	— Ky I
32182	Duke	— D
32183	Duke	Cox
32184	Duke	T
32185	5th Duke of Addison	— R R
32188	2nd Duke of Allendale	— T
32189	3rd Duke of Allendale	P S
32190	4th Duke Allendale	— Ky I
32191	5th Duke of Allendale	— M
32192	6th Duke of Allendale	— M
32193	7th Duke of Allendale	T
32194	8th Duke of Allendale	— T
32196	Duke Anderson	M
32198	Duke of Arlington	— P S
32199	Duke of Ashbrook	— P S
32200	Duke of Atchison	— M
32201	Duke of Avondale	— R R
32202	Duke of Avondale	P S
32203	2nd Duke of Avondale	M
32205	Duke of Baden	— M
32207	Duke Balder 6th	Ky I
32215	Duke Bell	— R R
32216	Duke of Belmont	— Wrong
32217	Duke of Bergen	— Cox
32218	Duke of Bird-in-hand	Daisy
32219	Duke of Blanchard 5th	— D
32220	2nd Duke of Boone	P S
32221	Duke of Buchanan	M
32222	Duke Buckner	— R R
32223	Duke of Butler 2nd	C
32226	Duke of Carey	— D
32227	Duke of Cass	— L R
32228	Duke of Cedar Lawn	— R R
32229	Duke of Clarence	Daisy
32230	Duke of Clark	— M
32232	2nd Duke of Columbus	L R

No.	Name	Code
32283	3rd Duke of Columbus	L R
32237	Duke of Cottage Grove	— P S
32238	Duke of Cottonwood	— L R
32239	3rd Duke of Cowassalon	— Cox
32240	Duke of Crawford	— L R
32241	Duke of Crawford	— L R
32242	Duke of Cross Creek	— R R
32243	Duke of Dane 2nd	— M
32244	Duke of Dane 3rd	— M
32246	Duke of Dixon	— R R
32247	4th Duke of Downs	— R R
32249	1st Duke of Edgewood	— L R
32250	Duke of Albert	— D
32251	Duke of Elford	— C
32252	Duke El Hakim	— D
32253	Duke of Elmendaro	Ky I
32254	Duke of Evergreen Farm	— R R
32256	3rd Duke of Fairview	T
32257	7th Duke of Fairview	M
32258	8th Duke of Fairview	— M
32259	6th Duke of Fenton	— Cox
32261	Duke of Flemington	— Cox
32263	Duke Forrest	— D
32264	Duke of Forest Hill	— M
32265	12th Duke of Forest Hill	Ky I
32266	Duke of Freehold	— Cox
32268	Duke of Genesee	L R
32269	Dan of Glenwood	— R R
32271	24th Duke of Goodness	— R R
32273	Duke of Grandview	— L R
32274	Duke of Granville	— Cox
32275	1st Duke of Greenwood	— M
32278	Duke of Hampden	— P S
32279	Duke of Hanover 2nd	— M
32280	7th Duke of Harlem	M
32281	8th Duke of Harlem	M
32283	Duke of Harrison	D
32284	1st Duke of Harvey	Ky I
32285	Duke of Hendon 4th	— R R
32286	Duke of Hendon 5th	— M
32288	12th Duke of Highland	— Cox
32291	Duke of Honor	P S
32293	Duke of Iowa County	— M
32295	Duke of Jamestown	L R
32296	Duke of Jefferson	Ky I
32299	Duke John	— R R
32302	Duke Joseph	— R R
32303	Duke of Juniper Hill	— Ky I
32304	Duke of Kansas	— Cox
32310	1st Duke of La Tache	Ky I
32311	Duke Lee	— D
32313	Duke of Linn	— M
32314	Duke of Linn	— R R
32316	Duke of Livingston	M
32317	1st Duke of Loamland	— M
32318	Duke of Lost Creek	M
32319	1st Duke of Lyon	— L R
32320	Duke of McDonald	L R
32321	Duke of McDonald 2nd	— R R
32322	Duke of McDonald 3rd	— D
32323	Duke of McDonald 4th	R R
32324	Duke of McDonald 5th	M
32326	Duke of McPherson	— P S
32327	Duke of Magenta	— Cox
32328	Duke of Mahtowa	— R R
32330	Duke of Maple Grove	M
32331	2nd Duke of Maple Grove	M
32332	Duke of Maplewood	P S
32333	5th Duke of Marion	M
32335	Duke of Media	— Ky I
32336	2nd Duke of Melleray	— M
32337	3rd Duke of Melleray	C
32339	Duke of Monroe	— R R
32340	Duke of Monroe	— Long-Horn
32341	Duke of Monroe	Ky I
32342	Duke of Montana	— L R
32343	Duke of Moonlight	P S
32344	Duke Morgan	— L R
32346	6th Duke of Moscow	— R R
32349	Duke of Nelson	M
32350	Duke of Northumberland	— Cox
32356	Duke of Oakland	Ky I
32357	4th Duke of Oakland	— R R
32358	24th Duke of Oakland	L R
32359	20th Duke of Onondaga	— Cox
32360	Duke of Orland	Ky I
32361	Duke of Orleans	— R R
32362	6th Duke of Osage	— Cox
32363	Duke of Osceola	Ky I
32364	Duke of Osceola	L R
32365	Duke of Oxford	— Daisy
32366	4th Duke of Oxford	— C
32368	Duke of Platte Valley	M
32369	Duke of Pleasant Hill	— C
32370	Duke of Pleasant Hill	— P S
32371	Duke of Pleasant Valley	M
32372	Duke of Pleasant View	— M
32374	2nd Duke of Portage	M
32375	3rd Duke of Post Road	— M
32376	Duke of Prentice	— M
32378	Duke of Railroad Farm	— D
32379	Duke Republic	— R R
32380	Duke of Red Oak	— R R
32381	Duke of Red Oak	M
32382	1st Duke of Richfield	Cox
32383	Duke of Richland	— Cox
32385	Duke of Richmond	— Long-Horn
32386	Duke of Riverview	M
32387	2nd Duke of Riverview	P S
32388	Duke of Roanoke	Ky I
32390	Duke of Rockingham	Ky I
32391	Duke of Rosedale 1st	— M
32392	Duke of Rosedale 2nd	— M
32393	Duke of Rush	— C
32394	Duke of Sac	— T
32395	Duke of Scott	— Ky I
32396	2nd Duke of Seneca	— M
32398	Duke of Sharon	— P S
32400	Duke of Sharon	P S
32401	Duke of Sharon 3rd	— D
32403	4th Duke of Skaneateles	— Cox
32404	5th Duke of Skaneateles	— Cox
32405	Duke of Springbrook	— Long-Horn
32406	Duke of Springbrook 13th	— R R
32407	Duke of Springbrook 14th	— R R
32408	Duke of Springbrook 16th	R R
32409	Duke of Springbrook 17th	— R R
32410	Duke of Springbrook 18th	— R R
32411	Duke of Springbrook 19th	— R R
32412	Duke of Springbrook 20th	— R R
32413	Duke of Springbrook 21st	— R R
32414	Duke of Springbrook 22nd	— P S
32415	Duke of Springbrook 23rd	— P S
32416	Duke of Springbrook 24th	— R R
32417	Duke of Springbrook 25th	— R R
32418	Duke of Springbrook 26th	— R R
32419	Duke of Springbrook 27th	— R R
32420	Duke of Springbrook 28th	— R R
32421	Duke of Springbrook 29th	— R R
32426	Duke of Stoughton 2nd	— R R

32427	Duke of Sunnyside ——D	32561	Ed Shipley —D
32429	2nd Duke of Tekamah —R R	32563	Edgar —R R
32431	22nd Duke of the Pines —R R	32565	Egoff —L R
32432	23rd Duke of the Pines —R R	32566	Elam —D
32433	24th Duke of the Pines —R R	32567	Elba Boy —T
32434	Duke of the Prairie —R R	32569	Ellicott Duke L R
32435	Duke of the Prairie D	32570	Ellicott Louanjo L R
32436	Duke of the Valley —P S	32575	Emperor Ky I
32438	Duke of Thorndale —Cox	32576	Emperor D
32439	Duke of Trumbull Ky I	32577	Emperor 7th —P S
32440	Duke of Trumbull Cox	32578	Enterprise —T
32441	Duke of Trumbull 2nd —L R	32579	Enterprise —R R
32442	Duke of Vernon Woods	32582	Euclid T
32446	Duke of Warren —M	32583	Eugenie's Duke —Cox
32447	2nd Duke of Washington M	32584	Eureka 3rd Cox
32449	Duke of Waterloo —Ky I	32585	Eureka 2nd Cox
32451	3rd Duke of Waveland L R	32587	Everton —Daisy
32454	Duke of West Plains —M	32589	Excelsior —R R
32456	Duke 6th of Wheatland —D	32591	Exchange M
32457	Duke 7th of Wheatland C	32592	Exchange 2nd M
32458	Duke 8th of Wheatland —Ky I	32593	Fabius —P S
32459	Duke 9th of Wheatland —R R	32594	Factotum —L R
32460	2nd Duke William —M	32595	Fairfax —M
32461	Duke of Windham —L R	32598	Fairfield Duke —M
32464	11th Duke of Windingvale —R R	32599	Fairy Duke of Jubilee —M
32465	1st Duke of Winnebago —Cox	32600	Falstaff M
32468	2nd Duke of Woodhill —Cox	32605	Farmer M
32470	Duke of Yarico —D	32606	Father Mathew P S
32471	3rd Duke of Yates Ky I	32610	Favorite —M
32472	Duke of Yates 14th —M	32611	Favorite —L R
32473	Duke of Yates 21st M	32612	Favorite 2nd —P S
32474	Duke of Yates 22nd —Cox	32613	Favorite 3rd —Ky I
32475	Duke of York —M	32614	Fearless —L R
32476	1st Duke of York —R R	32615	Felix —P S
32477	Dunglen Prince 2nd Ky I	32617	Fiat Ky I
32478	Dunstable Lad —M	32621	Filagree Gem 4th —M
32479	Dusky Darrell —Cox	32622	Filagree Gem 5th —M
32480	Dutch Bill M	32624	Firefly —Cox
32481	Earl 2nd —P S	32625	Fitz James L R
32484	Earl of Arborville —Cox	32627	Flave P S
32485	Earl of Athol —D	32628	Floral Monarch —M
32487	Earl of Bates —M	32629	Florentina's Double Duke —C
32489	Earl of Beaconsfield M	32630	Florid Duke Ky I
32498	Earl of Cedar Lawn —R R	32631	Floss Duke —R R
32500	Earl 2nd of Chelmsford —M	32632	Forest Duke —M
32501	Earl of Chesterfield —R R	32634	Fortune L R
32504	Earl of Cloverly —R R	32635	Fortune Junior Ky I
32505	Earl of Como —C	32636	Fragrant Duke —R R
32509	Earl Derby M	32638	Frank P S
32510	Earl Ducie —M	32639	Frank Crossley T
32511	Earl Dufferin —R R	32640	Frank Gloster L R
32515	Earl of Essex —T	32641	Frank Jackson M
32516	Earl Fitzwilliam —P S	32642	Franklin Duke 12th Ky I
32522	20th Earl of Greenbush T	32643	Franklin Duke 13th —L R
32523	21st Earl of Greenbush —P S	32644	Frank Lubbock —M
32524	22nd Earl of Greenbush —R R	32645	Frank Taylor L R
32525	23rd Earl of Greenbush D	32646	Frantic Duke —R R
32526	24th Earl of Greenbush —R R	32648	Frederick William 3rd —R R
32527	1st Earl of Greenside —Cox	32649	Freeborn —Ky I
32531	7th Earl of Kalamazoo Cox	32650	Freedom —Cox
32533	Earl of Little Indian T	32653	Gaudy Duke —P S
32534	Earl of Lockwood —D	32657	General —R R
32538	Earl of Lyndenwall M	32658	Gen. Bates L R
32543	2nd Earl of Oxford —Cox	32659	Gen. Cady —P S
32544	Earl of Pleasant View —Cox	32660	Gen. Carey —Cox
32550	Earl Thornapple 2nd —L R	32661	Gen. Cockburn L R
32556	Eclipse —M	32663	Gen. Custer M
32558	Eclipse M	32665	Gen. Desha —R R
32559	Eclipse —Ky I	32666	Gen. Doyle —L R
32560	Eclipse 3rd —R R	32667	Gen. Forrest R R

32668	Gen. Grant...................Cox	32771	Grand Prize.................— R R
32669	Gen. Grant...................— D	32774	Granger......................L R
32670	Gen. Grant...................L R	32775	Granger......................— L R
32671	Gen. Grant...................L R	32776	Grant........................— M
32672	Gen. Grant...................L R	32777	Grant........................— Ky I
32673	Gen. Grant...................L R	32778	Grant........................L R
32674	Gen. Harney..................— M	32780	Gray Jacket..................M
32676	Gen. Hopewell................— R R	32781	Great Republican.............— Cox
32677	Gen. Iles....................— M	32783	Grey Eagle...................— Cox
32678	Gen. Jackson.................P S	32786	Guardsman of Springbrook 1st— P S
32679	Gen. Kilpatrick..............— M	32787	Guardsman of Springbrook 2d— R R
32680	Gen. Lee.....................— P S	33788	Guardsman of Springbrook 3d— R R
32682	Gen. Logan...................— L R	32789	Guardsman of Springbrook 4th—R R
32683	Gen. Louan...................— R R	32790	Guelph.......................— Cox
32684	Gen. Lyons...................— M	32791	Gulnare's Son................— Daisy
32685	Gen. Mac.....................Ky I	32792	Gwinn........................— D
32686	Gen. Miles...................Ky I	32793	Gwynneth 2nd................— Ky I
32687	Gen. Mills...................— R R	32794	Hailstorm....................— M
32688	Gen. Mumford.................—T	32796	Hangtail.....................— L R
32691	Gen. Scott...................— D	32797	Hanover Hero................— M
32695	Gen. Stewart.................P S	32798	Hard Money..................Cox
32696	Gen. Todleben...............Woods	32799	Harold.......................— D
32697	Gen. Washington..............L R	32800	Harrington...................— R R
32698	Gen. Weaver..................— M	32805	Hayes........................— M
32702	Geneva Duke..................— Ky I	32807	8th Hazelwood Duke...........— C
32704	Geneva Lad 3rd...............M	32808	Heart Rose Madrid 3rd.......— Daisy
32708	George.......................— Cox	32809	Heathwood....................— Cox
32709	George.......................Cox	32811	Hector.......................D
32710	George.......................L R	32812	Hector.......................Woods
32711	George.......................Ky I	32814	Henry........................— R R
32712	George.......................— M	32815	Henry........................M
32713	George Vest..................— M	32816	Henry........................— Ky I
32714	George Washington............— M	32817	Henry........................Cox
32715	George Washington............Ky I	32818	Henry 2nd....................— M
32716	George Washington............Ky I	32819	Henry 3rd....................— D
32717	Gipsy Joe....................— Cox	32820	Henry Noacker...............Ky I
32718	Gladstone....................— R R	32821	Henry Ward Beecher..........P S
32719	6th Glen Count..............M	32822	Herbert Clapp...............L R
32720	7th Glen Count..............M	32823	Herman.......................Ky I
32722	Gloster......................— Cox	32825	Hero.........................— D
32723	Gloster Boy..................— Cox	32826	Hero of Maple Grove.........— Cox
32724	Gloster's Duke of Lawrence..— M	32827	Herod........................— M
32725	Gloster Star.................— Cox	32828	Herod........................L R
32726	Gold Dust....................— L R	32829	Hetto Duke...................— R R
32728	Golddust.....................— T	32830	Hiawatha.....................— C
32729	Golden Duke.................M	32831	Highflyer....................Ky I
32730	6th Golden Duke..............— M	32832	Highland Chief..............— D
32731	Golden King..................— P S	32833	Highland Chief..............— M
32732	Goldfinder...................— L R	32834	Highland Duke...............C
32733	Goldfinder...................— M	32836	Highland Duke...............— Cox
32734	Goldfinder...................D	32837	Highland Duke 2nd..........— Ky I
32735	Goldfinder 6th..............— Ky I	32840	Highland Lad................L R
32736	Gold Plait 2nd..............— L R	32843	Hillhurst Chief.............— M
32738	Goodness 2nd................— R R	32846	Hixon Duke..................M
32739	Goodness Cherub.............— P S	32847	Homer........................— Cox
32743	Gortschakoff................— M	32848	Homer Townley..............— M
32744	Governor.....................Ky I	32849	Honesty......................— P S
32745	Governor Bishop..............— Ky I	32851	Hooker.......................L R
32746	Governor General............— R R	32852	Hoosier Boy.................M
32747	Governor Hayes..............M	32853	Hoosier Dick................R R
32749	Governor Hubbard............L R	32854	Hopeful......................— R R
32751	Governor Phelps.............M	32855	Hopeful Star................— P S
32752	Governor Roberts...........— R R	32856	Hopewell.....................— M
32753	Governor Smith.............— R R	32857	Horatio 2nd.................— P S
32754	Governor Tilden............L R	32859	Howard.......................Ky I
32755	Grace's Duke................— M	32860	Howell Duke.................— Ky I
32762	Grand Duke of Milleray.....— M	32862	Hubback 2nd.................— R R
32763	Grand Duke of Mt. Hope......— M	32863	2nd Hubback.................— R R
32765	2nd Grand Duke of Oak Hill— R R	32864	Hubback 3rd.................— R R
32768	Grand Duke of Springfield...— M	32868	H. W. Beecher...............— D

SHORT-HORN CATTLE PEDIGREES.

No.	Name	Herd
32869	Idaho	Ky I
32870	Ida's Knight	M
32871	Ike Woodyard 2nd	Ky I
32875	Imperial Monarch	— M
32876	Imperial White Rose	R R
32878	Invermay Lad	— R R
32879	Invincible Duke 2nd	— M
32882	Iris Favorite	— M
32884	Isaac Hatch	— R R
32885	Ivanhoe	— Ky I
32888	Jack	Cox
32890	Jack M	P S
32895	January	M
32896	Jefferson	— Cox
32897	Jerome	— D
32898	Jessamine Duke	— M
32899	Jessie's Duke	— D
32900	Jim	— Long-Horn
32901	Jim Blaine	R R
32903	Jim Brooks	Ky I
32904	Jim Clay of Oakland	P S
32906	Jim Fisk	— M
32907	Jim Waddill	L R
32908	Joe	— D
32909	Joe	— M
32910	Joe Bigler	— R R
32912	Joe Johnston	M
32913	Joe Reynolds	Ky I
32914	Joe Schenck	T
32915	Joe Sharon	— D
32918	Joe Willet	— M
32919	John Brent	M
32920	John Bright	P S
32921	John Henry	Ky I
32922	John Hughes	— M
32924	John Morgan	Ky I
32925	Johnny Boggs	Ky I
32926	Johnny Bull	Ky I
32928	Johnny Sands	— D
32930	John O'Groat	— Cox
32931	John of Oakland	P S
32932	John R	Cox
32936	Josh Billings	— P S
32938	Jubilee Duke	— Ky I
32939	Jubilee Duke	M
32940	Judge Dillon	— D
32941	Judge Wellington	M
32942	Jugurtha	D
32943	Julia C's Duke	L R
32946	Juniper	T
32947	Junius	— L R
32951	Jupiter	— Cox
32952	Kalos 2nd of Oakland	— D
32953	Kansas	— P S
32957	Kentucky Joe	— L R
32958	King Bull	— Ky I
32960	King David	— R R
32961	King David	— M
32962	King Derby 4th	M
32963	King Edison	Cox
32964	King of England	— M
32966	King John	— R R
32967	King Otho	— Daisy
32970	2nd King of the Marys	— R R
32971	3rd King of the Marys	— R R
32975	King Tom	— Ky I
32976	King William	— M
32977	King William 2nd	Ky I
32978	Kirklevington 3rd	C
32985	Kirkpatrick	P S
32989	Knight of Ivanhoe	— L R
32991	Knight of St. George	L R
32992	Knight of Sharon	— M
32995	Laban	L R
32996	Lady's Duke	— M
32997	Lady's Duke	M
32999	Land Ranger 3rd	— Ky I
33000	Laura Ann's Breastplate	— T
33001	Leaverton	— L R
33002	Ledge Duke 1st	R R
33003	Legal Tender	M
33004	Leicester	— M
33005	Lemuel	Cox
33006	Lena's Duke	— M
33007	Leo	— R R
33008	Leon	— Cox
33009	Leon	— D
33010	Leonard	— M
33011	Leonard	Cox
33014	Leonidas of Oakland	Ky I
33015	LeRoy	P S
33017	Lewis Bryan	P S
33018	1st Liberty Duke	— D
33019	2nd Liberty Duke	— M
33020	3rd Liberty Duke	Ky I
33021	4th Liberty Duke	— D
33023	6th Liberty Duke	P S
33024	Lincoln	— D
33025	Linton	— M
33028	Leslie	— P S
33029	Little Ike	Ky I
33030	Little Jo	Cox
33031	Little John	Cox
33032	Little Tom	— Cox
33033	Little Tom	— M
33034	Little Mack	M
33035	Locomotive	— T
33036	Lofty Duke	M
33037	Logan	T
33038	Logan	— M
33039	Loguna	— P S
33041	Long Grove Earl	M
33042	Long John	— M
33043	Longstreet	Ky I
33045	Lord Absalom	M
33046	Lord Alfred	— R R
33048	Lord Bacon	— Cox
33049	Lord Baltimore 4th	— P S
33050	Lord Beaconsfield	L R
33051	Lord Beaconsfield of Milo	— R R
33053	Lord Byron	— M
33054	Lord Byron	Ky I
33055	Lord Byron	Ky I
33060	Lord Chatham, Jr	— M
33066	Lord Derby	L R
33068	Lord Dunmore 3rd	— R R
33069	Lord Ellington 4th	— Cox
33073	Lord Herbert	— L R
33074	Lord Heron	L R
33075	Lord Houghton	— Ky I
33082	Lord Lewis	— M
33083	Lord Lieutenant 5th	T
33084	Lord of Linn	— C
33085	Lord Lorne	— M
33087	Lord Mason of Trenton	Ky I
33091	Lord Milton	— M
33093	Lord Nelson	— Cox
33094	Lord Nelson	L R
33095	Lord Oxford	— L R
33097	Lord Perry	— Cox

11

33100	Lord Rodney	— M		33237	Master Maynard 1st	— C
33101	Lord of the Loudons	— R R		33240	Master Thorn	— D
33108	Lord Warwick	— D		33241	Master Wilderberg	M
33112	Lorne	R R		33242	Master Winthrop 2nd	— R R
33113	Lorne	— D		33243	Master Winthrop 3rd	— C
33114	Louan's Airdrie	— R R		33244	Matchem	— Cox
33115	Louan Chief	— R R		33245	Matilda's Thorndal 2nd	— R R
33116	Louan Duke	— R R		33246	Matt Embry	— M
33117	Louan Duke	— R R		33249	Mayflower	Ky I
33118	Louan Duke	D		33250	Mayflower 2nd	P S
33119	Louan Duke	— R R		33251	Mayflower 3rd	— L R
33122	Louan's Duke	— M		33252	Mayflower Prince	— M
33123	Louan Duke	— M		33253	Maynard's Duke	— C
33124	Louan Duke 2nd	— M		33255	Mazurka Duke	— Cox
33125	Louan Duke of Mt. Zion	— R R		33256	Mazurka Judge	— R R
33126	Louan Hotspur	— R R		33258	Mazurka Lad 2nd	— C
33128	Louanjo 2nd	— R R		33259	Mazurka Lad 3rd	— Daisy
33129	Louanjo 3rd	Ky I		33261	Mazurka Lad 5th	— M
33130	Louan Airdrie	— R R		33262	Mazurka's Oxford 8th	R R
33134	Loudon Duke 30th	— R R		33263	Mazurka's Oxford 9th	— Ky I
33141	Loudon Duke of Rush 2nd	D		33264	Mazurka's Oxford 10th	D
33142	Loudon Duke 3rd of Wabash	— R R		33265	Mazurka's Oxford 11th	Ky I
33144	Louis Napoleon	— P S		33266	Mazurka's Oxford 12th	Ky I
33145	Lucretius of Oakland	— R R		33267	Mazurka's Oxford 13th	Ky I
33146	Lulu's Duke	— P S		33268	Mazurka's Oxford 14th	Ky I
33147	Lumbago	— R R		33269	Mazurka's Oxford 15th	Ky I
33148	Lumberman	— R R		33271	Memnon	— Ky I
33157	Maidston Duke	— Cox		33272	Mercer	— Ky I
33158	Majestic	— M		33273	Meredith Duke	— L R
33161	Major	Ky I		33280	Midas	Cox
33162	Major	Ky I		33282	Miller	— Cox
33164	Major Bower of Mount Zion	— M		33283	Miller's Airdrie	— P S
33165	Major Cockburn	L R		33284	Milo Sheffielder	— D
33167	Major Coulter	R R		33285	Minglewood Lad	— C
33168	Major Kent	— Cox		33286	Mischief	M
33170	Major of Maple Grove	— L R		33288	Mistletoe Duke of Mt. Zion	— R R
33171	Major of Maple Grove 2nd	Cox		33289	Moderator	— L R
33172	Major of Maple Grove 3rd	— L R		33290	Modest Major	— L R
33173	Major of Maple Grove 4th	— L R		33292	Modoc Chief	D
33174	Major Morrill	M		33293	Mohawk	P S
33177	Major Renick	— Cox		33294	Molly's Duke	— M
33180	Major Townley 2nd	— Cox		33296	Monarch	— M
33181	Major Tuck	— R R		33299	Monmouth Lad	L R
33187	Manfred 2nd	— Cox		33300	Montage	— M
33188	Manhan	— Cox		33301	Montcalm	— R R
33191	Marion	— D		33303	Monti	Cox
33192	Mark Evans	P S		33304	Monticello	— R R
33195	Marquis	— D		33305	Moore's Duke	— Wrong
33197	Marquis	— R R		33306	Moreton Lad	— L R
33198	Marquis of Bluffdale	— D		33307	Morgan Duke	— Daisy
33199	3rd Marquis of Bute	— R R		33308	Morning Star	L R
33201	Marquis of Clinton	— L R		33309	Morning Star	— P S
33203	Marquis Gwynne	— Cox		33311	Moses	— P S
33204	Marquis of Lorne	Ky I		33312	Moses	— M
33209	Marquis of Mapledale	— D		33313	Mosstrooper	— P S
33210	Marshal	— M		33315	Moultrie Bellville	Ky I
33214	Mary's Prince	— M		33316	Moultrie Gamester	— M
33215	Mason	— R R		33317	Mowcher Bill	— R R
33216	Mason Duke	— R R		33319	Muscatoon of Edgewood	— M
33219	Master Airdrie	L R		33320	Musician 2nd	— Cox
33225	Master Airdrie 20th	— M		33322	Napoleon	P S
33226	Master Airdrie 21st	— M		33323	Napoleon	Ky I
33227	Master Airdrie 22nd	— Cox		33324	Nasby	Ky I
33228	Master Airdrie 23rd	— R R		33325	National	— R R
33229	Master Airdrie 24th	— R R		33327	Nelson	— P S
33230	Master Airdrie 25th	— R R		33328	Nelson	— Cox
33231	Master Alphonso	— M		33329	Nelson Boy 1st	— M
33232	Master Breckenridge	— M		33330	Nelson Duke	— T
33234	Master Frank	M		33331	Nanescah Chief	C
33236	Masterpierce	— R R		33332	Nero	— M

SHORT-HORN CATTLE PEDIGREES.

No.	Name	Herd
33333	Nero	Ky I
33334	Nero	— M
33335	Nero	P S
33336	Newham Prince	— R R
33337	Newtown Chief	— Ky I
33338	Newton Golddust	— L R
33340	New York	— D
33341	Niagara	— Cox
33342	Nicknacks	— L R
33343	Nightingale Boy	— Cox
33344	Noble	— Cox
33346	Noble Duke 2nd	— P S
33347	Noble Duke 3rd	— P S
33348	Noble Monarch	— M
33349	Nodaway Chief	— R R
33352	North Star	Ky I
33354	Oakland Lad	Ky I
33355	Oakland Lad	M
33356	Oakland Lad 3rd	— R R
33357	Octagon	L R
33358	Oddfellow	Ky I
33359	Ogden	— L R
33360	Olof	— M
33361	Oliver	— M
33362	Oliver Bloomfield	— Cox
33363	Oliver Goldsmith	— R R
33364	Oliver Perry	— R R
33365	Omaha Chief	— M
33366	Onarga Duke	Ky I
33367	Onarga Duke 2nd	— L R
33368	Onarga Duke 3rd	— Daisy
33369	One-Eyed Priest	— M
33371	1st Oneida's Duke of Melleray	— M
33373	3d Oneida's Duke of Melleray	— M
33374	Oneida Joe	Daisy
33376	Oneida Prince	— R R
33379	Oph Suyder	P S
33380	Orion	— Cox
33381	Orno	Ky I
33382	Orontes 2nd	— R R
33383	Orontes 3rd	— R R
33384	Orphan Boy	— M
33385	Orphan Boy	— T
33386	Orphan Boy	— Cox
33387	Orphan Boy 6th	— C
33388	Oscar	P S
33391	Osman Pasha	M
33392	Otho 2nd	Ky I
33393	Ottmar	— M
33394	Otsego	— Cox
33395	Overseer	— R R
33396	Oxford	— Cox
33401	Oxford Bloom	— L R
33403	Oxford Comet	— L R
33409	Oxford Holliday	— R R
33411	Oxford Julius	C
33412	Oxford King	— Cox
33413	Oxford Knight	— M
33414	Oxford Lad	— Cox
33415	Oxford Lad	— R R
33418	Oxford of Plum Grove	P S
33419	Oxford Prince	T
33424	Oxford Star	P S
33430	Ozark	— R R
33431	Ozark Duke	— D
33432	Panic	— M
33433	Panks	P S
33436	Paragon of the West	— R R
33437	Parson	Daisy
33438	Patrick	M
33439	Patterson Duke	— Daisy
33441	Pawne Chief	T
33443	Pearl	— Cox
33444	Pearl's Loudon Duke	— T
33445	Peavine	L R
33446	Penjerick	T
33447	Perfection	— M
33450	Peter Cooper	— Cox
33451	Peter Wink	L R
33452	Phil Sheridan	Ky I
33454	Phyllis' Oakland	— R R
33455	Pilgrim	Ky I
33456	Pilot	L R
33457	Pilot	Cox
33458	Pine Grove	— M
33459	Pine Knot	M
33460	Pinto	M
33461	Pierce 2nd	Ky I
33463	Pioneer	C
33466	Plevna	— L R
33467	Plumwood, Junior	— R R
33468	Plumwood W.	C
33469	Plumwood L. L.	R R
33470	Plumwood M. M.	— R R
33471	Plumwood N. N.	R R
33472	Plumwood O. O.	Daisy
33473	Plumwood P. P.	C
33474	Plumwood Q. Q.	C
33475	Plumwood R. R.	Ky I
33476	Plumwood Punch	— P S
33477	Pluto	L R
33478	Pollock	— P S
33479	Pontiac	— D
33480	Ponto	T
33481	Postmaster	— R R
33482	Powhatan	R R
33483	Powhatan	— L R
33484	Prairie Duke	— M
33486	Prairie Fire	— T
33487	President Hayes	— R R
33492	Pride of the Pasture	Cox
33495	Prince	— D
33497	Prince	— Cox
33498	Prince	— Cox
33499	Prince	L R
33500	Prince	L R
33501	Prince	L R
33502	Prince Albert	— Cox
33504	Prince Albert	L R
33505	Prince Albert	— Cox
33506	Prince Alfred	L R
33508	Prince Arthur	— Cox
33509	6th Prince of Australia	— Cox
33510	Prince Barmpton	— R R
33511	Prince Bismark	— D
33512	Prince Bismark	— M
33514	Prince Brown	M
33516	Prince Charles	Ky I
33517	Prince Charlie	— Cox
33518	Prince Cyrus	— L R
33519	Prince Derby	— D
33520	Prince Edward 2nd	— T
33521	Prince Edwy	— Cox
33524	Prince George	— Ky I
33525	Prince George 2nd	— L R
33526	2nd Prince of Glady	— M
33527	Prince of Golddust	— P S
33528	Prince Goodness	— Cox
33531	Prince of Hoosick	— Cox
33532	Prince of Idlewild	— P S

33533	Prince Imperial	— C	33627	Red Duke	M
33534	Prince Imperial	Ky I	33629	Red Duke	— R R
33538	Prince Leonard 1st	— M	33630	Red Duke	— C
33539	Prince Leonard 2nd	— M	33631	Red Duke 2nd	— P S
33540	Prince of Lewis	Ky I	33632	Red Duke 3rd	— P S
33541	Prince of Mecosta	— L R	33634	Red Eagle	— Ky I
33542	Prince Oxford	— R R	33636	Red Hope	— R R
33546	Prince of Seaham 2nd	— C	33637	Red Hunter of Oakland	P S
33547	Prince Sharon	— D	33638	Red Jacket	P S
33548	Prince Sodowsky	M	33639	Red Jacket	— Cox
33549	Prince of Sugar Grove	P S	33640	Red Jacket	— Daisy
33551	Princess Duke 2nd	— P S	33641	Red Jacket	— Cox
33552	Princess Duke 3rd	— P S	33642	Red Jacket	L R
33553	Prince of The River, Junior	— R R	33643	Red Jacket	— L R
33554	Prince of The Roses	— M	33644	Red Jenner's Grandson	— Cox
33555	Prince of The Valley	D	33645	Red Jim	Ky I
33556	Princeton	— R R	33646	Red June	P S
33561	Prince of Wildwood	— D	33648	Red Lad 2nd	— M
33563	4th Prince of Woodlawn	C	33649	Red Lion	Ky I
33564	6th Prince of Woodlawn	— R R	33650	Red Major	— C
33565	Prince of Willow Park	P S	33652	Red Oak	Ky I
33568	Prince of Yates 3rd	— M	33653	Red Oxford	P S
33569	Prince of Yates 4th	— M	33654	Red Prince 2nd	— R R
33570	Probability	— P S	33655	Red Ranger	— P S
33571	Professor	— L R	33658	Red Rover	— M
33573	Professor Underwood	— L R	33659	Red Rover	— L R
33574	Prohibitionist	M	33660	Red Rover	— Long-Horn
33576	Purvine's Favorite	M	33661	Red Royal	— R R
33577	Putnam	— M	33662	Red Star	— M
33578	1st Queen's Duke	— Ky I	33663	Red Starlight	— M
33579	Radical	— Cox	33664	Red Tempest	— D
33580	Ralph	— R R	33665	Red Wood	D
33581	Ralph Otley	— M	33666	Reed's Red Bull	— Long-Horn
33582	Ralston The Banker	R R	33667	Reformer	— L R
33583	Rambler	— D	33668	Regal Rose	— Cox
33585	Ranger	— Long-Horn	33670	Reginald 2nd	L R
33587	Ranger	M	33671	Renick's Airdrie 2nd	— Cox
33589	Rarus	P S	33672	Reno	Ky I
33591	Rattler	— M	33674	Renwick Duke	— T
33592	Rattler	T	33676	Reynold's Red Duke	— T
33593	Ravenswood	— L R	33677	Revenue	— L R
33594	Raymore	— R R	33678	Rhoda's Boy	— Cox
33595	R. B. Hayes	M	33679	Richard	— M
33596	Record	— M	33680	Richard	P S
33599	Red Barnpton	— R R	33682	Richard of Evergreen Hill	Cox
33600	Red Baron	— R R	33684	Richard Leslie	— Long-Horn
33601	Red Barton	P S	33686	Richmond	L R
33603	Red Blucher	Ky I	33687	Richmond	— M
33604	Red Buck	M	33688	Richwood	D
33605	Red Buck	Ky I	33689	Rimrock	M
33606	Red Bud	— Ky I	33690	Rising Sun	— L R
33607	Red Chief	Cox	33691	Roan Airdrie	— R R
33608	Red Chub	— M	33692	Roan Babraham	— M
33609	Red Cloud	— M	33693	Roan Barnpton	— R R
33610	Red Cloud	— L R	33694	Roan Charley	— L R
33611	Red Cloud	— T	33695	Roan Davy	— M
33612	Red Cloud	— P S	33698	Roan Duke	T
33613	Red Cloud	M	33699	Roan Duke	— P S
33614	Red Cloud	— L R	33700	Roan Duke	— Cox
33615	Red Cloud	— R R	33701	Roan Duke	D
33617	Red Cloud	— Cox	33702	Roan Duke	— C
33618	Red Comet	P S	33704	Roan Duke of Splendor	M
33619	Red Comet	L R	33705	Roan Gloster	P S
33620	Red Dick	— L R	33706	Roan John	— L R
33621	1st Red Duke	— Ky I	33707	Roan Lesgar	— Cox
33622	Red Duke	Ky I	33708	Roan Maids Duke	M
33623	Red Duke	— P S	33709	Roan Monarch	— M
33624	Red Duke	— Cox	33711	Roan Star	T
33625	Red Duke	— L R	33713	Robin Hood	— R R
33626	Red Duke	— R R	33717	Rob Roy	— R R

SHORT-HORN CATTLE PEDIGREES.

No.	Name	Sire
33720	Rockingham	— Daisy
33721	Rock River Lad 21st	— Cox
33722	Rock River Lad 22nd	— Cox
33723	Rock River Lad 23rd	— Cox
33724	Rock River Lad 24th	— Cox
33725	Rock River Lad 25th	— Cox
33726	Rock River Lad 26th	— Cox
33727	Rock River Lad 27th	— Cox
33728	Rock River Lad 28th	— Cox
33729	Rock River Lad 29th	— Cox
33730	Rock River Lad 30th	— Cox
33731	Rock River Lad 31st	T
33732	Rock River Lad 32nd	— Cox
33733	Rock River Lad 33rd	M
33735	Rock Spring Duke	— P S
33738	Roman	— M
33740	Romeo	— L R
33741	Romeo	— Cox
33742	Romeo	— M
33743	Romeo	— Cox
33744	Romeo	— Cox
33745	Romeo	M
33746	Romulus	— R R
33747	Romulus	— Daisy
33751	Roscoe	— Cox
33752	Roscoe	— Cox
33753	Roseberry	— M
33754	Rosebud	— M
33760	Rosy's Duke	Ky I
33762	Rover	M
33763	Rover	— D
33764	Rover	C
33765	Rover	— Cox
33766	Rover	L R
33767	Rover Boy	M
33768	Rowena's Napier	— Cox
33769	Royal	— Cox
33770	Royal Airdrie	P S
33772	Royal Briton 3rd	— M
33773	Royal Briton 4th	— R R
33774	Royal Briton 5th	— R R
33775	Royal Briton 6th	— L R
33776	Royal Briton 7th	— L R
33777	Royal Briton 8th	— L R
33778	Royal Chatham	— M
33780	Royal Crown	M
33781	Royal Dan	Cox
33782	Royal Defender	— L R
33786	Royal Gem	T
33787	Royal George 3rd	— M
33788	Royal Gloster	M
33789	Royal Henry	L R
33790	Royal Hubback	— L R
33791	Royal Hubback 2nd	— L R
33792	Royalist	Ky I
33793	Royal Jim	P S
33795	Royal Oakland 2nd	Ky I
33796	Royal Prince	— L R
33797	Royal Prince	T
33798	Royal Prince	— M
33800	Royal Prince	— R R
33802	Royal Punch	— P S
33803	2nd Royal Red Rose	— D
33804	3rd Royal Red Rose	T
33805	Royal Star	— Ky I
33806	Royal Star of Neponset	— M
33808	Ruby's Duke of Springwood	L R
33809	Rudolph Green	— R R
33811	Rutherford	— L R
33812	Rutherford 2nd	— L R
33813	Rutherford B	Ky I
33815	Saint Cloud	— R R
33816	Saint Elmo 5th	— R R
33817	Saint Louis	— R R
33818	Saint Nicholas	— Ky I
33819	Saint Patrick	— L R
33820	Saint Patrick	— L R
33821	Saint Patrick	Ky I
33822	Saint Patrick's Day	P S
33823	Salamander	— Daisy
33824	Salamander	— L R
33825	Sam	D
33826	Sam	— M
33827	Sam	T
33828	Sam Adams	— R R
33829	Sampson 2nd	M
33831	San Antonio	— M
33832	Sanantonio	Ky I
33833	Sancho Panza	— P S
33836	Saxon	— M
33837	Scipio	— Cox
33838	Scipio	— M
33839	Scipio 2nd	— M
33840	Scott	— M
33841	Scott	— R R
33843	Sebago	— L R
33844	Sedalia	Woods
33845	Senator	— M
33847	Senator Cockerell	— M
33853	Seth Thomas	M
33854	Shabona	— M
33855	Shaker Boy	Ky I
33856	Shanky	— M
33857	Shannon Lisgar	— Cox
33861	Sharon Red	— D
33863	Sharrett	— P S
33864	Shawnee	M
33865	Shenandoah	— R R
33866	Shenandoah Gloster	— Cox
33867	Shepherd	Ky I
33868	Shepherd Prince	Ky I
33869	Shere Ali	— R R
33870	Sheridan	P S
33871	Sheridan 2nd	L R
33872	Sheriff, Junior	— D
33873	Sheriff of Green River	P S
33874	Sherod 2nd	Ky I
33875	Shiree	— P S
33876	Shiroam	R R
33877	Shirock	— D
33878	Shyster	M
33883	Sir Archy	— Cox
33884	Sir Campbell	— P S
33885	Sir Charles	P S
33886	Sir Columbus	— Cox
33887	Sir Harry	— L R
33888	Sir Henry	— Cox
33890	Sir James	M
33892	Sir John	— M
33893	Sir Richard	— M
33895	Sir Rover	— M
33898	Sir Titus	— M
33899	Sir Tom	— D
33900	Sir Walter	— Cox
33902	Sir Walter Scott	— Cox
33904	Sir William	— T
33905	Sir William Drummond Stewart	D
33907	Sitting Bull	P S
33908	Sitting Bull	M
33909	Snowball	L R

33911	Snowdrop	Cox	34026	Valentine	Ky I
33912	Snowflake	— Cox	34027	Valentine	Ky I
33914	Snowflake	Cox	34028	Valley Cherub	— Cox
33916	Solon	— T	34029	Vanguard, Jr.	L R
33917	Son of Sharon	— L R	34031	Vermillion Duke	Wrong
33920	Specie	M	34034	Vich Jan Vohr	— Ky I
33921	Splendor	— M	34035	Victor	— L R
33924	Spread Eagle	D	34037	Victor	D
33927	Spurgeon	— R R	34038	Victor	P S
33928	Squire Mapleton	— Ky I	34039	Victor	— Cox
33930	Stanley	— R R	34040	Victor	L R
33931	Stanley	— R R	34041	Victor	P S
33933	Stanley 2nd	D	34042	Victoria's Duke	— R R
33934	Star	— P S	34043	Victoria's Duke	— R R
33935	Star Airdrie	C	34045	Victor Oxford	D
33937	Star Duke	— R R	34047	Vindex	— D
33938	Star Duke	— P S	34048	Vinne's Duke	— R R
33939	Star Duke	P S	34049	Visalia Duke	— P S
33940	Star Gazer	L R	34052	Vulcan	— Cox
33941	Star Gem	P S	34053	Wade Hampton	— M
33942	Star of Harristown	Ky I	34054	Wade Hampton	— R R
33943	Star Lewis	— R R	34055	Wade Hampton	T
33944	Starlight	— T	34056	Wade Hampton	— M
33947	Starlight	— L R	34057	Wade Hampton	— P S
33949	Star of Orange	— C	34058	Wade Hampton	— M
33950	Star of The West	— R R	34060	Walter James	M
33952	Steve Zollers	T	34061	Walter Scott	— P S
33953	Stock Farm Duke	M	34063	Ward Beecher	— R R
33954	Stockton Duke	L R	34064	War Eagle	— D
33955	Stoner	— M	34065	Washington	— Daisy
33956	Stonewall Jackson	— C	34074	Wauk	Cox
33959	Strawberry Duke	— Long-Horn	34075	Waunatoosa Chief	— P S
33963	Sucker Boy	— R R	34076	Waverly	— L R
33966	Suleiman Pasha	— M	34078	Wellington	P S
33968	Sweet Spring	— Ky I	34079	Welshman	L R
33970	Symmetry	— M	34080	Western King	— P S
33971	Symmetry's Duke of Scott	R R	34081	Western Lad	— P S
33972	Talbot	Cox	34082	Western Lad	— Ky I
33975	Tenny Boy	— M	34083	Western Lad	— Daisy
33977	Terror	— M	34085	Western Star	Ky I
33978	Telephone	— R R	34086	West Liberty	— M
33979	Telephone	P S	34088	White Cloud	— R R
33980	Tell	— P S	34090	White Monarch	— P S
33982	Texas Duke	P S	34092	White Prophet	Ky I
33983	Texas Star	Wrong	34093	White Stocking	— M
33984	Texican	Wrong	34094	White Stocking	P S
33985	The Admiral	M	34096	Wide-awake	— Cox
33989	The King	D	34097	Wide-awake Duke	— D
33993	Thomas	— Cox	34108	Wildwood Airdrie	— M
33994	Thomas Carr	L R	34109	Wiley	P S
33995	Thorndale	— C	34111	Wiley Oxford 3rd	— R R
33997	Thorndale Duke	— R R	34112	Wiley Oxford 3rd	M
33999	Thorndike	Ky I	34113	Wiley Oxford 4th	M
34000	Tilden	Ky I	34114	Wiley's Victor	— R R
34001	Tilden	— R R	34115	Willard	— M
34002	Tilton	— T	34116	William	— M
34004	Tippecanoe	L R	34117	William D.	— R R
34005	Tippoo Saib	— M	34118	William Long	— P S
34006	Todd Williams	Ky I	34119	William Oscar	M
34007	Tom	M	34120	William Tell	— R R
34008	Tom Dowley	— Cox	34121	Willie Airdrie	— Ky I
34009	Tom Ochiltree	— M	34123	Willow Boy	Ky I
34010	Tom Paine	— Long.Horn	34125	Windsor	Ky I
34011	Tom Vanmetre 2nd	— D	34126	Wiseacre	— D
34012	Tornado	— Cox	34128	Woodbine Duke	— C
34015	Trident	— Cox	34130	Yankee Boy	P S
34018	Trump	Cox	34132	York Jupiter	— Cox
34019	Twin Rosy Duke	— T	34133	Yorkshire	— L R
34022	Uncas	M	34134	Young Adams	— M
34025	Van Buren Duke	P S	34136	Young America	Cox

34137	Young America	—M	34255	King William	—R R
34138	Young Baron	—R R	34256	Lee	Ky I
34140	Young Bedford	P S	34257	Lettie's Airdrie	—M
34141	Young Belden	Ky I	34258	Linda's Rover	Cox
34142	Young Booth	—L R	34259	Logan	—Ky I
34143	Young Canefield	—M	34260	Louan's Duke of Airdrie	—R R
34144	Young Comet	—M	34261	Loudon Duke of Greenwood	—R R
34145	Young Crockett	M	34262	Louis	—Long-Horn
34149	Young Duke of Vermillion	—R R	34263	Marquis of Lorne	—T
34150	Young Gisbon	Ky I	34264	Mars Eleventh	—Daisy
34151	Young Gloster	—L R	34266	7th Meadow Duke	—M
34154	Young Lictor	—C	34267	Mitchel	—M
34155	Young Mapleton	—M	34268	Monarch 4th	Cox
34158	Young Oxford	—M	34270	Monroe	T
34159	Young Pearl	D	34271	Nannie's Duke	—R R
34160	Young's Prairie Diamond	—D	34273	Orontes Duke	—M
34161	Young Prince	—M	34277	Pearl Duke	—M
34162	Young Prince	—T	34278	Prince Leonard 5th	—M
34163	Young Richmond	—Ky I	34280	Reavis 2nd	—T
34164	Young Thorndale	—Cox	34281	Red Duke	M
34165	Young Sir Dimple 4th	—R R	34282	Road Agent	M
34166	Young Splendor	—Ky I	34283	Roan Boy	—M
34168	Zack Taylor	L R	34284	Roan Cherub	—M
34172	Ardamillan	Ky I	34286	Rover	—Cox
34173	Baker	T	34289	Rurik	Cox
34174	Ballantine	M	34290	Scotland Ben	—D
34177	Beecher	—Ky I	34292	Sitting Bull	M
34178	Ben Adhem	—M	34293	Solon	Ky I
34179	Billy Hawkins	—L R	34294	Solon Lad	—R R
34181	Blanco	—M	34295	Stockwell 2nd	—M
34182	Blondin	—Cox	34297	Thorndal Oxford 2nd	—C
34183	Blue Jeans	R R	34299	Thorndale Oxford 4th	—C
34184	Bolton 2nd	—P S	34301	Tilden	Ky I
34185	Brigham	M	34304	Waterman	Ky I
34192	Cheyenne	T	34305	White Cloud	—L R
34194	Clarion Duke	Ky I	34306	Wildair	—D
34195	Clarion Duke 2nd	Ky I	34308	Young Hoosier	
34196	Clinton Duke	—D	34309	Young Prince Louis	—R R
34199	Cottonwood Louanjo 7th	P S	34311	Aaron	—R R
34200	Cottonwood Louanjo 10th	M	34312	Abe Lincoln	—D
34201	Cottonwood Louanjo 11th	Ky I	34313	Accident	—R R
34202	Cottonwood Louanjo 12th	M	34314	Accident	—R R
34203	Cottonwood Louanjo 13th	P S	34315	Accommodation	—P S
34204	Cottonwood Louanjo 15th	M	34317	Acme	P S
34205	Cottonwood Louanjo 16th	P S	34319	Ada 5th's Duke	—R R
34206	Cottonwood Louanjo 17th	P S	34320	Adam Clark	—M
34210	Cypress Duke of Forest Hill	M	34321	Addie Treague's Kirklevington	—R R
34211	Cypress Lad	—M	34322	Admiral	—R R
34212	Dick Coopman	—Cox	34323	Admiral	—C
34213	Dick Prince	C	34324	Admiral 2nd	—P S
34215	2nd Duke of Alfred	L R	34325	Adonis	—Daisy
34217	Duke of Bourbon	—D	34326	Advance	Ky I
34218	Duke Clifton 3rd	—R R	34327	Advertiser	M
34219	Duke of Elmwood	—L R	34328	Aesop	—M
34220	32nd Duke of Goodness	—R R	34329	Afghan	—L R
34222	2nd Duke of Orland	Ky I	34330	Agate Peri Duke	—R R
34226	Duke of The Plains	M	34331	Agricola	P S
34230	Earl of Sprague	—Cox	34336	Airdrie Bully Boy	M
34233	Famous Rodney	—Cox	34337	Airdrie Chief	—C
34236	Genesee Lad	—R R	34339	Airdrie Duke	M
34238	Governor Hayes		34340	Airdrie Duke	—M
34240	Grand Duke of Goodness 2nd	—R R	34341	7th Airdrie Duke	M
34241	Granger	—R R	34342	8th Airdrie Duke	M
34242	Grenadier	—C	34344	Airdrie Duke of Elm Lawn	—R R
34244	Hercules	Ky I	34345	1st Airdrie Duke of Sandusky	—R R
34247	Howell	—P S	34347	Airdrie 1st of Hickory Grove	—R R
34250	Jim Clay	—R R	34348	Airdrie 2nd of Hickory Grove	—R R
34251	John M. Corse	Cox	34349	Airdrie Joe	—R R
34252	Jubilee Duke	—L R	34350	Airdrie's Lad	—R R
34253	Kansas Orphan	T	34353	Airdrie of Locust Lawn	M

No.	Name	Sire	No.	Name	Sire
34354	Airdrie McConnell	— P S	34470	Baron of Rivoli	L R
34355	Airdrie Maid's Duke	— R R	34472	Baron 1st of Spring Valley	— Cox
34357	Airdrie Oxford	M	34473	Baron 2nd of Spring Valley	— Ky I
34360	Airdrie Prince 2nd	Ky I	34474	Baron 3rd of Spring Valley	— Cox
34361	Airdrie Prince 3rd	Ky I	34475	Baron 4th of Spring Valley	— Cox
34362	Airdrie Rose's Oxford	— R R	34476	Baron Teague	— R R
34365	Airdrie Stuart 5th	— C	34477	Baron Thorndale 3rd	— L R
34366	Airdrie Thorndale	L R	34480	6th Baron of Vermillion	— L R
34367	Ajax	— T	34481	8th Baron of Vermillion	— L R
34368	Ajax	M	34482	Baron Wadsworth 4th	Cox
34369	Ajax of Maplewood	M	34483	Baron Wadsworth 5th	Ky I
34370	Albinus	— L R	34484	Baron Wadsworth 6th	Cox
34371	Alcibiades	— M	34486	Baron William	— R R
34372	Alderman	— R R	34487	Bashman	— L R
34373	Alex	P S	34488	Basil Duke 4th	— R R
34375	Alexis	— D	34489	Basilicus	— M
34377	Alhambra	— P S	34496	9th Bates of Oak Hill	— R R
34378	Alhenan	— Cox	34497	10th Bates of Oak Hill	— R R
34379	Alice's Duke	— P S	34498	12th Bates of Oak Hill	P S
34380	Allen	— L R	34500	Beaconsfield	— R R
34381	Almont	Ky I	34501	Beaconsfield	— Cox
34382	Almont	— Cox	34502	Beaconsfield	— M
34384	Alpha	— P S	34503	Beaconsfield	M
34386	Andrew Johnson	M	34504	Beaumont	— R R
34387	Andy	— M	34507	Beau Sharon	— D
34388	Animator	— P S	34508	Beauty's Trego	— M
34390	Annetta's Baron	— M	34509	Beaver Duke 4th	— P S
34391	Apple Jack	Ky I	34512	Beecher	— R R
34392	Appleton	— L R	34513	Beecher	M
34394	Archduke, Jr	Ky I	34514	Beech Gem	— Ky I
34396	Astolfo	— Cox	34519	Belle's Duke	Daisy
34400	Atlas	— Cox	34520	Bell Duke	— Long-Horn
34401	Antler	— Cox	34522	Bell Duke 2nd	— R R
34402	Augustus	— R R	34523	Belle Duke 3rd	Ky I
34403	Australia's Oxford	— Cox	34524	Belle Duke of Fairholme	— R R
34405	Babraham's Baron	— L R	34525	Belle Duke O	— R R
34406	Babraham's Royal Duke	— L R	34527	Bellman	— R R
34407	Baby Chief	— L R	34528	Belle's Oxford	— Ky I
34409	Badger Boy	— D	34529	Bell Punch	— C
34410	Badger Boy	— M	34531	Bellville Lad	— Long-Horn
34413	Balco	— L R	34532	Belmont	— L R
34414	Balco's Pride	— T	34533	Belmont	— Cox
34416	Bancroft	— D	34535	Belmont	P S
34417	Bandit	M	24536	Belted Knight	L R
34418	Banker	— L R	34537	Belton	L R
34419	Bannock	P S	34539	Belvidere	Ky I
34421	4th Barmpton Duke L	— R R	34541	Ben	L R
34422	Barney	M	34542	Ben	— M
34424	Barker	— M	34543	Ben	— R R
34425	Baron	— R R	34544	Ben Ali	T
34428	Baron Airdrie 3rd	— Long-Horn	34545	Ben Butler	Ky I
34429	Baron Argus	— R R	34546	Ben Butler	— P S
34430	Baron Booth 2nd	— R R	34547	Ben Butler	— M
34431	Baron Breastplate	— R R	34549	Ben Davis	— R R
34433	Baron Duke 7th	— T	34550	Ben Hill	— R R
34435	Baron of Cloverly	— M	34551	Ben 3rd of Maplewild	M
34436	Baron Dun	— C	34552	Ben 4th of Maplewild	M
34438	Baronet	— M	34553	Benton	Ky I
34442	Baron of Geneva	— T	34554	Benton Duke	L R
34444	4th Baron of Grass Hill	— Cox	34555	Benvolio	D
34445	5th Baron of Grass Hill	— Cox	34556	Beppo	— M
34446	2nd Baron of Grovedale	— Cox	34557	2nd Berthold	— M
34448	Baron Gwynne of Orchard	— Cox	34558	Bertram	— Long-Horn
34449	Baron Gwynne 2nd of Orchard	— Cox	34559	Bertram	— Ky I
34450	Baron Kinnellar 2nd	— R R	34561	Bettie's Duke 2nd	— M
34452	Baron Larry	— C	34563	Big Jim	M
34453	Baron Leonard 4th	— L R	34564	Billy	— L R
34458	Baron Moore	— T	34565	Billy Allen	— Cox
34462	Baron's Pride	Woods	34566	Billy Boy	— Cox
34464	Baron Richmond of Evergreen	Ky I	34567	Billy Curtis	L R

SHORT-HORN CATTLE PEDIGREES. 161

No.	Name	Herd
34568	Billy Duster	— Long-Horn
34569	Billy Jones	Cox
34570	Billy Jones	— M
34571	Bill Reynolds	— M
34572	Bill Ross	— M
34573	Bismark	M
34574	Bismark	— M
34576	Bismark	— T
34577	Bismark	— R R
34578	Bismark	— R R
34579	Bismark	— R R
34580	Black Hawk	— T
34581	Black Hills	— Ky I
34582	Blakie	— Cox
34583	Blaine	— R R
34584	Blaize	— R R
34585	Blizzard 1st	— M
34586	Blizzard 2nd	— M
34591	Blucher	— M
34592	Blucher	— Ky I
34593	Blucher	— Cox
34594	Blucher	— R R
34595	Boaster	M
34596	Bob	— R R
34597	Bob	M
34598	Bobbie Shaftoe	— Cox
34599	Bob Dixon	— M
34600	Bob Fisk	— P S
34601	Bob Ingersoll	— Cox
34602	Bob Ingersoll	— Cox
34603	Bob Ingersoll	— M
34604	Bob Ingersoll	— Long-Horn
34605	Bob Lee	Ky I
34606	Bob Lee	— L R
34607	Bob Miller	— T
34609	Bob Wiley	P S
34611	Bonanza	— T
34612	Bonanza	— L R
34613	Bonaparte	— R R
34614	Bonny Lad	Cox
34615	Bonnie Scotland 2nd	M
34618	Booth of Cedar Grove	— T
34619	Booth Duke	— C
34620	Booth of Sangamon Valley	— R R
34621	Boss Tweed	— Daisy
34622	Boston	— L R
34623	Bourbon	— D
34625	Bourbon Duke	— P S
34626	Bourbon Duke	— L R
34629	Bourbon Star 2nd	— D
34630	Bowery Boy	— Daisy
34631	Boxer	— L R
34632	Bracelet's Duke	— M
34633	Bradley	— L R
34636	Brazito	— T
34638	Breno	Ky I
34639	Bridesman	— R R
34640	Bridesman 2nd	P S
34641	Brigand	— C
34643	Bright Eyes Duke	— M
34646	Brilliant Lad	— P S
34647	Brockley Oxford	— R R
34648	Browning	— L R
34650	Byrant	— Cox
34651	Buckeye Boy	M
34652	Buckeye Lad	— R R
34653	Buckeye State	— M
34654	Buffalo Bill	— P S
34655	Bulbus	P S
34656	Bulldozer	— P S
34657	Burdette	— M
34658	Burley 2nd	M
34661	Burnside	— D
34662	3rd Burnside Duke	— D
34663	Burton Lad	Cox
34664	Buster Boy	L R
34669	Byington	Ky I
34670	Byron	R R
34671	Cadet	— L R
34672	Cæsar	Ky I
34673	Cæsar	P S
34674	Caleb	— T
34675	Calhoun 2nd	— D
34676	Caliph	— M
34677	Calla's Duke 2nd	— R R
34678	Calomel	— Cox
34679	Cambria Duke	— D
34682	Cambridge Duke of Geneva	— R R
34687	Canadian Chief	— Cox
34688	Canoga Prince	L R
34689	Canyon Duke	— P S
34690	Captain	— C
34695	Captain Fisher	M
34696	Captain George Leigh	— R R
34697	Captain Hall	M
34698	Captain Jack 6th	— M
34699	Captain Jack	— P S
34700	Captain Jack	— M
34701	Captain Jack	— M
34702	Captain Jack	— M
34703	Captain Jordon	— D
34704	Captain Mott	— M
34705	Captain Princeton	— C
34706	Captain Shaftoe	— M
34707	Captain Shortt	L R
34708	Captain Townley	M
34709	Captain Walsh	— M
34711	Carlos	— L R
34713	Carnation's Duke	— R R
34714	Caroline's Duke	— M
34715	Carrie's Airdrie	— R R
34716	Carson Lad	M
34717	Cashier	— D
34719	Cato	L R
34720	Cato	— Cox
34723	Cecrops	— T
34724	Centennial Jim	— M
34725	Centennial Lad	M
34728	Champion	— M
34730	Champion	Ky I
34731	1st Champion	— Cox
34732	Champion 2nd	— Cox
34733	Champion 3rd	— Cox
34734	Champion 4th	— Cox
34735	Charley	— M
34736	Charley	— P S
34737	Charlie	— R R
34738	Charlie Fisher	M
34739	Charley Foster	— R R
34742	Charming Prince	— R R
34744	Cherry's Duke	Ky I
34745	Cherry Lad 8th	— Cox
34746	Cherry Red	— C
34747	Chequest	— T
34749	Cherub 9th	M
34750	Cherub Duke	— Cox
34751	Chestnut Grove Dick	— M
34752	Chief	T
34753	Chief Joe	L R
34754	Chief Joseph	— L R

UNFASHIONABLE CROSSES IN

34755	Chief Mac-a-cheek	— M
34757	Chieftain	R R
34759	Chieftain	— M
34760	Chieftain	— Ky I
34764	Chimborazo 2nd	Cox
34765	Chippewa	— Cox
34766	Chrismore	— Cox
34767	Christmas Boy	— L R
34768	Christopher	— M
34769	Chromo	— M
34770	Chub	— M
34771	Chumleys Chief	R R
34773	Clarico	R R
34774	Clarion Duke	Daisy
34775	Clark Chief	R R
34776	Claude	— L R
34777	Claude Mathews	— D
34779	Claudius	— R R
34780	Clement	— Cox
34782	Clement	M
34783	Clifton	— L R
34784	Clifton Duke	M
34786	Climax	— L R
34788	Clirene	— M
34789	Colling	— L R
34790	Colonel	— Cox
34791	Colonel	— P S
34792	Colonel	— Cox
34793	Col. Barton	— Cox
34794	Col. Clifton	L R
34795	Col. Crockett	— M
34796	Col. D. M. Hannah	— P S
34797	Col. Dyer	— Cox
34798	Colfax	— Cox
34799	Col. Ed Lynch	T
34800	Col. Edward Prince	— T
34801	Col. Ellsworth	— L R
34802	Col. Fenton	— M
34803	Col. Foote	— T
34804	Col. Gilman	— D
34806	Col. Le Moyne	M
34807	Col. MacGregor	— R R
34808	Col. Mansfield	— R R
34809	Col. Morris	— R R
34810	Col. Payne	Cox
34812	Columbia Duke	— R R
34813	Columbus	— Cox
34815	Comet	— P S
34816	Comet	— L R
34817	Comet 1st	— T
34818	Comet 2nd	— T
34819	Comet of Maine Valley	L R
34820	Commander	— P S
34821	Commander 2nd	— L R
34822	Commander	P S
34823	Commander Punch	— P S
34824	Commissioner	— R R
34825	Commodore	P S
34826	Commodore	— C
34827	Commodore	— Cox
34830	Concord	— L R
34831	Conkling	— R R
34835	Constantina's Oxford 2nd	R R
34837	Corporal	M
34839	Coshocton	M
34841	Cottonwood Louanjo 8th	M
34842	Count Ariosto	— L R
34845	3rd Count of Oneida	— R R
34846	8th Count of Oneida	— M
34847	Cowlitz	M
34849	Credo	P S
34851	Cromwell	Ky I
34852	Crown Jewel	P S
34853	Crown Prince	P S
34854	Croxtou Airdrie	Daisy
34855	Crusader	Ky I
34856	Crystal Baron	— M
34858	Cypress Duke	M
34861	Cypress Duke of Sarpy	P S
34862	Czarowitz	— P S
34864	Dairyman	— Cox
34866	Daisy Boy	T
34868	Daisy's Duke	— D
34869	Daisy Duke 1st	— R R
34870	Daisy Duke 2nd	— R R
34871	Daisy Duke 2nd	— M
34872	Dan	Cox
34873	Dan	— C
34874	Dan Booth	— Cox
34875	Danby	— Cox
34876	Dandy	M
34877	Dandy Duke	— P S
34879	Daniel Boone	T
34881	Daniel Deronda	— R R
34882	Daniel Drew	— L R
34883	Dan Sickles	L R
34885	Danvers	P S
34887	Darby, Jr	M
34888	Darby Duke 8th	— R R
34889	Darby Duke 9th	R R
34890	Darby Duke 10th	— P S
34891	Darius	— R R
34892	4th Darlington of Rosemound	— T
34893	5th Darlington of Rosemound	—Cox
34894	6th Darlington of Rosemound	— C
34895	7th Darlington of Rosemound	— T
34896	8th Darlington of Rosemound	— M
34897	Dauntless	M
34899	Davis Duke	— P S
34900	Davy Clay	— M
34901	Davy Crocket	— L R
34902	Deacon	— R R
34903	Deacon Jones	— Daisy
34904	Dean	— M
34905	Decoration	— Cox
34906	Deerlick Duke 6th	— M
34910	Desoto	— C
34911	Dexter	— Cox
34912	Diamond	C
34914	Diamond	P S
34915	Diamond	M
34916	Dick	— R R
34917	Dick	P S
34918	Dick	Ky I
34920	Dick Campbell	— M
34921	Dickens	Cox
34922	Dick Johnson	Cox
34923	Dick Taylor	— P S
34924	Dick Taylor	— M
34925	Dick Taylor	— Daisy
34926	Dictator	M
34927	Dictator	— Daisy
34928	Dimple Duke	— M
34929	Dixon	—T
34931	Doctor	Cox
34932	Doctor	M
34933	Doctor Lowell	Ky I
34934	Doctor Macon	— D
34938	Doctor Shively	— L R
34939	Doctor of the Tree	M

SHORT-HORN CATTLE PEDIGREES.

No.	Name	Ref.
34940	Doctor Tom	Woods
34941	Dolly's Prince	M
34942	Dominix	Ky I
34943	Dom Pedro	— D
34944	Dom Pedro	— Ky I
34945	Dom Pedro	— P S
34947	Dom Pedro	Cox
34948	Dom Pedro	— Ky I
34949	Dom Pedro	— L R
34950	Dom Pedro 2nd	— P S
34952	Don	— P S
34953	Don Carlos	— M
34955	Donegal	L R
34956	Don John 2nd	— Cox
34957	Don Leo Airdrie	— Ky I
34958	Don Perie	M
34959	Dorado	— M
34960	Doras Duke	T
34961	Double John Martin	— M
34963	Douglass	— L R
34965	Duenna's Oxford	— R R
34966	Duff Duncan	— M
34967	Duke	— D
34968	Duke	P S
34969	Duke	— Cox
34970	Duke	M
34975	Duke Alexis	— Ky I
34976	Duke Alexis	P S
34977	Duke Alexis	Ky I
34978	12th Duke of Allendale	— Cox
34981	Duke of Arcola	— M
34982	1st Duke of Argentine	Cox
34983	Duke of Argyll	Ky I
34984	8th Duke of Armada	Cox
34985	6th Duke of Altaham	— M
34986	3rd Duke of Ashbrook	D
34987	4th Duke of Ashbrook	— P S
34988	5th Duke of Ashbrook	D
34989	6th Duke of Ashbrook	Cox
34990	7th Duke of Ashbrook	— P S
34993	Duke of Aubry	— M
34994	Duke of Avon	— Cox
34995	Duke of Bath	— Cox
34996	Duke of Bath 2nd	— Cox
34997	Duke of Bath 3rd	— Cox
34998	Duke of Bedford	— Ky I
34999	Duke of Bedford 4th	P S
35001	2nd Duke of Belvue	— M
35002	3rd Duke of Benton	— Ky I
35003	Duke of Berkeley	— M
35005	Duke of Blanchard	— R R
35006	Duke of Blanchard 6th	— M
35009	Duke of Bourbon	— C
35010	Duke of Bow Park	— R R
35011	Duke of Brant	— R R
35012	2nd Duke of Breadalbane	D
35013	Duke of Bristol	— P S
35014	Duke of Brunswick	— L R
35016	Duke of Burgundy	— M
35017	Duke of Butler 3rd	— D
35018	Duke of Butler 4th	— M
35019	Duke of Camebridge	— M
35021	Duke of Carimona	P S
35023	Duke of Carroll	Daisy
35024	Duke of Carsdale	— Cox
35025	Duke of Celina	Ky I
35027	Duke of Charter Oak	T
35028	Duke of Chartiers	L R
35029	2nd Duke of Chartiers	— M
35030	Duke of Clear Creek	— R R
35032	Duke of Clinton	— M
35033	2nd Duke of Clinton	T
35034	Duke of Clover Hill	— Ky I
35036	Duke of Concho	L R
35040	Duke of Dana	M
35041	Duke Darling	M
35043	Duke of Delaware	— L R
35048	Duke of Dunglow Farm 3rd	C
35049	Duke of Easton	M
35050	2nd Duke of Edgewood	— L R
35051	Duke of Eldred	P S
35052	3rd Duke of Elgin	Cox
35053	Duke of Elkhorn	— P S
35054	Duke of Elkrun	Ky I
35055	4th Duke of Elmwood	Ky I
35056	1st Duke of Essex	Ky I
35057	4th Duke of Exeter	L R
35059	1st Duke of Fairholme	— P S
35060	Duke of Fairview	— M
35061	Duke of Fairview	— R R
35062	9th Duke of Fairview	M
35064	Duke of Feudale	— L R
35065	3rd Duke of Fennimore	— C
35066	4th Duke of Fennimore	— C
35068	Duke of Florence	M
35069	Duke of Franklin	— M
35070	Duke of Franklin	M
35071	1st Duke of Franklin	Ky I
35072	2nd Duke of Franklin	Ky I
35073	Duke of Fremont	— P S
35074	15th Duke of Gabilan	— R R
35075	17th Duke of Gabilan	— R R
35077	21st Duke of Gabilan	Ky I
35078	23rd Duke of Gabilan	Ky I
35079	24th Duke of Gabilan	— R R
35081	27th Duke of Gabilan	Daisy
35083	Duke of Gaines	L R
35084	Duke of Gallatin	— R R
35085	Duke of Garth 2nd	— L R
35086	Duke of Geddes	M
35087	9th Duke's Gem	— R R
35089	Duke of Geneva	— M
35090	Duke Gladstone	— R R
35091	Duke of Glencoe	— P S
35092	Duke of Glenwood	— L R
35093	Duke of Goodlettsville	M
35094	26th Duke of Goodness	— R R
35095	30th Duke of Goodness	— R R
35097	48th Duke of Goodness	— R R
35098	51st Duke of Goodness	— R R
35099	52nd Duke of Goodness	— R R
35100	53rd Duke of Goodness	— R R
35101	Duke of Grand River	— L R
35102	19th Duke of Granville	— R R
35103	Duke of Greenlawn 1st	— M
35104	Duke of Greenlawn 2nd	— M
35105	Duke of Greenlawn 3rd	— M
35106	2nd Duke of Greenside	Ky I
35107	Duke of Greenwood Park	— L R
35108	5th Duke of Grovedale	— Cox
35109	Duke of Groveland	T
35110	Duke of Hamilton	— R R
35111	Duke of Hamilton	Daisy
35112	Duke of Hanover	— Ky I
35113	Duke of Hardindale	M
35114	Duke of Harford	— R R
35115	12th Duke of Harlem	T
35116	Duke of Harmony	L R
35117	Duke of Harrison	— Daisy
35118	2nd Duke of Harvey	Ky I

35119	8th Duke of Harvey............Ky I	35213	Duke of Oakland.......... — Daisy
35121	1st Duke of Heathwood .... — Cox	35214	Duke of Oakland 9th.......... — D
35123	Duke of Hickory Grove...... — R R	35215	20th Duke of Oakland ....L R
35124	Duke of High Blue........... — M	35216	Duke of Oaklandside..........Cox
35125	6th Duke of Highland..........L R	35217	1st Duke of Oak Shade...... — Ky I
35126	10th Duke of Highland..........L R	35218	2nd Duke of Oak Shade .... — D
35127	1st Duke of Hillside.......... — P S	35219	3rd Duke of Oak Shade........Ky I
35128	2nd Duke of Hillside..........Ky I	35220	4th Duke of Oak Shade.... — Ky I
35129	3rd Duke of Hillside..........Ky I	35221	6th Duke of Oak Shade.......... — D
35130	4th Duke of Hillside.............M	35222	7th Duke of Oak Shade........Ky I
35131	2nd Duke of Hinsdale.............M	35224	Duke of Oberlin ....Ky I
35132	Duke of Holden................. — M	35225	Duke of Ogle .... — M
35133	Duke of Honor............. — P S	35226	Duke of Old Town 2nd ......L R
35134	Duke of Hopewell........... — R R	35228	3rd Duke of Orleans ....Ky I
35135	Duke Imperial..................L R	35229	4th Duke of Orleans............P S
35139	1st Duke of Iowa .... — M	35230	5th Duke of Orleans...... — Cox
35140	2nd Duke of Iowa........... — M	35231	6th Duke of Orleans........ — R R
35141	3rd Duke of Iroquois.........Daisy	35232	Duke of Ottawa ..... — Long-Horn
35143	Duke of Jefferson...........M	35234	Duke of Oxford............ — Cox
35144	Duke John of Forked Creek... — M	35235	Duke of Oxford 3rd .... — R R
35145	5th Duke of Jonesville...... — R R	35237	Duke of Paris .... — P S
35146	11th Duke of Jonesville..... — R R	35239	Duke Philip of Hillside...... — R R
35148	Duke of Kansas .... — P S	35240	Duke of Pike .... — L R
35149	Duke of Kennedy ....M	35241	Duke of Pike 2nd............ — M
35151	1st Duke of Kenton........... — R R	35242	Duke of Plum Grove...........P S
35153	3rd Duke of Kenton........... — M	35243	Duke of Portage 3rd..........Ky I
35154	4th Duke of Kenton........... — R R	35244	1st Duke of Pulaski ....Ky I
35155	5th Duke of Kenton........... — R R	35245	2nd Duke of Pulaski ....Ky I
35156	Duke of Knox .... — Ky I	35246	3rd Duke of Pulaski........ — R R
35160	Duke of Lanark ....D	35247	4th Duke of Pulaski......... — R R
35161	Duke of Lansing .... — Ky I	35249	3rd Duke of Raisin .... — Ky I
35163	Duke of Lexington........... — R R	35250	Duke of Randall............ — P S
35164	Duke of Licking................M	35253	Duke of Rich Valley................T
35165	Duke of Ligonier............ — R R	35254	26th Duke of Ridgland ...... — L R
35167	Duke of Linwood............ — D	35255	30th Duke of Ridgeland...........M
35168	1st Duke of Littlestown.... — R R	35256	31st Duke of Ridgeland...........M
35169	3rd Duke of Locust Grove.... — M	35257	33rd Duke of Ridgeland...........M
35170	5th Duke of Locust Grove.... — M	35258	3rd Duke of Rio .... — P S
35171	7th Duke of Locust Grove.... — M	35259	2nd Duke of Rio ..... — M
35173	1st Duke of Lone Star........ — D	35261	Duke of Rockdale............ — L R
35174	2nd Duke of Lone Star......... — D	35262	Duke of Roscoe............. — M
35175	Duke Lorne....................P S	35263	2nd Duke of Rush .... D
35176	Duke of Lucas................Ky I	35264	Duke of Russell............. — Ky I
35177	Duke Lyle................ — R R	35273	Duke Sherman.............. — P S
35178	Duke of Magenta .... — L R	35274	Duke of Shopiere............ — Ky I
35180	Duke of Maine Valley ....L R	35275	Duke of Sidney .... — R R
35182	1st Duke of Maple Grove........C	35276	6th Duke of Skaneateles.... — Cox
35183	3rd Duke of Maple Grove.........M	35277	7th Duke of Skaneateles.... — Cox
35184	Duke of Marion ....M	35278	2nd Duke of Skara Glen.... — R R
35185	1st Duke of Marion...........R R	35279	3rd Duke of Skara Glen....... — D
35186	Duke of Marshall .... — M	35280	4th Duke of Skara Glen...... — M
35187	3rd Duke of Marlboro........ — P S	35281	5th Duke of Skara Glen ...... — D
35188	4th Duke of Marlboro........ — R R	35282	6th Duke of Skara Glen....... — C
35189	5th Duke of Marlboro........ — M	35283	Duke of Springbrook Farm.....L R
35190	6th Duke of Marlboro........ — P S	35284	Duke of Staffa C
35193	Duke of Mazomanie.......... — P S	35285	Duke of Steenrods........... — L R
35195	2nd Duke of Mendota .... — D	35286	2nd Duke of Steenrods........ — L R
35196	3rd Duke of Mendota......... — D	35287	Duke of Stephenson... — Long-Horn
35197	Duke of Miami............. — R R	35288	2nd Duke of Sunnyside........ — D
35198	Duke of Middlefield 2nd........P S	35289	Duke of Sutherland 2nd .... — R R
35199	Duke of Milwaukee .... — L R	35290	Duke of Sutherland A........ — P S
35200	Duke of Minglewood.............T	35291	Duke of Sutherland B...........P S
35201	Duke of Monmouth.......... — P S	35293	28th Duke of Tecumseh........Ky I
35202	Duke of Montebello..— Long-Horn	35294	Duke of the Tempest........ — L R
35203	Duke of Moreton........... — D	35296	Duke of the Hills..............M
35204	Duke of Moultrie .... — M	35297	Duke of the Oaks........... — Cox
35206	Duke of Mount Pleasant..... — P S	35298	Duke of the Ocean...........Daisy
35207	Duke of Muncie...............M	35299	25th Duke of the Pines....... — R R
35208	Duke of Nelson ....M	35300	26th Duke of the Pines...... — R R
35211	Duke of New Lyme ....M	35301	27th Duke of the Pines...... — R R

35302	28th Duke of the Pines	— R R	35406	Earl Lewis	— D
35304	Duke of the Valley	T	35407	3rd Earl of Liberty	— M
35305	Duke of Three Groves	— L R	35411	3rd Earl of Martin	Cox
35306	3rd Duke of Trumbull	M	35412	4th Earl of Martin	Cox
35307	4th Duke of Trumbull	M	35413	5th Earl of Martin	Cox
35310	1st Duke of Van Buren	T	35415	Earl of Montrose	— Cox
35311	Duke of Wabash	T	35419	Earl of Oakland	— R R
35312	Duke of Wabash	T	35421	Earl of Oxford	— Cox
35313	Duke of Wahoo	Ky I	35422	Earl of Oxford	— Cox
35320	Duke of Walnut Grove	— P S	35423	3rd Earl of Oxford	— Cox
35321	Duke of Walnut Nook	T	35424	1st Earl of Portage	M
35322	Duke of Warren	— R R	35427	Earl of Rochester	— C
35323	2nd Duke of Warren	P S	35428	Earl of Senham	— C
35324	3rd Duke of Warren	P S	35430	1st Earl of Springlake	Cox
35325	10th Duke of Waveland	— L R	35431	2nd Earl of Springlake	Cox
35326	Duke of Wayne	— R R	35432	3rd Earl of Springlake	Cox
35327	Duke of Wellington	M	35433	Earl of Sussex	— D
35329	Duke of Wellington	— L R	35436	Earl of Wild Rose	— C
35330	Duke of Wellington	— L R	35437	Earl of Wildwood	— D
35331	3rd Duke of West Lawn	— Cox	35438	Earl of Woodlawn	— M
35333	Duke 10th of Wheatland	C	35439	Earnest Christain	— Ky I
35334	Duke 11th of Wheatland	— Ky I	35440	Easter Boy	— T
35335	Duke 12th of Wheatland	— Ky I	35441	Ebenezer	— P S
35336	Duke 13th of Wheatland	C	35442	Eclipse	— D
35337	Duke 14th of Wheatland	— Ky I	35444	Edgwood Doctor	M
35339	Duke Wiley	L R	35446	Edwin Booth	— M
35340	12th Duke of Windingvale	— Daisy	35448	Egmont	— Ky I
35341	Duke of Winfield 2nd	— L R	35449	Eighteen-Eighty	— Ky I
35342	Duke of Winwood	— M	35450	Eighteen-Eighty	— L R
35343	Duke of Wisconsin	— R R	35454	Elvina's Goodness	— R R
35345	1st Duke of Woodland	— R R	35455	Emblem	— D
35347	2nd Duke of York	— R R	35456	Emperor	— Ky I
35348	Dunbar	— Cox	35458	Emperor	— C
35349	Dunlap	— Cox	35459	Emperor	Ky I
35350	Duncan	— R R	35463	English Boy	— D
35351	Duncan	D	35465	Ensign	— M
35352	Duncan Dunmore	— R R	35466	Erins Lad	— T
35353	Dunmore	M	35467	Ernesty	P S
35354	Dun's Royal Duke	Daisy	35470	Eudoras Napier	— R R
35355	Dutchman	R R	35471	Everton	— Cox
35356	Earl	Cox	35472	Example	Ky I
35358	Earl Airdrie	— Cox	35473	Exchange	— Cox
35362	Earl of Bridgewater	L R	35475	Eye-Out	— L R
35363	Earl of Brookside	— L R	35476	Fabius	Ky I
35365	Earl of Cedar	— R R	35478	Fair Boy of Syene	— R R
35366	Earl of Cedar Lawn	— R R	35480	Fairfax	— R R
35367	Earl of Cedar Lawn 3rd	— R R	35482	Fairy Duke of Hubbard	— L R
35368	Earl of Cedar Lawn 4th	— R R	35483	Falcon	L R
35375	Earl Derby 2nd	M	35484	Famous	— Daisy
35378	Earl of Dosie View	P S	35485	Fancy Boy	— P S
35379	2nd Earl of Dosie View	P S	35486	Fancy's Duke	— T
35381	Earl Duncan	— R R	35487	Fancy's Duke	Cox
35382	Earl Dunmore 2nd	— R R	35490	Fanny's Duke	— Ky I
35383	Earl Dunmore 3rd	— R R	35491	Fanny Hunt's Duke 2nd	— R R
35384	Earl Dunmore 4th	— M	35493	February Duke	M
35386	Earl of Easton	M	35494	Felix	— Cox
35390	Earl Gloster of Rush	— D	35495	Fenimore	— Cox
35391	2nd Earl Gloster of Rush	— Cox	35496	Fenton	— M
35392	6th Earl of Grass Hill	— Cox	35497	Ferdinand of Spring Branch	L R
35393	7th Earl of Grass Hill	— Cox	35498	Fidalgo 2nd	— M
35394	25th Earl of Greenbush	— P S	35499	Figure Seven	— Cox
35395	26th Earl of Greenbush	— L R	35500	Filagree's Duke	— R R
35396	27th Earl of Greenbush	— L R	35502	Fillmore	— T
35397	Earl Hamilton	Daisy	35504	Firefly	— P S
35399	Earl of Harlem	— Cox	35505	Flanker Atholl	— M
35401	Earl of Ivey	— C	35508	Florentia's Airdrie	— C
35402	8th Earl of Kalamazoo	Cox	35510	Flowery Duke	Ky I
35403	2nd Earl of Kent	— Cox	35511	Fluvius	Ky I
35404	1st Earl of Lake Grove	— D	35512	Fontenoy	M
35405	Earl of Lancaster	— M	35513	Forest	— R R

35514	Forest Duke — M	35608	Gen. Shields Ky I
35515	Forest Duke — D	35609	Gen. Sherman — R R
35517	Forester — R R	35611	Gen. Sherman — Cox
35518	Forest Lad — R R	35613	Gen. Sherman P S
35519	Fortune L R	35616	Gen. Taylor L R
35520	Fragrant Duke — Cox	35617	Gen. Thomas — M
35521	Francis Peabody — P S	35618	Gen. Thomas — R R
35522	Frank Cox	35619	Gen. Thomas — D
35523	Frank — Ky I	35621	Gen. Washington L R
35524	Frank Bedford — R R	35622	Gen. Weaver — M
35525	Frank Eberle — R R	35623	Gen. Wertz — T
35526	Frank Foster M	35624	Geneva — L R
35527	Frank Jessup — M	35625	Geneva Airdrie — R R
35528	Franklin L R	35626	Geneva Airdrie 2nd — R R
35529	Franklin — D	35627	Geneva Bates Daisy
35531	Frank Moulton 2nd — R R	35631	Geneva Earl — L R
35532	Frank Sutton L R	35632	Geneva of Elkhart — D
35533	Frantic Duke of Airdrie — M	35633	Geneva King P S
35534	Frantic of the Oaks — Cox	35636	Geneva's Prince — Cox
35535	Fred — R R	35637	Geneva Prince — M
35536	Fred Nye — D	35638	Geoffrey Weild — Cox
35537	Frederick Charles — Cox	35639	George Herbert — M
35539	Fremont — M	35640	George Martin P S
35541	Fremont — Cox	35641	George Thorndale 2nd — Cox
35542	Frenchy Johnson — Cox	35642	Gilderoy — P S
35543	Fry's Breastplate M	35643	Gip Elder Ky I
35544	Fulton — M	35644	Gipsy Duke Ky I
35545	Fulton Lad — R R	35646	Gladstone — L R
35546	28th Gaban — P S	35648	Glencoe — Cox
35547	Gaben of Cold Spring — P S	35649	Glencoe — Cox
35550	Gallant Duke, Junior — M	35650	Glendora's Oxford 2nd — R R
35551	Gambetta Ky I	35651	Glenmore M
35552	Gamester 2nd — M	35652	Gloster M
35553	Garcelon — M	35653	Gloster Duke — Daisy
35555	Garnet Airdrie M	35655	Gold Drop — R R
35556	Gem's Louanjo — Cox	35656	Golden Coin — R R
35561	General M	35657	Golden Crown — C
35562	General — R R	35660	Golden Prince L R
35564	Gen. Burnside M	35662	Gold Plait 3rd — L R
35565	Gen. Butler — R R	35665	Governor — T
35566	Gen. Custer M	35666	Governor — L R
35570	Gen. Custer Ky I	35667	Governor 2nd — P S
35571	Gen. Custer M	35668	Gov. Airdrie — M
35572	Gen. Dole D	35669	Gov. Bullock T
35573	Gen. Ewing — T	35670	Gov. Collum T
35575	Gen. Garfield M	35671	Gov. Cornell — Cox
35576	Gen. Grant — Ky I	35672	Gov. Dysart — D
35577	Gen. Grant — M	35673	Gov. Gear — M
35578	Gen. Grant — M	35674	Gov. Gear — P S
35580	Gen. Grant L R	35676	Gov. Gear — D
35581	Gen. Grant — P S	35677	Gov. Gwynne — Cox
35582	Gen. Grant — Ky I	35678	Gov. Hayes M
35583	Gen. Grant — M	35680	Gov. Morton — M
35587	Gen. Grant — Cox	35681	Gov. Phelps M
35589	Gen. Gwynne — Cox	35682	Gov. Sharon — P S
35591	Gen. Hayes — T	35683	Gov. Sprague — M
35592	Gen. Hayes P S	35684	Graceful Duke — R R
35593	Gen. Hook — R R	35686	Grand Airdrie 2nd — P S
35594	Gen. Hooker — D	35687	Grand Baron — Cox
35595	Gen. Jackson — T	35690	Grand Duke 11th M
35596	Gen. Lee M	35692	Grand Duke of Goodness — R R
35597	Gen. Logan D	35695	Grand Duke of Malleray — M
35598	Gen. Lyon L R	35697	2nd Grand Duke of Sharon P S
35599	Gen. Mead M	35699	2nd Grand Prince of Claro — R R
35600	Gen. Mende P S	35700	Grand River Chief — M
35601	Gen. Morgan — R R	35701	Grand River Duke — P S
35603	Gen. Scott — L R	35702	Granger P S
35604	Gen. Sigel Ky I	35703	Granger Ky I
35605	Gen. Sigel Ky I	35704	Granger — R R
35606	Gen. Sheridan M	35705	Granger — M

35706	Granger Duke	— R R	35795	Howard's Mazurka Duke	— P S
35707	Granger	T	35798	Hugo	— L R
35708	Granger	— P S	35799	Humboldt	L R
35709	Granger	— L R	35801	Humboldt	R R
35710	Granite 2nd	C	35803	Ike	M
35711	Grant	— Cox	35804	Illinois	— T
35712	Grant	— Ky I	35805	Ilus of Maplewild	— M
35713	Grant	P S	35809	Imperial Wild Rose	— L R
35715	Grant	— Cox	35810	Independence	— T
35716	Grant	— D	35812	Independent	— Cox
35718	Green Mountain Boy	— Cox	35814	Io Chesterford	— R R
35719	Guilford Chief	D	35815	Ionia Louanjo	— R R
35720	Gustavus	— L R	35816	Iosco	Ky I
35722	Guy's Duke	— R R	35819	Irad	M
35723	Guy Mannering	— R R	35820	Isaac	Woods
35725	Hacom	D	35821	Ishmael	Ky I
35726	Half Moon	— P S	35822	Ivanhoe	Ky I
35727	Hailstorm	— R R	35823	Jack	— M
35728	Hamilton	— Ky I	35824	Jackson	P S
35729	Hamlet	— L R	35825	Jackson	— Cox
35730	Hamlet Duke	— P S	35826	Jackson 2nd	— M
35731	Hamlet of Maine Valley	— R R	35827	Jacksonville Tilden	— M
35733	Hampton	— P S	35828	Jack Sprat	— Ky I
35734	Hannastown Comet	— R R	35829	Janus	— C
35735	Hanover Frank	Ky I	35830	Jason	— R R
35736	Hanover Hero 2nd	— M	35831	Jay Gould	— M
35737	Harold	Ky I	35832	Jay Gould	— M
35738	Harry	— M	35834	Jeff Davis	Woods
35739	Hayes	M	35835	Jericho	— R R
35741	Hayes	— Long-Horn	35836	Jerome	D
35742	Hayes	P S	35837	Jerry Doud	Ky I
35744	Hazeldell Romulus	— C	35838	Jester	— L R
35744	Hazeldell Remus	— C	35839	Jim	M
35745	Hector	— T	35840	2nd Jim Brown	— Ky I
35746	Hector	— T	35841	Jim Fisk	— R R
35747	Hector	— Ky I	35842	Jim Lang	— R R
35748	Hector 2nd	Cox	35844	Jimmie's Oxford of Syene	— P S
35750	Heir of Jason	— R R	35846	Jim Riley	— Cox
35752	Henderson	— P S	35847	Jim Russell	T
35755	Henri Loudon	— C	35848	Jim Stephens	M
35756	Henry Beecher	T	35849	Jim Watson	— P S
35757	Henry Dobson	— Ky I	35850	Joe	— L R
35758	Henry's Lancaster	— M	35851	Joe Airdrie 2nd	— L R
35759	Hermes	— T	35852	Joe Combs	— L R
35760	Hermit	M	35853	Joe Fletcher	— R R
35764	Hewitt	— M	35854	Joe Hooker	M
35766	Hicks	— M	35855	Joe Hooker	— L R
35767	Hidalgo	— M	35857	Joe Johnston 6th	— Cox
35768	High Jack	M	35858	Joe Johnston 7th	— Cox
35769	Highland Chief	— T	35859	Joe Knox	P S
35770	Highland Duke 2nd	P S	35860	Joe Lang	— R R
35771	Highland Duke	— M	35861	Joe McConnell	— M
35772	Highland Duke	— D	35862	Joe Nichols	— R R
35773	Highland Gem	— M	35863	Joe Scott	Ky I
35774	Highland Prince 2nd	— P S	35864	Joe Taylor	— C
35775	Hillhurst	— M	35865	Joe Varden of Maplewild	— M
35779	Hiram	— D	35867	John	Cox
35780	Hobart	Ky I	35868	John	M
35781	Hogarth	— L R	35869	John Brown	P S
35783	Homer	— M	35870	John Bryant	Ky I
35784	Homer P. Saxe	T	35871	John Decker	P S
35785	Honest	P S	35872	John Fremont	T
35786	Honest John	P S	35873	John Gillitt	M
35787	Honest John	— Cox	35874	John H.	M
35789	Hopeful	M	35875	Johnny Wiley	L R
35790	Hopeful	— T	35876	John R.	Ky I
35791	Horace	T	35877	John Sherman	— C
35792	Hotspur	— Cox	35878	John Sherman	— Cox
35793	Howard	— P S	35879	John Sherman	— L R
35794	Howard Granville	— P S	35880	Johnstown Lad	Cox

No.	Name	Code	No.	Name	Code
35881	Jolly Boy	Ky I	35981	Leinster	— Ky I
35882	Jordon	— M	35982	Leo	P S
35883	Joseph Scott	P S	35983	Leo	— R R
35884	Josh Billings	— D	35984	Leonard	— M
35885	Josie Duke	— R R	35985	Leopard	M
35887	Jubilee Boy	L R	35986	Le Roy	— M
35888	Jubilee Duke	Ky I	35989	Lexington	— M
35889	Jubilee Duke 2nd	— M	35990	Lexington McHenry	— R R
35890	Judge Bradley	M	35991	7th Liberty Duke	— L R
35891	Judge Foley	Ky I	35992	Lieut. Governor	— L R
35892	Judge Gould	— Cox	35993	Lightfoot	— Long-Horn
35893	Judge Lydgate	— Cox	35994	Lightheart	— L R
35894	Julian	Ky I	35995	Lilly's Duke	— Cox
35895	Julius	— D	35996	Lilla's Star	P S
35897	Junius	— M	35998	Lion	— Cox
35898	Jupiter	— D	36000	Little Dick	— L R
35899	Jupiter	— Ky I	36001	Little Jake	— L R
35901	Jupiter	— R R	36002	Little Monarch	— M
35903	Kansas Bill	— P S	36003	Little Travers	D
35904	Kansas Boy	P S	36004	Lochinvar	— L R
35905	Kansas Boy	— C	36005	Lock Lad	— Cox
35906	Kansas Orphan 2nd	T	36006	Locomotive 4th	— Daisy
35907	Kansas Orphan 3rd	T	36007	Locum	— R R
35908	Keepsake's Duke	T	36008	Lodi Chief	— M
35909	Keller	— P S	36009	Lofty	Ky I
35910	Kenneth	P S	36010	Logan	— M
35911	Kent	— L R	36011	Logan	— M
35912	Kentucky	— R R	36012	Logan Amateur	— D
35914	Kentucky Joe	L R	36013	Logan Chief	— M
35915	Kentucky Star	— P S	36014	Logan General	Ky I
35916	Keno	— M	36015	Logan Halkerston	— D
35917	Keno	— P S	36016	Logan Prince 2nd	— D
35918	Keokuk	— T	36017	Longfellow	D
35919	Keystone	L R	36018	Longfellow	Ky I
35920	Kickapoo	Ky I	36019	Longfellow	— M
35921	Kickapoo Ranger	M	36021	Lord Avenger	— Cox
35922	Kinderhook	— R R	36022	Lord Barington	— Cox
35923	King	— Ky I	36023	Lord Barrington	— R R
35924	King's Creek	— M	36024	Lord Barrington 3rd	— Daisy
35925	King David	Ky I	36027	Lord Beaconsfield	— L R
35926	King David, Jr	Ky I	36031	Lord Byron	— L R
35928	King Hiram	Ky I	36032	Lord Carnhurst	— M
35929	King John	M	36033	Lord Chatham 5th	— P S
35930	King's London Duke 7th	— R R	36034	Lord Colerain	— M
35931	King of Lowell	Ky I	36037	Lord Crisp	Ky I
35932	King Richard	— R R	36039	Lord Derby	— D
35934	3rd King of Prairie	Ky I	36040	Lord Dufferin	P S
35935	Kingsman	— R R	36043	Lord Ellington	— Cox
35936	Kingsville Prince	— M	36044	Lord Ellington 5th	— Cox
35938	King of the Valley	— Cox	36045	Lord Fairfax	— R R
35939	King William	— Cox	36046	Lord Garland	— R R
35941	Kirklevington Duke	— D	36047	Lord George	— R R
35948	Kitty's Baron	— M	36048	Lord Graham 3rd	— R R
35953	Knight of Genesee	L R	36052	Lord of Jersey	T
35956	Knightly Duke 2nd	— C	36053	Lord Lameach 3rd	— R R
35961	1st Knight of Waboo	Ky I	36057	Lord Lincoln	— M
35963	Kossuth	D	36059	Lord Raglan 2nd	— Cox
35964	Laclede Monarch	— P S	36060	Lord Ruber	— R R
35965	Ladrone	Ky I	36062	Lord of Springwood	L R
35969	Lafayette	— M	36064	Lord of the Manor 3rd	— M
35970	Lambertine	M	36065	Lord of the Valley	— M
35971	Lamine	P S	36066	Lord Varner	— M
35972	Lancaster	— C	36067	Lord of Vine Hill	— D
35973	Lancaster 2nd	— Ky I	36073	Lorne	Ky I
35974	Lancaster Volunteer	— Cox	36074	Lorne	— R R
35975	Last Chance	— R R	36075	Lost Switchey	— C
35976	Lawrence	— M	36077	Louan's Champion	— R R
35977	Lear	— R R	36078	Louan Duke	— D
35978	Le Clair	— M	36079	Louan Duke	— R R
35979	Leer Hency 2nd	— Cox	36080	Louan Duke	L R

SHORT-HORN CATTLE PEDIGREES. 169

36081	Louan Duke — P S		36183	Marquis of Bute 4th — C
36082	Louan Duke, Jr — C		36184	Marquis of Hazelhurst — M
36083	Louan Duke 1st — R R		36185	Marquis of Lorne — Cox
36084	Louan Duke 2nd — R R		36186	Marquis of Lorne — R R
36087	Louanjo Randolph — M		36187	Marquis of Waterford — R R
36088	Louan's Lord — R R		36189	Marshal Ney — P S
36089	Louan Prince 2nd — R R		36190	Marshfield King — R R
36090	Louan Prince of Randolph, Jr — M		36191	Mart — R R
36091	Loudon Airdrie — R R		36193	Mary's Airdrie — R R
36093	Loudon Decatur — R R		36194	Mary's Duke — P S
36094	Loudon Duke 14th — R R		36196	Mary's Orphan — M
36095	3rd Loudon Duke of Elmwood,— M		36201	Master — Cox
36096	2nd Loudon D. of Greenwood,— R R		36202	Master Airdrie — R R
36097	3rd Loudon D. of Greenwood,— R R		36203	Master Airdrie — R R
36098	4th Loudon D. of Greenwood,— R R		36205	Master Bates of Hickory Grove—R R
36102	Loudon Prince 3rd — Ky I		36206	Master Boy — Daisy
36105	Low Jack — M		36208	Master Hayes — M
36107	Lucien — Cox		36209	Master Hiram — M
36109	Lucretius Butterfly — R R		36211	Master Mayflower — R R
36111	Lucky — P S		36212	Master O'Conner — Cox
36112	Lucky Boy — L R		36213	Master Payne — D
36113	Lucky Duke — T		36214	Masterpiece — D
36114	Luke — P S		36215	Master Richmond — P S
36115	Lydia's Cherub — M		36217	Master of the Pines — R R
36116	Lydia's Duke — P S		36218	Master Winthrop 4th — Daisy
36117	Lydias Prince — C		36219	7th Master Wiseton — P S
36121	Marby — M		36220	8th Master Wiseton — P S
36122	Macbeth — Ky I		36221	Matchless — Ky I
36123	McCracken — P S		36222	Matchless — M
36124	McDonald Duke — M		36223	Matilda's Oxford 2nd, — Long-Horn
36125	McDonald Duke 2nd — R R		36225	Matt Foster — M
36126	McDonald Duke 3rd — L R		36226	Matt Logan 2nd — Ky I
36127	McDonald Duke 4th — Ky I		36227	Maude's Duke — Daisy
36128	McDonald Duke 5th — R R		36228	May Belle's Nimrod — D
36129	McDonald Duke 6th — P S		36229	May Boy — Cox
36110	McDonough Duke — M		36230	May Duke — Ky I
36131	MacWadsworth — D		36232	Mayflower of Leeds — P S
36132	Mae Glen Duke — P S		36233	2nd Mayflower Prince — M
36133	Magic — T		36234	Mayo — M
36134	Maggie's Beau — C		36235	Mazeena Duke — M
36136	Magna Charta — Ky I		36237	2nd Mazurka Duke — Cox
36137	Magnolia's Pride — Daisy		36238	Mazurka Lord — D
36138	Mahaska's Chief — Daisy		36239	Mazurka's Oxford 16th — D
36140	Maine Enterprise — M		36240	Mazurka's Oxford 17th — Ky I
36142	Major — M		36241	Mazurka's Oxford 18th — Ky I
36143	Major — Cox		36242	Mazurka Prince — Ky I
36145	Maj. Anderson — D		36244	Mazurka Sailor — R R
36146	Maj. Balco — M		36245	Mazurka Sheffielder — D
36148	Maj. Cooper — M		36246	Medea's Duke — M
36150	Maj. Davis — M		36247	Medina Duke — L R
36151	Maj. Gwynne — Cox		36249	Melbourne — P S
36152	Maj. Harper — M		36250	Memento's Airdrie — Daisy
36153	Maj. Jasper — R R		36251	Mercer Favorite — L R
36154	Maj. Kellogg — R R		36256	Milo — R R
36155	Maj. of Lake Park — Daisy		36259	Minister — R R
36156	Maj. Louan — Ky I		36260	Minnie's Baron — T
36157	Maj. Lynn — R R		36261	Minna Dole's Airdrie 2nd — M
36159	Maj. Maple — L R		36262	Minnie Lynn's Prince — P S
36160	Maj. Reno — P S		36265	Mister Favorite — M
36165	Malcolm — M		36267	Modoc — M
36166	Malden Duke — Ky I		36269	Modoc — P S
36168	Mammoth Duke — D		36270	Modoc — Cox
36172	Manfred 4th — Cox		36271	Mohawk — Cox
36173	Marathon — Cox		36272	Mollie's Duke — L R
36174	Marcus — M		36274	Monarch 2nd — Ky I
36175	Mariner's Oxford — R R		36275	Monarch of Boone — M
36176	Mark Twain — D		36276	Monarch of Galatin — R R
36177	Mark Twain's Grandson — L R		36278	Monarch of Maine Valley — P S
36178	Marmion — C		36279	Monarch of the Tree — M
36181	Marquis — C		36280	Monarch of the West — Cox

12

36282	Monitor	— M	36379	Oscar	P S
36283	Monitor	— M	36380	Oscar Dutton	— R R
36284	Moreau	— T	36381	Osceola Duke	Ky I
36285	Morning Star 2nd	M	36382	Osman Pasha	— P S
36286	Morning Star 3rd	M	36383	Othello	— P S
36288	Moscow	— Daisy	36384	Otley	— T
36289	Moses	— T	36385	Oto	L R
36290	Moses Bunker	— M	36386	Otoe Chief	— Daisy
36293	Motley	— Cox	36387	Otto Von Bismarck	— Ky I
36294	Moulton's Mazurka Duke	P S	36388	Ovid	Cox
36295	Moultrie Belleville	Ky I	36389	Oxford	R R
36296	Mountaineer	— C	36390	Oxford	— M
36298	Murdac	P S	36391	Oxford	— L R
36300	Muscatoon	T	36393	Oxford 6th	M
36301	Music's Airdrie	L R	36395	Oxford 8th	M
36302	Musket	M	36396	Oxford 9th	M
36305	Napier Duke	P S	36397	Oxford 10th	— P S
36306	Napoleon	— P S	36398	Oxford 11th	M
36307	Napoleon	— Cox	36399	Oxford 12th	M
36308	Napoleon	— Cox	36402	Oxford Beau	— Cox
36309	Nasby	— L R	36403	Oxford Beau	Daisy
36310	Nebrough of Woodland	D	36406	Oxford Boy	L R
36312	Nelly Bly's Nimrod	— P S	36407	5th Oxford Duke of Oak Shade	Ky I
36313	Nelson	L R	36408	Oxford Duke	— Cox
36315	Nelson Boy 2nd	— M	36409	Oxford Duke	— M
36316	Nelson Boy 3rd	— M	36411	Oxford Gloster	— Cox
36317	Nelson Maginnis	T	36413	Oxford of Lee Farm	L R
36322	Neptune	— P S	36414	Oxford Lynn	— D
36323	Nero	— P S	36416	Oxford 2nd of Plum Grove	— P S
36324	Nero	— Cox	36417	Oxford Prince 2nd	— M
36325	Nero	Cox	36418	Oxford Prince	— R R
36326	Nero	— M	36421	Oxford Royal	— C
36329	Nestor of Maplewild	— R R	36424	Oxford Wiley	Daisy
36332	Newburg Star	— M	36425	Palmer's Oxford 3rd	L R
36333	Newby's Prince Geneva	Daisy	36428	Paney Duke	T
36335	New Year's Day	— R R	36429	Paris	D
36336	New Year's Duke	— R R	36430	Parson	— Ky I
36337	New Year's Gift	P S	36432	Patio	— Cox
36338	New Years Lad	Cox	36433	Patriot	— P S
36340	Nimrod's Gem	— D	36434	Patriot of Knox	— R R
36341	Noble	— Cox	36435	Paul Colson	M
36342	Noble	— R R	36436	Peabody, Junior	M
36344	Noble Duke	— D	36437	Peacemaker	— P S
36345	Noble Duke	Cox	36439	Pearl Duke	— T
36346	Noble Grant 2nd	— Daisy	36441	Pedestrian	— D
36347	Null Prince	— R R	36442	Pedrick	— T
36348	Numa	— L R	36444	Pere	— Cox
36349	Oak Grove Richard	— C	36445	Perfect	L R
36350	Oakland	— L R	36446	Perfection	— M
36353	Oakland Duke	— R R	36447	Perfection	M
36354	Oakland Lad	Ky I	36448	Perfection	— L R
36355	Oakwood	— R R	36449	Perfection of Maine Valley	— M
36356	Oakwood 2nd	— T	36451	Pericles	— P S
36357	O'Connor	— P S	36455	Peri Lad	— R R
36358	O'Connor	— M	36457	Penrhyn	Ky I
36359	Ohio Boy	— P S	36458	Peter Cooper	— M
36360	Oliver	P S	36460	Petoskey	— R R
36361	Oliver	— M	36461	Petoskey 1st	— Cox
36362	Onarga Duke 4th	Ky I	36462	Phenomenon	— Cox
36363	Oneida	— Cox	36463	Philanthropist	— M
36364	Oneida	— L R	36465	Phyllis' Duke	— R R
36365	Oneida 2nd	P S	36466	Phyllis Duke	— R R
36367	Oneida Duke	— R R	36469	Pilot	Ky I
36369	Oneidas Duke of Dakota	— P S	36470	Pilot	— R R
36370	Oneida Duke of Goodness	— R R	36471	Pilot	L R
36372	Onondaga	— Cox	36472	Pilot	— Cox
36375	Orestes	Ky I	36473	Pilot	— L R
36376	Orondo	Ky I	36474	Pilot	— Cox
36377	Orphan Boy of Syene	— D	36475	Pilot	— Long-Horn
36378	Orrick	— M	36476	Pilot	— R R

36478	Pioneer — M	36584	Prince of Lanark — P S
36480	Plato — P S	36587	Prince Leonard 4th — M
36481	Plevna — P S	36588	Prince Lorain — Long-Horn
36482	Plowboy — P S	36590	Prince Louis — Cox
36483	Pluck — P S	36591	Prince of Madelia — P S
36484	Plumb Ky I	36592	Prince of Maine Valley — M
36485	Plumcreek Lad — M	36593	Prince Malone 1st — Cox
36486	Pluto — Long-Horn	36596	Prince of Millidgeville — Ky I
36487	Plumwood S S — R R	36597	Prince Napoleon — Cox
36488	Plumwood T T C	36598	Prince of Nelson — C
36489	Plumwood U U R R	36599	Prince Ney — L R
36490	Plumwood V V R R	36601	Prince of Orange — Ky I
36491	Plumwood W W R R	36603	Prince of Oxford — R R
36492	Plumwood X X — R R	36605	Prince of Oxford 2nd L R
36493	Plumwood Y Y Ky I	36608	Prince of Pine Grove — Cox
36494	Plumwood Z Z R R	36609	Princeps — Cox
36495	Plumwood A C C	36610	Prince Philip — L R
36496	Plumwood A D C	36612	Prince Regent 2nd — D
36497	Plumwood Lad F R R	36613	Prince Regent 3rd Ky I
36499	Poland Marquis of Bute — T	36614	Prince Regent 4th — D
36500	Pomp M	36615	Prince Regent 5th — M
36501	Pompey M	36616	Prince Regent 6th — L R
36502	Pontiac C	36617	Prince Regent 7th — M
36505	Post Master — M	36618	Prince Regent 8th P S
36506	Powell — L R	36619	Prince Regent 9th — M
36507	Powers P S	36620	Prince Regent 10th — M
36508	Prairie Chief P S	36622	Prince Regent 12th — M
36509	Prairie Duke — C	36623	Prince of Richland — R R
36510	Prairie Duke — Ky I	36624	Prince of Rich Valley — D
36511	Prairie Duke 3rd — Ky I	36628	Prince Rupert — Cox
36512	Prairie King — R R	36630	Prince of Sandusky R R
36513	Premier M	36631	Prince of Sharon 4th — Cox
36514	Premier M	36632	Prince of Sharon 5th — L R
36518	Pride's Duke of Airdrie — P S	36633	Prince of Sharon 6th — Cox
36520	Pride of Shields — Cox	36635	Prince of Springdale — D
36521	Pride of the Ledge M	36636	Prince of the Hills — D
36525	Prince 3rd — M	36637	Prince of the Realm — M
36526	Prince Airdrie — R R	36638	Prince of the Valley — L R
36527	Prince Albert M	36639	Princeton Duke — M
36528	Prince Albert — P S	36640	Prince of Wales — R R
36529	Prince Albert — L R	36641	Prince of Warren L R
36530	2nd Prince Albert — L R	36642	Prince of Wells — M
36531	Prince Albert — Ky I	36643	Prince of Wetona — L R
36532	Prince Albert L R	36644	Prince of Wetona 2nd — L R
36533	Prince Alfred — Cox	36645	Prince William — P S
36537	3rd Prince of Ashbrook D	36646	Prince William R R
36539	Prince Bismarck M	36647	Prince William — L R
36540	Prince of Brandywine — L R	36649	10th Prince of Wyaconda — M
36541	Prince Breastplate 2nd M	36650	11th Prince of Wyaconda M
36542	Prince of Brookfield — L R	36651	12th Prince of Wyaconda — P S
36543	Prince of Brookfield M	36654	Printanier — R R
36544	Prince of Buffalo L R	36656	Professor — L R
36549	Prince Edward 3rd P S	36657	Promise Ky I
36550	Prince of Elm Run — M	36658	Prospect M
36551	Prince of Fairview 2nd — R R	36659	Prospector — L R
36553	Prince of Franklin Ky I	36662	Puff — L R
36554	Prince of Franklin — Ky I	36663	Punch M
36555	Prince Frederick — Ky I	36664	Pure Gold M
36557	Prince Geneva 4th — M	36668	Quid-Sit — D
36558	Prince of Gentry — D	36669	Randolph M
36559	Prince George — R R	36670	Rand's Senator M
36560	Prince Goodness — R R	36671	Ranger — L R
36573	29th Prince of Herkimer — Cox	36672	Ranger — R R
36576	Prince Hope — M	36673	Ranger — D
36577	Prince of Hurlbut Ky I	36674	Ranger — Ky I
36578	Prince Imperial Ky I	36675	Raric — M
36579	Prince Imperial — L R	36676	Rarus — M
36580	Prince of Iowa Daisy	36679	Red Airdrie — D
36581	Prince of Jackson Ky I	36680	Red Airdrie L R
36583	3rd Prince of Kingsdale — D	36682	Red Airdrie 2nd — C

36684	Red Bear	L R	36764	Red Top	— Cox
36685	Red Ben	— Ky I	36765	Red Wing of Brookvale	— M
36686	Red Boy	— M	36766	Regent	— L R
36687	Red Boy	— R R	36767	Reform	— D
36688	Red Boy	— L R	36768	Reformer	Ky I
36690	Red Cherub	— M	36769	Reformer	— Cox
36691	Red Chesterford	— C	36770	Reliable	P S
36692	Red Chief	— P S	36771	Remus	— P S
36693	Red Chief	M	36772	Remus	M
36694	Red Cloud	L R	36773	Remus of Maplewild	— M
36695	Red Cloud	M	36775	Reno	— P S
36696	Red Cloud	Ky I	36776	Reno	— P S
36697	Red Cloud	— L R	36777	Reserve	Ky I
36698	Red Cloud	— D	36778	Resumption	— R R
36699	Red Cloud	Ky I	36779	Resumption	— L R
36701	Red Cloud	— L R	36780	Reuben	— L R
36702	Red Cloud	— Cox	36781	Reuben	P S
36703	Red David	Daisy	36782	Reuben	M
36704	Red Daisy Duke	Woods	36783	Revenue	— Ky I
36705	Red Dick	P S	36785	Richard 1st	— L R
36706	Red Duke	— D	36786	Richard 2nd	— L R
36707	Red Duke	M	36787	Richard 5th	— R R
36708	Red Duke	— M	36789	Ringgold 2nd	— Ky I
36709	Red Duke	R R	36790	Ringmaster	M
36710	Red Duke	— M	36792	Ripley	— D
36711	Red Duke	— M	36793	Rival	— D
36712	Red Duke	— M	36794	Riverton	— Cox
36713	Red Dean	Ky I	36795	Rivoli Boy	Daisy
36714	Red Duke	— R R	36797	Roan Boy	— Ky I
36716	Red Duke, Junior	— C	36799	Roan Duke	M
36717	Red Duke 2nd	P S	36801	Roan Duke	— R R
36718	Red Duke of Evergreen	Ky I	36802	Roan Duke	— L R
36719	Red Duke of Vine Hill	— M	36804	Roan Duke	— M
36720	Red Dutch	— R R	36805	Roan Duke	M
36721	Red George	— P S	36806	Roan Duke	— P S
36722	Red Hawk	M	36807	Roan Duke of Morgan	Ky I
36723	Red Jacket	P S	36808	Roan Lad	L R
36725	Red Jacket	— L R	36809	Roanoke	— T
36726	Red Jacket	— Cox	36810	Roan Peabody	P S
36727	Red Jacket 2nd	— R R	36811	Roan Prince	— Cox
36728	Red Jay	— R R	36813	Roan Renick	— T
36729	Red John	— P S	36816	Robert Lee	— M
36730	Red Knight	P S	36819	Robley	— R R
36731	Red Knight	— M	36820	Rob Roy	— Cox
36734	Red Knight of Oxford	— L R	36821	Rob Roy	P S
36735	Red Lancaster	— T	36822	Rob Roy	— T
36736	Red Lancaster's Oxford	— L R	36823	Rob Roy	L R
36737	Red Line	Cox	36824	Rob Roy	Ky I
36740	Red Marquis	— Ky I	36825	Rob Roy 2nd	— D
36741	Red Ranger	— M	36826	Rocket	— P S
36742	Red Rock	— R R	36827	Rock River Lad 34th	— Cox
36743	Red Rock	— Cox	36830	Romeo	— L R
36744	Red Rosecrans	P S	36831	Romeo	— M
36746	Red Rover	— L R	36833	Romulus	— P S
36747	Red Rover 2nd	— R R	36834	Romulus	M
36748	Red Rover	— Ky I	36836	Rouda	Ky I
36749	Red Rover	— R R	36838	Rosebud Duke	— R R
36750	Red Rover	— Ky I	36839	Rose Duke	Ky I
36751	Red Rover	— M	36840	Rosy Duke	M
36753	Red Rover 4th	L R	36841	Rosy Duke	— D
36754	Red Rover 5th	L R	36845	Rose's Duke	— R R
36755	Red Rover 6th	L R	36846	Rose Duke	— M
36756	Red Rufus	— Ky I	36847	Rose's Duke	— T
36757	Red Shakem	P S	36848	Rose Duke	— M
36758	Red Star	M	36849	Rose Duke	— Ky I
36759	7th Red Thorndale	M	36850	Rose Duke 2nd	— M
36760	8th Red Thorndale	M	36853	Roscoe	— Ky I
36761	9th Red Thorndale	M	36854	Roscoe	— M
36762	10th Red Thorndale	M	36855	Roscoe	— Cox
36763	11th Red Thorndale	L R	36857	Rough-And-Ready	— M

SHORT-HORN CATTLE PEDIGREES. 173

No.	Name	Code	No.	Name	Code
36858	Round Prairie Duke	M	36958	Sergeant Bates	M
36859	Rover	— P S	36963	Shakespeare	— M
36860	Rover Duke	P S	36970	Sharon Oxford	M
36861	Roving Boy	M	36971	Sharon Thorndale	— L R
36862	Roving Napier	— R R	36972	Sheedy	— M
36863	Rowena's Duke	— Daisy	36974	Shelby Duke	— D
36864	Rowsy Bower	M	36976	Sheridan	— M
36865	Roxbury 2nd	M	36979	Sheriff	— M
36867	Royal Airdrie 2nd	— P S	36980	Sherman	— M
36868	Royal Airdrie 2nd	— M	36981	Sherman	— Ky I
36869	Royal Arch	— Cox	36982	Sherman	— L R
36870	Royal Arch	Ky I	36984	Short Tail	M
36871	Royal Barmpton	— C	36986	Sigurd	Ky I
36873	Royal Bloomfield	— Cox	36987	Silver Coin	D
36874	Royal Booth	— D	36988	Silver Coin	— M
36876	Royal Booth 7th	— C	36989	Simon	— R R
36877	Royal Briton 2nd	Ky I	36990	Sinon	— R R
36879	Royal Commander	— D	36991	Sir Archy	L R
36884	Royal Dick	— P S	36992	Sir Benton	— P S
36886	Royal Duke	M	36993	Sir Bevis	— P S
36887	Royal Duke	— R R	36994	Sir Charles	M
36888	Royal Duke	— D	36995	Sir Charles	— Cox
36892	Royalist 2nd	— Cox	36996	Sir Franklin	— M
36894	Royal Lad 3rd	— M	36997	Sir George	M
36895	Royal Monarch	L R	36998	Sir Guy	— L R
36903	Royal Richard	— R R	36999	Sir Henry of Maine Valley	Ky I
36904	Royal Red	— C	37001	Sir John	— L R
36905	Royal Star	— D	37003	Sir Joseph	— L R
36906	Royal Sussex	M	37005	Sir Phillip	— P S
36907	Ruby's Duke	M	37006	Sir Robert Bruce	M
36909	Rushford Duke	— M	37007	Sir Spot	— Cox
36910	Rutherford B. Hayes	D	37009	Sitting Bull	— C
36911	Saginaw	— D	37011	Sitting Bull	— R R
36912	Saginaw Mazurka	— Cox	37012	Sitting Bull	— P S
36913	St. Croix	— L R	37015	Sleepy Tom	M
36914	St. Elmo	L R	37016	Sleepy Tom	— D
36915	St. Joe 2nd	— T	37017	Smokey	— Cox
36916	St. Julien	M	37018	Smuggler	M
36918	St. Nicholas	— L R	37019	Smuggler	Ky I
36919	Sam	Ky I	37020	Snow	— Cox
36920	Sam	— M	37021	Snowflake	P S
36923	Sam Covington	P S	37022	Sol	Cox
36924	Sam Ghrist	— M	37023	Solon	L R
36925	Sam Patch	D	37024	Son of Admiral	M
36926	Sam Patch	Ky I	37025	Son of Dexter	— Cox
36927	Sampson	— D	37029	Spectator	— M
36928	Samuel Sawyers	T	37030	Spotted Tail	M
36930	Samuel J. Tilden	— Cox	37031	Spotted Tail	Daisy
36931	Sam Tilden	— M	37032	Spotted Tail	C
36932	Samuel J. Tilden	— D	37033	Spotted Tail	Ky I
36934	Samuel J. Tilden	P S	37034	Spotted Tail	— R R
36935	Sam Tilden	— Cox	37035	Springdale Airdrie 2nd	— R R
36936	Sam Weller	— P S	37036	Springland Boy	— T
36937	Sam Wiley	— M	37037	Springland Lad	— T
36938	Sam Woods	— C	37040	Squire	— Cox
36940	Sarah's Earl 2nd	— Cox	37042	Standard	M
36941	Saxe Coburg 2nd	— P S	37043	Starbright	L R
36943	Saxon	M	37045	Star of Delavan	— Ky I
36944	Scioto Duke	— D	37046	Star Duke	— T
36945	Scotland	Ky I	37047	Star Duke	— P S
36946	Scottish Crown 2nd	— Cox	37048	Star Duke	Ky I
36947	Scottish Lad	— M	37050	Star Duke	Ky I
36950	Scotsman 3rd	— R R	37051	Star Duke	— M
36951	Sea Rover	— Cox	37053	Star Duke of Elkhart	— D
36952	Semper	— L R	37055	Starlight	L R
36953	Senator	Cox	37056	Starlight	— M
36954	Senator	— M	37057	Starlight	L R
36955	Senator Thurman	Wrong	37058	Starlight of Monticello	— M
36956	Seneca	— Cox	37060	Star of Oakland	P S
36957	Senor Conewango	— Cox	37061	Star of Oakland	— R R

37062	Star of Tama............L R	37148	Trump................— R R
37064	Statesman.............— M	37149	Tokio................— L R
37065	Stemwinder............— R R	37150	Tom..................M
37066	Stephen of Maplewild.....M	37151	Tom..................— Cox
37067	Stephenson............— P S	37152	Tom Boyd.............P S
37068	Sterling..............— R R	37153	Tom Matchem..........— R R
37072	Strafford.............— L R	37154	Tonga 1st.............R R
37073	Strathmore............— R R	37155	Tonga 2nd............— L R
37074	Strawberry Jim........— T	37156	Toots................— M
37075	Strawn's Airdrie.......— Daisy	37157	Tornado..............Ky I
37076	Success..............— M	37158	Toro Duke............— M
37078	Success..............— D	37159	Triermain............Daisy
37079	Sucker Boy 2nd........— Ky I	37160	Trimsharp.............— M
37080	Sugar Grove Boy.......— M	37163	Turk.................— M
37081	Sugar Run Lad.........R R	37164	Tymochtee............— Daisy
37082	Sultan................— M	37165	Uncle Abe............— L R
37083	Sultan Webawkan......— D	37166	Uncle Harry...........— D
37087	Summit Richard.......— R R	37167	Uncle Sam............D
37088	Summit Richard 2nd...— R R	37168	Underly Wild Eyes, Jr...— T
37089	Sunday...............— P S	37171	Valentine.............— Cox
37090	Sunday Lad...........— M	37173	Valentine.............L R
37091	Sunflower.............— D	37175	Valley Boy............M
37092	Sunshine..............— L R	37176	Valley Boy 2nd........M
37093	Sweepstakes...........M	37177	Valley Duke..........L R
37094	Sweepstakes...........P S	37178	Value................— L R
37095	Sylvia's Baron.........— Cox	37179	Vandal...............Ky I
37096	Symmetry.............Daisy	37180	Vermillion Prince......— P S
37097	Symmetrys Breastplate..R R	37181	Vernon...............Ky I
37098	Talmage..............Ky I	37182	Venerator 2nd........— M
37099	Tata's Duke...........— D	37183	Vespasian, Jr.........— P S
37100	Taurus...............— M	37184	Veto.................— R R
37101	Tawas................— D	37185	Veto.................P S
37102	Taylor Boy...........— R R	37186	Victor................M
37103	Tazewell J...........— Ky I	37187	Victor................— Ky I
37104	Tecumseh.............M	37188	Victor................M
37105	Tecumseh.............— M	37189	Victor................— L R
37106	Tecumseh.............— L R	37193	Victor Hugo...........— T
37107	Teeswater Prince......— T	37194	Victor Hugo...........— R R
37108	Teetotlar.............— M	37195	Vigilance.............— R R
37109	Telephone............— Cox	37199	Vincent..............— M
37112	Ten of Diamonds......— M	37201	Virgil................— L R
37113	Thanksgiving.........P S	37203	Viscount 3rd..........— C
37114	The Boss.............— T	37204	Viscount Moncontour...— T
37115	The Captain..........D	37205	Volunteer............— Cox
37116	The Cardinal.........— R R	37206	Voorhees.............T
37117	The General..........D	37210	Wade Hampton........— R R
37118	The General..........— Cox	37211	Wade Hampton........— M
37120	Theobald.............— Cox	37212	Wakarusa Chief.......— D
37121	The Parson...........— M	37214	Wallace..............L R
37121	The Priest............— M	37215	Walter Poe...........— M
37122	The Prince...........— R R	37216	Walworth's Champion..— T
37123	The Rajah............L R	37217	Wapello Chief.........— M
37124	The Red Prince.......M	37218	Wapsie Tom..........— Ky I
37125	The Red Prince 2nd...M	37220	Warren...............— L R
37126	The Squire...........M	37221	Warren Snow.........— R R
37127	The Sultan...........L R	37222	Warrior..............— Cox
37128	The Turk.............L R	37224	Washington 2nd.......M
37129	Thomas Bates........Ky I	37225	Washington Goodness..— R R
37131	Thorndale 2nd........— C	37226	Washington Stewart...Ky I
37132	Thorndale Chief......— D	37228	Waterloo.............M
37135	Thorndale Prince......— R R	37229	Waterloo 2nd.........— R R
37136	Thorndale Prince 2nd..— R R	37231	Water Prince.........— Cox
37137	Thorn Hill............L R	37232	Watts................— Ky I
37138	Tiberius..............— L R	37233	Waubansie of Oswego..— D
37139	Tilden................— M	37234	Weasel...............Daisy
37140	Tilden................— L R	37238	Wellington............— Ky I
37142	Tinker...............P S	37239	Wenona Prior.........Ky I
37143	Tip Richardson.......— Daisy	37241	Western Duke........— P S
37146	Trueman..............— R R	37243	Western Lad.........L R
37147	Truman Warren......P S	37244	Westview Chief.......Ky I

SHORT-HORN CATTLE PEDIGREES.

No.	Name	Herd
37245	White Cap	— R R
37246	White Chief	— L R
37247	White Cloud	— Ky I
37248	White Comet	— L R
37249	White Eyes	— R R
37250	White Prince	— D
37251	White Prince	— D
37252	White Remus	Cox
37254	Wild Boy	— M
37257	Wild Eyes	P S
37258	Wild Eyes of Elmsmere	Cox
37259	Wild Eyes Gloster	— Cox
37260	Wild Eyes Henry	— L R
37263	Wildwood Argus	— P S
37264	Wildwood Rover	— P S
37265	Wideawake	— D
37268	Wiley's Duke	T
37269	Wiley's Duke	— R R
37271	Wiley's Prince	T
37272	Wileys Victor	— R R
37273	Will	— Cox
37274	Will	Cox
37276	William A. Wheeler	— R R
37277	Willie Blackman	M
37279	Willow Boy 2nd	Ky I
37280	Winchester	— C
37283	Winfield Scott	— M
37287	Wiota	— P S
37290	Wood	— L R
37291	Woodbine Duke	— P S
37292	Woodbury	D
37293	World Beater	Ky I
37294	Yankee Boy	M
37295	Yankee Doodle	— R R
37296	Yellow Ben	— R R
37298	Young America	Cox
37300	Young Baron of Orchard Farm	— R R
37301	Young Bertram	— Ky I
37303	Young Bourbon of Blandinville	— P S
37304	Young Breastplate	M
37305	Young Champion	— M
37306	Young Chilton	— R R
37307	Young Clifton	M
37310	Young Hopewell	Daisy
37313	Young Mary's Boy	— P S
37314	Young Norfolk	— R R
37315	Young Oxford	L R
37316	Young Prince	L R
37317	Young Richmond	— M
37318	Young Sampson	M
37320	Young Sheriff, Jr	— D
37321	Young Stentor	— R R
37322	Young Tycoon	L R
37323	Young Wellington	M
37324	Young Wilmington	— R R
37325	Zack Chandler	— R R
37326	Zack Chandler	— M
37327	Zadak	Ky I
37330	Zulu	— P S
37370	Abel	— T
37371	Abercrombie	— T
37373	Abigail Duke 2nd	— R R
37374	Abigail Duke 3rd	— R R
37375	Abner	Ky I
37376	Abraham Boy	— L R
37377	Absolute Money	— Daisy
37380	Adair	— M
37382	Adam	M
37383	Adam	— L R
37385	Admiral	— P S
37388	Admiral	— Ky I
37391	Admiral Dawson	M
37392	Adolph	P S
37393	Aftou Boy	— Ky I
37396	Ahab	— M
37397	Airdrie 2nd	M
37400	Airdrie Duke	— D
37402	3rd Airdrie Duke	— D
37404	2nd Airdrie Duke of Manchester	— D
37406	2nd Airdrie Duke of Sandusky	D
37407	3rd Airdrie Duke of Sandusky	— M
37408	4th Airdrie Duke of Sandusky	— R R
37409	5th Airdrie Duke of Sandusky	— R R
37410	Airdrie Duke of Evergreens	— Cox
37411	Airdrie Duke of Evergreens 8th	— L R
37412	Airdrie Gem's Booth	— Cox
37413	Airdrie 3rd of Glen Echo	L R
37414	Airdrie Gooduess 2nd	— R R
37421	Ajax Airdrie	— Ky I
37422	Alaska	— Daisy
37423	Albert	— L R
37424	Albert	— R R
37425	Albert G. Porter	T
37426	Albert of Waveland	— R R
37427	Albia Boy	— D
37429	Albion 2nd	— M
37430	Albion Gwynne 2nd	— Cox
37431	Alcalde	M
37432	Alexander	P S
37434	Alexander	Ky I
37435	Alexander	P S
37436	Alexander 2nd	P S
37437	Alexander of Maine Valley	— L R
37438	Alex Shropshire	— D
37439	Alexis	L R
37440	Alexis	P S
37441	Alfred	— R R
37444	Alfred Alonzo	— Cox
37447	Allen Boy	— Cox
37448	Allen Duke	— L R
37450	Almont	— T
37453	Alphonso Duke	— R R
37454	Alva Clio	— Ky I
37455	Amboy	— M
37456	Ames	— T
37457	Ananias	— T
37458	Anda	— L R
37459	Andrew	L R
37460	Andrew	— T
37461	Angus	— L R
37462	Anna's Duke	— R R
37464	Annetta's Oxford	— M
37465	Ansel Sutton	P S
37466	Appanoose	— T
37467	Apollo	— P S
37469	Arabella's Duke	— R R
37470	Arad	P S
37471	Arcadia	Ky I
37472	Archdeacon	— Cox
37473	Archduke	— L R
37474	Archduke of Palmyra	— M
37475	Archelaus	— M
37477	Argyll of Jamestown	— Ky I
37479	Argyll 2nd of Riverside	— R R
37482	Arthur	— M
37483	Arthur	M
37484	Arthur	P S
37485	Arthur	— M
37486	Arthur	— Cox
37488	Arthur	— P S

No.	Name	Mark
37490	Ashton	— Daisy
37491	Ashton	— M
37498	Audubon	T
37499	Auglaize Duke	Ky I
37501	August Flower	Woods
37502	August Flower	Ky I
37506	Babe	— M
37509	Badger Boy	— L R
37510	Badger Boy	— T
37511	Badger Boy	— P S
37512	Badger Boy of Albion	P S
37513	Badger Duke	— M
37514	Badger State	— M
37518	Balder	— L R
37519	Bales	M
37520	Baltimore	— M
37521	Bangor	— Cox
37522	Banker	— M
37523	Banker 2nd	— M
37525	Barkis	— Ky I
37526	Barkis 2nd	— M
37527	Barmpton	Cox
37528	5th Barmpton Duke	— R R
37529	Barmpton Prince	— P S
37530	Barney Parsons	Daisy
37533	Baron Alaski	— R R
37535	Baron Barmpton	— R R
37537	Baron Bates	— L R
37544	Baron Belvedere	— Cox
37547	Baron of Bluffdale 6th	— Cox
37549	Baron Bly 3rd	— R R
37550	Baron Bly 4th	— Cox
37551	2nd Baron Booth of Woodlawn	— M
37552	Baron Boughton	— M
37553	Baron Brant	— R R
37555	Baron Bright Eyes	— L R
37562	Baron of Comodale 7th	— R R
37566	Baron Crunder	— L R
37568	Baron Cypress	— M
37569	Baron Duke	Ky I
37571	Baron French 2nd	— L R
37572	Baron of Geneva	— M
37573	6th Baron of Grass Hill	— Cox
37574	Baron Gunter	— R R
37576	5th Baron of Hilldale	— P S
37577	6th Baron of Hilldale	— M
37579	8th Baron of Hilldale	— M
37582	Baron Hubback 4th	— L R
37585	Baron Leslie	— R R
37586	Baron of Liberty	— D
37587	Baron Lind	P S
37592	6th Baron Mazurka	— R R
37600	Baron of Plumwood	— Ky I
37601	Barons Pride	Ky I
37604	5th Baron of Riverside	— Cox
37605	6th Baron of Riverside	— Cox
37608	Baron of Rosedale	— D
37614	Baron Steuben	M
37615	Baron Teague 2nd	— D
37617	Baron Thorndale 2nd	— Cox
37620	Baron Wellington 7th	— Cox
37621	Baron Woodlawn	— T
37626	Barrington Pride	— Cox
37627	Barrymore	D
37628	Bartlett	M
37629	Bass Lake Chief	— L R
37630	Batavia	— Cox
37631	Bates Duke	— M
37635	16th Bates of Oak Hill	— M
37636	Baxter	Ky I
37637	Bayard	— L R
37639	Beaconsfield	— Cox
37642	Beaugello	Ky I
37645	Beau Thorndale	— R R
37646	Beautiful Lad	Ky I
37648	Beauty's Knight	— P S
37649	Beaver	Ky I
37650	Beaver Duke 5th	— P S
37651	Beaver Duke 6th	— P S
37652	Becky's Duke	— R R
37653	Beecher	— Cox
37654	Beecher	P S
37655	Beecher	— L R
37657	Belle's Crown	Ky I
37658	Belle Duke	Ky I
37659	Belle's Duke	Daisy
37660	Belle's Duke	— P S
37661	Belle's Duke	Daisy
37664	Bell Duke	— P S
37665	Belle's Duke 2nd	Daisy
37668	Bell Duke of Chautauqua	— Cox
37672	Bell Duke of Irwin	Daisy
37673	3rd Bell Duke of Maplewood	Daisy
37678	Belle's Prince	— M
37679	Belle's Prince	R R
37682	Belus	— Cox
37686	3rd Belvedere of Rosemound	— Cox
37687	4th Belvedere of Rosemound	— Cox
37688	Ben	— L R
37689	Ben 2nd	T
37690	Ben Butler	— Cox
37691	Ben Butler	— M
37692	Ben Butler	— Long-Horn
37693	Ben Butler	— D
37694	Benedict	— D
37695	Ben Harrison	— M
37696	Ben Holt	— Ky I
37697	Benjamin F	— Cox
37698	Ben Morgan	T
37699	Ben Oakland	L R
37700	Beppo	P S
37701	Bernardo	L R
37702	Berry Hanks	— M
37704	Berwick	— Cox
37705	Beryl 2nd	Ky I
37706	Beulah's Airdrie	L R
37707	Billy	— T
37708	Billy	Ky I
37709	Bill	— Long-Horn
37710	Billy 2nd	— L R
37711	Bill Allen	D
37712	Billy Bell	— Ky I
37713	Billy Britton	M
37714	Bill Butler	M
37716	Billy Haven	D
37717	Bill Meeker	— D
37718	Billy Morgan	T
37719	Billy Pin	— D
37720	Billy Reed	— T
37721	Billy Sharon	M
37723	Bishop Ridley	Cox
37724	Bismarck	— R R
37725	Bismarck	M
37726	Bismarck	M
37727	Bismarck 2nd	Ky I
37728	Blaine	D
37731	Blake	D
37732	Bland	Ky I
37733	Blinkbonny Duke	— M
37734	Bloomfield	Ky I

37735	Bloomfield Airdrie	— R R		37819	Broderick 2nd	— R R
37738	Blucher	— L R		37820	Brokenhorn	Ky I
37739	Blue Jeans	— M		37822	Bruce	D
37740	Blue River Gem	L R		37823	Brunswick	— Cox
37741	Bluehead	— L R		37824	Brutus	— R R
37742	Blythedale Champion 1st	— L R		37825	Brutus	— L R
37743	Blythedale Champion 2nd	— L R		37826	Brutus	P S
37744	Blythedale Champion 3rd	— L R		37827	Brutus 2nd	P S
37745	Blythedale Sharon	— C		37829	Brutus Clay	— M
37746	Boanerges	— M		37830	Bryan Sweepstakes	— D
37747	Bob	Cox		37831	Bub Barmpton	— R R
37748	Bob	Ky I		37832	Buckeye	— P S
37749	Bobbin	— T		37833	Buckeye	— P S
37750	Bob Granger	— Ky I		37834	Buckeye Boy	— C
37751	Bob Hancock	L R		37835	Buckeye Duke	M
37752	Bob Ingersoll	— Cox		37836	Buckeye Lad	Ky I
37753	Bob Ingersoll	— M		37837	Buckingham Prince	L R
37754	Bob Ingersoll	— L R		37838	Buckner	— M
37755	Bob Newcomb	M		37839	Buffalo	— Cox
37756	Bob Sheffielder	— D		37840	Buffalo Bill	D
37757	Bob Straker	— T		37841	Bullion	— R R
37759	Bob White	— L R		37842	Bullwinkle	— R R
37760	Bodark	— T		37844	Burley	Cox
37761	Bold Robin	— P S		37845	Burley Boy	— M
37763	Bolivar	P S		37848	Burr Oak	— R R
37764	Bolivar	Ky I		37849	Burton Boy	— R R
37765	Bolton Duke	Ky I		37850	Business	L R
37766	Bonanza	— L R		37851	Buster	— M
37767	Bon Chief	— T		37852	Busti	L R
37768	Bonnie Duke	— R R		37853	Butcher	— M
37769	Bonnie Duke	— P S		37854	Butcher Boy	— M
37770	Bonny Scotland	— Ky I		37855	Buttercup's Duke 2nd	Daisy
37771	Boom	— Ky I		37856	Butterfly 5th	— Cox
37772	Boreas	— P S		37858	Buzzard	L R
37774	Boss Barmpton	— Daisy		37860	Byron 2nd	Cox
37775	Boston	P S		37861	Cabira	Ky I
37777	Boston	— T		37862	Cadet	— R R
37778	Boston Boy	M		37863	Cadiz Cannonball	— R R
37779	Boston Lad	— C		37864	Cæsar	— P S
37780	Bourbon	— R R		37865	California Monarch	— R R
37781	Bourbon	C		37866	Calla's Duke 3rd	— Cox
37783	Bourbon Lad	— Ky I		37867	Calumet Boy	— M
37784	Bourbon Star 2nd	— P S		37868	Calypso's Duke	T
37785	Boxer	— R R		37869	Cambria Duke	— P S
37786	Boy of Bristol	— P S		37873	Camden 5th	— M
37788	Bracelet's Chief	— M		37874	Camden 7th	— M
37789	Bradford	— P S		37875	Canadian Duke	— Cox
37790	Bragg Barmpton	— Daisy		37877	Captain	Cox
37791	Brave Lormelle	— Cox		37878	Captain	— M
37793	Breastplate	D		37883	Capt. Jack	M
37794	Breastplate, Jr	— C		37884	Capt. Jack	M
37795	Breastplate Louanjo 2nd	— L R		37885	Capt. Jack	M
37796	Breastplate Louanjo 3rd	— D		37886	Capt. Jay	Ky I
37797	Brick	— Cox		37887	Capt. Jinks	— D
37798	Brick Pomeroy	M		37888	Capt. Logan	— L R
37799	Brick Pomeroy	— R R		37889	Capt. Louan	— R R
37800	Brick Pomeroy	— L R		37890	Capt. of Mercer	— M
37801	Bride's Derby	— R R		37891	Capt. Nix	— M
37802	Brigadier	— P S		37892	Capt. Royal	— L R
37803	Brigham	— Long-Horn		37894	Capt. Scott	— P S
37804	Brigham Young	Ky I		37895	Capt. Shaftoe	— M
37806	Bright Duke	D		37898	Charlotta's Duke	— L R
37807	Bright Eye	— Cox		37899	Carl Schurz	— M
37811	Bright Eyes Gloster	— Cox		37900	Carl Schurz	L R
37812	Bright Hope	— M		37901	Carmine	— R R
37813	Brilliant	— R R		37902	Caroline's Battle Ax	— R R
37814	Brilliant of Maine Valley	L R		37903	Carroll Dick	— Cox
37815	Bristow	— R R		37904	Caroll Prince	— R R
37817	Brittannia Duke	— R R		37905	Cashier	— Cox
37818	Britton's Son	Ky I		37907	Casquet's Oxford B	— Cox

37909	Cassius	— R R	37995	Col. Judy	Ky I
37910	Cassius	— P S	37996	Col. Jupiter	— R R
37911	Cassius 2nd	— T	37997	Col. Keith	— Ky I
37912	Cato	— P S	38000	Col. Marsh	D
37914	Cawdor	T	38001	Col. Muir 3rd	— D
37915	Cedar Duke	— Ky I	38002	Col. Murray	— Ky I
37916	Cedar Duke 2nd	— Ky I	38003	Col. Newcombe	P S
37917	Cedar Prince	— P S	38005	Col. Prim	M
37918	Cedar Redham	— D	38006	Col. Sanders	— C
37920	Challenger	— Daisy	38007	Col. Scott	M
37921	Champaign Duke	— P S	38008	Col. Sims	P S
37922	Champion	— R R	38009	Col. Vest	— R R
37923	Champion	M	38010	Col. Warfield	— Woods
37924	Champion	L R	38011	Colony	T
37925	Champion	— P S	38012	Columbia Chief	— R R
37927	Champion 2nd	— Cox	38013	Columbus	— Cox
37928	Champion Duke	— M	38014	Columbus 2nd	— R R
37929	Chancellor	P S	38015	Comet	— P S
37930	Chaplet	— M	38016	Comet	— Long-Horn
37931	Charitys Tycoon	Ky I	38017	Comet	M
37932	Charles 1st	— P S	38019	Comet of Lee Side	— Cox
37933	Charles 2nd	— P S	38020	Comet of Maplewild	— R R
37934	Charles 3rd	— P S	38022	Comforts Wiley 2nd	— R R
37935	Charles Augustus	M	38025	Commander	— R R
37937	Charley Cook	M	38027	Commodore	— R R
37938	Charley Parks	— L R	38029	Commodore	— Cox
37939	Chauncey P	— C	38030	Commodore Nichols	— Cox
37940	Chautauqua Boy	T	38032	Commodore Vanderbilt	— M
37941	Chautauqua Marquis	L R	38035	Conowingo	— L R
37943	Cherry's Duke	— M	38036	Conrad	Ky I
37944	Cherry Lad 6th	— Cox	38038	Conscript	M
37945	Cherry Lad 7th	— M	38046	Constitution	— R R
37946	Cherry Prince	— M	38049	Cornelius	Ky I
37947	Cherub	— R R	38050	Cornell	— L R
37948	Cherub 2nd	— M	38051	Cornishite	— L R
37949	Cherub 3rd	— R R	38052	Coron	— P S
37950	Chester	— Cox	38054	Cortez	— L R
37951	Chester A. Arthur	— P S	38059	Count Hohenthal	— R R
37952	Chetopa	— M	38060	2nd Count of Lebanon	P S
37955	1st Chief of Fountaindale	— L R	38063	Country Gentleman	— M
37956	Chief Ouray	— T	38064	Cowan's Duke 2nd	M
37957	1st Chief of Seward	M	38065	Crawford Boy	M
37958	Chief Victoria	— T	38066	Crescent	— P S
37959	Chris Bana	P S	38068	Cripple	— R R
37960	Chris Flint	— M	38070	Crosstrees	— M
37962	Chubby	Ky I	38071	Crown Point	— D
37963	Cicero's Duke	D	38072	Crown Prince	— M
37964	Clarendon	L R	38073	Crown Prince	— L R
37965	Clark	— M	38075	Croxton of Calumet	Ky I
37966	Clark's Airdrie	M	38076	Crusader	— P S
37968	Claro of Rocky Ford	P S	38077	Crusader	M
37969	Clay	M	38080	Custer	— Daisy
37970	Clayton Duke	— R R	38081	Cyclone	— M
37971	Clifton 6th	— M	38082	Cyclone	M
37972	Clifton 7th	— M	38089	Dagon	— L R
37973	Clifton Duke	Ky I	38090	Dalilia's Prince	M
37974	Clifton Duke 2nd	— R R	38091	Dairyman	R R
37975	Climax	— Ky I	38092	Daisy Acomb	— Cox
37976	Climax Goodness	— R R	38093	Daisy Boy 1st	T
37977	Clinton Grand Duke	Wrong	38094	Daisy Boy 2nd	T
37978	Clipper	— T	38096	Daisy Duke	— R R
37979	Clover Charlie	— R R	38097	Daisy Duke	— Cox
37980	Clover Prince	— R R	38099	Dakota	— M
37982	Colonel	M	38100	Dakota	— Cox
37987	Col. Booth	— D	38104	Dandy	M
37989	2nd Col. Gloster	— Cox	38105	Dandy	M
37990	3rd Col. Gloster	— Cox	38106	Dandy Jim	— Cox
37991	4th Col. Gloster	— Cox	38107	Dandy Jim	M
37992	Col. Harper	— R R	38108	Daney	— R R
37993	Col. Jones	— M	38109	Daniel	— C

38110	Daniel Boone	— Ky I	38202	Doctor Tanner — M
38114	Dan O'Connell of Maine Valley, — M		38203	Dombey L R
38115	Dan Rice	— P S	38200	Dom Pedro Ky I
38116	Dan Rice	Cox	38207	Dom Pedro — Cox
38117	Dan West	— Cox	38208	Dom Pedro — D
38118	Darby Duke 11th	R R	38209	Dom Pedro — C
38119	Darby Duke 12th	— P S	38210	Dom Pedro 3rd — P S
38120	Darby Duke 13th	— R R	38211	Don — R R
38121	Darlington	Ky I	38213	Don — R R
38123	9th Darlington of Rosemound	— Cox	38214	Don Alphonso Ky I
38124	Dauntless	— Cox	38215	Donald — Cox
38126	Dave Lowman	Ky I	38216	Don Carlos — D
38127	Davinport	— R R	38217	Don Carlos — D
38128	Davinport 2nd	— M	38218	Don Colson — Cox
38129	Davy Jones	— P S	38219	Don Cupid — Cox
38130	Dave Rouner	— Long-Horn	38220	Don Dockrill — Cox
38181	Dave Ward	— Cox	38221	Don John — L R
38182	David Copperfield	P S	38222	Don Juan P S
38133	David Copperfield	— L R	38223	Don Juan — Cox
38135	Davy	M	38224	Don Morrison — M
38136	Deacon	— L R	38226	Dora R's Duke — D
38137	Dean	M	38227	Dott — Cox
38138	Defender, Jr	— R R	38228	Double Airdrie — L R
38139	De Kalb Duke	P S	38230	Double Major — Cox
38140	Delaware	— M	38232	Double Sharon Duke — M
38141	Delhi	P S	38233	Douglass R R
38143	Delmont	Ky I	38235	Dove's Duke — M
38145	Denver	— R R	38236	Dowdy — R R
38147	Derby 4th	— R R	38237	Dromio of Ephesus — Cox
38149	Derby Duke	— M	38238	Dromio of Syracuse — Cox
38150	Derby Orphan Boy	— D	38239	Drophorn — M
38151	Deronda	— Cox	38240	Druid Ky I
38152	De Soto Junior	P S	38241	Duchess' Duke — Woods
38153	Despot Duke	— L R	38242	Dudley of Augusta — Daisy
38155	Dexter 2nd	— M	38243	Dudley Prince — M
38156	Diadem	— Daisy	38244	Duenna's Oxford — R R
38157	Diamond	— R R	38245	Duke — Cox
38158	Diamond	— Cox	38246	Duke — Ky I
38159	Diamond	Ky I	38247	Duke L R
38163	Diamond	P S	38248	Duke — M
38167	Dick	M	38250	2nd Duke — R R
38168	Dick Cambria 3rd	Ky I	38251	Duke 2nd — M
38169	Dick Cambria 4th	Ky I	38252	Duke of Arbingdon — L R
38170	Dick Floyd	M	38253	1st Duke of Alameda — C
38171	Dick Highland 3rd	P S	38254	2nd Duke of Alameda — C
38172	Dick Orleans	— P S	38255	2nd Duke of Alameda D
38173	Dick Sutherland	M	38256	3rd Duke of Alameda — T
38174	Dick Taylor	D	38257	4th Duke of Alameda — T
38175	Dick Taylor	— R R	38258	Duke Alexis P S
38176	Dick Taylor	— P S	38259	Duke Alexis — Ky I
38178	Dictator	— R R	38260	Duke Alexis 2nd L R
38179	Dictator	— M	38261	Duke Alexis 3rd —"M
38180	Disco Chief	— M	38262	Duke of Allen —"M
38181	Dixie Duke	— R R	38263	Duke of Allen — Cox
38182	Dixie Duke	R R	38264	Duke of Allen — R R
38183	Dixon	P S	38265	19th Duke of Allendale — Cox
38184	Dixon	— L R	38266	30th Duke of Allendale — Cox
38185	Dixon	L R	38267	33rd Duke of Allendale — T
38186	Dodge	— T	38268	34th Duke of Allendale — T
38187	Doctor	— D	38269	7th Duke of Altaham — L R
38188	Doctor	— D	38270	Duke of Amboy — R R
38189	Doctor	— L R	38271	Duke of Arlington Cox
38190	Doctor A. C. Stevenson	— M	38272	5th Duke of Armada — Cox
38191	Doctor B	— R R	38273	10th Duke of Armada — Cox
38192	Doctor Ballard	M	38274	11th Duke of Armada L R
38193	Doctor Blanc	— R R	38275	Duke of Armstrong — R R
38194	Doctor Bolingbroke	Ky I	38276	Duke of Ascot M
38195	Doctor Bunker	— Cox	38280	7th Duke of Ashland — Woods
38200	Doctor Schliemann	— Cox	38285	Duke of Atwater — L R
38201	Doctor Tanner	D	38286	Duke of Auburn — M

38287	Duke of Avondale............— R R	38377	4th Duke of Forest Home........M
38288	Duke of Avondale............— M	38378	5th Duke of Forest Home...— L R
38289	2nd Duke of Avondale ....— M	38380	26th Duke of Gabilan........— R R
38290	Duke of Bath 4th............— Cox	38381	1st Duke of Ganderhook C
38291	Duke of Bath 5th ....— Cox	38382	Duke of Genesee............— Cox
38292	Duke of Bath 6th ....— Cox	38383	Duke of Geneva Centre ......— M
38294	Duke of Beaver.............— Ky I	38384	Duke of George ....M
38295	Duke of Bedford............— Ky I	38385	Duke of German............Ky I
38296	2nd Duke of Bedford ....M	38386	2nd Duke of German ....Ky I
38297	Duke of Bellaire ....D	38387	3rd Duke of German..........Ky I
38298	Duke of Belton ....— M	38389	Duke of Glendale ....— R R
38299	Duke of Berkeley.................M	38390	2nd Duke of Glendale.......— Ky I
38300	Duke of Berkshire........— L R	38394	49th Duke of Goodness...— R R
38301	Duke of Bluegrass................M	38395	55th Duke of Goodness......— R R
38305	Duke of Bradford............P S	38396	57th Duke of Goodness......— R R
38306	Duke of Brighten 2nd........— P S	38397	Duke of Gordon............— P S
38307	Duke of Brookside... — Long-Horn	38398	Duke of Grafton ....— Cox
38308	Duke Burruss................— M	38399	20th Duke of Granville......— R R
38309	Duke of Butler..............Ky I	38400	Duke of Greenfield ....M
38310	Duke of Butler............— R R	38401	Duke of Green Hill...........— D
38311	Duke of Cambridge...........— M	38402	Duke of Green Lawn 4th......— M
38313	Duke of Carnton 2nd.........— R R	38403	Duke of Green Lawn 5th.....— M
38314	Duke of Cass C	38404	3rd Duke of Green Valley...— Cox
38315	Duke of Cass ....— T	38405	Duke of Greenville, Jr.......— R R
38316	Duke of Champlain ....— L R	38407	Duke of Gwynne ....T
38317	Duke of Chase.............Ky I	38410	2nd Duke of Hamilton ....L R
38318	Duke of Chestnut Grove......— Ky I	38412	Duke of Hanover ....P S
38319	Duke of Chicago.............Ky I	38413	14th Duke of Harlem ....D
38321	Duke of Clark's Run..........Ky I	38414	11th Duke of Harvey ....Ky I
38322	Duke of Clarno ....— L R	38415	14th Duke of Harvey.........Ky I
38323	Duke of Clayton..............— T	38416	15th Duke of Harvey........Ky I
38324	Duke of Clinton..............— D	38418	4th Duke of Hazelhurst......— R R
38325	Duke of Clinton County ....P S	38419	Duke of Hazel Ridge..........T
38326	Duke of Clio...................T	38420	Duke of Henry..............— M
38327	4th Duke of Columbus..........L R	38421	Duke of Henry..............— M
38330	Duke of Council Bluffs......— P S	38422	Duke Herald................— Ky I
38331	Duke of Croxton ....Daisy	38423	1st Duke of Hickory Grove...— L R
38334	Duke Davis................— R R	38424	Duke of High Bridge........— R R
38337	Duke of Diamonds.........— Cox	38425	Duke of Highland ....T
38338	1st Duke of Dover............Daisy	38426	Duke of Highland ....Ky I
38339	2nd Duke of Dover...........Ky I	38427	Duke Hill....................T
38341	Duke of Eden ....M	38429	5th Duke of Hillside ....— Cox
38343	3rd Duke of Edgewood .....— P S	38430	6th Duke of Hillside ....Cox
38345	Duke of Elkhart.............Ky I	38431	Duke of Holland..........— P S
38346	2nd Duke of Elkhart.............T	38432	Duke of Hopewell..........— Cox
38347	Duke of Elkhorn ....M	38433	2nd Duke of Howland.......— R R
38350	Duke of Emerald Valley.....— R R	38434	Duke of Hubbard..........— L R
38352	2nd Duke of Ensley..........Ky I	38438	Duke of Iowa...............— M
38353	4th Duke of Erie..............— M	38439	Duke of Iowa ....— L R
38354	Duke of Evergreen ....— C	38440	Duke of Iowa................— M
38355	Duke of Expansion ....D	38441	Duke of Jamestown..........L R
38356	Duke of Fairchange........— L R	38443	Duke John 2nd.................M
38357	2nd Duke of Fairvale......— Cox	38444	Duke of Johnstown ....— M
38358	3rd Duke of Fairvale........— Cox	38448	6th Duke of Kenton ....R R
38360	5th Duke of Fairvale........— Cox	38449	8th Duke of Kenton ....R R
38361	6th Duke of Fairvale........— Cox	38450	9th Duke of Kenton ....R R
38362	Duke of Fairview............— Ky I	38451	Duke of LaHarpe...........— Ky I
38363	2nd Duke of Fairview ....Ky I	38452	Duke of LaHarpe............— M
38365	Duke's Favorite...............P S	38454	Duke of Lansing ....Ky I
38366	Duke of Fayette..............— D	38456	Duke of Laramie............— P S
38367	Duke of Fayette 2nd..........— D	38457	Duke of Laramie.........— Woods
38368	3rd Duke of Fayette............P S	38458	Duke of LaSalle ....— P S
38369	7th Duke of Fennimore.....— P S	38459	Duke of Leavenworth......— R R
38370	7th Duke of Fenton.. — Long-Horn	38460	Duke of Lebanon ....— R R
38371	Duke of Florence................M	38463	4th Duke of Lebanon........— R R
38372	2nd Duke of Forest Hill......— M	38464	Duke of Leroy.............— P S
38373	3rd Duke of Forest Hill......— L R	38465	Duke of Linden............— R R
38374	4th Duke of Forest Hill......— L R	38467	Duke of Lincoln..............— D
38375	2nd Duke of Forest Home....— Ky I	38468	Duke of Lincoln............— Cox
38376	3rd Duke of Forest Home ....— M	38469	Duke of Locust Grove............M

SHORT-HORN CATTLE PEDIGREES.

No.	Name	Code
38470	2nd Duke of Locust Lawn	— C
38471	Duke of London	— R R
38472	Duke of London	M
38474	Duke of Lone Oak	Ky I
38475	Duke Loudon	— M
38477	Duke McHenry	— L R
38478	Duke of Madison	— M
38479	Duke of Maple Grove	— L R
38481	Duke of Mapleton Park	— P S
38482	7th Duke of Marlboro	— M
38483	8th Duke of Marlboro	— D
38484	Duke of Marshland	P S
38486	3rd Duke of Mason	— Cox
38488	Duke of Mazomanie	P S
38489	Duke of Mecca	— D
38490	Duke of Medicine Creek	— Daisy
38491	Duke of Middlefield	P S
38493	Duke of Midway	— L R
38494	Duke of Milan	— P S
38495	Duke of Milledgeville	P S
38496	Duke of Monroe	T
38497	Duke of Montcalm	— L R
38499	Duke of Mounds	— R R
38500	1st Duke of Mound View	— Cox
38501	2nd Duke of Mound View	— C
38502	3rd Duke of Mound View	— Cox
38503	4th Duke of Mound View	— Cox
38504	5th Duke of Mound View	— Cox
38506	Duke of Nashua	— Ky I
38507	Duke of Nemaha	L R
38509	Duke of Norway	— T
38512	Duke of Oakland 2nd	— R R
38513	Duke of Oakridge	— L R
38514	Duke of Ohio	P S
38515	Duke of Omega	P S
38516	Duke of Onondaga	— Cox
38517	Duke of Orange	— Ky I
38518	Duke of Orland	— R R
38519	Duke of Orleans	— L R
38522	9th Duke of Orleans	— R R
38523	10th Duke of Orleans	Ky I
38524	Duke of Orville	— L R
38525	Duke Osceola	— L R
38534	Duke of Palmyra	— L R
38535	Duke of Paris	— Cox
38536	Duke of Paris	M
38537	Duke of Perryton	— P S
38539	Duke of Plumwood	— L R
38540	Duke of Putnam	— T
38541	Duke of Raisin	— R R
38542	Duke of Randolph	— M
38544	Duke of Richland	— R R
38545	Duke of Richland	— Cox
38546	2nd Duke of Richland	M
38547	Duke of Richmond	— L R
38548	5th Duke of Ridgevale	— L R
38549	34th Duke of Ridgeland	M
38550	35th Duke of Ridgeland	M
38551	Duke of Riverside	— M
38553	2nd Duke of Riverside	— R R
38554	3rd Duke of Riverside	— R R
38555	4th Duke of Riverside	— R R
38557	Duke of Rome	M
38558	Duke of Rosedale	— R R
38559	2nd Duke of Rosedale	— Cox
38560	3rd Duke of Rosedale	— M
38561	Duke of Rose Hill	— L R
38562	2nd Duke of Russell	— Cox
38564	Duke of Salem	— M
38566	Duke of Schoolcraft	M
38567	Duke of Schuyler	— M
38568	3rd Duke of Seneca	— Long-Horn
38509	Duke of Seward	— L R
38570	Duke of Sharon	— R R
38572	Duke of Sharon 7th	— R R
38574	Duke of Sherbrooke	Cox
38575	4th Duke of Shiawassa	Ky I
38576	Duke of Siddington	R R
38578	9th Duke of Skaneateles	— Cox
38579	7th Duke of Skara Glen	— M
38580	8th Duke of Skara Glen	C
38581	Duke of Sparta	P S
38582	Duke of Springbrood 29th	— R R
38583	Duke of Springdale	L R
38584	Duke of Spring Grove	— L R
38585	Duke of Spring Hill	R R
38586	Duke of Spring Lake	L R
38588	Duke of Sturgeon	— T
38589	Duke of Summit	— M
38590	Duke of Sunnyside 2nd	Ky I
38591	Duke of Sutherland C.	— P S
38592	Duke of Sutherland D.	— M
38593	Duke of Sutherland E.	P S
38594	Duke of Sutton	— Cox
38595	Duke of Taopi	C
38596	2nd Duke of Taopi	— Long-Horn
38598	29th Duke of the Pines	— R R
38599	30th Duke of the Pines	— R R
38601	Duke of the Rivers	— R R
38602	Duke of the Valley	— R R
38604	Duke of the West	— T
38605	Duke of the West	M
38606	Duke of Trenton	D
38607	3rd Duke of Trout Run	— L R
38608	8th Duke of Trout Run	— R R
38609	Duke of Troy 2nd	— Cox
38612	Duke of Tullamore	T
38613	Duke of Unadilla	— C
38614	Duke of Van Wert	— L R
38615	Duke of Vernon	— D
38616	5th Duke of Victor	— T
38617	14th Duke of Victor	— M
38618	16th Duke of Victor	— R R
38619	18th Duke of Victor	— R R
38620	19th Duke of Victor	— M
38621	Duke of Vinton	— P S
38622	Duke of Walnut	— Cox
38624	5th Duke of Wheatfield	— Ky I
38625	6th Duke of Wheatfield	— Ky I
38626	7th Duke of Wheatfield	— Ky I
38627	8th Duke of Wheatfield	— Ky I
38628	Duke of Wilderberg	— R R
38630	Duke of Woodson	— R R
38631	Duke of Wabash Valley	— Cox
38633	12th Duke of Walnut Hill	M
38634	Duke of Warren	— R R
38635	Duke of Watson	Ky I
38637	Duke of Wayland	— D
38638	Duke of Wayne	— L R
38639	Duke of Wellington	— Cox
38641	Duke 15th of Wheatland	— R R
38642	Duke 16th of Wheatland	— R R
38643	Duke 17th of Wheatland	— R R
38644	Duke Wiley	— R R
38645	Duke of Windsor	M
38646	Duke of Winnesheik	— R R
38648	Duke of Woodland	— P S
38649	Duke of Woodland	Daisy
38650	2nd Duke of Woodland	— P S
38651	2nd Duke of Woodland	— R R

38652	Duke of Woodlawn	— P S	38784	Engineer	— M
38655	Duke of Yates 25th	— M	38785	English	— M
38656	Duke of York	— L R	38786	English	— P S
38658	Duke of Yorkshire	— M	38788	Ensign	— P S
38659	Dumo	M	38790	Eskridge	— D
38660	Dunlap Duke	D	38791	Esquire	— L R
38661	Dunmore of Springdale	— R R	38793	Eula's Prince	— P S
38662	Dunn	— P S	38795	Eureka Boy	— Cox
38663	Durbin	— C	38796	Eureka 5th	Cox
38664	Durena	— Ky I	38799	Excelsior	M
38665	Dusty Miller	D	38800	Excelsior	— R R
38666	Dutch Lad	— R R	38801	Excelsior	— Ky I
38667	Dutchman	— M	38803	Exporter	P S
38668	Dykes	D	38804	Fairfax	P S
38669	Earl	— L R	38805	Fair View	M
38670	Earl	— Cox	38806	Fairy Duke	— R R
38671	2nd Earl of Allen	— Cox	38807	Falcon	— M
38677	Earl Barmpton	— R R	38808	Fall Pippin	— Cox
38687	5th Earl of Cedar Lawn	— R R	38810	Fancy Boy	Ky I
38688	6th Earl of Cedar Lawn	— R R	38811	Fancy Boy of Bluff Creek	— T
38689	7th Earl of Cedar Lawn	— R R	38812	Fancy Don	— L R
38691	2nd Earl of Conneaut	— R R	38813	Fancy's Duke	— P S
38694	Earl of Dee	P S	38815	Fanny's Duke	— R R
38695	Earl Derby 3rd	M	38817	Fashion Duke	— D
38706	3rd Earl of Goodness	— R R	38818	Fashion's Gloster	L R
38708	28th Earl of Greenbush	— P S	38821	Favorite	— R R
38709	29th Earl of Greenbush	— R R	38822	Favorite	P S
38710	30th Earl of Greenbush	M	38823	Favorite 2nd	— L R
38711	Earl of Green Meadow	— R R	38824	Favorite 3rd	— R R
38713	Earl of Hanover	— P S	38825	Favorite Boy	— M
38714	Earl of Hanover	P S	38826	Favorite Lad	— P S
38720	Earl of Maplewood	— P S	38827	Favorite of Plum Grove	— T
38722	Earl of Marshfield	— L R	38828	Fearful	— Ky I
38725	Earl of Perry	D	38829	Fear Not	— L R
38726	2nd Earl of Portage	M	38830	Feeder	T
38727	3rd Earl of Portage	M	38831	Felix	— D
38728	10th Earl of Raisin	— M	38833	Fidalgo 3rd	— L R
38729	11th Earl of Raisin	— M	38834	Field Marshal	— Ky I
38730	Earl of Rock Creek	P S	38835	Filagree Gem 8th	— R R
38731	Earl of Rock Run	P S	38837	Flathorn Duke	— P S
38733	Earl of Shannon	P S	38838	Flatrock Monarch	— R R
38736	4th Earl of Spring Lake	Cox	38839	Florentia's Duke	— C
38738	Earl Thornapple 3rd	— Cox	38840	Florentia's Duke	— C
38739	Earl of Waco	— M	38841	Flournoy	M
38742	Earl of Webster City	— D	38843	Fordland Dandy	P S
38743	Earl of Wheatland	C	38844	Forest	M
38745	Earnest Christain	— Ky I	38846	Forrester	M
38748	East Franklin	— L R	38847	Forester Duke	— R R
38749	Eben	Cox	38848	Forest Knight	— P S
38750	Ebenezer	— M	38850	Fountain Boy 7th	— R R
38752	Eclipse	Ky I	38851	Fra Lippi	— D
38754	Edgar A. Poe	— L R	38852	Frank	Daisy
38757	Edward	— P S	38854	Frank Coder	— R R
38758	Edward Lester	P S	38855	Frank Garfield	— P S
38760	Elder Dean	— C	38856	Frank of Hillside	— D
38761	El Dorado	M	38857	Frank Landers	— M
38762	El Dorado Lad	— P S	38858	Franklin	M
38763	El Dorado Napier	— M	38861	Frank West	Ky I
38764	Eli	M	38862	Frantic Storm	— T
38767	Elmwood Valentine	T	38863	Fred	T
38770	Elysian Boy	Ky I	38864	Fred	Ky I
38771	Emigrant 2nd	Ky I	38865	Fred	— Long-Horn
38773	Emma's Wellington	— R R	38866	Fred Douglass	— M
38775	Emperor	— R R	38867	Frederick	— P S
38777	Emperor	— L R	38868	Fred Grant 2nd	— Ky I
38779	Emperor 2nd	— P S	38869	Fred J. Shutt	— D
38780	Emperor 2nd	— Cox	38870	Fredlander	— R R
38781	Emperor 3rd	— Cox	38871	Fred Markle	Cox
38782	Endymion	M	38872	Fritz	Ky I
38783	Endymion	— Ky I	38873	Frontier E.	C

SHORT-HORN CATTLE PEDIGREES.

No.	Name	Code
38874	Frontier F.	R R
38875	Frontier G.	— R R
38876	Frontier H.	C
38877	Frontier K.	R R
38878	Frontier L.	C
38879	Frontier M.	C
38880	Frontier N.	L R
38881	Frosty	— R R
38883	25th Gaban	— P S
38884	26th Gaban	— P S
38885	29th Gaban	— P S
38886	30th Gaban	— P S
38887	Gallio	— M
38888	Garfield	— Cox
38889	Garfield	— L R
38890	Garfield	— Cox
38891	Garfield	M
38892	Garfield	— R R
38893	Garfield	R R
38894	Garfield	— M
38895	Garfield	P S
38896	Garfield	— M
38897	Garfield	— D
38898	Garfield	— D
38899	Garfield	— R R
38900	Garfield	— D
38902	Garfield	— T
38903	Garfield	— M
38904	Garfield	M
38905	Garfield	L R
38907	Garfield	M
38908	Garfield	— M
38910	Garfield	— C
38911	Garfield	L R
38912	Garfield	— M
38913	Garfield	— R R
38914	Garfield	— C
38915	Garfield	P S
38916	Garfield Duke	— M
38918	Garibaldi	— Cox
38921	Garland's Breastplate	— R R
38924	Garrard	— R R
38925	Garwin Prince	L R
38927	Gazelle Duke	— R R
38931	Gem's Prince	— R R
38933	General	— M
38934	General	— M
38936	Gen. Arthur	T
38937	Gen. Arthur	— Cox
38938	Gen. Arthur	— M
38939	Gen. Barnet, Jr.	— P S
38940	Gen. Bertrand	— D
38941	Gen. Boom	— M
38942	Gen. Cass	— M
38943	Gen. Clifton	L R
38944	Gen. Craig	M
38945	Gen. Custer 2nd	— Cox
38947	Gen. Custer 5th	— R R
38949	Gen. Gage	P S
38950	Gen. Garfield	— M
38951	Gen. Garfield	T
38952	Gen. Garfield	— Cox
38953	Gen. Garfield	— M
38955	Gen. Garfield	— M
38956	Gen. Garfield	— R R
38957	Gen. Garfield	— R R
38959	Gen. Garfield	— L R
38960	Gen. Garfield	— M
38962	Gen. Garfield	— T
38963	Gen. Garfield	— P S
38964	Gen. Garfield	M
38965	Gen. Garfield	— M
38968	Gen. Garfield	— R R
38969	Gen. Garfield	— P S
38970	Gen. Garfield	L R
38972	Gen. Garfield	P S
38973	Gen. Garfield	— T
38974	Gen. Garfield	— Cox
38977	Gen. Gibson	— R R
38978	Gen. Graff	Ky I
38979	Gen. Grant	— Cox
38980	Gen. Grant	M
38981	Gen. Grant	Ky I
38982	Gen. Grant	M
38984	Gen. Grant	— P S
38985	Gen. Grant	— Cox
38988	Gen. Gwynne	— Cox
38989	Gen. Hancock	— P S
38990	Gen. Hancock	— Cox
38991	Gen. Hancock	— M
38992	Gen. Hancock	— M
38993	Gen. Hancock	— R R
38994	Gen. Hancock	— M
38995	Gen. Hancock	L R
38996	Gen. Hancock	— R R
38997	Gen. Hancock	— P S
38999	Gen. Hancock	— R R
39000	Gen. Hancock	— T
39001	Gen. Hancock	— L R
39002	Gen. Hancock	— M
39003	Gen. Hancock	— T
39005	Gen. Hancock	— L R
39006	Gen. Hancock	— R R
39007	Gen. Hancock	— L R
39008	Gen. Hancock	— M
39009	Gen. Hancock	— T
39010	Gen. Hancock	— R R
39011	Gen. Hancock	— P S
39012	Gen. Hancock of Princeton	— Cox
39014	Gen. Henderson	— C
39015	Gen. Hood	M
39016	Gen. Hopewell 2nd	— M
39017	Gen. Howard	L R
39018	Gen. Howard	— D
39019	Gen. Jack	— Cox
39021	Gen. Jackson	— R R
39023	Gen. James	— R R
39024	Gen. Jim Shields	— M
39025	Gen. Jim Weaver	— R R
39029	Gen. Key	M
39030	Gen. Lafayette	— Ky I
39031	Gen. Lafayette	— M
39032	Gen. Lee	— P S
39033	Gen. Leslie	— T
39034	Gen. Logan	D
39035	Gen. McClellan	— Cox
39036	Gen. McGrant, Jr.	R R
39037	Gen. Marius	Ky I
39038	Gen. Mason	— D
39039	Gen. Miller	— D
39040	Gen. Pope	— D
39041	Gen. Potter	— Daisy
39042	Gen. Prim	— M
39043	Gen. Rice	— P S
39045	Gen. Richmond	— R R
39046	Gen. Roberts	— Cox
39047	Gen. Rose	— L R
39050	Gen. Scott	— M
39051	Gen. Scott	— Cox
39052	Gen. Sheridan	— T

No.	Name	Mark		No.	Name	Mark
39053	Gen. Sheridan	M		39138	Good One	— R R
39054	Gen. Sheridan	— Cox		39139	Governor	— Cox
39055	Gen. Sherman	P S		39140	Governor	M
39056	Gen. Sherman	— Ky I		39141	Governor	— R R
39057	Gen. Sherman	— Cox		39143	Governor	P S
39059	Gen. Thomas	— M		39144	Governor	— Long-Horn
39060	Gen. Thomas	— C		39145	Governor	— Cox
39061	Gen. Thornapple 3rd	— Cox		39146	Gov. Allen	— D
39062	Gen. Washington	— M		39147	Gov. Foster	— R R
39063	Gen. Weaver	— R R		39148	Gov. Garcelon	— D
39064	Gen. Weaver	— M		39149	Gov. Gear	L R
39065	Gen. Weaver	— R R		39150	Gov. Gear	— R R
39066	Gen. Weaver	— D		39152	Gov. Hampton	— M
39067	Gen. Weaver	— Daisy		39153	Gov. Hayes	P S
39068	Gen. Weaver	Ky I		39154	Gov. St. John	Cox
39069	Gen. Weaver	— T		39155	Gov. Tilden	— Cox
39070	Gen. Weaver	T		39156	Gov. Tilden	T
39071	Gen. Weaver	— M		39157	Gov. Vance	— R R
39072	Gen. Weaver	— D		39158	Gov. Wood	M
39073	Gen. Worth	— D		39159	Gramalda	Ky I
39074	Genesee	— Cox		39160	Grand Airdrie	— D
39076	Geneva of Bloomfield	— D		39161	Grand Airdrie of Valley Farm	Ky I
39077	Geneva Duke	— Cox		39162	Grand Barmpton	— R R
39081	George 2nd	P S		39164	Grand Chunk	— Cox
39082	George Garrison	Cox		39166	Grand Duke	M
39083	George Vest	— M		39172	Grand Duke Garfield	— Cox
39086	George Lee	— M		39174	Grand Duke of Mitchel	— R R
39087	George Vest	— P S		39175	5th Grand Duke of Oak Hill	P S
39088	George Washington	M		39177	7th Grand Duke of Oak Hill	— R R
39089	Gernard	— Cox		39180	Grand Duke of Wyandot	— D
39090	Gibbon	— Cox		39181	Grandeur	R R
39091	Gilbert	M		39182	2nd Grand Master	— P S
39092	Gil Blas	— T		39183	Grand Prince of Hazelwood	— Cox
39093	Gill Duke	— Cox		39185	Granger	— P S
39094	Gillette	— M		39186	Granger	M
39095	Gilt Edge	T		39187	Granger	M
39096	Gladiator	M		39188	Grant	— Daisy
39097	Gladiator	— Ky I		39189	Grant	L R
39100	Gladbrook Prince	— M		39190	Grant	P S
39102	Glenelg	Ky I		39191	Grant	M
39105	Gloster	L R		39193	Grant 2nd	— D
39106	Gloster 3rd	— Cox		39194	Gray Eagle	M
39107	Gloster of Armada	— Cox		39195	Greaser	— Long-Horn
39108	Gloster Boy	— Cox		39196	Great Duke of The West	— R R
39109	Gloster D. of The Evergreens	— L R		39197	Greeley	— M
39110	Gloster's Earl	— Cox		39198	Greenbacker	— D
39111	5th Gloster of Pine Grove	— Cox		39200	Greenwood Chief	— M
39112	6th Gloster of Pine Grove	— Cox		39201	Grenadier	— R R
39113	Gloster of Riverside	— R R		39202	Groveland Duke	— M
39114	Gold Digger	— M		39205	Gus Daniels	— M
39115	Golddrop 2nd	— M		39207	Gwendolin's Duke	— R R
39116	Golddrop 3rd	— M		39208	Gwynne Duke of Woodburn	— R R
39117	Golden	— M		39210	Gwynne's Pippin 2nd	— Cox
39118	Golden Bracelet	— M		39212	Hadley	— D
39119	Golden Crescent	— M		39216	Hancock	— T
39121	Golden King 7th	— Cox		39217	Hancock	R R
39122	Golden King 8th	— T		39218	Hancock	— P S
39124	Golden Prince 2nd	— R R		39219	Hancock	— M
39125	Golden Wreathe	M		39220	Hancock	— T
39126	Goldfinder	— D		39221	Hancock	P S
39127	Goldfinder	— D		39222	Hancock	— P S
39128	Goldfinder	P S		39223	Hancock	— Cox
39130	Goldfinder of Maine Valley	P S		39224	Hancock	— M
39131	Goldplait 4th	— L R		39225	Hancock	— R R
39132	Gokey	L R		39226	Hancock	— D
39133	Goodness 3rd	R R		39227	Hancock	— Ky I
39134	Goodness Bates	— Cox		39228	Hancock	— Ky I
39135	Goodness' Cherub 2nd	— P S		39229	Hancock	— L R
39136	Goodness Duke	— M		39230	Hancock Lad	— P S
39137	Good Sale	— P S		39231	Handy Andy	— M

39232	Hanlan	— Cox	39338	Iowa Boy	— R R
39233	Hanno	Ky I	39339	Iowa Boy	— M
39234	Hannibal	— Ky I	39340	Iowa Chief 2nd	M
39235	Hardee	— M	39341	Iowa Duke	— M
39236	Hardy	M	39343	Iron Duke	— M
39237	Harlan	— M	39344	Iron Duke	— L R
39240	Harry Warfield	— Daisy	39346	Island Duke	— Cox
39241	Harry Watson	— P S	39347	Island Duke 2nd	— Cox
39243	Hart Renick	— T	39348	Ivanhoe	— M
39244	Havelock	— M	39351	Ivanhoe Bates	— Ky I
39245	Hawkeye Logan	— R R	39352	Ivy's Son	— M
39246	Haw-Patch	D	39353	Jackson	— T
39247	Hawthorn	— M	39354	Jack Storm	— M
39248	Hayes	— M	39355	Jacques 2nd of Maplewild	— R R
39249	Hayes	— L R	39356	James A. Garfield	— R R
39250	Hazel Dell Duke	— R R	39357	James A. Garfield	L R
39251	Hazel Duke	M	39358	James A. Garfield	— Ky I
39254	Hector	— P S	39359	James A. Garfield	— Ky I
39255	Hector 4th	— M	39360	James A. Garfield	D
39256	Heir of Oakland 2nd	— R R	39361	James A. Garfield	— T
39257	Heir of Oxford	— R R	39362	James A. Garfield	— M
39259	Hendricks	Ky I	39363	James A. Garfield	— R R
39260	Henry Ward Beecher	T	39364	James B. Weaver	P S
39263	Hero	P S	39365	James Conkling	C
39265	Hero	— Ky I	39366	James Fitz James	P S
39268	Hesper	— R R	39367	James McKay	— T
39270	Hibernia 2nd	— P S	39368	James Morgan	T
39271	Hibernia Boy	— P S	39369	James Turtle	Ky I
39272	Highland Chief	— Cox	39371	Janesville Boy	— L R
39273	Highland Chief 2nd	T	39372	Jap	— Cox
39274	Highland Duke	P S	39373	Jasper	— L R
39275	Highlander	— P S	39374	Jasper Prince	— R R
39276	Highland Lad	D	39377	J. C. Flood	C
39277	Highland Napier	— Ky I	39378	Jean Val Jean	— P S
39282	Hillhurst of Woodbury	— R R	39379	Jeff	— C
39283	Hillson	— M	39380	Jefferson	M
39285	Hiram Abief	— R R	39381	Jerry Johnson	P S
39286	Hiram French	L R	39382	Jerry Myers	— D
39287	Hiram Price	— R R	39383	Jesse Rankin	— L R
39289	Holland	— R R	39386	Jim	— R R
39290	Holton's Sharon	— D	39387	Jim Blaine	Ky I
39291	Homer	— Cox	39389	Jim Blaine	Ky I
39295	Honest John	P S	39390	Jim Blaine	— L R
39296	Honest John	Ky I	39391	Jim Blaine	P S
39298	Hoosick	Cox	39392	Jim Blaine	P S
39300	Hopeful	— Long-Horn	39393	Jim Brownell	Cox
39301	Hopeful	— R R	39394	Jim Burns	M
39303	Hope's Tycoon	Ky I	39395	Jim Clay	— M
39305	Hornblower	Cox	39396	Jim Garfield	— L R
39306	Hornet	— M	39398	Jim Harkless	— L R
39307	Hotspur	— M	39399	Jim Laing	— T
39309	Howard	— M	39401	Jim Wilson	— T
39311	Howell Garfield	— Ky I	39405	Joe Bell 2nd	— T
39312	Hubback	— L R	39406	Joe Belleville	M
39315	Hugh Miller	P S	39407	Joe Byram	T
39316	Hugo	P S	39408	Joe Carson	T
39317	Hulburt's Pride	M	39409	Joe Dale of Maplewild	— M
39318	Hunter	— M	39410	Joe Daviess	— R R
39320	Huston	— L R	39411	Joe Downing	— R R
39321	Hutch	— D	39412	Joe Goodness	D
39322	Hyde's Comet	Cox	39414	Joe Pierce	C
39323	Il Frate	R R	39415	Joe Sayers	M
39328	6th Imperial Red Rose	— M	39416	Joe Scott	— R R
39329	Inca	— P S	39417	Joe Scott	— M
39331	Independence	Daisy	39418	Joe Scott 2nd	Ky I
39332	Independence Airdrie	— L R	39419	Joe Shoup	Ky I
39334	Invincible	— P S	39421	Joe Willet	— M
39335	Invincible	— Ky I	39423	John A. Logan	— L R
39336	Invincible 2nd	— M	39424	John A. Logan	D
39337	Ion Shaftoe	— D	39425	John Bright	M

13

No.	Name	Cross		No.	Name	Cross
39427	John Brown	— Cox		39544	Knight	— Cox
39428	Johnny Bull	T		39547	Knightly Wiley 2d of Evergreen,	Ky I
39430	John Ford	C		39548	Knightly Wiley 3d of Evergreen,	Ky I
39431	John Free	— R R		39553	Knox	R R
39432	John Gardner	D		39554	Kosciusko	— Cox
39434	John Hope	— M		39556	L. A. Cherub	— T
39435	John Knox	M		39557	Lad	— P S
39437	John Morgan 2nd	P S		39558	Lad of Waterloo	— L R
39438	John Morris	— Cox		39559	Laddie	— R R
39440	John Rose	— Daisy		39560	Laddie of Himrods	Cox
39441	John Routt	Ky I		39561	Lady Airdrie's Prince	P S
39443	John Sherman	— R R		39562	Lady Anna's Prince	— M
39446	John Smith	— P S		39563	Lady's Duke	M
39447	Johnson	— R R		39564	Lady's Duke	— Cox
39449	John Walker	M		39565	Lady's Duke	P S
39450	John Weehawken	— R R		39566	Lady's Duke	M
39451	Jonah	P S		39567	Lady's Knight	— R R
39452	Jonathan	P S		39568	Lad of the Lake	L R
39456	Josephus	— Cox		39569	Lafayette	— M
39457	Josephus	— L R		39570	Lafayette	— R R
39459	Joy	— P S		39571	Laird	Cox
39460	Jubilee Duke	— R R		39572	Lamartine 2nd	— M
39461	Jubila	— L R		39573	Lambert	— M
39462	Judas	— Cox		39574	Lamoni	— R R
39463	Judge Trimbal	— P S		39576	Lanning's Duke	— P S
39464	Judge Oxford	— R R		39577	Lander	— M
39466	Jules Margottin	— R R		39578	Laudable	M
39471	Julian	Ky I		39579	Laudable	— R R
39476	June Lad	— Ky I		39580	Laura Ascot's Muscatoon	— T
39477	Junior	— P S		39581	Laura's Duke	— M
39478	Junius	— M		39582	Laura's Kirk	M
39479	Junius	D		39586	Leap Year	M
39480	Junius 2nd	— M		39587	Le Bray	Ky I
39482	Jupiter 2nd	M		39588	Lee	— M
39483	Jupiter	— D		39589	Lee Schubert	— M
39484	Justice	— D		39590	Legal Tender	M
39486	Justice	— M		39591	Legal Tender	Ky I
39487	Justice 2nd	— M		39593	Legal Tender	— P S
39489	Kaiana Chief	Ky I		39595	Lenox	— M
39490	Kaiser	Ky I		39596	Leonard	D
39492	Kansas Boy	— M		39597	Leon Prince	— Cox
39493	Kansas Chief	— R R		39598	Leopard	Ky I
39494	Kansas Duke of Richmond	— R R		39599	Le Roy	L R
39495	Kansas Farmer	— M		39600	Le Roy	— Ky I
39496	Kate's Airdrie	— M		39601	Le Roy Duke	— M
39497	Kate's Duke	— Ky I		39603	Levy Star	— M
39498	Kaw Chief	— M		39604	Lewis	— Cox
39499	Kelsie	Ky I		39605	Lewis Patterson	M
39500	Keno	— M		39606	Lexicon	— T
39501	Kenoma	P S		39609	Libbie's Earl	T
39502	Kentucky Bill	— C		39611	Lilac's Duke	— Cox
39505	Kentucky Joe	— L R		39612	Lill's Mazurka	— P S
39506	Kentucky Joe 3rd	— L R		39613	Lincoln	— Cox
39507	Kickapoo	— R R		39614	Lincoln Sam	— D
39508	Kincade	— T		39615	Lind Duke	— M
39509	Kilpatrick	— M		39616	9th Linden	— M
39511	King	M		39617	Lion	L R
39512	King Charles	M		39618	Lion	— T
39514	King Oscar	— M		39619	Lionel	R R
39515	King Philip	— R R		39620	Little Monarch	— M
39516	King of Poland	L R		39621	Lizzie's Airdrie	— L R
39518	Kingston	— D		39623	Locomotive	— L R
39519	King of The Hills	— Cox		39624	Lodi	— Long-Horn
39524	Kinsley	Daisy		39626	Logan	P S
39525	Kirklevington Duke	— R R		39628	Logan	— Cox
39529	Kirklevington Lad	— R R		39630	Logan Boy	— C
39530	Kirklevington Lad	— R R		39631	Logan	— M
39540	Kirkwood	— R R		39632	Logan Duke	— Cox
39541	Kirkwood Hilpa	— P S		39633	Logan Duke	M
39542	Kit Carson	— P S		39634	London Chief	— L R

SHORT-HORN CATTLE PEDIGREES.

No.	Name	Code
39635	Lone Puritan	— L R
39636	Lonesome Jack	— Cox
39637	Lone Star	Ky I
39638	Lone Star	— Cox
39639	Longfellow	— M
39640	Longfellow	— P S
39641	Longfellow	— M
39642	Longfellow	M
39645	Lord Albion	— P S
39646	Lord Avondale	P S
39647	Lord Barmpton	— R R
39648	2nd Lord Barmpton of Wapsie	— R R
39650	Lord Barr	— Cox
39651	Lord Barrington of Hamburg	— R R
39652	Lord Beaconsfield	M
39653	Lord Beaconsfield	— T
39654	Lord Booth	— Ky I
39655	Lord Byron	— L R
39656	Lord Byron	D
39657	Lord Byron	— P S
39657½	Lord Chesterfield	— T
39659	Lord Cortland	— Cox
39662	Lord Derby 2nd	— D
39666	Lord Dunmore 3rd	— M
39669	Lord Edward	— P S
39670	Lord Eglintoun 2nd	C
39672	Lord Fairy	C
39675	Lord Graham 4th	— R R
39676	Lord Holland	M
39677	Lord John	P S
39682	Lord Leroy	— Cox
39683	Lord Larue	M
39685	Lord of Lynn 2nd	— C
39686	Lord of Maine Valley	L R
39687	Lord Marquis 3rd	— M
39688	Lord Marquis 4th	— M
39689	Lord Mar	— D
39691	Lord Mazurka	— R R
39692	Lord Napier	— R
39693	Lord Raglan	— Cox
39695	Lord Ruby of Maplewild	— R R
39696	Lord Russell	— Ky I
39700	Lord Strathallen 3rd	— Cox
39701	Lord Strathallen of Evergreen	Ky I
39703	Lord of the West	— Cox
39704	Lord Tom	— P S
39705	Lord Thornapple	— L R
39711	Lord Woodson	Ky I
39713	Lord Zeberman	— L R
39714	Los Osos Duke	— Daisy
39715	Lothair	— R R
39716	Lottery	— M
39717	Louan's Airdrie 2nd	Ky I
39718	Louan's Airdrie 3rd	Ky I
39719	Louan's Breastplate	— M
39720	Louan's Clifton	— R R
39721	Louan Duke	— R R
39722	Louan Duke	— R R
39723	Louan Duke	— M
39724	Louan Duke	— M
39725	Louan Duke	— R R
39726	Louan Duke	— R R
39727	2nd Louan Duke	— R R
39728	Louan Duke 3rd	— M
39729	Louan Duke Le Bon	— M
39730	Louan Duke of Cherry Grove	— R R
39731	Louanjo 2nd	— Long-Horn
39732	Louanjo 3rd	— R R
39733	Louanjo 4th	— R R
39734	Louanjo Medora	— R R
39735	Louan's Lad	— M
39736	Louan Lad	— R R
39737	Loudon Airdrie Duke	— D
39738	5th Loudon D. of Greenwood	— R R
39739	6th Loudon D. of Greenwood	— R R
39740	7th Loudon D. of Greenwood	— R R
39741	8th Loudon D. of Greenwood	— R R
39742	9th Loudon D. of Greenwood	— R R
39743	Loudon Duke of Marlboro	— R R
39744	Louis	— Cox
39745	Louis Oscar	— L R
39746	Louis of Pleasant Hill	— Cox
39747	Lucius	— R R
39748	Lucretius 2nd	— Cox
39750	Lucy's Duke	— D
39751	Ludlow	— L R
39756	Lymax	— R R
39757	Lyndon 2nd	Ky I
39759	Macbeth Clyde	— M
39760	McBride	— R R
39763	McDonald	M
39764	McDonald Duke 8th	— M
39765	McDonald Duke 9th	— T
39766	McDonald Duke 10th	Ky I
39767	McDonald Duke 11th	— C
39768	McDonald Duke 12th	Ky I
39769	McDonald Duke 13th	R R
39770	McDonald Duke 14th	— M
39771	McDonald Duke 15th	— R R
39772	Mack Clyde 2nd	M
39773	MacMahon	— M
39774	Maculus	— M
39776	Maggie's Breastplate	— R R
39777	Magic Clyde	— M
39778	Magistrate	— M
39780	Magnum Bonum	— R R
39781	Magruder	— Daisy
39782	Major	— M
39783	Major	L R
39784	Major	— M
39785	Major	Cox
39787	Major	— R R
39788	Major	— L R
39789	Major	Cox
39792	Maj. Anderson	— Cox
39793	Maj. Benton	— Ky I
39795	Maj. Booth	— T
39796	Maj. Clifton	— P S
39798	Maj. Elkhorn	— D
39799	Maj. Grant	— L R
39800	Maj. Grant	— D
39801	Maj. Hancock	— P S
39802	Maj. Hurley	— R R
39803	Maj. Ide	M
39804	Maj. 2nd of Lake Park	— Daisy
39805	Maj. 3rd of Lake Park	— Daisy
39807	Maj. Mack	— D
39808	Maj. Muller	— R R
39809	Maj. Nicolls	— R R
39810	Maj. Norton	— L R
39811	Maj. Rose	— T
39812	Maj. Rose	M
39813	Maj. Smith	— P S
39814	Maj. Stevens	— R R
39815	Maj. Sultan	L R
39817	Maj. Wiley	— Cox
39822	Mamie's Duke	— Cox
39823	Mandolin	T
39824	Manassah	T
39826	Maple Duke	— M

39827	Marbled Duke — L R	39946	Mazurka's Oxford 29th — M
39830	Marmaduke — M	39947	Mazurka's Oxford 30th — D
39831	Marmion — M	39948	12th Meadow Duke — M
39832	Marquis Ky I	39951	Melody's Duke — M
39833	Marquis Daisy	39953	Mendota Duke — L R
39834	Marquis — L R	39955	Mendota Prince — Cox
39835	Marquis M	39956	Mentor R R
39836	Marquis 2nd Ky I	39958	Merger — M
39837	Marquis 3rd Daisy	39959	Micawber — Ky I
39838	Marquis 4th Ky I	39962	Mick Dillon — P S
39839	Marquis 5th Ky I	39963	Mickado — Cox
39840	Marquis 6th Ky I	39964	Mike — D
39841	Marquis of Blue Mound M	39965	Mike Beaver T
39842	Marquis of Bluffdale 2nd — D	39967	Milksop — L R
39849	Marquis of Davis Ky I	39968	Miller's Sharon — D
39853	Marquis of Kankakee — C	39971	Minnesota Boy — C
39855	2nd Marquis of Locust Grove — M	39972	Minnesota P S
39856	Marquis of Lorne — M	39973	Minister of Emporia Ky I
39857	Marquis of Lorne — M	39974	Minor Ringgold L R
39858	Marquis of Lorne — D	39975	Missionary L R
39860	3rd Marquis of Maple Hill — R R	39976	Missourian — M
39862	Marquis of Palestine — C	39980	Mistletoe Duke — M
39863	Marquis of Poland L R	39982	Mitchel — D
39864	Marquis of Rose Hill — Cox	39983	Moderator — M
39866	Marquis of Townsend — D	39984	Modoc T
39869	Marrowbone Duke Ky I	39985	Modoc Chief — Cox
39870	Marshall — M	39986	Modoc Chief — R R
39872	Marshall Fairview — M	39987	Mohawk — Cox
39873	Marshall Lad — C	39988	Mohawk — L R
39875	Martina's Duke — C	39989	Mollie's Duke — R R
39876	Mary's Baron — R R	39990	Molly's Prince — L R
39877	Mary Belle's Don Ky I	39992	Monarch L R
39878	Mary's Breastplate — P S	39993	Monarch L R
39879	Mary's Duke — M	39995	Monarch 2nd P S
39881	Mary's Major — R R	39996	Monarch Junior — M
39885	Master Bertram Ky I	39997	Monarch of Augusta — R R
39886	Master Bob — Cox	39998	Monarch of Butler — M
39888	Master Charlie P S	39999	Monarch of Cooper — R R
39891	Master Joe — P S	40000	Monarch of Maple Grove — Cox
39894	Master Prince L R	40001	Monona Chief M
39895	Master Ralph — M	40002	Monroe Chief T
39904	Master Winfred — D	40003	Monta — R R
39905	Matchless Daisy	40004	Montgomery 2nd R R
39907	Matt Carpenter — L R	40005	Moody — M
39911	Maxey — L R	40006	Moonlight Ky I
39912	Maxey Boy — L R	40007	Moorefield — M
39913	Maximillian — M	40009	Moreton Duke — Long-Horn
39914	Maximus M	40010	Morgan Duke Ky I
39915	May Belle's Duke — C	40011	Morris Cox
39916	May Duke — L R	40012	Mortimer — M
39917	May Duke — L R	40013	Mortimer 2nd — M
39918	May Duke 2nd — M	40014	Moses — L R
39919	May's Favorite P S	40015	Moses Mansfield Cox
39920	Mayflower Ky I	40016	Moss Rose Duke — M
39921	Mayflower's Duke — Cox	40018	Moulton's Mazurka Duke 2nd, — P S
39923	3rd Mayflower Prince — M	40019	Moulton's Mazurka Duke 3rd, P S
39924	May King — C	40020	Moultrie George Ky I
39925	Maynard's Duke — C	40021	Mountaineer — Cox
39931	Mazurka Duke of Geneva — R R	40022	Mountain Yankee — Cox
39932	Mazurka's D. of Green Meadow — C	40023	Mozart — C
39934	Mazurka Earl 2nd — D	40024	Mulchmcho — M
39937	Mazurka of Oak Grove — L R	40025	Muddy Duke — P S
39938	Mazurkas Oxford 19th Ky I	40026	Muggins — P S
39939	Mazurka's Oxford 20th Ky I	40027	Muirkirk Boy — Cox
39940	Mazurka's Oxford 22nd D	40028	Mulberry Chief — M
39941	Mazurka's Oxford 23rd Ky I	40029	Multer's White Bull — R R
39942	Mazurka's Oxford 25th — Ky I	40031	Muscatine — M
39943	Mazurka's Oxford 26th T	40032	Music's Gloster L R
39944	Mazurka's Oxford 27th Ky I	40033	Music's Tycoon L R
39945	Mazurka's Oxford 28th R R	40035	Napoleon Ky I

No.	Name	Code	No.	Name	Code
40036	Napoleon	— D	40122	Oneida	M
40037	Napoleon	— Cox	40123	Oneida's Duke of Dakota 2nd	— R R
40038	Napoleon	L R	40124	Oneida's D. of Goodness 2nd	— R R
40039	Napoleon Bonaparte	— L R	40127	Oneida Prince 2nd	— Ky I
40040	Natt Head	— Cox	40128	Onondaga	— Cox
40041	Neal Dow	— Cox	40129	Onstot	D
40042	Nebraska King	— L R	40131	Ora Chief	P S
40043	Ned	Ky I	40132	Orange Duke	— R R
40044	Ned Forrest	— R R	40133	Orange Judd	L R
40045	Nellie's Baron	L R	40134	Orange Lad	— L R
40048	Nellie's Jupiter	— L R	40137	Orion	M
40049	Nellie's Oxford 1st	C	40139	Orion	— Cox
40050	Nelson	M	40140	Orion	Ky I
40052	Nelson Boy 4th	— M	40143	Orius	M
40054	Neosho	— M	40144	Orland	— L R
40055	Neptune	R R	40147	Orphan Boy	— P S
40056	Nereus	R R	40148	Orphan Boy	— R R
40057	Nero	— Cox	40149	Orphan Boy	P S
40059	New Year's Day	— P S	40150	Orphan Boy	— T
40060	New Year's Lad	M	40151	Orphan Duke	M
40061	New Years Profitable	— R R	40153	Orville	Ky I
40062	Ney	— M	40154	Oscar Shaw	C
40064	Nicati Duke 2nd	— P S	40155	Osman	— M
40065	Nicholas Nickleby	— L R	40156	Othello	— Ky I
40066	Nichols	— M	40157	Otis	Ky I
40067	Nicholson's London Duke	— R R	40159	Otto	M
40068	Niles	— R R	40160	Oxalis	— M
40069	Nimbus	M	40161	Oxford	— T
40070	Nimbus	— Ky I	40163	Oxford's Baron	— M
40071	Nimrod	— Ky I	40165	Oxford Bates 2nd	— R R
40074	Noble Duke	— L R	40166	Oxford of Bear Creek	— M
40075	Noble Duke	— T	40167	Oxford Bloom	— R R
40076	Noble Grant 3rd	— Daisy	40168	Oxford Boy	C
40077	Noble Romulus	— Woods	40169	Oxford Boy	— T
40078	Nodaway Chief	P S	40170	Oxford Boy	— D
40079	Nokomis	P S	40171	Oxford Boy 2nd	C
40084	Norfolk	— D	40175	Oxford Butterfly	— M
40086	North Star	— R R	40176	Oxford Chief	— M
40087	Norton	— M	40178	Oxford Duke	— T
40088	Norton's 4th Baron Lyndale	T	40180	Oxford Duke	— M
40089	Norton's 6th Baron Lyndale	M	40182	Oxford of English Farm	— L R
40091	Norton's 12th Baron Lyndale	T	40183	2nd Oxford of English Farm	— M
40092	Nortons 13th Baron Lyndale	— M	40184	Oxford's Geneva	— M
40093	Nortons 16th Baron Lyndale	M	40185	Oxford Grand	— Cox
40095	Nortons 19th Baron Lyndale	T	40190	Oxford King 2nd	— R R
40096	Nortons 21st Baron Lyndale	Ky I	40191	Oxford Lad	— T
40097	Nortons 23rd Baron Lyndale	— M	40198	Oxford Marquis	— Cox
40098	Nortons 24th Baron Lyndale	— R R	40200	Oxford Prince	— M
40099	Nottaway Chief	Cox	40202	Oxford Royal Duke	— Cox
40100	Oakdale	Cox	40203	Oxford of Springhill	— M
40101	Oak Grove Boy 3rd	— M	40205	Ozro Grant	— Daisy
40102	Oak Hill Prince	— P S	40206	Pandora's Republic	— R R
40103	Oakland	— T	40207	Paragon	— M
40104	Oakland	— T	40208	Paragon 2nd	— M
40105	Oakland Lad	M	40209	Paragon 4th	— M
40107	Oakley	P S	40210	Park Duke	P S
40108	Oakley	D	40211	Parnell	— R R
40109	Oak Ridge Duke	M	40212	Parole	Cox
40110	Observer	L R	40213	Parson Godman	Ky I
40111	Occident	Ky I	40214	Passano	— L R
40112	Occult	Ky I	40215	Pat Mulloy	P S
40113	Oddfellow	— Ky I	40216	Patriot	C
40114	Ogden Duke	— R R	40217	Paul	— R R
40115	Ohio	M	40219	Pawnee Chief	— P S
40116	Ohio Crown	— L R	40220	Peabody	P S
40117	Oklahoma Duke	— M	40222	Pearl	— P S
40118	Ola's Breastplate	— L R	40223	Pearl of Cottonwood	— M
40119	Old Bullion	— L R	40224	Pearl Duke	— M
40120	Oliver	M	40226	Pearl Duke	— D
40121	Oliver Cromwell	— R R	40227	Pearl Duke 2nd	— R R

40228	Pearl Prince — T	40320	Prairie Duke — R R
40229	Pearlwood Duke — R R	40321	Prairie Duke Ky I
40230	Peggy's Boy L R	40322	Prairie Duke M
40231	Poggy's Lad L R	40323	Prairie Duke — R R
40232	Peleus R R	40324	Prairie Duke 3rd — Ky I
40234	Percy — R R	40325	Prairie Eagle 2nd — R R
40237	Perfection Duke — M	40326	Prairie King L R
40238	Perfection Model — M	40327	Prairie Prince — C
40244	Peri Duke of Magnolia T	40330	President L R
40245	Peri Lad 2nd — R R	40332	President Garfield Ky I
40247	Pete Ky I	40333	President Hayes — L R
40248	Pete Ky I	40334	Preston L R
40250	Peter Cooper — T	40335	Pretender — R R
40251	Peter Cooper — L R	40336	Pride of Cayuga — Cox
40252	Peter G. L R	40337	Pride of Lone Jack — P S
40253	Pete Ilam M	40338	Primate M
40254	Peter McCool M	40339	Primrose — Long-Horn
40255	Peter McNelly — M	40340	Prince M
40256	Pete Mallet — T	40341	Prince M
40257	Phalanx Lad A. Cox	40342	Prince — Cox
40258	Phalanx Lad B. Cox	40343	Prince — T
40259	Phantom — Cox	40345	Prince — P S
40260	Phenomenon's Star — Cox	40346	Prince — M
40261	Phil — Ky I	40347	Prince L R
40262	Philip P S	40348	Prince — M
40263	Philip — Cox	40352	Prince of Airdrie — Cox
40264	Phil Kearney L R	40355	Prince Albert Ky I
40265	Phil Sheridan M	40356	Prince Albert — M
40266	Phil Stech — Cox	40357	Prince Albert — P S
40268	Phyllis Duke — R R	40358	Prince Albert — R R
40271	Piatt — R R	40360	Prince Albert — M
40272	Pickwick P S	40362	Prince Albert — L R
40273	Pills — P S	40363	Prince Albert — T
40275	Pilot — T	40364	Prince Alfred — P S
40276	Pilot 2nd M	40365	Prince Alfred — R R
40278	Pines Prince — R R	40367	Prince Arthur Cox
40279	Pioneer — M	40368	Prince Arthur M
40280	Pioneer — D	40374	Prince of Barmpton — C
40281	Piper — L R	40376	Prince of Bourbon — D
40282	Pirate — T	40379	Prince Caramel — D
40285	Placida's Airdrie — R R	40381	Prince Climax 6th — M
40286	Placida's Airdrie 2nd — R R	40383	2nd Prince of Edgewood M
40287	Plantagenet 4th L R	40384	Prince Edward Ky I
40288	Plato — D	40385	Prince Edward of Sonora — D
40289	Plato — M	40386	Prince Eugene — M
40290	Plato — Daisy	40387	Prince of Fair Lee P S
40291	Plato — R R	40390	P. Fred'k Charles of Mellington, M
40293	Pleasant Corner Duke — R R	40391	Prince George — M
40294	Plowboy — Wrong	40392	Prince George 2nd — M
40296	Plumwood A B C	40393	Prince of Grace Ky I
40297	Plumwood A E — R R	40394	Prince Gwynne 2nd — Cox
40298	Plumwood A F R R	40396	Prince of Hanover M
40299	Plumwood A G — R R	40397	Prince of Hanover 2nd M
40300	Plumwood A H C	40398	Prince Henry — R R
40301	Plumwood A I Ky I	40399	Prince Henry — P S
40302	Plumwood A J R R	40405	Prince Humbert L R
40303	Plumwood A K Ky I	40406	Prince Imperial — T
40304	Plumwood A L C	40407	Prince James Cox
40305	Plumwood A M R R	40408	Prince John of Vine Hill — R R
40306	Plumwood A N — R R	40409	Prince's Knight — P S
40307	Plumwood A O R R	40411	Prince Leopold — R R
40308	Plumwood A P — R R	40412	Prince Lorraine Cox
40409	Plumwood O O Daisy	40416	Prince of Maplewood — C
40310	Plumwood Duke — R R	40417	Prince of Maplewood — M
40311	Plumwood Lad D R R	40418	Prince Mononcue — M
40313	Plymouth Rock — M	40419	Prince of Montour L R
40314	Pontiac — Cox	40420	Prince Napoleon Cox
40315	Pontiff — M	40421	Prince of Newton — R R
40318	Porter L R	40422	Prince of Oakland — R R
40319	Portunus R R	40424	Prince of Oakland 2nd — R R

SHORT-HORN CATTLE PEDIGREES.

40426	Prince of Orleans	— Cox
40427	Prince Oxford 2nd	— C
40428	Prince of Palmyra	Ky I
40429	Prince of Plum Creek	— L R
40430	1st Prince of Quietude	— L R
40431	Prince Royal	P S
40437	Prince of Sharon 7th	— L R
40439	Prince of Stapleton	— Long-Horn
40440	Prince of Stark	— M
40442	Princeton	— R R
40443	Prince Victor	— R R
40445	Prince of Wales	L R
40446	Prince of Wales	— R R
40447	Prince of Walk Chalk	— L R
40448	Prince of Walnut Grove	Ky I
40449	Prince of Wayne	— P S
40450	13th Prince of Wyaconda	— T
40451	14th Prince of Wyaconda	— T
40452	15th Prince of Wyaconda	M
40457	Proctor	— Cox
40458	Professor	Ky I
40459	Profitable Duke	— R R
40460	Proper	— D
40461	Prospect Duke	— T
40462	Prospero	— P S
40463	Proteus	R R
40464	Proud Boy	— Cox
40465	Proud Duke of Atha	— R R
40467	Proud Prince	— L R
40468	Prudy's Duke	Ky I
40469	P. T. Barnum	D
40470	Ptolemy	— R R
40471	Punch	— M
40473	Punch's Watson	— P S
40474	Purdy	— C
40475	Pymosa	P S
40476	Queen's Airdrie	— D
40478	Queen's Duke	— Cox
40479	Queen's Duke	P S
40480	Queen's Duke	P S
40483	Queen's Fortunatus	— Cox
40485	Queens Imperial	— M
40486	Queen Mary's Duke	— M
40487	Quiver	— T
40489	Racket	— M
40491	Ralph	— Long-Horn
40492	Ralph	— M
40493	Ralph Moore	— D
40495	Rauger	— R R
40496	Ranger	P S
40497	Ranger Prince 2nd	— L R
40498	Ranger Prince 3rd	— L R
40499	Recorder	— L R
40500	Red Baron	— D
40501	Red Baron	— M
40502	Red Baron	— M
40503	Red Bird	— Cox
40504	Red Bird	— P S
40505	Red Bird	— D
40506	Red Boy	P S
40507	Red Boy	— Cox
40508	Red Boy	M
40509	Red Buck	— T
40510	Red Buck 2nd	— M
40512	Redbud Pontiff	— M
40513	Red Champion	— D
40514	Red Chief	M
40515	Red Chief	L R
40516	Red Chief of Rose	— Cox
40517	Red Cloud	Cox
40518	Red Cloud	L R
40519	Red Cloud	— M
40520	Red Cloud	— P S
40521	Red Cloud 2nd	— Cox
40522	Red Coleus	M
40523	Red Comet	M
40524	Red Derby	Ky I
40525	Redding	R R
40526	Red Doctor	Ky I
40527	Red Duke	C
40528	Red Duke	— C
40529	Red Duke	— R R
40530	Red Duke	— M
40531	Red Duke	— D.
40533	Red Duke	— P S
40534	Red Duke	— M
40535	Red Duke	Daisy
40536	Red Duke	— P S
40537	Red Duke	— M
40538	Red Duke	M
40539	Red Duke	P S
40542	Red Duke of Sutherland	— D
40543	Red Duke of Spring Grove	T
40544	2nd Red Duke of Vine Hill	— M
40545	3rd Red Duke of Vine Hill	— M
40546	Red Duke of Wayne	Ky I
40547	Red Earl	— M
40549	Red Favorite	— R R
40551	Red George	— D
40552	Red George 2nd	— D
40553	Red Gloster	P S
40554	Red Grand Airdrie	— P S
40555	Red Grant	L R
40556	Red Jacket	— M
40557	Red Jacket	— D
40558	Red Jacket	— Daisy
40559	Red Jacket	— L R
40560	Red Jacket	— P S
40563	Red Joe	— D
40564	Red John	— Ky I
40566	Red Knight	— P S
40567	Red Lad	— M
40568	Red Lad	— Cox
40569	Red Lad	M
40571	Red Lad 2nd	— M
40572	Red Lesley	— R R
40574	Red Mariner	M
40575	Red Oak	— Daisy
40576	Red Oak	— R R
40577	Red Oakland	— D
40578	Red Prince	— R R
40580	Red Prince	Ky I
40581	Red Prince 2nd	— R R
40582	Red Ranger	— P S
40584	Red Roman	— P S
40595	Red Rover	Ky I
40596	Red Rover	— R R
40598	Red Rover	— Cox
40599	Red Rover	— P S
40600	Red Rover	Ky I
40601	Red Rover	— M
40602	Red Royal Minister	— L R
40603	Red Senor	— L R
40604	Red Star	— R R
40607	16th Red Thorndale	M
40608	18th Red Thorndale	— M
40609	19th Red Thorndale	M
40610	Red Tycoon	— Cox
40611	Red Wellington	— D
40613	Reference	— L R

40614	Reformer	M	40709	Rock River Lad 42nd — Cox
40615	Reformer	— R R	40710	Rock River Lad 43rd — Cox
40616	Regishire	M	40711	Rock River Lad 44th — Cox
40617	Renick	M	40712	Rock River Lad 45th — Cox
40618	Renick	— Daisy	40713	Rock River Lad 46th — Cox
40620	Renick's Duke	T	40714	Rock River Lad 47th — Cox
40621	Renick's Highlander	— M	40715	Rock River Lad 48th M
40623	Renick of Orchard Farm	— R R	40716	Rock River Lad 49th — Cox
40625	Renton Prince	L R	40717	Rock River Lad 50th — Cox
40626	Reporter	Ky I	40718	Rock River Lad 51st — Cox
40627	Republican	— Daisy	40719	Rock River Lad 52nd — Cox
40628	Reserve	Ky I	40720	Rock River Lad 53rd — Cox
40629	Resumption	— M	40721	Rock River Lad 54th — Cox
40630	Resumption	D	40722	Rock River Lad 55th — Cox
40631	Resumption	— M	40723	Rock River Lad 56th — Cox
40632	Rhoda's Knight	— Cox	40724	Rock River Lad 57th — Cox
40633	Richard	— P S	40725	Rock River Lad 58th — Cox
40634	Richard 11th	— R R	40726	Rock River Lad 59th — Cox
40635	Richard 14th	— Ky I	40727	Rockwood Lad — Cox
40636	Richard B.	L R	40729	Roderick M
40637	Richard Cherry	— D	40730	Roderick Dhu — D
40638	Richard Lewis	— P S	40731	Roderick Dhu — Cox
40639	Richard Pansy	— Cox	40732	Rodman — M
40641	Richard Royal 3rd	P S	40733	Rodney L R
40642	Richard Sly	— M	40734	Rodolphus — M
40643	Richard Taylor	M	40735	Rohais Ky I
40644	Richland Duke	D	40736	Rolla — T
40646	Richmond	Ky I	40737	Rolla R R
40647	Rienzi	— M	40738	Romeo — Cox
40648	Ringgold	Cox	40740	Romley — M
40649	Ringgold	— M	40741	Romulus — Cox
40650	Rising Star	— Cox	40743	Rosalier Cox
40658	Roan Duke	— L R	40744	Roscoe — R R
40659	Roan Duke	Ky I	40745	Roscoe — L R
40662	Roan Duke	— Cox	40746	Roscoe — M
40663	Roan Duke	— L R	40747	Roscoe P S
40664	Roan Duke	M	40748	Roscoe — D
40665	Roan Duke	— P S	40749	Roscoe Conkling — M
40668	Roan Duke	— L R	40750	Roscoe Conkling — L R
40669	Roan Duke	Daisy	40751	Roscoe Duke — M
40670	Roan Duke 3rd	— R R	40752	Rose Barmpton — R R
40674	Roan Earl	— M	40759	Rosy's Duke Ky I
40675	Roan Major	L R	40760	Rose Duke — R R
40677	Roanoke	— R R	40763	Rose Duke of Burton — T
40678	Roan Oak	— R R	40764	Rose's Hillhurst — P S
40680	Roan Prince	Ky I	40765	Rose Hill Prince L R
40681	Roan Prince	M	40766	Rose's Lad — R R
40683	Roan Rover	Ky I	40770	Rough Lad — P S
40684	Roan Starlight	— M	40771	Rough Taylor — M
40685	Robert Barkley	M	40772	Rover L R
40686	Robert Burns	— M	40773	Rover M
40687	Robert Burns 2nd	— M	40774	Rover — P S
40688	Robert Earl	Ky I	40775	Rover — Cox
40691	Robert Lyle	— R R	40776	Rover — Cox
40692	Robin	Ky I	40777	Rover — L R
40693	Robin	— M	40778	Roving Lad M
40694	Robin 1st	M	40779	Rowdy Boy M
40695	Robin 2nd	M	40781	Royal Bates — Daisy
40696	Robin Grey	— Daisy	40782	Royal Briton 9th — L R
40697	Robin Hood	Ky I	40783	Royal Briton 10th — L R
40699	Robison	— T	40784	Royal Briton 11th — L R
40700	Rob Roy 3rd	— D	40785	Royal Briton 12th — R R
40701	Rockford Duke 3rd	P S	40786	Royal Briton 13th — R R
40702	Rockford Duke 4th	P S	40787	Royal Briton 14th — L R
40703	Rock River Lad 36th	— Cox	40790	Royal Chief — P S
40704	Rock River Lad 37th	M	40792	Royal Dick — Ky I
40705	Rock River Lad 38th	— Cox	40793	Royal Duke — Cox
40706	Rock River Lad 39th	— Cox	40794	Royal Duke — Cox
40707	Rock River Lad 40th	— Cox	40795	Royal Duke — P S
40708	Rock River Lad 41st	— Cox	40796	Royal Duke — M

40797	Royal Duke	— L R		40885	Scipio	— M
40798	Royal Duke	D		40886	Scipio	D
40799	Royal Duke	— M		40887	Scotsman	— R R
40800	Royal Duke	M		40890	Senator	— R R
40801	Royal Duke of Clarksville	— M		40891	Senator	Ky I
40802	2nd Royal Duke of Richland	— P S		40893	Senator	— T
40804	Royal Duke of Wadsworth	— L R		40894	Senator	— M
40806	Royal Elkhart	— Cox		40895	Senator	R R
40807	Royal Gem	— R R		40896	2nd Senator	— M
40808	Royal Gem 2nd	— Daisy		40897	Senator Bayard	Daisy
40810	Royal Grand Duke	— L R		40898	Senator of Waveland	— R R
40812	Royal Gwynne	Ky I		40901	Senor of Harmony	— M
40814	Royalist	Ky I		40902	Seventy-Three	— Cox
40815	Royalist 2nd	— Cox		40904	Seward Chief	P S
40816	Royalist 3rd	Cox		40905	Seymour	L R
40819	Royal Oakland 3rd	— M		40907	Shakespeare	— Cox
40821	Royal Peabody	M		40908	Shakespeare	— Ky I
40822	Royal Prince	D		40909	Shamrock	— M
40823	Royal Prince	R R		40910	Shamwalla	— M
40828	Royal Walker	C		40911	Shankland	— Cox
40829	Royal Williams	— Cox		40913	Sharon	M
40830	Rubicon	— Cox		40918	Sharon Duke	R R
40831	Ruby Duke	— R R		40919	Sharon Duke	Daisy
40832	Ruby's L'd Wiley of Maplewild	R R		40922	Sharon Duke of Kansas	— R R
40833	Ruby's Oxford	— M		40925	Sharon Prince	— R R
40834	Ruby's Prince	— L R		40926	Shelton	— Cox
40835	Rufus	— C		40927	Sheriff	— P S
40836	Rufus Bryant	— Long-Horn		40928	Sherman	P S
40837	Rupert	— M		40929	Sherman Duke	— L R
40839	Rustler	— T		40930	Short Head	— M
40840	Rutherford	— M		40933	Silver Bill	— D
40841	Saide's Duke	P S		40934	Silver Dale	— Cox
40842	Sagimon Chief	— P S		40935	Silver Dale	— Cox
40843	St. Anthony	M		40936	Simon	— T
40844	St. Clair	— Cox		40937	Simon's Duke	— D
40845	St. Elmo	— P S		40938	Sinclair	— R R
40847	St. Joe Chief	— D		40940	Sir Arthur	M
40848	St. John	— D		40941	Sir Henry	Ky I
40849	St. Julien	— R R		40942	Sir Henry	— L R
40850	St. Julien	— M		40943	Sir Henry	Ky I
40851	St. Lawrence	M		40944	Sir Henry	Ky I
40852	St. Nicholas	L R		40945	Sir Henry	— Long-Horn
40853	St. Patrick	— P S		40948	Sir Hugo	P S
40854	St. Valentine	M		40952	Sir Lawrence	— L R
40855	St. Valentine	Ky I		40953	Sir Leo	— L R
40856	St. Vincent	— M		40954	Sir Mack	— L R
40857	Salamander	— M		40955	Sirocco	— D
40858	Saline Lad	— D		40956	Sir Oscar	— M
40859	Sam	M		40959	Sir Robert Bruce	— M
40860	Sam	— Cox		40960	Sir Ruby of Maplewild	— R R
40861	Sam	— Ky I		40961	Sir Thomas	— R R
40862	Sam	P S		40963	Sir Walter	— L R
40863	Sambo	P S		40964	Sir Walter	P S
40864	Sambo	— L R		40965	Sir Walter	Ky I
40865	Sam Granger	M		40967	Sir William	— R R
40866	Sampson	— C		40968	Sir William	— R R
40867	Sampson	Ky I		40969	Sir William	— P S
40869	Sam Tilden	— M		40970	Sir Wm. Wallace	M
40870	Samuel	Ky I		40972	Sitting Bull	— M
40872	Sancho	— Cox		40973	Smith's Red Jacket	— P S
40873	Sankey	— M		40974	Snowball	— M
40874	Sanspariel Duke	— C		40976	Snowball	— Cox
40876	Santonine	D		40977	Snowball	— Cox
40877	Sarah 2nd's Duke	— Cox		40978	Snowball	— Cox
40878	Sarcoxie	— Cox		40981	Snowdrift	— L R
40879	Satelite 3rd	— M		40985	Sobieski	— Cox
40880	Sawyer	— Daisy		40986	Socrates	Ky I
40881	Saxon	— P S		40987	Solon	— Cox
40883	Schults	— M		40988	Solon 2nd	— R R
40884	Sciota Sharon	— R R		40989	Sonsie's Duke	— R R

No.	Name	Code	No.	Name	Code
40992	South Valley Duke	Ky I	41074	Tally Ho	— P S
40994	Spillman Ben Butler	— D	41075	Tamarack	— Ky I
40995	Spinogle	— M	41076	Tam O'Shanter	— P S
40996	Splendor	M	41077	Tam O'Shanter	— Cox
40997	Sportsman	Ky I	41082	Tebo	M
41000	Spring Brook A	— L R	41083	Tecumseh	— P S
41001	Spring Brook B	— L R	41084	Tecumseh	M
41002	Spring Brook C	— R R	41085	Tecumseh	P S
41003	Springfield Banker	L R	41088	Tempest Boy	M
41004	Springfield Duke	— M	41089	Tenbrœck	— R R
41005	Squire	— R R	41090	Testy	— Daisy
41007	Stair's Bull	— R R	41091	Texas Jack	— M
41008	Standard	— Ky I	41092	Thaddeus	— Cox
41009	Stanley	Ky I	41093	Thad Stevens	— P S
41010	Stanley	— Ky I	41095	The Boss	— L R
41011	Stanley	— R R	41096	The Boss	— Cox
41012	Stanley	M	41098	The Doctor	L R
41013	Star	— Long-Horn	41101	The Grand Sultan	— D
41014	Star	— Cox	41102	The Marshal	— P S
41015	Star	— Cox	41103	The Pirate	— Cox
41017	Star of Dana	T	41104	Thickset	L R
41018	Star Davis	P S	41105	Thompson	P S
41019	Star Duke	M	41107	Thorn Airdrie	M
41020	Star Duke	— Cox	41109	Thornton	— D
41021	Star of Hope	— Cox	41110	Tidy T	— M
41022	Starlight	L R	41111	Tiger of Milo	— Cox
41023	Starlight	— D	41112	Tilley's Duke	— M
41024	Starlight	Ky I	41113	Tilton 2nd	C
41025	2nd Star of Orange	— C	41114	Tim Bunker	P S
41026	Startler	— R R	41116	Tinker's Laddie	— Ky I
41027	Star of Tama	R R	41118	Tippecanoe	M
41028	Star of the West	Ky I	41119	Titus	— T
41029	Star of the West	P S	41120	Toby	T
41030	Star of Wetona	— Cox	41122	Tom	— L R
41031	Statesman	— P S	41123	Tom	Ky I
41032	Statesman	— R R	41124	Tom Boy	— R R
41033	Stephen	M	41125	Tom Buford	— M
41035	Stewart	L R	41126	Tom Corwin	— M
41036	Stewart's Duke 1st	M	41127	Tom Corwin	— Ky I
41037	Stock Farm Duke	M	41128	Tom Paine	P S
41038	Stoner 3rd	M	41130	Tom Valentine	D
41040	Stonewall	Ky I	41131	Tom Weston	— M
41041	Stonewall	M	41132	Tony Barmpton	— R R
41042	Stonewall	— L R	41134	Topliff	— Cox
41043	Stonewall of Cottonwood	— M	41135	Tornado	— R R
41044	Storm	— M	41136	Tornado	M
41045	Storm 3rd	M	41137	Tornado Chief	Cox
41047	Stunner	M	41138	Total Eclipse	— P S
41048	Styford	— M	41139	Tourgee	— D
41049	Subtility	— M	41140	Townsend Lad	— R R
41050	Success	L R	41141	Townley Gem, Jr	— R R
41052	Success	L R	41142	Trader	— Ky I
41053	Sugar Grove Boy	— D	41143	Tramp	M
41054	Sulky	— L R	41144	Tramp	T
41055	Sultan	— D	41145	Traveler	M
41057	Summit Duke of Springvale	— L R	41147	Triumph	— Cox
41058	Sunset	Ky I	41148	Triumph	— M
41059	Superb	— R R	41149	Troubadour Airdrie	— Ky I
41060	Superb	L R	41150	Tube Duke 3rd	— P S
41061	Surprise	— M	41151	Tube Duke 4th	— P S
41062	Surprise	Ky I	41154	Tuckaho	D
41063	Surveyor	Cox	41155	Turney Airdrie	M
41065	Swart's Duke of Springwood	— T	41156	Twin Boy	Ky I
41066	Sweepstakes	T	41157	Twin Star of Spring Grove	— P S
41067	Sweetcake Beaver	— Cox	41160	Uncas	— L R
41068	Sycamore	P S	41161	Uncle Sam	— M
41069	Sylvester of Maplewild	— M	41162	Uncle Sam	— M
41070	Symmetrys Breastplate	R R	41166	Uris	M
41071	Symmetry of Plumwood	M	41170	Valentine	— L R
41072	Talbot	— L R	41171	Valley Chief	— M

SHORT-HORN CATTLE PEDIGREES.

No.	Name	Code
41172	Valley Chief	D
41173	Valley Duke	— M
41174	Vampire	— M
41176	Vanderbilt 3rd	— D
41177	Vanderbilt of Plum Hollow	— D
41179	Van Stevens	M
41180	Van Wyck	M
41181	Vaulter	— D
41182	Velocipede	— Ky I
41187	Vermillion Prince 2nd	— P S
41188	Vermillion Prince 3rd	— Cox
41190	Vermont Boy	— Cox
41191	Vesper 2nd	— P S
41192	Vice Adam	M
41193	Vick	— L R
41194	Vicksburg	Cox
41196	Victor	Ky I
41197	Victor	— T
41198	Victor	— T
41199	Victor	R R
41200	Victor	R R
41201	Victor	Ky I
41202	Victor	— Cox
41203	Victor	— Cox
41204	Victor	Ky I
41205	Victor 2nd	— L R
41206	Victor A. of Maplewild	M
41207	Victor of Main Valley	L R
41213	Victoria's Pride	M
41214	Victorine's Prince	C
41216	Village	— P S
41219	Villa Nova Captain	— Cox
41221	Vinco Bright Eye	— M
41222	Vincent Keith	— D
41224	Volpone	— T
41226	Von Bismarck	— Cox
41227	Wabash	— M
41228	Wade Hampton	— P S
41231	Wade Hampton	— L R
41232	Walter Scott	L R
41233	Wanderer	L R
41234	Wappello Chief	— M
41235	Wapsie Duke	— R R
41236	Warfield	M
41237	Warlock	M
41238	Wasco	— M
41239	Washington	Ky I
41240	Washington Duke	— Ky I
41241	Washington	— M
41243	Washington Duke	— D
41244	Washington Duke 2nd	— Ky I
41245	Waterloo	— Cox
41250	Waterloo Prince	— Ky I
41251	Waterman 2nd	L R
41252	Waveland Duke	P S
41254	Weaver	M
41255	Weaver	— Daisy
41256	Wellington	P S
41259	Wellington	Ky I
41261	Wentworth 2nd	— L R
41263	Wesley Comet	M
41265	Western Duke	— M
41266	Weston Duke	— P S
41267	Western Lad	— D
41269	Westview Loudon	— M
41270	Whirlwind	C
41271	Whitefield Roan	— R R
41272	White Flauk	— M
41274	White Rover	Ky I
41275	White Star	— Ky I
41276	White Stockings	— L R
41277	White Stockings	— M
41278	Whitewater Lad	— M
41279	Whitewater Raspberry	— M
41280	Whoopsie	M
41281	Wild Eyes	M
41282	Wild Eyes	P S
41283	Wild Eyes of Armada	L R
41284	3rd Wild Eyes of Armada	L R
41287	Wild Eyes of Macomb	— Cox
41288	Wild Flower's Airdrie	— Cox
41289	Wild Flower's Duke	— Cox
41290	Wildwood Airdrie 5th	— M
41295	Wiley Oxford 13th	— P S
41296	Wiley Oxford 16th	M
41297	Wiley Oxford 17th	M
41298	Wiley Oxford 20th	P S
41299	Wiley Oxford 21st	P S
41300	Will Cody	M
41301	William Johnson	— Ky I
41302	Willow Wood A.	R R
41303	Wilton	— R R
41304	Wilton Duke	— P S
41305	Windom	— M
41306	Winfield	L R
41307	Winfield Scott	M
41308	Winfield Scott	— L R
41309	Winnebago	L R
41310	Winneshiek	— M
41315	Witch Major	— R R
41318	Wonder	— R R
41319	Woodbury Chief	— R R
41320	Woodland Duke	— M
41321	Woodland Duke	— M
41322	Woodlawn Mazurka	— P S
41323	Woolworth Duke	— P S
41324	Wooly Duke	— R R
41325	Worthy Chief	— M
41326	Wyatt	— Cox
41327	Yak	— M
41329	Yankee Sam	— L R
41331	Yankton	— P S
41332	Yaropolk	— D
41333	Yellow Rover	— M
41334	Yeoman	— L R
41336	Young Alex	Ky I
41337	Young Almont	D
41338	Young America	— T
41339	Young America	Cox
41340	2nd Young America	L R
41341	Young Aristocrat	— R R
41342	Young Athelstan	— M
41343	Young Baron	— R R
41346	Young Brigham	— M
41347	Young Brutus	— R R
41350	Young Clement	R R
41351	Young Duke	Ky I
41352	Young Duke	T
41353	Young Duke of Moundale	— L R
41354	Young Florestan	— Long-Horn
41355	Young Forester	L R
41357	Young General	— Ky I
41358	Young Giant	— M
41360	Young Ivanhoe	— T
41361	Young Knight	Cox
41362	Young Mary's Prince	— R R
41365	Young Oliver	— D
41367	Young Prince	Cox
41368	Young Prince	— M
41369	Young Red Jacket	— D

41370	Young Renick — R R	41515	3rd Berthold — P S
41371	Young Richard — D	41516	Billy — P S
41372	Young Rosy Man T	41517	Billy Boy Ky I
41373	Young Sandusky — D	41519	Billy King R R
41374	Young Senator — P S	41520	Billy Patterson — M
41376	Zeb T	41521	Billy Rocket L R
41378	Zeno — M	41522	Billy Taylor — Woods
41382	Zora's Duke — R R	41524	Bismarck Ky I
41383	Zoroaster — P S	41525	Bismarck — L R
41384	Zulu Chief — P S	41526	Bismarck Chief — P S
41428	Admiral of Melleray — M	41527	Black Hawk Boy T
41430	2nd Airdrie Bully Boy M	41528	Blanchard — D
41431	4th Airdrie Bully Boy M	41529	Blanco D
41432	5th Airdrie Bully Boy M	41530	Blanco P S
41435	Airdrie Lad — M	41531	Blanco — L R
41436	Airdrie Orphan Boy M	41532	Blucher — C
41437	Airdrie of Pleasant Hill — Cox	41533	Blyth — M
41440	Airdrie Royal 2nd D	41534	Bob — M
41443	Alddin M	41535	Bob Ingersoll D
41444	Albert — Ky I	41536	Bodie Ky I
41445	Aledo Duke — M	41538	Bonanza — D
41446	Alex M	41539	Bonny Bird — M
41447	Alexander — P S	41540	Bonny Duke — Cox
41448	Alixis — Cox	41541	Bonny Earl — Cox
41449	Alton — L R	41542	Boreas 2nd — L R
41451	Anoka Boy — R R	41545	Bourbon Prince 2nd — R R
41452	Archibald Cox	41546	Boxer P S
41453	Argonaut — M	41547	Bracelet's Duke — R R
41455	Arnold M	41550	Brayton — Cox
41456	Arthur — D	41552	Brides 3rd Duke — R R
41457	Arthur — M	41553	Bride's Gem 2nd — R R
41458	Arthur Hook Ky I	41554	Bright Eyes — M
41461	Audubon Ky I	41556	Bristol — L R
41462	A. W. Moore M	41557	Bristol Charley — P S
41463	Babraham's Duke of Oxford — Cox	41558	Bristow — D
41464	Babraham's Roan Duke — L R	41559	British Louanjo — R R
41466	Badger Boy — M	41560	Broken Horn — R R
41467	Barbecue P S	41562	Bruce — Long-Horn
41469	Barney — M	41563	Bruno L R
41471	Barney King — Ky I	41564	Bruere's Hope — R R
41472	Baron Ky I	41565	Brutus — M
41473	Baron M	41567	Buchanan — R R
41475	Baron Bates of Melleray — R R	41568	Buckeye — Cox
41477	Baron Grenville — D	41569	Buckeye Boy — D
41481	Baron Louanjo's Duplicate M	41570	Buckeye Minor — P S
41484	Baron May 2nd — D	41571	Bummer 2nd — M
41485	Baron Oxford 3rd — C	41572	Buncombe P S
41488	Baron Sheffielder — M	41573	Burdette P S
41490	Baron Wadsworth 7th Cox	41574	Burgoo P S
41491	Baron William 2nd — R R	41575	Busby P S
41492	Bascom P S	41578	Bushwhacker — Cox
41493	Bascom — L R	41579	Cadwallader — L R
41494	Bates 2nd — M	41580	Calhoun — R R
41495	Beau Plain — Ky I	41581	Calmar — P S
41496	Beaver Duke 2nd — P S	41582	Cambria Duke 4th — R R
41497	Beaver Lad — R R	41583	Cambria's Duke 10th — R R
41498	Beecher — P S	41587	Capt. Gillespie — M
41499	Belina Bull — M	41588	Capt. Highland P S
41500	Belina Bull 2nd — M	41589	Capt. Jack L R
41502	Bell Duke of Elkhart D	41590	Capt. Jack, Junior Ky I
41503	4th Bell Duke of Elkhart D	41591	Capt. Jenks — P S
41504	Bell Duke of Ridott — R R	41592	Capt. Leigh — Cox
41506	Belmont Ky I	41593	Capt. 2nd of Richland — P S
41508	Ben Adams D	41594	Capt. Taylor — Cox
41509	Ben Bolt — M	41595	Capt. Upright — M
41510	Ben Davis — P S	41597	Cash Down T
41511	Ben Franklin — Long-Horn	41599	Centennial Chief — D
41512	Ben Love — M	41600	Cetewayo — L R
41513	Benton Ky I	41601	Champaign Duke 2nd — P S
41514	Bernard Duke 2nd — M	41602	Champion L R

SHORT-HORN CATTLE PEDIGREES.

No.	Name	Mark
41603	Challinger	— M
41604	Charlie	— Ky I
41605	Charmer	— T
41606	Chatham	— M
41607	Chatham's Duke	— P S
41608	Chief Joseph	— D
41609	Chief Looking Glass	— D
41610	Chief of Oakland	— R R
41611	Chief Tecumseh	— M
41612	Chief White Bird	— Cox
41613	Cherry's Duke	Ky I
41614	Cherry Duke	— P S
41615	Cherry Duke	— P S
41616	Christmas Duke	— D
41618	Chub	— L R
41620	Clay Duke	— M
41621	Clay Gem	P S
41623	Clifton	— M
41624	Clifton	— R R
41626	Clovis	Cox
41629	Colonel	— Long-Horn
41630	Col. Crittenden	— M
41631	Col. Goshen	— M
41632	Col. Lothrop	— M
41633	Col. Napier 3rd	M
41634	Col. Norris	Ky I
41635	Col. Younger	Ky I
41636	Colorado	Cox
41638	Commodore	Ky I
41639	Comet	P S
41644	Conger	— M
41645	Conklin	P S
41646	Conqueror Chief	— P S
41647	Constable	M
41650	Convenience	— R R
41651	Conway Duke	— Ky I
41652	Corporal 8th	— Ky I
41653	Corporal Dick	— R R
41654	Cottrell Duke	Cox
41655	Councellor	— M
41656	Count Fosco	— M
41658	Count of Lebanon	P S
41659	Count of Magenta	— M
41660	9th Count of Oneida	— R R
41661	Count of Oxford	M
41662	Courtney	— Cox
41663	Cow Boy	— R R
41664	Cromwell	— Cox
41668	Cundiff's Duke	— M
41669	Cypress Duke 2nd	— Long-Horn
41670	Czar	— Cox
41671	Czar	— P S
41672	Czar of Sunnyside	— P S
41674	Daisy Lad	— L R
41676	Dalton Chief	— L R
41678	Dandy Pat	D
41679	Dan Kirwan	Ky I
41680	Dan Rice	M
41681	Daniel Flinn	— D
41682	Daniel Y	P S
41686	Dashing Dandy	— M
41687	Dave	— M
41688	David	— L R
41690	Dayton 2nd	— P S
41691	Deacon	— Long-Horn
41692	Deacon Joseph	Cox
41693	DeKalb	— M
41694	Delphos	— Long-Horn
41695	Demit	— P S
41697	Desha Duke	— Daisy
41698	Dexter Butterfly	Daisy
41700	Diamond	— L R
41701	Diamond 2nd	— L R
41702	Diamond Hill	— M
41703	Dick Long	— D
41704	Dick Renick	— D
41706	Dick Turpin	Ky I
41707	Dime	— Long-Horn
41709	Doctor	— M
41710	Doctor	— M
41711	Doctor of Labette	— D
41712	Doctor Luckett	— M
41713	Doctor Mazurka	— M
41714	Doctor Oakland	— M
41715	Doctor Prue	— M
41716	Doctor Robison	— L R
41718	Dom Pedro	— Cox
41719	Dom Pedro	— M
41720	Dom Pedro	— L R
41721	Don Carlos	— R R
41722	Donald Wiley	P S
41723	Don Sancho	— R R
41724	Don Juan of Livingston	— Ky I
41725	Donald	Cox
41726	Double Rosy Duke	— P S
41727	Douglas Dick	Ky I
41728	Duchess Duke	— R R
41730	Duchess Loudon Duke 4th	— R R
41731	Duchess Loudon Duke 5th	— T
41732	Duchess Loudon Duke 6th	— T
41733	Duck	— M
41737	Duke of Afton	L R
41738	Duke of Allen 2nd	— R R
41740	10th Duke of Ashland	— M
41742	Duke of Barry	— R R
41743	Duke of Bartondale	— Cox
41744	Duke of Benton	Cox
41745	2nd Duke of Benton	— T
41746	Duke of Brownsville	— R R
41749	2nd Duke of Cascade	L R
41752	Duke of Chautauqua	— L R
41753	Duke of Clayton	— L R
41754	Duke of Clinton	— M
41755	Duke of Compton	L R
41756	Duke of Cool Spring	M
41757	2nd Duke of Cool Spring	— M
41758	Duke of Corning	— R R
41760	Duke of Darby	— M
41761	Duke of Earl	— Cox
41762	Duke of Edinburg	— Cox
41764	Duke of Elmwood 3rd	— M
41765	Duke of Emmaton	Ky I
41766	Duke Fabius	Ky I
41767	Duke of Fraser 3rd	L R
41768	17th Duke of Glenflora	— R R
41769	Duke of Glenora	— Cox
41770	5th Duke of Glenwood	— Cox
41772	Duke of Greendale	— L R
41773	1st Duke of Grimsby	— D
41774	Duke of Groveland	— L R
41775	Duke Gwynne	— Cox
41776	Duke Gwynne	— Cox
41777	Duke of Hackberry	— Ky I
41778	Duke of Hancock	— P S
41779	11th Duke of Harlem	M
41780	17th Duke of Harlem	T
41781	18th Duke of Harlem	D
41782	Duke of Harrisburg	M
41783	Duke of Harrison	M
41784	5th Duke of Hazelhurst	— R R

No.	Name	Code		No.	Name	Code
41785	Duke of Hickory Grove 4th	— T		41883	4th Earl of Willow Street	— T
41788	Duke of Honeycreek	— T		41884	6th Earl of Willow Street	— T
41789	Duke of Honor	M		41885	7th Earl of Willow Street	T
41790	Duke of Hoosic	Cox		41886	Easter Bell's Wiley	— M
41791	Duke of Jackson	— Cox		41887	Easter Duke	— P S
41793	Duke of Jessamine	— M		41888	Echo	L R
41794	Duke of John	— M		41889	Edbrun Lad	L R
41795	Duke of Joy	— M		41891	Elba	L R
41800	Duke of Knox	M		41892	Elder	— Long-Horn
41801	Duke of Lafayette	— M		41893	Ellsworth	— L R
41805	Duke of Liberty	— L R		41895	Emperor	— M
41806	2nd Duke of Liberty	P S		41896	Emperor	— M
41807	2nd Duke of Lima	— L R		41897	Emperor	— M
41808	Duke of Linkville	— M		41898	Engineer	Ky I
41809	Duke Lookout	— M		41899	English	— D
41810	Duke of Loudon	D		41900	Ensign	— M
41811	Duke of Maplewood	M		41902	Equinox	— D
41812	Duke of Marengo	T		41903	Ernesty	P S
41813	Duke of Monterey	— R R		41905	Exemption	— Cox
41814	Duke of Muskingum	M		41906	Expectation	— P S
41815	3rd Duke of Newham	— M		41907	Extra	— M
41816	Duke of Noble County	D		41908	Fairholme Triumph	— L R
41817	Duke of Oakland	— D		41910	Fanny's Heir	— T
41818	Duke of Oldenburg	T		41911	Fannie's Prince	— P S
41819	Duke of Oxford	— Cox		41913	Fashion's Loudon Duke	— D
41820	Duke of Pearl Blossom 3rd	— R R		41914	Favorite	M
41822	Duke of Pleasant Lane	— P S		41915	Favorite	— C
41823	Duke of Pleasant View	— R R		41916	Favorite	— D
41824	3rd Duke of Putney	— Cox		41918	Ferdinand	L R
41825	Duke of Ravenna	— Cox		41919	Fidget's Hubback	— Cox
41826	Duke Renick	— R R		41920	Filagree Gem 9th	— R R
41828	Duke of Richland	— P S		41921	Fillmore	— T
41829	2nd Duke of Richland	— Cox		41923	Flora's Gloster	— M
41830	10th Duke of Ridgeland	— L R		41924	Forest Duke 2nd	— L R
41831	8th Duke of Ridgevale	— L R		41925	Fortune	— Ky I
41832	5th Duke of Rio	— P S		41926	Frank Adams	— Cox
41833	6th Duke of Rio	— P S		41927	Frank Barmpton	— R R
41834	7th Duke of Rio	— P S		41928	Frank Clay	M
41836	Duke of Rock	— L R		41929	Frank Forrester	— D
41837	Duke of Rome	M		41930	Frank Hall	— D
41839	Duke of Saginaw	Cox		41931	Frank Shepherd	T
41840	Duke of Second Creek	— R R		41932	Fred	— M
41842	Duke of Sheridan	Ky I		41933	Fred	— P S
41843	Duke of Spencer	— Cox		41934	Frederick	— L R
41844	2nd Duke of Springbrook	L R		41935	Freeville 2nd	— Cox
41845	Duke of Sugar Grove	— M		41936	Gaffer Green	— M
41847	Duke of Swan Creek	— M		41937	Garfield	M
41848	4th Duke of Townsend	M		41939	Garfield	— D
41849	Duke of Walnut	— M		41940	Garfield	— Cox
41850	Duke of Walnut Grove	— P S		41941	Garfield	R R
41853	Duke of Wayne	— Cox		41942	Garfield	— M
41854	Duke of Wellington	P S		41943	Garfield	Ky I
41855	Duke of Westmoreland	— D		41944	Garfield	— D
41856	Duke of Wheatland	— D		41945	Garfield	— Long-Horn
41860	Duke of Yates 28th	— Cox		41946	Garfield	M
41861	Duke of York	D		41947	Garfield	P S
41863	Duncan	— L R		41951	Gems Optimus	— Cox
41864	1st Earl of Bowne	— Cox		41953	Gen. Custer	P S
41865	Earl of Calumet	— R R		41956	Gen. Garfield	— Cox
41867	Earl of Compton	L R		41957	Gen. Garfield	— L R
41870	Earl of Dryden	Cox		41959	Gen. Garfield	— R R
41871	4th Earl of Grass Hill	— Cox		41961	Gen. Grant	— D
41872	Earl of Jackson	D		41962	Gen. Grant	Cox
41874	Earl of Melleray	— P S		41963	Gen. Grant	— C
41875	Earl of Oxford	— Cox		41964	Gen. Grant	— L R
41878	3rd Earl of Shopiere	M		41965	Gen. Grant	— R R
41879	5th Earl of Springdale	Cox		41967	Gen. Grant	— M
41880	6th Earl of Springlake	— L R		41968	Gen. Hancock	— T
41881	Earl of Encinal	M		41969	Gen. Hancock	L R
41882	Earl of White Pigeon	— P S		41970	Gen. Hancock	L R

SHORT-HORN CATTLE PEDIGREES.

No.	Name	Code
41972	Gen. Hooker	— M
41975	Gen. Logan	— D
41976	Gen. Mahone	L R
41977	Gen. Otley	— D
41978	Gen. Sherman	— R R
41979	Gen. Snowdon	Ky I
41981	Gen. Washington	— M
41982	Gen. Weaver	— D
41983	Gen. Weaver	M
41984	Geneva	Cox
41987	Geneva Lad of Willow Park	— M
41988	Geneva Lad of Willow Park 2nd	— M
41991	Geordie	— L R
41992	George Grimes	— P S
41994	Gigas	— D
41995	Glen	— L R
41996	6th Glen Count	M
41997	Gloster	— M
41999	Gloster Boy	— Cox
42000	Golden Duke	Ky I
42001	Golden Louanjo	— Cox
42002	Goldfinder	Cox
42003	Goodness	Ky I
42005	Gov. Culman	— M
42006	Gov. Foster	— R R
42008	Gov. Palmer	— M
42009	Gov. Porter	— T
42010	Gov. Potts	— D
42011	Gov. Tilden	— Cox
42012	Gov. Tilden	— M
42014	Grand Duke	L R
42015	Grand Duke of Goodness 2nd	— T
42016	Grand Duke of Goodness 3rd	— M
42017	Grand Duke of Highlands	— M
42019	2nd Grand Prince of Claro	— R R
42021	Grassland's Monarch	— R R
42024	Greeley	— M
42025	Grouty Duke	T
42026	Grundy	Ky I
42027	Grundy Duke	T
42028	Gumbo	— P S
42029	Half Moon	— M
42032	Hamlin	T
42033	Hancock	— D
42034	Hancock	— Cox
42035	Hancock	— M
42036	Hancock	— M
42037	Hancock Duke	P S
42038	Hankins Loudon Duke 4th	— R R
42039	Hanlan	— Cox
42040	Hannibal	T
42043	Harold	— R R
42044	Harrison Woods	— M
42045	Hays' Duke	Ky I
42046	Hector 7th	— M
42047	Hedge Row Duke	— L R
42048	Helianthus	— Cox
42049	Helmet	— P S
42051	Henrietta's Duke	M
42052	Henry	M
42053	Henry Cisco	— P S
42054	Henry's Duke 4th	L R
42055	Henry Franklin	L R
42056	Hercules	— R R
42057	Herkimer Chief	— L R
42059	Hero of Milleray	— M
42060	Highland Richard	— R R
42061	Highland Richard 2nd	— R R
42064	Holt	— M
42066	Honest John	Ky I
42067	Honest Tom	— L R
42068	Hoosic 2nd	Cox
42069	Hopefull	— L R
42071	Houghton	L R
42072	Hubback	— Cox
42073	4th Hubback	— M
42075	Hugh Custer	L R
42077	Humpty Dumpty	— Cox
42078	H. W. Beecher	— D
42079	Ike	— P S
42080	Imperial Duke	— Cox
42082	Imperial Oxford 2nd	P S
42084	Independence	— Cox
42085	Independence	— L R
42086	Independence	— Cox
42089	Ionia Goldfinder	— R R
42090	Iowa Chief	Daisy
42091	Iowa President	D
42092	Iroquois	— T
42094	Italian Duke	— Cox
42095	Jack	— Cox
42096	Jack Frost	— P S
42097	Jack Hayes	— R R
42098	Jack Lee	— P S
42099	Jack Rabbit	— L R
42100	Jacob Clay	L R
42101	Jacob of Hazelhurst	Daisy
42102	Jacobus	P S
42103	Jake	M
42104	James A	Cox
42105	James A	— Cox
42106	James A. Garfield	— P S
42107	James McHenry	— R R
42109	Jay Gould	— D
42110	Jerome	L R
42112	Jerome	— Ky I
42113	Jeweller	— Cox
42115	Jim Garfield	— R R
42116	Jim Garfield	Ky I
42117	Joaquin	— L R
42118	Joe Barmpton	— R R
42119	Joe Blackburn	L R
42121	Joe Hall	— Cox
42122	Joel Dexter	P S
42123	Joel Red	P S
42124	John	— R R
42125	John Barmpton	— R R
42126	John Barnum 2nd	L R
42127	John Bradley	Ky I
42128	John Bright 2nd	M
42129	John L.	— C
42130	John Monegan	M
42131	Joseph Clay	L R
42132	Josh Ward	Ky I
42134	Judge Burton	Ky I
42135	Judge Duncan	— R R
42136	Judge Parkinson	— R R
42139	Junius	— M
42140	Jupiter	Ky I
42141	Juno	— R R
42143	Kentucky Duke	— R R
42145	King Lear	T
42147	King Richard	— C
42148	King of Trumps	P S
42149	King Victor	Cox
42151	King William	— P S
42156	Lady's Duke	M
42159	Lauras Oxford	— T
42162	Leonard's Duke	— M
42163	Lexington	M

42164	Liberator	— T	42262	Neptune	Cox
42165	Liddie's Duke	— M	42263	Neptune Boy	Cox
42166	Lieutenant	— L R	42264	Newton	— R R
42167	Lill's Veto	— P S	42265	Niles Oxford	Daisy
42169	Lindsay	L R	42267	Nora	— Cox
42170	Linn Duke	P S	42268	Norwich Chief	D
42171	Little Bloomfield	— D	42269	Norwood 2nd	— P S
42172	Little Jack	— M	42270	Nota Bena	Cox
42173	Logan	— M	42271	Numa B	— L R
42174	Lord Baltimore 5th	T	42272	Oakland Duke	— M
42175	Lord Beresford	— Woods	42273	Oakland Lad 20th	— R R
42177	Lord Balmahay	— R R	42274	Oakwood	— Cox
42183	Lord Mayor	— M	42275	Odell	— D
42187	Lord Roscoe	D	42276	Oenanthe's Duke	— R R
42192	Lord York 3rd	— M	42277	Ole Bull	— R R
42193	Louan's Loudon Duke	— R R	42279	Onarga Prince	R R
42194	Loudon Clark 2nd	R R	42280	Oneida Junior	— Cox
42195	Loudon Duke 34th	— R R	42281	5th Oneida Duke of Melleray,	— R R
42197	Louis B	Ky I	42282	6th Oneida Duke of Melleray,	— R R
42198	Lowland Comet	— L R	42285	Orient	— R R
42199	Lucifer	— P S	42287	Oronte's Duke 2nd	— R R
42200	Lyman	Ky I	42288	Orphan Boy	— P S
42201	Lynn Lad	— R R	42289	Orphan Boy	M
42203	Major	— D	42290	Oshkosh	— Cox
42204	Major Bagstock	— C	42291	Otoe Chief	— P S
42206	Major Case	Cox	42292	Otley	Daisy
42207	Major Dill	M	42293	Oxford	L R
42208	Major Forest	— R R	42294	Oxford Cherub 13th	— M
42209	Major Jupiter	— R R	42295	Oxford Cherub 14th	— T
42210	Malcom Moss	Ky I	42296	Oxford Cherub 15th	M
42211	Marc Antony	M	42297	Oxford Cherub 16th	M
42212	Marius	— D	42299	Oxford Goodness	M
42213	Mark	— R R	42300	Oxford Gwynne	— Cox
42214	Mark Twain	M	42301	Oxford Gwynne 3rd	— Cox
42215	Marquette	L R	42303	Oxford J. 2nd	— M
42216	Marquis	— L R	42306	Oxford of Saline	— P S
42218	2nd Marquis of Blue Mound	M	42307	Oxford Sharon	— D
42219	Marquis of Lorne	— M	42308	Oxford's Sovereign	— R R
42220	Marquis of Melleray	— P S	42309	12th Oxford of Vermillion	— R R
42221	Marshal Maison	M	42310	Oxonian	— Cox
42222	Marshal Neil	L R	42311	Palmyra Duke	— L R
42223	Marshal Ney	— Cox	42312	Paris	— C
42224	Martin	Ky I	42313	Parole	— M
42225	Marvel	Cox	42315	Peach Hill	P S
42226	Mary's Duke 2nd	— R R	42316	Peach Hill 3rd	P S
42228	May's Breastplate	— M	42317	Pearl Duke	— T
42229	May Duke	Ky I	42325	Pertilla	— M
42230	May Duke	Ky I	42328	Phyllis' Oxford	— M
42231	May Duke	— M	42329	Piasa Bird	Cox
42232	Mayflower Grand Duke	— Cox	42330	Pilot	P S
42234	Mazurka Lad 3rd	— T	42331	Pilot 2nd	Ky I
42235	Mazurka's Oxford 21st	M	42332	Pine Hill Lad A	— D
42236	Mazurkas Oxford 24th	D	42333	Plato	Ky I
42237	Mazurkas Oxford 31st	Ky I	42334	Plato of Maine Valley	L R
42239	Menelaus	D	42335	Plumboy	— L R
42241	Milo	— M	42336	P. M. Lindsay	D
42242	Minneapolis	L R	42337	Pompey	— M
42243	Modoc	— M	42338	Pope	— M
42244	Modoc Chief 3rd	M	42339	Porter Prince	— Long-Horn
42245	Monitor	— C	42340	Pownal	— M
42246	Montana Lad	— Cox	42341	Prairie Chief	— Cox
42247	Montgomery Chief	— R R	42342	Prairie Duke	P S
42248	Montgomery Prince	— R R	42343	Premier	— R R
42249	Montcalm	— L R	42344	President Clay	L R
42252	Mortimer	Ky I	42345	President Garfield	Cox
42254	Moscow	— C	42346	President of Melleray	— R R
42255	Moses	— L R	42347	Priam	Ky I
42256	Moses	— M	42349	Prince	— Cox
42258	Napoleon	— L R	42350	Prince	— M
42261	Nellie's Cossack	— L R	42352	Prince	— L R

42353	Prince Albert	— D		42444	Red Rover	— M
42354	Prince Albert	Ky I		42445	Red Sheriff	— P S
42355	Prince of Aragon	T		42446	13th Red Thorndale	M
42356	Prince of Aragon 2nd	T		42447	Red Veto	P S
42357	Prince of Aragon 3rd	T		42448	Red Wiley 2nd	T
42358	Prince of Aragon 4th	T		42449	Reel Foot	— R R
42363	Prince Arthur	— Ky I		42450	Reform	— R R
42366	Prince Barmpton 3rd	— R R		42451	Regent	M
42367	Prince of Barrington	Cox		42452	Regular	— D
42368	Prince of Cedar Creek	T		42453	Regulator	— D
42369	Prince Chatham	M		42454	Remus	P S
42370	Prince of Columbus	— Cox		42455	Restless	— P S
42371	Prince of Denver	— R R		42456	Reveler 2nd	— M
42372	Prince Ellington	— P S		42457	Rex	Ky I
42373	Prince George	L R		42459	Richland	— Ky I
42374	Prince George 2nd	— R R		42461	Riverdale Booth	— Daisy
42375	Prince Goodness	— R R		42462	Roan Duke	— R R
42376	Prince Imperial	L R		42463	Roan Duke	— M
42377	Prince Joe	L R		42464	Roan Duke	Cox
42378	Prince John	— Ky I		42469	Roan Garfield	— M
42379	Prince Leboo	— Ky I		42470	Roan Prince	T
42382	Prince Malone 2nd	— Cox		42471	Roan Prince 2nd	— P S
42383	Prince of Melleray	— R		42472	Robert	— C
42385	Prince of New Auburn	— D		42473	Robert The Bruce	Cox
42386	Prince of Oak Grove	— M		42474	Rock Maple	— M
42390	4th Prince of Riverdale	— R R		42475	Rollin	M
42391	5th Prince of Riverdale	— R R		42476	Romeo	— D
42392	Prince Rudolph	— M		42477	Romeo	— M
42393	Prince of Valley Farm	Ky I		42478	Romeo	— R R
42395	Prince of Wales	Ky I		42479	Rosy Duke	— R R
42396	Prince of Wales	— Cox		42480	Rose Duke	— M
42397	Prince of Walnut Grove	M		42484	Rose's Lexington	— R R
42398	Prince of Waverly	— T		42485	Roses	P S
42399	Prince Williams	P S		42487	Ross Hammond	T
42401	Proctor Chief	P S		42492	Royal Commander	— R R
42402	Promise	M		42493	Royal Commander 2nd	M
42404	Queen's Breastplate 4th	— M		42494	Royal Duke	— L R
42405	Queen's Duke	M		42496	Royal Oxford	L R
42406	Queen's Duke	P S		42497	Royal Prince of Cass	— L R
42407	Queen's Kirklevington	M		42498	Russell	— M
42408	Queen's Reformer	P S		42499	Sailor	— M
42409	Racine	L R		42500	Sailor 2nd	— M
42411	Rattler	— Woods		42501	Saint Julian	Daisy
42412	Red Bill	Ky I		42502	Saint Julian	— P S
42413	Red Bill	— Ky I		42504	Saline Breadalbane	M
42414	Red Ben	Ky I		42505	Sam Hill	Ky I
42415	Red Boy	— M		42507	Sam Weller	— Cox
42417	Red Cloud	— L R		42508	San Antonio	Ky I
42418	Red Cloud	Cox		42509	Schorcher	— D
42419	Red Cloud	— R R		42510	Scottie Hillhurst	— M
42420	Red Cloud	— D		42511	Senator	— R R
42421	Red Diamond	— M		42513	Sharon Airdrie	— P S
42422	Red Dick	— Cox		42514	Sharon Duke	— R R
42423	Red Dick	— R R		42515	Sharon Duke	— R R
42424	Red Duke	— T		42516	Sharon Lad	— R R
42426	Red Duke	— P S		42517	Shelby Duke	M
42427	Red Hero	— R R		42518	Sheldon	— M
42428	Red Jacket	— P S		42519	Sherman	— Ky I
42429	Red Jacket	— R R		42520	Shirley's Airdrie	M
42430	Red Jacket	— L R		42523	Sigma	Ky I
42431	Red Jackson	— D		42524	Signet	— C
42432	Red King	Ky I		42525	Silverdale	— Cox
42433	Red Knight	L R		42526	Sim	— M
42434	Red Light	— R R		42527	Simon's Duke	— D
42435	Red Lion	M		42529	Sir Archie	— M
42437	Red Lion	— L R		42530	Sir Charles	— D
42438	Red River	— Cox		42531	Sir George	— M
42439	Red Rose Duke	— C		42533	Sir Henry of Empire	— D
42442	Red Rover	M		42534	Sir Henry of Empire 2nd	— D
42443	Red Rover	— L R		42536	Sir Thomas	— D

14

42587	Sir Walter	Cox
42589	Sky Lad	— R R
42540	Solon Chase	— M
42541	Son of Baron Bates 4th	— M
42542	Sophie's Duke	— L R
42544	Sparta Bill	— L R
42545	Spartan	— Woods
42546	Sportsman	Ky I
42547	Spotted Bill	L R
42549	Stalwart Duke	P S
42550	Star City Duke	— M
42551	Star City Duke 3rd	— Wrong
42552	Star City Lad	— M
42553	Star of Crane Valley	M
42554	Star Duke	Ky I
42555	Star Duke	Ky I
42556	Star Duke	— C
42557	Star of The Evening	L R
42559	Stately Hero 2nd	— Cox
42560	Stillwater Lad	— Cox
42561	Stonewall	— R R
42562	Success	M
42563	Success	— Cox
42565	Sultan	— L R
42566	Sultan 2nd	— Cox
42567	Sunlight	M
42568	Superb of Waveland	— P S
42569	Superior	— P S
42570	Sweepstakes of Locke	— L R
42573	Tamerlane	M
42574	Taurus Wiley	— R R
42578	Tempest	— M
42579	Templar	— L R
42582	Thomas Carlisle	L R
42583	Thomas Scott	— T
42585	Thompson's Airdrie	— R R
42590	Titus	— M
42591	Tobias Martin	Ky I
42593	Tom Cyrus	P S
42594	Tom Dowley 2nd	— L R
42595	Tom Platt	L R
42596	Tom Wallace	P S
42597	Tonga 3rd	— L R
42598	Tramp	T
42600	Trout	— D
42601	Turk	Ky I
42603	Turk	— P S
42605	Tutl	— R R
42606	Tycoon	— D
42607	Tyrone	L R
42609	Ulysses G	— Ky I
42611	Valley Duke 3rd	— M
42613	2nd Vandal	— T
42614	Veto 2nd	P S
42615	Victor Hugo	— M
42616	Victor Leo	M
42619	Waco	— D
42620	Wade Hampton	Ky I
42622	Wahkonsa Duke	— Cox
42623	Wahkonsa Duke 2nd	— Cox
42624	Wahnita's Duke	— R R
42625	Walker	Ky I
42627	Walnut Duke	— M
42628	Wapello Chief	— P S
42629	Warden Nabes	T
42630	War Eagle	— Cox
42631	Warren Stone	— Cox
42632	Washington Sharon	— R R
42637	Western	— Cox
42638	Westfield	— M
42639	White Boy	Cox
42640	White Stockings	L R
42642	2nd Wild Eyes of Armada	L R
42643	Wildwood	— R R
42644	Wiley Oxford 19th	— P S
42645	Wilkie	— D
42647	Willamette Chief	P S
42648	Will Johnson	— M
42649	Will Sibert	— P S
42650	Winneshiek Chief	— M
42653	Yaricon	— R R
42654	Young Baron 2nd	L R
42655	Young Duke	— M
42656	Young Duke	— M
42657	Young Dimple	— D
42658	Young Liberty	— D
42662	Young Prince	— D
42663	Young Reveler	— M
42664	Young Reveler 2nd	— M
42665	Young Reveler 3rd	— M
42666	Young Reveler 4th	— M
42667	Young Reveler 5th	— M
42668	Young Reveler 6th	— M
42669	Young Senator	— M
42670	Young Woodford	— R R
42671	Zechin of Fairland	L R
42672	Zero	— C
42676	Abidan	— P S
42677	Abner	— L R
42678	Abraham	— Cox
42680	Achilles	— M
42681	Achilles	Cox
42684	Adam A	M
42685	Add	— R R
42686	Addison Boy	— Cox
42688	Adonis	— R R
42689	Ad Sanders	— R R
42690	Affleck	— M
42691	Agnes' Oxford	— L R
42692	Alja Duke	Ky I
42696	Airdrie Belle	— P S
42697	Airdrie Bird	P S
42700	Airdrie Duke of Belleville	— Cox
42703	Airdrie Duke of Springvale	— L R
42704	Airdrie D. of Springvale 2nd	— L R
42707	Airdrie Hawkins	— T
42710	Airdrie Mason	— R R
42711	Airdrie's Peabody	M
42713	Airdrie Royal 2nd	D
42714	Airdrie of Saline	— P S
42717	Ajax Prince	— L R
42718	Alaric	— L R
42719	Alaska	— L R
42720	Albert	— Cox
42721	Albert	— D
42722	Albert 2nd	— D
42723	Albion 2nd	— Cox
42724	Albion 2nd	— L R
42725	Albion Nero	D
42726	Albolio	— Daisy
42729	Alexander	— L R
42733	Alpheus	— M
42734	Alphonso	— R R
42735	Alvin	— Cox
42736	Amanda Pierce's Oxford	C
42738	American	— Cox
42740	Anderson Minott	— P S
42742	Andrew Johnson	— M
42743	Andy Day	— M
42744	Andy Wise	M

SHORT-HORN CATTLE PEDIGREES.

42745	Annie's Climax	— R R
42747	Anthony Comstock of Lost Ranch	— M
42748	Apollo	— M
42750	Archie Moonlight	— P S
42751	Argus	— P S
42752	Aristides	— L R
42753	Armada	L R
42754	Armstrong	— L R
42755	Arnold's Duke	T
42757	Arthur	— R R
42758	Arthur	— M
42759	Arthur	— R R
42760	Arthur	L R
42761	Arubas Duke	— R R
42762	Ascot	— M
42769	Autumn Chief	— P S
42772	Bacchus	Ky I
42774	Baileys Breastplate	P S
42776	Baker Evans	Ky I
42777	Baldy	— D
42778	Ballard	— M
42779	Ballot	— T
42780	Bangor	L R
42781	Banker	— D
42782	Banker 3rd	— M
42783	Barnum Boy	L R
42785	Baron	— L R
42786	Baron	— Cox
42787	Baron	— R R
42788	Baron 2nd	— Cox
42789	Baron Acomb	— L R
42794	Baron Booth	— T
42796	Baron Carlos	D
42797	Baron Donahue	— T
42798	Baron Duke	— R R
42799	Baronet	— Cox
42800	Baron Geneva	— R R
42803	8th Baron Manlius	— Cox
42804	Baron of Maple Hill	— D
42808	Baron Napier	— R R
42810	Baron Oxford 5th	— R R
42815	Baron of Riverside	— P S
42816	7th Baron of Riverside	— Cox
42818	Baron 7th of Spring Valley,	— Cox
42819	Baron 8th of Spring Valley,	— Ky I
42820	Baron Stafford	Daisy
42821	Baron Steuben	M
42823	Baron Travare	— D
42825	Baron Wethersfield	— R R
42832	Bates Rose 2nd	— M
42834	Bayard	R R
42835	Bay State	— L R
42836	Beaconsfield	— Cox
42837	Beautiful Boy	Ky I
42838	Beaver	Cox
42839	Beecher	P S
42840	Beecher	Ky I
42841	Beecher	— Cox
42842	Beecher	Ky I
42843	Belcher	Cox
42845	Belina's Duke	— M
42848	Belle Climax Mary's Prince	— M
42849	Belle Climax's Prince	— M
42852	Belle's Goodness	— R R
42853	Belle's Duke	— M
42854	Belle's Duke	— M
42855	Belle's Duke 2nd	Daisy
42859	3rd Bell Duke of Lyndale	— R R
42860	2nd Bell Duke of Maple Hill,	— R R
42861	Bell Duke P	— R R
42865	3rd Bell Duke of Sandusky	— M
42866	4th Bell Duke of Sandusky	Ky I
42869	Bellemonte	— M
42870	Belle's Prince 2nd	R R
42873	Berton	— M
42874	Ben Bates	— L R
42875	Ben Bolt	— M
42876	Ben Breastplate	— M
42877	Ben Butler	— R R
42880	Ben Butler	L R
42881	Benedict	L R
42882	Ben Hunt	— R R
42883	Benomie	— D
42884	Ben Palmer	M
42885	Ben Wade	— M
42886	Berlin	— P S
42887	Bertram	— R R
42888	Bertram	— R R
42889	Bertram 2nd	— R R
42890	Bertram 3rd	— R R
42891	Bertram 4th	— R R
42892	Bertram 5th	— R R
42893	Bertram 6th	— R R
42894	Bertram of Maplewild	— R R
42897	Beulah's Duke 3rd	— R R
42898	Bij Blackmarr	— R R
42899	Billy Denman	M
42900	Bill Eaton	— Cox
42902	Billy Miller	— C
42905	Bill Sherman	— D
42906	Billy Sherman	D
42907	Billy Smith, Jr	Cox
42908	Billy Webb	— Ky I
42909	Billy Wilson	— R R
42910	Bingo	— T
42911	Bishop of Oxford	— Cox
42912	Bismarck	P S
42913	Bismasck	Ky I
42914	Bismarck	— M
42915	Bismarck	— R R
42916	Bismarck	— T
42917	Blanchard	— R R
42918	Blaze	— D
42920	Blossom's Mazurka Duke	— M
42921	Blucher	L R
42922	Blucher	M
42925	Bluemont Wiley	T
42926	Blue Racer	Ky I
42929	Blythedale Champion 4th	— L R
42930	Blythedale Champion 5th	— L R
42933	Bob	Ky I
42934	Bob Owen	M
42935	Bob Taylor	— D
42936	Bodine	— C
42937	Bojarde	— R R
42938	Bolivar	— L R
42939	Bolton Duke 2nd	— M
42940	Bonafide	— Cox
42941	Bonner 4th	— D
42943	Booth Favorite	— T
42944	Booth of Glasgow	— T
42946	Border Chief	— M
42947	Boreas	Ky I
42949	Boss Tweed	— D
42952	Bourbon Duke	P S
42953	Bourbon Duke	— R R
42954	Bourbon John	— R R
42956	Brandy	— R R
42957	Brandywine 2nd	— L R

No.	Name	Code
42958	Brandywine 3rd	P S
42959	Breadalbane 3rd	Ky I
42960	Breadalbane 4th	M
42962	Breastplate of Jasper	— R R
42963	Brick Pomeroy	— Cox
42964	Bridgeford	M
42965	Bright	— D
42966	Bright Duke	M
42967	Bright Eyes Duke	— M
42968	Bright Eyes Duke	— M
42970	British	P S
42974	British Prince	— L R
42975	Brilliant	— Cox
42976	Bristol Beecher	— P S
42977	Brokenhorn	— Ky I
42978	Brookfield Beau	— L R
42981	Brutus	M
42983	Buccaneer	— Cox
42984	Buck Baron	Ky I
42985	Buckeye Boy	— R R
42986	Buckeye Boy	— M
42987	Buckeye Duke 2nd	M
42988	Buckingham	— Cox
42989	Buckskin Joe	L R
42991	Bug	— P S
42992	Buffalo Duke 3rd	Ky I
42993	Bulldozer	— Daisy
42994	Burlingame	— Cox
42995	Burlington Lad	M
42997	Burr Oak	Ky I
42998	Buxton of Maine Valley	— M
42999	Cadet	— Long-Horn
43001	Caleb Heacock	M
43002	Calhoun 5th	— D
43003	Caliph 3rd	Ky I
43004	Calla's Duke	— R R
43007	Cambrian	— Ky I
43008	Cambridge Lad	— M
43009	Camilla's Duke	— M
43012	Canonicus	— R R
43013	Captain	— L R
43014	Captain	Ky I
43015	Captain	— Cox
43016	Capt. Ascot of Sugar Grove	— M
43017	Capt. Bates	— L R
43022	Capt. Dan	— Cox
43023	Capt. Derby	Cox
43024	Capt. Duke	— D
43025	Capt. Emerson	— P S
43026	Capt. Fry	D
43027	Capt. Hale	Ky I
43028	Capt. Jack	— P S
43029	Capt. Jack of Waynesfield	P S
43030	Capt. McConnell	— M
43031	Capt. Mack	M
43032	Capt. Moore 2nd	D
43033	Capt. Muller	— R R
43035	Capt. Richmond	— P S
43036	Capt. Steel	— R R
43038	Carolines Favorite	— R R
43040	Carl Lewis	— R R
43041	Carthage Bill	L R
43042	Catrina's Duke	— M
43043	Cato	— Ky I
43044	Cato	P S
43045	Cavalier	— R R
43046	Cayuga	Ky I
43047	Cayuga Duke	— Cox
43048	Cecil Lad	— M
43049	Cedar Airdrie	— P S
43050	Cedar Duke	— M
43053	Champaign Duke	— M
43054	Champion	M
43057	Champion	M
43060	Charlie B.	— P S
43061	Charles C.	— R R
43062	Charley Foster	— R R
43068	Chautauqua	— L R
43069	Chautauqua Chief	L R
43070	Cheesman	— M
43071	Cheney 3rd	— P S
43072	Cheney 4th	M
43073	Cherokee Duke	— M
43074	Cherry Boy	— M
43075	Cherry Duke	— R R
43076	Cherry Duke	— R R
43077	Cherry Duke	— Ky I
43079	Cherry Oxford 2nd	— Cox
43081	Chester	— Ky I
43084	Chester	— P S
43085	Chickasaw Chief	— Ky I
43086	Chico	P S
43087	Chief	— Cox
43088	Chief Bugler	— L R
43089	Chieftain	M
43090	Chieftain	— R R
43091	Chieftain of Richland	— P S
43092	Chief Yorke	— T
43093	Chilton	— M
43094	Chipco Louanjo	— R R
43095	Chris Reeder	— M
43096	Christmas	— R R
43097	Chub	— M
43099	Clear Creek Mounter	M
43101	Climax	— M
43102	Climax	Ky I
43104	Clinton Lad	L R
43105	Colfax	M
43106	Collier	— Cox
43107	Colonel	— L R
43108	Colonel	— R R
43109	Col. Airdrie	— R R
43110	Col. Arab	— L R
43111	Col. Barnpton	— R R
43112	Col. Bass	— P S
43115	Col. Custer	Cox
43116	Col. Dean	— Cox
43117	Col. Dick	P S
43118	Col. Garfield	— R R
43120	Col. Hooker	— Cox
43121	Col. Ingersoll of Lost Ranch	— M
43122	Col. Jubilee	— Ky I
43123	Col. Lee	— Cox
43124	Col. Plumwood	— R R
43125	Col. Powell	— M
43126	Col. Prim	— M
43127	Col. Sanford	— Cox
43128	Col. Sharp	— P S
43129	Col. Van Horn	— P S
43130	Col. Wells	— P S
43131	Col. Ward	T
43134	Columbus	— R R
43135	Columbus 3rd	— R R
43137	Comanche	— L R
43138	Comet	M
43140	Comet	Ky I
43141	Comet	— M
43142	Comet of Maine Valley	— R R
43147	Comfort's Wiley 8th	— Daisy
43150	Commodore	— L R

43151	Commodore 2nd — M	43256	Dexter — M
43152	Competitor P S	43257	Dexter Ky I
43153	Compromise — M	43258	Diamond Jo — M
43155	Comus 2nd — Cox	43260	Dick — Cox
43156	Concord — D	43261	Dickens Ky I
43157	Concord Chief — D	43262	Dick H. — M
43158	Conductor — M	43263	Dick Hill — R R
43160	Conqueror P S	43264	Dick Maxey — L R
43161	Conqueror — P S	43265	Dick Morris — M
43162	Conqueror — Cox	43266	Dick Oglesby — C
43163	Conservitor P S	43267	Dick Richard — Cox
43167	Constance Duke of Airdrie 2nd — L R	43268	Dick Turpin M
43171	Coral Duke Cox	43270	Dick Ward M
43172	Cornell Duke of Bethlehem — M	43271	Dime — D
43174	Cottage Duke 4th — R R	43272	Dionysius Ky I
43175	Cottonwood Louanjo 21st M	43273	Disappointment — P S
43176	Cottonwood Louanjo 27th M	43274	Dobbins Ky I
43177	Cottonwood Louanjo 28th M	43275	Doctor B. — L R
43178	Cottonwood Louanjo 29th — M	43276	Doctor Black — R R
43179	Cottonwood Louanjo 30th Ky I	43277	Doctor Cullen — M
43180	Cottonwood Louanjo 31st P S	43278	Doctor Franklin — M
43181	Council Bluffs Jim L R	43279	Doctor Gunn — C
43182	Count — M	43280	Doctor Highland — D
43183	Count 2nd — Ky I	43284	Dombey — Cox
43186	County Member M	43285	Dom Pedro — R R
43187	Cowan's Duke 3rd M	43287	Dom Pedro 2nd — C
43188	Cowboy — L R	43288	Dom Pedro 4th M
43189	Crabapple Duke — M	43289	Donald Duke — D
43190	Credit 2nd — R R	43290	Donald Duke 2nd C
43191	Crescent — D	43291	Donald Duke 3rd — R R
43192	Crimson Duke — R R	43292	Donald Duke 4th R R
43193	Crocus — L R	43293	Donald Duke 5th M
43195	Crown Chief P S	43294	Donald Duke 6th P S
43197	Crown Prince — M	43296	Don Blaine — M
43198	Crown Prince 2nd — P S	43297	Don Cassius — T
43199	Crown Prince of Oakwood — M	43298	Don Juan Ky I
43205	Cypress, Jr. M	43299	Don Juan L R
43206	Cyprus — Ky I	43301	Dot's Prince — M
43207	Czar — L R	43302	Double Duke of Airdrie — T
43208	Dacotah Prince P S	43303	Dragon — Cox
43210	Daisy's Baron — Cox	43305	Duchess Duke D
43211	Daisy's Breastplate Daisy	43307	Duke — R R
43212	Daisy Bull — M	43308	Duke — M
43213	Daisy Duke Ky I	43309	Duke P S
43218	Daisy's Red Rose Duke Ky I	43310	Duke — Ky I
43222	Dalton — R R	43311	Duke of Adair Daisy
43223	Damon — L R	43314	Duke Alexis — M
43224	Dan L R	43315	Duke Alexis — M
43225	Dan Able — T	43316	Duke Alexis 4th — M
43228	Dandy L R	43317	Duke Alexis 5th — M
43230	Dan Moore — M	43318	Duke of Alice P S
43231	Dan Tucker — Woods	43319	28th Duke of Allendale — T
43232	Daniel Boone M	43320	51st Duke of Allendale T
43233	Daniel Webster — M	43321	Duke of Almont — M
43234	Darley Cox	43322	Duke of Alpine 2nd P S
43238	Darby Dunmore — R R	43323	Duke Anderson of Denmark L R
43239	Darby Red — M	43324	Duke of Ashland — R R
43240	Dave Twin — L R	43325	Duke of Ashland — Cox
43241	David Ky I	43327	Duke of Australia — Cox
43243	David S. — M	43328	Duke Balco — R R
43244	Daylight — Cox	43329	Duke of Barrington — C
43245	Dayton 3rd — Cox	43331	Duke of Bath — D
43246	Deer Lick Duke 14th R R	43332	Duke of Beaconhall — M
43247	Deer Lick Prince — M	43333	Duke of Belmont — Wrong
43248	Defiance — P S	43334	Duke of Bennington — M
43249	De Kalb Cherub — M	43335	2nd Duke of Bennington M
43250	Dennis Kearney — P S	43336	Duke of Bloomington T
43252	Desmond — Cox	43338	Duke of Brandon C
43254	Detura's Duke C	43339	Duke Brumwell — L R
43255	Dexter — Cox	43340	Duke of Bunkerhill — R R

43341	Duke of Bunkerhill	— T	
43342	Duke of Burdette	— P S	
43343	Duke of Burlington	— Cox	
43344	Duke of Butler 5th	— D	
43350	Duke of Center Point	— P S	
43351	Duke of Chambers	— Cox	
43352	Duke of Chariton	— R R	
43354	Duke of Clemon's Grove	M	
43355	2nd Duke of Clemon's Grove	M	
43356	Duke Clifton 4th	— R R	
43357	Duke of Clinton County	— M	
43358	Duke of Colebrook	M	
43359	Duke of Connaught	L R	
43361	Duke of Cross Creek	— R R	
43362	2nd Duke of Cross Creek	L R	
43364	Duke of Darley	— L R	
43365	Duke of Dayton	M	
43366	Duke of Delaware	— R R	
43367	2nd Duke of Dereham Abbey	— Cox	
43368	Duke of Des Moines	— R R	
43369	Duke of Dix	— Cox	
43370	Duke of Dixie	— M	
43371	Duke of Doyle	T	
43372	Duke of Durham Center	— Ky I	
43373	5th Duke of Eastside	— M	
43374	4th Duke of Edgewood	— P S	
43375	Duke of Elder Park	— P S	
43377	2nd Duke of Eldora	— T	
43378	Duke of Elm Grove	— M	
43379	Duke of Elmwood	— D	
43380	Duke of Emerald Valley	— R R	
43381	Duke Equator	— P S	
43382	6th Duke of Evergreen Hill	— L R	
43383	7th Duke of Evergreen Hill	— L R	
43384	2nd Duke of Fairholme	— P S	
43385	3rd Duke of Fairholme	— P S	
43386	Duke of Fairview	— M	
43387	Duke of Farmdale	M	
43388	Duke of Farmington	L R	
43389	Duke of Fayette	D	
43391	5th Duke of Fayette	R R	
43392	6th Duke of Fayette	— T	
43396	10th Duke of Fayette	— T	
43398	Duke of Federal Hill	— R R	
43399	2nd Duke of Ferndale	— M	
43400	Duke of Fordland	P S	
43401	5th Duke of Forest Hill	— L R	
43402	7th Duke of Forest Hill	L R	
43403	8th Duke of Forest Hill	— M	
43404	4th Duke of Forest Home	— M	
43405	1st Duke of Forest Home	— Ky I	
43407	Duke of Frazer 2nd	L R	
43408	Duke Garfield	— L R	
43410	Duke of Gillam'	M	
43411	Duke of Gilman	— R R	
43412	Duke of Glencoe	Daisy	
43413	2nd Duke of Glen Rock	P S	
43414	2nd Duke of Gordon	— P S	
43415	Duke of Grape Grove	R R	
43417	Duke of Gratiot	— Cox	
43418	Duke Gwynne	— Cox	
43419	Duke Gwynne	— D	
43420	Duke of Halstead	— T	
43421	Duke of Hancock	— T	
43422	13th Duke of Harlem	T	
43423	16th Duke of Harlem	— M	
43424	Duke of Hastings 2nd	M	
43425	Duke Hawkins	— L R	
43426	2nd Duke of Highland	— M	
43427	3rd Duke of Highland	— M	
43428	9th Duke of Highland	L R	
43430	Duke of Hillside	— C	
43431	2nd Duke of Hoosier	— Cox	
43432	2nd Duke of Houston	— Cox	
43433	Duke of Iosco	— M	
43434	Duke J.	Ky I	
43435	Duke of Jamestown 2nd	— M	
43436	Duke of Jasper	— M	
43437	Duke of Jersyville	Ky I	
43438	2nd Duke of Jersyville	Ky I	
43439	Duke John	L R	
43440	Duke Kent	— D	
43441	7th Duke of Kenton	— R R	
43442	10th Duke of Kenton	— R R	
43443	11th Duke of Kenton	— R R	
43444	12th Duke of Kenton	— R R	
43445	13th Duke of Kenton	— R R	
43446	14th Duke of Kenton	— R R	
43447	15th Duke of Kenton	— R R	
43448	Duke of Kinsman	— M	
43449	Duke of Kisaway	— M	
43451	Duke of Lebanon	P S	
43452	6th Duke of Lebanon	— R R	
43453	7th Duke of Lebanon	— R R	
43454	8th Duke of Lebanon	— R R	
43455	Duke of Leesburg	— R R	
43456	Duke of Leroy	M	
43457	Duke of Lexington	— R R	
43458	Duke of Licking	— M	
43459	Duke of Licking 2nd	— M	
43460	Duke of Livingston	M	
43461	6th Duke of Locust Grove	— M	
43462	8th Duke of Locust Grove	— M	
43463	9th Duke of Locust Grove	— M	
43464	10th Duke of Locust Grove	— M	
43465	11th Duke of Locust Grove	— M	
43466	12th Duke of Locust Grove	— M	
43467	13th Duke of Locust Grove	— M	
43468	Duke of Lorain	— L R	
43470	Duke Loyal	Cox	
43471	Duke of Lucas	— R R	
43472	3rd Duke of Lucknow	L R	
43473	Duke of Main Valley	L R	
43474	Duke of Maple Grove	Ky I	
43475	2nd Duke of Maple Grove	— M	
43476	3rd Duke of Maple Grove	— M	
43477	Duke of Marion	M	
43478	Duke of Maryland	— Daisy	
43480	Duke of Maximillian	M	
43482	Duke of Mentor	— M	
43483	Duke Mepham	Ky I	
43484	Duke of Mill Creek	— M	
43485	Duke of Mina	— Cox	
43486	Duke of Mistletoe	— M	
43487	Duke of Monroe	— M	
43489	Duke of Mt. Pleasant	— L R	
43490	Duke of Nemaha	— Ky I	
43491	Duke of Ninnescah	T	
43494	Duke Oliver	— L R	
43495	Duke of Ontario	P S	
43496	Duke of Orange	— M	
43497	Duke of Orleans	— P S	
43498	15th Duke of Orleans	— Cox	
43499	10th Duke of Orleans	Ky I	
43500	2nd Duke of Osco	— M	
43501	Duke of Owens	— P S	
43503	Duke of Pataskala	— Daisy	
43504	Duke of Pearlmaid	— M	
43505	Duke of Pepsin	— L R	
43507	Duke of Pleasant Ridge	— M	

No.	Name	Herd
43508	Duke of Plymouth	— Cox
43509	Duke of Radcliffe	D
43510	Duke of Raritan	— Cox
43511	Duke of Reading	— Ky I
43512	Duke of Red Rose 24th	— C
43513	Duke 2nd of Richland	— P S
43514	Duke 3rd of Richland	— P S
43515	Duke of Richwoods	— R R
43516	Duke of Roanoke	— T
43517	3rd Duke of Rosedale	— Cox
43518	Duke of Rose Hill	P S
43519	Duke Royal	Cox
43520	1st Duke of Rubicon	— L R
43521	3rd Duke of Russell	— Ky I
43522	2nd Duke of Sac	Ky I
43523	Duke of Saline	P S
43524	Duke of Scotland	— M
43526	Duke of Sharon 2nd	— M
43527	Duke of Sharon 3rd	T
43529	2nd Duke of Sheldon	— P S
43530	Duke of Shenango	— R R
43531	Duke of Somerset	— L R
43532	Duke of Spring Valley	Cox
43533	2nd Duke of Spring Valley	Cox
43536	Duke of Stafford	Daisy
43539	Duke Sterling	— R R
43540	Duke of Stoner	— D
43543	Duke of Sullevan	— D
43544	Duke of Sullivan	M
43548	Duke of the Bluffs	Ky I
43549	Duke of the Forest	— L R
43550	31st Duke of the Pines	— R R
43551	32nd Duke of the Pines	— R R
43552	Duke of The Roses	M
43554	Duke of Thetford	P S
43555	Duke of The Valey	— P S
43556	Duke of Thorn	— Ky I
43557	Duke of Thorn 2nd	— M
43558	Duke of Thorn 3rd	— M
43559	Duke of Thorn 4th	— D
43561	Duke of Vanburen	P S
43562	Duke of Volga	— T
43564	Duke of Walnut	— L R
43565	Duke of Walnut 2nd	— L R
43566	Duke of Walnut 3rd	— L R
43567	Duke of Walnut 4th	— L R
43568	Duke of Walnut 5th	— L R
43569	Duke of Walnut 6th	— L R
43570	Duke of Warren	Ky I
43571	Duke of Watertown	— M
43572	Duke of Waverly	— T
43575	7th Duke of Waveland	— R R
43576	Duke of Wellington	L R
43577	Duke of Wellington	Ky I
43578	Duke of The West	D
43579	Duke of West Line	— C
43580	1st Duke of West View	— M
43581	Duke of West Virginia	— M
43583	1st Duke of Whitehall	— M
43584	2nd Duke of Whitehall	— T
43585	3rd Duke of Whitehall	— M
43587	Duke Wiley	— M
43589	1st Duke of Wixom	— D
43590	2nd Duke of Wixom	L R
43591	3rd Duke of Wixom	L R
43592	2nd Duke of Woodland	Daisy
43594	Dunglenna's Duke	— R R
43595	Dutch Boy	— R R
43596	Eagle Creek	— M
43597	Earl	M
43598	Earl	— Ky I
43599	Earl Airdrie	— M
43600	8th Earl of Cedar Lawn	— R R
43605	Earl of Cleveland	— M
43606	Earl of Clinton	L R
43607	3rd Earl of Conneaut	— R R
43608	Earl of Derby 4th	M
43609	Earl of Derby 5th	M
43610	Earl of Derby 6th	M
43611	6th Earl of Derby	— R R
43612	Earl Derby 7th	M
43613	Earl of Dover	— D
43614	Earl Duke of Rosedale	— Cox
43617	2nd Earlham Duke of Airdrie	— R R
43618	3rd Earlham Duke of Airdrie	— R R
43619	Earl of Hamilton	P S
43620	31st Earl of Greenbush	— Cox
43621	32nd Earl of Greenbush	— Cox
43622	33rd Earl of Greenbush	— Cox
43623	34th Earl of Greenbush	M
43624	35th Earl of Greenbush	— L R
43625	36th Earl of Greenbush	— L R
43626	37th Earl of Greenbush	— P S
43627	38th Earl of Greenbush	— L R
43628	Earl of Gun Plain	— M
43630	4th Earl of Lake Grove	— D
43631	5th Earl of Lake Grove	— D
43632	6th Earl of Lake Grove	— D
43633	7th Earl of Lake Grove	— D
43634	8th Earl of Lake Grove	— D
43635	Earl of Martin 7th	Cox
43636	Earl of Meadow Brook	M
43639	Earl of Orchard Place	— M
43640	Earl of Oseo 2nd	— M
43642	Earl of Raymond	— P S
43643	Earl of Richmond	— Cox
43644	Earl of Rose Lawn	— M
43645	10th Earl of Ruralusia	M
43646	11th Earl of Ruralusia	— Long-Horn
43649	Earl Vane 2nd	— R R
43650	Earl of Watertown	— M
43651	2nd Earl of Wheatland	— R R
43652	3rd Earl of Wheatland	— R R
43653	4th Earl of Wheatland	— D
43654	5th Earl of Wheatland	C
43655	Earl White Breast	— P S
43656	Earl of Woodlawn	— R R
43657	Echo	— L R
43658	Eclipse	Ky I
43659	Eclipse	— P S
43660	Eden Duke	— D
43664	Finesta	— R R
43665	Eli Perkins	— M
43666	Elkhorn Duke	M
43667	Ella's Mazurka	— R R
43668	Ellah's Young Waterloo	— R R
43669	Ellery	— Cox
43670	Emerald	T
43671	Emerald	M
43672	Emerald	— Ky I
43673	Emerald Lad	M
43674	Emery Moore	D
43676	Emmet	M
43677	Emmet of Maplewood	Ky I
43678	Emory	Ky I
43680	Emperor	M
43681	Empress' Bell Duke	— M
43682	Enoch Arden	— T
43683	Enterprise	P S
43684	Enterprise	— M

43685	Eric...M	43768	Gen. Arthur...— D
43686	Estella's Duke...D	43771	Gen. Beaver...— L R
43687	Eugene J. Hall...— Cox	43772	Gen. Brooks...T
43688	Eula's Prince 2nd...— P S	43773	Gen. Dick...M
43690	Excelsior...— Ky I	43774	Gen. Dix...— R R
43691	Excelsior 2nd...— M	43775	Gen. Drake...Ky I
43692	Excello Duke...— R R	43776	Gen. Garfield...L R
43693	Exile...Cox	43777	Gen. Garfield...— T
43694	Expansion Duke...— R R	43779	Gen. Garfield...— M
43695	Fairview 2nd...— Cox	43780	Gen. Garfield...— Cox
43696	Fairview Duke...— Ky I	43781	Gen. Garfield...— Cox
43697	Fairview Duke 2nd...R R	43782	Gen. Garfield...— Cox
43698	Fairy's Duke...Ky I	43783	Gen. Garfield...— D
43701	Fannie's Duke...— M	43786	Gen. Gifford...L R
43702	Fancy Boy...M	43787	Gen. Gloster...— Cox
43703	Fancy Boy 2nd...— P S	43788	Gen. Grant...— M
43706	Faro...— D	43789	Gen. Grant...— Cox
43707	Favorite...— T	43791	General H...— D
43708	Favorite...— M	43792	Gen. Hancock...— M
43709	Fearnaught...— R R	43793	Gen. Hancock...— P S
43710	Fear Not...— R R	43794	Gen. Hancock...Ky I
43711	Feather River Chief...— D	43795	Gen. Hancock...— P S
43712	Ferndale Lad...— M	43796	Gen. Hancock...— D
43713	Fifer...— T	43797	Gen. Hancock...T
43716	Filagree Star Duke 4th...— R R	43798	Gen. Hancock...— Ky I
43717	Filagree Star Duke 5th...— M	43799	Gen. Hopper...— T
43718	Financier...L R	43800	Gen. Lancaster...— R R
43719	Financier...— R R	43801	General Lee...— L R
43721	Five-Twenty, Jr...P S	43802	Gen. Logan...— R R
43722	Flora's Duke...— D	43803	Gen. Logan...— M
43724	Florio...— Wrong	43804	Gen. Martin...— D
43725	Fordland Laddie...P S	43806	Gen. Prince...T
43726	Forest Duke...— R R	43809	Gen. Scott...— M
43727	Forester Kunse...— R R	43810	Gen. Scott...— Ky I
43728	Forest King...— Daisy	43811	Gen. Van Wyck...— R R
43729	Founder...— T	43812	Gen. Walker...Ky I
43730	Four Aces...R R	43813	Gen. Wayne...M
43731	Foxhall...— P S	43814	Gen. Weaver...M
43732	Francisco...— P S	43815	Geneva...Ky I
43733	Frank...M	43819	Geneva Lad...Cox
43734	Frank...— Cox	43821	Geneva's Prince 2nd...— Cox
43736	Frank Boy...— M	43822	Geneva Thorndale...— D
43737	Frank Clifton...— M	43823	Geneva Wild Eyes of Bell Creek, — T
43738	Franklin...— Cox	42826	George Lord...— T
43739	Frank Steele...M	43827	George...— M
43740	Fred...— D	43828	George Hammond...M
43742	Frederick Lowell...— R R	43829	George Washington...— L R
43743	Freeville 3rd...— Cox	43830	Gideon...R R
43744	Fremont...Ky I	43831	1st Gift...— R R
43745	Fremont Lad...— M	43832	Gilford...— Cox
43746	Fremont Norton...Ky I	43833	Gipsy King...— T
43747	Fusileer...Daisy	43834	Gladiator...Ky I
43748	Gaban 19th...— P S	43835	Gladstone...— L R
43749	Gaban of Mazomanie...— P S	43836	Gladstone...— M
43750	Garfield...— C	43839	Glaucus...— L R
43751	Garfield...M	43840	Glenallen...— M
43752	Garfield...— C	43841	Glendale...— M
43753	Garfield...— R R	43842	Glendale...— L R
43754	Garfield...L R	43844	Gloster of Amada...— Cox
43755	Garfield of Waverly...— R R	43845	Gloster of Ionia...— Cox
43756	Garibaldi...T	43846	Gloster Prince...— R R
43757	Garland of Kirkwood...— P S	43847	Gold Bug...— P S
43758	Guth...L R	43848	Golddrop 5th...— R R
43759	Gazelle's Oxford...M	43849	Golddrop's Duke...— R R
43760	Gazelle...L R	43851	Gold Duke 2nd...Ky I
43762	Gem's Duke...— M	43853	Golden Gift...P S
43763	Gem's Duke...D	43854	Golden Prince...Ky I
43765	Gem of Oxford...— L R	43855	Golden Prince 1st...— M
43766	Gem Puzzle...— P S	43856	Golden Prince 4th...— T
43767	Gen. Adeline...P S	43857	Goldfinder...— R R

No.	Name	Code	No.	Name	Code
43858	Goldfinder	— M	43952	Highland Lad	— P S
43860	Good Luck	M	43953	Highland Laddie	— P S
43862	Good Intent Duke	— R R	43954	Highland Oxford	— R R
43863	Good Intent Duke 2nd	— T	43956	Hilpa's Duke	— D
43864	Good Intent Duke 3rd	— T	43959	Hilpa's Oxford 2nd	— L R
43867	Governor Bishop	M	43962	Holland Duke	— D
43868	Governor Hoyt	L R	43963	Homer	Ky I
43869	Governor of Nebraska	— R R	43964	Homeworth Belleville	— M
43870	Governor of Pleasant Hill	— Cox	43965	Honest Duke	Ky I
43871	Governor St. John	— Daisy	43966	Honest John	— D
43872	Governor Smith	— T	43967	Honest John 2nd	— Cox
43873	Governor Williams	— P S	43968	Honest Prince	Cox
43877	Grand Airdrie	— R R	43969	Hoosier Boy	M
43878	Grand Duke	— L R	43970	Hope of Atha's Mazurka	— M
43879	Grand Duke of Cherrywood	— P S	43971	Hopeful	M
43880	2d Grand Duke of Cherrywood	— P S	43972	Hopewell 2nd	— M
43884	Grand Sharon	— R R	43973	Hornet	— M
43885	4th Grandson of Minister	— M	43975	Huckleberry Bill	Ky I
43886	Grand Turk of Easton	L R	43976	Hudson Dennis	— Cox
43887	Granger	— Cox	43978	Hugo	Daisy
43888	Granger	— L R	43979	Humphrey Bull	— D
43889	Granger	M	43980	Huron Chief	— Cox
43890	Grant	— P S	43983	Independence	P S
43892	Gray Billy	— L R	43984	Independence	Ky I
43894	Great Eastern	M	43985	Inkapoda	Ky I
43897	Grinnell Baron	— D	43986	Inland Duke	— Ky I
43898	2nd Grinnell Baron	— D	43988	Ishmael	M
43899	Grundy Duke	T	43989	Ivanhoe	— Daisy
43900	Guilford Duke	D	43990	Jacques 2nd	M
43901	Guiteau	— Daisy	43991	Jake	— Cox
43902	Gwynne Duke	— Cox	43992	Jake	— M
43903	Gwynne's King		43993	Jake Ward	M
43904	Gwynne's Kirklevington	— Cox	43994	James T.	P S
43905	Ham	Ky I	43995	Jasper	M
43906	Hamlet of Maine Valley	— R R	43996	Jay Gould	— P S
43909	Hancock	— R R	43997	Jay Gould	— R R
43910	Hancock	M	43998	Jack Brag	M
43911	Hancock	T	43999	Jacksonville Leonard	— D
43912	Hancock	L R	44000	Jack Sheppard	— L R
43913	Hank Baker	— P S	44001	Jackson	— L R
43914	Hannibal	— Cox	44002	Jack Hudson	— R R
43916	Hans	— M	44003	Jacksonville Stanley	T
43917	Harp	P S	44004	Jeanot Bell	— D
43918	Harry of Maine Valley	— M	44005	Jeff Davis	— R R
43919	Hazelwood	L R	44006	Jefferson 2nd	M
43920	Headlight	P S	44007	Jefferson Frank	— R R
43922	Harts of Oak	— D	44008	Jefferson Reuben	— M
43924	Hector	— L R	44010	Jerry	— M
43925	Hector	— M	44011	Jerry	L R
43927	Hell Oh!	— L R	44012	Jesse	— L R
43928	Helm	— L R	44014	Jim Blaine	— R R
43929	Hendon Duke	— M	44015	Jim Blaine	— P S
43930	Henry	P S	44016	Jim Blaine	— P S
43931	Henry Adair	— R R	44018	Jim Howard	T
43932	Henry C.	— D	44019	Jim Mitchell	D
43933	Henry Clay	— R R	44020	Jim Willson	Ky I
43934	Henry Clay	— M	44021	Jim Young	— P S
43936	Henry Percy	L R	44022	Job	— Cox
43937	Hermann Forman	— D	44023	Jo Carson 2nd	T
43938	Hero	— P S	44025	Jo Stevens	Ky I
43941	Hero B.	— L R	44026	Joe Arthur	— Cox
43942	Herod 2nd	— M	44027	Joe Clinton	— R R
43943	Hero of Maine Valley	— R R	44028	Joe Cooper	Ky I
43944	Hero of Maplewood	— M	44029	Joe Ingham	— C
43945	Hickory	— R R	44030	Joe Johnson	— R R
43946	Hickory Pay	Ky I	44031	Joe P.	Ky I
43948	Highland Baron	M	44032	Joe Watson	— C
43949	Highland Chief	— P S	44033	John	M
43950	Highland Chief	— M	44035	John Alexander 2nd	D
43951	Highland Chief	— L R	44036	Johnny Bull of Brookvale	— M

No.	Name	Reg.
44038	John Finch	Ky I
44039	John Gilpin	— Cox
44040	John Glick	T
44041	John Growler	— M
44042	John Hailey	Ky I
44044	Johnny Meadows	— R R
44045	John Nelson 4th	Ky I
44047	John Wiley	— M
44048	John W. White	Ky I
44050	Josephus	P S
44051	Josephus	— P S
44054	Jules Grey	— M
44055	Junius	M
44056	Judah	M
44057	Judge F.	— M
44058	Judge Fremont	M
44059	Judge Porter	— L R
44060	Jupe	— M
44061	Jupiter	P S
44062	Jupiter	— D
44063	Jupiter	— L R
44064	Jupiter 2nd of Evergreen	Ky I
44065	Kalo	P S
44066	Kalo 2nd	P S
44068	Kansas Prince	Cox
44070	Kate Napier's Duke	— M
44071	Kedar	— M
44073	Kennedy's Oxford	— R R
44075	Kentucky Duke	M
44076	Khedive	— R R
44077	Killposey	Ky I
44078	King Charles 2nd	— M
44079	King Derby 5th	— M
44080	King George	— R R
44081	King John	— D
44082	King Lear	— R R
44084	King William	— T
44085	Kirk	— D
44094	Kirkwood	— R R
44095	Kirkwood 2nd	— R R
44096	Kirkwood Duke of Sharon	— L R
44097	Kit Carson	Daisy
44099	Knightly Blossom	— Cox
44104	Knightly Duke of Palmyra	Ky I
44105	Knightly S.	P S
44106	Knight of Sharon 2nd	— M
44107	Knight of the Plains	Ky I
44109	Knight of the Roses	— M
44110	Kris Kringle	— M
44111	La Crescent Duke of Lindale	— P S
44112	Lafayette	T
44114	Lansing Boy	— Cox
44115	Latouche	— R R
44116	Layton	— R R
44117	Leader	— M
44118	Lecture	P S
44119	Le Moine 2nd	— P S
44120	Le Moine 3rd	— P S
44121	Le Moine 4th	— P S
44122	Le Moine 5th	— P S
44123	Len T.	— P S
44124	Lentner Lad	— C
44125	Leo Chief	— D
44127	Leonidas	P S
44128	Leonidas	L R
44132	Levi	— R R
44133	Lew Bender	M
44135	Lewis Macbeth	Ky I
44136	Liberty Prince	— D
44138	Lime City Duke	— R R
44139	Lincoln	— M
44142	Linwood Duke	— D
44143	Little's Banker	Ky I
44144	Little Chief	Cox
44145	Little Greek Baron	T
44146	Little Sampson	— Cox
44147	Lieutenant Burnett	— L R
44149	Lockport	— C
44150	Lodi Lad	— M
44151	Logan	Ky I
44152	Logan	Ky I
44153	Logan 3rd	— P S
44154	Lonely Boy	Ky I
44156	Lookout	— R R
44157	Lord Baltimore	— P S
44159	Lord Barrington of Hamb'g 2nd	— C
44160	L'rd Barrington of Hamb'g 3rd	— R R
44161	Lord Beaconsfield	— Cox
44164	Lord Byron	— L R
44165	Lord Byron	L R
44166	Lord Byron	C
44167	Lord Byron	— D
44172	1st Lord Compton of Wyaconda	— T
44173	2nd Lord Compton of Wyaconda	M
44174	Lord Delaware	— P S
44176	Lord Ellington 6th	— Cox
44177	Lord Erne 3rd	— P S
44178	Lord George	— M
44179	Lord Graham 5th	— R R
44180	Lord of Grand Island	— Cox
44181	Lord Hamilton	— R R
44183	Lord Lanark	— Cox
44184	Lord Leroy 2nd	— Cox
44186	Lord Lieutenant 2nd	— R R
44188	Lord Lorne	Ky I
44189	Lord Lovell	P S
44190	Lord Mapleton	T
44192	Lord Monegan	M
44193	Lord Roscoe of Carl	T
44194	Lord Raine	— P S
44196	Lord Rossmore	— R R
44197	Lord Roscoe	P S
44201	Lord of The Manor	— Ky I
44203	Lord Wellington	P S
44208	Lotus Duke	— T
44209	Lou Airdrie's Duke	P S
44210	Louan Duke	— R R
44211	Louan's Duke	P S
44212	Louans Duke	— M
44213	Louanjo	— R R
44214	Louanjo 9th	— R R
44215	Louan Lad 2nd	— R R
44216	Louan's Madrid	— M
44218	Loudon Duke of Greenw'd 10th	— R R
44219	Loudon Duke of Greenw'd 11th	— R R
44220	Loudon Duke of Greenw'd 12th	— R R
44221	Loudon Duke of Greenw'd 13th	— R R
44222	Loudon Duke of Greenw'd 14th	— R R
44223	Loudon Duke of Oakdale	— M
44224	Loudon Duke of Oakwood	— R R
44225	Loudon Gloster	M
44226	Loudon Louan	— R R
44227	Loudon Mac	— R R
44228	Loudon Perfect	— R R
44229	Loudon Prince	— R R
44233	Loudon's Richmond	— R R
44234	Lucius	Ky I
44240	Lucy Princeton	— R R
44241	Lulu's Dexter	— M
44242	Lulu's Lad	— M

44243	Lydia's Boy — P S	44332	Master Macy — R R
44244	Lynden Chief D	44335	Master Washington — M
44245	Mac — M	44336	Mat Foster 2nd M
44246	McClellan — R R	44337	Mat S. — P S
44248	McClintock's Louan — D	44338	Mauntie — L R
44249	Macomb Prince — D	44339	Max — D
44250	McDonald Duke 14th M	44340	Max Cooper — M
44251	McDonough Duke — M	44341	Mayflowers Duke — L R
44252	Mack — M	44342	4th Mayflower Prince — M
44253	Mack Ky I	44343	Mazeppa Duke — M
44254	Mackenzie L R	44345	Mazurka Cambria — M
44255	Madam's Baron — L R	44347	Mazurka's Oxford 31st Ky I
44256	Madic's Duke — R R	44350	M Duke of Rose L R
44257	Madies Duke 2nd — R R	44351	14th Meadow Duke — M
44259	Maggie's Duke Daisy	44352	Meadow Farm Prince — D
44260	Maggies Duke 3rd M	44356	Mell Martin L R
44261	Magistrate — R R	44357	Melody 3rd's Madrid — M
44263	Major — R R	44358	Mentor — Daisy
44264	Major — M	44360	Meteor — Cox
44265	Major Bates P S	44361	Meteor Ky I
44266	Major Bimbo — Cox	44364	Midas T
44267	Major Buttercup — M	44365	Midland Chief M
44268	Major Croxton Daisy	44366	Miller D
44269	Major Crook — R R	44368	Milton — M
44270	Major Edwards T	44369	Minnie's Airdrie — Daisy
44271	Major Frank D	44370	Misfortune's Prince M
44272	Major Garwood M	44371	Miss Grace's Prince — Ky I
44273	Major Highland M	44372	Missouri Duke — M
44274	Major Hill of Maplewood Ky I	44374	Modoc — R R
44275	Major Kid — M	44375	Modoc M
44276	Major Leslie — P S	44376	Modoc D
44278	Major of Melleray — M	44378	Mollie's 4th Duke of Ridgevale — L R
44281	Major Sam — R R	44379	Monarch — D
44282	Major Van Campen Cox	44380	Monarch P S
44283	Major Wonn — T	44381	Monarch — R R
44284	Major Yates Cox	44383	Monarch of Chartiers L R
44285	4th Maple Grove Duke — M	44384	Moneyfinder — R R
44286	Maple Tim — M	44385	Monitor — D
44287	Mamie's Duke — Cox	44386	Monitor — T
44288	Mamie's 2nd Duke — Cox	44387	Monitor — Cox
44289	Maplewood Duke — R R	44388	Monitor — L R
44290	March — C	44389	Monitor — R R
44292	Margrave — Cox	44391	Monte — R R
44293	Mariscal P S	44393	Mordecai Ky I
44296	Mark Whipple — L R	44395	Moreton Chief P S
44297	Marmaduke — M	44397	Mose — M
44298	Marquis R R	44398	Moss Rose Cherub 4th M
44299	Marquis 7th Daisy	44399	Mozart M
44300	Marquis 8th P S	44401	Murillo Cox
44303	Marquis of Green Valley — P S	44402	Muscatoon — M
44305	Marquis of Lorne — L R	44404	Myron Duke — M
44306	Marquis of Lorne D	44405	Myrtle's Prince — R R
44307	Marquis of Lorne L R	44406	Napoleon Bonaparte — Ky I
44308	Marquis of Mapledale 2nd — D	44407	Nasby M
44309	Marquis of Mapledale 3rd — M	44409	Nebo — D
44310	Marquis of Pleasant Hill — Daisy	44410	Nebo — M
44311	Marquis of Ruralusia L R	44411	Nebraska Prince M
44312	M'quis of Springbrook—Long-Horn	44412	Nellie's Duke — P S
44313	Marquis of Sugar Grove 4th — M	44413	Neptune — R R
44314	Marquis of Sugar Grove 6th — M	44415	Neshannock — M
44315	Marquis of Sugar Grove 7th — Daisy	44416	Neshobee — Cox
44316	Martha's Son M	44417	Nestor — M
44317	Martial Duke — T	44419	Newton — M
44322	Mason — C	44420	New Year — M
44324	Massasoit — R R	44421	New Year's Profitable — R R
44325	Master Baca — D	44423	Nicholas — L R
44327	Master Garfield — M	44424	Nimbus — M
44328	Master of Glenwood — R R	44425	Nimbus — Cox
44329	Master Leslie — P S	44426	Nimrod's Gem 2nd — L R
44330	Master Melrose M	44427	Nipio — M

44428	Noah — Cox	44517	Paddy Mack — P S
44429	Nobby — Ky I	44518	Paragon Taylor — M
44431	Nobleman — Cox	44519	Parker R. — P S
44434	Nodaway Chief — M	44520	Pascarel — Cox
44436	Norman Porter — P S	44521	Patchoulie's Acomb — R R
44437	North Star — M	44522	Pat Lonergan Ky I
44438	Norton's 17th Baron Lyndale. M	44523	Pattarell — L R
44439	Norton's Kirklevington — Ky I	44524	Pattie Lad — Ky I
44440	Norton's 2nd Kirklevington — M	44525	Paul Boynton — R R
44442	Norton's 4th Kirklevington Ky I	44526	Paw Paw Chief Cox
44445	Norwood Star — R R	44527	Pearl — P S
44446	Oakland 3rd — M	44528	Pearl Duke 1st — M
44447	Oakland Duke — M	44529	Pearl Duke 2nd — M
44448	Oakland Lad P S	44530	Pecatonica Boy — M
44449	Oakland Lad — M	44531	Peerless 2nd — L R
44450	Oakland of Orange — R R	44532	Percival Ky I
44451	Oakland Prince — M	44533	Perfect — M
44452	Oakland Rose of Sharon — R R	44534	Perfection Chief — R R
44453	Oakland of Spring Branch — M	44537	Pet Baron — D
44454	Oakley 2nd T	44538	Peter — M
44455	Obed M	44539	Peter 2nd — M
44456	Oconto — D	44540	Peter 3rd — M
44457	Ohio Redchip — L R	44541	Peter Cooper — M
44459	Ole Bull — D	44542	Pete Ward M
44460	Olio — P S	44543	Petoskey — Ky I
44461	Oliver Cromwell — M	44549	Phyllis Duke 2nd — R R
44463	Onnetta — C	44550	Phyllis Gem — R R
44464	Onstot 2nd T	44552	Phil Sheridan — Cox
44465	Ontario — Cox	44553	Phil Sheridan — R R
44466	Ontario 2nd — P S	44554	Piedmont M
44467	Optimus Ky I	44555	Pike Bull — D
44469	Orion — R R	44556	Pilgrim — M
44471	Ornamental — Cox	44557	Pilgrim 2nd — M
44472	Orphan Boy — P S	44558	Pilot — P S
44473	Orphan Boy — M	44559	Pilot — M
44474	Orphan Dan M	44560	Pilot of Melleray — M
44475	Orphan's Geneva — M	44561	Pilot Springwood — M
44478	Osceola Duke L R	44562	Pinehill Lad A — D
44479	Ossian Ky I	44565	Pioneer 2nd — Ky I
44480	Ossowatomic Ky I	44566	Pixies Duke M
44481	Othello — C	44567	Placida's Airdrie 3rd — R R
44482	Otsego 2nd — Cox	44568	Pliny — Ky I
44483	Ottumwa Lad — P S	44569	Plumgrove Oxford — M
44484	Ouray M	44570	Plummer Duke M
44485	Ouray 2nd M	44571	Plumwood A Q C
44486	Overseer — R R	44572	Plumwood A R C
44487	Owings — M	44573	Plumwood A S R R
44488	Oxford — L R	44574	Plumwood A T — R R
44489	Oxford L R	44575	Plumwood A U R R
44490	Oxford 2nd L R	44576	Plumwood A V C
44491	Oxford 3rd L R	44577	Plumwood Roan — R R
44492	Oxford 4th L R	44578	Plumwood V V R R
44493	Oxford 22nd — P S	44579	Pluto — R R
44494	Oxford 24th M	44580	Polar Star Cox
44495	Oxford 25th — P S	44581	Pompey — C
44496	Oxford 26th — P S	44582	Pompey of Greenside — Cox
44497	Oxford 27th M	44583	Pontiac Cox
44499	Oxford Beautiful Ky I	44584	Pony Dick — D
44500	Oxford Bloom — L R	44586	Portage Duke — M
44501	Oxford Bloom 2nd — D	44587	Porter M
44502	Oxfords Babraham Duke — Cox	44589	Prairie Duke 3rd — M
44503	Oxford of Elkhart M	44590	Prairie Prince — D
44504	Oxford Freeville — Cox	44591	Prairie Prince of Springville M
44506	Oxford Gwynne — Cox	44592	Pre-Emption Ben — P S
44509	Oxford of Oakland — R R	44593	Prentice Duke T
44510	Oxford 2nd of Oakland — R R	44594	President Garfield P S
44511	Oxford Prince, Jr Ky I	44595	President Hancock M
44513	Oxford Roan — Cox	44596	Pretty Patsy — P
44514	Oxford Scipio — Cox	44597	Pride of Barrington Co
44515	Oxford of Sugar Grove — M	44598	Pride of Brimfield —

SHORT-HORN CATTLE PEDIGREES. 213

No.	Name	Herd
44599	Pride of Cobb River	— P S
44600	Pride of Eden	M
44601	Pride of Green	Ky I
44602	Pride of Podunk	— L R
44603	Prince	— Cox
44604	Prince	Ky I
44605	Prince	Ky I
44606	Prince	— D
44607	Prince	M
44608	Prince	Cox
44609	Prince 2nd	— D
44610	Prince A	— L R
44611	Prince Airdrie	— Daisy
44612	Prince Airdrie	— P S
44613	Prince Airdrie	— P S
44614	Prince Albert	L R
44615	Prince Albert	M
44616	Prince Albert	— M
44617	Prince Arthur	— Ky I
44618	Prince Arthur	Cox
44620	Prince Barmpton 2nd	— R R
44621	Prince Barrington	— R R
44622	Prince Baron	— Cox
44624	Prince of Burr Oak	Ky I
44625	Prince of Boulder	Ky I
44627	Prince Bruno	— D
44628	Prince Charles 7th	L R
44630	Prince of Clymer	L R
44632	Prince of Columbus	L R
44635	Princess Duke 4th	— P S
44636	Prince Dalton	— Ky I
44638	Prince Edward	M
44640	Prince of Emerald Valley	— D
44642	Prince George 3rd	— T
44644	Prince of Hamilton	Cox
44645	Prince Henry	— T
44648	Prince Imperial	Daisy
44649	Prince Imperial	— D
44650	Prince Imperial 2nd	M
44651	Prince Imperial 3rd	M
44652	Prince Imperial 4th	M
44653	Prince Imperial 5th	M
44654	Prince of Indiana	Ky I
44655	Prince John	— M
44656	Prince Kearsarge	— M
44658	Prince Knightley	— Cox
44660	Prince Loudon	— R R
44663	Prince of Maple Lodge	— D
44664	Prince of Marion 4th	— M
44665	Prince of Marion 5th	— M
44666	Prince of Marion 6th	— Ky I
44667	Prince Mason	— Daisy
44670	Prince of Orange	M
44671	Prince of Orange	— M
44672	Prince Otoe	— M
44673	Prince Oxford	— Cox
44674	Prince of Platte	Daisy
44675	Prince of Ray	— M
44676	2nd Prince of Rosedale	— Cox
44677	3rd Prince of Rosedale	— M
44678	Prince of Sportsfield	— L R
44679	Princeton's Logan	Ky I
44681	Prince of Viola	M
44682	Prince of Wales	— M
44683	Prince of Walnut Nook	T
44684	Prince of Waterloo	L R
44685	Prince of Watertown	— L R
44686	Prince of Waveland	— R R
44687	Prince William	— M
44688	16th Prince of Wyaconda	P S
44689	17th Prince of Wyaconda	— M
44690	19th Prince of Wyaconda	— P S
44691	21st Prince of Wyaconda	M
44692	Professor Pulse	— M
44694	Prudy's Duke 2nd	Ky I
44695	Publicola	— P S
44698	Pymatuning	Ky I
44699	Queen's Airdrie	— R R
44701	Queen's Duke	— M
44702	Queen's Dunmore	— R R
44703	Raccoon Creek Lad	— Ky I
44706	Ralph	D
44707	Ralph	— M
44708	Rambler	— Cox
44710	Ranger	— R R
44711	Ranger	— P S
44713	Rarus	— M
44714	Ravenswood	— M
44715	Raymond Monitor	L R
44717	Reber	— D
44718	Red Airdrie 3rd	Ky I
44719	Red Baron	— M
44720	Red Bear 2nd	L R
44721	Red Billy	— Cox
44723	Red Bird	— Cox
44724	Red Bonny	M
44725	Red Boy	— M
44726	Red Boy	— P S
44727	Red Briton	— P S
44728	Red Buck	L R
44729	Red Buck 3rd	L R
44730	Red Buck 4th	— M
44731	Redbud of Highland	— Ky I
44732	Red Chief	— Cox
44733	Red Cloud	L R
44734	Red Cloud	M
44735	Red Cloud Oakland 4th	Ky I
44736	Red Clover	— Daisy
44738	Red Comet	— M
44739	Red Dimple	— R R
44740	Red Duke	D
44741	Red Duke	D
44742	Red Duke	P S
44743	Red Duke	Ky I
44744	Red Duke	— Daisy
44745	Red Duke	— P S
44746	Red Duke	M
44747	Red Duke	T
44748	Red Duke	P S
44750	Red Duke of Walworth	— M
44751	Reddy Duke	— D
44754	Red Ike	— M
44755	Red Jack	D
44756	Red Jacket	P S
44757	Red Jim	— R R
44759	Red Lad	— M
44761	Red Mark	— T
44763	Red Prince	Ky I
44764	Red Prince	— T
44765	Red Raven 2nd	Ky I
44766	Red Rock	— M
44769	Red Rover	P S
44770	Red Rover	— Cox
44771	Red Sam	— Ky I
44772	Red Scarsdale	Ky I
44774	Red Simon	— M
44775	6th Red Thorndale	L R
44776	Red Warrior	L R
44778	Remus	Ky I
44784	Resolute	— L R

44785	Reuben	P S	44875	Royal Duke John	— L R
44786	Rex	— R R	44876	Royal Duke John 2nd	— M
44788	Rial	— Daisy	44877	Royal Duke John 3rd	— M
44790	Richard 3rd of Denmark	L R	44880	Royal Gwynne 2nd	Ky I
44791	Richard 3rd	— Ky I	44881	Royalist 3rd	— Cox
44792	Richland Chief	— M	44882	Royalist 4th	— Cox
44793	Richmond Duke	— Cox	44883	Royalist 5th	— Cox
44794	Rinaldo	— R R	44885	Royal Marion	— R R
44797	Ringwood	— T	44887	Royal Prince	—R R
44799	Riverton	— Ky I	44888	Royal Prince	Ky I
44801	Roan Charley	Ky I	44889	Royal Prince	— M
44802	Roan Duke	— R R	44895	Royal Sampson	— L R
44803	Roan Duke	L R	44897	Royal Star	— D
44804	Roan Duke	— Daisy	44898	Royal Stoneland	— D
44805	Roan Duke	T	44899	Royalton Chieftain	— Cox
44806	Roan Duke	Ky I	44900	Royalty	— T
44807	Roan Duke	— Cox	44902	Ruby	— M
44810	Roan Jupiter	Woods	44904	Ruby Duke	L R
44811	Roan Mark	— T	44905	Ruby Duke 2nd	L R
44812	Roan Marquis	— Long-Horn	44906	Rudolph	— M
44813	Roan Newbury	D	44907	Rufus January	— M
44814	Roanoke	—R R	44908	Ruler	P S
44815	Roan Prince	D	44909	Rural Duke	— R R
44816	Roan Prince	— T	44910	3rd Rural Lad	— Daisy
44817	Roan Prince	— P S	44911	Russia Duke	— M
44818	Roan Prince	M	44912	Rusty	— M
44819	Roan Prince	— Cox	44914	Sacramento Chief	T
44820	Roan Rupert	L R	44916	Sailor	M
44821	Roan Star	— Cox	44917	Sailor Boy	— M
44823	Robert Bruce	— R R	44918	St. Elmo	— L R
44825	Robert Lincoln	— M	44919	St. John's Lad	— Ky I
44826	Robin Gray	M	44920	St. Julien	Ky I
44827	Robin Hood	M	44922	St. Patrick	— M
44828	Robin Hood of Maine Valley	— M	44923	Salem Lad	— R R
44829	Rob Roy	— D	44924	Saline Rover	Ky I
44833	Rockingham	— T	44925	Sam	— D
44834	Rockingham	— P S	44926	Sam Daisy	— Daisy
44835	Rock River	M	44927	Sam Lengthy	M
44836	Rockwell	— P S	44929	Sam Patch	L R
44838	Rodman	— M	44930	Sample	— L R
44839	Rolla	— L R	44931	Sam Sodowsky	M
44840	Rome	M	44932	Sampson	— C
44841	Romeo	P S	44933	Sandstone Duke	P S
44842	Romeo	— P S	44934	Santa Anna	M
44843	Romeo	— P S	44935	Sarsfield	— T
44845	Roscoe	Ky I	44936	Saturn of Point Breeze	— L R
44846	Roscoe Conkling	— P S	44938	Schuyler Boy	— M
44847	Rosedale's Duke	— P S	44939	Scotch Lad	— M
44848	Rosedale Prince	— Cox	44941	Scotts Oneida	— R R
44849	Rosebud Duke	—R R	44942	Scott Ray	— M
44850	Rose Boy	— M	44944	Seek No Further	— Daisy
44851	Rose Duke	M	44946	Senator	M
44852	Rose's Duke	— T	44948	Senator Booth	P S
44853	Rose's Duke of Goodness	Ky I	44949	Senator Van Wyck	— M
44854	Rose's Hillhurst 2nd	— P S	44950	Seneca Chief	Ky I
44855	Rosy Knight	— M	44951	Serophina Prince	— Cox
44856	Rose Oxford	— T	44953	Seward Chief	— M
44858	Roswell	— Cox	44954	Seward King	— M
44859	Roswell 2nd	— Cox	44955	Seymour Chieftain	— Ky I
44860	Rough-and-Ready	— M	44956	Shakespeare	— R R
44862	Rover	M	44957	Shakespeare	— P S
44863	Rover	— Cox	44963	Sheldon Duke	— P S
44865	Rowena's Son	— L R	44964	Shelburn Duke 4th	P S
44867	Royal Briton 15th	— L R	44965	Shiawassee Joe	Ky I
44868	Royal Briton 16th	— L R	44966	Shiawassee Star	Ky I
44869	Royal Commander	— Ky I	44967	Shoreham Boy	— Cox
44870	Royal Duke	P S	44968	Short Creek Duke	— Long-Horn
44871	Royal Duke	P S	44969	Short Tail	— M
44872	Royal Duke	— Ky I	44970	Sidney	— M
44873	Royal Duke	— D	44971	Sidney of Leroy	— P S

SHORT-HORN CATTLE PEDIGREES. 215

No.	Name	Code	No.	Name	Code
44973	Silver Beauty	— C	45061	Theodore	M
44974	Signal	M	45062	Theodore Tilton	— D
44975	Sir Charles	— Cox	45063	The Senator	— R R
44976	Sir Charles	— R R	45065	Thomas Birch	— T
44977	Sir Charles	L R	45066	Thomas Booth	— T
44979	Sir Guy	Ky I	45068	Thornton	Cox
44980	Sir Guy	L R	45069	Thornton's Golddust	— M
44982	Sir Henry	Ky I	45071	Timberlake	— Ky I
44985	Sir Knox	— R R	45072	Tim Loomer	— P S
44986	Sir Leon	P S	45073	Toby	— M
44987	Sir Lorillard	— M	45074	Toby Custer	— R R
44990	Sir William	L R	45075	Toby Tyler	M
44991	Sir William C.	Ky I	45076	Tommy	— M
44993	Slosson	— D	45077	Tom Allen	— M
44994	Small Hopes	P S	45078	Tom Bailey 2nd	M
44995	Smuggler	— Cox	45081	Tom Bell	T
44996	Snowball	— Cox	45082	Tom Brown	L R
44997	Snowball	T	45083	Tom Corwin	— Ky I
44998	Snowdon Duke	T	45084	Tom Croxton	Daisy
44999	Snowdrop	— R R	45085	Tom Frahm	M
45000	Solomon	L R	45086	Tom Hendricks	— M
45001	Son of Oxford	— Cox	45087	Tom Hendricks	T
45001	Son of Oxford	— Cox	45088	Tom Marshall	— M
45007	Sparrell Lindell	— Cox	45089	Tom Moore of Emerald Valley	P S
45009	Spotted Chief	L R	45091	Tom Sawyer	— D
45010	Spotted Logan	— R R	45092	Tom Scott	— D
45011	Spotted Rambler	— Cox	45093	Tom Scott	M
45012	Spotted Tail	L R	45094	Tom Thumb	— C
45013	Spotted Tail	Ky I	45096	Topeka	— Daisy
45014	Spotted Tail	Ky I	45098	Tramper	M
45015	Spring Hill	— L R	45099	Trinket	— M
45016	Spring River Oxford	— Cox	45100	Trinket	— M
45017	Spring Vale Duke 2nd	Ky I	45101	Triple Louanjo	— L R
45019	Stanley	— R R	45102	Troilus	— Daisy
45020	Star	— R R	45103	Trumpet	C
45021	Star Duke 2nd	Ky I	45104	True's Barmpton	— R R
45022	Star Duke of Creamridge	P S	45105	Twilight	— R R
45023	Starlight	— D	45106	Twin Jim	M
45024	Star Mina	Ky I	45107	Twin Jim 2nd	M
45026	Star of the North	C	45108	Turkey Hill 2nd	P S
45029	Sterling	Ky I	45109	Tyro 2nd	Cox
45030	Steuben Lad	— R R	45110	Uncle Sam of Brookvale	— M
45031	Stillwater	— Cox	45111	Underedge Duke	— R R
45032	Stonewall	— P S	45112	University	— R R
45033	Stonewall Jackson	— Ky I	45113	Urbana Duke	— M
45034	Stuart	— Cox	45114	U. S. Grant	— P S
45035	Sullivan Duke	P S	45115	Valentine	Ky I
45036	Summit Richard	— R R	45116	Vanderbilt	— D
45037	Sunbeam's Duke	— Cox	45117	Vanderbilt	— M
45038	Superior Duke	— Ky I	45120	Vermont Boy	— Cox
45039	Supreme	— D	45122	Vick Taylor	D
45040	Sunrise	— Cox	45124	Victor	— M
45041	Sweepstakes	— R R	45125	Victor	L R
45042	Sweetzer	— R R	45126	Victor	L R
45043	Tahoe	— Daisy	45127	Victor	— L R
45044	Tally Ho	— P S	45129	Victor	— Cox
45045	Tammany Chief	P S	45130	Victor Chief	C
45046	Tantalus	— L R	45131	Victor Dee	— M
45047	Tarkio	— R R	45132	Victor of Emerald Valley	C
45049	Taylor Prince	— R R	45133	Victor Hugo	Ky I
45050	Taylor Prince	— R R	45134	Victorias Lad	— R R
45051	Tecumseh	— C	45135	Vignaux	T
45052	Tempest	P S	45136	Village Lad	— R R
45053	Tenbrœck	— P S	45137	Village Lad of Nebraska	— Cox
45054	Thad	— M	45138	Viola's Duke	— Cox
45055	Thanks	— L R	45139	Wabaunsee Lad	— D
45057	The Conquering Hero	M	45140	Wade Hampton	— L R
45058	The Knight	P S	45142	Walberg 2nd	Cox
45059	The Major	— R R	45143	Waldheim	Cox
45060	Theodore	— Cox	45144	Waldo	— P S

45145	Walter	R R	
45146	Walter	— Cox	
45147	Walter	— M	
45150	Warren Bates	— M	
45151	Warren Duke	R R	
45152	Washington	— Ky I	
45154	Washington	— P S	
45156	Washington Boy	— D	
45157	Washington Duke	— M	
45160	2nd Waterloo Duke	— P S	
45165	Watson's Duke	— M	
45166	Waveland Duke	P S	
45167	Weighty Bill	— Long-Horn	
45169	Western Star	— P S	
45170	Wetherfield Red	Ky I	
45172	White Buck	P S	
45173	White Duke	— Cox	
45175	Whitefoot Boy	M	
45176	Whitelaw Reid	— P S	
45177	White Prince	— D	
45178	White Stockings	M	
45179	White Stockings	— D	
45181	Whitewater Prince	— C	
45182	4th Wild Eyes of Armada	L R	
45183	Wild Guy	M	
45184	Wiley of Cloverdale	— M	
45187	Wiley Oxford 4th	Ky I	
45188	Wiley Oxford 7th	Ky I	
45189	Wiley Oxford 8th	— Ky I	
45190	Wiley Oxford 9th	— Ky I	
45191	Wiley Oxford 10th	— Ky I	
45192	Wiley Oxford 11th	— Ky I	
45195	Willowwood Beecher	R R	
45196	Willowwood Boy	— Daisy	
45197	Willowwood Oxford	— R R	
45199	Winfield Scott	— L R	
45200	Winfield Scott	— T	
45201	Wisdom	— Daisy	
45204	Woodland Boy	Cox	
45205	Worthy	— R R	
45207	Wyanoke	— Cox	
45209	Yorkshire Bell Duke	— L R	
45210	Yorktown	P S	
45212	Young America	— M	
45213	Young Anderson	— M	
45215	Young Boston	— C	
45217	Young Dimple	— R R	
45218	Young Doctor	— R R	
45219	Young Duke of Athol	— D	
45220	Young Fidgets Airdrie	D	
45222	Young Golden Duke	— M	
45223	Young Lad	— R R	
45224	Young Marquis	Daisy	
45225	Young Mary's Baron	— R R	
45226	Young Mary Duke	— M	
45233	Young Monona	— L R	
45234	Young Prince	Ky I	
45236	Young Snowdrop	Ky I	
45237	Young Tiger	— M	
45239	Zack Taylor	— D	
45240	Zaleucus	M	
45241	Zeb Belle	— D	
45242	Zero	— Ky I	
45243	Zero	D	
45244	Zero	— M	
45245	Zurock	L R	
45286	Abingdon	M	
45288	Adam	— D	
45290	Adelaides Duke	— P S	
45291	Admiral	— Cox	
45292	Admiral's Duke	M	
45293	Adonis	— M	
45298	Airdrie of Dover	— M	
45300	Airdrie Duke	— R R	
45303	Airdrie Lad	R R	
45306	Airdrie of Seward	— M	
45308	Airdrie's Sharon Duke	— M	
45311	Alaric	L R	
45312	Albert	— M	
45313	Albert McCall	D	
45314	Albert Porter	R R	
45315	Alexis	— M	
45316	Allison	— Cox	
45318	Alfred	— Long-Horn	
45319	Alfred of Melleray	— R R	
45320	Allen Prince of Texas	— M	
45321	All O. K.	— Long-Horn	
45322	Alp of the Solid South	— P S	
45324	Alphonso	— P S	
45325	Altamont	— L R	
45326	Altamont	— M	
45327	Alva	— L R	
45328	Anak	— R R	
45329	Andy Johnson	— D	
45333	Ann's Duke	— R R	
45335	Anthony	— M	
45336	April Fool	— L R	
45338	Archduke of Beacon Hall	— T	
45339	Argus	— Cox	
45340	Argyle	Cox	
45341	Armadale	L R	
45343	Arthur	— Ky I	
45344	Arthur Bailey	P S	
45345	Arthur's Success	L R	
45346	Artist	L R	
45348	Arundel	— L R	
45350	Ashton 2nd	— M	
45354	Augustine	— M	
45355	Autumn Lad 2nd	— P S	
45356	Autumn Lad 3rd	— P S	
45357	Avon Prince	Cox	
45358	Badger Duke 2nd	— M	
45359	Banker	— R R	
45360	Banker	Ky I	
45361	Bannack	— P S	
45362	Barber's Pride	— R R	
45363	Barnpton Duke 2nd	— R R	
45364	Barnpton Duke	— R R	
45365	Baron Acomb 4th	— M	
45366	Baron Atholl	— M	
45367	Baron Bly	— R R	
45368	Baron Booth of Catlin	— R R	
45369	Baron Breastplate	— R R	
45374	Baron De Kalb	— R R	
45375	Baron Duke 4th	— M	
45378	Baron Goodness	— R R	
45379	2nd Baron of Grovedale	— M	
45380	Baron Gwynne	— D	
45382	Baron of Helena	— P S	
45385	Baron J.	— R R	
45386	Baron of Lakeside	— Ky I	
45387	Baron Leslie	— R R	
45388	Baron of Lincoln	— Daisy	
45390	Baron Manlius 5th	— L R	
45391	Baron Marquis	— T	
45393	Baron of Oakland	P S	
45394	Baron Oxford	— M	
45396	Baron Piatt	— R R	
45397	Baron of Plumwood	— Ky I	
45399	Baron Rose	— R R	

SHORT-HORN CATTLE PEDIGREES. 217

45401	Baron Smithfield	— Cox		45490	Bob Ingersoll	— R R
45402	Baron Twilight	M		45491	Bob Jordan	— R R
45403	10th Baron of Vermillion	— L R		45493	Bold Nelson	— Cox
45404	11th Baron of Vermillion	— P S		45494	Bonanza	— L R
45405	12th Baron of Vermillion	— P S		45495	Bon Chief	— T
45406	13th Baron of Vermillion	— P S		45496	Bonnie Duke of Woolworth	— P S
45407	14th Baron of Vermillion	— M		45497	Bonnewell	— M
45408	Baron of Winfield	— P S		45498	Boone	— D
45409	Bashford	— Ky I		45499	Booth	M
45410	Bates Duke	— T		45500	Booth	Cox
45415	Bates Oxford	— R R		45503	Boss	— T
45418	Beauty's Napier	L R		45504	Boss Oxford	— Cox
45419	Beaver	— M		45506	Box-Toed Bill	— M
45420	Beck's Baron	— C		45507	Boyle Oxford	— P S
45422	Bedad	— L R		45508	Bracelet's Idol	— M
45424	Beecher	— P S		45509	Braden	— M
45425	Beecher	— M		45510	Breadalbane 5th	Ky I
45426	Beecher	P S		45511	Breadalbane 6th	— Ky I
45427	Beecher	L R		45512	Breadalbane 7th	— Ky I
45428	Beecher	— D		45513	Breadalbane 8th	— Ky I
45429	Beechwood Lad	— M		45514	Breadalbane 9th	— Ky I
45430	Bell Bates	— Cox		45515	Breadalbane 10th	— T
45433	Bell Betty's Duke	T		45516	Breadalbane 11th	— Ky I
45434	Bell Duke 2nd of Durham Park	— R R		45517	Breastplate	— M
45435	Bell Duke 3rd of Durham Park	— R R		45519	Brickbat	— M
45436	Bellcreek Chief Louan	— R R		45520	Bride's 3rd Duke	— R R
45437	Bell Duke of Freeport	— R R		45522	Bride's Underley	— R R
45438	Bell Duke of La Harpe	— Ky I		45523	Brigham	Ky I
45439	Bell Highland	— M		45524	Bright Boy	Ky I
45440	Belmont	— D		45525	Bright Eye's Duke	— M
45441	Belmont of Spring Branch	— M		45527	Brighton	Ky I
45442	Belvedere	R R		45528	Britton Boy	M
45444	Ben	— Cox		45529	Britt Trooper	— P S
45445	Ben Butler	— Cox		45530	Brutus	— Ky I
45447	Ben Heeler	Ky I		45533	Brutus of Melleray	— R R
45448	Benton Rose	— L R		45535	Bryson's Lad	Daisy
45449	Ben Wade	M		45536	Buckeye	Ky I
45452	Beres	— Cox		45537	Buckeye	— L R
45453	Berkshire Boy	— T		45538	Buckeye Boy	— L R
45455	Bertram 3rd	— R R		45541	Bulwer	— Cox
45456	Berwick	— L R		45542	Burk	Cox
45457	Bessie's Airdrie	— R R		45544	Buttercup 3rd	— Cox
45458	Bicker Boy	M		45545	Buttercup 4th	— Cox
45459	Bicker Lad	— Ky I		45547	Byron of Watkin's Glen	— M
45460	Biga	L R		45548	Cadet	— R R
45461	Big Casino	— P S		45549	Cadmus	— L R
45462	Bill Anderson	— L R		45550	Cæsar	— M
45463	Bill Bass	— M		45551	Caliph	— P S
45464	Billy Boy	Ky I		45552	Cameron	— M
45465	Billy Boy	— M		45553	Cameron Duke	P S
45466	Bilger	L R		45554	Cap	— D
45468	Bill Hatch	— D		45555	Capatina	— M
45469	Billy Pierce	C		45556	Captain Beck	— D
45470	Bill Sullivan	Daisy		45557	Capt. Braes	— P S
45471	Bishop Dudley	— Ky I		45558	Capt. Burns	L R
45473	Bismarck	— M		45559	Capt. Dee	— L R
45474	Bismarck	— L R		45560	Capt. Duke John	— L R
45475	Bismarck	— T		45561	Capt. Gay 2nd	— M
45477	Blaine	— M		45562	Capt. Gwynne	— M
45478	Blaize	— M		45563	Capt. Hall	— Ky I
45479	Blister	L R		45564	Capt. Harrison	D
45481	Bluegrass King	M		45565	Capt. Jack	— P S
45482	Blue River Oxford	D		45566	Capt. Jack	Ky I
45483	Bluff Sharon	— D		45567	Capt. Jack	L R
45484	Bob	T		45568	Capt. Jinks	— Ky I
45485	Bob	— D		45569	Capt. King	— R R
45486	Bob Blanc	— Ky I		45570	Capt. Lincoln	Ky I
45487	Bob Block	— P S		45572	Capt. of Melleray	— R R
45488	Bob Duncan	— P S		45573	Capt. Murphy	— P S
45489	Bob Ford	— Ky I		45574	Capt. Perda	— P S

15

No.	Name	Code	No.	Name	Code
45575	Capt. Row	Ky I	45675	Cyclone	— M
45576	Capt. Scott	Ky I	45676	Cyrus	— P S
45578	Carlton Duke	— M	45677	Dacotah	— L R
45579	Carnation Duke	— R R	45678	Dairyman	— D
45580	Carnation 5th's Duke	— M	45679	Daisy Duke	— L R
45581	Cash	— R R	45680	Daisy Duke	— P S
45582	Cashier	— R R	45683	Daisy Muscatoon	— C
45583	Cashier	— R R	45684	Dan	R R
45584	Casquet's Gwynne	— Cox	45685	Dan	Daisy
45586	Cassius Prince	L R	45686	Dan	Ky I
45588	Cayuga Chief	— M	45687	Dandy Jim	M
45590	Cedar Jim	— Cox	45688	Danny 2nd	— R R
45591	Centennial Duke	L R	45689	Daniel	T
45595	Champion of Cedar Springs	T	45690	Daniel Deronda	— P S
45596	Chandos	— M	45691	Dan Rice	— M
45597	Chariton Lad	— M	45692	Dan Rice	— L R
45599	Charley Ross	M	45693	Dauntless	— L R
45600	Chautauqua Beauty	L R	45694	Darby Duke 14th	— D
45601	Chautauqua Bill	L R	45695	Darby Duke 15th	— R R
45602	Cherry Duke	Ky I	45696	Darby Duke 16th	— P S
45603	Cherry Red	L R	45697	Darby Duke 17th	— P S
45604	Cherub of Oakland	P S	45699	David	— P S
45605	Chesnut's Breastplate	P S	45700	David Crockett	— Cox
45606	Chester	— Ky I	45701	Dayton Duke	— L R
45608	Chief	— C	45702	Deacon Smith	— L R
45609	Chief of River Styx	— D	45703	Decatur	Ky I
45610	Chief of Rock Creek	M	45704	Decorah Chief	— T
45613	Clarence	— T	45705	Defender	L R
45614	Clarendon	T	45706	Delaware	— Cox
45615	Claude	L R	45707	Delight 2nd's Duke	M
45617	Clearfield's Prince	— R R	45710	Delilah's Duke	— R R
45619	Clipper	— L R	45711	Delta's Duke	— P S
45620	Clinton Lad	Cox	45712	Denmark	— L R
45621	Clio Lad	— Ky I	45713	Dennie	— R R
45622	Coleman	— M	45715	Derby John	Cox
45625	Colonel	M	45716	Dervish	— R R
45626	Colonel	M	45717	Dewdrop	— D
45628	Col. Barmpton 2nd	— R R	45718	Dexter	— Cox
45629	Col. Foote	M	45719	Dexter	— Cox
45630	Col. Fox	Cox	45720	Diamond	— P S
45632	Col. Jones	— Woods	45724	Dick of Oldham	— L R
45633	Col. Judy	— R R	45725	Dick Rush	— C
45634	Col. McGee	M	45726	Dick Singleton	— R R
45635	Col. Matson	— M	45727	Dick Taylor 2nd	— M
45636	Col. Pike	— P S	45728	Dictator 2nd	P S
45637	Col. Reeves	— M	45729	Dillard Duke 2nd	— L R
45638	Colorado	— M	45732	Diomed	R R
45640	Columbus	R R	45734	Dr. Ballard	— R R
45641	Comanche Chief	— Cox	45735	Dr. Bender	L R
45643	Comet	— M	45736	2nd Dr. of Buena Vista	— C
45645	Commodore	— L R	45737	Dr. Dick	L R
45646	Commodore	— D	45738	Dr. Dick 2nd	— L R
45647	Commodore Perry	— P S	45741	Doddy O. Dan	— R R
45648	Conewango Lad 7th	— P S	45742	Dolce-Far	— D
45650	Conrad	— C	45743	Dolphus	— L R
45651	Cooley	— T	45744	Dombey	Ky I
45654	Cottage Star	Cox	45745	Don Carlos	— M
45655	Cottonwood Louanjo 24th	P S	45746	Dom Pedro	— P S
45659	Count Geneva	— Ky I	45747	Dom Pedro	— Ky I
45660	Count of Melleray	— P S	45748	Dom Pedro	— Cox
45661	Count of Riverdale	R R	45750	Double Sharon	— P S
45663	Creaght Diamond	— M	45751	Dover Boy	M
45664	Cream of the Valley	M	45752	Duchess Duke	— R R
45665	Crescent John	— T	45753	Duchess Duke 2nd	— Long-Horn
45666	Crescent H.	— L R	45754	Dudley George	— P S
45668	Crisp	— L R	45755	Duke	— M
45669	Crocket	— P S	45756	Duke	— R R
45671	Crowder	Ky I	45757	Duke 16th	T
45672	Crowdy	— P S	45758	Duke 17th	T
45674	Crumple	— P S	45759	Duke Airdrie	Ky I

SHORT-HORN CATTLE PEDIGREES.

No.	Name	Owner
45760	Duke of Airdrie 2nd	T
45762	3rd Duke of Alameda	— C
45763	Duke of Almont	Cox
45764	Duke of Andover	— L R
45765	Duke of Anthony	— C
45766	1st Duke of Argentine	— L R
45767	2nd Duke of Argentine	— L R
45768	Duke of Argyll	Woods
45769	12th Duke of Armada	— Cox
45771	15th Duke of Armada	— Cox
45772	Duke of Arndahl	— P S
45773	2nd Duke of Ashland	— Cox
45774	11th Duke of Ashland	— M
45775	12th Duke of Ashland	— M
45776	13th Duke of Ashland	— M
45777	14th Duke of Ashland	— Cox
45778	Duke of Audrian	— M
45779	Duke of Audubon	— L R
45782	Duke of Bacon Ridge	R R
45786	Duke of Bath 7th	— Cox
45787	Duke of Bath 8th	— Cox
45788	Duke of Bath 9th	— Cox
45789	Duke of Bath 10th	— Cox
45790	Duke of Berkshire	Cox
45792	Duke of Blue Mound	Ky I
45793	Duke of Brockhurst	— Cox
45794	Duke of Brockhurst 2nd	— Cox
45795	Duke of Brockhurst 3rd	— M
45796	Duke of Brockhurst 4th	— M
45797	Duke of Brooklyn	Ky I
45798	2nd Duke of Brownsville	— R R
45799	3rd Duke of Brownsville	— R R
45800	4th Duke of Brownsville	— R R
45801	5th Duke of Brownsville	— Ky I
45802	6th Duke of Brownsville	— R R
45803	Duke of Brownwood	M
45804	2nd Duke of Brownwood	M
45805	3rd Duke of Brownwood	M
45806	Duke of Burlingame	— D
45807	Duke of Bushnell	— R R
45808	Duke of Cambridge	M
45811	Duke of Canton	— P S
45812	Duke of Cascade	Ky I
45813	3rd Duke of Cascade	Ky I
45814	Duke of Clymer	— Cox
45815	Duke of Columbus	— Cox
45816	Duke of Constant 2nd	M
45817	Duke of Constant 3rd	M
45818	Duke of Cromwell	— L R
45819	Duke Cuyahoga	Ky I
45820	Duke of Doyle 2nd	T
45821	Duke of Dundee	L R
45822	Duke of Englewood	— M
45823	Duke of Erie	M
45824	5th Duke of Exeter	L R
45825	Duke of Fairview	P S
45826	3rd Duke of Fairview	Ky I
45828	3rd Duke of Forest Home	M
45829	4th Duke of Forest Home	M
45830	5th Duke of Forest Home	M
45831	6th Duke of Forest Home	M
45832	7th Duke of Forest Home	M
45833	8th Duke of Forest Home	M
45834	9th Duke of Forest Home	L R
45835	10th Duke of Forest Home	M
45836	11th Duke of Forest Home	M
45837	12th Duke of Forest Home	M
45838	13th Duke of Forest Home	L R
45839	14th Duke of Forest Home	M
45841	Duke of Fremont	— P S
45842	2nd Duke of Genesee	— M
45844	Duke of Gloster	— Cox
45847	Duke Grace	M
45848	6th Duke of Granville	— L R
45849	2nd Duke of Granville	Ky I
45850	3rd Duke of Greendale	— M
45851	Duke of Guilford	— L R
45852	Duke of Halleck	— R R
45853	Duke of Hampshire	— L R
45855	Duke of Hickory	— M
45856	Duke of Honey Creek	— P S
45857	Duke of Indian Hill	— Cox
45858	1st Duke of Isabella	— L R
45859	2nd Duke of Isabella	— Cox
45860	3rd Duke of Isabella	— M
45861	Duke of Jackson	— L R
45864	Duke of Kansas	— D
45865	Duke of Kewanee	— Cox
45866	Duke of Kirkwood	— P S
45867	Duke of Lakeside	— Cox
45868	Duke of Lanark	— L R
45869	Duke of Lancaster	— P S
45870	Duke of Lemonwier	— M
45871	4th Duke of Lenox	— M
45872	Duke of Leroy	— L R
45876	3rd Duke of Liberty	— D
45878	4th Duke of Lima	— L R
45880	Duke of Long Creek	— M
45881	1st Duke of Lowell	Ky I
45882	2nd Duke of Lowell	Ky I
45883	3rd Duke of Lowell	Ky I
45884	Duke of Lyons	— L R
45885	Duke of Macon	T
45886	Duke of Macon	— M
45887	Duke of Madison	— L R
45888	2nd Duke of Mahtowa	— R R
45889	Duke of Maple Lawn	— L R
45890	10th Duke of Marlboro	— D
45891	Duke of Middle River	Ky I
45893	Duke of Milo	— P S
45894	Duke of Modoc	— C
45896	Duke of Momence	— D
45897	Duke of Monroe	Ky I
45898	Duke of Montcalm	L R
45899	Duke of Montrose	— M
45900	Duke of Mulino	— T
45901	Duke of Mussey	Cox
45902	Duke of Parsons	— Ky I
45903	Duke of Pembroke	— M
45905	Duke of Pittsfield	— D
45908	Duke of Platt	— R R
45909	Duke of Plymouth	L R
45910	Duke of Primrose	L R
45911	Duke of Prospect Home	— M
45912	Duke of Pulaski	— M
45913	Duke of Neosho	— R R
45914	Duke of Nevin	— Cox
45915	Duke of New Berlin	Cox
45916	Duke of North River	— D
45920	Duke of Oneida	— Woods
45921	7th Duke of Osage	— P S
45923	Duke of Oxford	— M
45924	Duke of Richmond	— M
45925	Duke of Rich Valley	— M
45927	3rd Duke of Rock River Valley	P S
45928	2nd Duke of Rosewood	— L R
45929	3rd Duke of Roundhead	— M
45930	Duke of Ruralvale	— Ky I
45931	3rd Duke of Sac	
45932	Duke of St. Johns	— Cox

45933	Duke of Salem................ Ky I	46040	Empire Duke.............. — Ky I
45934	Duke of Seneca .... — D	46041	Emperor................... — P S
45935	Duke of Scott................ Ky I	46042	Emperor.................. — L R
45937	Duke of Sharon............. P S	46044	Emperor................... — M
45940	Duke of Shiloh............ — R R	46045	Emperor 8th.............. — P S
45943	9th Duke of Springdale...... — M	46046	Emperor of Melleray...... — M
45944	10th Duke of Springdale..... — M	46047	Emperor William.......... — C
45945	2nd Duke of Stark........... — M	46048	Endymion................. — D
45946	Duke of Steel Mount .... — P S	46049	Engineer................. — T
45947	Duke of Stephenson. — Long-Horn	46050	English................... Ky I
45948	Duke of Sterling........... — R R	46052	Ephraim.................. M
45950	Duke of Sugar Grove....... — R R	46054	Erybolme .... — P S
45956	26th Duke of Tecumseh...... Ky I	46055	Ettie Turner's Lad........ — R R
45957	Duke of the Plains......... — Cox	46056	Eudora Duke............. — P S
45958	Duke of the Valley......... — R R	46057	Eugene .... — P S
45959	Duke of Transfer............ — M	46058	Eureka................... M
45960	Duke Treble .... Daisy	46060	Ex-Baron................. — Cox
45962	3rd Duke of Troy.......... — Cox	46061	Excelsior................. Ky I
45964	5th Duke of Walnut Hill..... Ky I	46062	Excelsior................. — M
45965	Duke of Warren........... — R R	46065	Fargo.................... — R R
45966	Duke of Wayne 4th.......... — M	46066	Farmer................... — Cox
45968	Duke of Wellington........ P S	46067	Fashion.................. — L R
45969	Duke of Wellington 2nd ...... T	46069	Favorite.................. — T
45970	Duke of Westville......... — R R	46074	Flag Duke................ — Cox
45971	Duke of Wildcat............ — M	46075	Flashaway................ — R R
45972	Duke Wiley 2nd........... — R R	46078	Florida's 8th Duke......... — R R
45973	Duke Williams of Marion .... Ky I	46079	Forest King............... — M
45974	Duke of Wellingford......... — M	46080	Forest Lad................ — M
45975	Duke of Windsor.......... — L R	46081	Forest Lad 2nd............ — M
45976	4th Duke of Wixom .... L R	46082	Forest Lad 3rd............ — Daisy
45977	5th Duke of Wixom......... — D	46083	Fox...................... — R R
45978	2nd Duke of Woodlawn..... — R R	46084	Foxhall.................. — Cox
45979	2nd Duke of Woodland...... P S	46085	Frank.................... — M
45980	1st Duke of Wyandot...... — R R	46086	Frank.................... — M
45981	2nd Duke of Westview....... — M	46087	Frank.................... — L R
45982	Duke of Yorkshire......... — R R	46088	Frank Cambria .... — D
45983	Dunmore 1st............... — L R	46089	Frank Harper ....R R
45988	Durham Lad .... — M	46090	Frank King............... — D
45989	Duroc .... — L R	46091	Frank Leslie.............. — D
45990	Dutton .... — M	46092	Frank Leslie.............. — D
45991	Ead Rover .... — D	46093	Frank Scott..............M
45996	Earl Brutus............... — Cox	46094	Fred..................... — L R
45997	Earl Cato................ — Cox	46095	Fred..................... — T
46000	Earl of Clay............... M	46097	Frederick Mason .... — D
46003	7th Earl of Derby........... — R R	46098	Fred Goken .... — Ky I
46005	Earl of Erie .... — P S	46099	Freeburg Lad.............. T
46006	2nd Earl of Erie .... — P S	46100	Funder................... — Ky I
46008	Earlham Lad .... — P S	46101	Gallatin Prince .. .. — P S
46009	Earl of La Harpe.......... — P S	46102	Gamester 2nd.............. M
46010	2nd Earl of Lake Grove ..... — D	46103	Garf...................... — Cox
46011	Earl of Loudon............ — L R	46104	Garfield.................. P S
46013	Earl of Melleray........... — P S	46105	Garfield.................. — T
46014	2nd Earl of Oxford .... — Cox	46106	Garfield..................L R
46018	13th Earl of Ruralusia....... Ky I	46107	Garfield..................Cox
46020	Earl of Spring Hill........ — L R	46108	Garfield..................L R
46021	7th Earl of Springlake...... Cox	46109	Garfield.................. — R R
46022	Earl of Thornapple 4th..... — Cox	46110	Garfield.................. — Cox
46023	2nd Earl of Woodbine....... — R R	46111	Garfield ....Ky I
46025	Early..................... — M	46112	Garibaldi 2nd............. — D
46026	Earl of York.............. D	46113	Gay Boy................. — D
46027	Ebenezer................. — R R	46115	General................. — M
46028	Eclipse................... — P S	46116	Gen. Arthur............. — M
46029	Eclipse 2nd .... — P S	46117	Gen. Arthur............. — R R
46030	Edward................... M	46119	Gen. Barmpton........... — Daisy
46031	Ed White .... Cox	46120	Gen. Beauregard ....D
46034	Eli D. Gwynne............. — C	46121	Gen. Beaver.............. — R R
46036	Ellens Duke .... T	46122	Gen. Bristow............. — Cox
46037	Elmwood, Jr .... — M	46124	Gen. Carter..............Ky I
46038	Elmwood Valentine 2nd........ T	46125	Gen. Crocker............ — Ky I
46039	Empire................... — M	46126	Gen. Garfield............ — L R

SHORT-HORN CATTLE PEDIGREES.

No.	Name	Code
46127	Gen. Garfield	— M
46128	Gen. Garfield	— Ky I
46129	Gen. Garfield	C
46130	Gen. Garfield	— D
46131	Gen. Garfield	— Ky I
46133	Gen. Grant	— R R
46134	Gen. Grant	— D
46135	Gen. Grant	M
46136	Gen. Grant	— M
46137	Gen. Grant	M
46138	Gen. Grant	P S
46139	Gen. Grant 3rd	— D
46140	Gen. Grant of Elm Grove	— Ky I
46141	Gen. Hadley	— L R
46142	Gen. Hancock	— Cox
46143	Gen. Hancock	— P S
46145	Gen. Knox	Ky I
46146	Gen. Loring	— P S
46147	Gen. Scott	— T
46148	Gen. Shields	P S
46149	Gen. Stone	— Ky I
46150	Gen. Taylor	Ky I
46151	Gen. Worth	M
46153	Geneva of Elkhart	— D
46155	Geneva, Queen 2nd's Duke	M
46158	Geneva Wild Eyes of Tabor	— R R
46160	Gentle Bill	— P S
46161	Gordie	— Long-Horn
46162	George	T
46163	George	— M
46164	George	T
46165	George's Duke	— M
46166	George 1st of Sunnyside	T
46168	Gilman	— M
46169	Ginger	— L R
46171	Glasgow Duke	P S
46172	Glen Athol	— R R
46173	Glencoe	P S
46174	Glenwood 2nd	L R
46175	Gloster	— M
46176	Gold Button	— M
46178	Golddust	— M
46179	Golddust	— Cox
46180	Golddust 2nd	— M
46181	Golden Crown 2nd	— Cox
46182	Golden King 15th	— M
46183	Golden King 22nd	— Cox
46184	Golden King 23rd	— Cox
46185	Golden King 24th	— Cox
46186	Goldfinder	— L R
46187	Gold Medal	— R R
46188	Good Behavior	Ky I
46189	Good Intent Duke 4th	— R R
46190	Gould	— M
46191	Governor	— M
46192	Gov. Collum	M
46193	Gov. Daniel	— Ky I
46194	Gov. McKenzie	Cox
46195	Gov. Morton	— P S
46196	Gov. Ogley	M
46197	Gov. St. John	— C
46199	Grand Duke	T
46200	Grand Duke Alexis	M
46204	Grand River Bill	— R R
46206	Granger	— M
46207	Grant	— Long-Horn
46208	Grant 3rd	— D
46209	Granville Duke	— R R
46210	Grasshopper	— L R
46211	Greenbacker	— M
46212	Greenwood	— L R
46213	Greenwood Lad, Jr	M
46214	Greenville Lad	— D
46215	Grissim's Duke	— R R
46216	Grundy Duke	P S
46217	Guardsman of Neosho	— R R
46218	Guilford Imperial	Cox
46219	Guilford Emperor	D
46220	Halleck	— Long-Horn
46221	Hamilton	— Long-Horn
46222	Hamilton	— P S
46223	Hamilton	M
46225	Hancock	— C
46226	Hancock	— L R
46228	Hannibal Wilson	— T
46229	Hanson	D
46230	Harbinger	— P S
46232	Harbinger	— R R
46234	Hardin	— M
46236	Harold	— Cox
46238	Harvey	— T
46239	Heart of Oak	— M
46240	Hearts of Tipton	Ky I
46241	Hector	— L R
46242	Heir of Plumwood	M
46243	Henney Duke	P S
46244	Henry C	— P S
46245	Henry Fox	— D
46246	Henry Ward Beecher	— R R
46247	Hercules	— R R
46249	Hero	— Ky I
46251	Hero of Alma	— R R
46253	Hickory Jam	— M
46254	Highland Boy	M
46255	Highland Cherry's Duke	M
46256	Highland Chief	— R R
46257	Highland Duke	— Ky I
46258	Highland Duke 2nd	Cox
46259	Highland Duke 3rd	— Ky I
46260	Highgap Chief	— M
46261	Highland Lad	Ky I
46264	Hilpa's Airdrie	— L R
46266	Hindoo	— L R
46267	Hiyoo	— T
46268	Holiday	— P S
46269	Holiday	— D
46271	Honest John	— T
46272	Hoosier Boy	Ky I
46273	Hoosier Boy of Spring Branch	Ky I
46274	Hopeful	— D
46275	Hopeful	— D
46276	Hopeful	P S
46278	Hope's Mazurka	— M
46279	Horatio 2nd	— R R
46280	Hotspur	— L R
46281	Hudson Duke	— M
46284	Hurdle's Bull	— M
46285	Huron	— R R
46287	H. W. Beecher	L R
46288	Hylas	M
46289	Ichabod	L R
46290	Idlewild	P S
46291	Imperial Wild Rose	— L R
46292	Increase	— Daisy
46293	Independence	— M
46295	Independence	— R R
46296	Indian Chief	— R R
46298	Iowa	T
46299	Irish Jack	M
46300	Isaac Newton	T

46301	Ivanhoe 2nd	— P S	46383	Kiowa	— M
46302	Jack Frost	D	46384	Kirby	— D
46303	Jack Hopkins	— M	46389	Kirklevington Gwynne	— M
46304	Jackson	— P S	46395	Kit Carson	— L R
46305	Jake	P S	46396	Kitturah's Star Duke	— T
46306	Jake Markle	— Cox	46397	Knights Airdrie	P S
46307	James	T	46399	Knightley's Son	— Cox
46308	James A. Garfield	— L R	46400	Knight's Mark	P S
46309	James A. Garfield	T	46403	Knœffler	M
46311	James Baughman	— Ky I	46404	Kokomo	— P S
46312	January	Ky I	46405	Kosciusko	— D
46313	Jefferson	— M	46406	Kris Kringle	— Cox
46314	Jesse James	— L R	46407	Labau	M
46315	Jessie's Breastplate	— Cox	46409	Ladys Duke	Cox
46317	Jeweler	— L R	46411	Lafayette	— M
46318	Jim Snyder	M	46412	Lafayette	— D
46319	Job F.	— M	46413	Lagrange	M
46321	Jolly Boy	— Ky I	46414	Lair	R R
46323	Joe	M	46415	Lamar	M
46324	Joe Blackburn	— M	46417	Lanesboro Boy	— Cox
46325	Joe Bowers	— R R	46418	Lansing Lad	— Cox
46326	Jo Bowers	M	46419	Lawmaker	— R R
46327	Joe Harris	— D	46420	Lawndale	— R R
46328	Jo Johnston	— R R	46421	1st Laudable of Linn Grove	P S
46329	Joe Kelly	— L R	46422	Lawful	Cox
46330	Joe Murphy	C	46424	Leander	— M
46331	Joe Nelson 2nd	— L R	46427	Lee	— T
46332	Jo Phillips	Ky I	46428	Lee	— P S
46333	Jo Taylor	— R R	46429	Legal Tender	— R R
46335	John	L R	46430	Leonardo	— M
46336	John	— L R	46431	Leopold	— M
46337	Johnny	— L R	46432	Leroy	— M
46338	John Anderson	Ky I	46436	Lexington	M
46339	Johnny Boy	M	46437	Libey's Duke of Hendon	— M
46341	John Bright	— T	46438	Lightning	D
46343	John Ireland	— M	46441	Lily's Duke	— T
46344	John Norris	Ky I	46442	Limpsey Roy	— Cox
46345	John Oxford	— D	46443	Lincoln	T
46346	John Paragon	— R R	46444	Lincoln	— M
46347	John P. St. John	T	46445	Linden Lad	— D
46348	John Smith	M	46446	Linn Duke	P S
46350	Jonas	— D	46447	Linwood Lad	— R R
46351	Josh Billings	— P S	46448	Little Boone	— R R
46352	Josh Billings	M	46449	Little Sioux	— M
46353	Josh Billings	P S	46450	Locum	— Cox
46354	Joyful	— R R	46451	Logan	— M
46355	Jubilee Duke 4th	— R R	46452	Logan	Ky I
46356	Jubilee Duke 6th	— R R	46453	Logan Chief	— D
46358	Julius	Ky I	46454	Logan Duke	— M
46359	Jumbo	L R	46456	Longfellow	Ky I
46360	Jumbo	— M	46460	Lord Barnum of Denmark	L R
46361	Jumbo	Ky I	46461	Lord Bates	— R R
46362	Jumbo	L R	46462	Lord Beaconsfield of Vine Hill	— D
46363	Jumbo	— Cox	46464	Lord Benson	— L R
46364	Jumbo Duke	— R R	46467	Lord Byron	— M
46365	Junot	Cox	46468	Lord Cavendish	P S
46366	Jupiter	P S	46469	Lord Chatham 4th	— K I
46367	Jupiter	— R R	46471	Lord Compton	— C
46368	Jupiter	— M	46472	Lord Conkling	— M
46370	Kansas Duke	L R	46474	Lord Derby	Cox
46371	Kansas Orphan 3rd	T	46475	Lord Dorchester	L R
46372	Kenilworth	— L R	46480	Lord Ethelbert	— M
46373	Kenley Woods	— M	46481	2nd Lord Exeter	Ky I
46374	Kentucky Duke	— M	46482	Lord Fenwick	— Ky I
46375	Kinnellar's Prince	— R R	46484	Lord Granville	— Cox
46376	King Richmond	P S	46485	Lord Jay	— R R
46378	1st King of Wakarusa	— M	46487	Lord Murphy	— M
46380	King William	D	46489	Lord North	— Long-Horn
46381	King William	— Cox	46490	Lord Orline	P S
46382	Kinsman	— D	46491	Lord Sample	— M

46492	Lord Shelburne — Cox	46580	Matchless ...M
46496	Lord Roscoe L R	46581	Max — R R
46497	Lord Roscoe — M	46582	May Belle's Duke — C
46499	Lord Taylor — R R	46583	May Boy — L R
46500	Lord Thorpe — P S	46584	May Boy ...M
46502	Lord Yarico — M	46585	May Boy ...M
46503	Lord York 3rd ...M	46586	May Duke L R
46504	Lottie's Prince — L R	46587	May Duke — Cox
46505	Louan's Airdrie 2nd — D	46588	May Duke 3rd — M
46507	3rd Louan Duke — R R	46591	Maynard 2nd P S
46598	Louan's Duke of Vine Hill — R R	46594	Mazurka's Oxford 33rd Ky I
46509	Louan Guilford Duke — D	46595	Meadow King — L R
46510	Loudon Daisy	46596	Mecca — Ky I
46511	Loudon Clark 3rd R R	46597	Melody Gwynne's Prince — Cox
46512	London Duke of Lexington — P S	46599	Messala Boy — L R
46513	Loudon Duke of Lexington 2d — P S	46600	Mexico Clarence — Daisy
46514	Loudon Duke of Mackacheck — D	46602	Michigan Chief L R
46515	Louis 2nd Ky I	46605	Milestone — R R
46516	Louis 2nd — C	46609	Model Duke — R R
46517	Louis 3rd — C	46610	Modoc L R
46518	Louis 4th — R R	46611	Modoc Chief L R
46519	Louis 5th — R R	46612	Mollie's Duke — M
46520	Louis 6th — R R	46614	Monarch — P S
46521	Louis 7th — R R	46615	Monarch Ky I
46522	Louis 8th — R R	46616	Monarch — M
46523	Louis 9th — R R	46619	Money ...M
46524	Louis 10th — R R	46620	3rd Monona — P S
46526	Loyalty — M	46621	Monongahela Duke Cox
46527	Lucy's Prince — R R	46622	Monongahela Duke — T
46528	Lysander — R R	46623	Monopoly — P S
46530	McDonough Grand Red Rose — L R	46624	Monroe ...M
46531	McDonough Grand White Rose—L R	46625	Monroe Stewart — R R
46532	McIvor — M	46626	Montgomery — M
46533	Macon — R R	46627	Moreton L R
46534	Majestic 2nd — M	46628	Morgan Lad — Long-Horn
46535	Magic — M	46629	Morse P S
46537	Magistrate 25th — C	46630	Moses — P S
46538	Magistrate 27th — C	46632	Mountaineer 2nd — Ky I
46540	Major P S	46633	Mount Zion Lad — R R
46541	Major T	46634	Muccle John Ky I
46542	Maj. Allen Ky I	46635	Muezzin Duke — Cox
46543	Maj. Anderson — Cox	46637	Muscatoon 5th P S
46544	Maj. Barmpton — L R	46639	Napoleon P S
46545	Maj. Bedford — Ky I	46641	Nat Airdrie — D
46546	Maj. Belmont Ky I	46642	Neal Prince — T
46547	Maj. Clay — M	46643	Nebulous — Cox
46548	Maj. Dunn — P S	46646	Nettie Moore's Sonsie Duke — T
46549	Maj. Hill 11th Ky I	46647	Nero — L R
46550	Maj. Longfellow — Daisy	46648	Nero of Albion P S
46551	Maj. Russell P S	46649	Nevada — R R
46552	Maj. Upton Daisy	46650	Newman's Oxford — Cox
46554	Mameluke Clyde M	46651	Newsboy L R
46555	Mandan C	46654	Nimrod 2nd — D
46558	Manegold — M	46655	Noble Ky I
46559	Market Boy — M	46658	Nonesuch — M
46560	Mark Twain — L R	46659	North River Duke Ky I
46561	Marlin — M	46661	North Star of Middleton — R R
46562	Marmaduke — D	46662	Norton's 15th Baron Lyndale — D
46563	Marquart Ky I	46663	Norton's 20th Baron Lyndale,— Ky I
46564	Marquis of Ailsa Ky I	46664	Numa L R
46565	Marquis of Sugar Grove 2nd — M	46665	Numa C — M
46566	Marquis of Sugar Grove 8th — Ky I	46666	Nymphus — M
46567	Mars — L R	46667	Nymph Duke L R
46568	Marshalltown Duke — R R	46668	Oakland Lad 12th M
46570	Martial 2nd D	46669	Oakland Lad 14th M
46571	Master Airdrie 3rd — Cox	46670	Oakland Lad 19th — Daisy
46573	Master Darlington — M	46671	Oakland of Spring Branch 2nd M
46575	Masterman — R R	46672	Oakwood Lad — C
46578	Master Prince M	46673	Ole Bull — C
46579	Master Snowflake — L R	46674	Ole Bull M

UNFASHIONABLE CROSSES IN

No.	Name	Cross
46675	One Horn	— Ky I
46677	Onondaga Chief	— Cox
46686	Oriel	— L R
46687	Orphy's Boy of Springvale	— P S
46688	Osage Duke	— M
46689	Oscar Wilde	— M
46690	Oscar Wilde	— D
46691	Oscar Wilde	T
46693	Oscar Wilde	Ky I
46695	Oshawa	T
46697	Otis	— D
46698	Otoe	— R R
46699	Ouray	— Daisy
46701	Oxford 2nd	Ky I
46702	Oxford Boy	Cox
46709	Oxford's 3rd Grand Duke	— Cox
46710	Oxford's 4th Grand Duke	— Cox
46712	Oxford Gwynne Baronet 3rd	— L R
46713	Oxford Lad	— D
46714	Oxford Lad	T
46715	Oxford Prince	— C
46716	Oxford Prince 3rd	— R R
46717	Oxford Prince of Lambton	— D
46719	Oxford of Screbner Farm	— L R
46720	Parnell	— Ky I
46721	Parvenue	Cox
46723	Patrick	— L R
46725	Patriot 2nd	— Long-Horn
46726	Patterson's Woodhill	— Cox
46727	Paul	D
46728	Pawnee Chief	Ky I
46729	Pearl Duke	P S
46730	Pedro	— L R
46731	Peerless 3rd	— L R
46732	Peerless Duke	— R R
46733	Prosta Duke	— P S
46734	Peri Sharon	— C
46736	Perfection	— L R
46737	Perfection	— Ky I
46738	Perry Napier	— D
46739	Pete of Saline	— Cox
46740	Phil Sheridan	Cox
46741	Phil Sheridan, Jr.	— L R
46742	Phœbe's Earl of Constance	— T
46743	Phœnix Duke	— R R
46744	Phyllis Duke 3rd	— R R
46745	Phyllis Lad	— R R
46746	Pilot 2nd	P S
46747	Pinafore	Cox
46749	Pine Hill Lad J.	— D
46750	Pine Hill Star	— L R
46751	Pioneer Favorite	— M
46752	Plainfield	Cox
46753	Plebian	— D
46754	Pompey	— T
46756	Porter	— T
46757	Portland	T
46758	Powell's Duke	Ky I
46760	Prairie Prince	— M
46764	Prince	— Cox
46765	Prince	M
46766	Prince	— L R
46767	Prince	— Cox
46768	Prince	— Cox
46769	Prince	— M
46770	Prince	L R
46771	Prince Airdrie	— M
46772	Prince Albert	— Ky I
46773	Prince Albert 2nd	— L R
46774	Prince Alfred of Albion	P S
46775	Prince Albert of Pleasant Ridge	Ky I
46776	Prince Aleck	— L R
46778	Prince Arthur	— D
46780	Prince Arthur	— Cox
46781	Prince Arthur	— M
46782	Prince of Arragon 5th	T
46783	4th Prince of Ashbrook	D
46784	5th Prince of Ashbrook	D
46785	Prince Bob	— Cox
46786	Prince of Bridgeport	— Daisy
46787	Prince of Burnie	— M
46789	Prince Derby	— D
46790	Prince Duke	L R
46791	Prince Duke	— R R
46792	Prince Edward	— R R
46793	Prince Edward	Ky I
46794	Prince of Elkhorn	— M
46795	Prince of Fairfield	— Cox
46796	Prince Frederick	— P S
46797	Prince Geneva's Son	— C
46798	Prince George 3rd	— R R
46799	Prince George 4th	— T
46801	Prince of Hazel Ridge	P S
46802	Prince Hope 2nd	— M
46804	Prince John	L R
46805	Prince Louis	— Cox
46806	Prince of Mahaska	Daisy
46807	Prince Malone 3rd	— Cox
46808	Prince of Marion	— M
46809	Prince of Marion 2nd	— M
46810	Prince of Marion 3rd	— M
46813	Prince of Oak Ridge	M
46814	Prince of Orange	— L R
46815	Prince Regent	Ky I
46817	Prince of Salem	M
46818	Princess Duke 5th	— P S
46819	Prince of Sharon 9th	— L R
46820	Prince of Sharon 10th	— L R
46821	Prince of Sharon 11th	— Cox
46824	Prince Warren	— C
46825	Prince of Wales	— D
46826	Prince of Wales	— Cox
46827	Prince Wiley	— M
46828	Prince of Woodlawn	— R R
46829	Prince of York	— Ky I
46830	Progress	— R R
46831	Proud American	— D
46832	Proud Duke	— R R
46834	Proud Duke of Wilmington	Ky I
46835	Proud Taurus	— R R
46836	Publicola	— P S
46837	Punch	Ky I
46838	Purdy Jones	M
46839	Puritan	— M
46841	Queen's Airdrie	— R R
46843	Queen Breastplate 5th	— M
46844	Queen's Duke	— Ky I
46845	Quotation	— R R
46846	Rajah 2nd	M
46847	Rajah 3rd	M
46848	Rajah 4th	M
46851	Red	— M
46853	Red Airdrie	— M
46855	Red Bear 3rd	L R
46856	Red Buck 4th	— T
46857	Red Buck 5th	L R
46858	Red Buck 6th	— Cox
46859	Red Buck 7th	— D
46860	Red Buck 8th	— Cox
46862	Red Cliff	Ky I

No.	Name	Herd
46864	Red Cloud	— L R
46865	Red Cloud, Jr	— Cox
46866	Red Clymer	— L R
46867	Red Comet 2nd	M
46868	Red Dale	— P S
46869	Red Dick	— Ky I
46870	Red Duke	— P S
46871	Red Duke	— M
46872	Red Duke	— M
46873	Red Duke	— C
46874	Red Duke	— T
46876	Red Duke of Elm Grove	— Ky I
46877	Red Earl	L R
46878	Red Earl	— P S
46879	Red Fox	— D
46880	Red Fox 2nd	— D
46881	Red Gauntlet	— Cox
46882	Red Jacket	L R
46883	Red Jim	L R
46884	Red John	— L R
46885	Red Justice	— M
46886	Red Lad	— D
46891	Red Lion	— Cox
46892	Red Livington	— P S
46893	Red Lord	P S
46894	Red Monk	— Ky I
46895	Red Oak	— M
46896	Red Prince	L R
46897	Red Prince	— M
46898	Red Prince	— M
46899	Red Prince	Cox
46900	Red Prince	— L R
46901	Red Prince	— T
46902	Red Prince	Ky I
46903	Red Rover	— R R
46905	Red Rover	— P S
46906	Red Rose's Casquet	— C
46907	Red Sheffielder	— D
46908	Red Star of Oakland	P S
46909	Red Thunder	L R
46910	Red Victor	Ky I
46912	Reformer	— L R
46913	Reformer	— R R
46914	Regal Duke	M
46917	Renne	— Cox
46918	Reporter	— M
46919	Resolution	— L R
46920	Reuben Custer	— D
46921	Revenge	— Cox
46923	Reynolds	— Cox
46924	Riding Master	— R R
46925	Ridott Boy	L R
46926	Richard 2nd	— P S
46927	Richelieu	M
46931	Rising Sun	— P S
46932	R. Lee	— P S
46933	Roan Duke	— Cox
46934	Roan Duke	— P S
46936	Roan Duke 2nd	— L R
46939	Roan Earl	L R
46940	Roan Jay	Ky I
46941	Roan Jupiter	— Cox
46942	Roan Lad	— L R
46943	Roan Prince	L R
46944	Roan Prince	— M
46945	Roan Sharon	P S
46946	Roan Will	L R
46947	Robert Brook	Ky I
46949	Robert Dhu	Cox
46950	Robert M	— D
46951	Robert Smith 2nd	— L R
46952	Robinson Crusoe	— Cox
46954	Rob Roy	M
46955	Rob Roy 2nd	— M
46956	Rob Roy	— R R
46957	Rob Roy	— L R
46958	Rocket	— M
46960	Rockingham	— M
46961	Roderick	L R
46962	Roderick	T
46965	Roland	— M
46966	Roma's Waldberg	— Ky I
46967	Romeo	— Cox
46968	Romeo	— Cox
46969	Romeo	L R
46970	Roscoe	— Long-Horn
46972	Roscoe	— M
46973	Roscoe C	— M
46976	Roseberry	— M
46977	Rose Duke	— M
46979	Rose Duke	— Ky I
46980	Rosy Duke	— P S
46981	Rose Duke	— M
46983	Rosy Lad	— R R
46986	Roy	— M
46987	Royal	— D
46988	Royal Airdrie	— R R
46990	Royal Athelstane	M
46992	Royal Breastplate	— R R
46993	Royal Briton 17th	— L R
46994	Royal Briton 18th	— L R
46995	Royal Charles	— Cox
46997	Royal Dimple	— L R
46999	Royal Duke	— R R
47001	Royal Duke	— L R
47003	Royal Duke	L R
47004	Royal Duke	D
47005	Royal Duke of Sharon	C
47006	Royal Earl	— L R
47007	Royal Gallant	— M
47008	Royal George	M
47009	Royal George	L R
47010	Royal Goodness	Cox
47011	Royalist 4th	Cox
47013	Royal Maynard 2nd	Ky I
47016	Royal Oxford	Ky I
47017	Royal Prince	L R
47018	Royal Prince	M
47019	Royal Prince	— M
47022	Royal Star	— Cox
47026	Rouen	M
47027	Round Grove Marquis 2nd	T
47031	Rural Blanc	— R R
47032	Russell Gwynne	M
47033	Sachem	M
47034	St. Joseph	— Cox
47035	St. Nicholas, Jr	— L R
47036	St. Nicholas Baldur	— Ky I
47037	St. Patrick	— D
47038	Saladin	— R R
47039	4th Salem Prince	— R R
47040	Sam	L R
47041	Sam Houston	— R R
47042	Samuel J. Tilden	— M
47043	Sam Kirkwood	— D
47044	Sam Price	M
47045	Sam Snyder	— M
47046	Sampson	— P S
47048	Sam Weller	M
47049	Sam Wiley 2nd	C

47050	Sandy	Daisy		47139	Symmetrical Prince	— Cox
47051	Santa Claus	— D		47140	Tambour 2nd	— R R
47054	Scotland Thom	— M		47142	Taylor Bly	— T
47058	Senator	— M		47145	Tendoy	— P S
47059	Sensation	— Cox		47147	The Boss	— M
47060	Seraphina's Airdrie	— Cox		47148	The Doctor	— M
47062	Sharon Duke	— D		47149	The Earl	— P S
47063	Sharon Boy	L R		47150	The Governor	— R R
47064	Sharon King	— C		47151	Thomas Carlyle	M
47065	Sharon Prince	— C		47153	Thorndale Prince	T
47066	Shealor	C		47154	Thorndale Prince 2nd	— L R
47067	Sheffielder's Success	— D		47155	Thrasher	— L R
47068	Sidlaw Chief	— P S		47156	Tiger	P S
47069	Sigel	P S		47157	Timon	— M
47070	Silver Chief	— M		47158	Tip	Ky I
47071	Silverheels	— P S		47161	Tommy	— L R
47072	Silver Moon	— P S		47162	Tom Corwin	— D
47073	Silvernail	— D		47163	Tom Gant	— C
47074	Silvius	— M		47164	Tom King	— R R
47075	Simon	M		47165	Tom Mardis	Ky I
47077	Sir Arthur	R R		47166	Tom Scott	M
47078	Sir Curtis of Appleton	— C		47167	Tom Swan	Cox
47080	Sir Henry	T		47168	Tom Valentine	D
47081	Sir Julien	— R R		47169	Toronto	— D
47082	Sir Knight	— L R		47170	Trireman	M
47084	Sir Oxford	P S		47172	Troubadour	— M
47085	Sir Rodney	— D		47173	Tubal Cain	L R
47086	Sir Ralph	Ky I		47175	Tuberose Duke	— L R
47087	Sir Spot 2nd	— Cox		47179	Twilight	— M
47088	Sir Stanley	— Cox		47180	Tyrone	— L R
47089	Sir Titus Sault	— Cox		47182	Union Duke	— P S
47090	Sir William M. Lardin	Ky I		47186	Valentine	M
47091	Smuggler	P S		47187	Valentine Duke	— R R
47092	Smuggler 2nd	Ky I		47188	Valley Duke	— M
47093	Snowball	— P S		47190	Valley Prince	— Cox
47094	Snowflake	D		47191	Valley Prince	M
47095	Somonauk	— Cox		47192	Vanderbilt	— R R
47096	Son of Duke	— M		47194	Valois	— M
47099	Son of Lexington	— D		47195	Varga	— R R
47100	Sophrona's Duke 2nd	— M		47198	Vespasian	— L R
47101	South Fork Lad	— D		47199	Vicksburg	— M
47103	Spanker of La Paz	— M		47200	Victor	— Ky I
47106	Splendid	— M		47201	Victor	— M
47107	Starr	— M		47203	Victor of Cedar Springs	T
47108	Starr of Castle Grove	— M		47204	Victor Hugo	— M
47109	Star Duke	L R		47206	Victoria Lad	M
47110	Star of Granger	— L R		47207	Victor of Lyons	— L R
47111	Star of Hope	— P S		47208	Victor of Oakland	P S
47112	Starkey Pride	Cox		47210	Vigor	— D
47115	Star of Oakland 2nd	— D		47212	Volunteer	— T
47116	Star of the Union	— Cox		47214	Wade Hampton	— T
47117	Star of the West	— P S		47215	Wade Hampton	L R
47118	Stem Winder	— P S		47217	Waldberg 2nd	P S
47119	Stentor	M		47218	Wadden	P S
47120	Stewart's Airdrie	— R R		47219	Walnut Grove Chief	M
47121	Stewart's Don Airdrie	— M		47220	Wapello Boy	— D
47122	Stewart's Duke of Marengo	— R R		47221	Ward's Bull	— Cox
47123	Stillwater	— L R		47222	Warren Lexington	— R R
47124	Stonehill Jackson	— D		47223	Warwick	— Cox
47125	Stonewall	— M		47225	Washington Duke 2nd	— M
47127	Sucker Boy	Ky I		47230	Waudema	— R R
47128	Sultan	L R		47231	Waxenhorn's 2nd Duke	P S
47129	Sultan	— R R		47233	Welbourn 2nd	— M
47131	Sunfish	— M		47234	Weldon Duke	— Ky I
47133	Superior Lad of Bell Creek	— Ky I		47235	Weldon Gem	— Ky I
47134	Surprise Duke	— L R		47236	Well Bee	— P S
47135	Sutherland	— M		47237	Western Boy	— P S
47136	Sycum	T		47238	White Chief	Ky I
47137	Sycum 2nd	T		47239	White Comet	— P S
47138	Sylvanus of Pleasant Ridge	Ky I		47240	White Stockings	— R R

No.	Name	Herd	No.	Name	Herd
47241	White Tail	— C	47343	Alexander	M
47243	Wild Cat	— Cox	47344	Alexander	— D
47245	5th Wild Eyes of Armada	L R	47345	Alfonzo	— R R
47246	6th Wild Eyes of Armada	L R	47346	Alfred	— M
47247	Wild Eyes Gloster 1st	L R	47348	Allan Bane	Ky I
47250	Wiley Duke	— P S	47350	Allen Gibson	M
47251	Wiley Morris	— R R	47351	Almon	P S
47252	Wiley Oxford 5th	Ky I	47352	Althea Bull	— M
47253	Wiley Oxford 6th	Ky I	47353	Al West	— M
47255	Wildwood Airdrie	— M	47354	Amendment	— D
47256	Wilfred	— R R	47355	American Boy	— D
47257	Wilkins Micawber	— R R	47356	American Boy	— Cox
47258	Wilna	— M	47357	Andrew	— M
47260	William Tibbs	P S	47358	Andy Johnson	— Ky I
47261	William Vance	— P S	47359	Annawan	— Daisy
47262	Willow Grove Lad	L R	47360	Annie's Duke	— Ky I
47263	Winchester	— R R	47361	Anthony	— Cox
47264	Winnebago Chief	— C	47362	Arizona	Ky I
47265	Wonder	— R R	47363	Apollo	Ky I
47266	Woodside Earl of Springwood	Cox	47364	April Prince	— M
47267	Woodson	Daisy	47365	Arabella's 2nd Mayflower	— R R
47268	Woolworth Duke 2nd	— R R	47366	Arabi Pacha	— M
47269	Woolworth Duke 3rd	— R R	47368	Archimedes	— L R
47271	Yankee Prince	Ky I	47369	Archy	— T
47273	Yorktown	— L R	47370	Aristides	— R R
47274	Young Admiral	M	47371	Arnold	— R R
47276	Young America	P S	47372	Arthur	— M
47277	Young Baron	— R R	47376	Athlete	— Cox
47278	Young British Flag	— L R	47378	Auglaize Charley	P S
47280	Young Comet of Middleton	Cox	47379	Auglaize Dick	P S
47282	Young Earl of Spring Lake	— Cox	47380	Augustus	— D
47284	Young Hickory	— L R	47381	Aztec	— P S
47285	Young Mary's Beau	— D	47382	Baden Duke 6th	M
47287	Young Oxford	— Cox	47383	Baden Duke 7th	P S
47288	Young Stuart	— M	47384	Baden Duke 8th	P S
47290	Young Twilight	— M	47385	Baden Duke 9th	P S
47291	Zeb Dun 3rd	— M	47386	Baden Duke 10th	M
47292	Zeb Dun 4th	— M	47387	Baden Duke 11th	M
47293	Zenadia's Duke	— L R	47388	Baden Duke 12th	P S
47304	Aaron Arslan	— M	47389	Baden Duke 13th	— L R
47305	Abaris	— Cox	47390	Baden Duke 14th	M
47306	Abe	P S	47391	Baden Duke 15th	M
47307	Abner Sharon	— Daisy	47392	Ball	— P S
47309	A. C. R.	— M	47393	Banker	— Daisy
47310	Acton	— M	47394	Banker	L R
47311	Adam	Cox	47397	Banquo	— R R
47312	Adam	— L R	47399	Barmpton Prince	— Cox
47313	Adelaide's Victor	— D	47401	Barnett	Ky I
47314	Adjutant	— M	47402	Barnum	— M
47315	Admiral	— L R	47403	Baron	— M
47317	Admiral Lad	Cox	47404	Baron Airdrie	— Cox
47318	Adonis	— M	47405	Baron of Audubon	— M
47319	Adonis 3rd	— T	47409	Baron Duke 8th	— M
47320	Adrer	L R	47410	Baron of Cedar Hill	Daisy
47321	Agnes' Duke	— L R	47413	Baron Gwynne 2nd	— Cox
47322	Aguila	Ky I	47414	Baron Gwynne of Oakland	— R R
47323	1st Airdrie Bully Boy	— L R	47416	Baron Kinellar 3rd	— R R
47327	Airdrie's Hilpa	— P S	47417	Baron Kinellar 4th	— R R
47328	Airdrie Lad 2nd	— P S	47418	Baron Lewis 5th	Ky I
47330	Airdrie Prince 2nd	L R	47422	Baron Louan	— Cox
47331	Airdrie Prince 3rd	L R	47423	8th Baron Manlius	— Cox
47332	Ajax	— C	47426	Baron Oakland's Duke	— T
47333	Ajax	— Ky I	47427	Baron Payne	— D
47334	Ajax	— L R	47428	Baron Polk	— P S
47336	Alaska	L R	47429	Baron Richmond	— C
47337	Albert 3rd	— D	47430	Baron Rothchild	— D
47338	Albert Martin	— L R	47433	Baron Thorndale	M
47340	Alcimedon	— M	47434	Baron of Wapsie	— P S
47341	Alex	— M	47435	Barrett	P S
47342	Alexander	— M			

47436	Barrington Duke 3rd of Bluff Creek .... L R	47527	Bixby .... D
47437	Barrington Duke 4th of Bluff Creek .... — T	47528	Blackwater .... Woods
47438	Barrington Duke 5th of Bluff Creek .... — Long-Horn	47530	Blitzer of Spring Valley .... Cox
		47531	Blooming Prairie Duke— Long-H'n
		47533	Bloom's Royalist .... — Cox
47443	Battleax 3rd .... — M	47534	Blucher .... — D
47444	Battle Royal of Sunnyside ... — R R	47535	Blucher .... — R R
47445	Baxter .... — D	47536	Blue Prince .... — R R
47447	Beaconsfield 2nd .... — Cox	47537	Blue Valley Bates .... M
47448	Beaconsfield 4th .... — Cox	47538	Bluff Duke .... — M
47449	Beaconsfield 5th .... — Cox	47540	Bob .... Ky I
47450	Beau Lewis .... — R R	47541	Bob Bean .... — R R
47451	Beaumont 2nd .... — C	47542	Bobbie .... — Cox
47452	Beaumont 3rd of Spring Valley, Cox	47543	Bob Ingersoll .... Ky I
47454	Beech Duke .... — M	47544	Bob Moore .... — M
47455	Beecher .... — M	47545	Bob White .... — Cox
47456	Beecher .... M	47546	Bob White .... — M
47457	Beecher of Dell Rapids ...... — M	47547	Bogardus .... — L R
47458	Begale .... Cox	47548	Bois Gilbert .... — L R
47459	Bell Boy .... Cox	47549	Bolivar .... — L R
47461	Belle Duke .... — Cox	47550	Bolivar .... — Cox
47462	Belle Duke 2nd .... Ky I	47551	Bolton Duke 3rd .... — M
47463	Belle Duke 2nd .... — R R	47552	Bolus .... — Cox
47467	Bell Duke of Cambridge .... — Cox	47553	Bonanza .... Cox
47468	Bell Duke of Milford .... — R R	47554	Bonanza 2nd .... D
47469	Bell Duke of Oakland .... — L R	47557	Bonnie Airdrie .... — P S
47470	Bell Duke Q. .... — R R	47559	Booth .... Cox
47471	Bell Duke of Stephenson ..... M	47560	Booth of Oakland .... — Cox
47472	Bell Duke of Stillwater ..... L R	47561	Borrito .... — M
47474	Bell Gwynne 2nd .... — Cox	47562	Boss of Bell Creek .... — R R
47475	Bell Gwynne 3rd .... — Cox	47563	Boss Bright Eyes .... — Cox
47476	Bellman .... — Cox	47564	Bossworth .... — R R
47477	Bell Oxford .... — R R	47565	Bourbon Duke .... Woods
47479	Bellvador .... — R R	47566	Brampton Boy .... Ky I
47481	Belmont .... Cox	47567	Brazos .... — Ky I
47482	Belted Will .... M	47569	Bride's Gem .... — R R
47483	4th Belvedere .... — M	47570	Brigham .... — Ky I
47484	5th Belvedere .... — M	47571	Brigham .... Ky I
47489	10th Belvedere of Rosemound — Cox	47572	Brigham .... — R R
47490	Ben .... L R	47573	Brigham Young .... — L R
47491	Ben Bolt .... — M	47574	Brigham Young .... — L R
47492	Ben Butler .... — Cox	47576	Bright Boy .... — M
47493	Ben Butler .... L R	47577	Bright Eyed Lad .... — L R
47494	Ben Butler .... — Cox	47578	Bright Eyes Boss .... — Cox
47495	Ben Butler .... — Cox	47580	Brooke .... — Cox
47496	Ben Davis .... P S	47581	Brooke 3rd .... — Cox
47497	Ben Frederick .... — M	47582	Brookside Lad 3rd .... — D
47501	Ben LeClaire .... — T	47583	Bruno .... — L R
47503	Benton County Lad .... — M	47584	Brutus .... — R R
47504	Ben Wiley .... — D	47586	Buchanan .... — Cox
47506	Bernhardt .... — R R	47587	Buckeye .... Cox
47507	Berry Hanks 2nd .... — M	47588	Buckeye Duke 3rd .... M
47508	Beethoven .... — L R	47589	Buckeye Lad .... L R
47509	Bilboa .... — R R	47590	Buckeye Lad .... — Cox
47510	Bill .... L R	47591	Buckeye Prince .... Cox
47511	Bill Ferguson .... — L R	47592	Buckeye Prince 2nd .... — P S
47513	Billy .... — D	47593	Bulger .... — M
47514	Billy Boy .... — Cox	47594	Burget .... — P S
47515	Billy Boy .... — L R	47595	Burly Jim .... — Ky I
47516	Billy Boy .... L R	47596	Burnie's Clay .... — R R
47517	Billy Boleyn .... L R	47597	Burnside .... — T
47518	Billy Cummings .... — P S	47598	Bushrod ....
47519	Billy DeBuvy .... M	47599	Busti Duke .... — Cox
47521	Billy Leslie .... — P S	47600	Butcher .... — M
47522	Billy Mason .... Cox	47601	Butler Duke .... — R R
47523	Billy Weeks .... — D	47603	Byron .... — R R
47524	Billy Winters .... — Ky I	47604	Cadet Taylor .... — P S
47525	Bismarck .... — R R	47605	Cadmus .... — L R
47526	Bitter Sweet .... — Cox	47607	Calhoun 6th .... — D
		47608	Caliph 2nd .... — D

No.	Name	Herd
47609	Calvert	— Ky 1
47611	Cambria Duke of Bluff Creek	— Long-Horn
47612	Cambridge Duke	— P S
47613	Candor Duke	C
47614	Cap Airdrie	Ky I
47615	Captain	— Cox
47617	Capt. Boabdil	— M
47618	Capt. Bogardus	— Ky I
47620	Capt. Cobb	— M
47621	Capt. Doubledick of Spring Valley	Cox
47623	Capt. Hubbell	L R
47624	Capt. Jenks	— T
47625	Capt. Moore	M
47626	Capt. Twiggs	M
47627	Capt. V.	P S
47628	Capt. Wiggs	M
47629	Carl	— Ky I
47630	Carlos	— L R
47631	Carlyle	— Daisy
47633	Cassandra's Duke	— C
47634	Cassius	— D
47635	Cassius	— M
47636	Cato 2nd	— R R
47637	Cedar Bill	— L R
47638	Centreville Duke	— T
47639	Challenge	— M
47640	Challenger	— M
47643	Champion	Cox
47644	Champion	M
47645	Champion	— M
47646	Champion Duke	M
47647	Champion of the Valley	— M
47648	Chance	— Cox
47649	Changeable	— Cox
47650	Charles	— M
47651	Charles	P S
47652	Charlie	— R R
47653	Charley A.	— D
47654	Charley Clay	— R R
47655	Charmer 2nd	— Ky I
47657	Chester	P S
47658	Chester	— M
47659	Chesteto	— R R
47660	Chicaskia Chief	— M
47661	Chief of Jackson	— R R
47662	Chieftain	— R R
47663	Chieftain	— R R
47664	Chieftain	D
47665	Christmas Day	— Cox
47668	Cicero	— R R
47669	Clackamas	— M
47672	Clifton Duke 2nd	Daisy
47673	Clifton Lad	Cox
47674	Clifton Napier's Duke	— M
47675	Climax	— L R
47676	Climax	— P S
47677	Climax	— M
47678	Clinton Lad	— Ky I
47679	Clymer	— Cox
47680	Cola	D
47682	Collins	C
47684	Colonel	P S
47686	Col. Buford	— M
47687	Col. Crawford	— L R
47688	Col. Curry	— M
47689	Col. Devosse	— L R
47690	Col. Forde	— L R
47691	Col. Fred	— Cox
47692	7th Col. Gloster	— Cox
47693	Col. Judy	Ky I
47694	Col. Judy	— D
47695	Col. King	— M
47696	Col. Louan	M
47698	Col. Stephenson	T
47699	Col. Wagram	— L R
47700	Col. Wm. A. Stone	L R
47701	Colorado Boy	Ky I
47702	Columbus	— C
47703	Columbus	— L R
47704	Columbus Lad	L R
47705	Comet	— M
47706	Comet	— M
47707	Comet	L R
47709	Comet	R R
47710	Comet	L R
47711	Comet	— L R
47712	Commander	— M
47713	Commander	— M
47715	Commodore	— L R
47716	Commodore	M
47718	Commodore Richmond 2nd	— R R
47719	Como	— Cox
47720	Con	— P S
47721	Conger	— R R
47722	Congressman	— Cox
47723	Conkling	P S
47724	Conkling	— L R
47726	Conqueror of Waveland	— T
47727	Constance Duke 2nd of Maple Lawn	— L R
47728	Copley Strife	— L R
47729	Copper Bottom	— Cox
47730	Copperfield	M
47731	Cortez	— R R
47732	Cortland	— Cox
47733	Corydon	— M
47734	Cossack	T
47735	Counsellor of Waveland	— T
47736	County Member 2nd	Ky I
47737	Cowboy of Linn	— P S
47738	Cowslip's Duke	— P S
47739	Crawford Duke	— D
47740	Crocket	— P S
47741	Crossings Duke	— M
47742	Crowfoot	— L R
47743	Crown Prince	— M
47745	Crusader	— Ky I
47746	Cuyahoga Rover	Cox
47747	Cyclone	— D
47748	Cy Hamil	— M
47749	Cypress Duke	Ky I
47750	Cyrus	— M
47751	Daily Duke	— Cox
47756	Dakota Boy	— P S
47757	Dakota Chief	P S
47758	Damon	— L R
47759	Dan	Ky I
47760	Dan	— Cox
47761	Dandy	Cox
47762	Dandy Jim of Maple Grove	— Cox
47763	Daniel	— D
47764	Daniel	— C
47765	Daniel Boone	— C
47766	Daniel O'Conner	— P S
47767	Daniel Webster 2nd	— D
47769	Danny	— M
47770	Dante	— D
47771	Darby Chief	P S

47772	Darwin	Cox	47866	18th Duke of Ashland — M
47773	Dashwood	— P S	47867	3rd Duke of Avondale — M
47775	Davie Deset	— P S	47868	Duke of Bavaria — Long-Horn
47777	Decker	— M	47870	Duke of Beason D
47778	Defiance 1st of O. K.	— M	47871	Duke of Berlin L R
47779	Delight's Duke	M	47872	2nd Duke of Blooming Prairie D
47782	Derby Prince	Cox	47873	Duke of Brookfield — L R
47784	De Soto 3rd	P S	47874	7th Duke of Brownsville — R R
47785	Dexter	M	47875	8th Duke of Brownsville — R R
47788	Dick	— M	47876	2nd Duke of Bunker Hill — R R
47789	Dick	T	47877	Duke of Cambridge — Cox
47790	Dickey Dobbins	— D	47879	Duke of Carlingford — D
47791	Dick Grey	— M	47880	Duke of Cedar Croft — D
47792	Dick Seaton	— M	47881	8th Duke of Chico — P S
47793	Dick Taylor	— Cox	47882	11th Duke of Chico — M
47794	Dick Williams	Ky I	47883	13th Duke of Chico L R
47796	Dick Willis	Ky I	47884	15th Duke of Chico — P S
47799	Dixie	— M	47885	16th Duke of Chico — P S
47800	Dixie Duke	Cox	47886	17th Duke of Chico — P S
47801	Dobbin	— M	47887	21st Duke of Chico — M
47803	Doc King	M	47888	26th Duke of Chico — P S
47804	Doc Odbert	— P S	47889	28th Duke of Chico M
47805	Doc Odbert 2nd	— M	47890	29th Duke of Chico M
47807	Dr. Allison	— P S	47891	30th Duke of Chico M
47808	Dr. Barnett	T	47892	2nd Duke of Clinton — M
47809	Dr. Dee	— P S	47893	3rd Duke of Clinton — M
47810	Dr Green	P S	47894	4th Duke of Clinton — M
47811	Dr. Sprague	— R R	47895	Duke of Cloverdale — D
47812	Dolly's Prince	— Cox	47897	Duke's Comet L R
47813	Dolphin	— L R	47899	Duke of Condit — L R
47814	Dominion Lad	— R R	47900	Duke of Connaught M
47815	Dom Pedro	— R R	47901	Duke of Connaught Ky I
47816	Dom Pedro	— P S	47903	2nd Duke of Cortland Ky I
47817	Dom Pedro	D	47904	Duke of Crawford — D
47819	Dom Pedro	— L R	47905	Duke of Cressbrook — D
47821	Dom Pedro	— C	47906	Duke of Cross Creek 3rd L R
47822	Don	— M	47907	Duke of Cross Creek 4th — D
47823	Don	— Cox	47910	Duke of Delphos Ky I
47824	Donald	— L R	47911	Duc DeMorny — C
47825	Donald Duke 7th	— D	47912	Duke of Douglas —Long-Horn
47826	Donald Duke 8th	R R	47913	Duke of Dover — C
47827	Donald Duke 9th	M	47914	2nd Duke of Earl — Cox
47828	Donald Duke 10th	M	47917	Duke of Edinburg — M
47829	Donald Duke 11th	— D	47918	Duke of Ellington — L R
47830	Donald Duke 12th	— R R	47920	6th Duke of Erie — M
47831	Donald Duke 13th	R R	47921	7th Duke of Erie — M
47833	Don John	— L R	47922	8th Duke of Evergreen — L R
47834	Don Juan	— M	47923	10th Duke of Evergreen — M
47835	Don Martin	— R R	47924	Duke of Fairfield 5th — M
47836	Dorr	L R	47925	4th Duke of Fairview P S
47837	Double Bell Duke	— L R	47926	Duke of Fontanelle — M
47839	Dow of Attica	— L R	47927	Duke Fashion — L R
47841	Drain	— P S	47928	Duke of Fayette — R R
47843	Druid	— P S	47929	2nd Duke of Fayette L R
47844	Dublin Duke	— D	47930	10th Duke of Forest Hill L R
47845	Dudley	— C	47931	11th Duke of Forest Hill — M
47846	Duke	P S	47932	4th Duke of Fraser L R
47847	Duke	— Cox	47933	Duke of Geddes — Cox
47848	Duke	— Ky I	47934	Duke of Glenwood — R R
47849	Duke	— Cox	47935	Duke of Green Ky I
47850	Duke 7th	— Ky I	47936	2nd Duke of Greenfield M
47854	Duke of Adams	M	47937	3rd Duke of Greenfield M
47855	6th Duke of Alameda	D	47938	Duke of Greenwood — D
47856	Duke of Alderville	— M	47939	2nd Duke of Greenwood — M
47857	Duke of Alexis	— M	47941	Duke of Gruby Knolls L R
47859	Duke of Alva	— M	47943	Duke of Harmony — T
47860	Duke of Andover	— Ky I	47944	1st Duke of Harper — M
47861	4th Duke Annabella	— R R	47945	Duke of Hastings 4th — P S
47864	Duke of Antrim	— P S	47946	Duke Celena of Prickly Pear, — Ky I
47865	Duke of Arlington	Ky I	47947	2nd Duke of Hickory Grove — P S

SHORT-HORN CATTLE PEDIGREES.

No.	Name	Code	No.	Name	Code
47949	Duke of Highland	— M	48034	5th Duke of Plum Grove	— M
47950	2nd Duke of Highland	— M	48035	6th Duke of Plum Grove	— M
47951	4th Duke of Highland	— M	48037	Duke of Portage	— M
47952	13th Duke of Highland	— Cox	48038	Duke of Portage	— L R
47953	Duke of Hillfarm	T	48039	Duke of Prairie View	— L R
47954	2nd Duke of Hillfarm	T	48040	Duke Prince	— L R
47955	Duke of Hillsboro	— Daisy	48041	6th Duke of Pulaski	— R R
47956	Duke of Hillsdale	— M	48042	Duke of Randboro	L R
47957	Duke of Hilo	— Cox	48043	Duke of Rawson	— D
47958	3rd Duke of Houston	— Cox	48044	Duke of Redwood	Ky I
47959	4th Duke of Houston	T	48045	2nd Duke of Redwood	Ky I
47960	1st Duke of Iverness	— L R	48046	3rd Duke of Redwood	P S
47962	Duke of Ionia	M	48047	Duke 4th of Richland	— P S
47965	Duke of Jefferson	L R	48049	2nd Duke of Ridgvale	— L R
47966	2nd Duke of Jefferson	L R	48050	13th Duke of Ridgevale	Cox
47967	Duke of Jelloway	M	48051	Duke of Riverdale	— Daisy
47968	Duke of Jericho	— L R	48052	Duke of Sharon	Cox
47969	Duke Jim	— Long-Horn	48054	4th Duke of Shiloh	M
47970	3rd Duke John	— L R	48055	5th Duke of Shiloh	M
47971	Duke Kent	— D	48056	10th Duke of Skaneatles	— Cox
47976	4th Duke of Lapwing	— M	48057	Duke of Slipperyrock	— L R
47977	Duke of La Salle	— P S	48058	Duke of Sparsewood 9th	— R R
47978	Duke of Lawndale	— D	48059	Duke of Spring Hill	M
47979	2nd Duke of Lawndale	— Ky I	48060	2nd Duke of Stafford	Daisy
47980	Duke 9th of Lebanon	— R R	48061	3rd Duke of Stafford	Daisy
47981	10th Duke of Lebanon	— R R	48062	Duke of Stone House	L R
47982	Duke of Lexington 2nd	— R R	48063	Duke of Sublette	— R R
47983	Duke of Licking 3rd	— M	48064	Duke of Sullivan	— P S
47984	Duke of Lincoln	— D	48065	4th Duke of Swansea	— M
47984½	6th Duke of Linwood	L R	48068	Duke of Tabo	— C
47985	7th Duke of Linwood	Ky I	48069	Duke of Tallmadge	— M
47986	Duke of Logan	— Cox	48070	Duke of Taylor's Run	— D
47987	Duke of McLean	M	48071	Duke of the Fort	— L R
47988	Duke of Madison	— R R	48073	Duke of the Union	— D
47989	Duke of Maine Valley	— M	48074	Duke of the Valley	M
47992	3rd Duke of Manchester	— D	48075	Duke of the West	— P S
47993	Duke of Mansfield	— L R	48076	Duke of Uinta	— P S
47994	Duke of Maple Grove 2nd	— Cox	48077	Duke Valentine	— R R
47995	Duke of Maplewood	— L R	48078	Duke of Wabash Valley 2nd	T
47996	Duke of Marion	— R R	48081	8th Duke of Walnut Hill	— Ky I
47997	12th Duke of Marlboro	— R R	48082	Duke of Warren	— P S
47998	14th Duke of Marlboro	— M	48083	Duke of Warren 2nd	Ky I
47999	Duke of Miami	— M	48084	2nd Duke of Watson	Ky I
48000	Duke of Mill Creek	— L R	48085	3rd Duke of Waverly	— D
48001	Duke of Monmouth	— P S	48086	Duke West	P S
48002	Duke of Montgomery	— D	48089	Duke of West Point	— C
48003	Duke of Montgomery	— M	48091	4th Duke of White Hall	— M
48005	Duke of Moultrie 2nd	— M	48092	5th Duke of White Hall	C
48009	Duke of Nebraska	— R R	48094	Duke Wiley 2nd	— M
48010	Duke of New York	— Cox	48096	Duke of Willowdale	— P S
48011	Duke of Northfield	— Cox	48097	Duke of Wilmont 2nd	— L R
48012	Duke of Northumberland 2nd	— D	48098	Duke of Wilmont 3rd	— L R
48013	Duke of Oakland 10th		48099	Duke of Winchester	— Cox
48014	Duke of Orchard Hill	Cox	48100	6th Duke of Wixom	L R
48015	Duke of Orleans	L R	48101	7th Duke of Winton	— D
48016	Duke of Orville	Ky I	48103	Duke of Yates 29th	M
48017	Duke of Oxford 10th	R R	48104	Duke of York	L R
48018	2nd Duke of Palestine	— T	48105	Duke of York	— T
48019	3rd Duke of Palestine	M	48106	Dunbar Duke	— L R
48020	4th Duke of Palestine	— T	48107	Duncan	— Daisy
48021	5th Duke of Palestine	— T	48108	Dunglenna's Duke	— Daisy
48022	1st Duke of Pecatonica	L R	48109	Du Page	— M
48024	1st Duke of Phelps	L R	48111	Dursee	P S
48025	2nd Duke of Phelps	— P S	48112	Dutton	— Cox
48028	2nd Duke of Pittsfield	P S	48115	Earl Brownell	— P S
48029	1st Duke of Pleasant Valley	Cox	48118	Earl of Clinton	— Ky I
48030	2nd Duke of Pleasant Valley	Cox	48119	2nd Earl of Clinton	L R
48031	Duke of Plum Grove	— D	48120	2nd Earl of Clinton	L R
48032	2nd Duke of Plum Grove	— R R	48122	Earl of Denton	D
48033	3rd Duke of Plum Grove	— M	48123	Earl Derby 10th	M

48124	Earl of Dryden 3rd	L R
48126	Earl of Erve	— Cox
48128	39th Earl of Greenbush	M
48130	41st Earl of Greenbush	— L R
48132	43rd Earl of Greenbush	M
48133	44th Earl of Greenbush	— L R
48135	Earl of Louan	M
48138	Earl of Marion	— P S
48139	Earl of Marr	— Ky I
48140	Earl of Onondaga	— Cox
48142	Earl of Richland	— D
48143	Earl of Sigourney	— D
48145	Earl Wayne	— P S
48146	Earl of Westford	L R
48147	Ebenezer	— R R
48148	Eckert's Duke	D
48149	Eclipse	L R
48150	Edward Gray	— M
48151	Effie's Geneva	— T
48154	Elias Brown 2nd	Ky I
48155	Elkhorn	Ky I
48156	Emperor	— Ky I
48159	Emperor 2nd	M
48161	Enoch	— L R
48162	En Regle	Cox
48163	Enterprise	— D
48164	Equal	— L R
48168	E. Whitney	— M
48169	Evening Duke	— Cox
48171	Extra Billy Smith	Cox
48172	Ezera	— L R
48173	Famous	— M
48174	Fancy Boy 3d of Bluff Creek	— T
48175	Fancy Boy of Bluff Creek 2d	— T
48176	Fancy's Champion	— L R
48177	Fannie's Duke	— P S
48178	Fannie's Duke	— L R
48179	Fanny Fern's Duke	Ky I
48180	Farley	— M
48181	Favorite	M
48182	Favorite	— D
48186	Fidalgo	— L R
48187	Filagree Gem 5th	M
48188	Filagree Gem 9th	— M
48190	Firefly 2nd	— L R
48192	Five Mile Duke	— D
48193	Flat Woods Rover	— M
48194	Fletchers Duke	— Cox
48195	Fletcher Duke 2nd	Cox
48196	Florine's Duke	— M
48197	Forest Duke 3rd	— R R
48198	Forester	— R R
48201	Fourth of July	M
48203	Frank	Ky I
48205	Frank Gentry	— T
48206	Frank Leslie	— P S
48207	Franklin	P S
48208	Franklin Duke 7th	— C
48209	Frantic Duke	— Cox
48210	Frantic Prince	L R
48211	Fred	— Cox
48212	Fred Grant	M
48213	Frederick the Great	M
48214	Frelinghuysen	— P S
48215	French Creek Billy	— Cox
48216	Frontier Lad	— P S
48217	Gamester of Bell Creek	— T
48218	Garfield	P S
48219	Garfield	— Daisy
48220	Garfield	— D
48221	Garfield	— M
48223	Gem's Prince	— R R
48224	Gen. Arthur	— Cox
48225	Gen. Arthur	— Cox
48226	Gen. Bly	— R R
48227	Gen. Bunker	— M
48228	Gen. Burnside	— Cox
48229	Gen. Canby	— M
48230	Gen. Dumont	— D
48231	Gen. Forest	— C
48232	Gen. Garfield	T
48233	Gen. Garfield	— T
48234	Gen. Garfield	— L R
48235	Gen. Garfield	— Cox
48236	Gen. Gideon	— M
48237	Gen. Grant	P S
48238	Gen. Grant	M
48239	Gen. Grant	— L R
48240	Gen. Hancock	Ky I
48241	Gen. Hancock	— Cox
48242	Gen. Hancock	— C
48243	Gen. Jim Beaver	— M
48244	Gen. Joe Hooker	P S
48245	Gen. Lawler	— M
48246	Gen. Lee	— R R
48247	Gen. Link	— M
48248	Gen. Lyon	D
48249	Gen. Harop	L R
48250	Gen. Prather	Ky I
48251	Gen. Scott 2nd	— R R
48253	Gen. Sherman	Ky I
48254	Gen. Stark	Cox
48255	Gen. Sigel	M
48256	Gen. Taylor	— M
48258	Gen. Thornton	— M
48259	Gen. Washington 2nd	Ky I
48260	Genesee Duke	L R
48261	Geneva 3rd	— Cox
48262	Geneva Booth	— T
48268	Geneva of Bell Creek	M
48272	Gentle Prince	— L R
48273	George	— Cox
48274	George	— M
48275	George D.	M
48276	George M.	M
48277	George V. Lawrence	R R
48278	George Washington	— C
48279	George Washington 2nd	— Ky I
48280	George of Woodpecker Ridge	— P S
48281	George Thorndale 2nd	— Cox
48282	Gideon	L R
48283	Gideon 2nd	T
48284	Gill Duke 2nd	— Cox
48285	Gillette	P S
48287	Gipsy Duke	Ky I
48288	Girard	— Cox
48289	Gladstone	— L R
48290	Gladstone	— L R
48291	Glamorgan	Ky I
48292	Glencoe Chief	Ky I
48293	Glendale Boy	— P S
48294	Glenwood	— Cox
48297	Gloster of Constantine	— Cox
48298	Goforth	— M
48299	Gold Drop 2nd	— P S
48300	Gold Drop 6th	— C
48301	Gold Drop 7th	— M
48302	Gold Dust	— P S
48303	Gold Dust 2nd	— M
48305	Golden Duke	— R R

48306	Golden King 20th	— Cox		48401	Independence	— L R
48307	Golden Prince 10th	— M		48402	Ingersoll	— P S
48308	Golden Prince 11th	— T		48403	Ingomar	Woods
48309	Golden Prince 12th	T		48404	Iowa Chief	— P S
48310	Golden Prince 13th	T		48405	Ira	L R
48311	Golden Prince 14th	T		48406	Iroquois	P S
48312	Golden Prince 15th	— T		48407	Iroquois	— Cox
48313	Golden Prince 16th	— T		48408	Isaac B.	— M
48315	Gordius	— M		48409	Isabel's Joe	— M
48316	Gordon	L R		48410	Island Prince	— Cox
48317	Governor	— D		48411	Ivanhoe	— R R
48318	Governor	P S		48412	Jack	— L R
48319	Governor	— D		48413	Jack	— T
48320	Gov. Begole	L R		48414	Jack	— M
48322	Gov. Crittenden	M		48415	Jack Arthur	— M
48323	Gov. Glick	— M		48416	Jack Biddle	— C
48324	Gov. Glick	— P S		48418	Jack Frost	P S
48326	Gov. Jerome	— M		48419	Jack Robinson	M
48327	Gov. Porter	— M		48420	James C.	L R
48328	Gov. Pastor	M		48421	James Campbell	— M
48329	Gov. Sherman	P S		48423	Jamestown, Jr	— L R
48330	Gov. Thayer	— D		48424	Jay Gould	— D
48331	Grand Chief	— Long-Horn		48425	Jay Gould	— D
48332	Grand Duke	— R R		48426	Jay Hubbell	— T
48333	Grand Duke	— R R		48427	Jayisee	— P S
48336	3d Grand Duke of CherryWood	— P S		48428	J. B. Meginnis	— L R
48337	Grand Duke of Fruitland	— Daisy		48429	Jere Boggs	— P S
48340	Grant	— T		48430	Jerry	D
48341	Green Ridge Lad	— M		48431	Jerry Burch	L R
48342	Grover Cleveland	— Cox		48432	Jersey Smith	— Long-Horn
48344	Gulliver	— M		48433	Jesse James	— M
48345	Gulnare Prince	— R R		48434	Jesse James	— M
48347	Hamilton	— M		48435	Jessie's Duke	Ky I
48348	Hancock	— P S		48436	Jester	— R R
48349	Hannibal	— L R		48437	Jim Bell	Daisy
48351	Happy Harry	— P S		48438	Jim Blaine	T
48354	Harry Bailey	M		48439	Jim Blaine O.	Ky I
48355	Harvard Lad	— P S		48440	Jim of Maine Valley	Ky I
48356	Haskins	— R R		48441	Jim Moore	— M
48357	Heber Kimball	— D		48442	J. L. Williams	— Ky I
48359	Hector	Cox		48443	Joab Clay	— R R
48360	Hector	— P S		48446	Joe	— Cox
48361	Hector Duke	— Cox		48447	Joe Beatty	— R R
48362	Hendon	L R		48449	Joe Davis	L R
48363	Henry Beecher	— P S		48450	Joe Ecret	— Daisy
48364	Henry Newby	M		48451	Joe Hooker	M
48365	Henry Ward	— L R		48452	Joe Johnson	Ky I
48366	Hercules	M		48454	Joe Orford	— Cox
48367	Herman	Cox		48455	Joe Scott	M
48368	Hermes	— R R		48456	John Bender	M
48369	Hero	P S		48458	John Corbin	— C
48370	Hero	— M		48461	John Heim	L R
48371	Hero	— T		48462	John Kilsey	— R R
48372	Hero	— M		48463	John Harlan	— M
48373	Hero of Albion	Ky I		48464	John O'Connor	— T
48375	Hickman	— M		48465	John O'Groat	— Cox
48377	Highland Dexter	— M		48466	John R.	— M
48378	Highland Duke	M		48467	John Sherman 2nd	— D
48380	Hiram Weeks	— D		48468	Johnstown Lad	— M
48382	Hopeful	— Daisy		48469	Johnstown Lad 2nd	Cox
48384	Hopeful	Cox		48470	Jolly Lad	Cox
48385	Hopewell 3rd	— M		48471	Jonetta	— R R
48386	Hopewell 4th	— Daisy		48472	Joseph	— Cox
48387	Hopewell 5th	— Ky I		48474	Joshua	— Cox
48390	Hubback, Jr	— Cox		48476	Jubilee Duke 3rd	— R R
48394	Hunter	— P S		48478	Judge	— R R
48395	Idlewild	— Cox		48479	Judge	— M
48396	Illehee	— T		48480	Judge Davis	L R
48397	Imperial Duke	— R R		48481	Judge Willets	— R R
48400	Independence	— T		48482	Judson	— T

48483	Judson Duke — P S	48580	Leland — M
48484	Jules Grevy 2nd — M	48581	Lentner Lad 2nd — C
48485	Julia's Duke — R R	48582	Leo D
48486	Julius Cæsar Ky I	48583	Leo — M
48487	Jumbo P S	48585	Leon — M
48488	Jumbo — L R	48586	Leonardo — M
48490	Jumbo Cox	48587	Leonidas — M
48491	Jumbo L R	48590	Leopold — Cox
48492	Jumbo M	48591	Leslie Fayler — R R
48493	Jumbo — Cox	48592	Le Sueur Duke M
48494	Jumbo L R	48593	Lewis — R R
48495	Jumbo Cox	48594	Lewis — M
48496	Jumbo M	48596	Lexington — D
48497	Jumbo — Cox	48597	Lick Fork Duke — Cox
48498	Jumbo — Cox	48600	Lilly Duke P S
48499	Jumbo 2nd — Cox	48601	Lind Duke 2nd — M
48500	Jumbo of Hornby — L R	48602	Little Giant Cox
48502	Jupiter Woods	48603	Little Sam — M
48503	Jupiter — R R	48604	Little Washington — M
48504	Jupiter Duke — M	48605	Locomotive — D
48505	Kadara — M	48606	Locust Grove Prince — M
48506	Kalo 3rd P S	48607	Lodi 2nd — Long-Horn
48507	Kansas Boy — R R	48608	Lodwick Cox
48508	Kansas Duke Ky I	48609	Logan — T
48510	Kentucky Champion M	48611	Long Beard — P S
48513	Khedive L R	48612	Longfellow — T
48514	King Arthur — M	48613	Longfellow of Woodlawn —Long-H
48515	King Bess Ky I	48615	Lord Baron 2nd Ky I
48516	King of Butler County Ky I	48616	Lord Barrington 3rd — C
48517	King Cyrus Ky I	48618	Lord Barrington 4th of Brighton—T
48518	King David — R R	48620	Lord Beaconsfield — T
48519	King Duke 2nd — L R	48621	Lord Derby 2nd — R R
48520	King Duke John — L R	48622	Lord Drumore — L R
48521	King of Maine Valley P S	48623	Lord Ducie — Cox
48522	King of Meadow Side — M	48626	Lord Geneva — Cox
48523	King Pharaoh — Ky I	48627	Lord Henry — Cox
48524	King of Plum Hollow — M	48628	Lord Lamech of Monmouth — T
48526	King Oscar D	48629	Lord of Linn — C
48527	King of the Meadows — T	48630	Lord Lucas C
48528	Kings Washington Airdrie — R R	48632	3rd Lord Ramsden — R R
48529	Kinsman Ky I	48636	Lord Valentine — Cox
48531	Kirklevington Lad — M	48637	Lord Wellington Ky I
48534	Kirklevington Phyllis' Duke — M	48639	Lorena's Duke P S
48536	Kisers Cherub — R R	48641	Louan's Champion — R R
48537	Kishon Cox	48642	Louan's Chief — M
48538	Kitty's Juno — D	48643	Louan's Chief — R R
48541	Knightley Blossom 2nd — Cox	48644	Louan Dick — R R
48548	Knight of Prairie 3rd — R R	48645	Louan Duke — R R
48550	Laban Cox	48646	Lonan's Duke — M
48552	Lad of Elmwood — T	48647	Louan Duke of Westbrook — R R
48553	2nd Lad of Elmwood — C	48648	Louanjo Lad — P S
48554	Lad of Maine Valley L R	48649	Louan Knight Ky I
48555	Lad of Rockland — M	48650	Louan's Major — R R
48556	Lady's Duke — T	48651	Loudon Chief — R R
48558	Lafayette Ky I	48653	Loudon Duke of Dover — M
48561	Lanark Boy L R	48654	Loudon Duke 2nd of Earlville Cox
48562	Lapsley — L R	48655	Loudon Duke of Elmwood — M
48563	Las Casas — M	48656	Loudon D. of Greenwood 15th — R R
48564	Latimer — R R	48658	Loudon Duke of Peru — R R
48565	Landau M	48660	Loudon's Marquis Ky I
48567	Law Ky I	48661	Loudon's Prince — R R
48568	Lawrence — C	48663	Loudon Rose Duke — R R
48569	Lawson 2nd Woods	48664	Louis — M
48570	Leander — T	48665	Lucas Lad — M
48571	Leander — Ky I	48666	Lucius — Cox
48573	Leandro — M	48669	Lucy Duke M
48574	Le Boeuf Duke — Cox	48670	Lurk P S
48575	Le Claire Duke — P S	48671	Luther — D
48577	Lee Cox	48672	Luther 2nd T
48578	Lee — C	48673	Luther 3rd T

SHORT-HORN CATTLE PEDIGREES.

No.	Name	Code
48674	Mabel's Oxford	M
48675	Mack	M
48676	McDill's Shaftoe	— Ky I
48677	McDowell Duke	— M
48679	Macgregor	— R R
48680	McMahon	Ky I
48682	Madison Duke	— P S
48685	Magnolia Duke	— C
48686	Majesty	M
48687	Major	— P S
48688	Major	L R
48689	Major	— Cox
48690	Major	— Daisy
48692	Major Duke of Goodness	— R R
48693	Maj. Fairman	M
48695	Maj. K.	— R R
48696	Maj. K. 2nd	Ky I
48698	Maj. of Maple Grove 2nd	— Cox
48699	Maj. Mack 2nd	— D
48700	Maj. of New Castle	— R R
48701	Maj. Oxford	— P S
48702	Maj. Taylor of Oakland	— D
48703	Maj. Trickey	P S
48704	Maudane Lad	— M
48705	Manistee	L R
48706	Maquoketa's Pride	— L R
48707	Marcus	— R R
48709	Marion Chief	— P S
48710	Marion Leslie	— M
48711	Marion Leslie 2nd	— M
48712	Marion Leslie 3rd	Ky I
48713	Marion Leslie 4th	— M
48714	Marion Leslie 5th	— P S
48715	Marion Leslie 6th	— P S
48716	Mark	L R
48717	Mark	M
48718	Mark	— P S
48719	Marlboro Duke	— P S
48721	Marquis 2nd	Ky I
48722	Marquis of Dover	— Cox
48723	Marquis of Lorne	— Cox
48724	Marquis of Rosewood	— M
48725	Marshal	— Ky I
48726	Marshall Duke	— P S
48727	Marshal of Maine Valley	— R R
48728	Marshal Ney	— R R
48734	Master Airdrie 5th	— Cox
48735	Master Bates	— Cox
48739	Master Hiram 2nd	— M
48743	Master Rose	— P S
48744	Master Van Tromp	— Cox
48745	Master Wiseton	— P S
48746	Mat	— D
48749	Matthew	Cox
48750	Maud's Duke	— R R
48751	May Duke	Woods
48753	Mayflower Chief	D
48754	Mayflower of Fennimore	— C
48755	Mayflower of Oakland	— R R
48756	5th Mayflower Prince	— M
48758	Meadow Lad	— Cox
48759	Merrimac	— R R
48761	Millbrook	— M
48762	Miller of the Dee	— P S
48763	Miller's Duke	— M
48764	Milo Chief	T
48765	Miltiades	L R
48766	Milton Lad	P S
48767	Minnie's Independence Duke	— T
48768	Minnies Lad	— T
48769	Missouri Duke	— P S
48770	Mitchell's Duke	— Daisy
48772	Mohawk	L R
48773	Molly's Duke 2nd	— M
48774	Molly's Duke 3rd	— M
48775	Mollie's 5th Duke	— L R
48777	Monarch	— P S
48783	Money Maker	— M
48784	Monitor of Maple Grove	— L R
48785	Monk	— Ky I
48787	Montana	T
48788	Monterey	P S
48789	Montezuma	— P S
48790	Montrose	— M
48791	Montville Duke	— Cox
48792	Moody	P S
48793	Moonlight	— M
48794	Morning Duke	— Cox
48795	Mortimer Monroe	M
48796	Moscow Duke	Ky I
48797	Moses	Cox
48798	Moundale Duke	— C
48799	Mountaineer	— R R
48800	Mount Shasta	— M
48801	Mozart	— Cox
48802	Mozart	— D
48803	Mucklewee	— P S
48804	Muggins	— L R
48806	Murdock	— D
48807	Music's Gloster	L R
48809	Napier Royal	— R R
48810	Napoleon	— C
48811	Nane	Ky I
48812	Nat Peterson	— T
48813	Nebraska Chief	— T
48814	Nebraska Chief	— P S
48815	Ned	— Cox
48816	Ned	— Cox
48817	Nelson	— D
48818	Nelson	Ky I
48819	Nelson Boy 5th	— M
48820	Nelson Boy 6th	— M
48821	Neosho	— D
48823	Nero	— M
48824	Nero	Cox
48825	Newton Duke	Ky I
48826	New Year's Day	Ky I
48827	Nichol's Favorite	— Cox
48828	Nickel	— D
48829	Nickel 2nd	— Cox
48830	Nickle Plate	— Cox
48831	Nimbus Duke	— M
48832	Noah	— C
48833	Noble	— M
48834	Noble	M
48836	Noble of Maine Valley	L R
48838	Norton	P S
48839	Norton Duke	— Cox
48840	Norway	— L R
48841	Nubian	— M
48842	Oakfield Boy	— Cox
48843	Oak Hill Lad	Ky I
48844	Oakland Boy	P S
48846	Oconto	— L R
48847	Odell Duke	— T
48850	Oliver Twist	P S
48851	Olympus	L R
48852	Orange Boy	Ky I
48854	Orbus	Ky I
48856	Orphan Lad	— M

48857	Orwell	— Cox	
48858	Oscar Wilde	— Cox	
48859	Oscar Wilde	— Cox	
48860	Oscar Wilde	— D	
48861	Oscar Wilde	— T	
48862	Oscar Wilde	— Cox	
48863	Othello	— R R	
48864	Otisco Lad	— Cox	
48865	Otsego	L R	
48866	Otselic Duke	— Cox	
48867	Otselic Prince	— Cox	
48868	Owlsborough	L R	
48869	Oxford, Jr.	— Ky I	
48872	Oxford Bell's Prince	— Cox	
48873	Oxford Boy	— T	
48874	Oxford Boy 2nd	— Cox	
48875	Oxford Chief	C	
48876	Oxford Duke	— Cox	
48878	Oxford's 2nd Grand Duke	— Cox	
48879	Oxford of Highland	— P S	
48880	Oxford Lad	— M	
48881	Oxford Lad	M	
48882	Oxford Lad 2nd	— Cox	
48883	4th Oxford Lad	— Cox	
48884	5th Oxford Lad	— Cox	
48885	3rd Oxford of Oakland	— R R	
48886	Oxford Prince	— Cox	
48888	Oxford Prince	— C	
48889	Oxford Prince 2nd	— R R	
48891	Oxford Roan	— Cox	
48894	Parnassus	Cox	
48895	Pat Airdrie	Ky I	
48896	Patrick Henry	— Ky I	
48897	Paul	— C	
48898	Paul Ecton	— R R	
48900	Paul Myron	Ky I	
48903	Pearl Prince	— C	
48904	Pedro	L R	
48905	Pedro	— M	
48906	Pedro	P S	
48907	Pedro	— P S	
48908	Peep-O-Day	P S	
48909	Peleg	— Ky I	
48910	Perfection	— P S	
48911	Perfection	P S	
48912	Pegasus	— L R	
48913	Peri	T	
48914	Peri Constance Duke 2nd	— R R	
48915	Peri's Prince	— L R	
48917	Perrine	— D	
48918	Petroleum	R R	
48919	Philip	— M	
48920	Philip Ray	P S	
48923	Pilot	Ky I	
48924	Pilot	P S	
48927	Pinkerton	— D	
48928	Pitsburg	— T	
48929	Plato	— L R	
48930	Pleasant Grove Duke	— L R	
48931	Pleasant Valley Duke	— M	
48932	Plumwood	— R R	
48933	Plumwood Andrews	— L R	
48934	Plumwood A W	R R	
48935	Plumwood A X	R R	
48936	Plumwood A Y	R R	
48937	Plumwood A Z	R R	
48938	Plumwood B A	— R R	
48939	Plumwood B C	Daisy	
48940	Plumwood B D	— R R	
48941	Plumwood B E	C	
48942	Plumwood B F	R R	
48943	Plumwood B G	C	
48944	Plumwood B H	R R	
48945	Plumwood Duke	— L R	
48946	Plumwood Roan	— M	
48947	Ponce De Leon	— R R	
48948	Pony Duke	— Cox	
48951	Portage	— R R	
48952	Portage Duke 2nd	— M	
48953	Portage Lad	— P S	
48954	Portage Starlight	— P S	
48956	Porter	— P S	
48957	Portland	— D	
48958	Prairie Boy	— M	
48959	Prairie Duke	Cox	
48960	Prairie King	— M	
48961	Prairie Lad	— P S	
48962	Prairie Prince	— M	
48963	President	— Ky I	
48964	President Arthur	L R	
48965	Pride of Othello	— M	
48966	Pride's Prince of Orange	P S	
48967	Pride of the Patch	M	
48968	Pride of the Summit	Ky I	
48969	Primus	— Cox	
48970	Primus	— Cox	
48973	Prince	— Cox	
48974	Prince	— Cox	
48976	Prince	M	
48977	Prince Airdrie	— P S	
48978	Prince Albert	— P S	
48979	Prince Albert	— Cox	
48980	Prince Albert	— C	
48981	Prince Albert	— R R	
48982	Prince Albert 2nd	M	
48983	Prince Albert 2nd	— Cox	
48984	Prince Albert 3rd	— Daisy	
48986	Prince Alden	L R	
48988	Prince Arthur 2nd	— Cox	
48989	Prince Arthur 3rd	— Cox	
48990	Prince Arthur 4th	— Cox	
48991	Prince of Ashbrook	D	
48992	6th Prince of Ashbrook	D	
48993	Prince of Avondale	Ky I	
48994	Prince Barmpton W.	— R R	
48997	Prince of Cambridge	— L R	
48998	Prince of Caudor	— Cox	
48999	Prince of Clinton	— Cox	
49000	Prince Colfax	— D	
49002	Prince Edward	— C	
49003	Prince of Ellington	— M	
49004	Prince Ellington	T	
49010	Prince Imperial	— Cox	
49012	Prince of Leicester	— Cox	
49014	Prince Louan 2nd	— R R	
49015	Prince Loudon 2nd	— R R	
49017	Prince of Maine Valley	L R	
49018	Prince of Maplewood	— P S	
49019	Prince of Maquoketa	— L R	
49020	Prince of Miami	T	
49022	Prince of New Castle	— M	
49023	Prince Oxford	— P S	
49024	2nd Prince of Plum Creek	Ky I	
49025	Prince of Royalty	— T	
49026	Princess Oxford	— Cox	
49027	Prince of Scotland	Ky I	
49028	Prince Sharon	— R R	
49029	Prince Sweyn	— T	
49030	Prince of the West	— M	
49031	Princeton	P S	

SHORT-HORN CATTLE PEDIGREES.

No.	Name	Herd
49032	4th Prince of the Valley	— M
49034	Prince of Wales	— D
49035	Prince of Wales	M
49036	Prince of Wayne	— D
49037	Prince of Wheatland	— M
49038	Prince Wiley	— R R
49040	Prince William of Albion	Ky I
49041	Prince of Winterset	Ky I
49043	8th Prince of Woodlawn	C
49044	9th Prince of Woodlawn	C
49045	Prize Boy	— R R
49046	Proctor Knott	M
49047	Prodigy	— D
49049	Prudent	— Ky I
49050	Publican	— M
49052	Putnam	— T
49053	Quantum	— R R
49054	Queen's Duke	Ky I
49055	Queen's Duke	— R R
49056	Queen's Duke 2nd	— R R
49057	Queen's Own	— M
49058	Racquet	Ky I
49059	Radiate	— D
49061	Rambler	— L R
49064	Ranger	— Cox
49065	Ranger	— R R
49066	Rawhide Duke	M
49067	Rayado	— M
49068	Rear Admiral	Cox
49069	Red Airdrie	— Ky I
49070	Red Airdrie 6th	— M
49072	Red Bank	— T
49074	Red Beauty	P S
49075	Red Benton	D
49076	Red Buck	Ky I
49077	Red Bud	P S
49078	Red Chunk	L R
49079	Red Chunk 2nd	— M
49080	Red Cloud	— M
49081	Red Cloud	— L R
49084	Red Cloud	— Cox
49085	Red Cloud	— P S
49086	Red Cloud 2nd	P S
49087	Red Cloud 3rd	P S
49089	Red Darby	— M
49090	Red Dick	— D
49091	Red Duke	— M
49092	Red Duke	— L R
49093	Red Duke	P S
49094	Red Duke	— Cox
49095	Red Duke	— Cox
49096	Red Duke	P S
49097	2nd Red Duke	— P S
49098	Red Duke of Vine Hill	— M
49099	Red Gauntlet	— M
49101	Red Jacket	— Cox
49102	Red Jacket	— M
49103	Red Jacket 2nd	P S
49105	Red Jim	— P S
49106	Red Knight	— Cox
49107	Red Lad	— Cox
49108	Red Manchester	M
49109	Red Mariner 2nd	— Cox
49111	Red Muscatoon	— C
49112	Red Pilot	M
49115	Red Prince	— Cox
49116	Red Raven 3rd	M
49117	Red Raven 6th	M
49119	Red Rover	— Cox
49120	Red Rover	— M
49121	Red Rover	— R R
49122	Red Rover	— Cox
49123	Red Rover	T
49124	Red Rover	— M
49125	Red Rover	— R R
49126	Red Royal	— C
49127	Red Ruby's Duke	L R
49128	Red Taylor	— R R
49129	Red Tom	— Cox
49131	Redwood Booth	— P S
49132	Redwood Lord	— Ky I
49133	Reginald	M
49134	Remus	— M
49135	Remus	— M
49136	Renick	M
49141	Rex	— Cox
49142	Richard 13th	— R R
49143	Richard Pansy 2nd	— Cox
49144	Richard Taylor 2nd	— D
49145	Richard of Waverly	— Cox
49146	Richart	— M
49148	Ridge Prairie	— D
49150	Ringgold	M
49151	R. L. Raymond	— M
49152	Roan Airdrie	— P S
49154	Roan Derby 2nd	— T
49156	Roan Duke	— M
49157	Roan Duke	— Daisy
49158	Roan Duke	— C
49159	Roan Duke	— R R
49160	Roan Duke	D
49161	Roan Duke of Millwood Park	— M
49163	Roan Prince	— Ky I
49164	Roan Veto	P S
49165	Robert Bruce	L R
49166	Robert Emmet	— P S
49167	Robert Emmet	— T
49168	Robert Louan	— R R
49169	Rob Highland	P S
49170	Robin Adair	L R
49171	Robinson Crusoe	— Cox
49172	Rob Roansides	— P S
49175	Rock Creek	T
49176	Rockland	— L R
49177	Rockwood	— M
49178	Roderick	— M
49180	Roger	— M
49181	Rodgers Duke	— L R
49182	Rokeby	— R R
49184	Rolla	D
49185	Rolla Duke	— R R
49187	Romeo	— M
49188	Romeo	— Cox
49189	Romeo	— D
49190	Romulus	— M
49191	Romulus 2nd	M
49192	Roscoe	— M
49193	Roscoe	— P S
49194	Roscoe	— Daisy
49195	Roscoe	— L R
49196	Roscoe Conkling	— D
49198	Rosebud Lad	— R R
49199	Rose Duke	T
49200	Rose 14th's Duke	— M
49201	Rosemound Duke	— Cox
49202	2nd Rosemound Duke	— C
49203	Rosewood	— R R
49207	Rosy Lad	— R R
49210	Rover	Ky I
49211	Rover	— Cox

49212	Rowdy Boy	— P S	
49215	Rower	M	
49216	Rowland	— M	
49217	Royal	— L R	
49219	Royal Bengal	— T	
49220	Royal Doctor W.	M	
49221	4th Royal Doctor W.	— M	
49222	5th Royal Doctor W.	— Ky I	
49223	Royal Duke	— R R	
49225	Royal Duke	M	
49227	Royal Gem	— T	
49228	Royalist	Ky I	
49229	Royal James	— R R	
49231	Royal Lad	— L R	
49235	Royal Oscar	Cox	
49236	Royal Oxford	— Cox	
49237	Royal Oxford 2nd	L R	
49238	Royal Prince	Ky I	
49239	Royal Prince	— L R	
49240	Royal Prince	— C	
49241	Royal Prince 3rd	— C	
49242	Royal Prince 4th	— C	
49244	Royal Star	Cox	
49245	Royal of Villa Nova	M	
49249	Royal Wychlery	— Cox	
49250	R. S. Blount	L R	
49251	Rubicon	Cox	
49252	Ruby	— Ky I	
49253	Ruby	Ky I	
49256	2d Ruby's Prince of Wyaconda	— M	
49257	Rufe Whitis	— Long-Horn	
49258	Rufus	C	
49259	Rugby	L R	
49260	Rustan	M	
49261	Rustic	— P S	
49262	Rustler	— D	
49264	Saberson's 2nd Earl of Shopiere	L R	
49265	Sage of Dale	Ky I	
49266	Sailor Boy	Ky I	
49267	St. Jacob	— P S	
49268	St. Jacob 2nd	— P S	
49269	St. John	M	
49271	St. Joseph	— D	
49272	St. Julien	Ky I	
49273	St. Julien	P S	
49274	St. Lawrence 2nd	— M	
49275	St. Patrick	R R	
49276	St. Patrick	— Cox	
49277	12th Salem Prince	— R R	
49278	Sam	D	
49279	Samuel	— M	
49280	Sam Brady	M	
49281	Sam Dudley	— R R	
49282	Sam Hillman	— D	
49283	Sam Kirkwood	M	
49284	Sampson	L R	
49285	Sam Rivers	— M	
49287	Sancho	— L R	
49288	Sangamah	— R R	
49289	Sankey Smith	— R R	
49290	San Pablo	— M	
49292	Saturn	Cox	
49293	Saturn	— R R	
49294	Saucy Jack	Ky I	
49295	Sawyer Duke	— Ky I	
49296	Saxon	— D	
49297	Scotchman	— R R	
49298	Scott	— M	
49299	Senator	M	
49300	Senator	— M	
49301	Senator	— R R	
49302	Senator	— R R	
49303	Senator	— Cox	
49305	Sergeant	— Ky I	
49306	Seward Chief 2nd	— M	
49307	Seward Chief 3rd	— M	
49308	Sexton	— R R	
49309	Shaker Boy	M	
49310	Shannon Boy	L R	
49311	Sharon Bell	M	
49315	Shawnee Chief	— L R	
49316	Sheridan	— P S	
49317	Sheriff	— Long-Horn	
49319	Shiawassee Lad	— R R	
49320	Shultz	Ky I	
49321	Siam	M	
49322	Sid	— C	
49323	Silenus	— R R	
49324	Silvania Duke	— C	
49325	Silver Creek's Wonder	— Daisy	
49326	Silver Simon	— D	
40327	Sim Curd	— C	
49328	Simon Cameron	— Daisy	
49329	Simpson	— M	
49330	Sir Alfred	— R R	
49331	Sir Arthur	— M	
49333	Sir Day	— M	
49334	Sir Frederick	P S	
49335	Sir Garnet	L R	
49336	Sir George	L R	
49338	Sir Henry	— R R	
49339	Sir Henry	Ky I	
49340	Sir Henry	T	
49341	Sir Isaac	Ky I	
49343	Sir Kenneth	— T	
49346	Sir Niegel	— L R	
49348	Sir Thomas	— Cox	
49349	Sir Walter Scott	— R R	
49350	Sir Walter Scott 2nd	— Cox	
49351	Sir William	— R R	
49352	Skookum	— T	
49353	Smith Bull	— L R	
49354	Smithville Favorite	— L R	
49356	Snowball	— D	
49357	Snowball	— Cox	
49359	Solon	— Cox	
49360	Solon	— Cox	
49361	Spartan	T	
49362	Spello	P S	
49363	Sperry's Duke	— M	
49364	Spillman Rock	— D	
49366	Spotted Boy	P S	
49367	Spotted Duke	— L R	
49368	Spotted Jim	M	
49369	Springfield Banker 2nd	L R	
49370	Springfield Boss	— M	
49371	Springfield Lad	— M	
49373	Springwood Champion	— L R	
49375	Squire of Maine Valley	L R	
49376	Squire Mapleton	— Ky I	
49377	Stanley of Maine Valley	— R R	
49378	Stanton	— Ky I	
49379	Star	M	
49380	Star Duke	Ky I	
49381	Starlight	— T	
49382	Star of the West	— M	
49383	Stephen	— P S	
49384	Sterling's Fancy	— L R	
49385	Stillwater Duke	— Cox	
49388	Stonewall Jackson	— R R	

49390	Strawn	L R
49391	Strawn	– P S
49392	Stub	– Cox
49393	Stumpy Tail	– D
49394	Sucker Boy	– D
49396	Sundown	– M
49397	Sunlight	M
49398	Superior Briton	– R R
49399	Surprise	– D
49400	Swansea Boy	– P S
49401	Sweepstakes 2nd	– P S
49402	Tama	Cox
49403	Tarleton	– C
49404	Taurus	Cox
49405	Tecumseh	P S
49406	Tecumseh	– P S
49407	Tenant	– R R
49409	The Doctor	– P S
49410	The Grove Boy	– L R
49411	Themistocles	– Cox
49412	Theodore Bates	– L R
49418	Thomas	M
49419	Thorndale Duke	– C
49423	Tiger	– Cox
49426	Tincher	D
49427	Toby of Maine Valley	– M
49429	Tom	M
49431	Tom Noble	– Ky I
49432	Tom Prince	C
49433	Tom Ragan	– D
49434	Tom Reno	– D
49435	Tom Roy	– Ky I
49436	Tonitah	– Cox
49437	Tony	P S
49439	Tornado	– M
49446	Triumph	– Cox
49447	Triumph of Maine Valley	Ky I
49449	Tudor	L R
49450	Tusculum	Cox
49451	Ulysses G. 2nd	– Ky I
49452	Una's Rover	T
49453	Uncle Sam	P S
49454	Undine's Oxford	– Cox
49455	Union Chief	– M
49456	Union Village	– R R
49457	Updike	– P S
49458	Uriah Heap	– T
49459	Valentine	– M
49461	Vanderbilt of Sullivan	– M
49462	Vanguard	– Cox
49464	Van Wyck	– R R
49465	Vastine	– M
49466	Velvet Chaff	– M
49467	Vermont	– P S
49468	Vermont Boy	– P S
49470	Vernon Lad	– L R
49471	2nd Vernon Lad	– L R
49472	Veteran	Ky I
49473	Veto	– Ky I
49474	Veto 3rd	P S
49475	Victor	Cox
49476	Victor	– P S
49477	Victor	– Daisy
49478	Victor	– L R
49480	Victor	– L R
49481	Victor	– P S
49484	Victor Gillett	M
49485	Victor of Waveland	– T
49486	Victorio	– P S
49487	Vina Curley	T
49488	Virginia's Pride	– C
49490	Wade Hampton	– Long-Horn
49491	Wallace	– R R
49492	Walter Scott	– P S
49493	Walt Moore	M
49494	Wapello	M
49495	Wapsie Bill	Cox
49496	Ward Beecher	– M
49497	Ward Beecher	– M
49498	Warden Nobes 2nd	T
49499	Warden Nobes 3rd	T
49502	Warrior	– T
49504	Washington Duke	– P S
49505	Waterloo Prince	– R R
49506	Watseka Duke	– M
49507	Webster	– M
49508	Welcome Duke	– R R
49510	Western Duke	– P S
49511	White Knight	T
49512	White Stockings	L R
49513	White Stockings	– M
49514	Whiteland	– D
49515	7th Wild Eyes of Armada	L R
49516	8th Wild Eyes of Armada	L R
49517	Wild Eye of Bell Creek	– M
49519	3rd Wild Eyes of Macomb	– Cox
49520	Wild Eyes of Madelia	– P S
49524	Wild Irishman	– P S
49527	Wiley's Duke	– M
49529	Wiley Oxford 12th	– Ky I
49530	Wilhoit	– P S
49531	William H. Niece	– D
49532	William Rufus	– R R
49533	Willovize	– R R
49534	Winfield	M
49535	Winterfold 2nd	– Cox
49536	Wixom	– Ky I
49537	Wolcott	T
49538	Woodford Boy	– R R
49539	Woodson	– R R
49541	Wycliffe	P S
49542	Wyoming	– L R
49544	Yankee Boy	– D
49545	Yamma	Ky I
49546	Yearkit	– P S
49547	Yellow Jacket	– M
49548	Young Abe	– Cox
49549	Young Aristocrat	M
49550	Young Baron	– P S
49551	Young Ben 2nd	D
49552	Young Bletsoe	– M
49553	Young Comet	– M
49554	Young Commander	– M
49556	Young Gloster	M
49557	Young Hopeful	– T
49558	Young Mary's Duke	– Ky I
49560	Young Oxford	– M
49562	Young Tornado	M
49563	Young Warren	– D
49564	Ypsi Chief	– R R
49565	Zera	– L R
49566	Zohauk	D
49567	Bismarck	– Cox
49568	Buffalo Jim	– Ky I
49569	Duke of Chestnut	M
49570	Duke of Kent	– Long-Horn
49571	2nd Duke of Kent	– Long-Horn
49572	Duke of Morgan	M
49573	Erk of Parsons	– Ky I
49574	3rd Glen Airdrie Duke	D

49575 Granger .... — D
49576 Jumbo .... — M
49577 Prince Imperial .... — T
49578 Rutherford .... — Cox
49579 Tom Boyd .... — L R
49580 William .... — Long-Horn
49581 Young Conant .... — Long-Horn

www.ingramcontent.com/pod-product-compliance
Lightning Source LLC
Chambersburg PA
CBHW031740230426
43669CB00007B/423